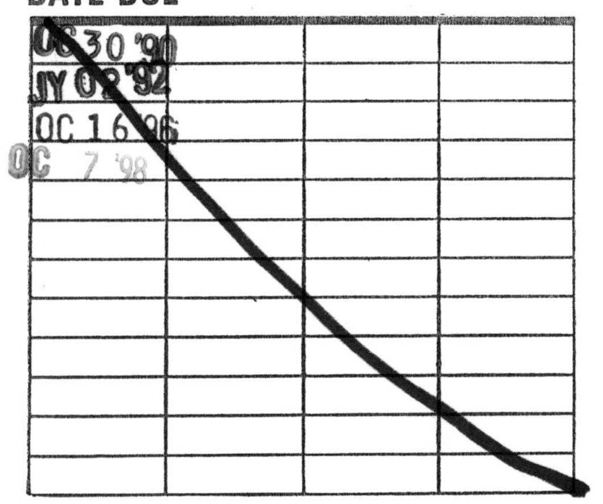
DATE DUE
OC 30 '90
JY 02 '92
OC 16 '96
OC 7 '98

COMPLETE BOOK OF 1989 BASEBALL CARDS

Louis Weber, C.E.O.
Publications International, Ltd.
7373 North Cicero Avenue
Lincolnwood, Illinois 60646

This edition published by:
Beekman House
Distributed by Crown Publishers, Inc.
225 Park Avenue South
New York, New York 10003

Manufactured in U.S.A.

h g f e d c b a

ISBN: 0-517-67428-9

Contributing writers: Tom Owens and H.R. Ted Taylor. Special thanks to AU Sports Memorabilia, Skokie, Illinois.

Page 4 photo of Orel Hershiser: J. Daniel/ALLSPORT USA; page 6 photo of Kirk Gibson: Don Smith/ALLSPORT USA; page 7 photo of Jose Canseco: Robert Hagan/ALLSPORT USA; page 8 photo of Tony Gwynn: Diane Johnson/ALLSPORT USA; page 9 photo of Wade Boggs: John Swart/ALLSPORT USA; page 10 photo of Frank Viola: B. Schwartzman/ALLSPORT USA; page 11 photo of Dennis Eckersley: Dave Stock/ALLSPORT USA; page 12 photo of John Franco, Stephen Dunn/ALLSPORT USA; page 13 photo of Mark McGwire: Otto Greule/ALLSPORT USA

BEEKMAN HOUSE

CONTENTS

Orel Hershiser

It's no secret that baseball card collecting is one of the fastest growing hobbies of today. The popularity of baseball is at an all-time high, and there's no better way to appreciate the sport than through baseball cards.

The *Complete Book of 1989 Baseball Cards* can help prepare you for the upcoming season. The publication is an innovative step in the hobby. For the first time, collectors will have an in-depth profile of more than 600 different players who could be key performers for their clubs. Each of these players' 1989 cards are shown, giving every fan an early preview of the best possible hobby investments.

Everyone can benefit from the *Complete Book of 1989 Baseball Cards.* Casual followers of baseball will want 1988 and career statistics to help predict the top teams and stars of 1989. Collectors will value the expert investment advice for each player's cards. Each profile has a rating of the best 1989 card. We've used several criteria to rate the cards, including the technical quality, aesthetics, and composition of the photo; integration of the photo into the card design; and the presentation of information on the back of the card. Hobbyists should take these factors into account when ranking the 1989 cards.

What can collectors expect from the 1989 season? For starters, more cards will be available than ever before. Those increased choices may sound great, but collectors unable to obtain every new card set produced will need to know which products hold the greatest potential for investment. Fleer, Donruss, and Score will each produce 660-card sets in 1989, while Topps will return with a 792-card set. These four card issues, which were the most popular collecting and investing choices of 1988, are the focus of this publication.

Other sets are available. The 3-D Sportflics cards return, but they've not been accepted as mainstream yet. Upper Deck plans a 1989 set with counterfeit-proof holograms on the backs. Only dealers will carry these sets, limiting their investment potential. All four major companies issue fall update sets; several produce 33- and 44-card boxed sets, which aren't as popular as the four regular sets. Still, players with good reviews in this publication will be the best choices in any set.

The booming baseball card hobby can be fun and profitable for any educated collector. In the 1960s and early '70s, collectors paid little attention to individual players. Most merely wanted to accumulate complete sets. Star and rookie cards were unheard of. Now, the hobby has exploded. Baseball cards are marketed in specialty shops and large conventions that often draw more than 10,000 collectors a day. Baseball cards are a new investment commodity, right beside stocks and bonds or gold and silver.

That's why the information in this publication is so important. Anyone can become a successful investor with only a little effort. It's possible to build an impressive collection on a small budget. Remember, those high-priced star cards of today once could be bought for only a few cents.

The principle of supply and demand determines the market prices of cards for individual players. When certain cards are available to the collecting public in smaller quantities (such as the 1988 Fleers), the price for any cards from those sets will be slightly higher. The 1988 Donruss cards were more readily available, but the cards numbered 600 to 660 were harder to find, except in complete sets assembled at the factory. Even a common player from that scarce series can be worth three times as much as other ordinary cards from the Donruss set.

Kirk Gibson

Ordinarily, a collector has an equal chance of acquiring any card when purchasing a pack from the candy store. Although all major card companies keep their production numbers a closely guarded secret, it's assumed that equal numbers of all cards are printed. Even when there aren't equal numbers, the disparity is usually not as great as the '88 Donruss high-number series. Therefore, the only difference between the card of an All-Star and a benchwarmer is popularity. The usual card supply of superstars like Don Mattingly and Wade Boggs just can't satisfy their millions of fans. When that happens, prices of those cards increase.

Baseball cards are sold in several types of packages. The best-known is the wax pack (sold in waxed paper), which has cost 40 to 45 cents in the past. Anywhere from 15 to 17 cards come in each package. It's inaccurate to call all baseball cards "bubblegum cards," because Topps is the only manufacturer that includes gum in each package. Fleer includes a team logo sticker in each pack, Donruss offers three jigsaw puzzle pieces, and Score has a three-dimensional trivia card.

Wax packs are sold 36 to the box. It's possible to get discounts on wax pack boxes from dealers. Also, companies will use sales incentives like cards printed on wax pack boxes or special card inserts available only in selected wax packs.

Score won points with collectors by creating a poly-bag package to replace the wax pack. The poly-pack has to be torn open and cannot be resealed. This prevents retailers from tampering with the selection of cards inside and resealing the pack.

Each of the four major companies sells "economy packs" of cards known as cellos (for the cellophane-package wrapping). You'll get a larger number of cards for a lower per-unit price than wax packs. Collectors can get sneak peeks at cards through the see-through packaging, often getting to view both the top and bottom cards in the pack. Also, it's sometimes possible to predict the cards in the middle of a pack by cracking the company's "code." Because the cards in cello packs are mechanically collated, it's possible to detect the sorting patterns after studying a couple of boxes worth of cellos. Keep each opened pack in its original order and jot down the numerical sequences. Then, by seeing the top and bottom cards on future packs, it'll be possible to estimate the middle cards in the package, too.

This system works best with rack packs, packages of three cellophane pockets of cards that are often displayed vertically on store racks. Rack packs will reveal six cards in the pack, three top and three bottom cards. Remember that different collating methods will be used for rack packs and cellos, but the code-cracking procedure works the same. Unlike wax or cello packs, it's highly unlikely that a rack pack can be tampered with and resealed. Never buy entire boxes of packs without opening a couple of test packages beforehand to see if the assortment is reasonable. Use dealers you know and trust when buying assortments of cards.

Buying complete sets of cards isn't so convenient when a collector wants to speculate on individual cards. A complete set will guarantee you one of every card, but no more than 200 of those individual cards will ever have any potential investment value. Sometimes, complete sets may seem easier to obtain than individual packages. For instance, major retail outlets offered complete sets of 1988 baseball cards from all manufacturers. These cards were collated into complete sets at the card factory. Fewer large retail markets offered wax packs.

None of the card assortments will be good for investing unless a hobbyist takes calculated gambles. Study the sports pages just like a Wall Street tycoon would scan the stock market section of the newspaper. Follow the long-term progress of players who might be good card investments. Even players with average abilities may be great card investments if they get a lot of publicity. Some popular managers, such as Whitey Herzog and Sparky Anderson, were mediocre players during their careers in the 1950s. However, their older cards are popular now because of their famous second careers. Also, off-the-field news can influence card values. Colorful sports announcers like Joe Garagiola and Bob Uecker have hotly pursued cards from their playing days in the 1950s and '60s. Look for daily clues from the

Jose Canseco

media to determine who might be tomorrow's superstars.

More insight into individual players can be found in various baseball magazines. These publications may take deeper looks into a player's career and rank him against his contemporaries and other accomplished players from baseball's past. During the preseason, a flood of baseball magazines will hit the newsstands. These once-a-year publications include team-by-team scouting reports and try to forecast the futures of many newcomers.

Don't think that an investor should monitor only the major leagues. Each year, several unknown faces will debut with many clubs. Informed hobbyists are acquainted with each rookie's collegiate and minor league record to know what potential each young player holds.

Hobby-oriented newspapers and magazines can be helpful, too. Many collectors guard their investment strategies, but clues to top investments can be gathered from various advertisements. After the 1988 World Series, numerous hobbyists began seeking the cards of postseason star Orel Hershiser. Some prepared traders started selling Hershiser's cards when his popularity was at its highest. Looking at both the buying and selling ads helped determine a standard market price for his cards. Some hobby papers provide regular price guides that supposedly monitor price increases in certain cards. These guides are only of limited use, however. They seldom account for regional interest in cards. Wisconsin fans, for instance, might have to pay area dealers double for cards of Brewer heroes Robin Yount and Paul Molitor.

The only investment-worthy card of the 1980s is a Mint one. Today's picky retailers and collectors won't accept anything less. Just because the card is fresh out of a wax pack, don't assume it's Mint. The hobby's grading standards, which vary in definition slightly with different collector publications, classify Mint cards as ones with four square, sharp corners. Many 1988 Score cards out of poly-packs were cut improperly in the factory and had fuzzy edges. (However, the company immediately recalled these damaged cards.) All the major companies have these problems from time to time. Because millions of cards are produced yearly, the quality suffers occasionally. Cards like these, although unharmed by human hands, are still considered less valuable than pristine specimens. Rounded corners are a major blemish for any card intended for resale.

Tony Gwynn

Any other minor production flaws, such as gum stains, ink streaks, or paper creases, will lower the grade and value of the card as well. Collectors expect Mint cards to have well focused photographs, free of imperfections. The photo on a Mint card is centered so that all four borders seem equal in width. Again, an off-center photo is a flaw that occurs before the card is shipped out of the factory, so collectors should beware of this problem when buying singles.

Ordinarily, it's a relatively simple process to grade a card, if you know what you're looking for. However, when you buy a dealer-assembled assortment of cards, don't assume the cards are all Mint. It's easy to accidentally or purposely insert a few battered cards in the middle of a Mint stack being sold in a plastic container. Likewise, if you're going to buy just one star card that is housed in a plastic protector, it's best to see the card up close, out of its packaging. Dealers unwilling to accommodate serious buyers don't deserve your business. Cards with even some of these minor flaws can lose more than one-third of their value instantly.

When the cards you've obtained pass your scrutiny, you're ready to preserve your acquisitions. A variety of durable plastic cases are available in hobby publications or from merchants for keeping those cards Mint. Get a container that keeps cards tightly enclosed, so your investments don't slop around and deteriorate over time. Don't make the mistakes youngsters made decades ago. Keeping cards stored loosely in a shoe box, or tightly trussed up with rubber bands can destroy cards quickly.

How do you handle the sale of a card of a future Hall of Famer? Very carefully! Some superstars will keep climbing in value forever. Unless you truly need the cash, reconsider your sale. Pete Rose is a sure bet for the Hall of Fame. Cards from his playing career will always be big sellers. Their values may never level off. You won't see big gains, but the gains will be consistent.

"Star" cards, cards of veteran players at a crossroads in their careers, are tougher calls to make. If a player over 30 years old has the first great season of his career, you may want to sell quickly for a short-term profit. Try to project the long-term success of a sudden star. Was his success a one-time affair? Can he last another decade? Will his lifetime stats remain memorable or perhaps earn him a spot in the Hall of Fame? If a player's future seems shaky, sell while there is still marginal interest in his card.

A pitcher may prove the most baffling card investment. Many hurlers may have pitched up to four years in college and possibly a few more seasons in the minors before making a major league debut. Several pitchers each year are permanently sidelined by arm injuries, simply because they've been active for so long. Unlike hitters, who can succeed anywhere, a great pitcher is helpless without a competent team behind him.

Another sometimes-befuddling area is rookie cards. In the past, investors have been stuck with hundreds of cards of J.R. Richard, Mark Fidrych, or Ron Kittle, three electrifying rookies who never lived up to their initial billings. These cards, once big sellers, now are only lukewarm in popularity. Investors unwilling to take modest profits missed out on any real gains. However, many rookie cards keep appreciating in value. In 1988, the two most popular rookie cards were those of Mark Grace and Gregg Jefferies. Both passed the $3 mark by the end of the World Series. With their continued success in 1989, those cards might double in price. If you've recouped your initial investment on a lot of one player's cards with a partial sale, go ahead and be daring with the remainder. Generally, though, investors feel that tripling your investment is good enough. The final decision rests on your sense of adventure.

Don't despair, though, if one of your investments starts losing some of its appraised value. An example is Dwight Gooden. His cards dropped steadily in price when he entered drug rehabilitation. Patient investors kept their cards, and the values rebounded when Gooden did. Realize that even if the market for some of your investments had dried up, you'll find a buyer somewhere. The price may be smaller, but you'll still get those cards sold. Bay area dealers in California can always sell cards of Giants and A's players, long after the world has found other players to idolize. Make the regional connection with your nonsellers by studying hobby paper advertisements.

Collectors and investors can obtain cards from numerous sources these days. Retail stores either carry complete sets of cards or one of the three previously discussed types of assorted packages. Hobby stores, which are popping up in both large and small communities across the nation, cater strictly to the collector and will offer more

Wade Boggs

options. Hobby stores, mail-order hobby dealers, or sellers at a baseball convention all sell individual cards. Expect any kind of hobby dealer to want a profit on his cards, due to his labor and other expenses. It's safe to assume that 1989 cards of nondescript players will start selling at prices of 3 to 5 cents each.

Many dealers sell their cards by mail. This is a good alternative for collectors living far away from hobby stores or conventions. The only drawback here is postage and handling costs, along with not seeing the merchandise beforehand.

When you decide what sources you'll use to obtain individual cards, it's time to make a want list. This preparation can be valuable. Make a simple list detailing which cards you want to speculate on and how much you want to pay. Being focused on a goal helps avoid making needless impulse buys, and your research will win you respect from retailers. Giving the impression that you can't be fooled may win you a better bargain with a dealer.

Think about how committed you'll be to your investments. If you find a promising player who has 1989 cards selling at three cents, it would be easy to invest in a couple hundred cards. However, trying to buy 200 cards of Jose Canseco might be an expensive proposition. You'll find that few merchants will market 1989 cards of individual players in 50- and 100-card lots. However, buying large quantities of certain players will get you better discounts.

If you've acquired hundreds or even a few thousand 1989 cards looking for certain players, you may have lots of trading material. When trading, consult price guides first to know current market values. Don't expect a dealer to trade you for the full estimated value of your cards. Dealers are trying to make money on every transaction, and they may give you only 25 to 50 percent of a card's worth. Buy from and sell to people you're familiar with to avoid hassles.

Newcomers to the hobby may wonder how investors actually make money from their cards. It's easy to open a price guide and appraise your own hoard of cards for a certain value. However,

Frank Viola

getting money for those cards may be another matter.

The first tip smart investors pass along is not to be greedy. Suppose one of your card investments gains 10 cents in value only a week after you made your move. It's easy, but perhaps foolish, to believe that the card will be worth a dollar more in ten more weeks. Card values change as fast as the stock market. A prolonged slump, career-ending injury, or numerous personal problems may quickly erase all value that player's card has gained. Does that mean to sell your entire investment stock fast?

Not really. Such a method would become too predictable and wouldn't bring much profit. Instead, try a more varied approach. Suppose you've invested $5 in 100 5-cent cards of a certain player. When you notice that his cards are worth a dime, you could sell off half your supply to regain your initial investment. Then, if your dreams come true and the card becomes a $2 item by season's end, you still have 50 cards to strike it rich with. When selling, the comments about trading with dealers will apply, too. Exceptions include desperate needs for certain cards. After any World Series, many dealers will want to build up their inventory of cards from the winning team.

Selling in the fall, directly after a World Series can be a profitable move. Everyone on a world championship team gets added respect, which translates into higher card prices. It might be wise to sell those cards before spring, when that same team could wind up in the cellar. Cards of postseason award winners, such as Rookies of the Year, Cy Young winners, or Most Valuable Players, see dramatic upswings in their card values immediately after they win their awards. Keep in mind that regional interest can benefit you when selling cards. East Coast collectors quite likely would pay much more for cards of any player on the Boston Red Sox, New York Mets, or New York Yankees.

If the 1988 season was any indication of things to come, the 1989 campaign should bring more excitement to all fans. Last season in the American League, the Oakland A's looked like a future dynasty by dominating the entire American

Dennis Eckersley

League with more than 100 wins. Team leader Jose Canseco won the league's MVP honors by surpassing the coveted "40/40" in both home runs and stolen bases. A has-been starting pitcher named Dennis Eckersley spent an entire season in the bullpen. He found new life, leading the American League with 45 saves. The A's had the A.L.'s third straight Rookie of the Year in shortstop Walt Weiss.

The dethroned world champion Minnesota Twins did get one small blessing. Their finest hurler, Frank Viola, led the major leagues with 24 wins, earning his first Cy Young award. Outfielder Kirby Puckett batted a blistering .356 in 158 games, but he lost the league batting crown to perennial champ Wade Boggs. Boggs bagged the title with a .366 effort.

Boston won the A.L. East in the last week of the season, after battling New York, Milwaukee, and Toronto all season long. This struggle indicates that the division will be wide open in 1989. The Red Sox are looking forward to another banner season from Mike Greenwell, who established his talent in 1988 with a year of 22 homers, 119 RBIs, and a .325 average.

The mighty A's looked helpless in the World Series against the upstart Los Angeles Dodgers, a team that many sportswriters scoffed at when the season began. The Dodgers, who claimed a World Series crown in just five games, produced Most Valuable Player in former Detroit Tiger Kirk Gibson. However, the biggest newsmaker on the Cinderella team was pitcher Orel Hershiser. Hershiser captured the Cy Young Award with 23 wins, 15 complete games, eight shutouts, and a record-breaking feat of 60 scoreless innings pitched.

The Cincinnati Reds battled the Dodgers for a pennant most of the season. In the end, their only lasting victories were a Rookie of the Year award for third baseman Chris Sabo, a scrappy player cast in the mold of Reds great Pete Rose, and a Fireman of the Year award for reliever John Franco. Newcomer Danny Jackson finished a close second in the Cy Young balloting. Jackson, a former Kansas City Royal, tied Hershiser with 23 wins.

John Franco

Hurlers like Hershiser stymied all the league's hitters in 1988. Only five full-time players hit .300 or better. San Diego Padres star Tony Gwynn won the N.L. batting title with a paltry .313 mark, his lowest since his 1983 rookie season.

The excitement of baseball only partially explains the enormous appeal of baseball cards. Ever since baseball cards made their debut in packages of cigarettes 101 years ago, someone somewhere has wanted to collect these unique slabs of cardboard. Since then, baseball cards have been premiums in a variety of products, ranging from breakfast cereal to hot dogs to dog food. In fact, a haircutting salon chain produced its own baseball card set in 1988. However, remembering that baseball cards start out as worthless pieces of cardboard may help collectors keep their hobby in perspective. Only the phenomenal demand from a baseball-crazy public keeps baseball cards valuable.

Perhaps collectors see a deeper-than-money value in baseball cards. These tiny squares, with dazzling photography, detailed statistics, and condensed biographies, give detailed insight into a player's career. Baseball cards capture moments of time and preserve the history of the sport, something any baseball fan, young or old, can appreciate.

The most important element in collecting or investing in baseball cards is enjoyment. Either activity can be a low-cost pastime. You can earn big dividends with some investments, but your losses don't have to be astronomical if you invest wisely. So be daring, but don't forget to have fun in your hobby pursuits. Good luck!

Mark McGwire

SHAWN ABNER

	BA	G	AB	R	H	2B	3B	HR	RBI	SB
1988	.181	37	83	6	15	3	1	2	5	0
Life	.215	53	130	11	28	6	1	4	12	1

POSITION: Outfield
TEAM: San Diego Padres
BORN: June 17, 1966 Hamilton, OH
HEIGHT: 6'1" **WEIGHT:** 190 lbs.
BATS: Right **THROWS:** Right
ACQUIRED: Traded from Mets with Kevin Mitchell and Stan Jefferson for Kevin McReynolds, Gene Walter, and Adam Ging, 12/86

While the San Diego faithful are not ready to write Abner off quite yet, it's apparent that if he doesn't make it soon he's not going to. Padre fans thought Abner would be a long-term fixture in the outfield when he hit .298 for Las Vegas and drove in 85 runs in 1987. But the rap against him has always been his lack of power; he only managed 11 homers at Las Vegas in '87 and hit but three there in '88. Abner hit .254 at Las Vegas in '88, while hitting only .181 in the bigs. Abner has plenty of talent and is still young, and he could become the impact player that the Padres are looking for.

Abner's first card appeared in the 1985 Topps set (First Draft Picks) and sells for 40 cents. His 1989 card will open in the 15- to 20-cent range. Our pick for his best 1989 card is Donruss.

JIM ACKER

	W	L	ERA	G	SV	IP	H	R	BB	SO
1988	0	4	4.71	21	0	42.0	45	22	14	25
Life	24	33	4.07	264	26	567.2	285	257	217	281

POSITION: Pitcher
TEAM: Atlanta Braves
BORN: September 24, 1958 Freer, TX
HEIGHT: 6'2" **WEIGHT:** 212 lbs.
BATS: Right **THROWS:** Right
ACQUIRED: Traded from Blue Jays for Joe Johnson, 7/86

Acker had little success in a brief season with the Atlanta Braves in 1988. He shared the woes of the rest of the pitching staff, going winless in 21 appearances. Acker was successful in 1987, tallying four wins and 14 saves in 114 innings. He appeared in a career-best 68 games in 1987. His professional career began in the Braves' organization in 1980, but he was drafted by the Blue Jays in 1983. There, he had a sparkling 7-2 mark with ten saves and a 3.23 ERA in 1985. If Acker is healthy and gets more work in 1989, his pitching form should improve.

Acker's 1989 cards will be three cents or less. Don't invest in his cards until the Braves team itself looks like it might win a few games in 1989. Our pick for his best 1989 card is Topps.

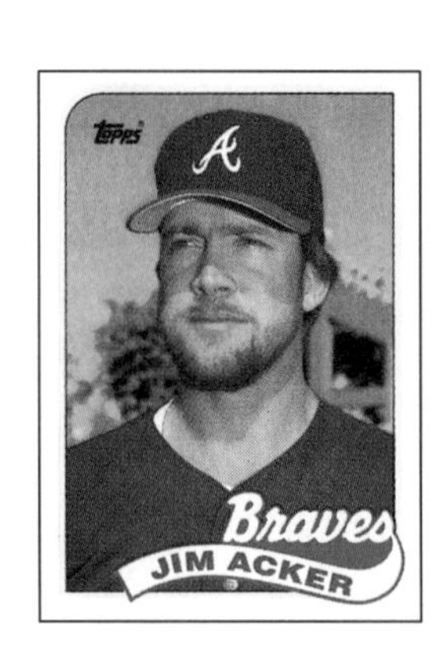

JUAN AGOSTO

	W	L	ERA	G	SV	IP	H	R	BB	SO
1988	10	2	2.26	75	4	91.2	74	23	30	33
Life	20	13	3.62	273	22	309.1	301	124	126	149

POSITION: Pitcher
TEAM: Houston Astros
BORN: February 23, 1958 Rio Piedras, Puerto Rico
HEIGHT: 6′2″ **WEIGHT:** 190 lbs.
BATS: Left **THROWS:** Left
ACQUIRED: Signed as a free agent, 4/87

Agosto had the winningest season of his career with the 1988 Houston Astros. The tall lefty registered the lowest ERA (2.26), the most appearances (75), and the most wins (ten) of his eight-year major league career. Agosto's ERA was the lowest on the 1988 Astros, and his number of appearances was the highest. He tied for second in the league in appearances. He bounced around in the White Sox system from 1981 through '86. Agosto was called up from the Astros' Triple-A team in July 1987, and he has stayed with the team since then. If Agosto keeps pitching so well, he'll be with them for years to come.

Agosto had a great year in 1988, but it was his first successful season ever. Don't invest in his common-priced cards in 1989, until he proves that last season wasn't a fluke. Our pick for his best 1989 card is Topps.

LUIS AGUAYO

	BA	G	AB	R	H	2B	3B	HR	RBI	SB
1988	.250	50	140	12	35	4	0	3	8	0
Life	.240	472	910	126	219	36	9	33	96	5

POSITION: Infield
TEAM: Cleveland Indians
BORN: March 13, 1959 Vega Baja, Puerto Rico
HEIGHT: 5′9″ **WEIGHT:** 195 lbs.
BATS: Right **THROWS:** Right
ACQUIRED: Signed as a free agent, 12/88

Aguayo became the chief utility man for the 1988 New York Yankees, filling in wherever the need existed. Valued primarily for his fine fielding and versatility, he had a decent year at the plate, too. Although he didn't match his homer-hitting feats of last year, Aguayo hit a solid .250. In 1987 with the Phillies, Aguayo pounded out a career-best 12 homers. Before that, he never had more than six round-trippers in a single season. Aguayo may not have a starting role for the 1989 Indians, but he'll surely be filling in where fans least expect.

Cards of journeymen infielders normally don't climb in value. Aguayo's cards are no exception. Don't indulge in his 1989 cards, which should be priced at three cents. Our pick for his best 1989 card is Score.

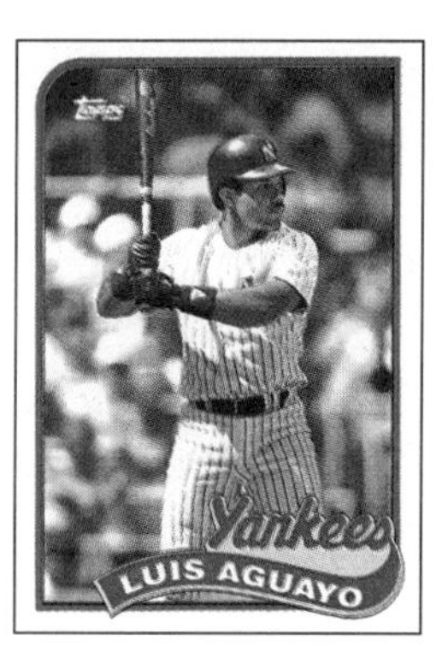

MIKE ALDRETE

	BA	G	AB	R	H	2B	3B	HR	RBI	SB
1988	.267	139	389	44	104	15	0	3	50	6
Life	.285	349	962	121	274	51	5	14	126	13

POSITION: Outfield
TEAM: Montreal Expos
BORN: January 29, 1961 Carmel, CA
HEIGHT: 5′11″ **WEIGHT:** 185 lbs.
BATS: Left **THROWS:** Left
ACQUIRED: Traded from Giants for Tracy Jones, 12/88

The Expos created a full-time outfield job for Aldrete by trading Tracy Jones one on one for him. Aldrete in 1988 played in 139 games and hit a respectable .267, with 50 RBIs. He is a natural first baseman, but Will Clark had that spot locked down long before Aldrete came up. Although the Giants shuffled Aldrete around at four positions until 1988, the three-sport high school star persevered, hitting .325 with nine homers and 51 RBIs in 1987. In 1986, he hit .250 in a half season with the Giants. With another year of experience and a permanent position, Aldrete will be a key component in Montreal's 1989 pennant drive.

Aldrete's 1989 cards will sell as commons. If he wins a batting title or propels the Expos back to first place, his cards will quadruple in price in a matter of weeks. Our pick for his best 1989 card is Topps.

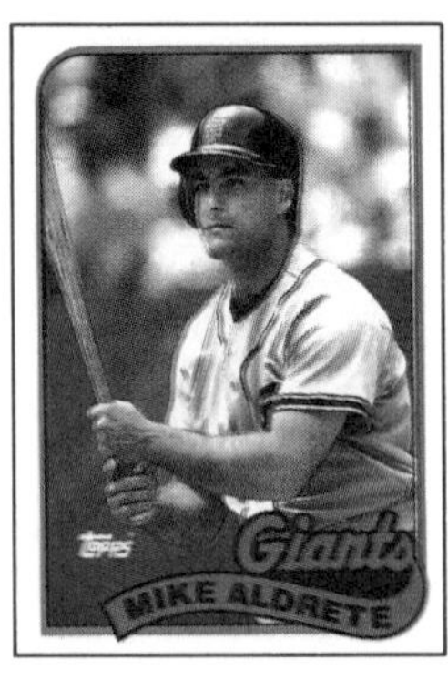

DOYLE ALEXANDER

	W	L	ERA	G	CG	IP	H	R	BB	SO
1988	14	11	4.32	34	5	229.0	260	110	46	126
Life	188	156	4.04	528	93	3143.0	3131	1411	902	1433

POSITION: Pitcher
TEAM: Detroit Tigers
BORN: September 4, 1950 Cordova, AL
HEIGHT: 6′3″ **WEIGHT:** 200 lbs.
BATS: Right **THROWS:** Right
ACQUIRED: Traded from Braves for John Smoltz, 8/87

In his 18th major league season, Alexander looked as strong as ever. He led the Tigers in innings pitched, and he won 14 games for the second straight season. Just in time for Detroit's 1987 pennant run, the Tigers pulled a shrewd trade by rescuing Alexander from the Braves. The Tigers were concerned mostly with getting some pitching security for those crucial final weeks. However, after repeating his 1987 heroics, Alexander seems able to pitch for several more big league seasons. This season should be a special one for Alexander, who seems ready to achieve the 200-win horizon.

Alexander's cards will sell as commons in 1989. They could bring short-term gains when he wins his 200th and finally gets some attention for his long, successful career. Our pick for his best 1989 card is Score.

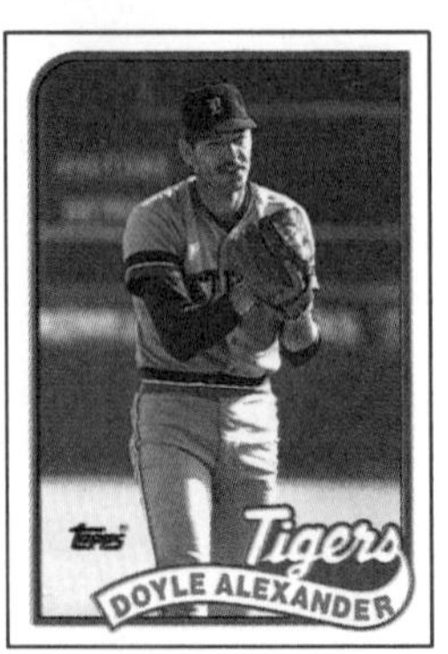

LUIS ALICEA

	BA	G	AB	R	H	2B	3B	HR	RBI	SB
1988	.212	93	297	20	63	10	4	1	24	1
Life	.212	93	297	20	63	10	4	1	24	1

POSITION: Second base
TEAM: St. Louis Cardinals
BORN: July 29, 1965 Santurce, Puerto Rico
HEIGHT: 5′9″ **WEIGHT:** 185 lbs.
BATS: Both **THROWS:** Right
ACQUIRED: First-round pick in 6/85 free-agent draft

Alicea had a mid-season shot at the Cardinal second base job in 1988, but major league pitching proved a little bit too much for him. At Triple-A Louisville in 1988, Alicea batted .277. He opened 1987 at Arkansas, and after hitting .270 he was moved up to Louisville. There he hit .305 in 29 games. The Cardinal first-round pick in 1985 should be ready to challenge Jose Oquendo for the starting second sacker job. At one time St. Louis had doubts about Alicea because of his penchant for mistakes. He seems to have overcome these problems, however, and should be a key player for the Cardinals for years to come.

Alicea was in the 1988 Donruss Rookies set, and his 1989 cards will open in the 25-cent range. Our pick for his best 1989 card is Score.

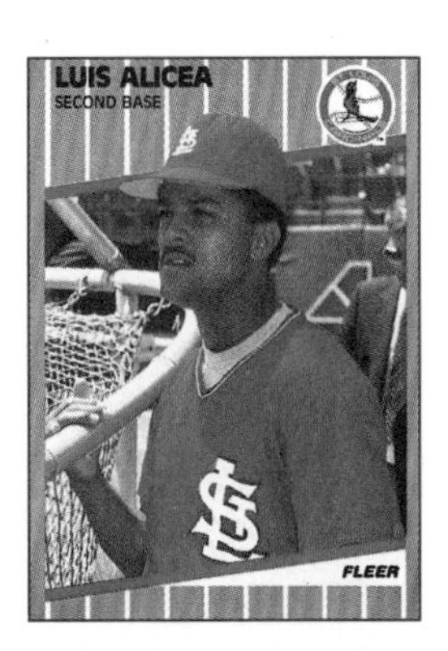

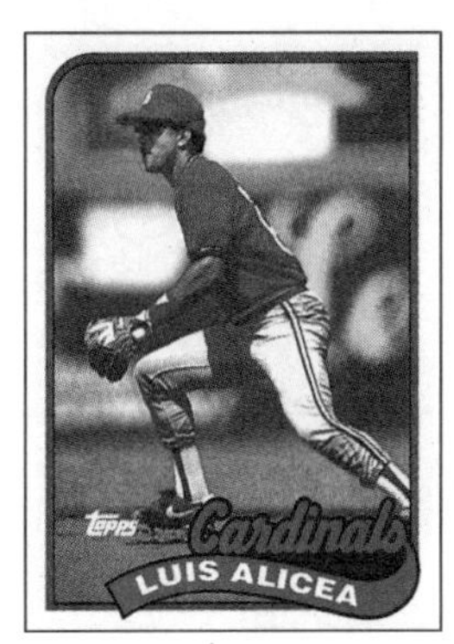

ANDY ALLANSON

	BA	G	AB	R	H	2B	3B	HR	RBI	SB
1988	.263	133	434	44	113	11	0	5	50	5
Life	.251	284	881	91	221	24	3	9	95	16

POSITION: Catcher
TEAM: Cleveland Indians
BORN: December 22, 1961 Richmond, VA
HEIGHT: 6′5″ **WEIGHT:** 215 lbs.
BATS: Right **THROWS:** Right
ACQUIRED: Second-round pick in 6/83 free-agent draft

Allanson, in his third season with the Cleveland Indians, caught more games than ever before. In 133 games, he hit five homers, one more than his previous two seasons. His 50 RBIs were among the best efforts of American League catchers. He also had a solid .263 average. At 6′5″, Allanson is one of the largest catchers in major league baseball. Despite his size, he is an adept fielder. He became the Indians' number-one catcher in 1988, and he has solidified the backstop position for the Tribe. With his new-found power and the opportunity to be Cleveland's starting catcher in 1989, Allanson could have his best season ever.

Allanson's cards are priced as commons. Although his 1988 season looked promising, his past record doesn't merit investment in his cards yet. Our pick for his best 1989 card is Topps.

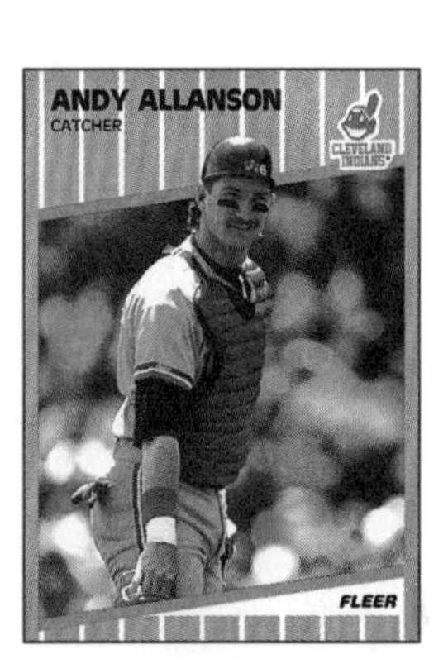

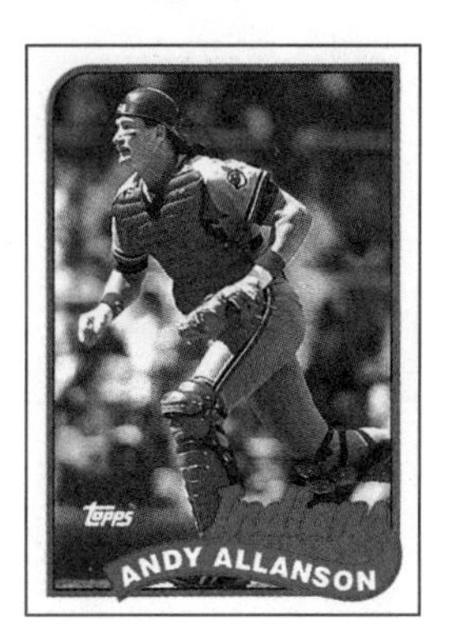

ROBERTO ALOMAR

	BA	G	AB	R	H	2B	3B	HR	RBI	SB
1988	.266	143	454	84	145	24	5	9	41	24
Life	.266	143	454	84	145	24	5	9	41	24

POSITION: Second base
TEAM: San Diego Padres
BORN: February 5, 1968 Salinas, Puerto Rico
HEIGHT: 6′ **WEIGHT:** 155 lbs.
BATS: Both **THROWS:** Right
ACQUIRED: Signed as a free agent, 2/85

Despite batting .360 in spring training with the Padres, Alomar started 1988 in Triple-A. It didn't take long, though, for San Diego to recall him, and he quickly became the regular second baseman. Alomar is still prone to fielding lapses, but when he does make the plays they are nothing short of brilliant. He hit around the .260 mark for the '88 Padres. Signed by San Diego as a 17-year-old free agent, Alomar was shifted to shortstop in 1987 at Double-A Wichita. He made a smooth transition and batted .319 with 12 homers, 68 RBIs, and 43 stolen bases. His father, Sandy, is a Padre coach, and his brother, Sandy, Jr., is a prospect at catcher.

Alomar's 1989 cards will sell for about 50 cents. They figure to appreciate nicely. Our pick for his best 1989 card is Topps.

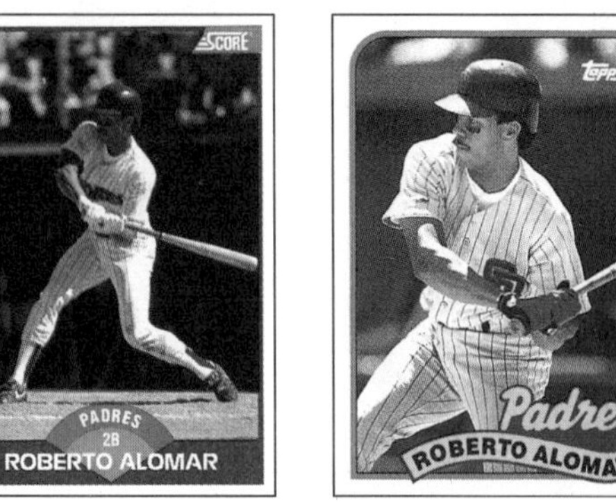

SANDY ALOMAR

	BA	G	AB	R	H	2B	3B	HR	RBI	SB
1988	.000	1	1	0	0	0	0	0	0	0
Life	.000	1	1	0	0	0	0	0	0	0

POSITION: Catcher
TEAM: San Diego Padres
BORN: June 18, 1966 Salinas, Puerto Rico
HEIGHT: 6′5″ **WEIGHT:** 200 lbs.
BATS: Right **THROWS:** Right
ACQUIRED: Signed as a free agent, 2/83

Rated as the top big league prospect in the Pacific Coast League in 1988 by *Baseball America,* Alomar suffered a knee injury late in the season, precluding a preview glimpse of him in a San Diego uniform. The rifle-armed catcher already has other major league teams beating a path to the Padre front office in hopes of a trade. And no wonder: Alomar just came off his best pro season, batting .297, with 16 home runs and 71 RBIs. His brother, Roberto, is the Padre second baseman. The best part is that Sandy is only 22 years old. In 1987, he hit .307 at Double-A Wichita. Alomar could help make the Padres a surprise contender.

Alomar could be the hottest rookie of 1989, and his cards will open at $1 or more. If he lives up to his potential, that price could double. Our pick for his best 1989 card is Donruss.

JOSE ALVAREZ

	W	L	ERA	G	SV	IP	H	R	BB	SO
1988	5	6	2.99	60	3	102.1	88	34	53	81
Life	5	6	3.04	68	3	112.0	96	38	55	87

POSITION: Pitcher
TEAM: Atlanta Braves
BORN: April 12, 1956 Tampa, FL
HEIGHT: 5′11″ **WEIGHT:** 175 lbs.
BATS: Right **THROWS:** Right
ACQUIRED: Signed as a free agent, 8/86

One of the biggest surprises of the 1988 season for the Braves had to be relief pitcher Jose Alvarez. Alvarez was a 32-year-old rookie with only eight games of major league experience. He proceeded to pitch in 60 contests, finishing 23 of them. Alvarez delivered a 2.99 ERA, the best on the square for full-time pitchers. His strikeout total was among the best for N.L. relievers. Alvarez was drafted originally by the Braves in the early 1980s, then released. Somehow, he failed to stick with three other major league teams. Despite his late start, Alvarez could be the best news the Braves bullpen will have in 1989.

Alvarez could be a real workhorse for the Braves in 1989. Expect his cards to be about a nickel, but don't buy until Alvarez can repeat his success this season. Our pick for his best 1989 card is Topps.

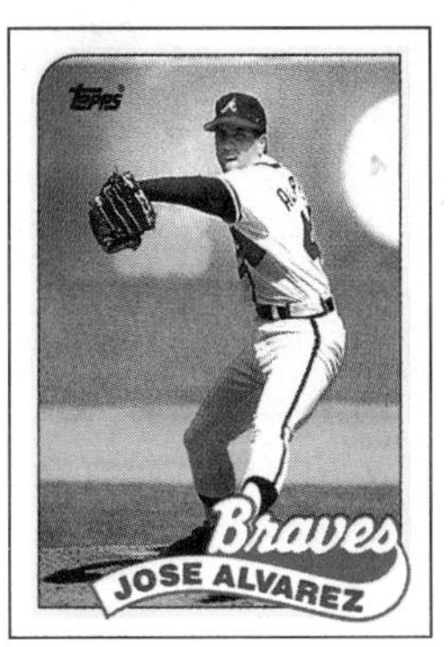

LARRY ANDERSEN

	W	L	ERA	G	SV	IP	H	R	BB	SO
1988	2	4	2.94	53	5	82.2	82	27	20	66
Life	23	24	3.58	409	24	636.0	638	253	203	411

POSITION: Pitcher
TEAM: Houston Astros
BORN: May 6, 1953 Portland, OR
HEIGHT: 6′3″ **WEIGHT:** 205 lbs.
BATS: Right **THROWS:** Right
ACQUIRED: Signed as a free agent, 5/86

Andersen maintained his status as one of the Houston Astros' top middle relievers in 1988. Andersen finished 25 of the 53 games in which he appeared in 1988, the third best on the team. His ERA remained below three, and his win-loss mark was on the negative side for only the second time in his major league career. In 1987, he was 9-5, all in relief, with a 3.45 ERA and five saves. Andersen has been active in professional baseball since 1971. He made his major league debut with Cleveland in 1975, and has since pitched with the Mariners and Phillies.

Middle relief men like Andersen get little acclaim. In fact, he has gotten more publicity from his colorful remarks and sense of humor. Unfortunately, the future looks bleak for anyone investing in his 1989 common-priced cards. Our pick for his best 1989 card is Donruss.

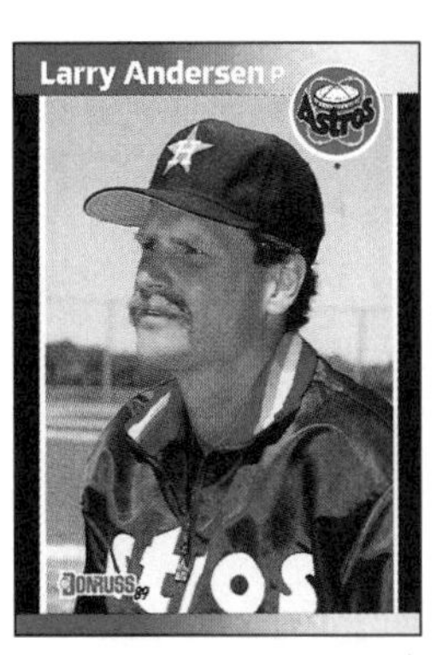

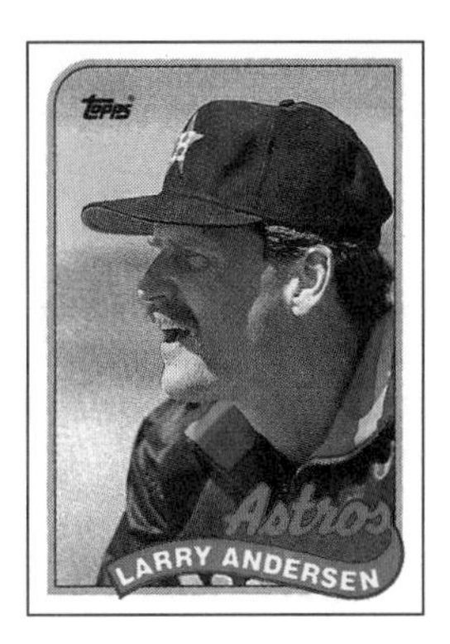

ALLAN ANDERSON

	W	L	ERA	G	CG	IP	H	R	BB	SO
1988	16	9	2.45	30	3	202.1	199	70	37	83
Life	20	15	3.67	55	4	299.0	325	139	77	137

POSITION: Pitcher
TEAM: Minnesota Twins
BORN: January 7, 1964 Lancaster, OH
HEIGHT: 5′11″ **WEIGHT:** 169 lbs.
BATS: Left **THROWS:** Left
ACQUIRED: Second-round pick in 6/82 free-agent draft

Anderson came into his own this year for the Twins. He was 16-9 with a 2.45 ERA. The lefthander also pitched 202⅓ innings, walking only 37 batters while striking out 83. His year was a turnaround from his 1987 performance. At Triple-A Portland, Anderson was 4-8 with a 5.60 ERA. He did win one game in two starts in the majors last season, but his ERA was an astronomical 10.98. At Portland in '88, he was 1-1 with a 1.26 ERA before he was called up to Minnesota for good. He should move into the number-two pitching slot behind teammate Frank Viola, giving the Twins two tough lefthanders at the top of their rotation.

Anderson's 1989 cards will be in the commons box. If you risk a buck on them, they might pay some dividends if he has a good season and the Twins climb back to the top of the A.L. West. Our pick for his best 1989 card is Topps.

BRADY ANDERSON

	BA	G	AB	R	H	2B	3B	HR	RBI	SB
1988	.212	94	325	31	69	13	4	1	21	10
Life	.212	94	325	31	69	13	4	1	21	10

POSITION: Outfield
TEAM: Baltimore Orioles
BORN: January 18, 1964 Silver Spring, MD
HEIGHT: 6′1″ **WEIGHT:** 175 lbs.
BATS: Left **THROWS:** Left
ACQUIRED: Traded from Red Sox with Curt Schiller for Mike Boddicker, 8/88

One of Boston's most highly regarded minor league prospects, Anderson was dealt to the Orioles in mid-season 1988. He reported to Baltimore and became the Orioles center fielder. Anderson batted .294 for Double-A New Britain in 1987, with six homers, seven steals, and 35 RBIs. After he was moved up to Triple-A Pawtucket, he hit .380. In 1986, Anderson played at Class-A Winter Haven, where he stole a team-high 44 bases while batting .319 in 126 tilts. Although he didn't tear up the A.L. for Baltimore, he did steal 10 bases. His batting average should improve with experience. Anderson will be one of the key blocks as the Orioles rebuild in 1989.

Anderson's 1989 cards should open in the 35-cent range. Those prices could come down if he starts slowly in '89. Our pick for his best 1989 card is Score.

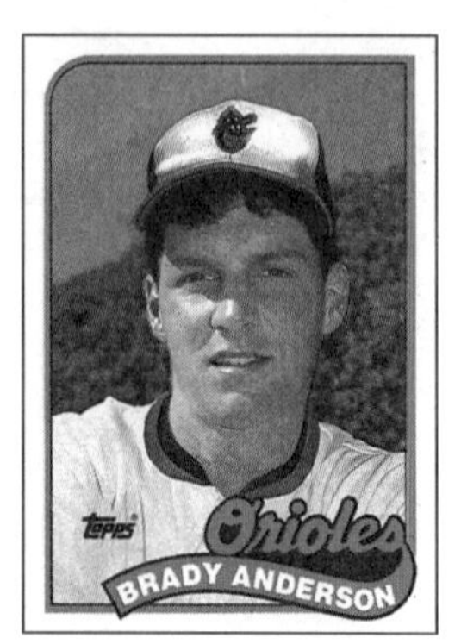

DAVE ANDERSON

	BA	G	AB	R	H	2B	3B	HR	RBI	SB
1988	.249	116	285	31	71	10	2	2	20	4
Life	.232	575	1476	181	343	57	9	12	102	44

POSITION: Infield
TEAM: Los Angeles Dodgers
BORN: August 1, 1960 Louisville, KY
HEIGHT: 6′2″ **WEIGHT:** 184 lbs.
BATS: Right **THROWS:** Right
ACQUIRED: First-round pick in 6/81 free-agent draft

Anderson was a valuable asset to the 1988 Dodgers when shortstop Alfredo Griffin was injured. A utility infielder since 1983, he had a fine offensive year at the plate, hitting .249 in limited duty. His average was the highest since 1984, his first full year with the team. That season, he hit .251 and looked like a possible starter. Anderson, an able performer at second base, shortstop, or third, made only five errors all season long. He has been plagued by chronic back problems throughout his career, which has limited his playing time. If he's back at full strength in 1989, Anderson will be sure to see lots more playing time.

Nonstarters like Anderson don't make good investment prospects. His 1989 cards will be priced at three cents or less. Besides, Anderson's frequent injuries might end his career prematurely. Our pick for his best 1989 card is Score.

LUIS AQUINO

	W	L	ERA	G	CG	IP	H	R	BB	SO
1988	1	0	2.79	7	1	29.0	33	15	17	11
Life	2	1	3.79	14	1	40.1	47	23	20	16

POSITION: Pitcher
TEAM: Kansas City Royals
BORN: May 19, 1964 Santurce, Puerto Rico
HEIGHT: 6′ **WEIGHT:** 155 lbs.
BATS: Right **THROWS:** Right
ACQUIRED: Traded from Blue Jays for Juan Beniquez, 7/87

Aquino smoked opponents at Triple-A Omaha in 1988, and the Royals hope that he can do the same in the big leagues in 1989. He won eight games in 16 starts with Omaha, with three losses. He compiled a 2.85 ERA, had 93 strikeouts, and gave up 50 bases on balls in 129 innings. After a late-season call-up, Aquino was 1-0, with a 2.79 ERA for the Royals. In 1986, he played briefly for the Blue Jays, going 1-1 with a 6.35 ERA, all in relief. He will have to work hard to crack the tough Kansas City rotation in 1989. But Aquino could give the Royals a long-relief man and part-time starter.

Aquino's 1989 cards should open in the 5- to 15-cent range. Wait to see if he can pitch consistently on the major league level before buying. Our pick for his best 1989 card is Topps.

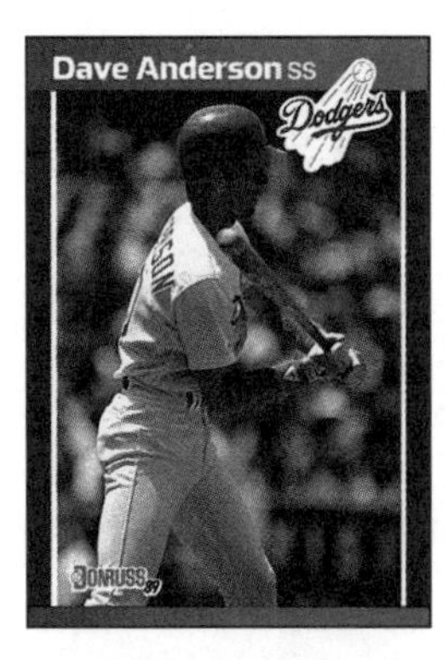

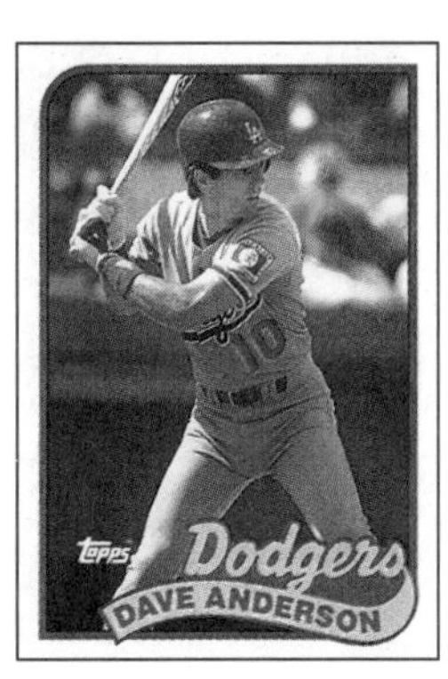

TONY ARMAS

	BA	G	AB	R	H	2B	3B	HR	RBI	SB
1988	.272	120	368	42	100	20	2	13	49	1
Life	.252	1372	4962	592	1250	197	38	240	785	18

POSITION: Designated hitter
TEAM: California Angels
BORN: July 2, 1953 Anzoatequi, Venezuela
HEIGHT: 6′1″ **WEIGHT:** 224 lbs.
BATS: Right **THROWS:** Right
ACQUIRED: Signed as a free agent, 7/87

Armas was just a part-time player for the 1988 California Angels, but he was one of their best hitters. Armas had one of his best power-producing seasons since his time with the Red Sox in 1985, and his .272 average was his best since 1980. Armas was a feared power hitter in the early '80s before he was hobbled by leg injuries. He hit more than 20 home runs from 1980 to 1985, with his biggest season coming in 1984 (.268, 43 homers, and 123 RBIs). He also has three previous 100-RBI seasons to his credit. Don't expect him to be a starter in 1989, but expect him to be popping a few more homers for the Angels.

Armas' career stats aren't that stunning when averaged over 13 seasons. Look for his cards at a nickel apiece in 1989. With the Angels youth movement, his playing time should decrease. Our pick for his best 1989 card is Topps.

JACK ARMSTRONG

	W	L	ERA	G	CG	IP	H	R	BB	SO
1988	4	7	5.79	14	0	65.1	63	44	38	45
Life	4	7	5.79	14	0	65.1	63	44	38	45

POSITION: Pitcher
TEAM: Cincinnati Reds
BORN: March 7, 1965 Neptune, NJ
HEIGHT: 6′5″ **WEIGHT:** 210 lbs.
BATS: Right **THROWS:** Right
ACQUIRED: First-round pick in 6/87 free-agent draft

It's difficult not to call Armstrong "The All-American Boy" after the radio hero of the same name. Physically, he's hero size, and he has the credentials for stardom. At Nashville in 1988, Armstrong split ten decisions in 120 innings, striking out 116. The Reds were anxious to get a first-hand look at him, and he finished the season in Cincinnati. He showed flashes of what was to come, including a late season two-hit shutout. He pitched at Billings in '87, where the righty went 2-1 with a 2.66 ERA. Promoted to Double-A Vermont that year, he went 2-1 with a 3.03 ERA. Armstrong seems destined to be a part of the Cincinnati starting rotation in 1989.

Armstrong's 1989 cards will open in the 25- to 40-cent range. Wait to see if he can whittle down his ERA before buying. Our pick for his best 1989 card is Score.

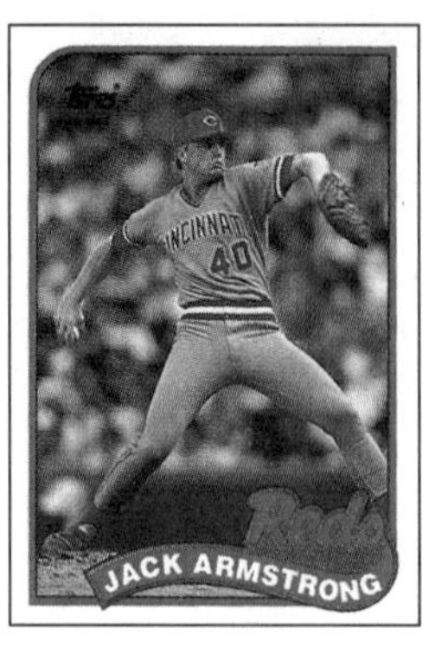

ALAN ASHBY

	BA	G	AB	R	H	2B	3B	HR	RBI	SB
1988	.238	73	227	19	54	10	0	7	33	0
Life	.246	1348	4062	393	1000	182	12	90	510	7

POSITION: Catcher
TEAM: Houston Astros
BORN: July 8, 1951 Long Beach, CA
HEIGHT: 6'2" **WEIGHT:** 195 lbs.
BATS: Both **THROWS:** Right
ACQUIRED: Traded from Blue Jays for Joe Cannon, Pedro Hernandez, and Mark Lemongello, 11/78

Ashby shared the catching duties with Alex Trevino for the 1988 Houston Astros. Ashby, who spent his tenth season with Houston in 1988, saw a real drop in offensive productivity compared to last year. In 1987, he played in 125 games, hitting 14 homers and 63 RBIs, both personal highs. One highlight in Ashby's career is catching three no-hitters while with the Astros. His pro career began in 1969, and his first major league experience was in 1973 with the Cleveland Indians. He played in Toronto in 1977 and 1978 before becoming a fixture in Houston. Although he has never put up great numbers, Ashby has been a dependable backstop for the Astros, and he has a good arm.

Ashby might be a platoon catcher in 1989. If he is, it will sap the investment potential from his 1989 cards, which will sell at a nickel or less. Our pick for his best 1989 card is Topps.

PAUL ASSENMACHER

	W	L	ERA	G	SV	IP	H	R	BB	SO
1988	8	7	3.06	64	5	79.1	72	27	32	71
Life	16	11	3.43	177	16	202.1	191	77	82	166

POSITION: Pitcher
TEAM: Atlanta Braves
BORN: December 10, 1960 Detroit, MI
HEIGHT: 6'3" **WEIGHT:** 195 lbs.
BATS: Left **THROWS:** Left
ACQUIRED: Signed as a free agent, 7/83

Assenmacher rebounded from shoulder problems and ineffectiveness to enjoy one of his best seasons ever with the 1988 Braves. He set career highs in wins (eight), appearances (64), and strikeouts (71). He is Atlanta's top lefty in the bullpen. In 1987, Assenmacher only earned two saves and one win. His first season with Atlanta, 1986, was one of his most memorable. He went 7-3 with seven saves in 61 games. His ERA (2.50) was third-best among league relievers that year, trailing only Todd Worrell and Jesse Orosco. Assenmacher is one of the Braves' brightest hopes on a sometimes mysterious pitching staff.

Assenmacher's 1989 cards will be a nickel or less. His success is even more impressive, considering the Braves' poor record during the last few years. His cards are a worthwhile investment. Our pick for his best 1989 card is Fleer.

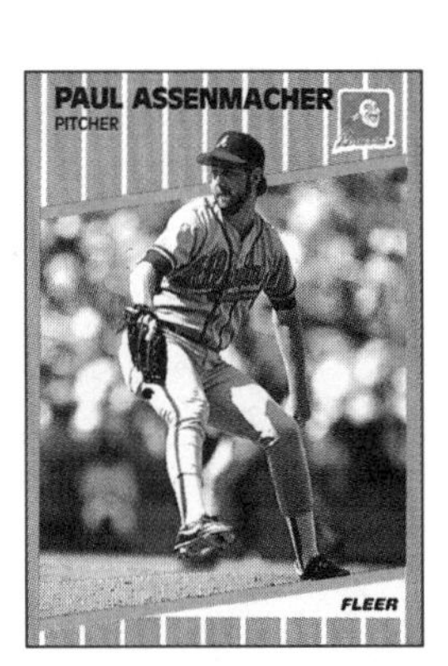

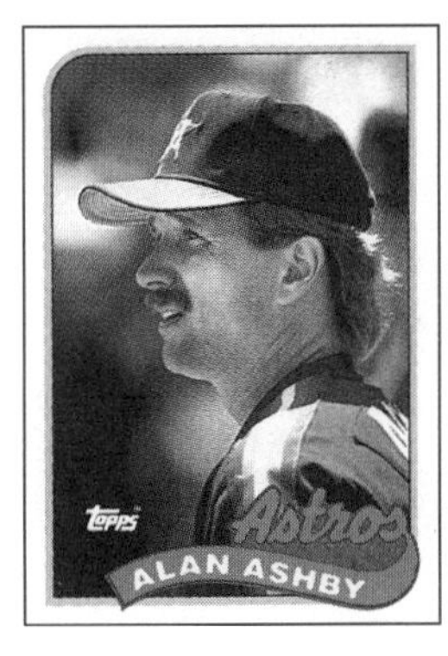

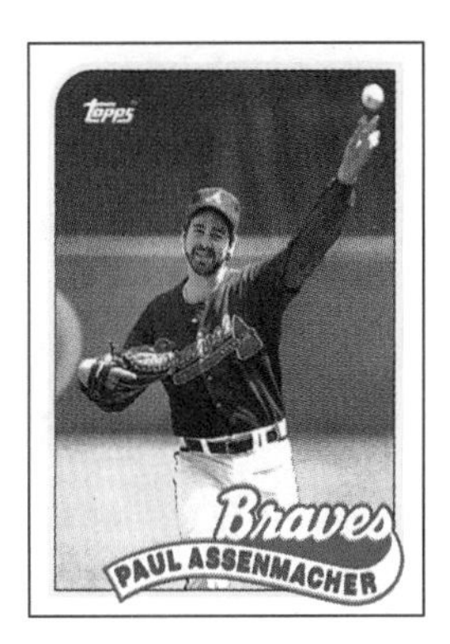

KEITH ATHERTON

	W	L	ERA	G	SV	IP	H	R	BB	SO
1988	7	5	3.41	49	3	74.0	65	29	22	43
Life	33	38	3.98	310	24	527.1	498	246	202	336

POSITION: Pitcher
TEAM: Minnesota Twins
BORN: February 19, 1959 Mathews, VA
HEIGHT: 6′4″ **WEIGHT:** 200 lbs.
BATS: Right **THROWS:** Right
ACQUIRED: Traded from A's for Eric Broersma, 5/86

Even though he appeared in ten fewer games than last season, Atherton nearly duplicated his 1987 season for last year's Minnesota Twins. In both 1987 and 1988, Atherton attained identical 7-5 records. He lowered his ERA by more than a point in 1988, and he saved three games as opposed to two in 1987. He made 49 appearances in 1988, pitching 74 innings. Atherton is a durable hurler. The last time he appeared in less than 50 games was his 29-game debut with the Oakland Athletics in 1983. Atherton is an able set-up man, but he gets overshadowed by the work of team stopper Jeff Reardon.

Atherton's cards are commons, selling for a nickel or less. Middle relievers seldom achieve much acclaim, so Atherton's cards would be unlikely choices for investment purposes. Our pick for his best 1989 card is Donruss.

DON AUGUST

	W	L	ERA	G	CG	IP	H	R	BB	SO
1988	13	7	3.09	24	6	148.1	137	55	48	66
Life	13	7	3.09	24	6	148.1	137	55	48	66

POSITION: Pitcher
TEAM: Milwaukee Brewers
BORN: July 3, 1963 Mission Viejo, CA
HEIGHT: 6′3″ **WEIGHT:** 190 lbs.
BATS: Right **THROWS:** Right
ACQUIRED: Traded from Astros with Mark Knudson for Danny Darwin, 8/86

Another member of the talented 1984 U.S. Olympic baseball team, August made it to the majors in 1988. His performance was a key factor for the resurgent Brewers. His 13 wins were tied for second highest among the club's starters, and he had a 3.09 ERA. August is not a power pitcher, but his control is excellent. He gave up only 48 bases on balls in 148⅓ innings of work in '88, while striking out 66 batters. He was 10-9 in 1987 at Triple-A Denver, with 91 strikeouts in 179 innings. He split the 1986 season between Tucson and Vancouver, with a combined record of 10-11. August should give the Brew Crew 150-plus quality innings a year for seasons to come.

August's 1989 cards will sell in the 20-cent range. Be prudent at that price. Our pick for his best 1989 card is Topps.

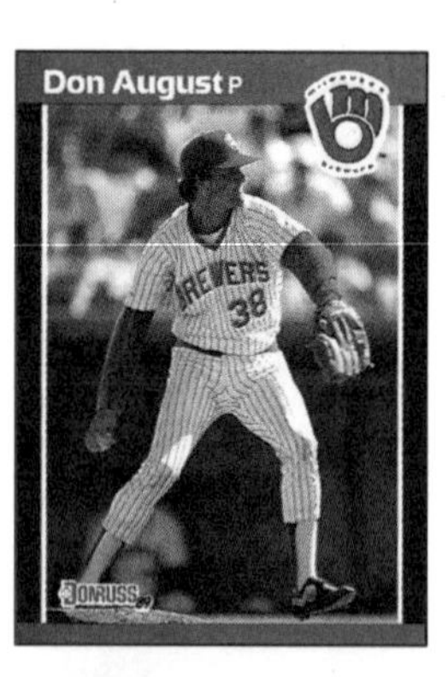

WALLY BACKMAN

	BA	G	AB	R	H	2B	3B	HR	RBI	SB
1988	.303	99	294	44	89	12	0	0	17	9
Life	.283	765	2369	359	670	95	14	7	165	106

POSITION: Second base
TEAM: Minnesota Twins
BORN: September 22, 1959
Hillsboro, OR
HEIGHT: 5′9″ **WEIGHT:** 160 lbs.
BATS: Both **THROWS:** Right
ACQUIRED: Traded from Mets with Mike Santiago for Jeff Baumgartner, Toby Nivens, and Steve Gasser, 12/88

Backman will get a fresh start with Minnesota. Formerly one half of the Mets' second base platoon, he had been battling Tim Teufel for playing time for the past three years. In 1988, Backman saw action in 99 games and batted .303. In 1987, he appeared in 94 contests and hit just .250. What had frustrated him was that in his last season as a full-timer, 1986, he batted .320 in 124 games. His lack of power kept him out of the Mets lineup; his career home run total, dating back to 1980, is seven. He hit .333 in the 1986 World Series for New York. Now that Backman is playing for the Twins, he should be considered a vital part of the roster.

Backman's cards are in the commons box along with all the other utility infielders. There's a chance of their appreciating in value. Our pick for his best 1989 card is Topps.

SCOTT BAILES

	W	L	ERA	G	SV	IP	H	R	BB	SO
1988	9	14	4.90	37	0	145.0	149	79	46	53
Life	26	32	4.83	138	13	378.0	417	203	136	178

POSITION: Pitcher
TEAM: Cleveland Indians
BORN: December 18, 1961
Chillicothe, OH
HEIGHT: 6′2″ **WEIGHT:** 175 lbs.
BATS: Left **THROWS:** Left
ACQUIRED: Traded from Pirates for John LeMaster, 7/85

The Cleveland Indians didn't know what to do with Bailes in 1988; sometimes he was used as a starter, and other times he appeared as a reliever. His 9-14 record is evidence of that bouncing around. Bailes made his Cleveland debut in 1986, and he finished the year with a respectable 10-10 mark with seven saves. Even though Bailes has a lifetime losing record, those outcomes may have been reversed if he had pitched for a contending team. Once the Indians define his role, Bailes may be one of the finest pitchers on the team.

Bailes will have modest statistics as long as he's bounced back and forth between the bullpen and the starting rotation. Until he has a winning record in either capacity, avoid investing in his common-priced cards. Our pick for his best 1989 card is Topps.

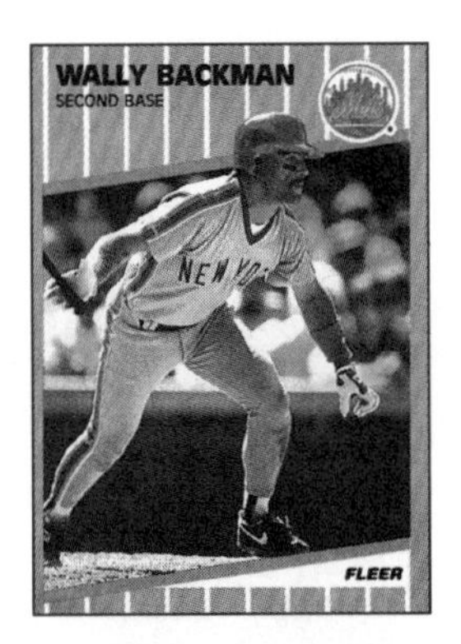

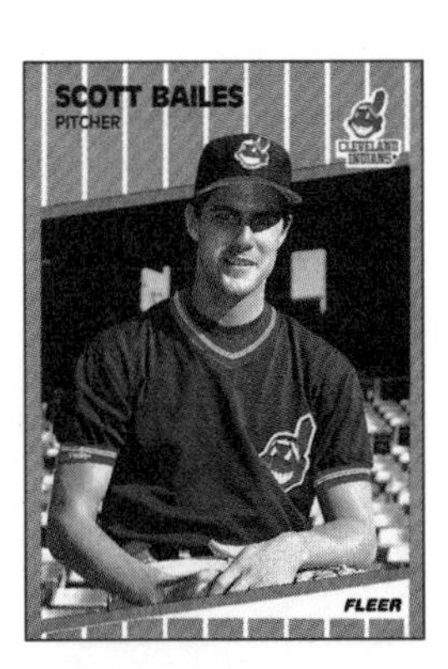

HAROLD BAINES

	BA	G	AB	R	H	2B	3B	HR	RBI	SB
1988	.277	158	599	55	166	39	1	13	81	0
Life	.286	1282	4858	606	1391	247	43	173	763	90

POSITION: Outfield; designated hitter
TEAM: Chicago White Sox
BORN: March 15, 1959 Easton, MD
HEIGHT: 6′2″ **WEIGHT:** 195 lbs.
BATS: Left **THROWS:** Left
ACQUIRED: First-round pick in 6/77 free-agent draft

Baines suffered through slumps with the rest of the Chicago White Sox in 1988, but he remained the team's best all-around player. A veteran club leader now entering his tenth big league season, Baines supplied the Sox with some offensive sock last year. He led the team in games played (158), average (.277), hits (166), doubles (39), and RBIs (81). The speedy fly-catcher was one of the A.L.'s finest outfielders in 1988, making only two errors all season. You can be sure that if the White Sox ever contend for a pennant, the many talents of Harold Baines will spark the process.

Baines' cards will be 10 cents or less in 1989. At that price, they're wise investments that should bring immediate payoffs, especially if Baines helps the Sox return to the .500 level. Our pick for his best 1989 card is Score.

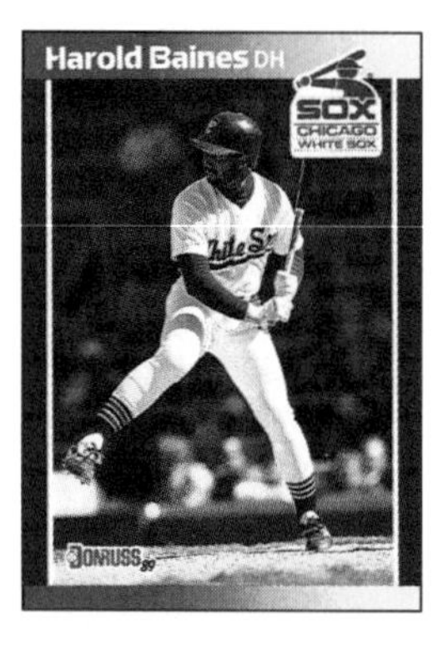

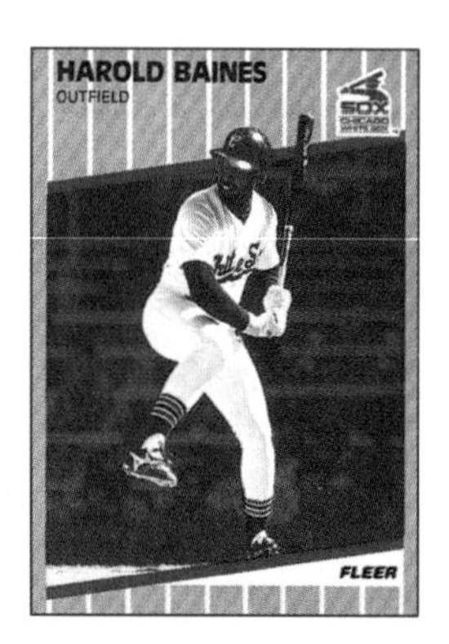

JEFF BALLARD

	W	L	ERA	G	CG	IP	H	R	BB	SO
1988	8	12	4.40	25	6	153.1	167	75	42	41
Life	10	20	5.01	39	6	223.0	267	126	77	68

POSITION: Pitcher
TEAM: Baltimore Orioles
BORN: August 13, 1963 Billings, MT
HEIGHT: 6′2″ **WEIGHT:** 205 lbs.
BATS: Left **THROWS:** Left
ACQUIRED: Fourth-round pick in 6/85 free-agent draft

Ballard was a nonroster player when he was invited to the Orioles' 1988 spring training camp. His preseason performance earned him a spot on the parent club, and he went on to tie teammate Dave Schmidt for the team's lead with eight wins. Ballard's modest record doesn't reflect his six complete games or one shutout. In addition, remember that Ballard and nine of his teammates had losing records on the last-place Orioles. Ballard, a big lefty who throws a fastball, curve, slider, and forkball, could become a mainstay for the Orioles if he can curtail the number of walks he surrenders.

Ballard's 1989 cards will sell as commons. He could be a consistent winner if the Orioles get back on track in 1989. Pick up a few of his cards at a nickel or less. You might be surprised with the results. Our pick for his best 1989 card is Donruss.

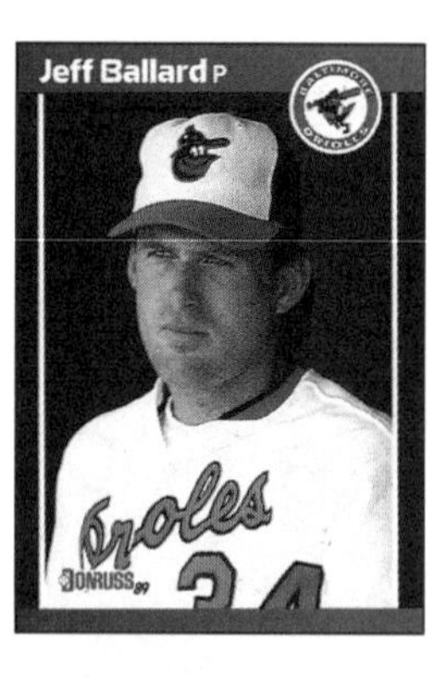

SCOTT BANKHEAD

	W	L	ERA	G	CG	IP	H	R	BB	SO
1988	7	9	3.07	21	2	135.0	115	29	43	76
Life	24	26	4.02	72	4	405.1	404	181	117	196

POSITION: Pitcher
TEAM: Seattle Mariners
BORN: July 31, 1963 Raleigh, NC
HEIGHT: 5′10″ **WEIGHT:** 175 lbs.
BATS: Right **THROWS:** Right
ACQUIRED: Traded from Royals with Steve Shields and Mike Kingery for Danny Tartabull and Rick Luecken, 12/86

Mariners fans feel that Bankhead is making the Tartabull trade look better every season. Tartabull was one of the Mariners' best young power hitters who was sacrificed to obtain much-needed pitching. Bankhead is providing just that. His record isn't so bad, considering that the Mariners lost 22 one-run games. The young righty, a member of the 1984 U.S. Olympic team, won a career-high nine games in 1987. At age 25, Bankhead could be a promising member of an ever-improving Mariners staff.

The Mariners could be vastly better in 1989, and Bankhead could be one reason why. If the team scores some runs for him, he could win 20 games. Bankhead's cards are priced as commons, and they could yield some surprise dividends if the team fares well this season. Our pick for his best 1989 card is Topps.

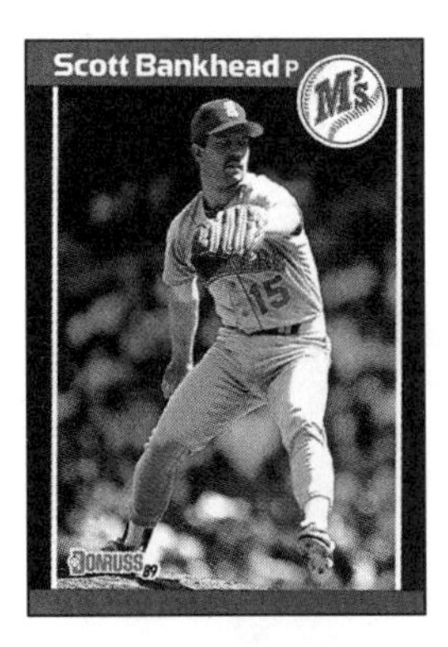

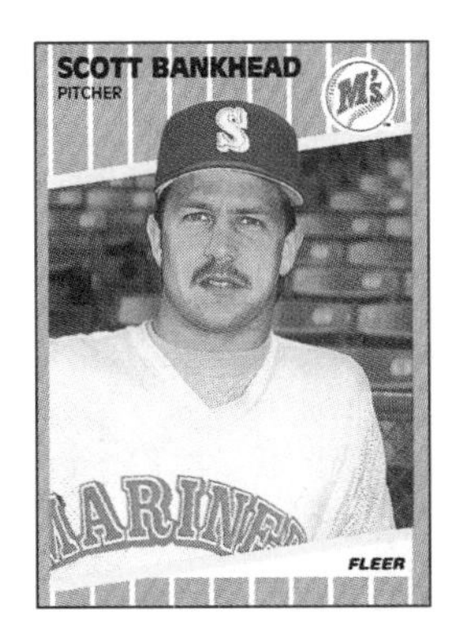

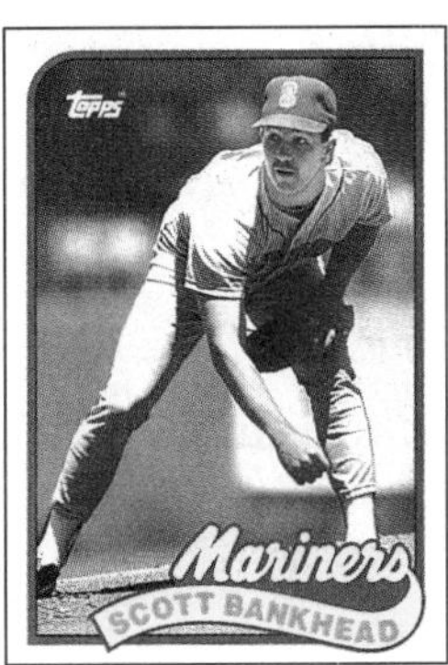

FLOYD BANNISTER

	W	L	ERA	G	CG	IP	H	R	BB	SO
1988	12	13	4.33	31	2	189.1	182	102	68	113
Life	129	141	4.01	365	62	2250.1	2169	1110	797	1642

POSITION: Pitcher
TEAM: Kansas City Royals
BORN: June 10, 1958 Pierre, SD
HEIGHT: 6′1″ **WEIGHT:** 202 lbs.
BATS: Left **THROWS:** Left
ACQUIRED: Traded from White Sox with Dave Cochrane for Melido Perez, John Davis, Chuck Mount, and Greg Hibbard, 12/87

Bannister became the fourth starter the 1988 Royals needed so badly. He went 12-13 with Kansas City, with a modest 113 strikeouts. That is quite a change from his 1982 season, when he led the A.L. with 209 Ks. Last season could have just been a one-year slump that comes from adjusting to a new team. Since he began his career, Bannister has been recognized as a hard thrower. Unfortunately, he's never been the consistent winner people expected, winning 16 games only twice in his career. Maybe playing with the Royals, a yearly contender, will be a boost for Bannister in 1989.

Bannister's 1989 cards will sell for a nickel or less. The low price makes Bannister's cards an attractive gamble. Speculators should be prepared to sell quick for small, guaranteed returns. Our pick for his best 1989 card is Topps.

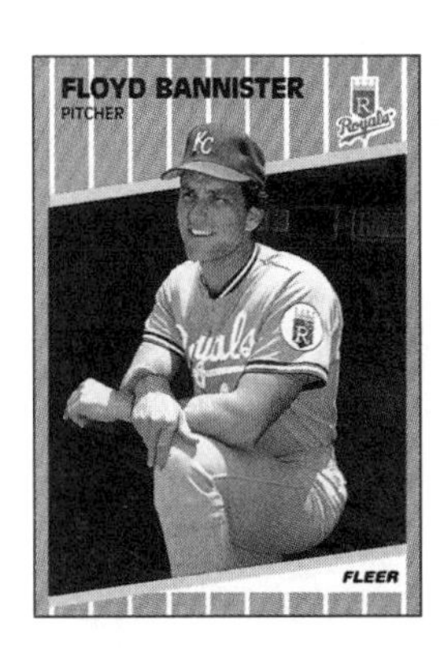

JESSE BARFIELD

	BA	G	AB	R	H	2B	3B	HR	RBI	SB
1988	.244	136	468	62	114	21	5	18	56	7
Life	.266	1010	3383	522	903	158	27	174	516	55

POSITION: Outfield
TEAM: Toronto Blue Jays
BORN: October 26, 1959 Joliet, IL
HEIGHT: 6′1″ **WEIGHT:** 200 lbs.
BATS: Right **THROWS:** Right
ACQUIRED: Ninth-round pick in 6/77 free-agent draft

Barfield had his worst season in the last four years for the 1988 Blue Jays. The veteran outfielder had 18 homers, 56 RBIs, and a .244 average, which is respectable in most circles. However, Barfield hadn't been below 20 homers or a .250 average since 1984. Big things were expected from Barfield following his stellar 1986 campaign. Barfield won his first American League home run crown with 40 round-trippers. He also had 108 RBIs and a .289 average. His totals dipped slightly to 28 homers and 84 RBIs in 1987. Expect a big comeback from the 29-year-old slugger in 1989.

Card investors can profit from Barfield's slump. His 1989 cards might be as low as a dime—a great investing price. Barfield has another decade of play ahead of him, and he'll have several good seasons on tap. Our pick for his best 1989 card is Topps.

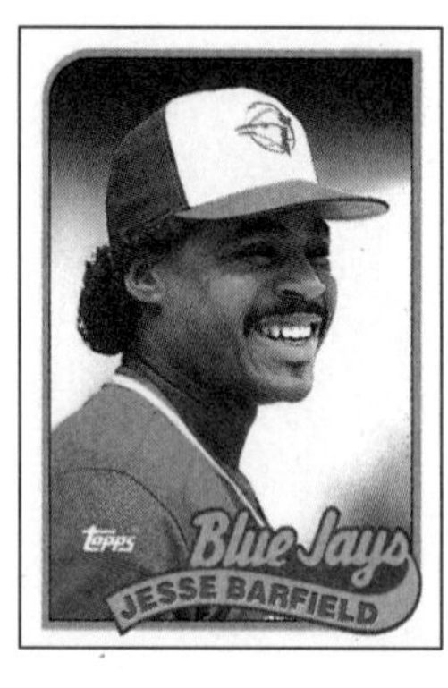

MARTY BARRETT

	BA	G	AB	R	H	2B	3B	HR	RBI	SB
1988	.283	150	612	83	173	28	1	1	65	7
Life	.283	781	2867	371	813	140	9	16	271	48

POSITION: Second base
TEAM: Boston Red Sox
BORN: June 23, 1958 Arcadia, CA
HEIGHT: 5′10″ **WEIGHT:** 175 lbs.
BATS: Right **THROWS:** Right
ACQUIRED: Signed as a free agent, 6/79

Barrett enjoyed one of his most productive seasons with the 1988 pennant-winning Red Sox. He only missed 12 games, and he drove in 65 runs, his most ever. Barrett's .283 average matched that of the whole Red Sox team combined, which led the American League. Barrett is a competent fielder, too. In 1988, he made just seven errors. In his five seasons as Boston's starting second baseman, he has proven his worth as one of the team's most consistent clutch players. Barrett will be a major contributor in the Red Sox' 1989 pennant defense.

Barrett may get overlooked playing with stars like Wade Boggs. Barrett's 1989 cards are bargains at less than a nickel. Those prices could double if he hits .300 and the Red Sox repeat. Our pick for his best 1989 card is Fleer.

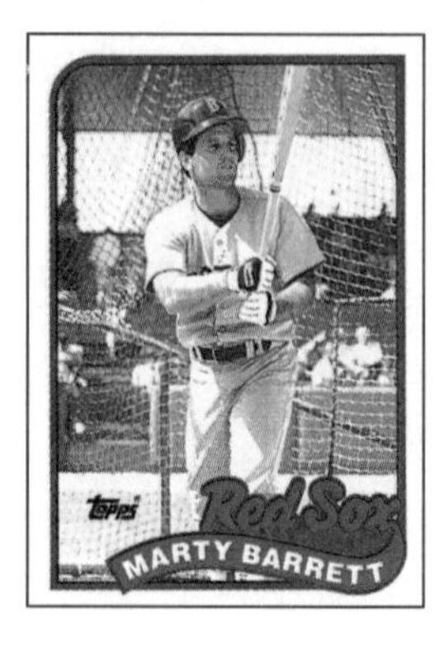

KEVIN BASS

	BA	G	AB	R	H	2B	3B	HR	RBI	SB
1988	.255	157	541	57	138	27	2	14	72	31
Life	.272	860	2822	359	768	142	25	73	352	100

POSITION: Outfield
TEAM: Houston Astros
BORN: May 12, 1959 Redwood City, CA
HEIGHT: 6′ **WEIGHT:** 180 lbs.
BATS: Both **THROWS:** Right
ACQUIRED: Traded from Brewers with Frank DiPino and Mike Madden for Don Sutton, 8/82

Kevin Bass continued to be one of the Astros' most consistent power hitters in 1988. Bass didn't match his 1987 total of 19 homers, but he swatted 14 round-trippers, second only to Glenn Davis. Bass has 59 homers in the past four seasons. His average dipped a bit to .255, but he maintained his RBI production again in 1988. He has had at least 65 RBIs for four consecutive years. He preserved his reputation as a slick fielder, making only six miscues in 157 games. Bass is an underrated star who does his job quietly but consistently.

Expect 1989 cards of Bass to be a nickel or less. Bass could break loose with a power explosion in 1989 and drive in 100-plus runs. If so, his card values would soar. Our pick for his best 1989 card is Topps.

JOSE BAUTISTA

	W	L	ERA	G	CG	IP	H	R	BB	SO
1988	6	15	4.30	33	3	171.2	171	82	45	76
Life	6	15	4.30	33	3	171.2	171	82	45	76

POSITION: Pitcher
TEAM: Baltimore Orioles
BORN: July 24, 1964 Bani, Dominican Republic
HEIGHT: 6′2″ **WEIGHT:** 195 lbs.
BATS: Right **THROWS:** Right
ACQUIRED: Drafted from Mets, 12/87

After languishing for seven years in the Mets' minor league system (never higher than Double-A), Bautista made a lasting impression on the 1988 Baltimore Orioles, leading the team in innings pitched. His six victories may seem small by some standards, until one remembers that the most wins for any Orioles pitcher last season was eight. Bautista also contributed three of the staff's 16 complete games. The Orioles had great respect for Bautista because he was the first player the team had claimed in the major league draft since 1977. He'll get the chance to improve in 1989.

Even though Bautista is just 24 years old, he's been playing professional baseball since 1981. Don't invest in his commons cards until he posts a complete winning season in the majors. Our pick for his best 1989 card is Donruss.

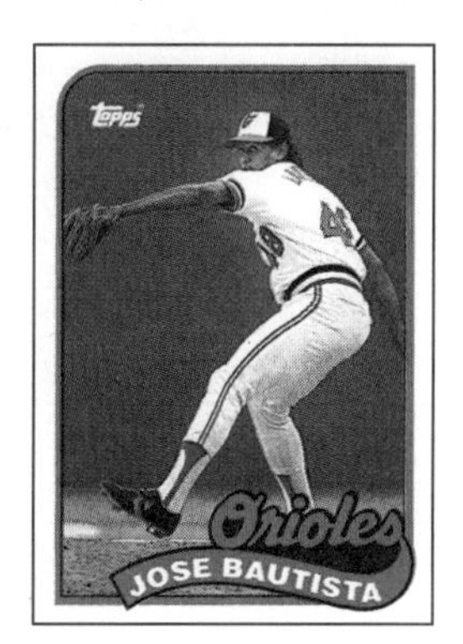

DON BAYLOR

	BA	G	AB	R	H	2B	3B	HR	RBI	SB
1988	.220	92	264	28	58	7	0	7	34	0
Life	.260	2292	8198	1230	2135	366	28	338	1276	285

POSITION: Designated hitter
TEAM: Oakland A's
BORN: June 28, 1949 Austin, TX
HEIGHT: 6'1" **WEIGHT:** 210 lbs.
BATS: Right **THROWS:** Right
ACQUIRED: Signed as a free agent, 2/88

Baylor is one of baseball's good luck charms. In the past three seasons, he has been with three teams: Boston (1986), Minnesota (1987), and Oakland (1988). Each year his teams have gone to the World Series, which should say something about his positive influence. Baylor was only a part-time player in 1988, but he still whacked seven homers and 34 RBIs. Baylor helps his clubs any way he can. He's baseball's active hit-by-pitch leader. In his career, Baylor has been more than just a good player. He's been a team player.

Baylor's 1989 cards might be his last. Expect them to sell for a nickel or less. Considering that Baylor is at best a long shot for the Hall of Fame, his cards have little hope for short-term gains. Our pick for his best 1989 card is Topps.

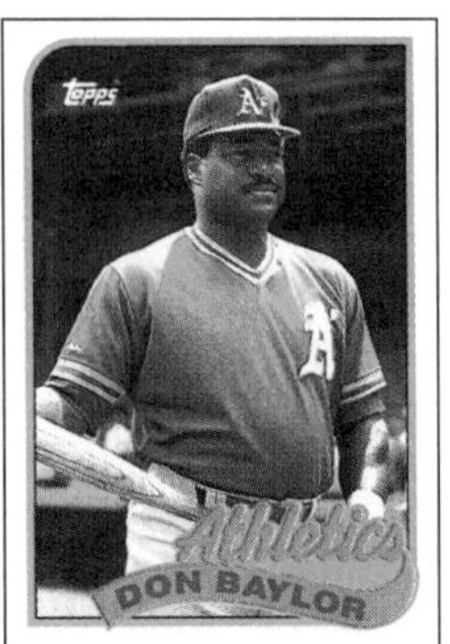

STEVE BEDROSIAN

	W	L	ERA	G	SV	IP	H	R	BB	SO
1988	6	6	3.75	57	28	74.1	75	34	27	61
Life	53	54	3.27	416	138	825.2	713	331	356	678

POSITION: Pitcher
TEAM: Philadelphia Phillies
BORN: December 6, 1957 Methuen, MA
HEIGHT: 6'3" **WEIGHT:** 195 lbs.
BATS: Right **THROWS:** Right
ACQUIRED: Traded from Braves with Milt Thompson for Ozzie Virgil and Pete Smith, 12/85

Bedrosian, the 1987 National League Cy Young winner, backed up his dream season with another admirable outing in 1988. The righty recorded 28 saves and had a 3.75 ERA. Although the Phillies remained stuck in last place most of the season, Bedrosian kept pitching with gusto. He was the only member of the Phillies bullpen to have double figures in saves. Bedrosian was a record-setter when it came to converting consecutive save opportunities. In 1987, his Cy Young year, he recorded 40 saves while registering a 2.83 ERA. At age 31, he could be an N.L. relief star for the next decade.

Bedrosian's 1989 cards should be available for less than 10 cents each. Many relievers have self-destructed from overwork, so investing in their cards can be risky. Invest a few dollars in low-priced Bedrosian cards, then sell when he reaches the quarter mark. Our pick for his best 1989 card is Score.

TIM BELCHER

	W	L	ERA	G	CG	IP	H	GS	BB	SO
1988	12	6	2.91	36	4	179.2	143	27	51	152
Life	16	8	2.82	42	4	213.2	173	32	58	175

POSITION: Pitcher
TEAM: Los Angeles Dodgers
BORN: October 19, 1961 Mt. Gilead, OH
HEIGHT: 6'3" **WEIGHT:** 210 lbs.
BATS: Right **THROWS:** Right
ACQUIRED: Traded from A's for Rick Honeycutt, 8/87

Acquired by L.A. late in 1987 in a trade for Rick Honeycutt, Belcher pitched his way into the starting rotation in 1988. He won 12 games in 1988 for the world champion Dodgers, kept his ERA under 3.00, and had more than 150 Ks. He was named the N.L.'s top rookie pitcher by *The Sporting News.* In 1987, after going 9-11 with Triple-A Tacoma, he was 4-2 with a 2.38 ERA for the Dodgers. The A's first signed Belcher away from the Yankees in 1984 in a free-agent deal. Twice he was a number-one draft choice: first in 1983, picked by the Twins; then in 1984, picked by the Yankees. The righty was an 11-game winner for the A's Huntsville club in 1985.

Belcher's 1989 cards will open in the 15- to 20-cent range. Wait to see if he repeats his '88 stats before stocking up. Our pick for his best 1989 card is Topps.

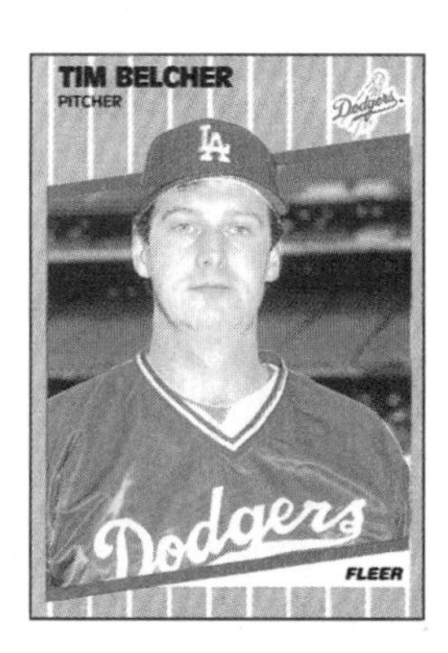

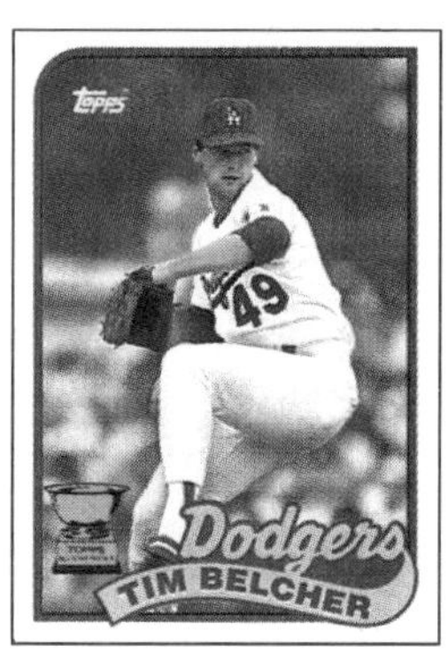

BUDDY BELL

	BA	G	AB	R	H	2B	3B	HR	RBI	SB
1988	.241	95	323	27	78	10	1	7	40	1
Life	.280	2371	8913	1147	2499	421	56	201	1103	55

POSITION: Third base
TEAM: Houston Astros
BORN: August 27, 1951 Pittsburgh, PA
HEIGHT: 6'2" **WEIGHT:** 200 lbs.
BATS: Right **THROWS:** Right
ACQUIRED: Traded from Reds, 6/88

Bell was a popular addition to the 1988 Houston Astros. After he stopped Houston's revolving door at third base, this talented veteran gave stability to the infield. Bell, a fine fielder and contact hitter, was active in 95 games in 1988. His .241 average was way below his normal average, usually in the .270s. He spent the early years of his career with the Texas Rangers and the Cleveland Indians before joining the Reds in mid-1985. In 1986, Bell responded with 20 homers, 75 RBIs, and a .278 average. Bell should be a great boost to the 1989 Astros simply by playing there a full season.

Bell's 1989 cards will be a nickel or less. Bell could be only four seasons away from 3,000 hits, which makes his cards good long-term investments. Our pick for his best 1989 card is Topps.

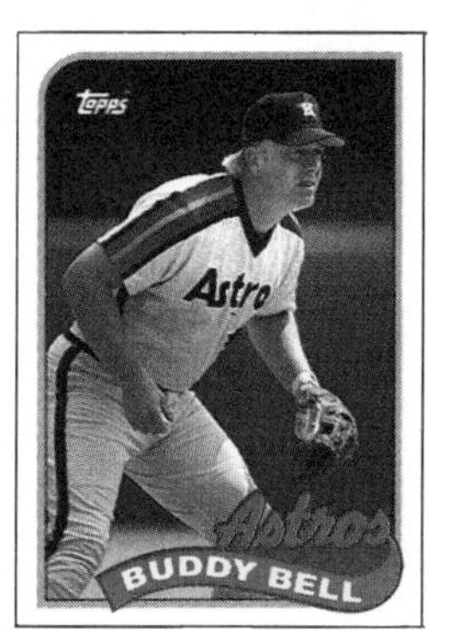

GEORGE BELL

	BA	G	AB	R	H	2B	3B	HR	RBI	SB
1988	.269	156	614	78	165	27	5	24	97	4
Life	.287	886	3353	486	963	171	30	163	550	52

POSITION: Outfield
TEAM: Toronto Blue Jays
BORN: October 21, 1959 San Pedro de Macoris, Dominican Republic
HEIGHT: 6′1″ **WEIGHT:** 190 lbs.
BATS: Right **THROWS:** Right
ACQUIRED: Drafted from Phillies, 12/80

Bell, the 1987 American League MVP, hit a tailspin in 1988. In 1987, he clobbered 47 homers and 134 RBIs, and batted .308. His '88 homer totals fell by 50 percent to 24, and his average was stuck in the .260s, while driving in 97 runs. Bell's unfortunate 1988 season would have been fine for other hitters; the entire Toronto offense slumped early in 1988. Initial turmoil brewed in Toronto early in 1988, when the team tried to make Bell a full-time designated hitter. Settling on one regular position for Bell in 1989 may help him return to his MVP form.

Due to his power slippage, Bell's 1989 cards should sell for 25 cents. That's a decent price, assuming that Bell will be a happy and healthy MVP-caliber player again in 1989. If the Blue Jays regain their winning ways, the price of his cards will spiral upward. Our pick for his best 1989 card is Topps.

JAY BELL

	BA	G	AB	R	H	2B	3B	HR	RBI	SB
1988	.218	73	211	23	46	5	1	2	21	4
Life	.222	116	350	40	78	16	2	5	38	6

POSITION: Shortstop
TEAM: Cleveland Indians
BORN: December 11, 1965 Pensacola, FL
HEIGHT: 6′1″ **WEIGHT:** 180 lbs.
BATS: Right **THROWS:** Right
ACQUIRED: Traded from Twins with Curt Wardle and Jim Weaver for Bert Blyleven, 8/85

Bell is seen as the Indian shortstop of the future, but he couldn't lock up the job based on his 1988 performance. He struck out 53 times, roughly once in every four at-bats. His fielding wasn't much better: He committed ten errors in 73 games. Bell needs to come closer to his grand debut in 1986. During a five-game trial, he had five hits in 14 at-bats for a .357 average. Bell's year-long slump could be attributed to age. Only 23, he has gotten an early start on a big league career. Bell's future will be limited, though, unless he polishes his hitting and fielding skills.

The Indians have shown interest in Bell, but he hasn't come through yet. Until he does, his cards aren't good investments, even at their current prices of a nickel or less. Our pick for his best 1989 card is Donruss.

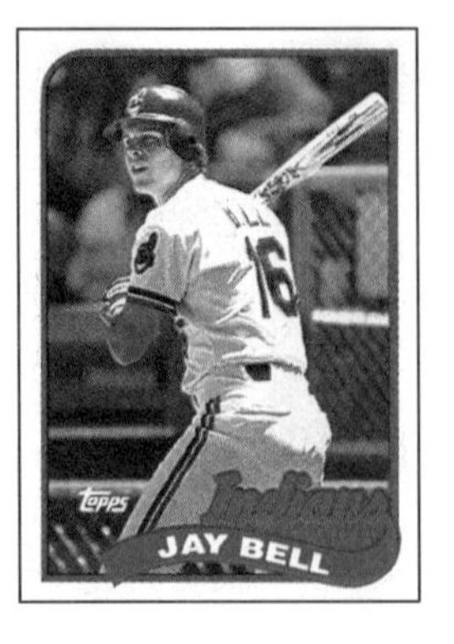

RAFAEL BELLIARD

	BA	G	AB	R	H	2B	3B	HR	RBI	SB
1988	.213	122	286	28	61	0	4	0	11	7
Life	.219	370	843	95	185	9	9	1	58	29

POSITION: Shortstop
TEAM: Pittsburgh Pirates
BORN: October 24, 1961 Puerto Nuevo Mao, Dominican Republic
HEIGHT: 5′8″ **WEIGHT:** 150 lbs.
BATS: Right **THROWS:** Right
ACQUIRED: Signed as a free agent, 7/80

Belliard hit only .213 for Pittsburgh last season, overshadowing the fact that he led N.L. shortstops in fielding (.977), the first Pirate to do so since Tim Foli did it in 1980. Belliard divided 1987 between Pittsburgh and Double-A Harrisburg, where he hit a career-high .338 in 37 games. He played in 117 games for the Pirates in 1986, hitting only .233. Belliard has hit only one home run in 843 major league at-bats. He was the Eastern League All-Star shortstop in 1983, hitting .263, but he hasn't shown much since then. Without an improved bat in 1989, Belliard will continue to look over his shoulder.

Belliard's cards will be commons as long as he hits under .250. His cards are not a good investment. Our pick for his best 1989 card is Score.

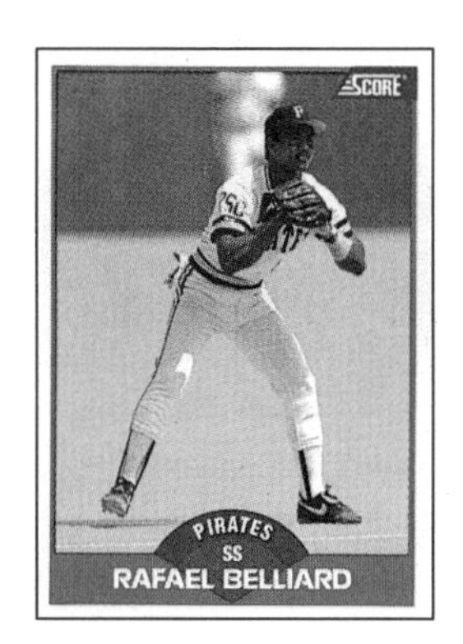

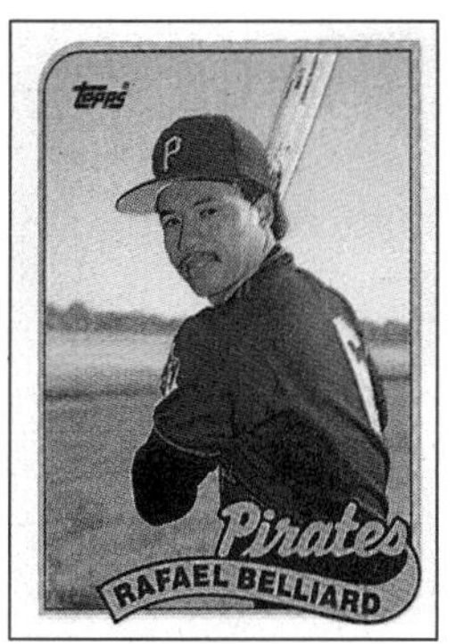

BRUCE BENEDICT

	BA	G	AB	R	H	2B	3B	HR	RBI	SB
1988	.242	90	236	11	57	7	0	0	19	0
Life	.244	916	2718	202	665	95	6	17	254	12

POSITION: Catcher
TEAM: Atlanta Braves
BORN: August 18, 1955 Birmingham, AL
HEIGHT: 6′2″ **WEIGHT:** 195 lbs.
BATS: Right **THROWS:** Right
ACQUIRED: Fifth-round pick in 6/76 free-agent draft

Backup catcher Benedict saw only part-time duty in 1988 with the Atlanta Braves. Still, his 90-game effort of a .242 average and 19 RBIs was a big boost from his discouraging 1987 campaign. In 1987, Benedict played in a career-low of 37 games, hitting .147. Benedict is a two-time All-Star (in 1981 and 1983). In 1983, he played in 134 games, hitting .298. While he doesn't hit for much power, he is a strong contact hitter who seldom strikes out (only 234 times in his career). He is an accomplished fielder with a strong throwing arm. Benedict will be a dependable reserve for the 1989 squad.

Benedict's 1989 cards will be three cents or less. Based on Benedict's lifetime statistics and backup status, his cards aren't sound investments. Our pick for his best 1989 card is Donruss.

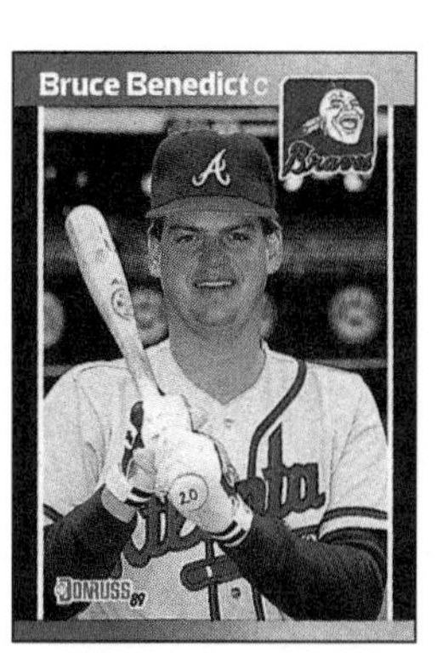

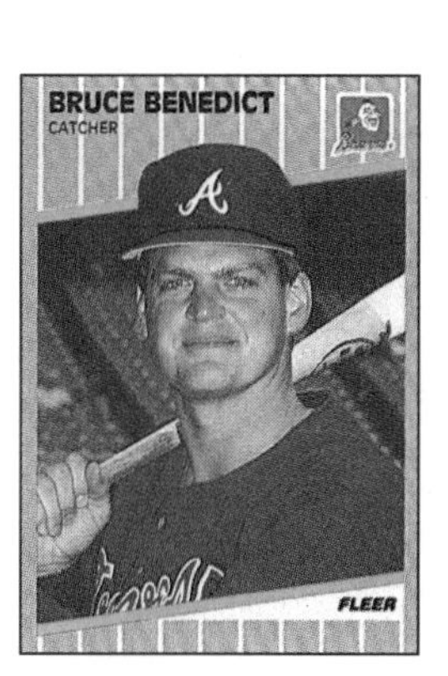

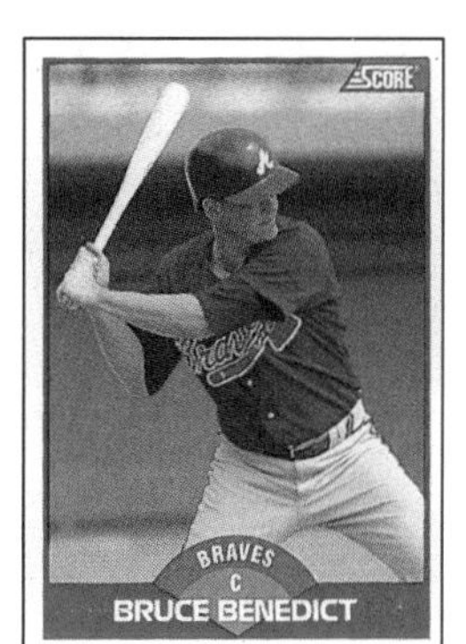

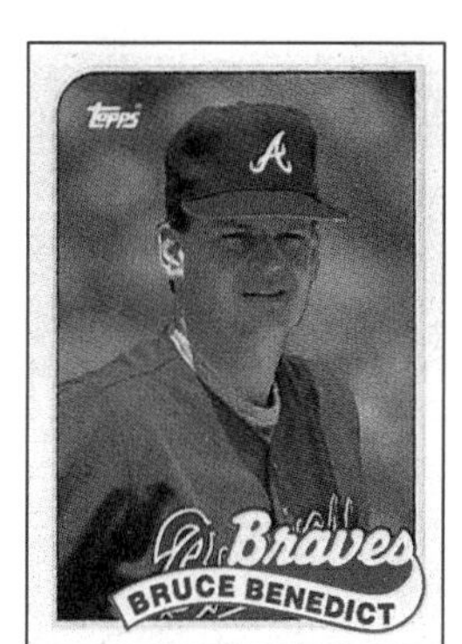

TODD BENZINGER

	BA	G	AB	R	H	2B	3B	HR	RBI	SB
1988	.254	120	405	47	103	28	1	13	70	2
Life	.262	193	628	83	165	29	2	21	113	7

POSITION: Outfield; first base
TEAM: Boston Red Sox
BORN: February 11, 1963 Dayton, KY
HEIGHT: 6′1″ **WEIGHT:** 185 lbs.
BATS: Both **THROWS:** Right
ACQUIRED: Fourth-round pick in 6/81 free-agent draft

In his first full season with Boston, Benzinger was a vital part of the team's divisional championship. He didn't match his rookie year average of .278, but he managed to set career highs in every offensive category. He clubbed 13 homers and 70 RBIs, and his power stats should continue to climb. Benzinger's downfall in 1988 was his 80 strikeouts, approximately one for every five at-bats. His versatility makes him a choice addition on the Red Sox. He's a switch-hitter capable of playing first base or the outfield. Benzinger should get more playing time in 1989, and his statistics should continue to improve with more experience.

Benzinger is a potential All-Star, playing for a winning team. That combination means that his 1989 cards, which could sell as high as a quarter, will be great investments. Our pick for his best 1989 card is Topps.

JUAN BERENGUER

	W	L	ERA	G	SV	IP	H	R	BB	SO
1988	8	4	3.96	57	2	100.0	74	44	61	99
Life	46	46	3.99	287	11	857.0	733	380	443	707

POSITION: Pitcher
TEAM: Minnesota Twins
BORN: November 20, 1954 Aguadulce, Panama
HEIGHT: 5′11″ **WEIGHT:** 215 lbs.
BATS: Right **THROWS:** Right
ACQUIRED: Signed as a free agent, 1/87

Berenguer was busy in 1988, appearing in 57 games. His workload was second only to Jeff Reardon's 63 appearances. Berenguer, who went 8-1 with the 1987 world champion Twins team, tallied an 8-4 mark in 1988. He has become an effective set-up man for Minnesota. He finished 27 games for the Twins last season. Berenguer was a starting pitcher earlier in his career. He posted a career-best 11-10 record with the 1984 Detroit Tigers, including two complete games and a shutout. But his bullpen success in two seasons with Minnesota will keep Berenguer in relief for the rest of his career.

Berenguer's lack of career wins or saves has kept him from gaining more recognition. His 1989 cards are commons, selling at three cents or less. Due to his modest career statistics, avoid investing in his cards. Our pick for his best 1989 card is Score.

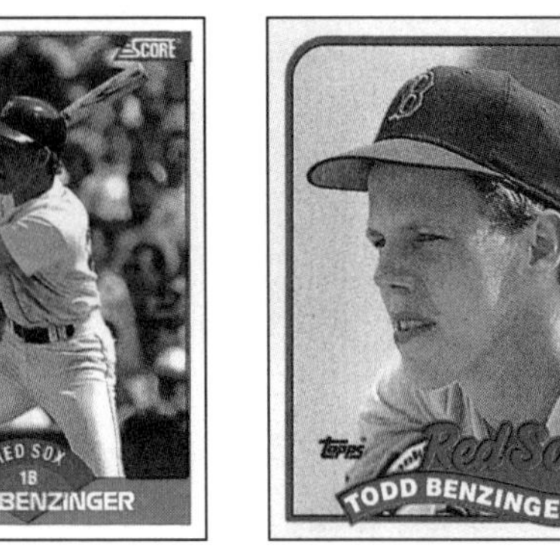

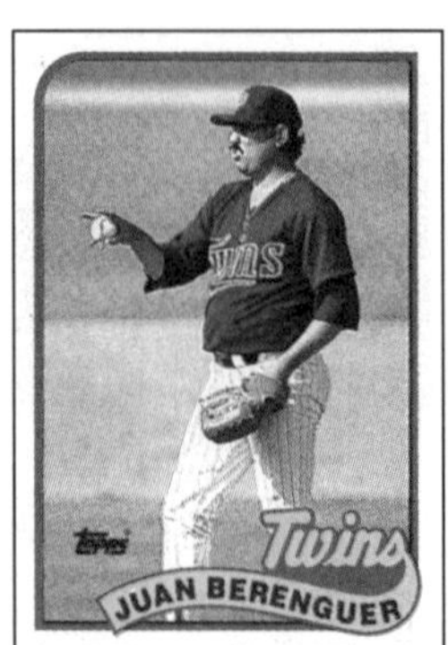

DAVE BERGMAN

	BA	G	AB	R	H	2B	3B	HR	RBI	SB
1988	.294	116	289	37	85	14	0	5	35	0
Life	.258	939	1714	213	442	64	13	37	187	13

POSITION: First base; outfield
TEAM: Detroit Tigers
BORN: June 6, 1953 Evanston, IL
HEIGHT: 6′2″ **WEIGHT:** 190 lbs.
BATS: Left **THROWS:** Left
ACQUIRED: Traded from Phillies with Willie Hernandez for Glenn Wilson and John Wockenfuss, 3/84

When the 1988 Detroit Tigers needed to fill a gap, they did it with Bergman's help. As the Tigers juggled their lineup throughout the season, he served well as a first baseman, designated hitter, and pinch hitter. His average was second on the club only to Alan Trammell's. In 1984, Bergman played in 120 games for the world champions, hitting .273. He is also valued as a fielder. During the entire 1988 season, he committed only four errors while playing more than one position. He is one of baseball's finest utility players. Bergman succeeds when his team needs it the most.

Bergman's 1989 cards will be priced at under a nickel. They'll never increase in value until Bergman lands a starting role or makes headlines with some dramatic pinch hits. Our pick for his best 1989 card is Donruss.

DAMON BERRYHILL

	BA	G	AB	R	H	2B	3B	HR	RBI	SB
1988	.259	95	309	19	80	19	1	7	38	1
Life	.252	107	337	21	85	20	1	7	39	1

POSITION: Catcher
TEAM: Chicago Cubs
BORN: December 3, 1963 South Laguna, CA
HEIGHT: 6′ **WEIGHT:** 210 lbs.
BATS: Right **THROWS:** Right
ACQUIRED: First-round pick in 1/84 free-agent draft

Rated the best defensive catcher in the American Association a year ago, Berryhill took over as the Cubs regular catcher in 1988, replacing longtime receiver Jody Davis. Berryhill hit close to .260, and he showed some power, hitting seven home runs and knocking in 38 runs. He hit .206 in 1986 at Double-A Pittsfield. In 1987, Berryhill's .287 average, 18 home runs, and 67 RBIs at Triple-A Iowa encouraged the parent club to call him up for a late-season look. The Cubs liked what they saw both offensively and defensively, and he went to spring camp with a shot at winning the job. The rest is history.

Berryhill's 1989 cards should open in the 20- to 25-cent range. They should appreciate nicely, considering he is a young, good-hitting receiver. Our pick for his best 1989 card is Topps.

CRAIG BIGGIO

	BA	G	AB	R	H	2B	3B	HR	RBI	SB
1988	.211	50	123	14	26	6	1	3	5	6
Life	.211	50	123	14	26	6	1	3	5	6

POSITION: Catcher
TEAM: Houston Astros
BORN: December 14, 1965
Kings Park, NY
HEIGHT: 5′11″ **WEIGHT:** 180 lbs.
BATS: Right **THROWS:** Right
ACQUIRED: First-round pick in 6/87 free-agent draft

Biggio was Houston's first choice in the June 1987 draft. Less than a year later he was on the Astros roster. The promotion came too soon, though, and Biggio struggled to bat around the .200 level. At Triple-A Tucson in 1988, he hit .320, with three homers, 39 RBIs, and 19 stolen bases. In 1987, Biggio hit .375 for Asheville in 64 games. He had nine home runs among his 81 hits and drove in 49 runs. Ironically, some feel that Biggio's ultimate position will be somewhere other than catcher, pointing out that Dale Murphy made it to the majors as a catcher but became a superstar as an outfielder.

Biggio has all the tools and all the right intangibles. His 1989 cards, which should open at about 25 cents, would be good long-term buys at that price. Our pick for his best 1989 card is Donruss.

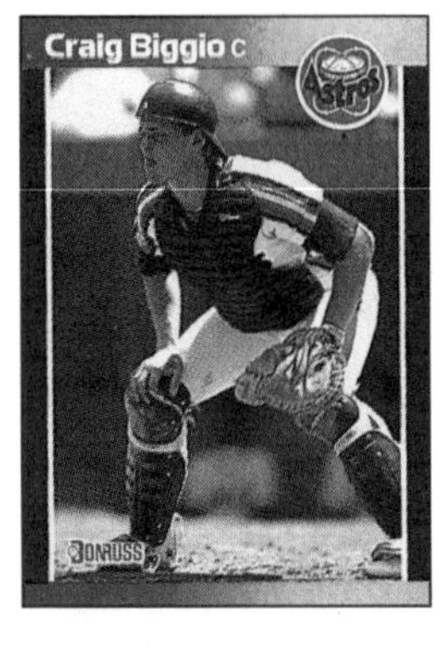

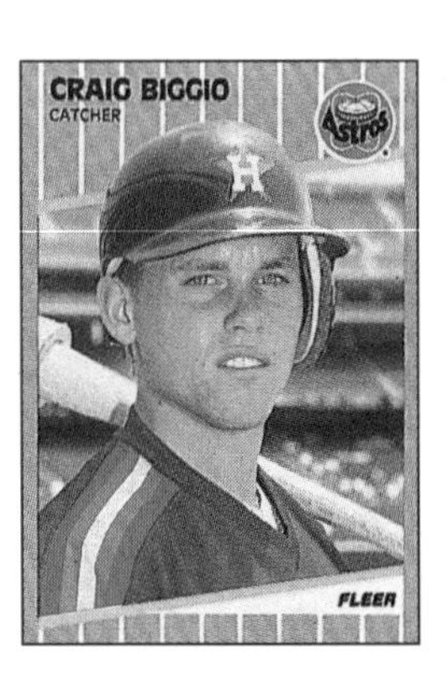

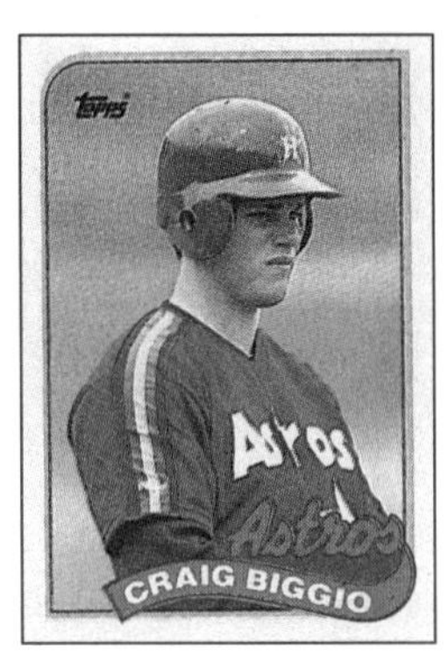

MIKE BIRKBECK

	W	L	ERA	G	CG	IP	H	R	BB	SO
1988	10	8	4.72	23	0	124.0	141	65	37	64
Life	12	13	5.04	40	1	191.0	228	107	68	102

POSITION: Pitcher
TEAM: Milwaukee Brewers
BORN: March 10, 1961 Orville, OH
HEIGHT: 6′2″ **WEIGHT:** 185 lbs.
BATS: Right **THROWS:** Right
ACQUIRED: Fourth-round pick in 6/83 free-agent draft

Birkbeck, who had brief tours of duty with the Brewers in 1986 and 1987, distinguished himself with his best season ever in 1988. He achieved a 10-8 mark last season, which was the third best on the club. Birkbeck pitched 124 innings in 23 appearances, surpassing his previous two seasons combined with the Brewers. His fine control was evident in 1988, as his strikeout total nearly doubled the number of walks that he allowed. He progressed rapidly through the Brewer minor league system. Because of his improvement, Birkbeck is sure to get serious consideration as the team's fifth starter in 1989.

Despite Birkbeck's ten wins in 1988, his ERA remained high at 4.72. Although his cards will be priced as commons in 1989, Birkbeck's performance has yet to give investors much reason to buy his cards. Our pick for his best 1989 card is Topps.

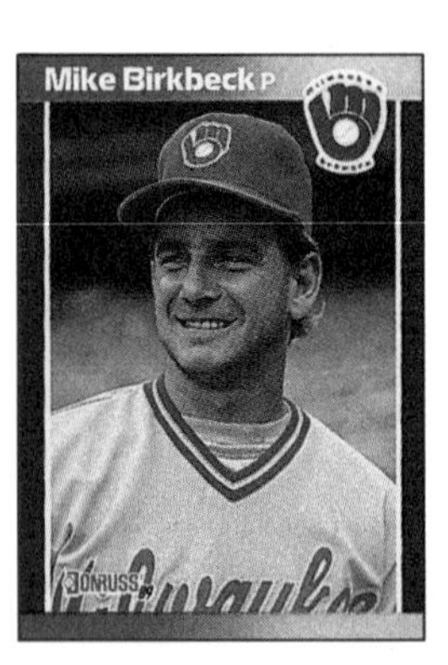

TIM BIRTSAS

	W	L	ERA	G	SV	IP	H	R	BB	SO
1988	1	3	4.20	36	0	64.1	61	30	24	38
Life	11	9	4.24	67	0	207.2	187	98	119	133

POSITION: Pitcher
TEAM: Cincinnati Reds
BORN: September 5, 1960 Pontiac, MI
HEIGHT: 6'6" **WEIGHT:** 235 lbs.
BATS: Left **THROWS:** Left
ACQUIRED: Traded from A's with Jose Rijo for Dave Parker, 12/87

Birtsas has been a perennial prospect who still has not lived up to his potential. Traded from the A's to Cincinnati prior to the 1987 season, the giant lefty appeared in 36 games for the 1988 Reds, mostly in relief, going 1-3. He also went 1-3 in an eight-game stint at Triple-A Nashville. At Triple-A Tacoma in 1987, Birtsas was impressive with a 7-2 record and a 3.12 ERA. Birtsas won ten games for the A's in 1985, but a series of injuries relegated him to the minor leagues for the next two campaigns. Lefthanders are notoriously late developers, and Birtsas still has the time and potential for big league stardom.

His 1989 cards are in with the commons. Buy a few bucks worth and put them in your "futures" box. Our pick for his best 1989 card is Score.

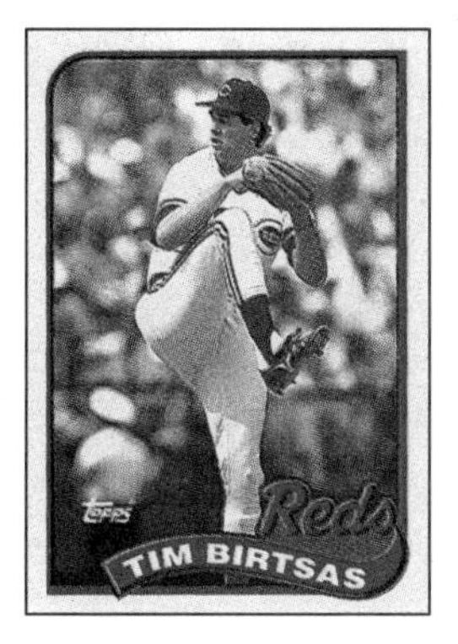

BUD BLACK

	W	L	ERA	G	SV	IP	H	R	BB	SO
1988	4	4	5.00	33	1	81.0	82	45	34	63
Life	58	60	3.80	234	11	1037.2	1003	438	315	552

POSITION: Pitcher
TEAM: Cleveland Indians
BORN: June 30, 1954 San Mateo, CA
HEIGHT: 6'2" **WEIGHT:** 180 lbs.
BATS: Left **THROWS:** Left
ACQUIRED: Traded from Royals for Pat Tabler, 6/88

The Indians gave up one of their finest hitters to bolster their pitching staff in 1988, and they chose Black for that mission. He worked in relief, appearing in 33 games and finishing nine of them. His ERA was one of his highest ever, partially due to serving up eight home runs. Black is a former starter, registering a sparkling 17-12 effort in 1984. His greatest season as a reliever came in 1986, when he had five wins, nine saves, and a 3.20 ERA. Black has the ability to benefit the Indians as a starter or reliever, which will be a big boost for the Tribe in 1989.

Because of his lifetime losing record, Black's 1989 cards will sell for a nickel or less. Until he distinguishes himself either starting or in relief, refrain from investing in his cards. Our pick for his best 1989 card is Donruss.

JEFF BLAUSER

	BA	G	AB	R	H	2B	3B	HR	RBI	SB
1988	.239	18	67	7	16	3	1	2	7	0
Life	.241	69	232	18	56	9	4	4	22	7

POSITION: Shortstop
TEAM: Atlanta Braves
BORN: November 8, 1965 Los Gatos, CA
HEIGHT: 6′ **WEIGHT:** 170 lbs.
BATS: Right **THROWS:** Right
ACQUIRED: First-round pick in 6/84 free-agent draft

Blauser is an example of a talented player who regresses because he's rushed up the ladder too fast. Blauser was so impressive in 1987 spring training that he was almost the Atlanta opening day shortstop. He was sent down to Triple-A Richmond, where he hit a lowly .177. Demoted again, this time to Double-A Greenville, he regained some confidence, hitting .289, with 13 homers and 52 RBIs. At Richmond in 1988, he batted .284 with five homers before getting a late-season recall to the big club. Although Atlanta's 1988 shortstop, Andres Thomas, had a pretty good season in 1988, Blauser will be given a chance to start on the Braves in 1989.

Blauser's 1989 cards will open in the 10- to 15-cent category. That is a good price for long-term investment. Our pick for his best 1989 card is Topps.

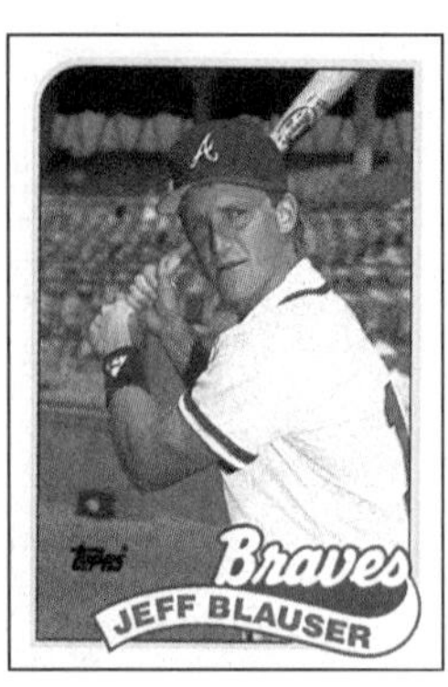

BERT BLYLEVEN

	W	L	ERA	G	CG	IP	H	R	BB	SO
1988	10	17	5.43	33	7	207.1	240	125	51	145
Life	254	226	3.25	611	231	4462.2	4094	1792	1224	3431

POSITION: Pitcher
TEAM: California Angels
BORN: April 6, 1951 Zeist, the Netherlands
HEIGHT: 6′3″ **WEIGHT:** 205 lbs.
BATS: Right **THROWS:** Right
ACQUIRED: Traded from Twins with Kevin Trudeau for Mike Cook, Rob Wassenaar, and Paul Sorrento, 11/88

Righthanded ace Blyleven didn't manage a spectacular performance in 1988, but he did add a few more tallies to his Hall of Fame resume. He won ten games for the Twins while losing 17, compiling a 5.43 ERA. In 1987, the Twins' championship season, he went 15-12; he was 1-1 in the World Series, striking out 12 in 13 innings. In his 19th full season, Blyleven was second in the team for strikeouts (trailing only Frank Viola) with 145. His strikeout total topped a good many younger hurlers, including all the moundsmen on four other A.L. staffs. If the 37-year-old Blyleven can maintain this pace for four more seasons, he'll surpass 300 wins and 4,000 strikeouts, assuring himself a spot in Cooperstown.

Blyleven's 1989 cards will be priced around a dime apiece; investors will gain long-term rewards when Blyleven gains Hall of Fame induction. Our pick for his best 1989 card is Topps.

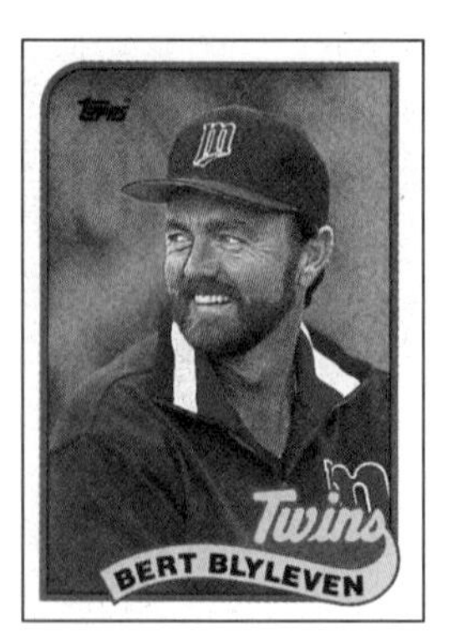

MIKE BODDICKER

	W	L	ERA	G	CG	IP	H	R	BB	SO
1988	13	15	3.39	36	5	236.0	234	89	77	156
Life	86	76	3.66	205	54	1362.2	1283	554	470	882

POSITION: Pitcher
TEAM: Boston Red Sox
BORN: August 23, 1957 Cedar Rapids, IA
HEIGHT: 5′11″ **WEIGHT:** 185 lbs.
BATS: Right **THROWS:** Right
ACQUIRED: Traded from Orioles for Brady Anderson and Curt Schiller, 8/88

Boddicker was a main reason why Boston won their division in 1988. Acquired in mid-season by the Red Sox, he won 13 crucial games for the BoSox, adding five complete games and one shutout. His best year ever was in 1984, when he went 20-11 with a 2.79 ERA, marks that topped the A.L. Boddicker has been a workhorse, logging more than 200 innings during each of the past five seasons. He has 14 career shutouts and 54 complete games. During 1989, his first full season in Boston, Boddicker can reestablish himself as one of the American League's finest hurlers.

Boddicker has had losing seasons in three of the last four years. However, his new surroundings could help him change that. Buy his 1989 cards at a nickel, then cash in when Boston repeats or when Boddicker wins 20 games. Our pick for his best 1989 card is Score.

JOE BOEVER

	W	L	ERA	G	SV	IP	H	R	BB	SO
1988	0	2	1.77	16	1	20.1	12	4	1	7
Life	1	3	3.62	54	1	76.2	77	31	28	53

POSITION: Pitcher
TEAM: Atlanta Braves
BORN: October 4, 1960 St. Louis, MO
HEIGHT: 6′1″ **WEIGHT:** 200 lbs.
BATS: Right **THROWS:** Right
ACQUIRED: Traded from Cardinals for Randy O'Neal, 7/87

In 1988, Boever made the Triple-A All-Star team while he was hurling for Richmond. At Richmond, he notched 22 saves and a 6-3 record, with a 2.14 ERA. In 1987 at Triple-A Louisville, Boever appeared in 43 games and earned 21 saves. He had a 3.43 ERA, while going 3-2 with 79 strikeouts and only 27 walks. *Baseball America* picked him as the best relief pitcher in the American Association in '87. He moved up to Atlanta late in the 1987 campaign and made 14 relief appearances. This past season he also made a late-season visit to Atlanta and recorded an ERA under 2.00. Boever has good control and a wicked curve, and he should add value to the Atlanta bullpen.

Boever's 1989 cards will be in the 10- to 20-cent range. Don't invest a lot of money in his cards. Our pick for his best 1989 card is Donruss.

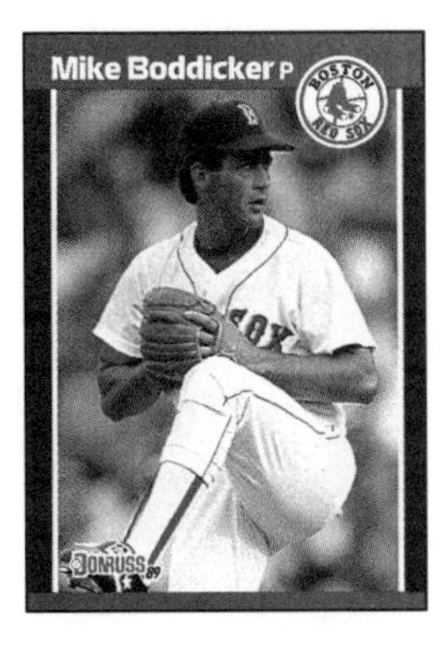

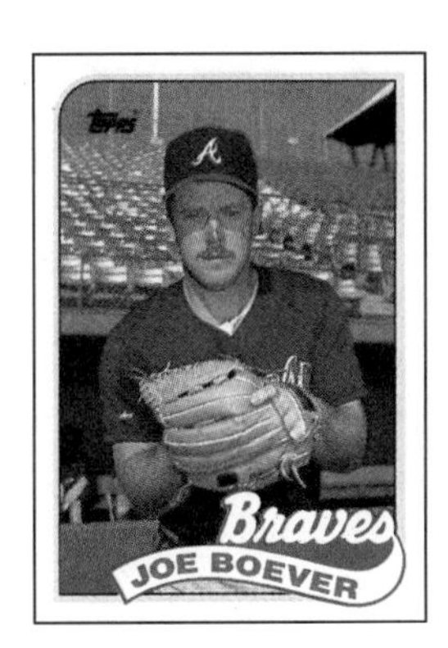

WADE BOGGS

	BA	G	AB	R	H	2B	3B	HR	RBI	SB
1988	.366	155	584	128	214	45	6	5	58	2
Life	.356	1027	3913	710	1392	263	29	61	469	12

POSITION: Third base
TEAM: Boston Red Sox
BORN: June 15, 1958 Omaha, NE
HEIGHT: 6′2″ **WEIGHT:** 190 lbs.
BATS: Left **THROWS:** Right
ACQUIRED: Seventh-round pick in 6/76 free-agent draft

It may not be surprising to learn that Boggs won his fourth A.L. batting title in five seasons in 1988. It is shocking, though, to view the high averages he has registered those years. Boggs' 1988 title was complemented by a season of 214 hits, 125 walks, and a stunning on-base percentage near .500! His power totals dropped from a career high of 24 homers and 89 RBIs in 1987 to five homers and 58 RBIs in '88. He was a key contributor to Boston's A.L. East title in 1988. All that's left for Boggs to achieve on his way to several all-time records is batting .400 for a season and winning a World Series.

Boggs' 1989 cards will sell for slightly more than $1. That price won't bring any immediate gains, but profits will come after he gains Hall of Fame membership. Our pick for his best 1989 card is Score.

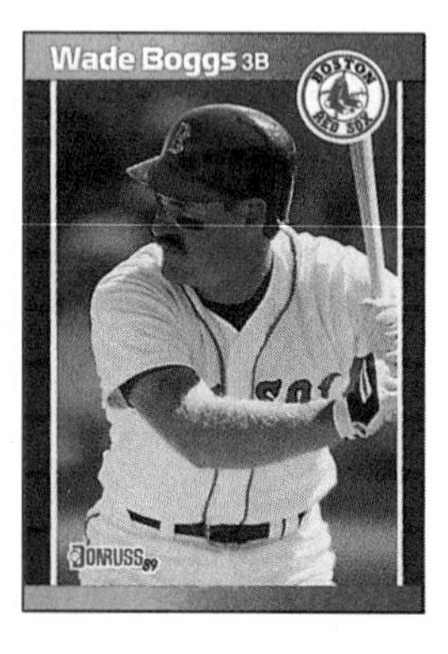

BARRY BONDS

	BA	G	AB	R	H	2B	3B	HR	RBI	SB
1988	.283	144	538	97	152	30	5	24	58	17
Life	.258	407	1502	268	388	90	17	65	165	85

POSITION: Outfield
TEAM: Pittsburgh Pirates
BORN: July 24, 1964 Riverside, CA
HEIGHT: 6′1″ **WEIGHT:** 185 lbs.
BATS: Left **THROWS:** Left
ACQUIRED: First-round pick in 6/85 free-agent draft

Bonds, a young, hard-hitting outfielder with plenty of speed, developed into a leader for the surprising Pirates. In 1988, he slugged 24 homers, with 58 RBIs and 97 runs scored. He started his career fast, slugging 41 homers in his first two seasons for the Bucs. Only Dick Stuart and Hall of Famer Ralph Kiner started faster for Pittsburgh. After spending only one and a half seasons in the minors, Bonds won a starting job in the Pirate outfield in 1986. His father is Bobby Bonds, former major league outfield star. Barry has a chance to have as long and productive a career as his father.

Barry's cards were priced as commons in 1988, and his 1989 cards should be the same. Load up on them, because as his home run and stolen base production increases, so will his card values. Our pick for his best 1989 card is Topps.

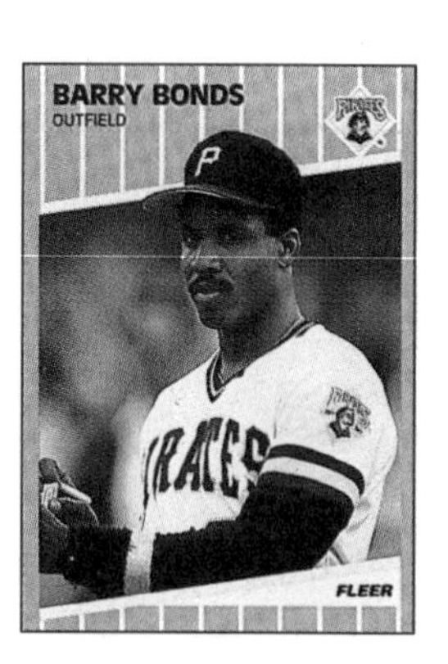

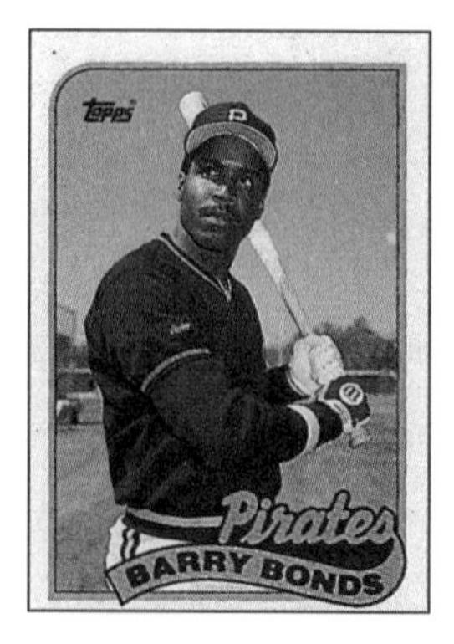

BOBBY BONILLA

	BA	G	AB	R	H	2B	3B	HR	RBI	SB
1988	.274	159	584	87	160	32	7	24	100	3
Life	.277	438	1476	200	409	81	14	42	220	14

POSITION: Third base
TEAM: Pittsburgh Pirates
BORN: October 4, 1964 San Diego, CA
HEIGHT: 6′3″ **WEIGHT:** 210 lbs.
BATS: Both **THROWS:** Right
ACQUIRED: Traded from White Sox for Jose DeLeon, 7/86

Bonilla followed up a promising first year with the Bucs by having a great '88. He became a full-time third baseman and won a berth on the N.L. All-Star team. This converted outfielder set career highs in both home runs and RBIs in 1988. In 1987, his first full year with the Pirates, Bonilla hit .300 with 15 homers and 77 RBIs. His 1988 homer total set a club record for switch-hitters. Bonilla first signed with the Pirates as a free agent in 1981, when he was discovered at a European baseball clinic. He is another of the Pirate building blocks who should help the Bucs challenge the Mets for the N.L. East crown in 1989.

Outside of Pittsburgh, Bonilla's 1989 cards should sell as commons. Despite his fielding weaknesses, Bonilla's slugging should keep him known for years to come. At a nickel apiece, his cards are worth accumulating. Our pick for his best 1989 card is Topps.

GREG BOOKER

	W	L	ERA	G	SV	IP	H	R	BB	SO
1988	2	2	3.39	34	0	63.2	68	24	19	43
Life	5	6	3.76	142	1	234.0	245	98	106	106

POSITION: Pitcher
TEAM: San Diego Padres
BORN: June 22, 1960 Lynchburg, VA
HEIGHT: 6′6″ **WEIGHT:** 245 lbs.
BATS: Right **THROWS:** Right
ACQUIRED: Tenth-round pick in 6/81 free-agent draft

Booker was an active middle man for the 1988 San Diego Padres. He tallied 34 appearances (the third highest on the team) and finished 11 of those games. The most encouraging sign about Booker's 1988 campaign was his regained control. In three of his major league seasons, his walks have exceeded his strikeouts. In 1988, Booker fanned 43 and walked just 19. In 1987, he appeared in 44 games, notching a 3.90 ERA. He had control problems, walking 30 and striking out only 17. Middle relievers are some of the most overlooked players, simply providing the opportunity for a relief ace to come in. Booker hasn't gotten much credit for his career, a fact that could change in 1989.

Booker, if he finishes more games in 1989, might get more attention. Until then, his 1989 common-priced cards will be unappealing investments. Our pick for his best 1989 card is Topps.

BOB BOONE

	BA	G	AB	R	H	2B	3B	HR	RBI	SB
1988	.295	122	352	38	104	17	0	5	39	2
Life	.253	2093	6723	635	1699	287	24	104	774	34

POSITION: Catcher
TEAM: Kansas City Royals
BORN: November 19, 1947
San Diego, CA
HEIGHT: 6′2″ **WEIGHT:** 210 lbs.
BATS: Right **THROWS:** Right
ACQUIRED: Signed as a free agent, 11/88

Boone continued his ironman catching streak with the Angels in 1988, once again playing in more than 100 games (122), and catching his 2,000th career game early in the season (a major league record). This 41-year-old wonder posted his highest batting average over the past six seasons in 1988, hitting .295. Boone shows no signs of slowing down or decreasing abilities, despite the workload he's welcomed for years. In 1987, Boone played in 128 games, hitting .242. If he ever gives up his starting job, now with the Royals, he may be an eventual inductee to the Hall of Fame, mainly due to his perseverance.

Boone's 1989 cards will be commons, priced at five cents and less. Short-term profits are unlikely, although his possible Hall of Fame election could bring long-term dividends. Our pick for his best 1989 card is Fleer.

PAT BORDERS

	BA	G	AB	R	H	2B	3B	HR	RBI	SB
1988	.273	56	154	15	42	6	3	5	21	0
Life	.273	56	154	15	42	6	3	5	21	0

POSITION: Catcher
TEAM: Toronto Blue Jays
BORN: May 14, 1963 Columbus, OH
HEIGHT: 6′2″ **WEIGHT:** 190 lbs.
BATS: Right **THROWS:** Right
ACQUIRED: Sixth-round pick in 6/82 free-agent draft

Borders became the Blue Jays' number-two catcher in 1988, batting close to .280 with five home runs in limited action. He broke into the big leagues with a bang, however, getting three hits and driving in five runs against the Royals last April. He hit .242 at Triple-A Syracuse before being called up. Originally an infielder, he played first, second, and third base in the minors. He was converted to catcher in 1986. In 1986, Borders batted .328 at Kinston and .353 with Knoxville. He was the South Atlantic League's RBI leader at Florence in 1984 and was MVP of the league All-Star game that season.

Borders should challenge for the starting slot behind the plate for the Blue Jays this year. His 1989 big league cards should open in the 15- to 20-cent range. Our pick for his best 1989 card is Topps.

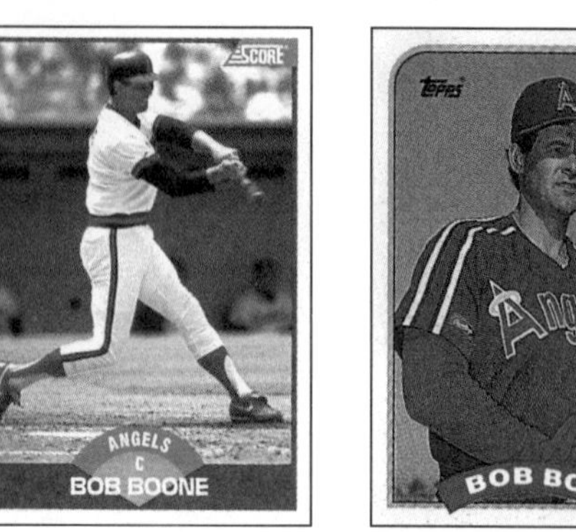

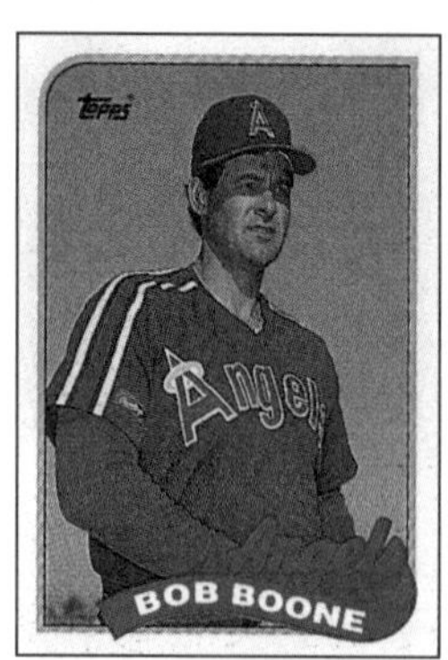

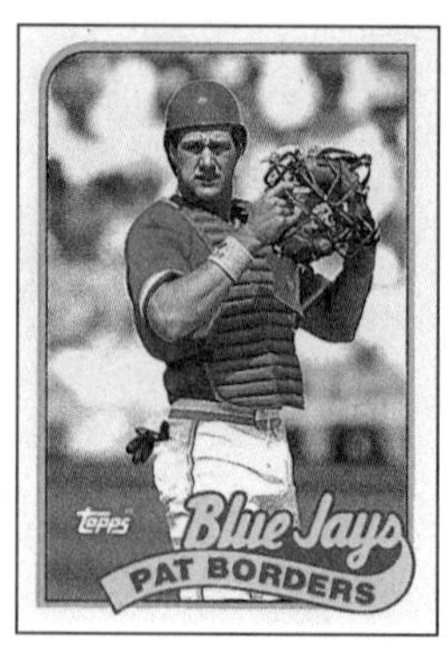

CHRIS BOSIO

	W	L	ERA	G	CG	IP	H	R	BB	SO
1988	7	15	3.36	38	9	182.0	190	80	38	84
Life	18	27	4.52	94	11	382.2	418	209	101	263

POSITION: Pitcher
TEAM: Milwaukee Brewers
BORN: April 3, 1963 Carmichael, CA
HEIGHT: 6'3" **WEIGHT:** 235 lbs.
BATS: Right **THROWS:** Right
ACQUIRED: Second-round pick in 1/82 free-agent draft

If any major league pitcher experienced bad luck in 1988, it had to be reliever Bosio. He entered last season with a lifetime mark of 11-12 in two previous years with the Brewers. Last season, however, Bosio had the league's worst mark. He "led" all hurlers with an 11-game losing streak, which lasted from May 21 through August 26. His ERA was a respectable 3.36, and he managed to finish 15 of the 38 games he appeared in. Bosio's six saves were also a career high. Provided he receives consistent offensive support in 1989, Bosio could become a solid reliever for Milwaukee.

Bosio's 1989 cards will sell for a nickel or less. Despite the low prices, it might be wise to refrain from investing in his cards for now. Wait and see if his losing streak was a fluke or an omen of future troubles. Our pick for his best 1989 card is Fleer.

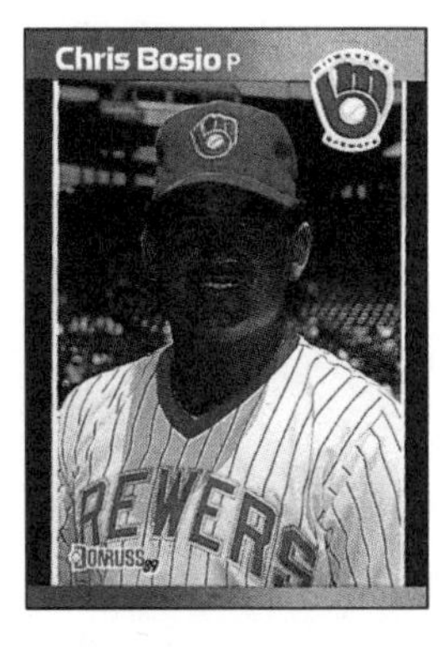

DARYL BOSTON

	BA	G	AB	R	H	2B	3B	HR	RBI	SB
1988	.217	105	281	37	61	12	2	15	31	9
Life	.237	394	1132	145	268	60	9	33	100	44

POSITION: Outfield
TEAM: Chicago White Sox
BORN: January 4, 1963 Cincinnati, OH
HEIGHT: 6'3" **WEIGHT:** 195 lbs.
BATS: Left **THROWS:** Left
ACQUIRED: First-round pick in 6/81 free-agent draft

Boston's fifth big league season was one of his best ever with the ChiSox. He hit a career-high 15 homers and 31 RBIs in 1988. Boston's nine stolen bases were second highest on the team. This former top-round draft pick had an anemic batting average (.217), but he connected with power when he connected. Nearly half of his hits were for extra bases. He has a lot of potential, but he has never proven that he can play every day in the major leagues. Boston could see more playing time in 1989 if he can revive his batting average.

Boston's 1989 cards will be three cents or less. He was third on the team in homers, and the Sox hope that he'll increase that total. If he does, his card values will rise. Therefore, we recommend picking up a small quantity of his cards. Our pick for his best 1989 card is Topps.

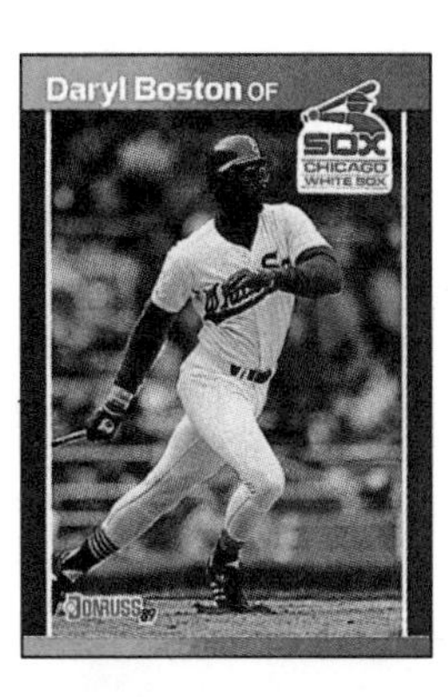

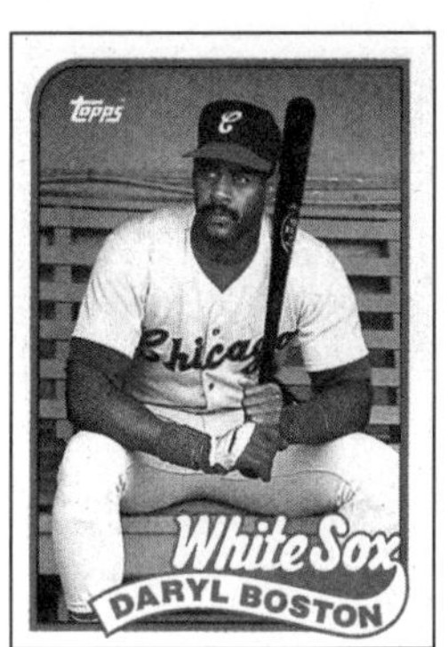

DENNIS BOYD

	W	L	ERA	G	CG	IP	H	R	BB	SO
1988	9	7	5.34	23	1	129.2	147	82	41	71
Life	57	54	4.14	142	39	957.2	1010	489	240	545

POSITION: Pitcher
TEAM: Boston Red Sox
BORN: October 6, 1959 Meridian, MS
HEIGHT: 6′1″ **WEIGHT:** 150 lbs.
BATS: Right **THROWS:** Right
ACQUIRED: 16th-round pick in 6/80 free-agent draft

Lingering injuries stopped Dennis "Oil Can" Boyd from getting in a full season's work with the 1988 Boston Red Sox, but the lanky righthander did show the ability to win again. Boyd only got into seven games in 1987, but made 23 starts in 1988. The flamboyant hurler led the 1986 Red Sox into the World Series with a 16-10 performance, his finest career effort. He is an often-quoted, much-heralded personality who is well known to most fans. All Boyd needs now is to avoid injuries in 1989 and show that he can survive the rigors of an entire season.

Boyd's minor fame is perhaps ironic, considering that his lifetime record is barely above .500. His 1989 cards will be a nickel. Don't consider investing until the doubts about Boyd's health are removed. Our pick for his best 1989 card is Score.

PHIL BRADLEY

	BA	G	AB	R	H	2B	3B	HR	RBI	SB
1988	.264	154	569	77	150	30	5	11	56	11
Life	.293	761	2728	423	799	142	31	63	290	118

POSITION: Outfield
TEAM: Baltimore Orioles
BORN: March 11, 1959 Bloomington, IN
HEIGHT: 6′ **WEIGHT:** 180 lbs.
BATS: Right **THROWS:** Right
ACQUIRED: Traded from Phillies for Ken Howell and Gordon Dillard, 12/88

Bradley has a chance to help Baltimore regain its winning ways. Dealt from Seattle to the Phillies before the 1988 season, he struggled up to the All-Star break before regaining the stroke that had him among lifetime .300 hitters. Bradley eventually hit .264 for the Phillies. He hit .301 for Seattle in 1984, .300 in 1985, and .310 in 1986. He hit a career high 26 home runs in 1985. The 29-year-old flychaser is a valuable commodity. A former all-conference quarterback at Missouri, Bradley is an outstanding athlete and should be a solid performer for a long time.

Bradley's cards, despite his obvious talents, still languish in the 10-cent range. Because he's not a long-ball hitter, it'll take a batting title or some other outstanding performance to push him into the star price category. Our pick for his best 1989 card is Donruss.

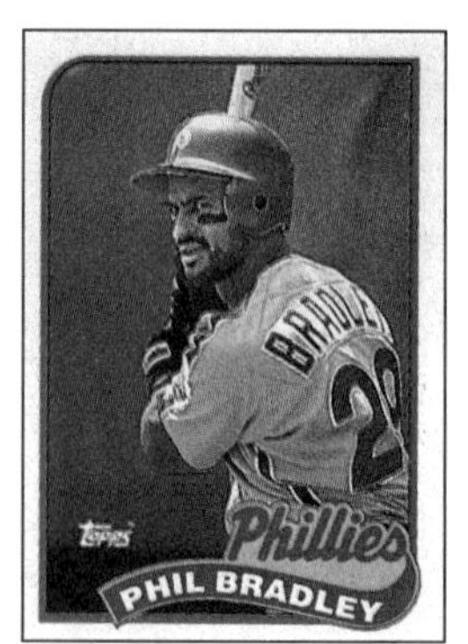

SCOTT BRADLEY

	BA	G	AB	R	H	2B	3B	HR	RBI	SB
1988	.257	103	335	45	86	17	1	4	33	1
Life	.270	310	967	106	261	43	6	14	107	2

POSITION: Catcher
TEAM: Seattle Mariners
BORN: March 22, 1960 Essex Falls, NJ
HEIGHT: 5′11″ **WEIGHT:** 185 lbs.
BATS: Left **THROWS:** Right
ACQUIRED: Traded from White Sox for Ivan Calderon, 6/86

Bradley wound up as the Mariners' starting catcher for most of 1988, and he responded with an adequate performance. He played in 103 games, the most in his career. Bradley seems to get more playing time due to his lefthanded hitting, an added benefit from a catcher. He doesn't have exceptional power, but his average is better than that of most second-string backstops. However, it is his defensive ability that keeps him employed. If Bradley can maintain his RBI totals, he could eventually land a starting catcher's job sometime in the future.

So far, Bradley's stats are typical for a second-string player. Although his cards sell as commons, they aren't worthy of investment as long as Bradley is not in a starting position. Our pick for his best 1989 card is Donruss.

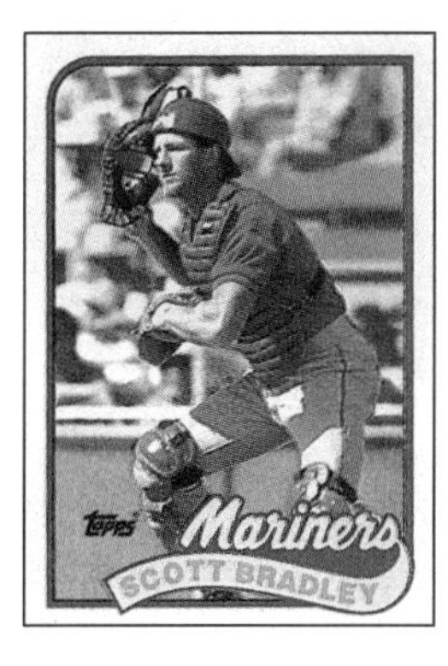

GLENN BRAGGS

	BA	G	AB	R	H	2B	3B	HR	RBI	SB
1988	.261	72	272	30	71	14	0	10	42	6
Life	.260	262	992	116	258	50	9	27	137	19

POSITION: Outfield
TEAM: Milwaukee Brewers
BORN: October 17, 1962 San Bernardino, CA
HEIGHT: 6′3″ **WEIGHT:** 210 lbs.
BATS: Right **THROWS:** Right
ACQUIRED: Second-round pick in 6/83 free-agent draft

Braggs was on the verge of having his finest season ever in 1988 before injuries ended his year prematurely. He is one of the brightest hopes for future Brewer teams, and he proved worthy of such admiration during the opening weeks of the 1988 season. His fast start signaled that he'd be sure to erase his previous highs of 13 home runs, 77 RBIs, and a .269 batting average, all set in 1987. Braggs has all the offensive and defensive tools needed to become a future star. An injury-free season in 1989 could be his best ever, and it could help the Brewers capture their division.

Buy all of Braggs' cards you can get for a dime or less. He would be a highly touted star if he played for the Yankees or Mets. Braggs could achieve long-deserved recognition with his 1989 performance. Our pick for his best 1989 card is Topps.

MICKEY BRANTLEY

	BA	G	AB	R	H	2B	3B	HR	RBI	SB
1988	.263	149	577	76	152	25	4	15	56	18
Life	.270	268	1030	140	278	51	8	32	117	32

POSITION: Outfield
TEAM: Seattle Mariners
BORN: June 17, 1961 Catskill, NY
HEIGHT: 5'10" **WEIGHT:** 180 lbs.
BATS: Right **THROWS:** Right
ACQUIRED: Second-round pick in 6/83 free-agent draft

Brantley earned his full-time starting status in 1988 and registered some impressive credentials at the end of his first full big league season. His 15 home runs and 56 RBIs were complemented by 18 stolen bases. Brantley played the outfield well, committing only five errors in 149 games. In 1987, Brantley hit for a .302 average with 14 home runs and 54 RBIs. The Mariners are on the verge of becoming a winning ball club, and they need Brantley's abilities to do so. He gives Seattle speed, defense, and power. In time, his skills will sharpen, and he'll become a legitimate star.

Brantley's cards should sell for a nickel or less in 1989. He seems to have all the required skills, and his cards should make steady gains in value as he receives more recognition. Our pick for his best 1989 card is Fleer.

SID BREAM

	BA	G	AB	R	H	2B	3B	HR	RBI	SB
1988	.264	148	462	50	122	37	0	10	65	9
Life	.263	543	1708	207	449	109	8	45	236	32

POSITION: First base
TEAM: Pittsburgh Pirates
BORN: August 13, 1960 Carlisle, PA
HEIGHT: 6'4" **WEIGHT:** 215 lbs.
BATS: Left **THROWS:** Left
ACQUIRED: Traded from Dodgers with R.J. Reynolds and Cecil Espy for Bill Madlock, 6/85

After starting strong, Bream's stats were down in 1988. He hit .264 with ten home runs and 65 RBIs for the Pirates. He was fourth in the N.L. with 37 doubles. The former Dodger was second among N.L. first basemen in fielding (.995), behind Houston's Glenn Davis. Bream also shared N.L. Player of the Week honors with Will Clark for June 20 to 26. In 1986, Bream clubbed 16 homers and 77 RBIs; in 1987, he hit 13 round-trippers and 65 RBIs. The Pirates hope that this downward spiral stops. A solid player, Bream is still looking for that break-out season to show what he can really do.

Not a high-demand card, the 28-year-old Bream could still become a bona fide star. His cards are worth holding as a speculative investment. Our pick for his best 1989 card is Score.

BOB BRENLY

	BA	G	AB	R	H	2B	3B	HR	RBI	SB
1988	.189	73	206	13	39	7	0	5	22	1
Life	.251	811	2505	310	628	114	6	90	324	44

POSITION: Catcher
TEAM: San Francisco Giants
BORN: February 25, 1954 Coshocton, OH
HEIGHT: 6′2″ **WEIGHT:** 205 lbs.
BATS: Right **THROWS:** Right
ACQUIRED: Signed as a free agent, 6/76

Brenly endured the worst slump of his big-league career during the 1988 season. He had been averaging 18 homers and 137 games a season during the past four years. In his limited appearances in 1988, Brenly accomplished little. He struck out approximately once every five times at bat, hitting only .189. In 1987, the sure-handed receiver led all major league catchers with 83 assists, and he batted .267 with 18 homers and 51 RBIs. The Giants would like to see that kind of production again. Early in his career, he filled in at first base, third base, and the outfield. Brenly will need a strong comeback to keep his starting job in 1989.

Brenly's 1989 cards will be a nickel or less. See how healthy he is, and how well he rebounds from his slump before investing. Our pick for his best 1989 card is Score.

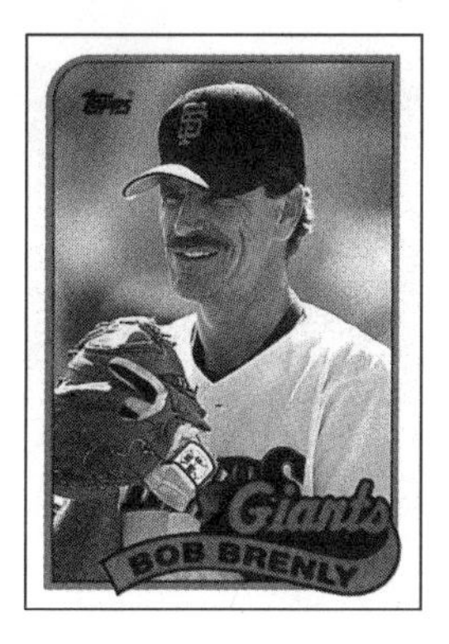

GEORGE BRETT

	BA	G	AB	R	H	2B	3B	HR	RBI	SB
1988	.306	157	589	90	180	42	3	24	103	14
Life	.312	2013	7691	1233	2399	488	117	255	1231	161

POSITION: First base
TEAM: Kansas City Royals
BORN: May 15, 1953 Glen Dale, WV
HEIGHT: 6′ **WEIGHT:** 200 lbs.
BATS: Left **THROWS:** Right
ACQUIRED: Second-round pick in 6/71 free-agent draft

Brett showed his pride and determination in 1988. He rebounded from nagging injuries to post a banner year. He hit .306 and slugged 24 homers and 103 RBIs while playing first base on a full-time basis. He was named the A.L.'s top first baseman by *The Sporting News.* Brett rebounded from injury-plagued seasons in 1986 and 1987, and he handled being moved from third base to first with no problem. Going into 1989, he is set to reach the coveted 3,000-hit plateau in four more seasons, if he avoids injury. If the Royals want to dethrone the A's for the divisional crown in '89, they'll need another standout performance from Brett.

Brett can count on eventual membership in the Hall of Fame. His 1989 cards should start out at 35 cents each. Buy them fast. The price will go up quickly if the Royals seriously contend for the pennant. Our pick for his best 1989 card is Topps.

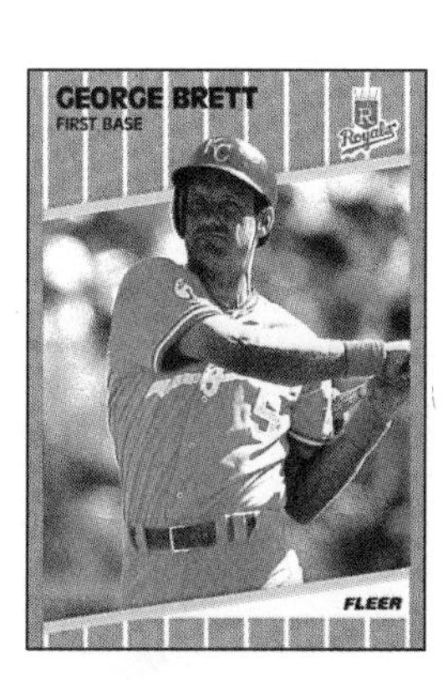

GREG BRILEY

	BA	G	AB	R	H	2B	3B	HR	RBI	SB
1988	.250	13	36	6	9	2	0	1	4	0
Life	.250	13	36	6	9	2	0	1	4	0

POSITION: Outfield; second base
TEAM: Seattle Mariners
BORN: May 24, 1965 Bethel, NC
HEIGHT: 5′9″ **WEIGHT:** 170 lbs.
BATS: Left **THROWS:** Right
ACQUIRED: First pick in secondary phase of 6/86 free-agent draft

After starting out as a second baseman, the fleet Briley was switched to the outfield in 1988. The move seemed to agree with him. At Triple-A Calgary last season he batted .313 and showed some power with 11 home runs and 66 RBIs. His 139 hits were second best on the team, and he swiped 27 bases. He got a late-season recall to Seattle on the strength of his fine Pacific Coast League stats. Briley hit .250 with the M's. He played with Double-A Chattanooga in 1987, and he was impressive with a .275 average, seven homers, 34 stolen bases, and 61 RBIs. Briley has a good shot to make the Mariners in 1989.

Briley's 1989 cards should open in the 15- to 20-cent range. Considering his potential, they are a good buy. Our pick for his best 1989 card is Topps.

GREG BROCK

	BA	G	AB	R	H	2B	3B	HR	RBI	SB
1988	.212	115	364	53	77	16	1	6	50	6
Life	.244	752	2402	329	587	98	6	90	354	30

POSITION: First base
TEAM: Milwaukee Brewers
BORN: June 14, 1957 McMinnville, OR
HEIGHT: 6′3″ **WEIGHT:** 205 lbs.
BATS: Left **THROWS:** Left
ACQUIRED: Traded from Dodgers for Tim Crews and Tim Leary, 12/86

Brock, who missed 47 games in 1988, was unable to put together the type of season the Brewers expect from him. Last season's six homers were his fewest in the last six seasons, and his .212 average was his worst since 1982. The Brewers traded two pitchers for Brock in 1986, which seemed like a steal. In his first full Brewer season, Brock had 13 homers, 85 RBIs, and a .299 average. Prior to 1987, his previous best was .251 in 1985. Brock is ripe for his first banner year as a slugger. The Brewers need some heavy hitting from him in 1989 to challenge in the competitive A.L. East.

Always a good hitter, Brock has never bested 21 homers or 66 RBIs in the big leagues. His cards will sell for a nickel each in 1989. A modest investment could reap big rewards if Brock slugs the Brewers to their first pennant since 1982. Our pick for his best 1989 card is Topps.

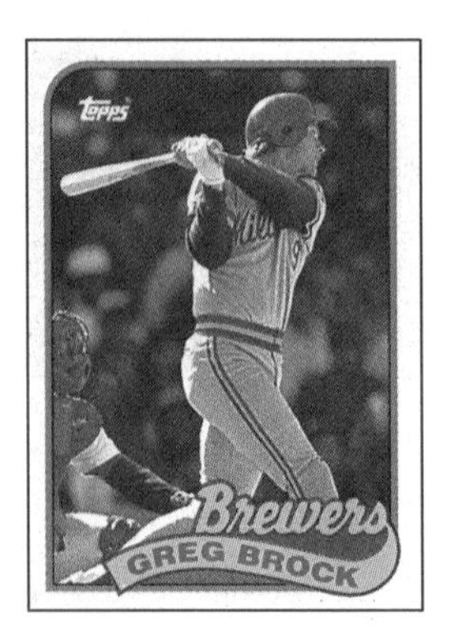

TOMMY BROOKENS

	BA	G	AB	R	H	2B	3B	HR	RBI	SB
1988	.243	136	441	62	107	23	5	5	38	4
Life	.246	1206	3543	445	871	162	38	66	397	85

POSITION: Infield
TEAM: Detroit Tigers
BORN: August 10, 1953
Chambersburg, PA
HEIGHT: 5′10″ **WEIGHT:** 175 lbs.
BATS: Right **THROWS:** Right
ACQUIRED: First-round pick in 1/75 free-agent draft

Brookens contributed to the Tigers in 1988, filling in wherever needed. Primarily a third baseman, he has always been with the Tigers. Although his batting average was two points higher in 1988 than 1987, Brookens' other statistics fell drastically. The Tigers got 13 home runs and 59 RBIs from him in 1987 en route to a pennant. Due to the Tigers' acquisition of infielders Keith Moreland and Chris Brown from the Padres, Brookens may have to fight harder than ever for playing time. The Tigers are aware of Brookens' versatility and power, however. You can bet he'll help out the 1989 Tigers.

Brookens is a steady but unspectacular player. His cards are economically priced at a nickel or less, but they represent a gamble considering his cloudy future. Our pick for his best 1989 card is Topps.

HUBIE BROOKS

	BA	G	AB	R	H	2B	3B	HR	RBI	SB
1988	.279	151	588	61	164	35	2	20	90	7
Life	.277	1050	3972	431	1099	194	28	89	539	49

POSITION: Outfield
TEAM: Montreal Expos
BORN: September 24, 1956
Los Angeles, CA
HEIGHT: 6′ **WEIGHT:** 178 lbs.
BATS: Right **THROWS:** Right
ACQUIRED: Traded from Mets with Mike Fitzgerald, Herm Winningham, and Floyd Youmans for Gary Carter, 12/84

A shortstop for most of his nine years in the big leagues, Brooks became an outfielder for the Expos last season. While he wasn't crazy about the idea, he went along with the plan and saw action in 151 games—39 more than in 1987, when he was strictly a shortstop. In 1988, Brooks belted a career-high 20 home runs and had 90 RBIs. Both numbers were second best on the Expos. He was having a career year in 1986, batting .340, when he broke his wrist and missed the last two months of the season. Brooks will be an essential element in Montreal's 1989 season.

Brooks is a marginal star player. His cards are not highly recommended as long-term investments. Currently they sell in the 10- to 20-cent range. Our pick for his best 1989 card is Topps.

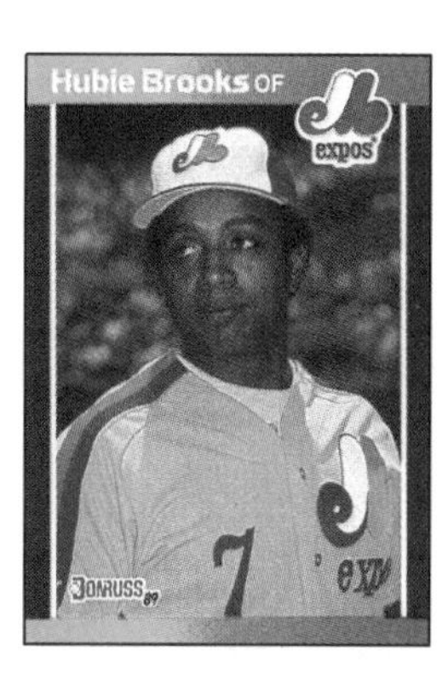

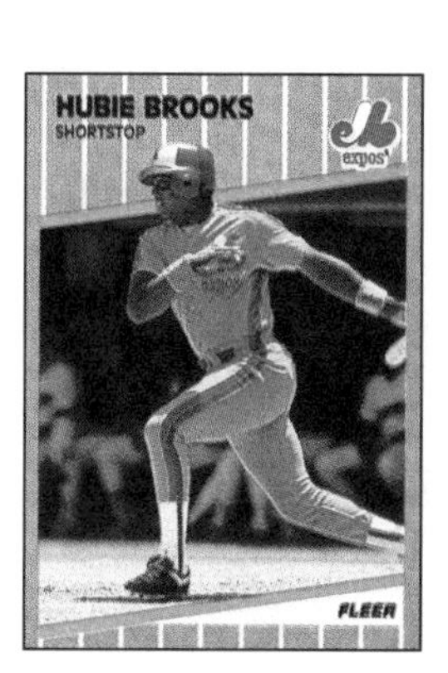

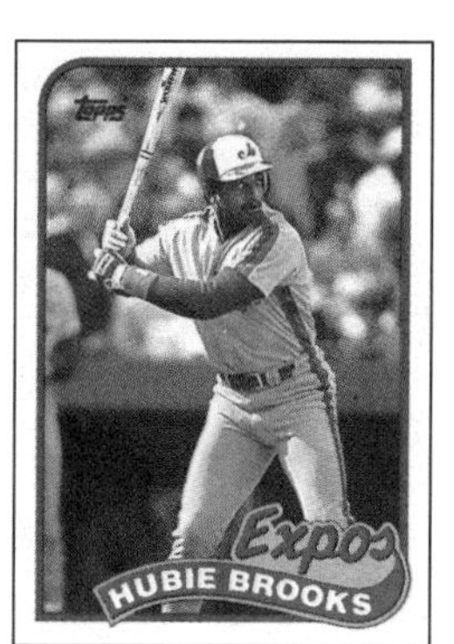

BOB BROWER

	BA	G	AB	R	H	2B	3B	HR	RBI	SB
1988	.224	82	201	29	45	7	0	1	11	10
Life	.244	230	513	95	125	18	3	15	57	26

POSITION: Outfield
TEAM: New York Yankees
BORN: January 10, 1960 Queens, NY
HEIGHT: 6′ **WEIGHT:** 190 lbs.
BATS: Right **THROWS:** Right
ACQUIRED: Traded from Rangers for Bobby Meachem, 12/88

Brower's sophomore season was a definite letdown from his encouraging 1987 major league debut. During 82 games in 1988, Brower didn't post any memorable statistics. His 1987 season was more upbeat, featuring 14 home runs, 46 RBIs, and a .261 batting average. Brower does have above-average speed, as evidenced by his ten steals in 1988. With some of the great Yankee outfielders ahead of him, it's unlikely that Brower will see a lot of playing time. However, his speed and defense are two assets that could help him keep a spot on the 1989 roster.

Brower's 1989 cards may not be as exciting as his 1988 issues. Fleer placed his picture on Jerry Browne's card, which was later corrected. That mistake sells for around $1.50. Brower's '89 cards will sell for a nickel. Don't invest in his cards until Brower repeats his 1987 stats. Our pick for his best 1989 card is Topps.

CHRIS BROWN

	BA	G	AB	R	H	2B	3B	HR	RBI	SB
1988	.235	80	247	14	58	6	0	2	19	0
Life	.272	432	1466	161	399	58	6	38	180	21

POSITION: Third base
TEAM: Detroit Tigers
BORN: August 15, 1961 Jackson, MS
HEIGHT: 6′2″ **WEIGHT:** 210 lbs.
BATS: Right **THROWS:** Right
ACQUIRED: Traded from Padres with Keith Moreland for Walt Terrell, 10/88

Brown will try to win a starting position with his third different team, the Tigers, in 1989. Brown had a subpar 1988 season with San Diego. Another injury-marred season limited his appearances to 80 games. Brown's stamina has been questioned in many circles because he's never played more than 131 games in a single major league season. His longest season came in 1985 with the San Francisco Giants, when he hit 16 homers and 61 RBIs, batting .271. Brown, at age 27, should have a long career to look forward to. But first he'll have to prove that he's not an injury-prone liability to the Tigers.

Brown's 1989 cards should be a nickel or less. Daring investors may want to gamble on a few of his cards. Brown has a high lifetime average, and a different league might give his career new life. Our pick for his best 1989 card is Topps.

KEITH BROWN

	W	L	ERA	G	CG	IP	H	R	BB	SO
1988	2	1	2.76	4	0	16.1	14	5	4	6
Life	2	1	2.76	4	0	16.1	14	5	4	6

POSITION: Pitcher
TEAM: Cincinnati Reds
BORN: February 14, 1964 Redding, CA
HEIGHT: 6′4″ **WEIGHT:** 205 lbs.
BATS: Right **THROWS:** Right
ACQUIRED: 21st-round pick in 6/86 free-agent draft

Brown is another of the good young pitchers that the Reds have. He started out the 1988 season with Double-A Chattanooga, going 7-1 with a 1.59 ERA in eight games. He was quickly promoted to Triple-A Nashville, finishing second in the American Association pitching race with a 1.90 ERA. Brown was 6-3 for Nashville, fanning 43 and walking 28. A graduate of California State–Sacramento, Brown broke into professional baseball in 1986 by going 4-1 at Sarasota (0.95 ERA), 2-0 at Billings (2.11 ERA), and 1-1 at Vermont (5.14 ERA). In 1987, he spent the whole year at Cedar Rapids. He was 13-4 with a league-leading 1.59 ERA and 86 strikeouts in 124⅓ innings. Brown looks like he is ready to make his mark.

Brown's 1989 cards will start out in the 25-cent range. His future looks good, but pitchers are always risky short-term investments. Our pick for his best 1989 card is Fleer.

JERRY BROWNE

	BA	G	AB	R	H	2B	3B	HR	RBI	SB
1988	.229	73	214	26	49	9	2	1	17	7
Life	.263	217	692	95	182	27	8	2	58	34

POSITION: Second base
TEAM: Cleveland Indians
BORN: February 13, 1966 Christiansted, Virgin Islands
HEIGHT: 5′10″ **WEIGHT:** 165 lbs.
BATS: Both **THROWS:** Right
ACQUIRED: Traded from Rangers with Pete O'Brien and Oddibe McDowell for Julio Franco, 12/88

Browne's quest to be the Ranger second baseman of the future was sidetracked in 1988. Playing in only 73 games, his 1988 statistics tailed off from his impressive 1987 big league debut. In 1987, Browne hit .271, with six triples, 38 RBIs, and 27 stolen bases. His 1988 totals weren't close to what he accomplished in his first season with the Rangers. Browne may have to battle to get into the starting lineup for the Indians. Still, he has the potential to be a vital member of the Tribe.

Don't forget that Browne is just 23 years old. With some additional major league seasoning, he could sprout into a solid, every-day player. Browne's cards, priced as commons, could yield small profit returns if he wins a spot in the Tribe lineup. Our pick for his best 1989 card is Donruss.

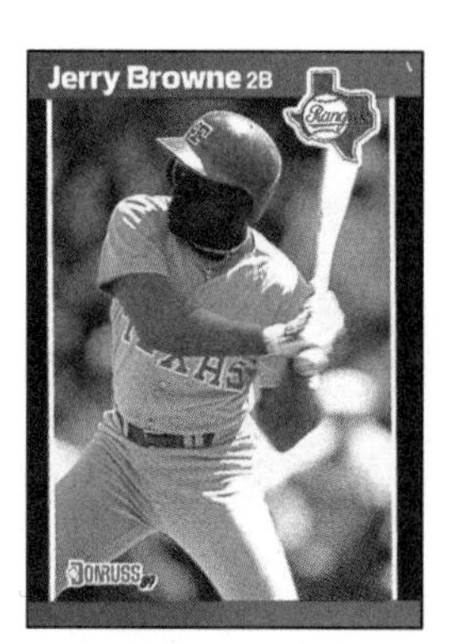

TOM BROWNING

	W	L	ERA	G	CG	IP	H	R	BB	SO
1988	18	5	3.41	36	5	250.2	205	98	64	124
Life	63	40	3.81	148	17	961.2	900	443	273	557

POSITION: Pitcher
TEAM: Cincinnati Reds
BORN: April 28, 1960 Casper, WY
HEIGHT: 6′1″ **WEIGHT:** 190 lbs.
BATS: Left **THROWS:** Left
ACQUIRED: Ninth-round pick in 6/82 free-agent draft

Browning looked like a 20-game winner throughout 1988, as he battled back from a two-year slump. The southpaw hurled a perfect game late in the season as the Reds contended for the pennant. In 1986 and 1987, Browning's ERA swelled, and his record went from a sophomore effort of 20-9 in '85 down to 14-13 and 10-13. That bought Browning a trip back to the minor leagues. His turnaround was major in 1988—18-5 with a 3.41 ERA. He finished second to teammate Danny Jackson in most pitching departments, signaling that the two moundsmen will be a dynamic duo in 1989. They will need to be for the Reds to escape the second-place finishes that have dogged them for the last four seasons and win a title.

Browning's 1989 cards will be priced at less than a nickel. If Browning does win 20 games in 1989, the price of his cards could triple overnight. Our pick for his best 1989 card is Topps.

TOM BRUNANSKY

	BA	G	AB	R	H	2B	3B	HR	RBI	SB
1988	.245	143	523	69	128	22	4	22	79	16
Life	.249	1056	3820	521	952	175	17	187	548	52

POSITION: Outfield
TEAM: St. Louis Cardinals
BORN: August 20, 1960 Covina, CA
HEIGHT: 6′4″ **WEIGHT:** 215 lbs.
BATS: Right **THROWS:** Right
ACQUIRED: Traded from Twins for Tommy Herr, 4/88

In 1988, Brunansky was an offensive savior who led the otherwise discouraged Cardinals in home runs (22), RBIs (79), bases on balls (79), and least errors (only one miscue in 143 games, a Gold Glove-caliber effort). One of only a handful of major leaguers to notch 20 or more home runs for seven consecutive seasons, Brunansky boosted his batting average from .183 at the time of his pick-up by the Cards to a season-ending mark of .245. Because he hits in spacious Busch Stadium, Brunansky's power-hitting potential isn't readily apparent from his stats. Still, his exploits will continue to refurbish a team starved for hitters since the departure of Jack Clark.

A consistent and personable player, Brunansky will be better appreciated if the Cardinals make strides, or if he moves to a top team. Watch for a slow climb from the nickel asking price for Brunansky's 1989 cards. Our pick for his best 1989 card is Topps.

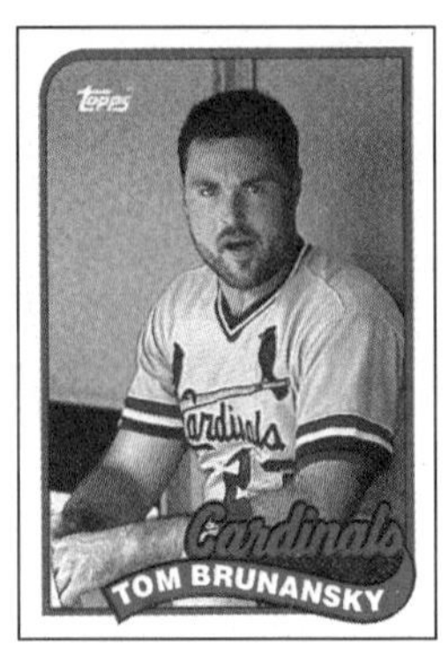

BILL BUCKNER

	BA	G	AB	R	H	2B	3B	HR	RBI	SB
1988	.249	108	285	19	71	14	0	3	43	5
Life	.291	2416	9178	1066	2669	494	48	172	1189	182

POSITION: Designated hitter; first base
TEAM: Kansas City Royals
BORN: December 14, 1949 Vallejo, CA
HEIGHT: 6′1″ **WEIGHT:** 182 lbs.
BATS: Left **THROWS:** Left
ACQUIRED: Signed as a free agent

Buckner, in his 20th major league season, still managed to make a sizable contribution to the success of the 1988 Royals. Even in a part-time position, Buckner was an efficient hitter. His average was the lowest since 1975, when playing with the Dodgers. The Angels gave up on Buckner after only one season in 1987, and it's uncertain if the Royals will find room for the veteran in 1989. But Buckner is 331 hits away from the coveted 3,000-hit plateau, and it seems that he'll want to be chipping away at the mark somewhere this season.

Buckner, 39, could last a few more years in the A.L. Incredibly, Buckner's cards are still less than a nickel. Smart investors could find possible long-term gains in Buckner's cards if he gets close to 3,000 hits and draws consideration for the Hall of Fame. Our pick for his best 1989 card is Fleer.

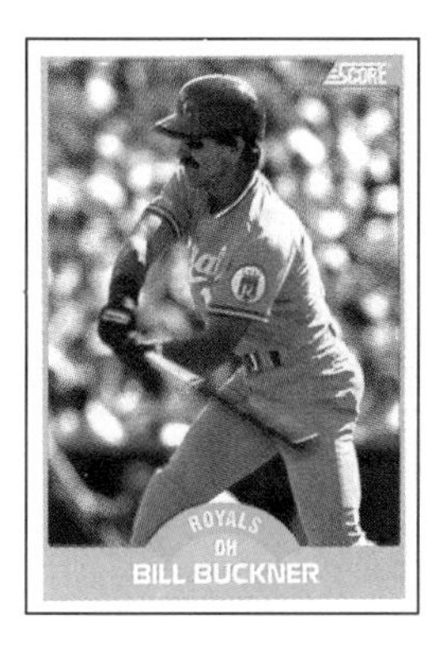

STEVE BUECHELE

	BA	G	AB	R	H	2B	3B	HR	RBI	SB
1988	.250	155	503	68	126	21	4	16	58	2
Life	.241	513	1546	184	372	66	9	53	183	12

POSITION: Third base
TEAM: Texas Rangers
BORN: September 26, 1961
Lancaster, CA
HEIGHT: 6′2″ **WEIGHT:** 190 lbs.
BATS: Right **THROWS:** Right
ACQUIRED: Fifth-round pick in 6/82 free-agent draft

Buechele's third season as the Rangers third baseman was memorable. He belted 16 homers and a career high of 58 RBIs. His average was his best ever at .250. He missed only six games in 1988, and appeared to be the team's most dependable third baseman since Buddy Bell. Buechele's rise to the Rangers was reasonably quick: He spent only a couple of years in the minor leagues. He was named the league MVP when playing at Triple-A Oklahoma City in 1985. As long as Buechele keeps his average up and is lucky enough to stay free of injuries, he should be a Ranger regular for seasons to come.

Buechele's 1989 cards should sell for a nickel or less. His cards are questionable investments. He's never hit above .250 or more than 20 homers in a season, basic requirements to be a star third baseman. Our pick for his best 1989 card is Topps.

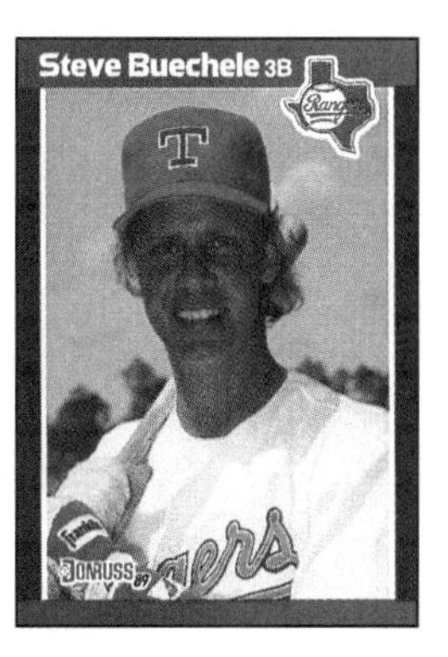

JAY BUHNER

	BA	G	AB	R	H	2B	3B	HR	RBI	SB
1988	.215	85	261	36	56	13	1	13	38	1
Life	.216	92	283	36	61	15	1	13	39	1

POSITION: Outfield
TEAM: Seattle Mariners
BORN: August 13, 1964 Louisville, KY
HEIGHT: 6′3″ **WEIGHT:** 205 lbs.
BATS: Right **THROWS:** Right
ACQUIRED: Traded from Yankees with Rick Balabon for Ken Phelps, 7/88

One of the smartest trades the Mariners made in 1988 was the acquisition of Jay Buhner. Buhner was a talented outfielder with no place to go in the Yankee organization. The Mariners welcomed having a talented prospect on the team, and Buhner responded with 13 homers and 38 RBIs. Buhner's biggest problem in 1988 was strikeouts. He fanned 93 times, roughly once for every three at-bats. His defense was superior, with only three errors all season. An entire season with the Mariners in 1989 should give Buhner the needed confidence to blossom.

Buhner appeared in the 1988 Donruss set, and that card sold for 50 cents after the World Series. His 1989 cards are bargains at 20 cents or less. If Buhner's first full season is full of home runs, those rookie cards will soar to a dollar. Our pick for his best 1989 card is Topps.

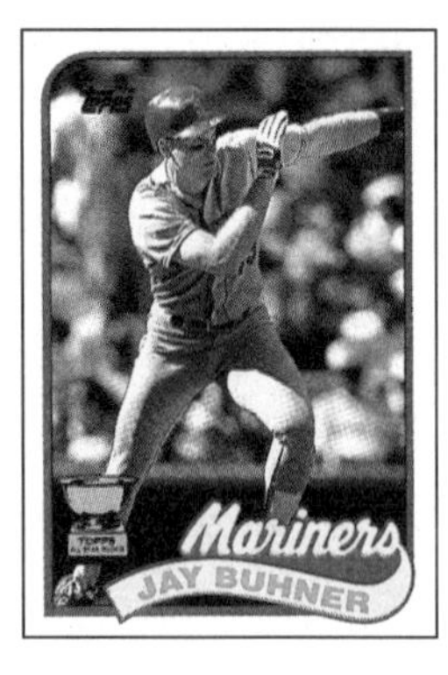

DeWAYNE BUICE

	W	L	ERA	G	SV	IP	H	R	BB	SO
1988	2	4	5.88	32	3	41.1	45	29	19	38
Life	8	11	4.06	89	20	155.1	132	74	59	147

POSITION: Pitcher
TEAM: California Angels
BORN: August 27, 1957 Lynwood, CA
HEIGHT: 6′ **WEIGHT:** 185 lbs.
BATS: Right **THROWS:** Right
ACQUIRED: Signed as a free agent, 11/85

Buice didn't get a chance to repeat his dazzling debut season in 1988. Injuries allowed him to appear in only 32 games, compared to 57 appearances during 1987. Buice saved 17 games in 1987 to lead the Angels. Last year, another rookie, Bryan Harvey, assumed Buice's place as the bullpen ace. Even in a shortened season, Buice notched twice as many strikeouts as walks. Buice's pro career began in 1977, including stints in the Oakland A's and Cleveland Indians organizations. If he can recapture his 1987 abilities, Buice's accomplishments will stand out on a team that is hungry for pitching.

Buice's 1989 cards will sell for about a nickel each. At age 31, Buice has had only one good season. Due to his late big league start, it will be tough for him to gain lasting acclaim. Our pick for his best 1989 card is Score.

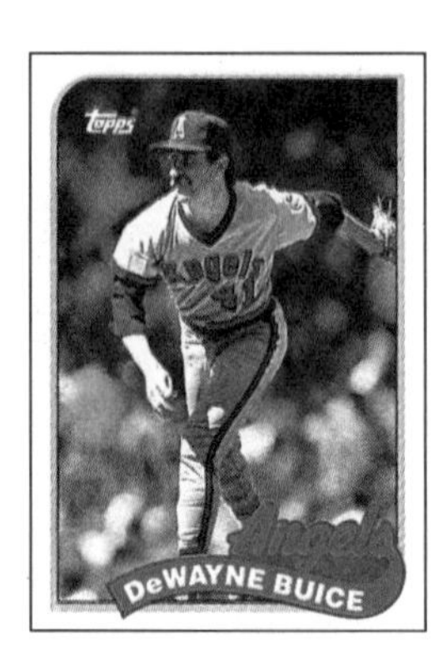

TIM BURKE

	W	L	ERA	G	SV	IP	H	R	BB	SO
1988	3	5	3.40	61	18	82.0	84	36	25	42
Life	28	16	2.46	262	48	394.2	337	123	132	269

POSITION: Pitcher
TEAM: Montreal Expos
BORN: February 19, 1959 Omaha, NE
HEIGHT: 6′3″ **WEIGHT:** 205 lbs.
BATS: Right **THROWS:** Right
ACQUIRED: Traded from Yankees for Pat Rooney, 12/83

Burke has saved 36 games over the past two years for the Expos, a fact very often overlooked when fans talk about N.L. firemen. Last season, the 29-year-old righthander went 3-5 with a 3.40 ERA in 61 outings. His 18 saves were tops on the team. In 1987, Burke was a perfect 7-0 in 55 games with an incredible 1.19 ERA and only 64 hits allowed in 91 innings. He saved 18 games that year as well. In 1986, he was 9-4 with a 2.39 ERA in 78 games in his rookie season with the Expos. Burke could become the Expo stopper in 1989.

Burke's cards are a notch above commons, selling in the 10-cent range. For the moment, that's about all they're worth. If he becomes a stopper, the value of his cards could increase. Our pick for his best 1989 card is Donruss.

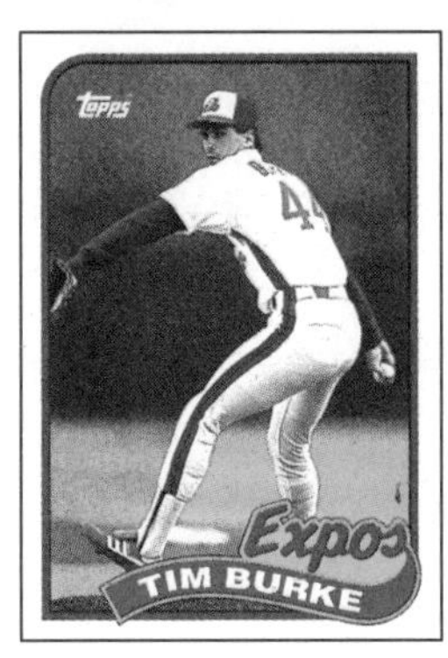

ELLIS BURKS

	BA	G	AB	R	H	2B	3B	HR	RBI	SB
1988	.294	144	540	93	159	37	5	18	92	25
Life	.283	277	1098	187	311	67	7	38	151	52

POSITION: Outfield
TEAM: Boston Red Sox
BORN: September 11, 1964 Vicksburg, MS
HEIGHT: 6′2″ **WEIGHT:** 175 lbs.
BATS: Right **THROWS:** Right
ACQUIRED: First-round pick in 1/83 free-agent draft

In only his second full season in the majors, Burks was one of the offensive centerpieces of the 1988 Boston Red Sox. Burks set career highs in hits (159), batting average (.294), doubles (37), triples (5), and RBIs (92). He had 25 steals to lead the team. In 1987, he hit .272, with 20 homers, 30 doubles, 59 RBIs, and 27 stolen bases. Burks is a young, multitalented star who can do it all. In 1988, he proved he could beat the "sophomore jinx" and demonstrated he could hit for average. Boston should remain an offensive powerhouse for years, and the all-around talents of Burks should help the Red Sox to several more titles.

Burks' 1989 cards will be anything but cheap, selling at the 50-cent level. If he continues his dramatic improvements in 1989, however, those prices could double by year's end. Our pick for his best 1989 card is Score.

TODD BURNS

	W	L	ERA	G	CG	IP	H	R	BB	SO
1988	8	2	3.16	17	2	102.2	93	38	34	57
Life	8	2	3.16	17	2	102.2	93	38	34	57

POSITION: Pitcher
TEAM: Oakland A's
BORN: July 6, 1963 Maywood, CA
HEIGHT: 6′2″ **WEIGHT:** 185 lbs.
BATS: Right **THROWS:** Right
ACQUIRED: Seventh-round pick in 6/84 free-agent draft

Burns began the 1988 season at Triple-A Tacoma but was beckoned to Oakland in mid-year, despite a .500 record and an ERA close to 4.00. Burns quickly rewarded manager Tony LaRussa's confidence by winning seven of his first nine decisions. He ended the season at 8-2. In 1985, he was 8-8 at Class-A Madison; at Double-A Huntsville near the end of the season, the righty was 3-0 with a 1.19 ERA. He spent both the 1986 and 1987 seasons going back and forth between Huntsville and Triple-A Tacoma; in 1987, he earned seven saves for Huntsville and had an ERA under 3.00. Burns looks like a solid choice as a fifth starter and long relief.

Burns' 1989 cards will open in the 25- to 30-cent range. He has good potential and his cards should be a solid investment. Our pick for his best 1989 card is Topps.

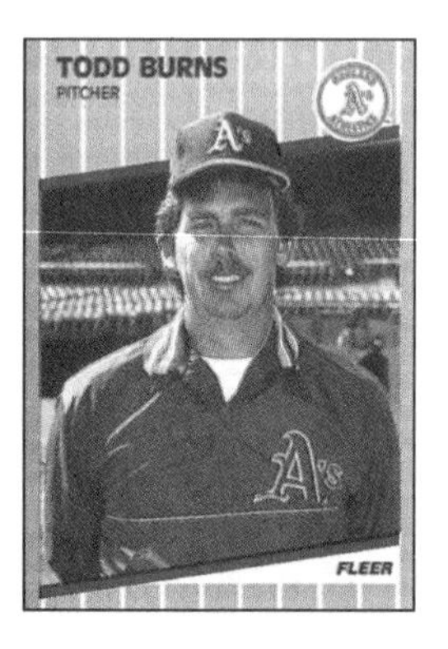

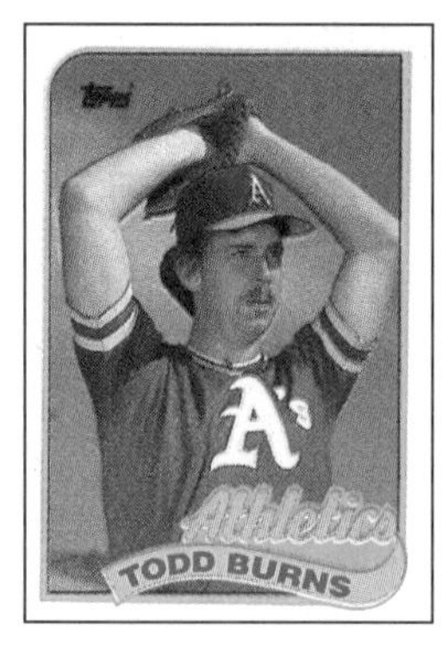

RANDY BUSH

	BA	G	AB	R	H	2B	3B	HR	RBI	SB
1988	.261	136	394	51	103	20	3	14	51	8
Life	.250	777	2081	275	520	109	20	68	289	27

POSITION: Designated hitter; outfield
TEAM: Minnesota Twins
BORN: October 5, 1958 Dover, DE
HEIGHT: 6′1″ **WEIGHT:** 185 lbs.
BATS: Left **THROWS:** Left
ACQUIRED: Second-round pick in 6/79 free-agent draft

Bush played in more games than ever before for the Twins in 1988, and he responded with one of his best offensive seasons ever. Bush powered a career-high 14 home runs in 136 games. His 51 RBIs were the most since 1983, his first full year with the Twins. The Twins use Bush sometimes at designated hitter to get his powerful bat in the lineup. However, Bush is anything but a defensive liability in the outfield. If Bush gets to stick to just one role in 1989, be it the outfield or DH, his hitting might prosper even more.

Bush needs to increase either his average or homers before he'll gain attention as a potential star. His 1989 cards will be commons. Investment will be a gamble until Bush reaches his full offensive potential. Our pick for his best 1989 card is Score.

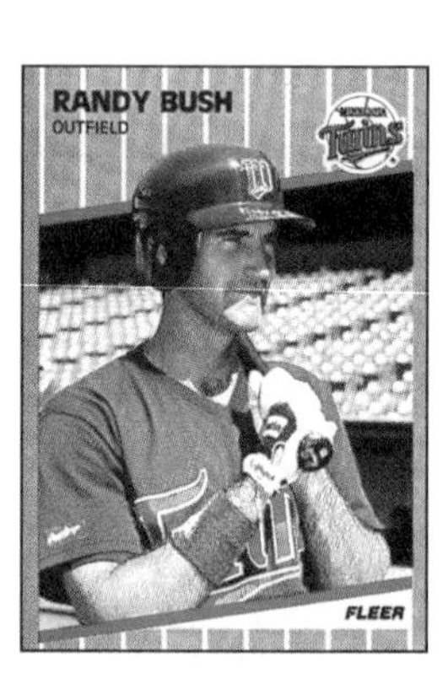

BRETT BUTLER

	BA	G	AB	R	H	2B	3B	HR	RBI	SB
1988	.287	157	566	109	163	27	9	6	43	43
Life	.281	1046	3785	642	1064	147	70	32	282	276

POSITION: Outfield
TEAM: San Francisco Giants
BORN: June 15, 1957 Los Angeles, CA
HEIGHT: 5′10″ **WEIGHT:** 160 lbs.
BATS: Left **THROWS:** Left
ACQUIRED: Signed as a free agent, 12/87

Butler returned to the National League in style in 1988 by joining the San Francisco Giants. Butler first came up with the Braves in 1982, but spent four seasons with Cleveland. Butler proved to be a valuable addition to the Giants in 1988. He missed just five games and was an offensive threat all year. He ended the season on a high note, whacking nine doubles and two triples the last two months of the season. His on-base percentage was among the league's best at .393. Butler is a multi-talented player who will be a great aid to the 1989 Giants.

Butler's 1989 cards are a steal at a nickel. He'll never be a homer-hitting demon, but he'll find lots of ways to win a ball game. Invest in his cards while they're cheap. Our pick for his best 1989 card is Topps.

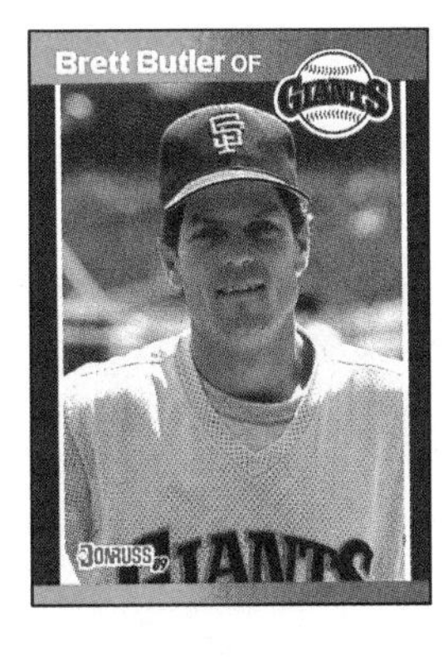

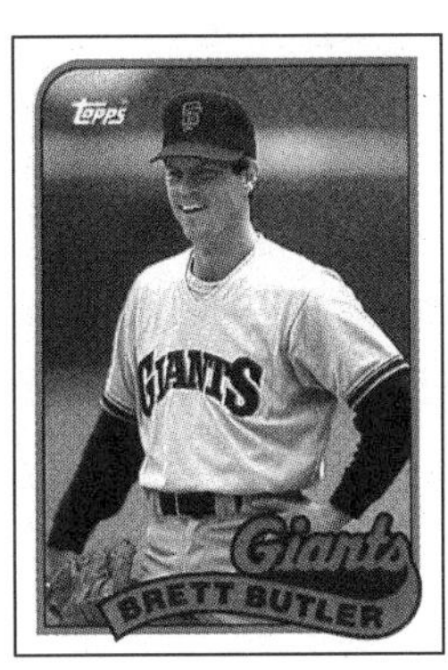

IVAN CALDERON

	BA	G	AB	R	H	2B	3B	HR	RBI	SB
1988	.212	73	264	40	56	14	0	14	35	4
Life	.267	345	1204	188	321	76	7	53	162	22

POSITION: Outfield
TEAM: Chicago White Sox
BORN: March 19, 1962
Fajardo, Puerto Rico
HEIGHT: 6′1″ **WEIGHT:** 205 lbs.
BATS: Right **THROWS:** Right
ACQUIRED: Traded from Mariners for
Scott Bradley, 6/86

Missing 89 games ruined Calderon's chances to come close to duplicating his exciting 1987 season. The hapless White Sox were electrified by Calderon's hitting in 1987. He blasted 28 homers and 83 RBIs while hitting a tidy .293. In 1988, however, prolonged absences hurt both his own statistics and the team's record. After bouncing around in the Mariner farm system for several years, it looked like Calderon had found his chance for fame with the White Sox. In 1989, he'll have to prove that he can play on an every-day basis and that he can return to the caliber of his 1987 efforts.

Calderon's 1989 cards should be back to a nickel. Because he has enjoyed only one stellar season, his ability is a question mark. Gamblers will invest in his cards, then quickly sell if he begins banging dozens of homers again. Our pick for his best 1989 card is Fleer.

KEN CAMINITI

	BA	G	AB	R	H	2B	3B	HR	RBI	SB
1988	.181	30	83	5	15	2	0	1	7	0
Life	.227	93	286	15	65	9	1	4	30	0

POSITION: Third base
TEAM: Houston Astros
BORN: April 21, 1963 Hanford, CA
HEIGHT: 6′ **WEIGHT:** 200 lbs.
BATS: Both **THROWS:** Right
ACQUIRED: Third-round pick in 6/84 free-agent draft

Caminiti remains one of the Houston Astro possible solutions for their third base problem. The Astros obtained veteran Buddy Bell in mid-season of 1988, but Bell is 37 and seems like a short-term solution. Caminiti hit a lackluster .181 in 83 at-bats for Houston in '88. But he hit .272 at Triple-A Tucson, with five homers, 66 RBIs, and 13 stolen bases. He made the jump from Double-A to the Astros in mid-1987 and played in 63 games. He hit a respectable .246 with three homers and 23 RBIs. If Caminiti continues to improve, he could be the Astro hot-corner man for years to come.

Look for Caminiti's 1989 cards to be a nickel or less. If you risk a few bucks, that could be a good long-term buy. Our pick for his best 1989 card is Topps.

MIKE CAMPBELL

	W	L	ERA	G	CG	IP	H	R	BB	SO
1988	6	10	5.89	20	2	114.2	128	81	43	63
Life	7	14	5.54	29	3	164.0	169	110	68	98

POSITION: Pitcher
TEAM: Seattle Mariners
BORN: February 17, 1964 Seattle, WA
HEIGHT: 6′3″ **WEIGHT:** 210 lbs.
BATS: Right **THROWS:** Right
ACQUIRED: First-round pick in 6/85 free-agent draft

Campbell came to the A.L. in 1988 heralded as the best pitcher and prospect to come out of the Pacific Coast League. The righty started the season in Seattle's starting rotation, but was disappointing and eventually was returned to Calgary to straighten out his problems. He dazzled his Triple-A opponents in 1987 with a 15-2 record, a 2.77 ERA, and 130 Ks in 163 innings. He was recalled late in the '87 season and appeared in nine games and fanned 35 in 49⅓ innings of work. Not an overpowering pitcher, he does have good movement on his fastball and spots the ball well. Campbell should find a spot on the M's rotation in 1989.

Until Campbell reestablishes himself, look for his 1989 cards in the commons box. At commons prices, you should stock up on them. Our pick for his best 1989 card is Score.

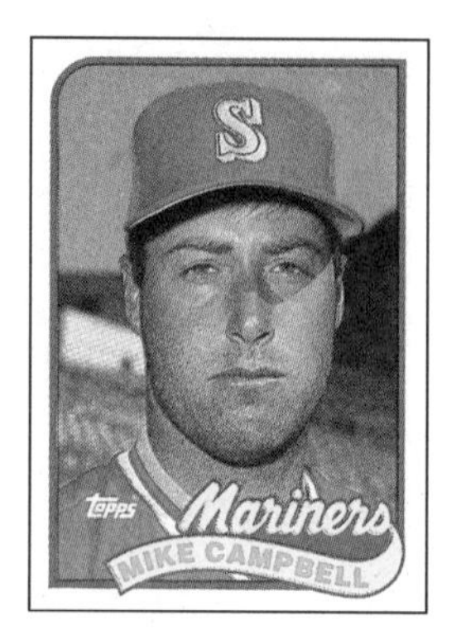

SIL CAMPUSANO

	BA	G	AB	R	H	2B	3B	HR	RBI	SB
1988	.218	73	142	14	31	10	2	2	12	0
Life	.218	73	142	14	31	10	2	2	12	0

POSITION: Outfield
TEAM: Toronto Blue Jays
BORN: December 31, 1966 Mono Guayabo, Dominican Republic
HEIGHT: 6′ **WEIGHT:** 160 lbs.
BATS: Right **THROWS:** Right
ACQUIRED: Signed as a free agent, 11/83

Campusano's 1988 rookie season wasn't the success everyone hoped for. The Blue Jays planned to install Campusano as a regular outfielder and move George Bell to the designated hitter slot. Bell publicly protested the move, which put even more pressure on the rookie. Campusano appeared in 73 games, but his hitting didn't reflect his full ability. He only hit .210 in 62 at-bats at Triple-A Syracuse in '88. At the age of 22, he is still relatively inexperienced. But with his talent, Campusano will improve with every season.

Campusano is a strong prospect who could inherit a full-time job if one of the Blue Jay sluggers (and their hefty contracts) get traded. At a dime or less, his 1989 cards would be strong investments. Our pick for his best 1989 card is Score.

JOHN CANDELARIA

	W	L	ERA	G	CG	IP	H	R	BB	SO
1988	13	7	3.38	25	6	157.0	150	69	23	121
Life	164	102	3.23	398	53	2302.2	2170	922	523	1481

POSITION: Pitcher
TEAM: New York Yankees
BORN: November 6, 1953 Brooklyn, NY
HEIGHT: 6′7″ **WEIGHT:** 225 lbs.
BATS: Right **THROWS:** Right
ACQUIRED: Signed as a free agent, 1/88

Candelaria immediately emerged as the ace of the Yankee staff during his first season with the team. He paced the Yankees with a 13-7 season. Those wins were the most for Candelaria since his 1983 season with the Pirates, when he went 15-8. He broke in with Pittsburgh in 1975 and spent 11 seasons there. His best year ever was with the 1977 Pirates, when he went 20-5 with a league-leading 2.34 ERA. Candelaria might have 200 wins by now, if he hadn't missed nearly the whole 1981 season with injuries, and hadn't been solely a relief pitcher in 1985.

Many investors will shun Candelaria's 1989 cards in favor of rookies. His cards will be commons and are good investments. If Candelaria leads the 1989 Yankees to the World Series, watch his card values jump. Our pick for his best 1989 card is Donruss.

TOM CANDIOTTI

	W	L	ERA	G	CG	IP	H	R	BB	SO
1988	14	8	3.28	31	11	216.2	225	86	53	137
Life	43	44	3.86	117	37	758.2	752	372	278	459

POSITION: Pitcher
TEAM: Cleveland Indians
BORN: August 31, 1957
Walnut Creek, CA
HEIGHT: 6′3″ **WEIGHT:** 205 lbs.
BATS: Right **THROWS:** Right
ACQUIRED: Signed as a free agent, 12/85

Candiotti rebounded from a 1987 slump and resumed his role as one of the Indians' finest starters. He bounced back from an awful 7-18 mark in 1987 to go 14-8 in 1988 with 11 complete games and a shutout. The Tribe will need another great effort from Candiotti in 1989. His first season in Cleveland, 1986, was marked by a 16-12 effort and a league-leading 17 complete games. Candiotti has been one of Cleveland's most rugged moundsmen. He's hurled more than 200 innings for three straight years. With the aid of his knuckler, Candiotti may be a central part of the Cleveland staff for many years.

Candiotti's 1989 cards should be about a nickel apiece. Based on his fame as one of the league's few knuckleball artists, his cards could be good investments if he keeps winning. Our pick for his best 1989 card is Topps.

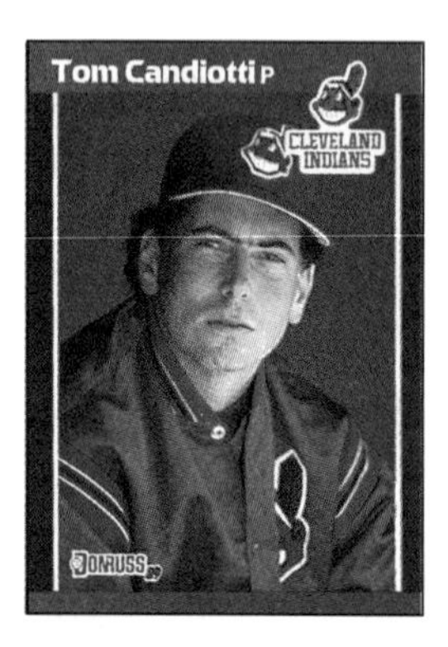

JOSE CANSECO

	BA	G	AB	R	H	2B	3B	HR	RBI	SB
1988	.307	158	610	120	187	34	0	42	124	40
Life	.270	503	1936	302	522	101	4	111	367	71

POSITION: Outfield
TEAM: Oakland A's
BORN: July 2, 1964 Havana, Cuba
HEIGHT: 6′3″ **WEIGHT:** 215 lbs.
BATS: Right **THROWS:** Right
ACQUIRED: 15th-round pick in 6/82 free-agent draft

After being overshadowed by Mark McGwire's rookie home run efforts in 1987, Canseco took center stage again for the '88 Athletics. He earned an elite spot in baseball history, becoming the only athlete to ever hit 40 home runs and steal 40 bases in a single season. He set career highs in both categories. He led the A's in hits and runs as well, indicating that he is becoming a complete ballplayer. He led the team to its first pennant of the decade. He was the 1986 A.L. Rookie of the Year and the 1988 A.L. Most Valuable Player. If the A's become a divisional dynasty, they'll probably have Canseco to thank.

Canseco's potential is unlimited. His cards might be in the $1.50 range in 1989. If he has another fine year, his card prices could double by World Series time. Our pick for his best 1989 card is Score.

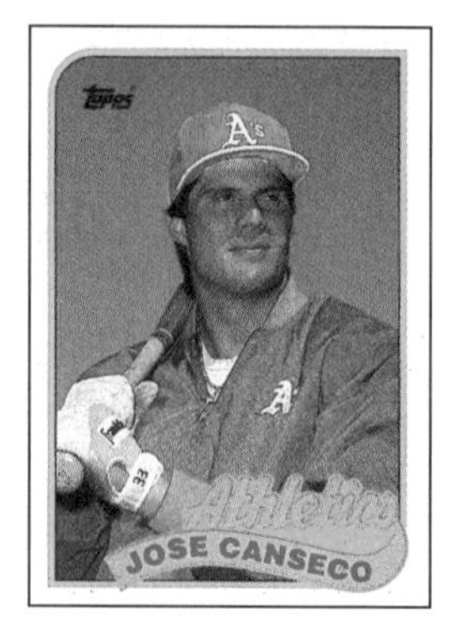

DON CARMAN

	W	L	ERA	G	CG	IP	H	R	BB	SO
1988	10	14	4.29	36	2	201.1	211	101	70	116
Life	42	35	3.77	204	7	647.1	584	295	235	442

POSITION: Pitcher
TEAM: Philadelphia Phillies
BORN: August 14, 1959
Oklahoma City, OK
HEIGHT: 6'3" **WEIGHT:** 190 lbs.
BATS: Left **THROWS:** Left
ACQUIRED: Signed as a free agent, 8/78

Carman's stock diminished a bit in 1988 as he suffered his first losing season in a Philadelphia uniform, going 10-14 in 32 starts with a 4.29 ERA. In 1987, he won 13 games against 11 losses, emerging as one of the N.L.'s most reliable performers. He had spent most of his big league career as a reliever until the Phillies made him a starter in late 1986. That year, the lefthander tossed eight perfect innings at San Francisco in August, only to lose it in the ninth. Carman appeared in 71 games as a reliever in his 1985 rookie year, going 9-4 with a 2.08 ERA. He was 10-5 in 1986 while relieving in 36 games and starting 14 others.

Carman's cards are a cut above commons, selling for between 10 and 15 cents. Unless the 29-year-old becomes a 20-game winner, there is no investment potential here. Our pick for his best 1989 card is Donruss.

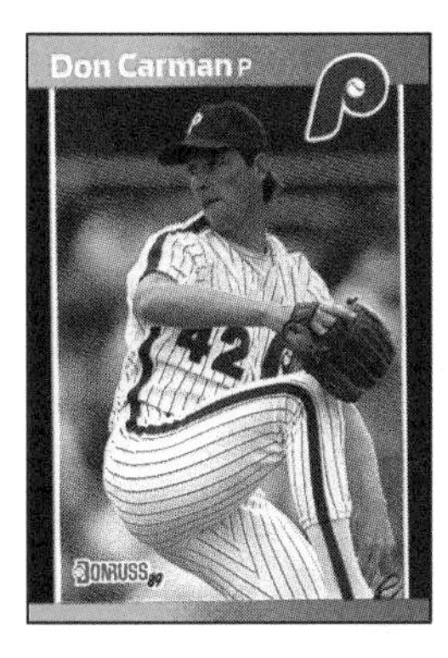

CRIS CARPENTER

	W	L	ERA	G	CG	IP	H	R	BB	SO
1988	2	3	4.72	8	1	47.2	56	27	9	24
Life	2	3	4.72	8	1	47.2	56	27	9	24

POSITION: Pitcher
TEAM: St. Louis Cardinals
BORN: May 5, 1965 St. Augustine, FL
HEIGHT: 6'1" **WEIGHT:** 185 lbs.
BATS: Right **THROWS:** Right
ACQUIRED: First-round pick in 6/87 free-agent draft

Carpenter stepped off the University of Georgia campus right into the starting rotation of Triple-A Louisville and promptly won his first six decisions. A shoulder problem, feared to be a slight tear of the rotator cuff, ended 1987 on a down note for him. In 1988, Carpenter spent time on the big league roster, going 2-3, with a 4.72 ERA. At Louisville, he started 13 games, going 6-2 with a 2.87 ERA and 45 strikeouts in 88 innings. The MVP of the 1987 Pan American Games, he has an 88-mph fastball and is working on his breaking ball and changeup. Carpenter, an All-American at Georgia, has great potential.

Carpenter's 1989 cards should open in the 20- to 25-cent range. At that price, wait to see if he makes the Cards' starting rotation before investing. Our pick for his best 1989 card is Donruss.

MARK CARREON

	BA	G	AB	R	H	2B	3B	HR	RBI	SB
1988	.556	7	9	5	5	2	0	1	1	0
Life	.381	16	21	5	8	2	0	1	2	0

POSITION: Outfield
TEAM: New York Mets
BORN: July 19, 1963 Chicago, IL
HEIGHT: 6′ **WEIGHT:** 170 lbs.
BATS: Right **THROWS:** Left
ACQUIRED: Seventh-round pick in 6/81 free-agent draft

Though he's been in the Mets farm system since 1981, Carreon is still regarded as an outstanding prospect. He had a strong spring in 1988 and was disappointed when he failed to make the Mets. Returning to Triple-A Tidewater, where he hit .312 in 1987 and .289 in 1986, Carreon wondered what he had left to prove. And perhaps in 1988 he proved that he had some long-ball punch in his bat. He hit 14 homers, a career high, and 55 RBIs. On the down side, however, his batting average fell to .263. In nine games with the '87 Mets, he batted .250. He is the son of Camilo Carreon, who spent eight seasons in the majors.

Carreon's 1989 cards should sell for about 20 cents. They're good buys for the long term at that price. Our pick for his best 1989 card is Fleer.

GARY CARTER

	BA	G	AB	R	H	2B	3B	HR	RBI	SB
1988	.242	130	455	39	110	16	2	11	46	0
Life	.267	1958	7041	941	1879	321	30	302	1128	36

POSITION: Catcher
TEAM: New York Mets
BORN: April 8, 1954 Culver City, CA
HEIGHT: 6′2″ **WEIGHT:** 210 lbs.
BATS: Right **THROWS:** Right
ACQUIRED: Traded from Expos for Hubie Brooks, Mike Fitzgerald, Herm Winningham, and Floyd Youmans, 12/84

A superstar for many years with both the Expos and the Mets, Carter is now approaching the down side of a rewarding All-Star career. In fact, Carter was the N.L. All-Star catcher for seven straight seasons. Carter batted only .242 in 130 games this year with 11 home runs and 46 RBIs, yet there was little doubt that with Carter the Mets were a better ball club. In 1987, Carter reached the 1,000-RBI plateau; he hit the 300-homer plateau in 1988. Certain to be elected to the Hall of Fame one day, Carter will probably be able to extend his career by playing more first base or the outfield in 1989.

Carter's cards are actively collected and will hold their value until he achieves the Hall of Fame. At that point they'll double or triple in value. His 1989 cards will be at the 10- to 20-cent level. Our pick for his best 1989 card is Score.

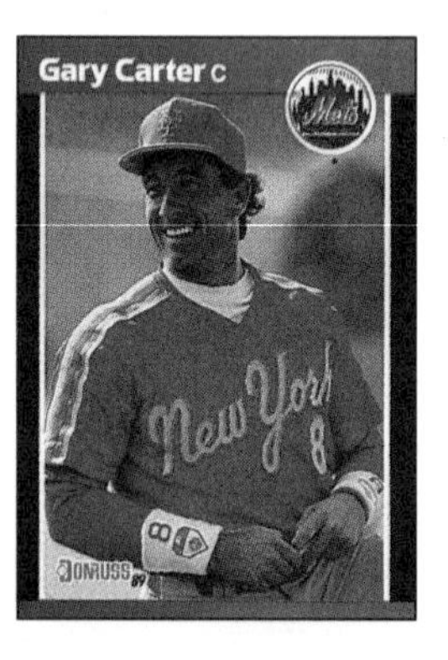

JOE CARTER

	BA	G	AB	R	H	2B	3B	HR	RBI	SB
1988	.271	157	621	85	168	36	6	27	98	27
Life	.274	700	2656	378	727	133	19	116	426	114

POSITION: Outfield
TEAM: Cleveland Indians
BORN: March 7, 1960
Oklahoma City, OK
HEIGHT: 6′3″ **WEIGHT:** 215 lbs.
BATS: Right **THROWS:** Right
ACQUIRED: Traded from Cubs with Mel Hall and Don Schulze for Rick Sutcliffe, Ron Hassey, and George Frazier, 6/84

For the third straight season, Carter remained as one of the American League's most fearsome sluggers. His production figures for last season—.271 average, 27 homers, 98 RBIs, 27 stolen bases—were right on track with 1987's tallies. He hit .264, with 32 home runs, 106 RBIs, and 31 stolen bases in '87. The Indians still sputtered in the divisional race in 1988, but Carter submitted his usual All-Star-quality stats. In 1989, Carter might make his first strong challenge for a league home run title. He is the key to any hopes that the Tribe has of competing for a divisional crown in the tough A.L. East.

Carter's cards still sell for less than a dime apiece. The current values are great invitations for investment. Those prices could exceed 50 cents if Carter wins a homer crown or if the Indians become contenders. Our pick for his best 1989 card is Topps.

CARMEN CASTILLO

	BA	G	AB	R	H	2B	3B	HR	RBI	SB
1988	.273	66	176	12	48	8	0	4	14	6
Life	.256	464	1152	156	295	54	4	47	152	14

POSITION: Outfield
TEAM: Cleveland Indians
BORN: June 8, 1958 San Francisco de Macoris, Dominican Republic
HEIGHT: 6′1″ **WEIGHT:** 190 lbs.
BATS: Right **THROWS:** Right
ACQUIRED: Drafted from Phillies, 12/78

Being a part-time player is tough on many major leaguers, but Castillo has made an art out of being a fourth outfielder. His run-producing abilities weren't at their fullest in 1988, but he still hit a respectable .273 in 66 games. Castillo came up with career-high totals of 11 home runs in 89 games last year. Previously, he had hit 11 homers in only 67 games in 1985. Castillo may never be a full-time player for the Indians, but he gives the team vital righthanded power and steady defense when called upon.

As long as he stays in Cleveland, Castillo seems destined for second-string status the rest of his career. His cards are priced as commons, but cards of pinch-hitters and substitute outfielders seldom have any investment possibilities. Our pick for his best 1989 card is Donruss.

JUAN CASTILLO

	BA	G	AB	R	H	2B	3B	HR	RBI	SB
1988	.222	54	90	10	20	0	0	0	2	2
Life	.217	196	465	60	101	11	5	3	35	18

POSITION: Infield
TEAM: Milwaukee Brewers
BORN: January 25, 1962 San Pedro de Macoris, Dominican Republic
HEIGHT: 5′11″ **WEIGHT:** 155 lbs.
BATS: Right **THROWS:** Right
ACQUIRED: Signed as a free agent, 10/79

Castillo wasn't an offensive powerhouse for the 1988 Brewers, but he filled in at whatever position he was needed. His determination can be measured by the six seasons he spent in the minors before he got his break with the Milwaukee club in 1986. During the next season, Castillo played in 116 games. He hit three homers, had 28 RBIs, and stole 15 bases. Like most other light-hitting infielders, he would have a hard time breaking into the starting lineup of the Brewers' infielders. However, Castillo's dependable glovework could be an asset for the Brewers in 1989.

At age 27, Castillo has yet to distinguish himself after two seasons in Milwaukee. Since his first professional season in 1980, he's batted better than .300 only once. His cards are priced as commons, but they are unwise investments. Our pick for his best 1989 card is Donruss.

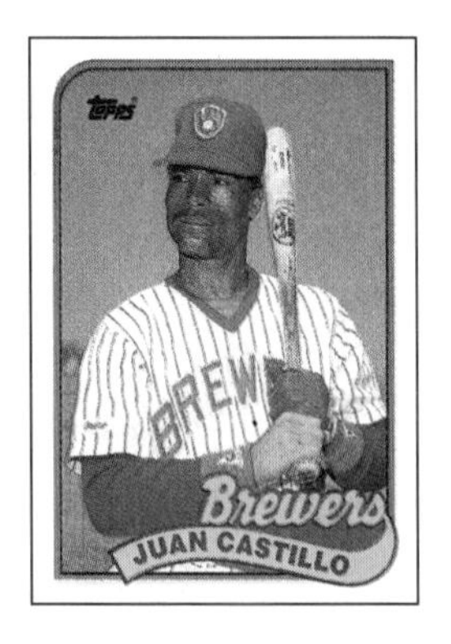

JOSE CECENA

	W	L	ERA	G	SV	IP	H	R	BB	SO
1988	0	0	4.78	22	1	26.1	20	16	23	27
Life	0	0	4.78	22	1	26.1	20	16	23	27

POSITION: Pitcher
TEAM: Texas Rangers
BORN: August 20, 1963 Ciudad Obregon, Mexico
HEIGHT: 5′11″ **WEIGHT:** 180 lbs.
BATS: Right **THROWS:** Right
ACQUIRED: Drafted from Phillies, 12/86

Injuries kept Cecena from becoming an impact player in 1988, but the Rangers remain very high on him. In limited big league action in '88, he earned a save and fanned 27 in 26⅓ innings. Drafted from the Phillies' farm system in 1986, Cecena had an 8-4 record with a 3.34 ERA and 66 strikeouts for Clearwater that year. It's a mystery why the Phillies didn't protect the righty. At Tulsa in 1987, he was converted to a reliever and fanned 61 batters in 61 innings while going 3-3. He pitched his way onto the Ranger roster this past spring by keeping his strikeout-per-inning ratio going. Cecena has a chance to be a reliever for the Rangers.

Cecena's 1989 cards should open in the 10- to 15-cent range. If he starts to rack up saves, his card prices will increase. Our pick for his best 1989 card is Fleer.

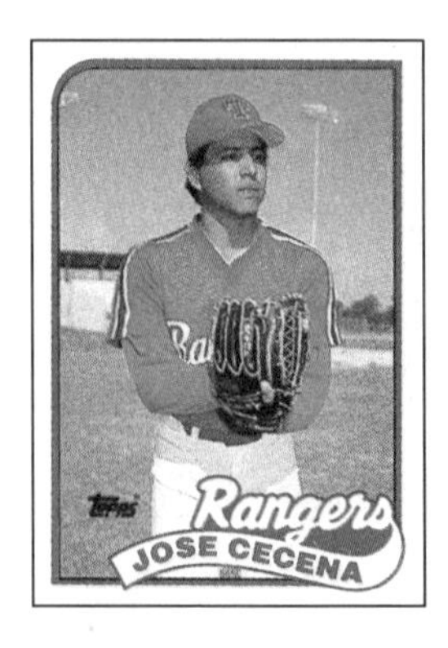

RICK CERONE

	BA	G	AB	R	H	2B	3B	HR	RBI	SB
1988	.269	84	264	31	71	13	1	3	27	0
Life	.241	1055	3344	325	805	151	14	50	354	4

POSITION: Catcher
TEAM: Boston Red Sox
BORN: May 19, 1954 Newark, NJ
HEIGHT: 5′11″ **WEIGHT:** 185 lbs.
BATS: Right **THROWS:** Right
ACQUIRED: Signed as a free agent, 4/88

Cerone joined the Boston Red Sox in 1988 and helped them capture a pennant. Cerone was picked up by Boston mostly as a glove man to fill in for starting catcher Rich Gedman. Cerone, however, wielded a potent bat in 1988. His .269 average, three homers, and 27 RBIs were some of his best accomplishments in years. Cerone's best effort ever was with the 1980 Yankees. He batted .277, with 14 homers and 85 RBIs. Even at age 34, Cerone is a capable fielder and should be around for several more seasons.

Cerone might not match his glory years as a Yankees starter, but he'll surely carry on as a backup backstop somewhere. Still, Cerone's 1989 cards aren't worth investing in, even at their prices of three cents or less. Our pick for his best 1989 card is Score.

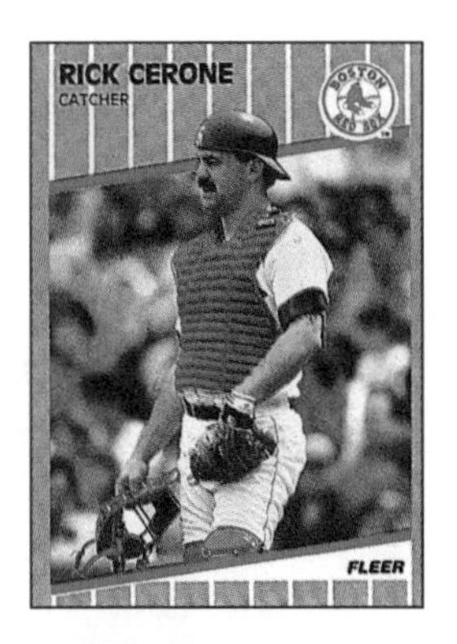

JOHN CERUTTI

	W	L	ERA	G	SV	IP	H	R	BB	SO
1988	6	7	3.13	46	1	123.2	120	56	42	65
Life	26	17	3.96	128	2	427.0	424	211	152	251

POSITION: Pitcher
TEAM: Toronto Blue Jays
BORN: April 28, 1960 Albany, NY
HEIGHT: 6′2″ **WEIGHT:** 200 lbs.
BATS: Left **THROWS:** Left
ACQUIRED: Second-round pick in 6/81 free-agent draft

Cerutti wasn't an inadequate pitcher with Toronto in 1988, but he did suffer from bad luck. He lowered his ERA by more than a point in 1988, but he was saddled with a 6-7 record. Last year, despite a 4.40 ERA, he went 11-4. In 1986, his ERA floated above four again, but his record was 9-4. He will be battling for a spot in the Toronto bullpen in 1989, due to the fine seasons submitted by fellow lefty relievers Jeff Musselman and David Wells. But Toronto will be able to count on Cerutti for long relief and occasional starting duty in 1989.

Cerutti's cards are commons, priced at a nickel or less. His past record isn't outstanding, and he likely won't gain any acclaim until his role with the Blue Jays is better defined. Our pick for his best 1989 card is Fleer.

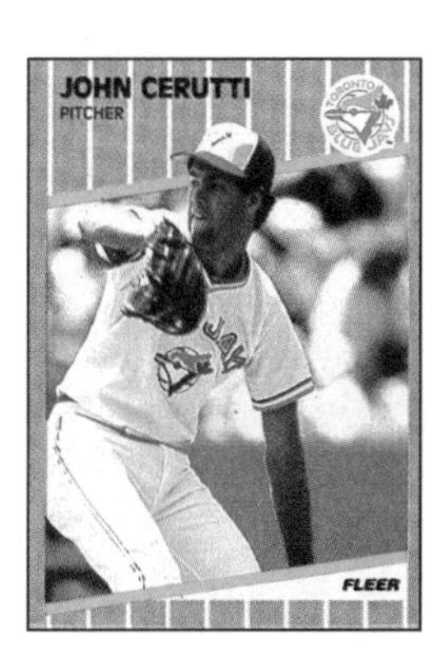

NORM CHARLTON

	W	L	ERA	G	CG	IP	H	R	BB	SO
1988	4	5	3.96	10	0	61.1	60	27	20	39
Life	4	5	3.96	10	0	61.1	60	27	20	39

POSITION: Pitcher
TEAM: Cincinnati Reds
BORN: January 6, 1963 Ft. Polk, LA
HEIGHT: 6′3″ **WEIGHT:** 195 lbs.
BATS: Both **THROWS:** Left
ACQUIRED: Traded from Expos with Tim Barker for Wayne Krenchicki, 3/86

Charlton is a hard-throwing lefty with good control pitches. He was an 11-game-winner for Triple-A Nashville in 1988, starting 27 games and completing eight of them. He also was recalled to Cincinnati for a ten-game cameo appearance, going 4-5 with a 3.96 ERA. At Nashville, Charlton struck out 161 batters in 182 innings; for the Reds he whiffed 39 more—200 Ks for the year. He found success at Double-A Vermont in 1986, going 10-6 with a 2.83 ERA. In 1987 at Nashville, he was only 2-8 but saw limited action that year. If Charlton can maintain his control, he could find a spot in the Cincinnati rotation in 1989.

Charlton's 1989 cards should open in the 10- to 15-cent range. That rate is too high for investment purposes. Our pick for his best 1989 card is Donruss.

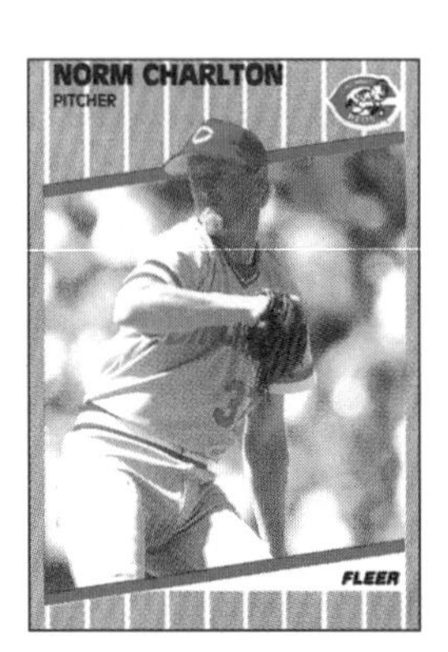

JOHN CHRISTENSEN

	BA	G	AB	R	H	2B	3B	HR	RBI	SB
1988	.263	23	38	5	10	4	0	0	5	0
Life	.225	76	294	36	66	16	2	5	33	3

POSITION: Outfield
TEAM: Minnesota Twins
BORN: September 26, 1960 Downey, CA
HEIGHT: 6′3″ **WEIGHT:** 205 lbs.
BATS: Right **THROWS:** Right
ACQUIRED: Signed as a free agent, 1/88

After having little success with the Mets or the Mariners, Christensen got a shot with the 1988 Minnesota Twins. He filled in wherever he could, as a pinch-hitter, defensive replacement, and occasional starter. In 23 games, Christensen batted a healthy .263. Previously, Christensen hit .242 in 53 games with the 1987 Mariners. Christensen came up through the Met system, and played in 51 games with the 1985 team. His paltry .186 average banished him to Triple-A for the rest of the season. After seven professional seasons of part-time work, Christensen's future doesn't look hopeful.

Based on his past bad luck, it seems unlikely that Christensen will play full time. Even getting a spot on the roster might be tough in 1989. Christensen's 1989 cards, priced as commons, are not worthy of investment. Our pick for his best 1989 card is Fleer.

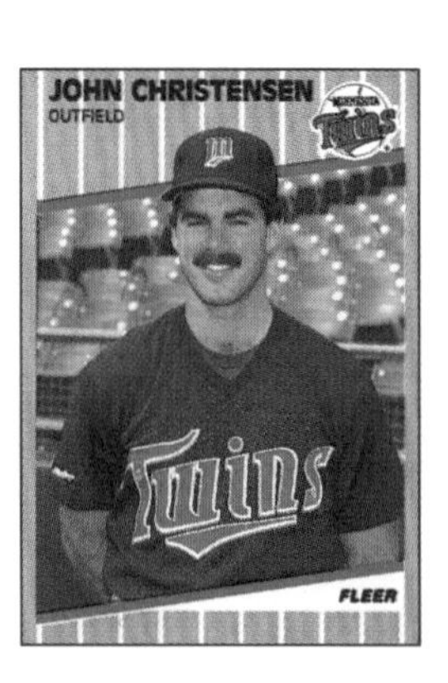

JIM CLANCY

	W	L	ERA	G	CG	IP	H	R	BB	SO
1988	11	13	4.49	36	4	196.1	207	106	47	118
Life	128	140	4.10	352	73	2206.0	2185	1104	814	1237

POSITION: Pitcher
TEAM: Toronto Blue Jays
BORN: December 18, 1955 Chicago, IL
HEIGHT: 6′2″ **WEIGHT:** 185 lbs.
BATS: Right **THROWS:** Right
ACQUIRED: Selected from Rangers in expansion draft, 11/76

Clancy, an original member of the Blue Jays, saw his production slip a bit in 1988, posting a losing record (11-13) for the first time since 1984. To cure his slump, Toronto used him in spot relief work, during which he picked up a save and finished five games. The veteran hurler is a durable member of the Blue Jay staff, having pitched more than 200 innings in four of the last six seasons. A return to form by Clancy could be the boost the Blue Jays need to win the American League East.

Clancy is saddled with a losing record. His cards will never make gains in value unless he wins 20 games or the Blue Jays make the World Series. Until then, his common-priced cards are risky investments. Our pick for his best 1989 card is Topps.

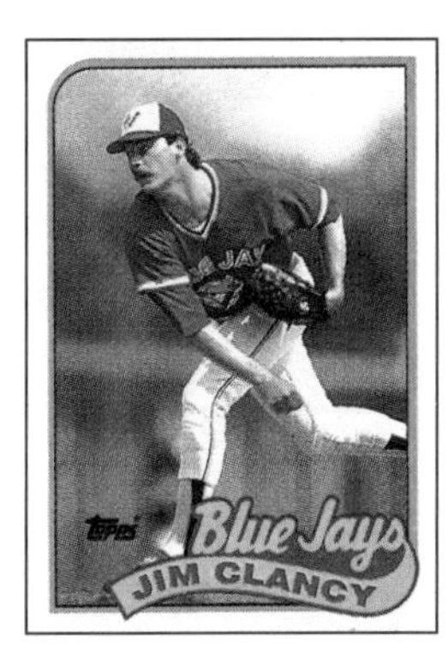

DAVE CLARK

	BA	G	AB	R	H	2B	3B	HR	RBI	SB
1988	.263	63	156	11	41	4	1	3	18	0
Life	.249	110	301	32	75	10	1	9	39	2

POSITION: Outfield
TEAM: Cleveland Indians
BORN: September 3, 1962 Tupelo, MS
HEIGHT: 6′2″ **WEIGHT:** 200 lbs.
BATS: Left **THROWS:** Right
ACQUIRED: First-round pick in 6/83 free-agent draft

Clark seems ready to make his mark. *Baseball America* had rated him as the third best big league prospect in the American Association in 1987, and he opened the 1988 season with the Indians. After a disappointing start, Clark was sent out to Triple-A Colorado Springs, where he hit .247, with four home runs and 31 RBIs. For the Tribe in '88, he hit .263 and three homers. At Triple-A Buffalo in 1987, Clark punished American Association hurlers with a .340 batting average, 30 homers, and 80 RBIs. He has a strong arm and played college ball at Jackson State University. After two partial seasons with the Tribe, Clark figures to become a permanent fixture in 1989.

Clark's 1989 cards will open in the 10- to 15-cent range, a great price for investing. Our pick for his best 1989 card is Topps.

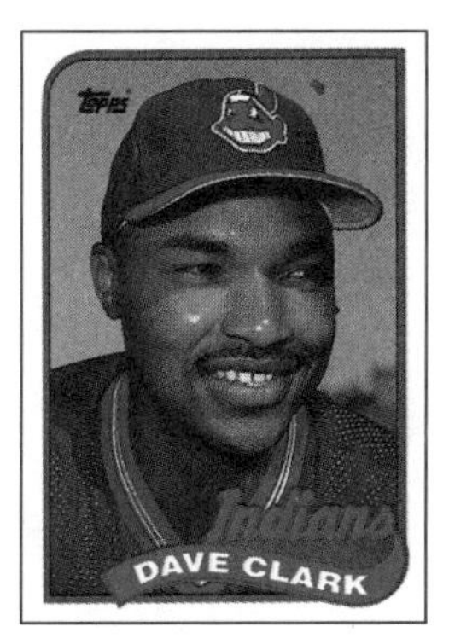

JACK CLARK

	BA	G	AB	R	H	2B	3B	HR	RBI	SB
1988	.242	150	496	81	120	14	0	27	93	3
Life	.273	1516	5320	876	1453	272	36	256	904	66

POSITION: First base
TEAM: San Diego Padres
BORN: November 10, 1955
New Brighton, PA
HEIGHT: 6′3″ **WEIGHT:** 205 lbs.
BATS: Right **THROWS:** Right
ACQUIRED: Traded from Yankees with Pat Clements for Lance McCullers, Jimmy Jones, and Stan Jefferson, 10/88

Clark, a 13-year veteran, goes to the Padres with a familiar role: offensive savior. He said that he feels like a National Leaguer, and the N.L. pitchers probably lost a few nights' sleep. He had his first taste of A.L. pitching in 1988 and passed all tests. While he didn't match his incredible offensive totals of 1987, he slugged 27 home runs and 93 RBIs. In '87, Clark crushed 35 homers and amassed 106 RBIs and 93 runs for the Cardinals. His explosive bat could make any team a contender, and the Padre fans have good reason for high hopes in 1989.

Clark's 1989 cards might soar to 50 cents each if he opens well. Don't pay more than a dime for his cards, though. If he survives a second straight season without major injury, he'll win more believers. Our pick for his best 1989 card is Score.

JERALD CLARK

	BA	G	AB	R	H	2B	3B	HR	RBI	SB
1988	.200	6	15	0	3	1	0	0	3	0
Life	.200	6	15	0	3	1	0	0	3	0

POSITION: Outfield
TEAM: San Diego Padres
BORN: August 10, 1963 Crockett, TX
HEIGHT: 6′4″ **WEIGHT:** 190 lbs.
BATS: Right **THROWS:** Right
ACQUIRED: 12th-round pick in 6/85 free-agent draft

Clark, selected in the 12th round, managed to steal the spotlight at Triple-A Las Vegas in 1988 from three former first-round-pick outfielders—Shawn Abner, Shane Mack, and Stanley Jefferson. Clark hit .301 in '88, the fourth time in four years he's hit over .300. *Baseball America* picked him as the eighth-best prospect in the Pacific Coast League in 1988. At Double-A Wichita in 1987, he batted .311, with a career-high 18 home runs and 95 RBIs. He hit .325 for Spokane in the Northwest League in 1985. In 1986, he hit .303 at Class-A Reno. Clark has the size and the batting stroke to be a long-ball threat in the majors.

Clark's 1989 cards should open at 25 cents. We see him as a good investment. He hits for average, and he has good power. Our pick for his best 1989 card is Fleer.

TERRY CLARK

	W	L	ERA	G	CG	IP	H	R	BB	SO
1988	6	6	5.07	15	2	94.0	120	39	31	39
Life	6	6	5.07	15	2	94.0	120	39	31	39

POSITION: Pitcher
TEAM: California Angels
BORN: October 10, 1960
Los Angeles, CA
HEIGHT: 6′1″ **WEIGHT:** 200 lbs.
BATS: Right **THROWS:** Right
ACQUIRED: Signed as a free agent, 2/86

Although Clark began the 1988 season at Triple-A Edmonton, the Angels soon realized that he belonged in the California starting rotation. Clark finished last season at the .500 mark. He was signed as a free agent by California after seven years in the Cardinal farm system. His first season in the Angels organization in 1986 at Double-A Midland resulted in a 9-4 record, a 3.29 ERA, and 66 strikeouts in 90⅓ innings of work. In 1987, the righthander moved up to Edmonton and fashioned an 8-9 record and a 3.84 ERA. He has good control, as evidenced by the 31 bases on balls he allowed in 94 innings for the '88 Angels. Clark should continue to be a factor in the Angel rotation.

Clark's 1989 cards will open in the 25- to 30-cent range. For the moment, his cards are not outstanding investments. Our pick for his best 1989 card is Score.

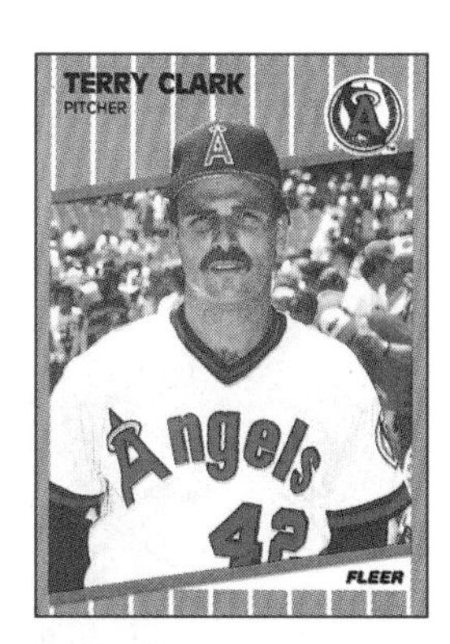

WILL CLARK

	BA	G	AB	R	H	2B	3B	HR	RBI	SB
1988	.282	162	575	102	162	31	6	29	109	9
Life	.292	423	1512	257	442	87	13	75	241	18

POSITION: First base
TEAM: San Francisco Giants
BORN: March 13, 1964 New Orleans, LA
HEIGHT: 6′1″ **WEIGHT:** 190 lbs.
BATS: Left **THROWS:** Left
ACQUIRED: First-round pick in 6/85 free-agent draft

Will "The Thrill" Clark was one of the Giants' most dependable players in 1988, leading the N.L. with 109 RBIs. He helped the Giants to a divisional crown in 1987 with a super sophomore season of 35 homers, 91 RBIs, and a .308 average. Again in 1988, he led the team in doubles (31) and homers (29). Clark was named as the N.L. top first baseman by *The Sporting News.* A member of the 1984 Olympic team, he hit .429 with three homers in five games. At age 25, Clark will be starring at first base for the Giants for years to come.

Clark's many talents are no secret to those fans who will buy his 1989 cards at 60 to 70 cents each. Speculators won't see short-term profits at these prices. Still, the price is a worthwhile buy. Our pick for his best 1989 card is Topps.

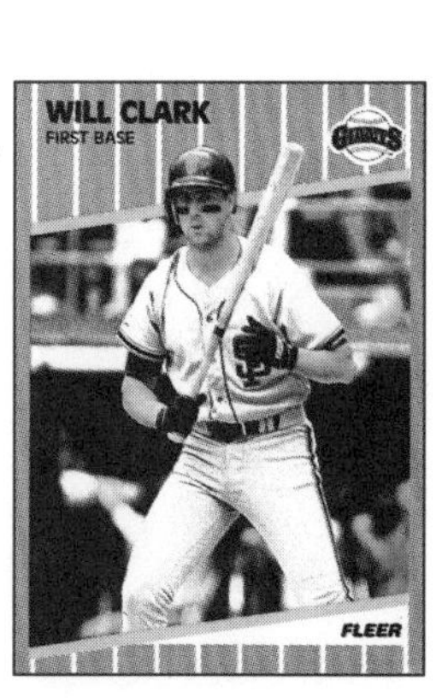

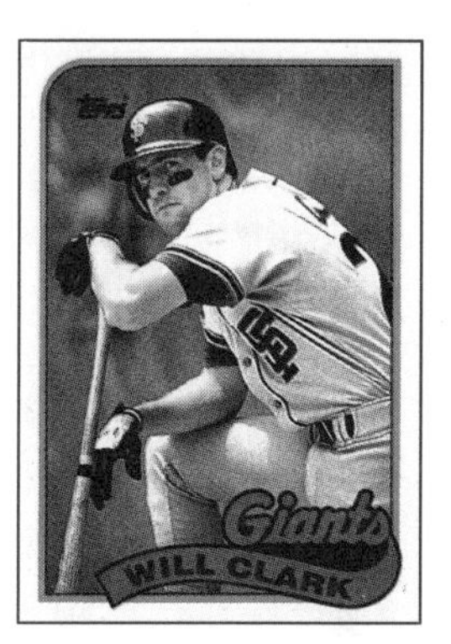

ROGER CLEMENS

	W	L	ERA	G	CG	IP	H	R	BB	SO
1988	18	12	2.93	35	14	264.0	217	93	62	291
Life	78	34	3.05	140	50	1031.1	873	375	278	985

POSITION: Pitcher
TEAM: Boston Red Sox
BORN: August 4, 1962 Dayton, OH
HEIGHT: 6′4″ **WEIGHT:** 205 lbs.
BATS: Right **THROWS:** Right
ACQUIRED: First-round pick in 6/83 free-agent draft

Clemens fell short in his bid for three straight Cy Young awards, but the righty still achieved admirable totals in 1988. In revenge for last season, he beat Seattle's Mark Langston in the league strikeout derby, ending with 291 Ks. Clemens, 18-12, just missed his third straight 20-win season. He was just a few Ks shy of reaching 1,000 career strikeouts. Clemens had a 2.93 ERA, and he hurled 264 innings. Most importantly, he made major contributions to Boston's capture of first place. In 1987, Clemens was 20-9 with an incredible 18 complete games. At age 26, Clemens is averaging yearly accomplishments which rank him as a future Hall of Famer.

Because Clemens missed the Cy Young, his 1989 cards will sell at 60 to 75 cents, a dandy price. If he becomes the A.L.'s best pitcher again, those cards could reach the $1.50 level. Our pick for his best 1989 card is Score.

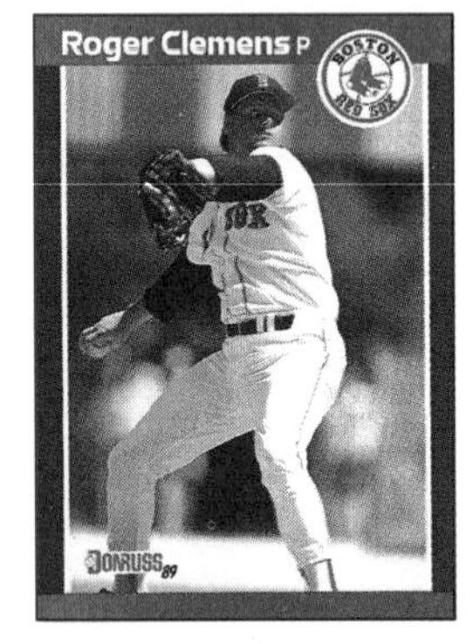

PAT CLEMENTS

	W	L	ERA	G	SV	IP	H	R	BB	SO
1988	0	0	6.48	6	0	8.1	12	8	4	3
Life	8	9	3.88	194	12	245.2	242	110	106	106

POSITION: Pitcher
TEAM: San Diego Padres
BORN: February 2, 1962 McCloud, CA
HEIGHT: 6′ **WEIGHT:** 180 lbs.
BATS: Right **THROWS:** Left
ACQUIRED: Traded from Yankees with Jack Clark for Lance McCullers, Jimmy Jones, and Stan Jefferson, 10/88

Clements might be an added bonus in the trade that brought Jack Clark to the San Diego Padres. Clements didn't accomplish much in 1988, but he notched a career best of seven saves in 1987 with the Yankees. He appeared in a career high of 65 games with the 1986 Pirates. His first major league season was spent with the Angels in 1985. Clements registered a perfect 5-0 mark with one save in 41 appearances. He only began relieving in 1984. The Padres believe that he can bounce back and recapture his rookie year form. Lefty relievers are always in demand, so the Padres will give Clements lots of opportunity.

Expect Clements' 1989 cards to sell for three cents or less. At this point, monitor his progress in 1989 before investing. Our pick for his best 1989 card is Topps.

VINCE COLEMAN

	BA	G	AB	R	H	2B	3B	HR	RBI	SB
1988	.260	153	616	77	160	20	10	3	38	81
Life	.262	609	2475	399	649	67	38	7	150	407

POSITION: Outfield
TEAM: St. Louis Cardinals
BORN: September 22, 1961
Jacksonville, FL
HEIGHT: 6′ **WEIGHT:** 170 lbs.
BATS: Both **THROWS:** Right
ACQUIRED: Tenth-round pick in 6/82 free-agent draft

The 1985 N.L. Rookie of the Year, Coleman slowed down only a bit for the Cardinals after stealing more than 100 bases during his first three seasons. Nevertheless, he led the N.L. in stolen bases (81) again in 1988, the fourth time in his four-year career. Coleman hit .260, with 77 runs scored and 20 doubles. His on-base average dipped from .358 in 1987 to .313 in '88. In 1987, he hit .289 with 109 stolen bases and 121 runs scored. He swiped 145 bases during his first full season of minor league ball in 1983, a pro record. Each year, Coleman's total steals surpass the number of stolen bases by entire teams.

Despite Coleman's blazing speed, he has never hit .300 in the majors. His 1989 cards will open at about 30 cents. Until his batting improves, don't invest more than a quarter apiece in his cards. Our pick for his best 1989 card is Donruss.

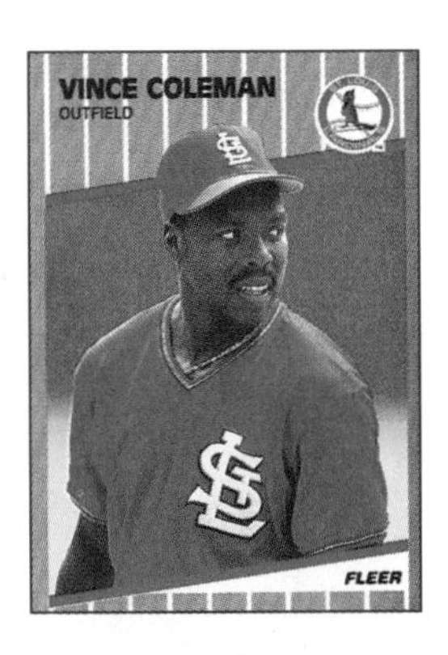

DARNELL COLES

	BA	G	AB	R	H	2B	3B	HR	RBI	SB
1988	.292	55	195	32	57	10	1	10	34	3
Life	.245	460	1489	185	365	80	6	47	212	13

POSITION: Third base; outfield
TEAM: Seattle Mariners
BORN: June 2, 1962 San Bernardino, CA
HEIGHT: 6′1″ **WEIGHT:** 185 lbs.
BATS: Right **THROWS:** Right
ACQUIRED: Traded from Pirates for Glenn Wilson, 6/88

Coles returned to the Mariners, his original team, at the midpoint of the 1988 season. He's returned as a more versatile, talented player, as evidenced by last year's stats. He batted .292 with ten homers and 34 RBIs, all in just 55 games. Coles is a solid fielder at third base or the outfield, so he gives the Mariners options. He hit a career-high 20 homers and 86 RBIs with the 1986 Tigers. The Mariners seem delighted to add some punch to their lineup and must be dreaming about the stats Coles may rack up in a full 1989 season.

Coles hasn't captured much attention, since he's bounced from team to team. His 1989 cards will sell as commons. Buy them up. At age 26, Coles may become a Mariner mainstay and a power-hitting celebrity. Our pick for his best 1989 card is Donruss.

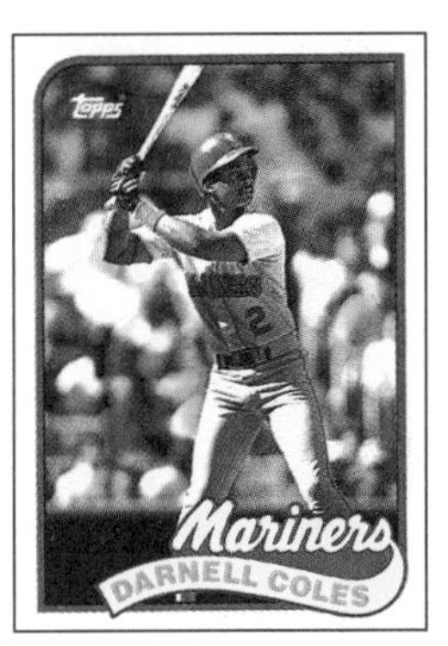

DAVE COLLINS

	BA	G	AB	R	H	2B	3B	HR	RBI	SB
1988	.236	99	174	12	41	6	2	0	14	7
Life	.273	1524	4743	643	1297	182	52	32	363	385

POSITION: Outfield
TEAM: Cincinnati Reds
BORN: October 20, 1952 Rapid City, SD
HEIGHT: 5′10″ **WEIGHT:** 175 lbs.
BATS: Both **THROWS:** Right
ACQUIRED: Signed as a free agent, 1/88

Collins returned to the Cincinnati Reds in 1987 after a five-year absence. In 1988, he spent most of his time as pinch-hitter and substitute outfielder, participating in 99 games. His average was the lowest since 1977, when he played with the Seattle Mariners. In 1987, he hit .294 in limited duty with the Reds. Other teams Collins has served in his 14-year career include the California Angels (1975 to '76), the Reds (1978 to '81), New York Yankees (1982), Toronto Blue Jays (1984), Oakland Athletics (1985), and Detroit Tigers (1986). Collins, who once stole as many as 79 bases in one season, swiped just seven in 1988.

Collins will wind up his career as a reserve outfielder. His 1989 cards, priced at three cents or less, don't merit investment due to his substitute status. Our pick for his best 1989 card is Score.

DAVE CONCEPCION

	BA	G	AB	R	H	2B	3B	HR	RBI	SB
1988	.198	84	197	11	39	9	0	0	8	3
Life	.267	2488	8723	993	2326	389	48	101	950	321

POSITION: Infield
TEAM: Cincinnati Reds
BORN: June 17, 1948
Argua, Venezuela
HEIGHT: 6′1″ **WEIGHT:** 200 lbs.
BATS: Right **THROWS:** Right
ACQUIRED: Signed as a free agent, 9/67

Concepcion began his career in 1970 and spent his 19th consecutive season with the Cincinnati Reds in 1988. In his prime, he was a great shortstop. Now the team's chief utility infielder, he even pitched 1⅓ innings last season, allowing just two hits and no runs, while striking out one. Concepcion, a nine-time All-Star, had a stellar season in 1987. Serving as a part-time second baseman, he hit .319 with one homer and 33 RBIs. He has played in four World Series contests and has a cumulative average of .266.

Concepcion's 1989 cards should be a nickel or less. While they show no chances for short-term gains, they might have long-term potential. He could be a long shot for the Hall of Fame, based mainly on his longevity. Our pick for his best 1989 card is Fleer.

DAVID CONE

	W	L	ERA	G	CG	IP	H	R	BB	SO
1988	20	3	2.22	35	8	231.1	178	67	80	213
Life	25	9	2.85	67	9	353.1	294	127	137	302

POSITION: Pitcher
TEAM: New York Mets
BORN: January 2, 1963 Kansas City, MO
HEIGHT: 6′1″ **WEIGHT:** 180 lbs.
BATS: Left **THROWS:** Right
ACQUIRED: Traded from Royals for Ed Hearn and Rick Anderson, 3/87

Cone, a fireballing Mets righty, battled teammate Dwight Gooden for most wins all season, but led the club in strikeouts in 1988. Cone was 20-3, with a 2.22 ERA and 213 Ks in 231⅓ innings. His winning percentage and low ERA earned him a berth on the 1988 All-Star team. His 1988 effort was a real turnaround from his so-so Mets debut in 1987. He was 5-6 in '87, with a 3.71 ERA, 68 strikeouts, and 44 walks in 99⅓ innings. Cone is no youngster; he toiled for five years in the Kansas City minor league system before getting his break in New York. He is now a vital element of the Met pitching staff.

Cone's 1989 cards could bring up to 25 cents, which would make a questionable investment. After only one winning season to his credit, Cone isn't a proven superstar. Following his 1989 season, that could change quickly. Our pick for his best 1989 card is Topps.

DENNIS COOK

	W	L	ERA	G	CG	IP	H	R	BB	SO
1988	2	1	2.86	4	1	22.0	9	8	11	13
Life	2	1	2.86	4	1	22.0	9	8	11	13

POSITION: Pitcher
TEAM: San Francisco Giants
BORN: October 4, 1962 Lamarque, TX
HEIGHT: 6′3″ **WEIGHT:** 185 lbs.
BATS: Left **THROWS:** Left
ACQUIRED: 18th-round pick in 6/85 free-agent draft

Cook had a good 1988, and his prospects for 1989 are promising. An 11-game winner at Triple-A Phoenix in 1988, he got a late-season recall to San Francisco. His first outing resulted in a two-hit shutout. In 1987, *Baseball America* called the young lefty the pitcher with the best control in the Double-A Texas League. At Shreveport that year, Cook had a 9-2 record and 2.13 ERA. He fanned 98 and walked only 20 in 105⅔ innings of work. He's another of those good University of Texas hurlers—Bruce Ruffin, Calvin Schiraldi, and Roger Clemens went there. If Cook follows them, the Giants have a real winner on their roster.

Cook's 1989 cards should open in the 20-cent range. That's too high a price for short-term investing. Our pick for his best 1989 card is Donruss.

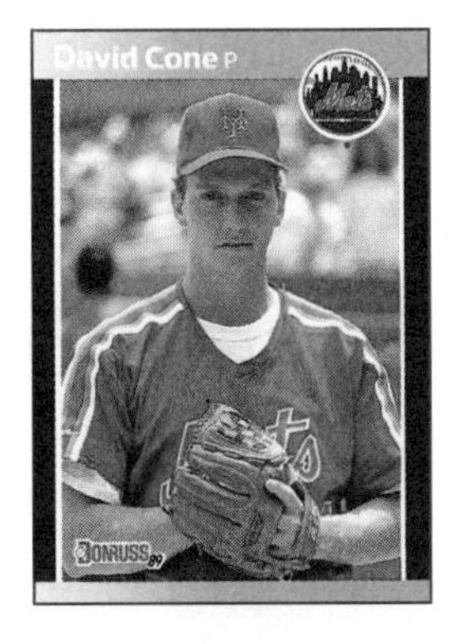

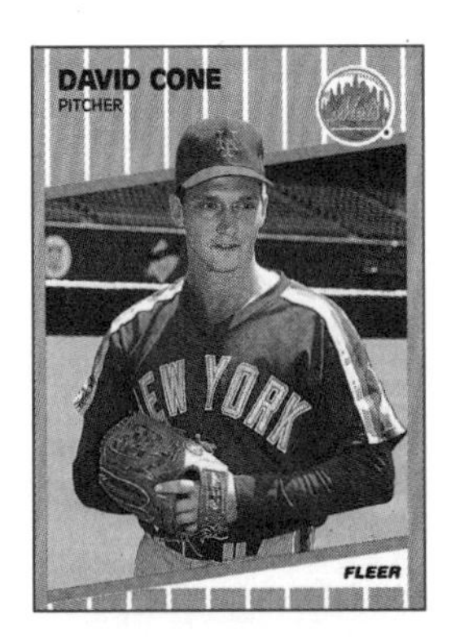

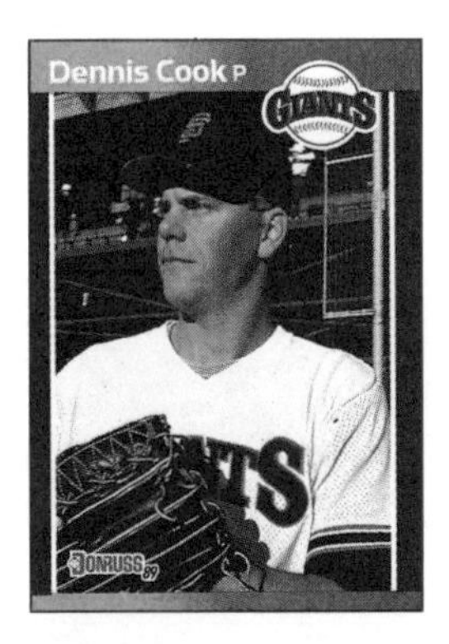

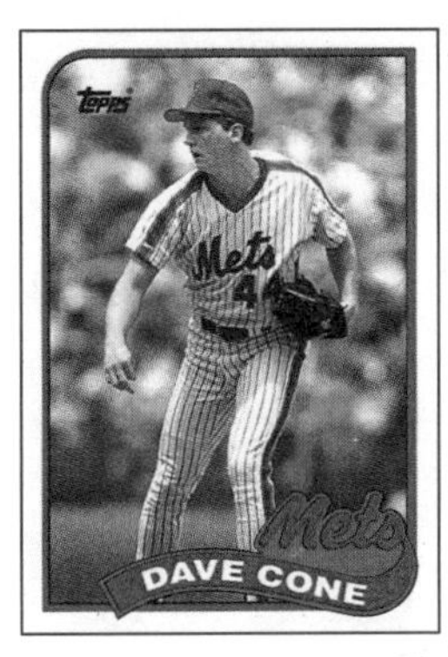

JIM CORSI

	W	L	ERA	G	SV	IP	H	R	BB	SO
1988	0	1	3.80	11	0	21.1	20	10	6	10
Life	0	1	3.80	11	0	21.1	20	10	6	10

POSITION: Pitcher
TEAM: Oakland A's
BORN: September 9, 1961
Newtonville, MA
HEIGHT: 6'1" **WEIGHT:** 210 lbs.
BATS: Right **THROWS:** Right
ACQUIRED: Signed as a free agent, 4/87

Corsi became the Triple-A Tacoma Tigers closer in 1988, and he responded with 16 saves and a 2.75 ERA, fanning 48 in 59 innings. He then got a late-season call from the front-running A's and continued to impress. Oakland signed Corsi as a free agent early in the 1987 season, and the righty rewarded their faith by going 3-1 at Class-A Modesto and 8-1 in Double-A at Huntsville with ten saves combined. The A's are his third organization. The Red Sox cut him after he won only two games in 1986 for their Double-A club. He first signed with the Yankees in 1982. If Corsi progresses further, he has a solid chance of being in the Oakland bullpen in 1989.

Corsi's 1989 cards should open in the 10- to 15-cent range. Don't buy huge quantities at that price. Our pick for his best 1989 card is Fleer.

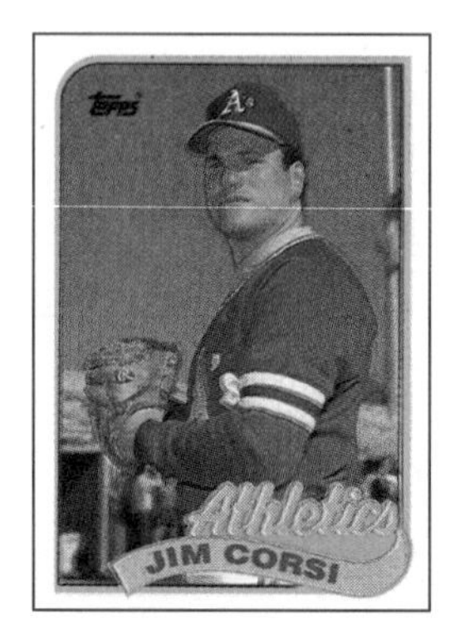

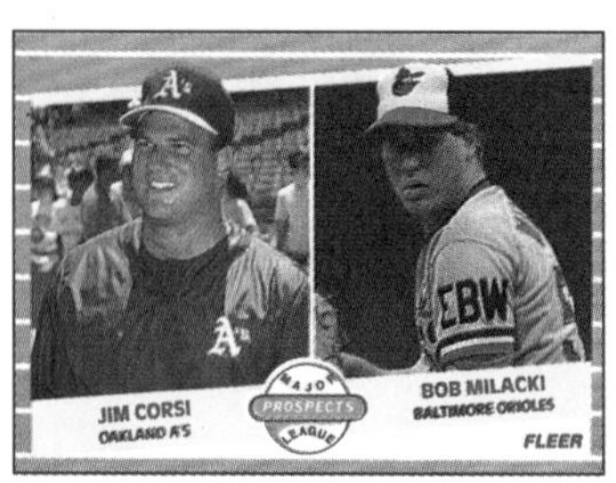

JOHN COSTELLO

	W	L	ERA	G	SV	IP	H	R	BB	SO
1988	5	2	1.81	36	1	49.2	44	15	25	38
Life	5	2	1.81	36	1	49.2	44	15	25	38

POSITION: Pitcher
TEAM: St. Louis Cardinals
BORN: December 24, 1960
Oceanside, NY
HEIGHT: 6'1" **WEIGHT:** 180 lbs.
BATS: Left **THROWS:** Right
ACQUIRED: 25th-round pick in the 6/83 free-agent draft

Costello was one real ray of sunshine in an otherwise disappointing 1988 for the Cardinals. He finished the season with an ERA below 2.00, the best on the Red Bird staff. At Triple-A Louisville in '88, Costello racked up 11 saves and kept his ERA at 1.84. He divided 1987 between Double-A Arkansas, where he went 5-2, and Triple-A Louisville, where he was unbeaten in two decisions. After beginning 1988 at Louisville, he was quickly recalled to St. Louis. Pitching at Class-A Springfield in 1985, Costello's won-lost record was 8-13, but he chalked up a career-high 127 strikeouts (against only 60 walks). He went 8-2 at Class-A St. Petersburg in 1986.

His 1989 cards will open in the 25- to 30-cent range. Despite a promising 1988, wait until he chalks up a few saves in 1989 before buying. Our pick for his best 1989 card is Fleer.

HENRY COTTO

	BA	G	AB	R	H	2B	3B	HR	RBI	SB
1988	.259	133	396	50	100	18	1	8	33	27
Life	.256	375	817	110	209	37	1	15	73	44

POSITION: Oufield
TEAM: Seattle Mariners
BORN: January 5, 1961
New York, NY
HEIGHT: 6′2″ **WEIGHT:** 180 lbs.
BATS: Right **THROWS:** Right
ACQUIRED: Traded from Yankees with Steve Trout for Lee Guetterman, Clay Parker, and Shane Taylor, 12/87

Cotto enjoyed one of the best seasons of his career with the 1988 Mariners. He played in 133 games, the most ever, and he logged some impressive hitting statistics. Cotto had only seven career homers in his four previous seasons; he hit eight in 1988. His 33 RBIs were another personal best. Cotto is a defensive wizard in the outfield, as evidenced by his two errors in 1988. His 27 stolen bases were second highest on the team, and he was caught stealing only three times. Cotto was one of Seattle's biggest surprises in 1988. He could be a starter in 1989

Cotto's cards will be three cents or less in 1989. He had a great 1988, and could be a star on this season's squad. Invest while prices are still low. Our pick for his best 1989 card is Donruss.

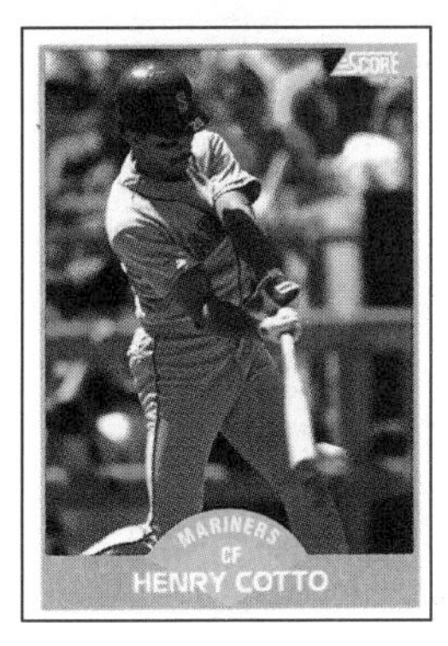

DANNY COX

	W	L	ERA	G	CG	IP	H	R	BB	SO
1988	3	8	3.98	13	0	86.0	89	40	25	47
Life	56	56	3.40	152	21	985.2	991	434	297	493

POSITION: Pitcher
TEAM: St. Louis Cardinals
BORN: September 21, 1959
Northampton, England
HEIGHT: 6′4″ **WEIGHT:** 230 lbs.
BATS: Right **THROWS:** Right
ACQUIRED: 13th-round pick in 6/81 free-agent draft

Cox was on the disabled list during much of 1988. He saw action in 13 games. He compiled a 3-8 record, his worst mark since joining the team in 1983, but he did notch a respectable 3.98 ERA. Cox also missed a month of the pennant-winning 1987 season, but he still was the Cards' big-money hurler. He pitched a complete game to clinch the pennant and a shutout against the Giants to win the N.L. playoffs that year. He had an 11-9 record and a 3.88 ERA in 1987. A comeback from Cox could help the Cardinals turn it around in 1989.

Cox has a big arm, but at 29 he hasn't won 100 games in his career yet. His 1989 card values are just a slice above commons with little growth potential. Our pick for his best 1989 card is Fleer.

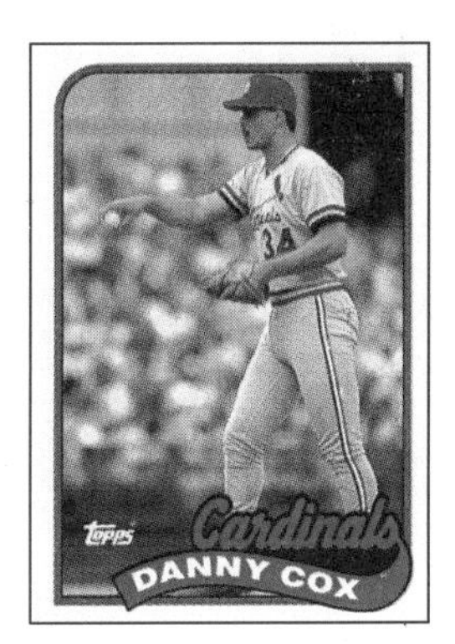

CHUCK CRIM

	W	L	ERA	G	SV	IP	H	R	BB	SO
1988	7	6	2.91	70	9	105.0	95	38	28	58
Life	13	14	3.33	123	21	235.0	228	98	67	114

POSITION: Pitcher
TEAM: Milwaukee Brewers
BORN: July 23, 1961 Van Nuys, CA
HEIGHT: 6′ **WEIGHT:** 170 lbs.
BATS: Right **THROWS:** Right
ACQUIRED: 17th-round pick in 6/82 free-agent draft

Crim followed up his 1987 debut with another fine season of relief for the Milwaukee Brewers. In 1988, he topped the American League with 70 appearances, finishing 25 of those contests. He was second only to Brewer relief ace Dan Plesac in many categories. The tireless Crim was second on the 1987 Brewers with his 3.67 ERA. He was 5-4 in '87, racking up 12 saves. His future looks promising after back-to-back successes in his first two major league seasons. Avoiding exhaustion will be Crim's greatest challenge in 1989.

Crim could be one of the relief stars of the immediate future, but he has not yet received national attention. Priced at a nickel or less, his 1989 cards could be real sleepers if he saves a pennant for Milwaukee this year. Our pick for his best 1989 card is Fleer.

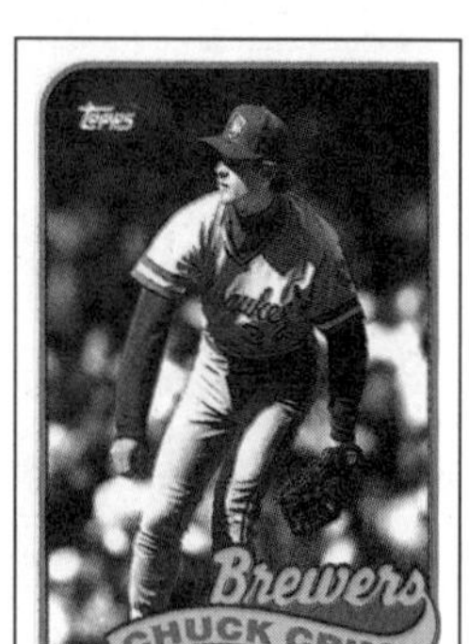

STEVE CURRY

	W	L	ERA	G	CG	IP	H	R	BB	SO
1988	0	1	8.18	3	0	11.0	15	10	14	4
Life	0	1	8.18	3	0	11.0	15	10	14	4

POSITION: Pitcher
TEAM: Boston Red Sox
BORN: September 13, 1965 Winter Park, FL
HEIGHT: 6′6″ **WEIGHT:** 217 lbs.
BATS: Right **THROWS:** Right
ACQUIRED: Seventh-round pick in 6/84 free-agent draft

Curry, Triple-A Pawtucket's top hurler in 1988, should make the jump to Fenway Park in 1989 if all the indications we see are true. Curry fashioned an 11-9 record in '88, with a 3.08 ERA and 110 strikeouts in 146 innings of work. Late in the season he saw limited, if unspectacular, duty with the big club. In 1987, the righthander was 11-12 with Pawtucket, with a 3.81 ERA and 112 Ks in 184 innings. He was 11-9 at Double-A New Britain in 1986, starting a string of three consecutive 11-win seasons. At Winter Haven in 1985, he was 9-10 with a 3.69 ERA; he was 6-4 at Elmira in 1984. Curry is a cannon-armed hurler who should be ready for the big time in '89.

Curry should crack the BoSox starting rotation. His 1989 cards will open in the 15- to 20-cent range. That's too expensive for investing. Our pick for his best 1989 card is Fleer.

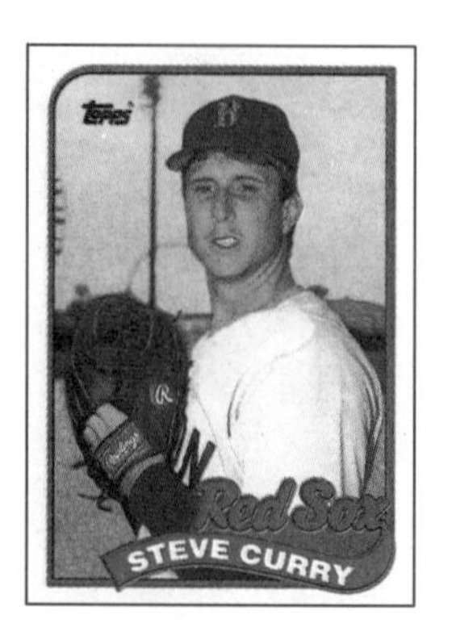

KAL DANIELS

	BA	G	AB	R	H	2B	3B	HR	RBI	SB
1988	.291	140	495	95	144	29	1	18	64	27
Life	.311	322	1044	202	325	63	6	50	151	68

POSITION: Outfield
TEAM: Cincinnati Reds
BORN: August 20, 1963 Vienna, GA
HEIGHT: 5′11″ **WEIGHT:** 185 lbs.
BATS: Left **THROWS:** Right
ACQUIRED: First-round pick in 6/82 free-agent draft

Daniels suffered a slump from his 1987 stats in '88, but he still was one of the Reds' most dependable hitters last season. He hit 18 homers (second only to Eric Davis), and he had 64 RBIs in 1988. Although he hit just .291, he kept his career average above .300. Daniels, who missed considerable time in 1987 due to knee surgery, played in a career-high 140 games in 1988. His 27 stolen bases, another career high, ranked fourth on the team. Daniels is a polished fielder as well. His many talents make him a valuable commodity for Cincinnati. Daniels could have his best season ever in 1989.

The secret is spreading that Daniels could be a future superstar. His 1989 cards should sell for 20 cents or more. Buy them at that price, because they will rise in value. Our pick for his best 1989 card is Topps.

RON DARLING

	W	L	ERA	G	CG	IP	H	R	BB	SO
1988	17	9	3.25	34	7	240.2	218	97	60	161
Life	73	41	3.36	174	20	1174.1	1028	493	472	838

POSITION: Pitcher
TEAM: New York Mets
BORN: August 19, 1960 Honolulu, HI
HEIGHT: 6′3″ **WEIGHT:** 195 lbs.
BATS: Right **THROWS:** Right
ACQUIRED: Traded from Rangers with Walt Terrell for Lee Mazzilli, 4/82

Darling maintained his high lifetime winning percentage and improved his overall statistics with a solid showing in 1988. The righthander lowered his ERA nearly one entire point as he enjoyed a brief encounter with the possibility of a 20-game win season. He went 17-9 with a 3.25 ERA. He was second on the pitching-rich Mets team in complete games and shutouts, and he increased his innings pitched in 1988. He has won 12 or more games for the Mets for five consecutive seasons. Darling may not have the same flamethrowing gift as David Cone or Dwight Gooden, but his dependability makes him a valuable member of the Met staff.

Darling's 1989 cards should be available for 10 cents or less. Not even age 30, Darling has several years ahead of him to become a big winner. Our pick for his best 1989 card is Fleer.

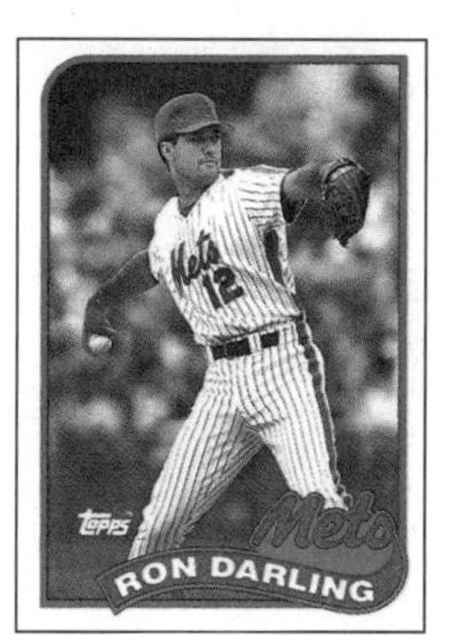

DANNY DARWIN

	W	L	ERA	G	CG	IP	H	R	BB	SO
1988	8	13	3.84	44	3	192.0	189	86	48	129
Life	89	101	3.59	372	44	1628.2	1548	744	517	1052

POSITION: Pitcher
TEAM: Houston Astros
BORN: October 25, 1955 Bonham, TX
HEIGHT: 6′3″ **WEIGHT:** 190 lbs.
BATS: Right **THROWS:** Right
ACQUIRED: Traded from Brewers for Don August and Mark Knudson, 8/86

Darwin was kept busy by the 1988 Astros, serving both in starting and relief assignments. He had three complete games, eight wins, nine games finished, and three saves in 1988. The veteran righty has been alternating between the starting rotation and the bullpen since he broke in with the Texas Rangers in 1978. Darwin had his greatest season in 1980 with Texas; he went 13-4, with a 2.62 ERA and eight saves, all of which remain as his personal bests. He has pitched at least 180 innings for six consecutive seasons. Darwin's presence will be a solidifying factor for the 1989 Astros pitching staff.

Darwin's stats would be more impressive if he spent his career in one role, starter or reliever. As they are, it's a risk to invest in his 1989 common-priced cards. Our pick for his best 1989 card is Topps.

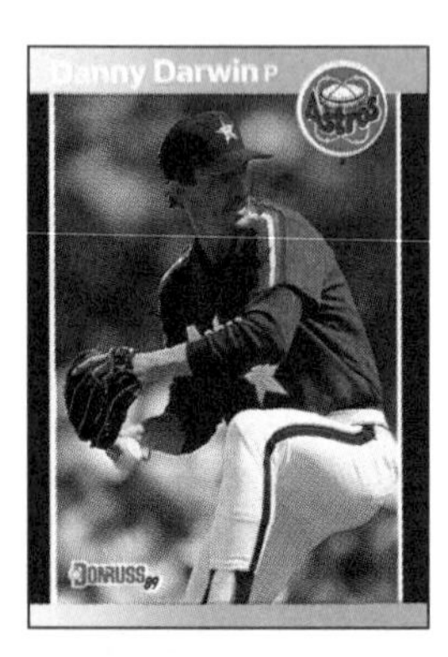

DOUG DASCENZO

	BA	G	AB	R	H	2B	3B	HR	RBI	SB
1988	.213	26	75	9	16	3	0	0	4	6
Life	.213	26	75	9	16	3	0	0	4	6

POSITION: Outfield
TEAM: Chicago Cubs
BORN: June 30, 1964 Cleveland, OH
HEIGHT: 5′8″ **WEIGHT:** 160 lbs.
BATS: Both **THROWS:** Left
ACQUIRED: 13th-round pick in 6/85 free-agent draft

Dascenzo took the Wrigley Field faithful by storm late last season, when he batted close to .500 in his first seven games (getting 11 hits in 24 at-bats). He spent most of the 1988 campaign at Triple-A Iowa, where he batted .295 and was the team leader in hits with 149. While not a long-ball hitter, this swift center fielder did hit six home runs and drove in 49. He batted .306 at Double-A Pittsfield in 1987. His first pro stop was in 1985 at Geneva, where he batted .333 in 70 contests. He hit .327 the next year at Winston-Salem. Dascenzo could solve the Cubs problems as a lead-off hitter and center fielder.

Dascenzo's 1989 cards should open at 30 to 40 cents. If he makes the Cubs, his cards' value will increase. Our pick for his best 1989 card is Score.

DARREN DAULTON

	BA	G	AB	R	H	2B	3B	HR	RBI	SB
1988	.208	58	144	13	30	6	0	1	12	2
Life	.209	198	517	56	108	19	1	16	57	7

POSITION: Catcher
TEAM: Philadelphia Phillies
BORN: January 3, 1962
Arkansas City, KS
HEIGHT: 6′2″ **WEIGHT:** 190 lbs.
BATS: Left **THROWS:** Right
ACQUIRED: 25th-round pick in 6/80 free-agent draft

A perennial prospect who spends lots of time on the disabled list, Daulton, at age 27, is at the crossroads of his career. He could end up as the Phillies' number one catcher in 1989 or hunting for a new line of work. Daulton's first big league experience came during a two-game cameo appearance for the 1983 Phillies. He saw some action with the big club in 1985 and 1986, and he caught 53 games in 1987 and batted .194. In 1988, he was hitting .208 when he punched out a water cooler and broke his hand.

Daulton's career is on hold at the moment, and his cards are commons. If lightning strikes, he could become a star, and his card values would escalate. However, don't bet the ranch. Our pick for his best 1989 card is Donruss.

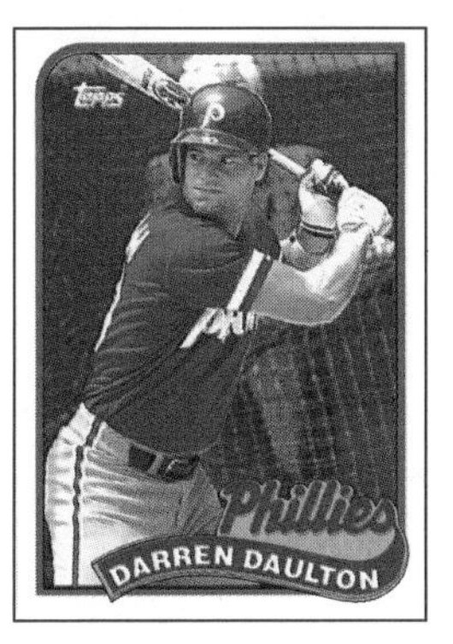

ALVIN DAVIS

	BA	G	AB	R	H	2B	3B	HR	RBI	SB
1988	.295	140	478	67	141	24	1	18	69	1
Life	.278	739	2682	377	769	146	8	110	435	7

POSITION: First base
TEAM: Seattle Mariners
BORN: September 9, 1960 Riverside, CA
HEIGHT: 6′1″ **WEIGHT:** 190 lbs.
BATS: Left **THROWS:** Right
ACQUIRED: Sixth-round pick in 6/82 free-agent draft

Davis continued his seesaw success in 1988. Last season, his offensive stats slid considerably from his admirable work of 1987 (.295, 29 homers, 100 RBIs). In 1988, his RBI count dropped by more than 30 to 69, and his homer output declined to 18. However, his average was solid (.295), and his on-base percentage (.412) was third finest in the league. In five seasons, he has surpassed 100 home runs—not bad for a solid on-base hitter. This isn't the first time Davis has battled minor slumps and won. After winning the A.L. Rookie of the Year award in 1984, his production slacked off the next two seasons before he made his 1987 comeback.

Cards of Davis and other members of the often overlooked Mariners are inexpensive. At a nickel for a 1989 card, another Davis comeback could pay tidy short-term dividends. Our pick for his best 1989 card is Topps.

CHILI DAVIS

	BA	G	AB	R	H	2B	3B	HR	RBI	SB
1988	.268	158	600	81	161	29	3	21	93	9
Life	.267	1032	3748	513	1001	173	23	122	511	104

POSITION: Outfield
TEAM: California Angels
BORN: January 17, 1960
Kingston, Jamaica
HEIGHT: 6'3" **WEIGHT:** 200 lbs.
BATS: Both **THROWS:** Right
ACQUIRED: Signed as a free agent, 1/88

Davis was a welcome addition in 1988, his first year with the California Angels. He was a main cog in the Angels' offense with 21 homers and 93 RBIs (tops on the Angel team). Davis achieved his 1,000th hit to wind up the season on a high note. His success was mostly offensive in 1988. Davis led all American League outfielders with 19 errors. The Angels are likely to excuse the miscues, due to his enormous run production. If the Angels make a serious run at the pennant in 1989, Davis will be a main factor in the effort.

Davis may never rack up Hall of Fame-quality statistics, but he could become one of the A.L.'s top hitters. Buy his 1989 cards at a nickel, then sell when he makes the All-Star team. Our pick for his best 1989 card is Topps.

ERIC DAVIS

	BA	G	AB	R	H	2B	3B	HR	RBI	SB
1988	.273	135	472	81	129	18	3	26	93	35
Life	.273	509	1657	357	452	69	14	108	312	191

POSITION: Outfield
TEAM: Cincinnati Reds
BORN: May 29, 1962 Los Angeles, CA
HEIGHT: 6'2" **WEIGHT:** 175 lbs.
BATS: Right **THROWS:** Right
ACQUIRED: Eighth-round pick in 6/80 free-agent draft

Many players only dream of enjoying the "slump" that Davis went through in 1988. In 1987, Davis had a .293 average, with 37 home runs, 100 RBIs, and 50 stolen bases. Last season, however, he reached only 26 homers and 93 RBIs, and his average dipped 20 points. He also stole 35 bases. In 1986, Davis swiped 80 bases while hitting 27 home runs. The fleet outfielder may one day be the first National Leaguer to join Jose Canseco in the "40-40" club in home runs and stolen bases. He is no slouch in the outfield, twice robbing Jack Clark of home runs in consecutive games in 1987. If Davis restores his offensive clout to its 1987 level, he could help the Reds to their first pennant of the 1980s.

The 1989 Davis cards should sell in the $1 price range. If he puts together an MVP-quality season and the Reds contend in 1989, those prices could double by year's end. Our pick for his best 1989 card is Topps.

GLENN DAVIS

	BA	G	AB	R	H	2B	3B	HR	RBI	SB
1988	.271	152	561	78	152	26	0	30	99	4
Life	.262	579	2124	296	557	109	5	110	365	11

POSITION: First base
TEAM: Houston Astros
BORN: March 28, 1961
Jacksonville, FL
HEIGHT: 6′3″ **WEIGHT:** 210 lbs.
BATS: Right **THROWS:** Right
ACQUIRED: First-round pick in secondary phase of 1/81 free-agent draft

Davis remains as the one constant power threat for the Astros. In 1988, he surpassed 20 home runs for the fourth straight year and tallied his third consecutive season of 90-plus RBIs. His 31 home runs in 1986 broke a 1972 club record of 29 set by Lee May. Davis, originally an outfielder, was first drafted by the Baltimore Orioles in 1979. For the Astros, he has hit 20 or more homers four years in a row. He raised his average to the .270-plus level in '88, and he is becoming a better defensive player. If he continues to improve, he can challenge for honors as the best first baseman in the league.

Davis, after three full seasons in the majors, also may be ready to challenge for a league home run title, even though he plays in the immense Astrodome. His cards are a smart investment at 15 cents each. Our pick for his best 1989 card is Donruss.

JODY DAVIS

	BA	G	AB	R	H	2B	3B	HR	RBI	SB
1988	.230	90	257	21	59	9	0	7	36	0
Life	.251	992	3326	352	836	159	11	123	470	7

POSITION: Catcher
TEAM: Atlanta Braves
BORN: November 12, 1956
Gainesville, GA
HEIGHT: 6′3″ **WEIGHT:** 210 lbs.
BATS: Right **THROWS:** Right
ACQUIRED: Traded from Cubs for Kevin Coffman and Kevin Blankenship, 9/88

Davis, the Cub backstop for eight seasons, will battle Ozzie Virgil for the starting catcher spot for the 1989 Braves. Davis is a power hitter. He is also a great defensive catcher: He handles pitchers well, has a strong arm, and is fearless blocking the plate. Relegated to backup duty for much of 1988, he hit .230, with seven homers and 36 RBIs. In the five previous seasons, he averaged 20 home runs and 72 RBIs a season. His best season was in 1983, when he hit .271, with 24 homers, 84 RBIs, and 31 doubles. Davis is also durable, averaging 139 games caught from the seasons 1982 to 1987. Davis will be a steadying influence on the rebuilding Braves.

Davis' 1989 cards will be a slice above commons. He probably won't play full-time anymore, making his cards questionable investments. Our pick for his best 1989 card is Donruss.

JOHN DAVIS

	W	L	ERA	G	SV	IP	H	R	BB	SO
1988	2	5	6.64	34	1	63.2	77	58	50	37
Life	7	7	4.86	61	3	107.1	106	71	76	61

POSITION: Pitcher
TEAM: Chicago White Sox
BORN: January 5, 1963 Chicago, IL
HEIGHT: 6′7″ **WEIGHT:** 215 lbs.
BATS: Right **THROWS:** Right
ACQUIRED: Traded from Royals with Melido Perez, Chuck Mount, and Greg Hibbard for Floyd Bannister, 12/87

Davis, one of the tallest pitchers in baseball, had only mild success with the 1988 White Sox. He had two wins, one save, and finished ten of the 34 games he appeared in. He was one of the key rookies the White Sox wanted when they traded away Floyd Bannister. The White Sox were impressed with Davis' 1987 debut with the Royals. In his first 27 games, he went 5-2 with two saves and a 2.27 ERA. Both in 1987 and 1988 Davis walked more batters than he struck out. If he finds some control, Davis could be a great asset to the 1989 White Sox.

Rookie cards of Davis from 1988 sell for about a quarter each. His 1989 cards will be a nickel or less. Don't invest until Davis cures his control problem. Our pick for his best 1989 card is Score.

MARK DAVIS

	W	L	ERA	G	SV	IP	H	R	BB	SO
1988	5	10	2.01	62	28	98.1	70	24	42	102
Life	36	62	4.00	346	41	765.2	692	373	309	662

POSITION: Pitcher
TEAM: San Diego Padres
BORN: October 19, 1960 Livermore, CA
HEIGHT: 6′4″ **WEIGHT:** 200 lbs.
BATS: Left **THROWS:** Left
ACQUIRED: Traded from Giants with Mark Grant and Chris Brown for Dave Dravecky, Craig Lefferts, and Kevin Mitchell, 7/87

Davis was a top-notch reliever in 1988, his first full year with the Padres. The lefthander ranked among league leaders in saves all season long with 28, and logged a 2.01 ERA. Davis finished more than 50 games for the Padres, a mark of a quality closer. In 1986, he had 90 strikeouts in $84\frac{1}{3}$ innings pitched; in 1985, he had 131 Ks in $114\frac{1}{3}$ innings. Again in 1988, Davis' strikeout totals exceeded his innings pitched (102 Ks in $98\frac{1}{3}$ innings). In mid-1987, Davis was part of a six-player swap with the Giants. It appears that Padre fans may view him as their biggest dividend in 1989.

Davis' 1989 cards should sell for a nickel or less. Due to the lack of recognition relievers for losing teams receive, it's possible that Davis will labor in obscurity. Investing in his cards cannot be advised. Our pick for his best 1989 card is Topps.

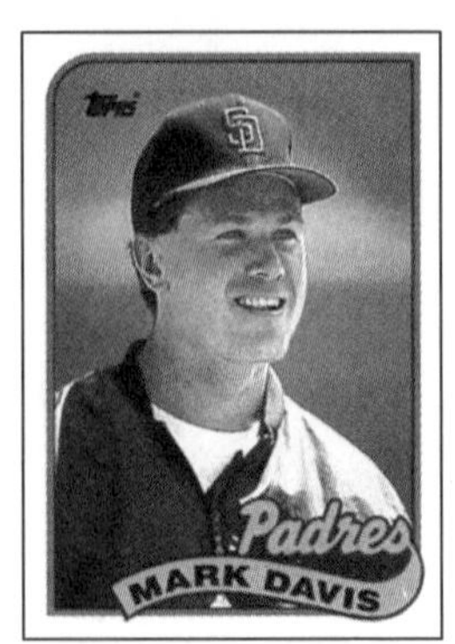

MIKE DAVIS

	BA	G	AB	R	H	2B	3B	HR	RBI	SB
1988	.196	108	281	29	55	11	2	2	17	7
Life	.260	896	2826	398	735	154	15	86	352	128

POSITION: Outfield
TEAM: Los Angeles Dodgers
BORN: June 11, 1959 San Diego, CA
HEIGHT: 6′3″ **WEIGHT:** 185 lbs.
BATS: Left **THROWS:** Left
ACQUIRED: Signed as a free agent, 12/87

Davis atoned for a poor 1988 season with the Los Angeles Dodgers by his play in the World Series. Davis served as the team's designated hitter in Oakland. His fifth-game home run was a crucial blow that allowed the Dodgers to clinch their world championship. Davis escaped Oakland after 1987 by free agency, and was expected to be a major force on the Dodgers. Fans were naturally disappointed with Davis in 1988, after he had hit 84 homers in a five-year stint with the Athletics. Davis may win back a starting job in 1989.

Smart investors should be buying Davis' 1989 cards at less than a nickel. If Davis gets to play a full season in 1989, he should hit well. The better he hits, the higher his card values soar. Our pick for his best 1989 card is Fleer.

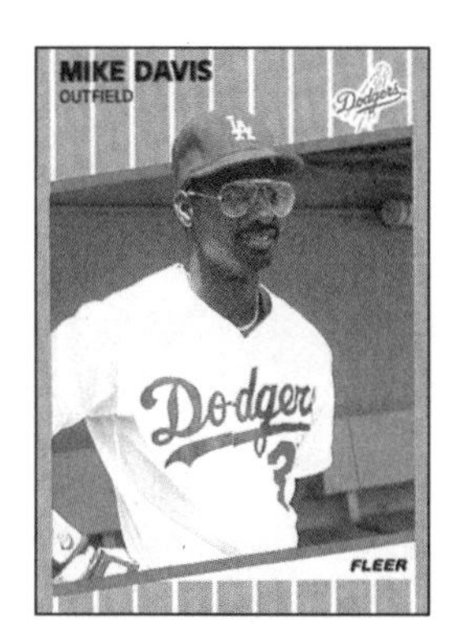

STORM DAVIS

	W	L	ERA	G	CG	IP	H	R	BB	SO
1988	16	7	3.70	33	1	201.2	211	86	91	127
Life	73	55	3.79	213	28	1149.2	1128	525	420	678

POSITION: Pitcher
TEAM: Oakland A's
BORN: December 16, 1961 Dallas, TX
HEIGHT: 6′4″ **WEIGHT:** 200 lbs.
BATS: Right **THROWS:** Right
ACQUIRED: Traded from Padres for Dave Leiper, 8/87

One of baseball's best comebacks in 1988 belonged to pitcher Storm Davis. He split his 1987 season between the Padres and the Athletics, going 3-8 with a miserable 5.23 ERA. Just when his future looked doubtful, Davis rebounded with a career-high 16-7 mark in 1988 in 200 innings (the most he had worked since 1984). He had only one complete game in 1988, mostly because relief ace Dennis Eckersley bailed out all starters. Only 27, he began his pro career with Baltimore, pitching there from 1982 to 1986. With the mighty A's offense behind him, Davis might be able to win 20 games for the first time ever in 1989.

Cards of Davis should be available for a dime or less in 1989. Take a chance here. If he wins 20, his cards could reach a quarter. Our pick for his best 1989 card is Topps.

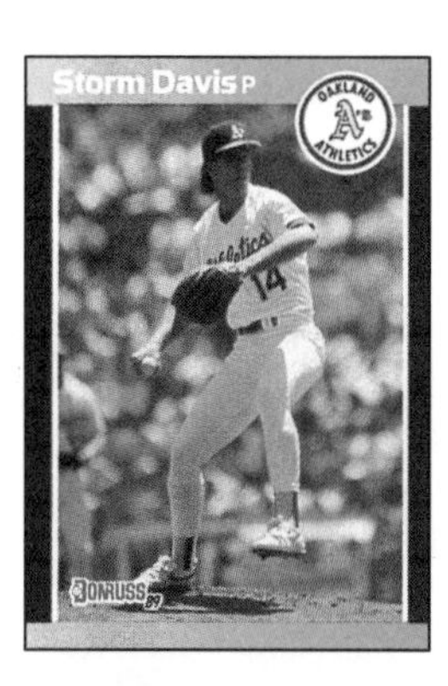

ANDRE DAWSON

	BA	G	AB	R	H	2B	3B	HR	RBI	SB
1988	.303	157	591	78	179	31	8	24	79	12
Life	.282	1753	6840	996	1932	350	77	298	1054	276

POSITION: Outfield
TEAM: Chicago Cubs
BORN: July 10, 1954 Miami, FL
HEIGHT: 6′3″ **WEIGHT:** 195 lbs.
BATS: Right **THROWS:** Right
ACQUIRED: Signed as a free agent, 3/87

After just two seasons, Dawson remains as the hub of the Chicago Cubs. In 1987, he was the first player ever from a last-place team to win an MVP award. His 49 home runs, 137 RBIs, and seventh career Gold Glove win became bright spots in the club's dismal season. Unfortunately, Dawson's 1988 accomplishment of surpassing 20 home runs for the ninth time in his career seemed pale in comparison. He hit .303, with 24 homers and 79 RBIs in '88. He is the Expos' all-time leader in home runs and RBIs. If Dawson continues his current pace, he'll belt more than 400 homers.

Dawson should play at least five more seasons in homer-friendly Wrigley Field. Because he has a chance at the Hall of Fame, his 1989 cards purchased at current values of 25 cents will reap long-term dividends. Our pick for his best 1989 card is Topps.

KEN DAYLEY

	W	L	ERA	G	SV	IP	H	R	BB	SO
1988	2	7	2.77	54	5	55.1	48	20	19	38
Life	25	38	3.77	246	25	420.0	430	210	156	310

POSITION: Pitcher
TEAM: St. Louis Cardinals
BORN: February 25, 1959 Jerome, ID
HEIGHT: 6′ **WEIGHT:** 180 lbs.
BATS: Left **THROWS:** Left
ACQUIRED: Traded from Braves with Mike Jorgensen for Ken Oberkfell, 6/84

Dayley's 2.77 ERA was the third best on the Cardinal staff last season. He also notched five saves in 54 relief appearances. Used sparingly, usually to get one or two tough outs, he has been an asset to the St. Louis bullpen since coming over to them from Atlanta in June 1984. At the beginning of his career he was a starter, but following elbow surgery in 1984, he has become one of the toughest lefthanded relievers in the game. Dayley's career high in saves was 11 for the Cards in 1986, and he went 9-5 with four saves in 1987. With Todd Worrell, Dayley helps make the Card bullpen one of the toughest in the N.L.

Dayley's cards are typical of most relievers; they are not actively collected as investment pieces and generally will not appreciate. Our pick for his best 1989 card is Donruss.

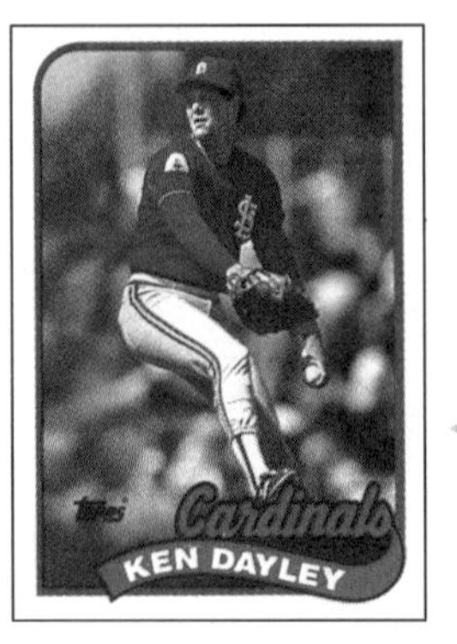

ROB DEER

	BA	G	AB	R	H	2B	3B	HR	RBI	SB
1988	.252	135	492	71	124	24	0	23	85	9
Life	.234	494	1618	244	379	61	6	95	274	27

POSITION: Outfield
TEAM: Milwaukee Brewers
BORN: September 29, 1960 Orange, CA
HEIGHT: 6′3″ **WEIGHT:** 210 lbs.
BATS: Right **THROWS:** Right
ACQUIRED: Traded from Giants for Dean Freeland and Eric Pilkington, 12/85

Deer traded a few home runs for a few more hits in 1988. He was saddled with the dubious honor of leading the A.L. in 1987 with 186 strikeouts. However, he became a bit more selective in 1988 and cut his whiffs to 153, which tied Pete Incaviglia for the A.L. lead. The good news is that Deer's average shot up 14 points, and he kept knocking in lots of runs. If he could cut his strikeouts down to around 100, Deer might be the league's most ferocious hitter. Until then, he'll continue to be an all-or-nothing type of hitter.

Deer has a low career batting average, and his offensive productivity is unpredictable. His 1989 cards may sell for a dime, but his stats don't merit much reason to invest in his cards. Our pick for his best 1989 card is Donruss.

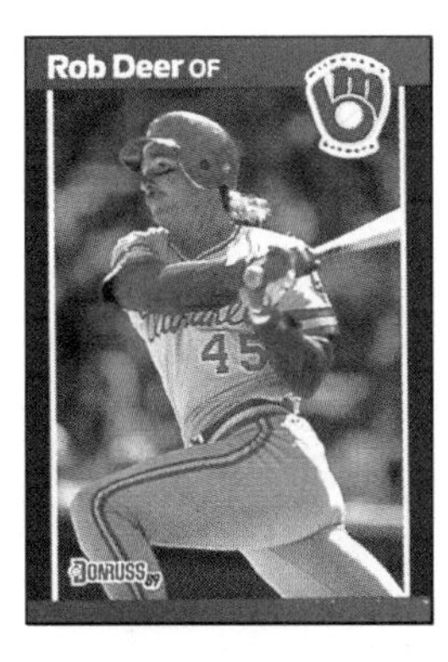

JOSE DeLEON

	W	L	ERA	G	CG	IP	H	R	BB	SO
1988	13	10	3.67	34	3	225.1	198	95	86	208
Life	45	65	3.86	165	15	989.2	801	462	470	860

POSITION: Pitcher
TEAM: St. Louis Cardinals
BORN: December 20, 1960 La Vega, Dominican Republic
HEIGHT: 6′3″ **WEIGHT:** 195 lbs.
BATS: Right **THROWS:** Right
ACQUIRED: Traded from White Sox for Lance Johnson and Ricky Horton, 2/88

DeLeon came back to the N.L. last year and was the top winner on the Cardinal staff. He went 13-10 in 34 starts for St. Louis, with a 3.67 ERA. His 208 strikeouts were third best in the league, 20 behind leader Nolan Ryan. DeLeon's strength has been a great breaking ball, but he has always had control problems—last year he walked 86. Still, the deal that brought him from the White Sox was a plus for the Red Birds. In 1987 for the ChiSox, he was 11-12 in 31 starts, with a 4.02 ERA, 153 Ks, and 97 bases on balls in 206 innings. DeLeon has the talent to win 20 games and to lead the N.L. in Ks.

DeLeon's cards are selling in the 10- to 15-cent range. He has big-season potential, but speculation on his cards for a big increase is still a risk. Our pick for his best 1989 card is Topps.

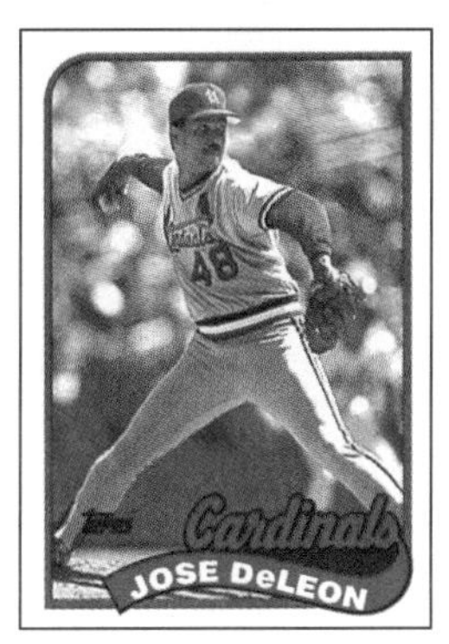

LUIS de los SANTOS

	BA	G	AB	R	H	2B	3B	HR	RBI	SB
1988	.091	11	22	1	2	1	1	0	1	0
Life	.091	11	22	1	2	1	1	0	1	0

POSITION: First base
TEAM: Kansas City Royals
BORN: December 29, 1966
San Cristobal, Dominican Republic
HEIGHT: 6′5″ **WEIGHT:** 195 lbs.
BATS: Right **THROWS:** Right
ACQUIRED: Second-round pick in 6/84
free-agent draft

De los Santos has the size and the range to be an excellent major league first baseman. Over the past three seasons, he has also shown the potential to become a solid hitter. In 1988 at Omaha, he batted .301 with 29 doubles, two homers, and 67 RBIs. During a late-season call to Kansas City, he hit only .091 in 22 at-bats. Originally a shortstop, he made his presence felt in 1986, when he batted .303 with 84 RBIs for Double-A Memphis. De los Santos may fill a utility role with the Royals in 1989, playing first and short.

De los Santos eventually should add long-ball punch to his arsenal, the only missing ingredient he needs for superstardom. His cards should be rewarding long-term investments, and in 1989 will open in the 25- to 30-cent range. Our pick for his best 1989 card is Donruss.

BOB DERNIER

	BA	G	AB	R	H	2B	3B	HR	RBI	SB
1988	.289	68	166	19	48	3	1	1	10	13
Life	.262	797	2296	348	602	87	16	22	139	214

POSITION: Outfield
TEAM: Philadelphia Phillies
BORN: January 5, 1957
Kansas City, MO
HEIGHT: 6′ **WEIGHT:** 160 lbs.
BATS: Right **THROWS:** Right
ACQUIRED: Signed as a free agent, 12/87

An 11-year pro, with parts of nine years in the majors, Dernier returned to the Phillies as a free agent after the close of the 1987 season. Though he hit well over .300 for most of the 1988 campaign, a late-season slump saw him finish at .289, which was still the third best average on the club. The Phils originally signed him as a free agent in 1977. After spending 1982 and '83 with the Phillies, Dernier was dealt to the Cubs. He batted .278 in 1984 and a career-high .317 in 1987. An outstanding defensive center fielder, Dernier is at his best as a platoon player.

Dernier's cards are not high demand items and never will be. Expect to pay no more than a dime for any of them. Our pick for his best 1989 card is Score.

JIM DESHAIES

	W	L	ERA	G	CG	IP	H	R	BB	SO
1988	11	14	3.00	31	3	207.0	164	77	72	127
Life	34	26	3.65	87	5	513.0	452	225	195	366

POSITION: Pitcher
TEAM: Houston Astros
BORN: June 23, 1960 Massena, NY
HEIGHT: 6′4″ **WEIGHT:** 225 lbs.
BATS: Left **THROWS:** Left
ACQUIRED: Traded from Yankees with Neder de Jesus Horta and Dody Rather for Joe Niekro, 9/85

Deshaies didn't have a remarkable season in 1988 with the Astros, but his losing mark didn't tell the whole story. He had three complete games and two shutouts, and he kept his ERA at 3.00 (his lowest ever). Deshaies matched his 11 wins from 1987, and ran his string of double-digit winning seasons to three. He pitched 207 innings through 31 games, his pro career best in seven years. He set a modern record on September 23, 1986, at Houston, when he struck out eight consecutive Dodgers he faced during the beginning of the game. Deshaies could have his best season ever in 1989.

Deshaies has been winning consistently since 1986, and could get more victories with an increased workload like he carried in 1988. His cards are an enticing investment for 1989 at a nickel or less. Our pick for his best 1989 card is Topps.

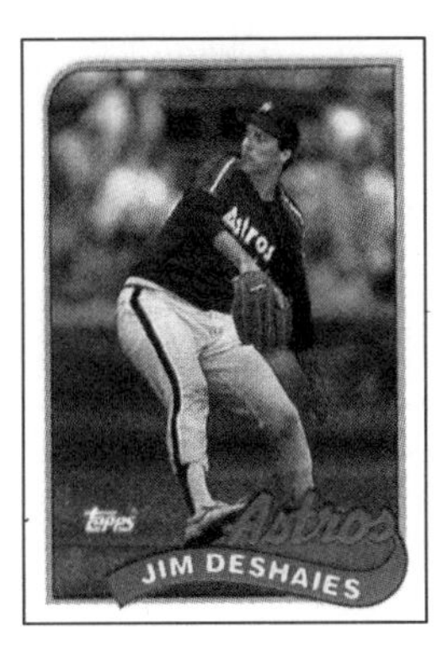

ORESTES DESTRADE

	BA	G	AB	R	H	2B	3B	HR	RBI	SB
1988	.149	36	47	2	7	1	0	1	3	0
Life	.182	45	66	7	12	1	0	1	4	0

POSITION: First base
TEAM: Pittsburgh Pirates
BORN: May 8, 1962 Santiago, Cuba
HEIGHT: 6′4″ **WEIGHT:** 210 lbs.
BATS: Right **THROWS:** Right
ACQUIRED: Traded from Yankees for Hipolito Pena, 4/88

Destrade is looking to unseat Sid Bream at the Pirate first base post in 1989. At Triple-A Buffalo in 1988, Destrade hit .271, with 12 homers and 42 RBIs. He showed promise in the Yankee organization at Triple-A Columbus in 1987, hitting 25 homers, a team-high 26 doubles, and driving in 81 runs. Late in the season, he was called up to New York, where he batted .263 in 19 trips to the plate. At Triple-A Columbus in 1986, he had hit 19 round-trippers when a broken ankle derailed his season after 98 games. The Yankees signed him as a free agent in 1981, and Destrade is running out of time career-wise to prove himself.

Destrade can hit for power, and he should find a place to play. His 1989 cards will open in the 5- to 15-cent range—a little too high. Our pick for his best 1989 card is Topps.

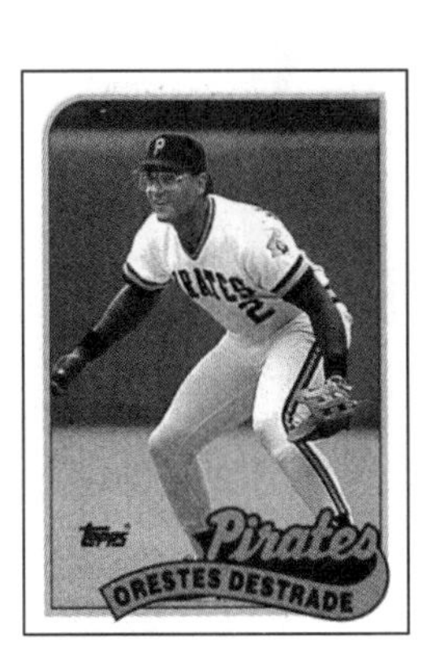

MIKE DEVEREAUX

	BA	G	AB	R	H	2B	3B	HR	RBI	SB
1988	.116	30	43	4	5	1	0	0	2	0
Life	.175	49	97	11	17	4	0	0	6	3

POSITION: Outfield
TEAM: Los Angeles Dodgers
BORN: April 10, 1963 Casper, WY
HEIGHT: 6′ **WEIGHT:** 195 lbs.
BATS: Right **THROWS:** Right
ACQUIRED: Fifth-round pick in 6/85 free-agent draft

A solid year at Triple-A Albuquerque in 1988 (.340 average, 13 home runs, and 76 RBIs) should finally project Devereaux into the Dodger picture. Slated to open with the big club in 1987, he ended up with Double-A San Antonio and fell out of the Dodger plans. He had a fine year in '87, hitting .301 with 26 homers and 91 RBIs. Rival managers have commented that Devereaux was a better prospect than players whom the Dodgers had placed ahead of him. He joined the Dodgers in late-season 1987 and 1988. Devereaux has the ability to be a star in the majors.

It appears that Devereaux has now earned another long look and will get that opportunity in the Dodger outfield corps this spring. His 1989 cards will open in the 15- to 20-cent range. Our pick for his best 1989 card is Donruss.

BO DIAZ

	BA	G	AB	R	H	2B	3B	HR	RBI	SB
1988	.219	92	315	26	69	9	0	10	35	0
Life	.257	950	3142	321	807	157	5	86	444	9

POSITION: Catcher
TEAM: Cincinnati Reds
BORN: March 23, 1953 Caracas, Venezuela
HEIGHT: 5′11″ **WEIGHT:** 205 lbs.
BATS: Right **THROWS:** Right
ACQUIRED: Traded from Phillies with Greg Simpson for Tom Foley, Alan Knicely, and Fred Toliver, 8/85

Diaz saw his average drop more than 50 points with the 1988 Reds. He was the team's starting catcher in 1986 and 1987, but he got into less than 100 games in 1988. He hit just .219, but still contributed ten homers and 35 RBIs. Diaz hit .270 in 1987, with 15 homers and 82 RBIs. He began his career with the 1977 Red Sox. His best overall season was in Philadelphia in 1982, hitting .288, with 18 homers and 85 RBIs. Diaz, at age 36, may not have the stamina to catch a full season. However, his hitting still seems healthy.

Although the 1989 cards of Diaz will be three cents or less, they aren't good investments. He is an aging catcher with less than 1,000 career games, and he may not last more than three more seasons. Our pick for his best 1989 card is Topps.

MARIO DIAZ

	BA	G	AB	R	H	2B	3B	HR	RBI	SB
1988	.306	28	72	6	22	5	0	0	9	0
Life	.305	39	95	10	29	5	1	0	12	0

POSITION: Shortstop
TEAM: Seattle Mariners
BORN: January 10, 1962 Humacao, Puerto Rico
HEIGHT: 5′10″ **WEIGHT:** 170 lbs.
BATS: Right **THROWS:** Right
ACQUIRED: Signed as a free agent, 12/78

Insiders see Diaz and Edgar Martinez as key players in the M's infield in 1989. Diaz hit .300 in a brief stay with Seattle in 1988—it was the second time he'd been recalled late in the season from Triple-A Calgary and topped the .300 mark. Diaz batted .329 for Calgary in 1988. In 1987 at Calgary, Diaz hit .282 with four homers, 17 doubles, and 52 RBIs; he was voted the Pacific Coast League's best defensive shortstop. In 1986, he hit .282 for Calgary. After three Triple-A seasons, Diaz's time seems to have come.

Diaz's 1989 cards will open at 15 cents. That is a good price for a young shortstop with a good bat. Our pick for his best 1989 card is Topps.

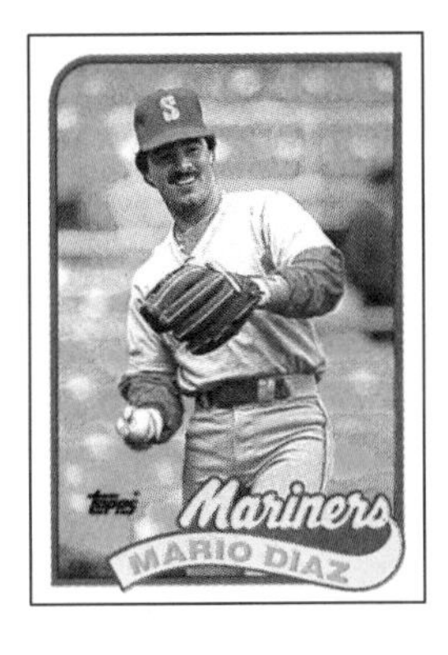

MIKE DIAZ

	BA	G	AB	R	H	2B	3B	HR	RBI	SB
1988	.237	40	152	12	36	6	0	3	12	0
Life	.247	239	683	70	169	27	2	31	102	1

POSITION: Outfield
TEAM: Chicago White Sox
BORN: April 15, 1960 San Francisco, CA
HEIGHT: 6′2″ **WEIGHT:** 200 lbs.
BATS: Right **THROWS:** Right
ACQUIRED: Traded from Pirates for Gary Redus, 9/88

Diaz was acquired to add some much-needed power to Chicago's lineup. He managed only three homers for his new club, but he was coming off his finest hitting season ever in 1987. In his last year with the Pirates, Diaz smacked 16 homers and 48 RBIs in just 103 games. Prior to 1988, his career home run percentage was 6.1, an Aaron-like number. He is a talented utilityman who can play catcher, first base, third base, and the outfield. He'll serve the White Sox in many ways in 1989.

Cards of Diaz from 1989 sets will be selling at three cents or less. Because he has never had a starting job, no one really knows his full capabilities. Until he does become a starter, don't invest in his cards. Our pick for his best 1989 card is Topps.

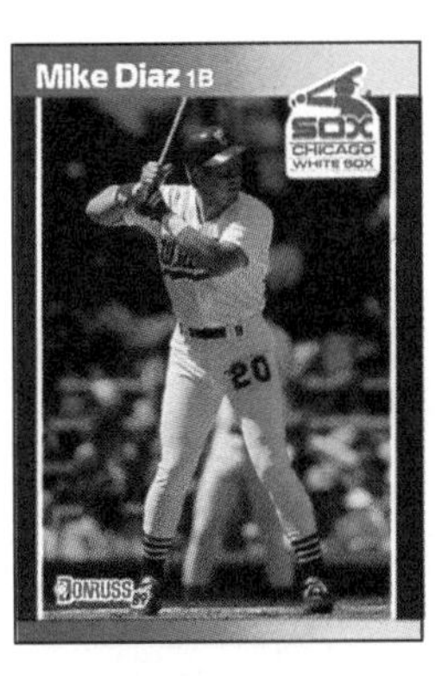

ROB DIBBLE

	W	L	ERA	G	SV	IP	H	R	BB	SO
1988	1	1	1.82	37	0	59.1	43	12	21	59
Life	1	1	1.82	37	0	59.1	43	12	21	59

POSITION: Pitcher
TEAM: Cincinnati Reds
BORN: January 24, 1964 Bridgeport, CT
HEIGHT: 6′4″ **WEIGHT:** 230 lbs.
BATS: Left **THROWS:** Right
ACQUIRED: First pick in secondary phase of 6/83 free-agent draft

Dibble saw considerable playing time in the second half of the 1988 season with the Reds. He didn't get a save because he was used mostly in middle relief for Cincy, but he did end up with the second-best ERA on the Red staff (1.82) in 59⅓ innings. At Triple-A Nashville in '88, he rolled up 13 saves in 31 games (with a 2-1 record and 2.31 ERA). In 1987 with Nashville, Dibble appeared in 44 games, getting four saves with a 2-4 record and a 4.72 ERA. He struck out 51 batters and walked 27. The Reds look forward to having Dibble in the bullpen for an entire season in 1989.

Dibble's 1989 cards will open in the 15- to 20-cent range. Even though he is a good prospect, that price is expensive for a middle reliever. Our pick for his best 1989 card is Topps.

FRANK DiPINO

	W	L	ERA	G	SV	IP	H	R	BB	SO
1988	2	3	4.98	63	6	90.1	102	54	32	69
Life	20	35	3.91	365	53	503.2	478	247	209	409

POSITION: Pitcher
TEAM: Chicago Cubs
BORN: October 22, 1956 Syracuse, NY
HEIGHT: 5′10″ **WEIGHT:** 175 lbs.
BATS: Left **THROWS:** Left
ACQUIRED: Traded from Astros for Davey Lopes, 7/86

DiPino appeared as a relief pitcher for the Cubs in 63 games last season, earning six saves and going 2-3 in 90⅓ innings, with a 4.98 ERA. Generally used as the set-up man in the Cub bullpen, he is highly valuable as a lefty setting the stage for closer Goose Gossage, a righthander. DiPino's best season in the major leagues was in 1983 with the Astros. He racked up 20 saves in 53 appearances, ending with a 3-4 record and a 2.65 earned run average. In 1984, he notched 14 saves, and it looked like he would remain the lefthanded short relief man. DiPino may have found his niche as a long reliever.

DiPino is found in the commons. There is little investment interest in pitchers who are the set-up pitchers. Our pick for his best 1989 card is Score.

JOHN DOPSON

	W	L	ERA	G	CG	IP	H	R	BB	SO
1988	3	11	3.04	26	1	168.2	150	69	58	101
Life	3	13	3.62	30	1	181.2	175	86	62	105

POSITION: Pitcher
TEAM: Boston Red Sox
BORN: July 14, 1963 Baltimore, MD
HEIGHT: 6′4″ **WEIGHT:** 205 lbs.
BATS: Left **THROWS:** Right
ACQUIRED: Traded from Expos with Luis Rivera for Spike Owen and Dan Gakeler, 12/88

Dopson will look for a starter role with the BoSox. He moved in to the Expos starting rotation in 1988. His 3-11 record was disappointing, but his 3.04 ERA was encouraging. In 1985, he had a 25-scoreless-inning streak for Triple-A Indianapolis. He ended that year at 4-7, with a 3.78 ERA. Dopson began 1987 on the disabled list following arthroscopic surgery on his shoulder; he pitched in 21 games for Double-A Jacksonville, going 7-5 with a 3.80 ERA. Dopson was bothered by a sore shoulder for most of the 1986 season; he was 0-3 in four games at Indianapolis. The Boston brass is very high on Dopson.

Because of his shoulder, Dopson is still more of a suspect than a prospect. For the time being his 1989 cards, at a dime apiece, cannot be considered prime investment material. Our pick for his best 1989 card is Donruss.

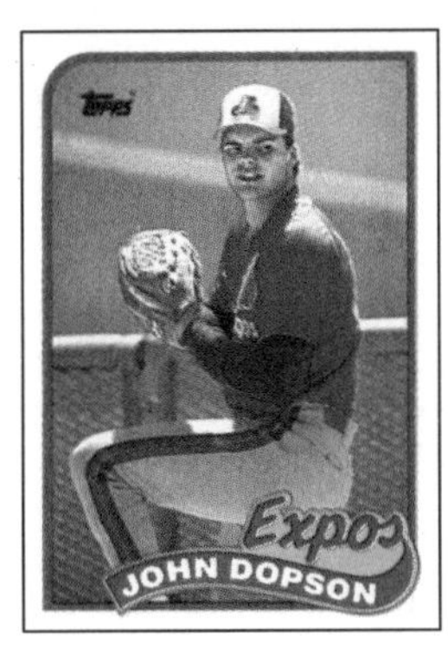

BILL DORAN

	BA	G	AB	R	H	2B	3B	HR	RBI	SB
1988	.248	132	480	66	119	18	1	7	53	17
Life	.272	914	3413	497	929	134	31	55	314	151

POSITION: Second base
TEAM: Houston Astros
BORN: May 28, 1958 Cincinnati, OH
HEIGHT: 6′ **WEIGHT:** 175 lbs.
BATS: Both **THROWS:** Right
ACQUIRED: Sixth-round selection in 6/79 free-agent draft

Doran, the 1987 Astro MVP, saw his 1988 campaign marred by injuries. As a result, the popular second baseman missed 30 games after having played in all 162 in 1987. Despite his shortened '88 season, Doran managed to hit .248 with seven homers, 53 RBIs, and 17 stolen bases. Those are respectable numbers, but they only hint at Doran's real ability. In 1987, for example, he posted career-high marks of .283, 16 homers, and 79 RBIs. Last year's Astros team battled the Dodgers for first place throughout August. If a healthy Doran contributes his usual quality effort in 1989, the Astros could be contenders down to the wire.

Due to Doran's lack of production in 1988, his 1989 cards will sell as commons. Some investors might overlook his potential, but smart collectors will wait for Doran to regain his full talent in 1989. Our pick for his best 1989 card is Topps.

RICH DOTSON

	W	L	ERA	G	CG	IP	H	R	BB	SO
1988	12	9	5.00	32	4	171.0	178	103	72	77
Life	106	97	4.13	269	53	1677.0	1660	851	668	895

POSITION: Pitcher
TEAM: New York Yankees
BORN: January 10, 1959 Cincinnati, OH
HEIGHT: 6′ **WEIGHT:** 203 lbs.
BATS: Right **THROWS:** Right
ACQUIRED: Traded from White Sox with Scott Nielsen for Dan Pasqua, Mark Salas, and Steve Rosenberg, 11/87

Dotson tied Rick Rhoden for second in wins for the 1988 Yankees. He went 12-9 during the season, his first in New York. His best season ever was with the 1983 White Sox, when he carved out a 22-7 record. Dotson's worst season followed in 1986. His 17 losses were the most of any A.L. pitcher that year. In his ten big league seasons, Dotson has never kept his ERA under 3.00. His 1988 ERA, at 5.00, was his second-worst ever. However, with the mighty Yankees offense supporting him, Dotson should be a big winner if he pitches well in 1989.

Dotson has average stats for a ten-year starter. But his 1989 cards will be a nickel or less, a good price for investing. He has won at least ten games in seven seasons. That success should continue in 1989. Our pick for his best 1989 card is Score.

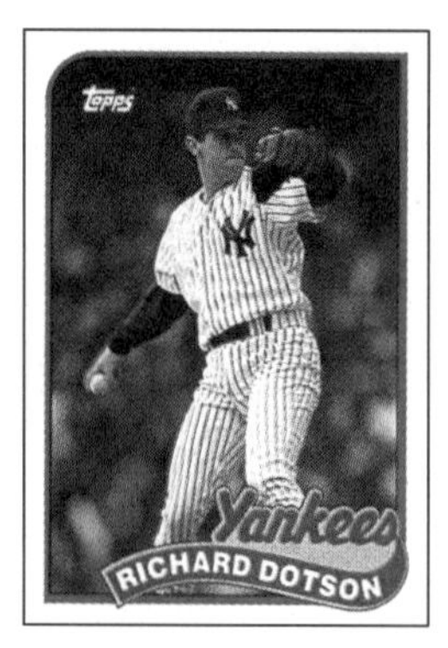

BRIAN DOWNING

	BA	G	AB	R	H	2B	3B	HR	RBI	SB
1988	.242	135	484	80	117	18	2	25	64	3
Life	.264	1876	6252	953	1653	282	22	220	875	48

POSITION: Designated hitter; outfield
TEAM: California Angels
BORN: October 9, 1950 Los Angeles, CA
HEIGHT: 5′10″ **WEIGHT:** 190 lbs.
BATS: Right **THROWS:** Right
ACQUIRED: Traded from White Sox with David Frost and Chris Knapp for Bobby Bonds, Rich Dotson, and Thad Bosley, 12/77

Even though he played in 20 games less than last season, Downing nearly repeated his previous hitting exploits for the 1988 Angels. His 25 home runs were tops on the team, although they were far fewer than he hit last year. In 1986, Downing drove in a career-high 95 RBIs. He's the Angel all-time leader in that category. Recognized for his odd-looking hitting stances, he began his career as a catcher. In the outfield, he went without an error in 1988. Now, even at age 38, he's still an important ingredient in the future hopes of the Angels.

Playing for the Angels hasn't helped Downing achieve recognition. His 1989 cards will sell at a nickel or less. Unless he could help the Angels win a pennant, there isn't much promise in investing in his cards. Our pick for his best 1989 card is Score.

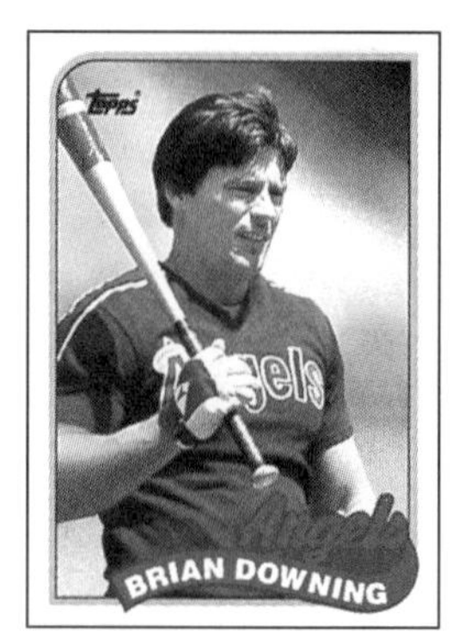

KELLY DOWNS

	W	L	ERA	G	CG	IP	H	R	BB	SO
1988	13	9	3.32	27	6	168.0	140	67	47	118
Life	29	22	3.34	82	11	442.1	403	179	144	319

POSITION: Pitcher
TEAM: San Francisco Giants
BORN: October 25, 1960 Ogden, UT
HEIGHT: 6′4″ **WEIGHT:** 200 lbs.
BATS: Right **THROWS:** Right
ACQUIRED: Traded from Phillies with George Riley for Al Oliver and Renie Matin, 9/84

Downs enjoyed the most prosperous season of his young career as a member of the 1988 San Francisco Giants. Fresh off a 12-9 outing in 1987, he posted a career-best 13-9 mark. He enjoyed full-time status in the starting rotation in 1988, after getting sent to the bullpen in 1987 to make room for newly acquired Rick Reuschel. Downs etched a team-leading three shutouts in 1988, and his six complete games trailed only Reuschel. Downs struck out 118 batters in '88, and he walked only 47 in 168 innings of work. In 1987, he racked up 137 Ks in 186 innings. Based on his past achievements, Downs looks like a future 20-game winner.

The 1989 issues of Downs should cost a nickel or less. Stock up on his cards. He could be truly successful soon. Our pick for his best 1989 card is Fleer.

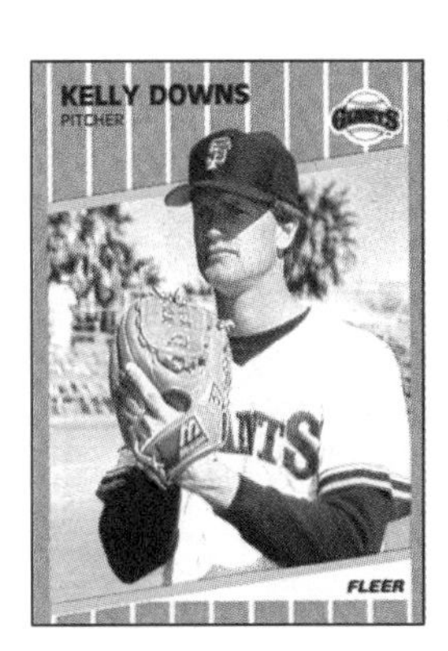

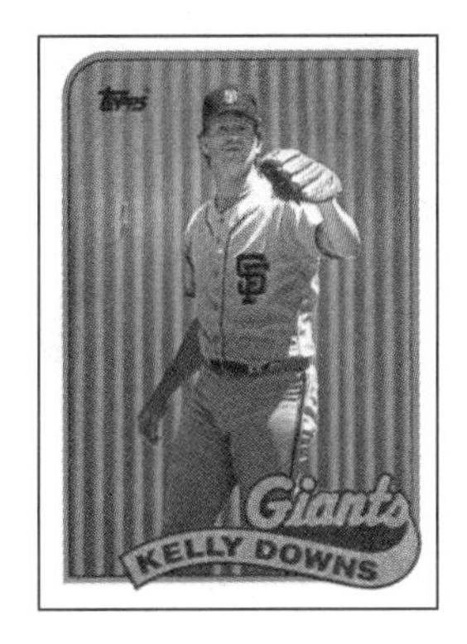

DOUG DRABEK

	W	L	ERA	G	CG	IP	H	R	BB	SO
1988	15	7	3.08	33	3	219.1	194	83	50	127
Life	33	27	3.60	89	4	527.1	485	233	146	323

POSITION: Pitcher
TEAM: Pittsburgh Pirates
BORN: July 25, 1962 Victoria, TX
HEIGHT: 6′1″ **WEIGHT:** 185 lbs.
BATS: Right **THROWS:** Right
ACQUIRED: Traded from Yankees with Logan Easley and Brian Fisher for Rick Rhoden, Cecilio Guante, and Pat Clements, 11/86

Drabek had a great season in 1988, leading the Pirates in wins. A 15-game winner for the Bucs in 1988, he fashioned a 3.08 ERA in 32 starts, along with 127 strikeouts and only seven losses. Drabek was the Bucs' leader in starts and strikeouts in 1987 while compiling an 11-12 record to go with a 3.88 ERA. After starting the 1986 season at Triple-A Columbus, he was summoned to Yankee Stadium, where he was 7-8 in 21 starts for the Bronx Bombers. At Double-A Albany in 1985, he was 13-7 with a 2.99 ERA, and he led the Eastern League in strikeouts, with 153. With a strong season in 1989, Drabek could become the Pittsburgh staff ace for years to come.

Drabek looks like the real thing. Build a supply of his cards, which should sell in the 20- to 25-cent range. Our pick for his best 1989 card is Topps.

DAVE DRAVECKY

	W	L	ERA	G	CG	IP	H	R	BB	SO
1988	2	2	3.16	7	1	37.0	33	19	8	19
Life	62	57	3.13	224	28	1049.2	960	416	311	553

POSITION: Pitcher
TEAM: San Francisco Giants
BORN: February 14, 1956
Youngstown, OH
HEIGHT: 6′1″ **WEIGHT:** 200 lbs.
BATS: Right **THROWS:** Left
ACQUIRED: Traded from San Diego with Craig Lefferts and Kevin Mitchell for Chris Brown, Keith Comstock, Mark Davis, and Mark Grant, 7/87

Injuries virtually wiped out Dravecky's 1988 season with the Giants. He got into just seven games and posted a 2-2 record. He had played a crucial role in helping the Giants to their 1987 divisional title. He went 7-5 with four complete games and three shutouts after joining the Giants in July. Dravecky had a brilliant two-hit victory versus the Cardinals in the 1987 National League Championship Series. He had pitched nearly five years with the Padres before joining San Francisco. His best previous season was a 14-10 mark in 1983. Dravecky can be quite effective when healthy.

Dravecky's past stats, however, aren't stunning. Due to his age and his lack of work last season, wait and see how he fares in early 1989 before investing in his newest common-priced cards. Our pick for his best 1989 card is Fleer.

CAMERON DREW

	BA	G	AB	R	H	2B	3B	HR	RBI	SB
1988	.188	7	16	1	3	0	1	0	1	0
Life	.188	7	16	1	3	0	1	0	1	0

POSITION: Outfield
TEAM: Houston Astros
BORN: February 12, 1964 Boston, MA
HEIGHT: 6′5″ **WEIGHT:** 215 lbs.
BATS: Left **THROWS:** Right
ACQUIRED: First-round pick in 6/85 free-agent draft

Drew drew rave notices at Triple-A Tucson in 1988, with his .356 batting average and 70 RBIs. The only note of concern was his lack of power, which limited him to only four homers. He was the first pick of the Astros in 1985, surprising some who knew him as an outstanding basketball player at the University of New Haven. At Asheville in '86, he was dazzling, hitting .326 with 26 homers and 116 RBIs. At Double-A Columbus in 1987, he made the league All-Star team. He hit .278 with 17 homers and 70 RBIs. Drew could be the hard-hitting outfielder that the Astros have been seeking for years.

Drew's 1989 cards will open in the 35- to 40-cent range, a good long-term buy. He has a good stick, and his power stats will improve. Our pick for his best 1989 card is Fleer.

ROB DUCEY

	BA	G	AB	R	H	2B	3B	HR	RBI	SB
1988	.315	27	54	15	17	4	1	0	6	1
Life	.255	61	102	27	26	5	1	1	12	3

POSITION: Outfield
TEAM: Toronto Blue Jays
BORN: May 24, 1965
Toronto, Ontario
HEIGHT: 6'2" **WEIGHT:** 175 lbs.
BATS: Left **THROWS:** Right
ACQUIRED: Signed as a free agent, 5/84

Just what the Toronto fans needed: a native Canadian to root for. Exactly where the Toronto-born Ducey is going to play isn't certain, but the talent he's displayed makes a strong case for finding a spot for him. Ducey played with Triple-A Syracuse in 1988, batting .256 with seven homers and 42 RBIs. In 1987 at Syracuse, he hit .284 with ten homers and 60 RBIs, before getting a late-season look in Toronto. In 1986, Ducey began the year at Class-A Ventura, where he batted .327 with 12 homers and 32 RBIs. He was then promoted to Double-A Knoxville, where he impressed with a .306 mark, 11 homers, and 58 RBIs.

Ducey has a world of talent and could challenge for top rookie honors. His 1989 cards will open in the 25-cent range, a good price for a top prospect. Our pick for his best 1989 card is Topps.

MIKE DUNNE

	W	L	ERA	G	CG	IP	H	R	BB	SO
1988	7	11	3.92	30	1	170.0	163	88	88	70
Life	20	17	3.48	53	6	333.1	306	154	156	142

POSITION: Pitcher
TEAM: Pittsburgh Pirates
BORN: October 27, 1962 South Bend, IN
HEIGHT: 6'4" **WEIGHT:** 190 lbs.
BATS: Right **THROWS:** Right
ACQUIRED: Traded from Cardinals with Andy Van Slyke and Mike LaValliere for Tony Pena, 4/87

Another of the good young pitchers that the Pirates have been stockpiling over the past few years, Dunne came to Pittsburgh in the Andy Van Slyke deal in 1987. Dunne was an effective starter in '87, going 13-6 in 23 starts with a 3.03 ERA. In 1988, he had 28 starts and ended up 7-11 with a 3.92 ERA. On the plus side, the Pirates were 15-13 in the games he started, though he wasn't always around for the victory. Dunne was the Cardinals' first pick in the June 1984 draft; he was also a member of the 1984 Olympic team. Pittsburgh figures to be in the playoff hunt for the next several years, and Dunne will be a potent weapon in the Pirate arsenal.

Dunne's 1985 Topps Olympic card already sells for $2.00. His 1989 cards will open in the 15-cent range. Our pick for his best 1989 card is Donruss.

SHAWON DUNSTON

	BA	G	AB	R	H	2B	3B	HR	RBI	SB
1988	.249	155	575	69	143	23	6	9	56	30
Life	.250	474	1752	215	438	90	16	35	164	66

POSITION: Shortstop
TEAM: Chicago Cubs
BORN: March 21, 1963 Brooklyn, NY
HEIGHT: 6'1" **WEIGHT:** 175 lbs.
BATS: Right **THROWS:** Right
ACQUIRED: First-round pick in 6/82 free-agent draft

Dunston has been something of a disappointment to the Cubs, because he hasn't developed as quickly as they would have liked. He missed almost half of the 1987 season due to injuries and batted .246 in 95 games with just five home runs and 22 RBIs. In 1988, Dunston stayed healthy and saw action in all but seven of the Cub games, batting .249 with nine home runs and 56 RBIs. Dunston was second on the club with six triples and had seven game-winning hits. He is erratic in the field, making spectacular plays and booting the easy ones. Dunston still has talent and may put together a great season in 1989.

Initially Dunston's cards started out in the star category. Their value, however, has dropped, and we don't recommend a heavy investment in them. Our pick for his best 1989 card is Topps.

LENNY DYKSTRA

	BA	G	AB	R	H	2B	3B	HR	RBI	SB
1988	.270	126	429	57	116	19	3	8	33	30
Life	.279	488	1527	260	426	92	16	27	140	103

POSITION: Outfield
TEAM: New York Mets
BORN: Febuary 10, 1963 Santa Ana, CA
HEIGHT: 5'10" **WEIGHT:** 160 lbs.
BATS: Left **THROWS:** Left
ACQUIRED: 12th-round pick in 6/81 free-agent draft

Dykstra energizes the Mets much in the way Pete Rose used to rev up the Reds as a player. Dykstra is an exceedingly tough out and will foul off pitches endlessly to work a hurler for a walk. He'll bunt for a hit, dive for a sinking liner, do anything he can to motivate the club. Last season Dykstra hit .270 for New York in 126 games, with eight homers, 33 RBIs, and five game-winning hits. Half of the Mets center field platoon—with Mookie Wilson—Dykstra hit .295 in 1986 and .285 in 1987. Dykstra is a fan favorite in New York.

If Dykstra becomes an every-day player, which is likely, his card values could accelerate. For now, just hold on to any Dykstra cards you have. Our pick for his best 1989 card is Fleer.

DENNIS ECKERSLEY

	W	L	ERA	G	SV	IP	H	R	BB	SO
1988	4	2	2.35	60	45	72.2	52	20	11	70
Life	161	138	3.61	490	64	2684.1	2552	1162	652	1810

POSITION: Pitcher
TEAM: Oakland A's
BORN: October 3, 1954 Oakland, CA
HEIGHT: 6'2" **WEIGHT:** 195 lbs.
BATS: Right **THROWS:** Right
ACQUIRED: Traded from Cubs for David Wilder, 4/87

Relief artist Eckersley had a great record-setting season in 1988, helping the A's win the division. In a sense, the righty has started a second career. He won more than 150 games and hurled a no-hitter during his many years as a starter. After being traded to the A's in 1987, manager Tony LaRussa placed Eckersley in the bullpen. After collecting 16 saves in 1987, he became baseball's best stopper last season, entering the coveted 40-save circle with 45 saves. He also had a 2.35 ERA and a 4-2 record. While many older pitchers quietly end their careers in the bullpen, Eckersley has found a new life as an A's reliever.

Eckersley's cards may reach 15 cents in 1989, too high a price for investment purposes. Regardless of his 1988 effort, his age works against him. Our pick for his best 1989 card is Score.

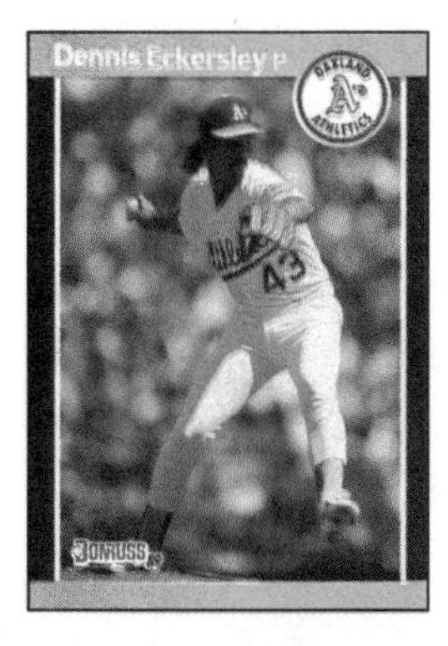

MARK EICHHORN

	W	L	ERA	G	SV	IP	H	R	BB	SO
1988	0	3	4.19	37	1	66.2	79	32	27	28
Life	24	18	2.98	202	15	398.1	334	139	138	306

POSITION: Pitcher
TEAM: Toronto Blue Jays
BORN: November 21, 1960 San Jose, CA
HEIGHT: 6'3" **WEIGHT:** 200 lbs.
BATS: Right **THROWS:** Right
ACQUIRED: Second-round pick in 1/79 free-agent draft

Eichhorn would have had a hard time topping his 1987 performance with the Toronto Blue Jays, but most mere mortals would have, too. The rugged reliever set a team record with 89 appearances for the Blue Jays in 1987, going 10-6 with four saves and a 3.17 ERA. In 1988, he pitched in 37 games, but went 0-3 with one save and a 4.19 ERA. Eichhorn appeared in 69 games in 1986, and he led the A.L. with 14 relief wins. He has pitched professionally for ten seasons, three with the Blue Jays and seven in the minors. If Eichhorn is healthy, he'll see lots more work for the 1989 Toronto squad.

Eichhorn's 1989 cards should be about a nickel each. See if he makes a sufficient comeback in 1989 before investing anything in his cards. Our pick for his best 1989 card is Topps.

JIM EISENREICH

	BA	G	AB	R	H	2B	3B	HR	RBI	SB
1988	.218	82	202	26	44	8	1	1	19	9
Life	.243	174	445	48	108	24	2	7	52	12

POSITION: Outfield; designated hitter
TEAM: Kansas City Royals
BORN: April 19, 1959 St. Cloud, MN
HEIGHT: 5′11″ **WEIGHT:** 195 lbs.
BATS: Left **THROWS:** Left
ACQUIRED: Signed as a free agent, 10/86

Eisenreich endured a small slump from his 1987 debut with the Royals, but he remained as one of baseball's most inspiring success stories. He made his major league debut with the 1982 Minnesota Twins. Eisenreich's .303 effort in 34 games made him look like a future regular for the team. However, a nervous disorder plagued his career to such an extent that he retired in June 1984. After sitting out the next two years, he attempted a comeback with the Royals. It took only two months of minor league ball to prove that Eisenreich could handle the majors again.

Eisenreich may never be a great player, but he's one of baseball's most admired. His cards are common-priced, and could pay big dividends if he has a full season of success. Our pick for his best 1989 card is Score.

KEVIN ELSTER

	BA	G	AB	R	H	2B	3B	HR	RBI	SB
1988	.214	149	406	41	87	11	1	9	37	2
Life	.215	173	446	45	96	14	1	9	38	2

POSITION: Shortstop
TEAM: New York Mets
BORN: August 3, 1964 San Pedro, CA
HEIGHT: 6′2″ **WEIGHT:** 180 lbs.
BATS: Right **THROWS:** Right
ACQUIRED: Second-round pick in 1/84 free-agent draft

Elster has all the tools to be a great one. He was named the best defensive shortstop and the number-one big league prospect in the Triple-A International League in 1987 by *Baseball America.* In 1988, Elster was the starting Met shortstop. He batted only .214, but he hit nine homers with 37 RBIs. At Triple-A Tidewater in 1987, Elster hit .310, with eight homers, seven triples, 33 doubles, and 74 RBIs. He had four hits in ten at-bats during a late-season call-up in '87 with New York. Elster has outstanding fielding ability—good hands, good arm, outstanding range—and he's sure to become a solid big league hitter in the years to come.

Elster's cards should be a good buy. Expect to pay 20 to 25 cents for his 1989 editions. Our pick for his best 1989 card is Topps.

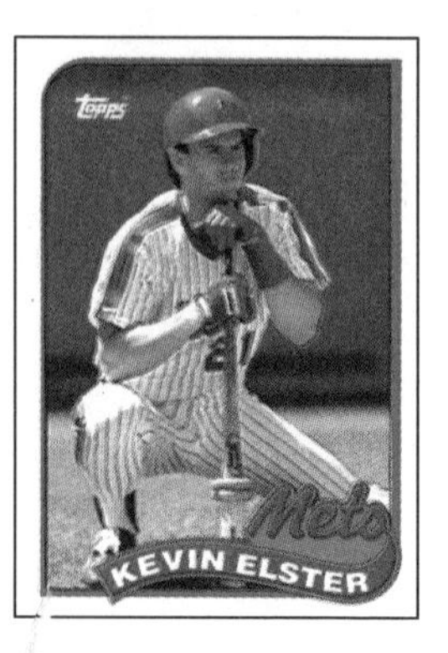

JIM EPPARD

	BA	G	AB	R	H	2B	3B	HR	RBI	SB
1988	.283	56	113	7	32	3	1	0	14	0
Life	.287	64	122	9	35	3	1	0	14	0

POSITION: First base; outfield
TEAM: California Angels
BORN: April 27, 1960 South Bend, IN
HEIGHT: 6′2″ **WEIGHT:** 180 lbs.
BATS: Left **THROWS:** Left
ACQUIRED: Purchased from A's, 1/87

During the winter of 1986, California searched for quality minor leaguers to bolster their farm clubs. The Angels acquired Eppard from Oakland, who had given up on him despite a .274 batting average at Triple-A Tacoma in '85. In 1987, he led the Triple-A Pacific Coast League with a .341 batting average and 94 RBIs. He didn't open the 1988 season with the Angels, despite batting .333 for them late in the 1987 season. Eppard returned to Edmonton and was batting .262 when the Angels recalled him. As a reward for their confidence, he batted close to .300 in the second half of the season. Eppard appears to have found a home in Anaheim.

Eppard's 1989 cards will open in the 10- to 15-cent range. Those prices could bring good dividends if he finds a starting spot for the Angels. Our pick for his best 1989 card is Score.

NICK ESASKY

	BA	G	AB	R	H	2B	3B	HR	RBI	SB
1988	.243	122	391	40	95	17	2	15	62	7
Life	.245	647	2104	255	515	94	16	92	319	17

POSITION: First base
TEAM: Cincinnati Reds
BORN: February 14, 1960 Hialeah, FL
HEIGHT: 6′3″ **WEIGHT:** 215 lbs.
BATS: Right **THROWS:** Right
ACQUIRED: First-round pick in 6/78 free-agent draft

Esasky maintained his power production in 1988 with Cincinnati, homering in double figures for his sixth straight year. He clubbed 15 homers and 62 RBIs in 1988, while batting .243. In the past, he has reached highs of 22 homers (in 1987) and 66 RBIs (in 1985). Esasky's two biggest problems have been injuries and the platoon system. He once was shuffled between first and third base before it was decided he could play first regularly. These factors have stopped him from playing more than 125 games in any season. If Esasky can play healthy in 150 games, he might prove himself in 1989.

Esasky's cards should be a nickel or less in 1989. Although he doesn't have a great career average, Esasky is a constant long-ball threat. His cards are fair investments. Our pick for his best 1989 card is Topps.

CECIL ESPY

	BA	G	AB	R	H	2B	3B	HR	RBI	SB
1988	.248	123	347	46	86	17	6	2	39	33
Life	.243	157	366	51	89	18	6	2	40	35

POSITION: Outfield
TEAM: Texas Rangers
BORN: January 20, 1963 San Diego, CA
HEIGHT: 6'3" **WEIGHT:** 195 lbs.
BATS: Both **THROWS:** Right
ACQUIRED: Traded from Pirates for Mike Dotzier, 4/87

Espy finally got his big break with the 1988 Texas Rangers. He tied for the most stolen bases on the team, with 33. His speed helped defensively; he made only three errors all season. Espy seemed doomed to the minors forever after working more than three seasons for a 20-game trial with the Dodgers in late 1983. Three more years of the minors followed. He appeared in 14 games for the 1987 Rangers, but went hitless in eight at-bats. Luckily, Espy got another chance in 1988, and seems to be a front-runner for a starting job in 1989.

Espy seems to be a Vince Coleman-type player capable of lots of excitement. Espy's 1989 rookie cards could go for at least 15 cents. If you can get them cheaper, do it. He could be ready for a big future. Our pick for his best 1989 card is Topps.

DWIGHT EVANS

	BA	G	AB	R	H	2B	3B	HR	RBI	SB
1988	.293	149	559	96	164	31	7	21	111	5
Life	.272	2236	7761	1287	2114	429	66	346	1183	70

POSITION: Outfield
TEAM: Boston Red Sox
BORN: November 3, 1951 Santa Monica, CA
HEIGHT: 6'3" **WEIGHT:** 205 lbs.
BATS: Right **THROWS:** Right
ACQUIRED: Fifth-round pick in 6/69 free-agent draft

Most players would have trouble matching a single-season effort of 34 homers, 123 RBIs, and a .305 batting average, but Evans came close. Although his 1987 totals were hard to beat, Evans stayed around the .300 mark all season long in 1988, and he drove in 111 runs. Evans also obtained his 2,000th hit in 1988, his 17th season with the Red Sox. He has hit at least 20 home runs for eight consecutive seasons. Evans may not get the media recognition of superstar teammates like Wade Boggs or Roger Clemens, but he proved in 1988 that he'll keep pace with the best in baseball.

Because the Red Sox are a star-laden team, Evans' cards have been somewhat overlooked. Pick up his 1989 cards at the inexpensive rate of 10 to 15 cents each. Our pick for his best 1989 card is Topps.

STEVE FARR

	W	L	ERA	G	SV	IP	H	R	BB	SO
1988	5	4	2.50	62	20	82.2	74	25	30	72
Life	22	23	3.61	212	31	436.2	401	187	179	362

POSITION: Pitcher
TEAM: Kansas City Royals
BORN: December 12, 1956 Cheverly, MD
HEIGHT: 5′11″ **WEIGHT:** 190 lbs.
BATS: Right **THROWS:** Right
ACQUIRED: Signed as a free agent, 5/85

Farr had the best year of his career for the 1988 Royals. He filled a void in the Royal bullpen created when Dan Quisenberry was released. Farr gained a team-leading 20 saves, his highest career total. He won five games, and he lowered his ERA from 1987's 4.15 mark to a tidy 2.50. He finished 49 of the games he appeared in. The Indians released Farr after he had a tough 3-11 season in 1984. In 1989, Farr will have to prove that he's a talented stopper and that his 1988 success wasn't a fluke.

Farr had an admirable season in 1988, his first in five years in the majors. At age 32, it'll be difficult for him to accumulate any meaningful career stats. His 1989 cards, priced at 15 cents or more, should be avoided. Our pick for his best 1989 card is Donruss.

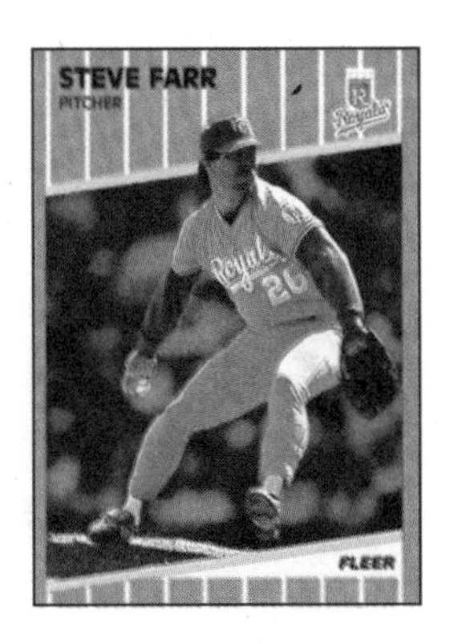

JOHN FARRELL

	W	L	ERA	G	CG	IP	H	R	BB	SO
1988	14	10	4.24	31	4	210.1	216	106	67	92
Life	19	11	4.03	41	5	279.1	284	135	89	120

POSITION: Pitcher
TEAM: Cleveland Indians
BORN: August 4, 1962
Monmouth Park, NJ
HEIGHT: 6′4″ **WEIGHT:** 210 lbs.
BATS: Right **THROWS:** Right
ACQUIRED: Second-round pick in 6/84 free-agent draft

Farrell, after only a brief ten-game trial, turned out to be one of the Indians' finest starting pitchers in 1988. His 14 victories tied for second on the Tribe. He had an unspectacular minor league career, but got a late-season chance to join the Tribe in 1987. He made the most of it, going 5-1 with one complete game and a 3.39 ERA in just ten games. Farrell added four more complete games to his career stats in 1988. He was a pleasant surprise in 1988. A second fine season in 1989 by Farrell could help make the Indians contenders again.

Farrell's 1988 rookie cards sold for about a quarter. Expect his second-year cards to start at 15 cents in 1989. Don't make rash investing decisions until Farrell demonstrates he can win in the majors for a second year. Our pick for his best 1989 card is Fleer.

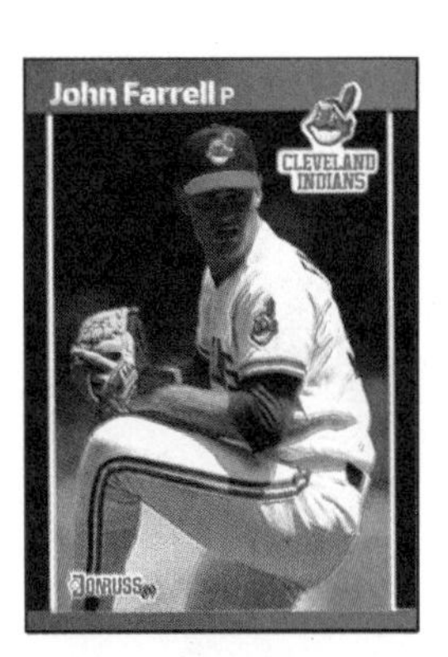

FELIX FERMIN

	BA	G	AB	R	H	2B	3B	HR	RBI	SB
1988	.276	43	87	9	24	0	2	0	2	3
Life	.265	66	155	15	41	0	2	0	6	3

POSITION: Infield
TEAM: Pittsburgh Pirates
BORN: October 9, 1963
Mao, Dominican Republic
HEIGHT: 5′11″ **WEIGHT:** 170 lbs.
BATS: Right **THROWS:** Right
ACQUIRED: Signed as a free agent, 6/83

It looks like 1989 will be the year that Felix "The Cat" Fermin will become a fixture in Pittsburgh. He spent most of 1988 at Triple-A Buffalo, where he played outstanding shortstop—a long-time trouble spot for the Pirates. Fermin played for Pittsburgh in 1987, hitting a respectable .250 in 68 at-bats. Most of his 1987 was spent at shortstop for Double-A Harrisburg, where he batted .268. Though he doesn't hit the long ball, he can be dangerous on the base paths—having stolen 40 bases in 84 games in 1986 for Prince William. Fermin could be the shortstop that the Pirates needed.

Fermin's 1989 cards will open in the 5- to 10-cent range. He should make a strong bid to be the opening-day shortstop. Our pick for his best 1989 card is Donruss.

SID FERNANDEZ

	W	L	ERA	G	CG	IP	H	R	BB	SO
1988	12	10	3.03	31	1	187.0	127	69	70	189
Life	55	40	3.33	134	9	813.2	607	326	349	774

POSITION: Pitcher
TEAM: New York Mets
BORN: October 12, 1962 Honolulu, HI
HEIGHT: 6′1″ **WEIGHT:** 220 lbs.
BATS: Left **THROWS:** Left
ACQUIRED: Traded from Dodgers with Ross Jones for Carlos Diaz and Bob Bailor, 12/83

Fernandez started 31 games in 1988 and finished with a 12-10 record, a 3.03 ERA, and 189 strikeouts in 187 innings. In 1987, the big lefthander was 12-8, with a 3.81 ERA and 134 strikeouts in 156 innings. Fernandez's best season in the majors was 1986, when he was 16-6, with a 3.52 ERA and 200 Ks in 204⅓ innings. El Sid, as Mets fans call him, has been a steady, but not spectacular, hurler for the Mets. Getting the work required for stardom is difficult on a staff that includes Dwight Gooden, David Cone, and Ron Darling. But Fernandez is an excellent hurler who could help the Mets notch many championships.

Fernandez might leap into the headliner category, but collectors have taken a wait-and-see attitude toward his cards. His 1989 cards will be in the 5- to 10-cent range. Our pick for his best 1989 card is Donruss.

TONY FERNANDEZ

	BA	G	AB	R	H	2B	3B	HR	RBI	SB
1988	.287	154	648	76	186	41	4	5	70	15
Life	.299	727	2744	362	820	140	35	25	274	90

POSITION: Shortstop
TEAM: Toronto Blue Jays
BORN: August 6, 1962 San Pedro de Macoris, Dominican Republic
HEIGHT: 6′2″ **WEIGHT:** 165 lbs.
BATS: Both **THROWS:** Right
ACQUIRED: Signed as a free agent, 4/79

In 1988, Fernandez produced a close copy of his 1987 season, aside from injury. He suffered a drop in batting average from his career high .322 in 1987 to .287 in 1988. However, he led the 1988 Blue Jays in at-bats and doubles, and he had 70 RBIs. Fernandez has scored at least 70 runs for four consecutive seasons, and he has 65 or more RBIs three straight years. His fielding remained strong, as he maintained his reputation as one of the league's top glove men. After four years as Toronto's starting shortstop, Fernandez can reach the 1,000-hit plateau with another good year in 1989.

Fernandez's 1989 cards should be plentiful at a nickel apiece. Buy them up. If Toronto ever enters a World Series, the world will be clamoring for Fernandez cards at a quarter apiece. Our pick for his best 1989 card is Topps.

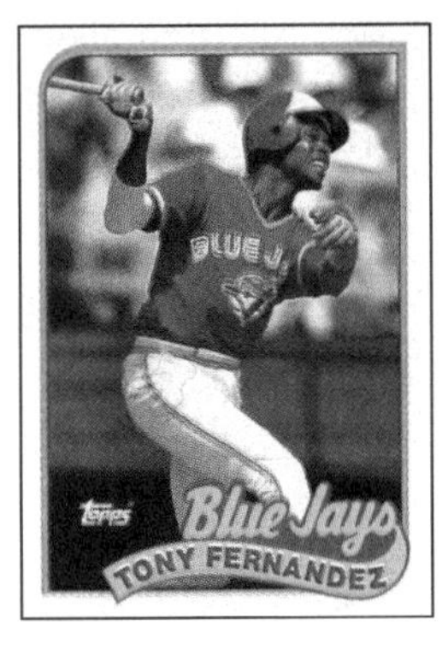

BRUCE FIELDS

	BA	G	AB	R	H	2B	3B	HR	RBI	SB
1988	.269	39	67	8	18	5	0	1	5	0
Life	.273	54	110	12	30	6	1	1	11	1

POSITION: Outfield
TEAM: Seattle Mariners
BORN: October 6, 1960 Cleveland, OH
HEIGHT: 6′ **WEIGHT:** 185 lbs.
BATS: Left **THROWS:** Right
ACQUIRED: Traded from Tigers, 1987

Fields has made a career out of being an outstanding prospect. Now at age 28, he'll likely make the grade with Seattle as a designated hitter and spare outfielder. There's little doubt that he can hit, twice winning minor league batting titles, in 1985 and 1986. Acquired by the Mariners for 1988, he began the year at Calgary, batting .336 when the M's beckoned. He hit .269 for Seattle. In 1987, he hit .305 for Triple-A Toledo and stole 24 bases. He batted .368 at Nashville—then a Detroit farm club—in 1986. He hit .323 at Birmingham in 1985. Fields could help make the Mariners a better team in 1989.

Fields has the ability to hit above .300. Though old for a prospect, his 1989 cards, which will open as commons, could be a bargain. Our pick for his best 1989 card is Topps.

CHUCK FINLEY

	W	L	ERA	G	CG	IP	H	R	BB	SO
1988	9	15	4.17	31	2	194.1	191	95	82	111
Life	14	23	4.18	91	2	331.1	333	166	148	211

POSITION: Pitcher
TEAM: California Angels
BORN: November 26, 1962 Monroe, LA
HEIGHT: 6′6″ **WEIGHT:** 220 lbs.
BATS: Left **THROWS:** Left
ACQUIRED: First-round pick in 1/85 free-agent draft

Finley got a taste of the 1988 Angels' starting rotation after spending two years in the team's bullpen. His 1988 performance wasn't great, but his nine wins ranked third in the club and his 111 strikeouts only trailed team ace Mike Witt (who had 133). Finley's record doesn't reflect his two complete games, either. He made 33 appearances as a reliever in 1987. His career skyrocketed in 1986, when he was called up from his Class-A team in May. Once Finley adapts to the regimen of starting, he could be a much-improved hurler in 1989.

Finley's career record explains why his cards will be priced as commons in 1989. He's a long shot as an investment, but with only four years of pro experience at age 26, he's sure to get better with time. Our pick for his best 1989 card is Topps.

JOHN FISHEL

	BA	G	AB	R	H	2B	3B	HR	RBI	SB
1988	.231	19	26	1	6	0	0	1	2	0
Life	.231	19	26	1	6	0	0	1	2	0

POSITION: Outfield; third base
TEAM: Houston Astros
BORN: November 8, 1962 Fullerton, CA
HEIGHT: 5′11″ **WEIGHT:** 185 lbs.
BATS: Right **THROWS:** Right
ACQUIRED: Ninth-round pick in 6/85 free-agent draft

Fishel was batting close to .300 for Triple-A Tucson in 1988 when the call came to report to the parent Astros. While the long-ball hitting youngster didn't tear up the N.L. for the balance of the season, it appears likely that he's up in the majors to stay. In Double-A at Columbus in 1987, he hit a career-high 24 homers and drove in 88 runs. Fishel played at Auburn in 1985, where he batted .261 in 77 games, chipping in with nine home runs and 42 RBIs. At Osceola in '86, he hit .269, with 83 RBIs and 12 circuit blows. Fishel may be the RBI man that the Astros are searching for.

Fishel may find a spot in the Astro lineup in '89. His 1989 cards will probably open in the 15- to 20-cent range. Our pick for his best 1989 card is Fleer.

BRIAN FISHER

	W	L	ERA	G	CG	IP	H	R	BB	SO
1988	8	10	4.61	33	1	146.1	157	78	57	66
Life	32	28	4.22	187	7	526.2	524	270	195	335

POSITION: Pitcher
TEAM: Pittsburgh Pirates
BORN: March 18, 1962 Honolulu, HI
HEIGHT: 6′4″ **WEIGHT:** 210 lbs.
BATS: Right **THROWS:** Right
ACQUIRED: Traded from Yankees with Doug Drabek and Logan Easley for Rick Rhoden, Cecilio Guante, and Pat Clements 11/86

A member of the Yankee alumni club in Pittsburgh, Fisher came over to the steel city in the Rick Rhoden deal in November 1986. He went 11-9 as a combination starter and reliever in his first N.L. season. In 1988, Fisher was 8-10 with a 4.61 ERA in 33 games, 22 of them starts. He was 2-9 with one save in 11 relief outings. He won his first three starts for the Bucs in 1988, becoming the first Pirate hurler to do so since Doc Ellis turned the trick in 1973. Fisher was 4-4 for the Yankees in 55 games in 1985 and 9-5 for them in 1986 in 62 contests. Fisher is a solid performer for the Pirates.

Fisher's 1989 cards will be commons. He is not superstar material, and his card values will never gain premium prices. Our pick for his best 1989 card is Donruss.

CARLTON FISK

	BA	G	AB	R	H	2B	3B	HR	RBI	SB
1988	.277	76	253	37	70	8	1	19	50	0
Life	.270	2038	7228	1108	1953	346	44	323	1098	116

POSITION: Catcher
TEAM: Chicago White Sox
BORN: December 26, 1947
Bellows Falls, VT
HEIGHT: 6′2″ **WEIGHT:** 217 lbs.
BATS: Right **THROWS:** Right
ACQUIRED: Signed as a free-agent, 3/81

Injuries squelched what looked like a great season for Fisk in 1988: Despite playing in less than 100 games, he belted 19 home runs and 50 RBIs. It was a frustrating and familiar story for Fisk: In the last three years, he's spent nearly an entire season on the disabled list. Despite his injuries, Fisk is averaging more than 66 RBIs a season in eight years with the ChiSox. He is only the third catcher in history to compile 300 home runs, 1,000 RBIs, and 1,000 runs scored. If Fisk plays in 1989 without injuries, he'll keep adding to those records.

Fisk's 1989 cards should start at 15 cents. That's a good price for someone who has an outside shot at the Hall of Fame if he can continue his accomplishments for one or two more seasons. Our pick for his best 1989 card is Fleer.

MIKE FLANAGAN

	W	L	ERA	G	CG	IP	H	R	BB	SO
1988	13	13	4.18	34	2	211.0	220	106	80	99
Life	155	124	3.88	385	100	2445.0	2458	1144	787	1367

POSITION: Pitcher
TEAM: Toronto Blue Jays
BORN: December 16, 1951
Manchester, NH
HEIGHT: 6′ **WEIGHT:** 195 lbs.
BATS: Left **THROWS:** Left
ACQUIRED: Traded from Orioles for
Oswald Pereza, 8/87

At one time, it seemed that leg injuries might snuff out Flanagan's career. His questionable health might have been the reason the Orioles unloaded him in 1987. However, he put those fears to rest when, at age 36, he led the Blue Jays in innings pitched. The veteran lefty hadn't gone more than 200 innings since 1983. Flanagan's 13-13 mark ended a streak of three losing seasons. The winner of the 1979 Cy Young Award, he has been pitching professionally since 1973. During 1989, his 15th big league outing, Flanagan could be the incentive the Blue Jays need to capture a pennant.

At Flanagan's age, it's unlikely that he'll be able to assemble Hall of Fame-quality statistics. But his common-priced cards could show some short-term gains if he could win 20 games again. Our pick for his best 1989 card is Score.

SCOTT FLETCHER

	BA	G	AB	R	H	2B	3B	HR	RBI	SB
1988	.276	140	515	59	142	19	4	0	47	8
Life	.271	855	2722	359	737	122	22	16	259	54

POSITION: Shortstop
TEAM: Texas Rangers
BORN: July 30, 1958
Fort Walton Beach, FL
HEIGHT: 5′11″ **WEIGHT:** 172 lbs.
BATS: Right **THROWS:** Right
ACQUIRED: Traded from White Sox with
Ed Correa and Jose Mota for
Dave Schmidt and Wayne
Tolleson, 11/85

Fletcher proved again in 1988 that he might be one of the most underrated shortstops in the American League. He was fourth on the Rangers in batting, and he made only 11 errors all season long. Fletcher is an accomplished contact hitter. He struck out only 34 times in 515 at-bats, an average of only once in every 15 plate appearances. Fletcher's finest season ever was 1986, his first with the Rangers, when he hit .300. In 1987, he drove in a career-high 63 runs. With all that ability, how much longer can Fletcher remain unknown?

Fletcher's 1989 cards are underpriced as commons. Shortstops like Alan Trammell and Cal Ripken receive more acclaim because they've played on winning teams during their careers. If Texas even finished at .500 in 1989, Fletcher's cards could double in value. Our pick for his best 1989 card is Topps.

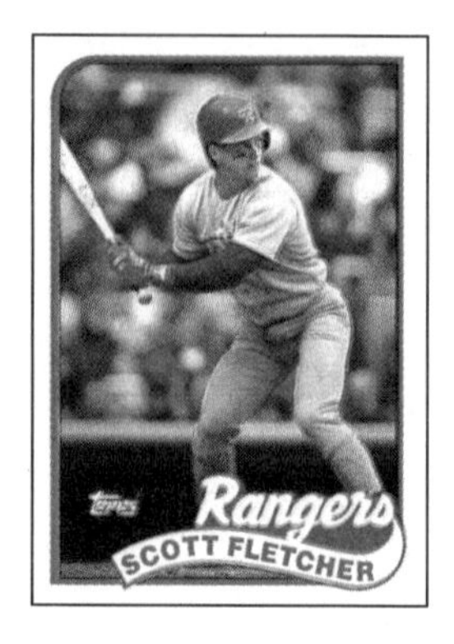

TOM FOLEY

	BA	G	AB	R	H	2B	3B	HR	RBI	SB
1988	.265	127	377	33	100	21	3	5	43	2
Life	.260	599	1545	151	402	79	14	19	153	24

POSITION: Shortstop
TEAM: Montreal Expos
BORN: September 9, 1959
Fort Benning, GA
HEIGHT: 6′ **WEIGHT:** 180 lbs.
BATS: Left **THROWS:** Right
ACQUIRED: Traded from Phillies with Larry Sorensen for Dan Schatzeder and Skeeter Barnes, 7/86

A valuable role player, Foley is the kind of a player you want on your ball club. The Expos have been happy to have the versatile infielder on their club since acquiring him from the Phillies in July 1986. Originally signed by the Reds in 1977, Foley performs with workmanlike efficiency. He batted .253 for the Reds in 1984; and the Phils, badly in need of a shortstop, traded Bo Diaz for him in August 1985. Foley batted .240 for the two clubs that year and .266 in 1986. In 1987, he hit a career-high .293 for Montreal and batted .265 in 127 games this past year. Foley should continue to earn his pay for the Expos for years.

Foley's value as a utility man does not translate into card values. He's not a good baseball card investment. Our pick for his best 1989 card is Score.

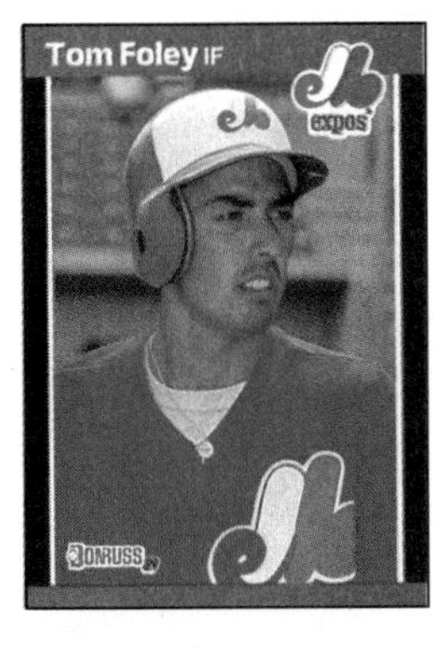

CURT FORD

	BA	G	AB	R	H	2B	3B	HR	RBI	SB
1988	.195	91	128	11	25	6	0	1	18	6
Life	.256	277	582	75	149	32	7	6	76	31

POSITION: Outfield
TEAM: St. Louis Cardinals
BORN: October 11, 1960 Jackson, MS
HEIGHT: 5′10″ **WEIGHT:** 150 lbs.
BATS: Left **THROWS:** Right
ACQUIRED: Third-round pick in 6/81 free-agent draft

The Cardinals have been expecting big things from Ford since they signed him back in 1981, but last season he was a major disappointment. In 1988, he had a .195 batting average in 91 games, with six stolen bases. Ironically those numbers come on the heels of 1987, when he batted .285 for the N.L. pennant winners. Ford stole 11 bases in '87 and scored 32 runs. He has been up and down between Triple-A Louisville and the majors almost every year since 1984. Ford has gone from a prospect to a suspect, and he has to prove that he belongs with the Cardinals in 1989.

A swift, singles-hitting, base-stealing outfielder fits the Cardinal offensive strategy, and that's why Whitey Herzog has stuck with him. Collectors, on the other hand, have relegated his cards to the commons box. Our pick for his best 1989 card is Fleer.

BOB FORSCH

	W	L	ERA	G	CG	IP	H	R	BB	SO
1988	10	8	4.29	36	1	136.1	153	73	44	54
Life	164	131	3.70	461	67	2686.2	2644	1251	786	1093

POSITION: Pitcher
TEAM: Houston Astros
BORN: January 13, 1950 Sacramento, CA
HEIGHT: 6'3" **WEIGHT:** 215 lbs.
BATS: Right **THROWS:** Right
ACQUIRED: Traded from Cardinals for Denny Walling, 9/88

After playing in 15 straight seasons with the St. Louis Cardinals, Forsch was traded to the Houston Astros in hopes of aiding their futile drive to take first place away from the Dodgers. While the team failed, Forsch succeeded. He posted a combined 10-8 mark in 36 appearances in 1988, while he started and relieved for the Astros. Going into the 1988 season, he was third on the all-time win list for St. Louis. Forsch has always been one of the best-hitting pitchers in the National League. He had 12 career homers through 1987. Forsch is a versatile veteran who will lend leadership and experience to the 1989 Astros staff.

Forsch could receive recognition if the Astros win the N.L. West in 1989. At a nickel or less, his common-priced 1989 cards are a good investment. Our pick for his best 1989 card is Donruss.

JOHN FRANCO

	W	L	ERA	G	SV	IP	H	R	BB	SO
1988	6	6	1.57	70	39	86.0	60	18	27	46
Life	38	22	2.37	333	116	447.1	383	139	174	307

POSITION: Pitcher
TEAM: Cincinnati Reds
BORN: September 17, 1960 Brooklyn, NY
HEIGHT: 5'10" **WEIGHT:** 175 lbs.
BATS: Left **THROWS:** Left
ACQUIRED: Traded from Dodgers with Brett Wise for Rafael Landestoy, 5/83

Franco went from a contender to the top in 1988, leading the N.L. in saves with 39. Cincinnati fans hope that the southpaw closer can lead the Reds to the top in 1989. Franco had an incredible season in '88, notching a 1.57 ERA while striking out 46 batters in 86 innings and going 6-6. In 1987, Franco had 32 saves, and he was 8-5 with a 2.52 ERA. He had 12 relief wins in 1985. He hasn't had a season-ending ERA over 3.00 in five years of pitching. He uses a wide assortment of pitches, and he challenges all hitters he faces. At age 28, Franco could be the Cincinnati stopper for years to come.

Franco's 1989 cards will open at 5 to 15 cents. Investing in his cards could be a bit tricky, so wait to see how he starts 1989 before paying those prices. Our pick for his best 1989 card is Topps.

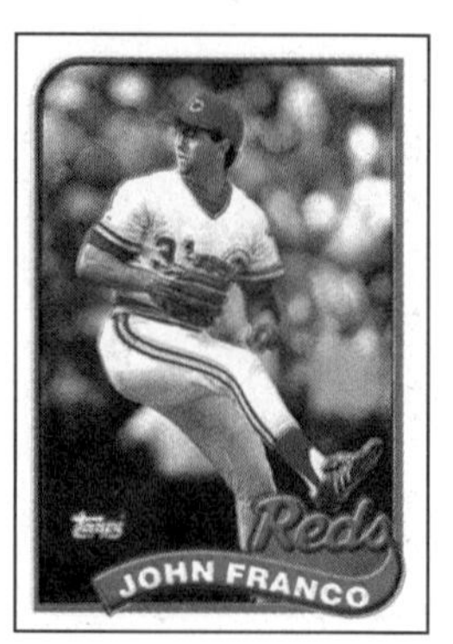

JULIO FRANCO

	BA	G	AB	R	H	2B	3B	HR	RBI	SB
1988	.303	152	613	88	186	23	6	10	54	25
Life	.295	914	3590	504	1059	157	31	45	432	131

POSITION: Shortstop
TEAM: Texas Rangers
BORN: August 23, 1961 San Pedro de Macoris, Dominican Republic
HEIGHT: 6′ **WEIGHT:** 160 lbs.
BATS: Right **THROWS:** Right
ACQUIRED: Traded from Indians for Oddibe McDowell, Pete O'Brien, and Jerry Browne, 12/88

In July of 1988, Franco seemed to own A.L. pitching. He was the talk of the league from July 3 to July 27, when he compiled a 22-game hitting streak. He hit above .300 for the third straight season (.303) and was the Tribe's leader both in hits and average last year. He and Joe Carter were the only Indians to steal more than 20 bases in 1988 (Franco was caught stealing 11 times). He is not a power hitter, but he showed a little pop in his bat in '88. Franco's speed, combined with his steady fielding and improving hitting, make him a fixture at short for the Rangers for years to come.

The Tribe didn't contend for the pennant in 1988, so fine players like Franco got overlooked. His 1989 cards will be less than a nickel, a bargain price. Our pick for his best 1989 card is Donruss.

TERRY FRANCONA

	BA	G	AB	R	H	2B	3B	HR	RBI	SB
1988	.311	62	212	24	66	8	0	1	12	0
Life	.281	615	1494	136	420	64	5	13	120	10

POSITION: First base; designated hitter
TEAM: Cleveland Indians
BORN: April 22, 1959 Aberdeen, SD
HEIGHT: 6′ **WEIGHT:** 175 lbs.
BATS: Left **THROWS:** Left
ACQUIRED: Signed as a free agent, 4/88

Serving both as a designated hitter and backup first baseman in 1988, Francona led the Indians in hitting. Francona's .311 average was the third-best in his eight-year major league career. The son of former major leaguer Tito Francona, Terry broke in with the Expos in 1981. He played in more than 100 games both in 1983 and 1985, and appeared to be the Expo starting first baseman until Andres Galarraga came along. At age 29, he is far from being a washed-up veteran. Francona should be an important member of the Indian bench in 1989.

Francona's 1989 cards should be selling at three cents or less. His stats aren't enticing enough to prompt investment in his cards. If he did win a starting job with the Indians, his cards might become a better gamble. Our pick for his best 1989 card is Score.

WILLIE FRASER

	W	L	ERA	G	CG	IP	H	R	BB	SO
1988	12	13	5.41	34	2	194.2	203	129	80	86
Life	22	23	4.74	71	7	375.2	369	218	144	194

POSITION: Pitcher
TEAM: California Angels
BORN: May 26, 1964 New York, NY
HEIGHT: 6′3″ **WEIGHT:** 200 lbs.
BATS: Right **THROWS:** Right
ACQUIRED: First-round pick in 6/85 free-agent draft

Fraser was a converted starter for the 1988 Angels. He served as a swing man in both starting and relief roles in 1987, his first full year in the majors. In 1988, his 12 wins were second on the California staff, only behind 13-game winner Mike Witt. The gopher ball haunted Fraser during 1988, spoiling what might have been a fine record. Instead, Fraser yielded a league-leading 33 home runs to opposing batters last season. In 1987, he was 10-10, with a 3.92 ERA, three relief wins, and one save. At age 24, he has a total of only four pro seasons worth of experience. Fraser will become a better pitcher with seasoning.

Fraser's 1989 cards are priced as commons. Don't invest until Fraser can prove that he can post a winning record. Our pick for his best 1989 card is Fleer.

MARVIN FREEMAN

	W	L	ERA	G	CG	IP	H	R	BB	SO
1988	2	3	6.10	11	0	51.2	55	36	43	37
Life	4	3	5.19	14	0	67.2	61	40	53	45

POSITION: Pitcher
TEAM: Philadelphia Phillies
BORN: April 10, 1963 Chicago, IL
HEIGHT: 6′6″ **WEIGHT:** 200 lbs.
BATS: Right **THROWS:** Right
ACQUIRED: Second-round pick in 6/84 free-agent draft

Freeman is an enigma. In the past three years, he has gone from outstanding pitching prospect to hopeless case and back again. The Phillies gave the righty another chance late in 1988, and he rewarded their confidence with some solid performances. How confusing is the Freeman case history? He tossed a seven-inning one-hitter against the Mets and a seven-inning two-hitter against the Giants late in the '88 campaign, but he also went 8-15 with a 5.20 ERA the past two seasons in the minors. He was 13-6 in 1986 at Double-A Reading. Freeman has a ton of talent, and he could be a key member of the 1989 Phillies.

Freeman's 1989 cards should sell for five cents. Watch that price climb if he becomes the solid big leaguer the Phils hope for. Our pick for his best 1989 card is Donruss.

TODD FROHWIRTH

	W	L	ERA	G	SV	IP	H	R	BB	SO
1988	1	2	8.25	12	0	12.0	16	11	11	11
Life	2	2	4.30	22	0	23.0	28	11	13	20

POSITION: Pitcher
TEAM: Philadelphia
BORN: September 28, 1962
Milwaukee, WI
HEIGHT: 6′4″ **WEIGHT:** 195 lbs.
BATS: Right **THROWS:** Right
ACQUIRED: 13th-round pick in 6/84 free-agent draft

Frohwirth made the jump from Double-A to the majors in late 1987 and realized a lifelong dream of being teamed with his pitching idol, Kent Tekulve. Frohwirth began 1988 in Philadelphia, but was sent down to Triple-A Maine when he had some control problems. The righthander got back on track and was Maine's ERA leader (2.27) and had 13 saves. At Double-A Reading in 1987, Frohwirth had a 1.86 ERA, 19 saves, 44 strikeouts, and just 13 walks in 58 innings. Promoted to Maine, he added four more saves in 17 games, with a 2.51 ERA. Frohwirth could be the 1989 Philadelphia short-relief pitcher.

Frohwirth is a side-armer and displays the same easy motion that has kept Tekulve in the big leagues for 16 years. Frohwirth's 1989 cards will be in the 30-cent range. Our pick for his best 1989 card is Score.

GARY GAETTI

	BA	G	AB	R	H	2B	3B	HR	RBI	SB
1988	.301	133	468	66	141	29	2	28	88	7
Life	.260	1077	3914	522	1019	214	16	166	598	62

POSITION: Third base
TEAM: Minnesota Twins
BORN: August 19, 1958 Centralia, IL
HEIGHT: 6′ **WEIGHT:** 185 lbs.
BATS: Right **THROWS:** Right
ACQUIRED: Selected in secondary phase of 6/79 free-agent draft

Gaetti's 1988 totals (28 homers and 88 RBIs) nearly matched his dazzling output of 1987 (31 home runs and 109 RBIs). However, he boosted his batting average nearly 40 points (from .265 in 1987), quite an accomplishment for any free-swinging power hitter. Gaetti, the 1987 American League Championship Series MVP, has been a familiar face at third base for the Twins for several years now. He has hit 20 or more homers in six out of his seven full seasons in the major leagues. If he can keep his power figures up while bolstering his once-fair batting average, Gaetti will gain universal acclaim as one of baseball's best "hot corner" men.

Gaetti's 1989 cards should sell at 10 cents or less. If he helps restore the Twins to win a World Series in 1989, however, those prices will climb quickly. Our pick for his best 1989 card is Donruss.

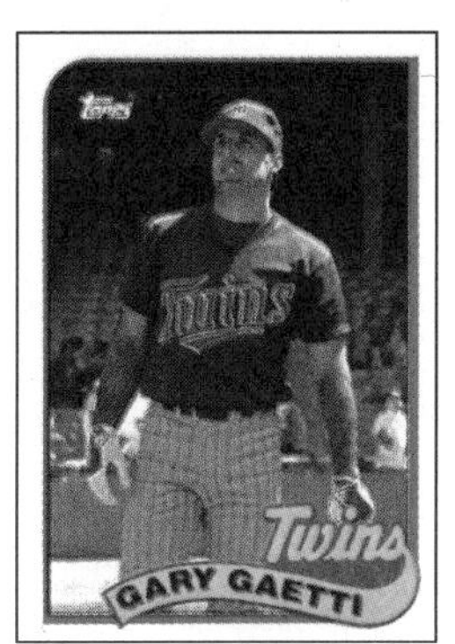

GREG GAGNE

	BA	G	AB	R	H	2B	3B	HR	RBI	SB
1988	.236	149	461	70	109	20	6	14	48	15
Life	.244	568	1691	240	412	86	22	38	168	43

POSITION: Shortstop
TEAM: Minnesota Twins
BORN: November 12, 1961
Fall River, MA
HEIGHT: 5′11″ **WEIGHT:** 175 lbs.
BATS: Right **THROWS:** Right
ACQUIRED: Traded from Yankees with Ron Davis and Paul Boros for Roy Smalley, 4/82

Gagne demonstrated that he's not a typical weak-hitting shortstop. Although his average slipped a bit, he produced a career-best 14 homers. The one-time New York Yankee will begin his fifth straight year as the starting shortstop for the Twins in 1989. Gagne's speed helps him handle the tough chore of fielding the Metrodome's fast artifical turf grounders. He also swiped a personal high of 15 bases in 1988. He is a dependable, every-day type of player. If Gagne can eliminate his high number of strikeouts (110 in 1988), he'll have a strong chance of becoming a perennial .300 hitter.

Gagne will gain national attention once again if the Twins return to the top. Expect his 1989 cards, now worth no more than a nickel, to double in value if Minnesota reclaims its division. Our pick for his best 1989 card is Donruss.

ANDRES GALARRAGA

	BA	G	AB	R	H	2B	3B	HR	RBI	SB
1988	.302	157	609	99	184	42	8	29	92	13
Life	.291	433	1556	219	453	96	11	54	228	27

POSITION: First base
TEAM: Montreal Expos
BORN: June 18, 1961
Caracas, Venezuela
HEIGHT: 6′3″ **WEIGHT:** 230 lbs.
BATS: Right **THROWS:** Right
ACQUIRED: Signed as a free agent, 1/79

Galarraga demonstrated his first superstar-quality season in 1988. His .300-plus season average was only points behind batting champion Tony Gwynn's. Galarraga also had 29 home runs and 92 RBIs. He set various career bests for himself, and led the Expos in games played, at-bats, hits, doubles, homers, and RBIs. Unfortunately, he was among the league leaders in strikeouts, an incident that will become more rare as he becomes a more experienced, disciplined hitter. He seems to have come into his own as a brawny slugger with a good average. When the Expos make a serious pennant run in the future, Galarraga's heavy hitting will fuel their drive.

Galarraga's 1989 cards should start selling at 15 cents each. That's a great investment price, considering that his cards could top 50 cents if he wins any hitting awards. Our pick for his best 1989 card is Topps.

DAVE GALLAGHER

	BA	G	AB	R	H	2B	3B	HR	RBI	SB
1988	.303	101	347	59	105	15	3	5	31	5
Life	.285	116	383	61	109	16	4	5	32	7

POSITION: Outfield
TEAM: Chicago White Sox
BORN: September 20, 1960 Trenton, NJ
HEIGHT: 6′ **WEIGHT:** 180 lbs.
BATS: Right **THROWS:** Right
ACQUIRED: Signed as a free agent, 1/88

At age 28, Gallagher finally arrived in the major leagues to stay in 1988, when the White Sox called him up from Triple-A Vancouver. In his first big league tilt, Gallagher hit an 11th-inning home run to beat Toronto. Gallagher's average stayed right around the .300 mark all season, ending at .303, with five homers. He broke into baseball with the Cleveland organization and spent four years in their farm system. The Tribe called him up in 1987, and after 15 games sold him to Seattle. Seattle farmed him out, and he played 75 games at Triple-A Calgary, hitting .306. Gallagher seems destined to start in the ChiSox outfield in 1989.

Gallagher's cards will open the 1989 season in the commons box. His cards are worth keeping an eye on. Our pick for his best 1989 card is Topps.

MIKE GALLEGO

	BA	G	AB	R	H	2B	3B	HR	RBI	SB
1988	.209	129	277	38	58	8	0	2	20	2
Life	.223	297	515	71	115	21	1	5	47	3

POSITION: Infield
TEAM: Oakland A's
BORN: October 31, 1960 Whittier, CA
HEIGHT: 5′8″ **WEIGHT:** 160 lbs.
BATS: Right **THROWS:** Right
ACQUIRED: Second-round pick in 6/81 free-agent draft

Gallego filled in anyplace he could for the 1988 Athletics. His batting average wasn't the greatest, but he did a fine defensive job of substituting in various roles. Equally talented as a shortstop or second baseman, he made just eight errors all season long. He hit .209 in 277 at-bats, with two home runs in 1988. Gallego's time with the Athletics is well-earned. He toiled in the minor leagues for four straight years beginning in 1981. With the departure of Glen Hubbard, last season's starting second baseman, Gallego could have a chance at a full-time job in 1989.

Gallego has never batted .300 in eight professional seasons. It shouldn't be surprising then that his 1989 cards will sell for three cents or less. Based on his career, his cards shouldn't be in demand. Our pick for his best 1989 card is Score.

RONNIE GANT

	BA	G	AB	R	H	2B	3B	HR	RBI	SB
1988	.259	146	563	85	146	28	8	19	60	19
Life	.260	167	646	94	168	32	8	21	69	23

POSITION: Second base
TEAM: Atlanta Braves
BORN: March 2, 1965 Victoria, TX
HEIGHT: 6′ **WEIGHT:** 172 lbs.
BATS: Right **THROWS:** Right
ACQUIRED: Fourth-round pick in 6/83 free-agent draft

Gant began the year in the minors in 1988, but the Southern Association's All-Star second sacker in 1987 was soon a Brave. With Atlanta, Gant hit .259, with 19 homers and 60 RBIs. He has been an All-Star at most of his minor league stops. Gant had a brief stay with the Braves during '87 and hit .265. That stint followed a .247 season at Double-A Greenville, where he had 14 homers, 82 RBIs, and 24 stolen bases. He had his top season in 1986 at Durham, when he was the league leader in home runs (26) and total bases (271); Gant was named Atlanta's "Minor League Player of the Year."

Gant's 1989 cards are a very good buy at 25 cents. He is a great hitter and good fielder, and he should be the Atlanta second baseman for years to come. Our pick for his best 1989 card is Topps.

JIM GANTNER

	BA	G	AB	R	H	2B	3B	HR	RBI	SB
1988	.276	155	539	67	149	28	2	0	47	20
Life	.275	1356	4675	554	1287	197	25	44	444	89

POSITION: Second base
TEAM: Milwaukee Brewers
BORN: January 5, 1954 Eden, WI
HEIGHT: 5′11″ **WEIGHT:** 175 lbs.
BATS: Left **THROWS:** Right
ACQUIRED: 12th-round selection in 6/74 free-agent draft

Gantner found that his 13th season in the majors was a lucky one. After playing only half of the Brewers games in 1987 due to injuries, he was back at full strength in 1988. He hit .276, his highest mark since 1983. He trailed only teammates Paul Molitor and Robin Young in most offensive categories. When Gantner is healthy, he is one of the most dependable players the Brewers have. He's a steady glove man and has never hit lower than .254 in the last ten seasons. Even at age 35, Gantner should be patrolling second base for the Brewers for at least another five years.

Unless Gantner can approach the 2,000-hit plateau, it's unlikely that he'll gain any lasting stardom. His cards sell for a nickel or less. Our pick for his best 1989 card is Topps.

WES GARDNER

	W	L	ERA	G	CG	IP	H	R	BB	SO
1988	8	6	3.50	36	1	149.0	119	61	64	106
Life	12	15	4.48	116	1	277.0	270	150	122	207

POSITION: Pitcher
TEAM: Boston Red Sox
BORN: April 29, 1961 Benton, AR
HEIGHT: 6′4″ **WEIGHT:** 195 lbs.
BATS: Right **THROWS:** Right
ACQUIRED: Traded from the Mets with Calvin Schiraldi, John Christensen, and LaSchelle Tarver for John Mitchell, Chris Bayer, Bob Ojeda, and Tom McCarthy, 11/85

Gardner, Boston's leading reliever in 1987, had mixed success with the 1988 Red Sox. Gardner had a team-best ten saves in 1987, but he earned only two in 1988. However, the tall righty raised his record from 3-6 in 1987 to 8-6 during last season. Gardner spent two seasons with the Mets in 1984 and 1985, but had little luck in 30 games. Gardner was one key component in the trade that convinced the Red Sox to ship established starter Bob Ojeda to New York. Because Lee Smith has become a one-man bullpen for the Red Sox, a comeback by Gardner in 1989 would be a real relief.

Gardner's 1989 cards will sell for a nickel or less. Because he's played only two seasons with the Red Sox, investors are advised to judge Gardner's play in 1989 before making a decision. Our pick for his best 1989 card is Topps.

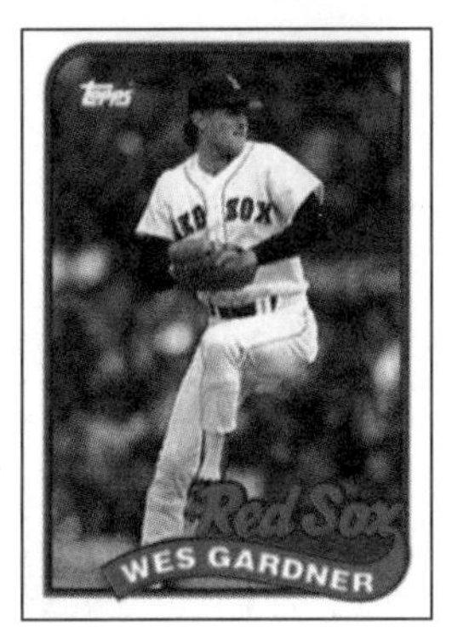

SCOTT GARRELTS

	W	L	ERA	G	SV	IP	H	R	BB	SO
1988	5	9	3.58	65	13	98.0	80	42	46	86
Life	42	36	3.25	283	48	564.1	451	232	288	496

POSITION: Pitcher
TEAM: San Francisco Giants
BORN: October 30, 1961 Urbana, IL
HEIGHT: 6′4″ **WEIGHT:** 205 lbs.
BATS: Right **THROWS:** Right
ACQUIRED: First-round pick in 6/79 free-agent draft

Garrelts led the Giants in saves for the fourth straight season in 1988. He matched his career high of 13 saves, first achieved in 1985. His strikeout totals are consistently among the highest for any N.L. reliever. Garrelts is the top reliever the Giants have. However, he's never pulled down more than 13 saves a season, which isn't a lot compared to the work of stoppers from other teams. Garrelts hasn't always been a reliever. In 1986, he started 18 games (completing two of them) before getting his relief role back. In the last five years, he has remained free of injuries. Garrelts' durability will be an asset to the 1989 Giants pitching staff.

Garrelts' 1989 cards are priced at about a nickel each. The cards don't show the promise of short-term gains in value. Our pick for his best 1989 card is Fleer.

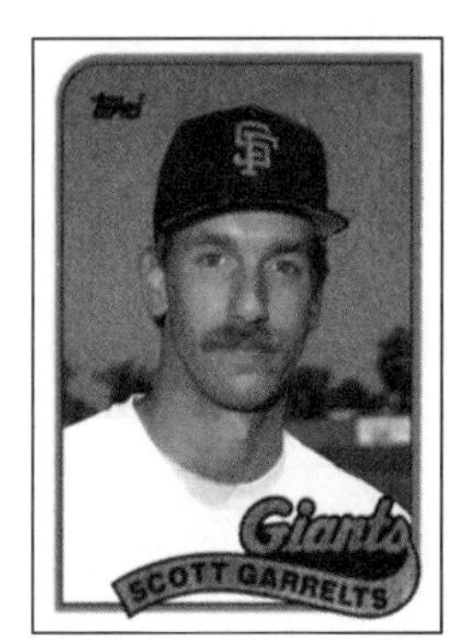

RICH GEDMAN

	BA	G	AB	R	H	2B	3B	HR	RBI	SB
1988	.231	95	299	33	69	14	0	9	39	0
Life	.265	803	2581	288	683	155	12	79	340	3

POSITION: Catcher
TEAM: Boston Red Sox
BORN: September 26, 1959
Worcester, MA
HEIGHT: 6′ **WEIGHT:** 215 lbs.
BATS: Left **THROWS:** Right
ACQUIRED: Signed as a free agent, 8/77

Injuries continued to take their toll on Gedman in 1988. The starting Red Sox catcher, who inherited the job after Carlton Fisk left, failed to play in 100 games for the second straight season. Gedman, once viewed as one of Boston's best power hitters, added nine homers and 39 RBIs to the team effort in 1988. His only problem is his age. In 1981, he was one of the American League's top rookies. Now, seven seasons later, Gedman has averaged only about 115 games per year. No one doubts his talents as a catcher or hitter. The only uncertainty is Gedman's physical ability to catch a full season.

Gedman's cards are commons, sold at a nickel or less. Due to doubts about his stamina and his future, his cards are risky investments. Our pick for his best 1989 card is Topps.

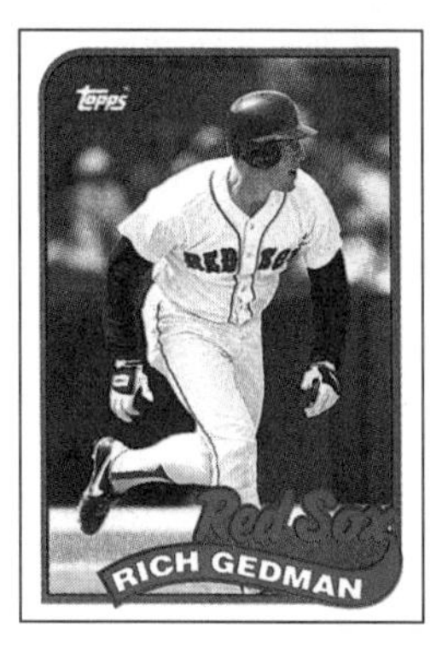

KEN GERHART

	BA	G	AB	R	H	2B	3B	HR	RBI	SB
1988	.195	103	262	27	51	10	1	9	23	7
Life	.221	215	615	72	136	22	3	24	64	16

POSITION: Outfield
TEAM: Baltimore Orioles
BORN: May 19, 1961 Charleston, SC
HEIGHT: 6′1″ **WEIGHT:** 195 lbs.
BATS: Right **THROWS:** Right
ACQUIRED: Fifth-round pick in 6/82 free-agent draft

Gerhart showed only glimpses of his power potential in 1988, his second full year with the Orioles. After sitting out nearly the final two months of the 1987 season due to a broken wrist, he managed to play in only 11 more games in 1988. Gerhart's 1987 injury ended what might have been a banner season. He had hit .301 with seven homers and 22 RBIs in the 22 previous games before getting hit in the right hand. He finished the year with 14 home runs and 34 RBIs. The team could use Gerhart's power hitting, especially if he could stay free of injuries throughout the season.

Gerhart's past career has been marred by slumps and injuries. Due to his past professional problems and his uncertain future, Gerhart's 1989 cards aren't good purchases, even at 3 to 5 cents each. Our pick for his best 1989 card is Topps.

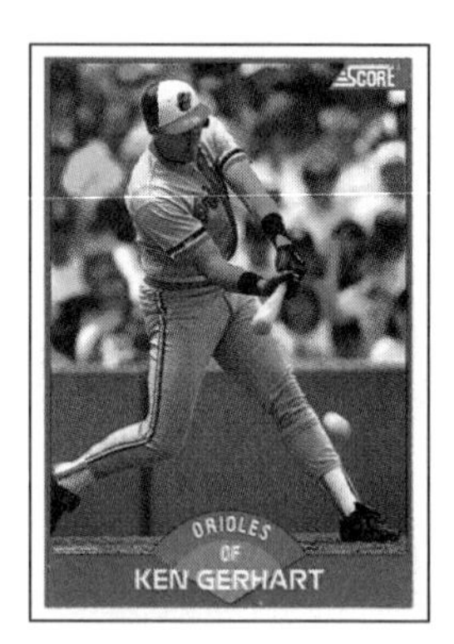

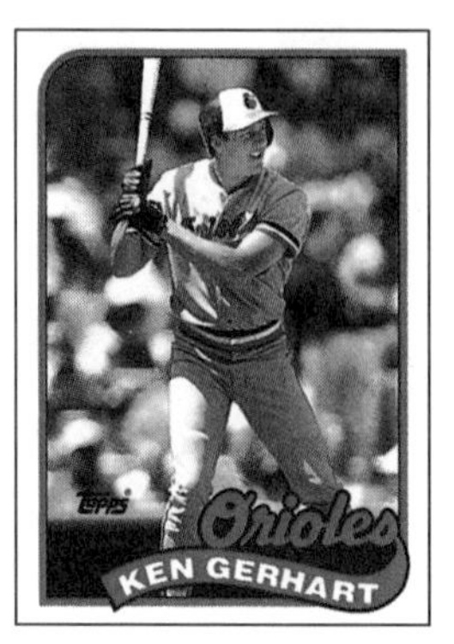

KIRK GIBSON

	BA	G	AB	R	H	2B	3B	HR	RBI	SB
1988	.290	150	542	106	157	28	1	25	76	31
Life	.278	1043	3752	634	1042	168	36	175	575	197

POSITION: Outfield
TEAM: Los Angeles Dodgers
BORN: May 28, 1957 Pontiac, MI
HEIGHT: 6′3″ **WEIGHT:** 215 lbs.
BATS: Left **THROWS:** Left
ACQUIRED: Signed as a free agent, 2/88

Most fans have a two-word explanation of why the Dodgers won the World Series in 1988: Kirk Gibson. In his ninth full major league season, the 1988 N.L. Most Valuable Player became the nucleus of a once-streaky Dodger offense. Gibson, injury free for the first time in three seasons, surpassed the 20-homer, 20-steal mark for the fifth consecutive year in 1988. Gibson was the MVP of the American League Championship Series in 1984, and went on to hit .333 with two homers and seven RBIs as the Tigers won the World Series.

Gibson gained considerable national attention in his first season with the pennant-winning Dodgers. Based on his 1988 postseason performance, his cards may exceed the 25-cent mark. Our pick for his best 1989 card is Topps.

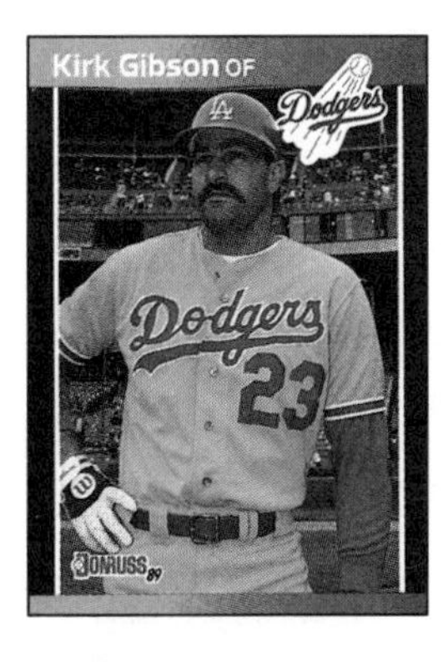

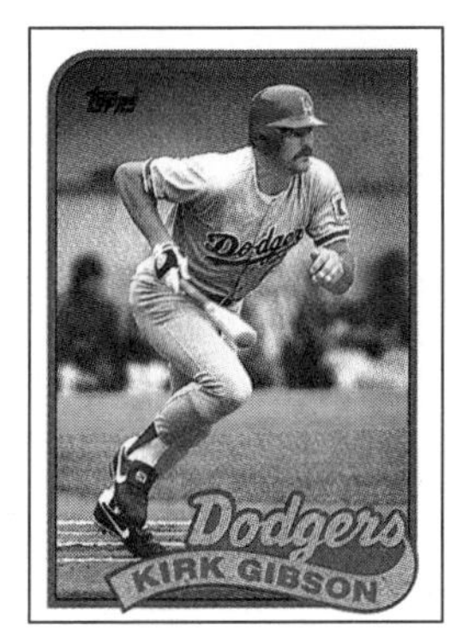

DAN GLADDEN

	BA	G	AB	R	H	2B	3B	HR	RBI	SB
1988	.269	141	576	91	155	32	6	11	62	28
Life	.272	610	2272	356	617	103	19	35	210	147

POSITION: Outfield
TEAM: Minnesota Twins
BORN: July 7, 1957 San Jose, CA
HEIGHT: 5′11″ **WEIGHT:** 180 lbs.
BATS: Right **THROWS:** Right
ACQUIRED: Traded from Giants for David Blakely, Jose Dominguez, and Ray Velasquez, 3/87

Gladden enjoyed some new-found power with the 1988 Minnesota Twins. He pounded out 11 homers and 62 RBIs, both career highs. This speedy outfielder continued to lead the Twins in stolen bases, swiping 28. His fielding continued to be top-notch, as he committed only three errors in 141 games. Gladden is a true team player. He even pitched for his 1988 club, throwing one inning of relief. After a scoreless one-inning stint, he wound up with a 0.00 ERA, the lowest on the team. Gladden is a multi-talented player and a real boost to the Twins.

Gladden's cards are commons, sold at less than a nickel. Last season could have marked a turning point in his career. Judging from his many talents, Gladden could be a decent investment. Our pick for his best 1989 card is Donruss.

TOM GLAVINE

	W	L	ERA	G	CG	IP	H	R	BB	SO
1988	7	17	4.56	34	1	195.1	201	111	63	84
Life	9	21	4.76	43	1	245.2	256	145	96	104

POSITION: Pitcher
TEAM: Atlanta Braves
BORN: March 25, 1966 Concord, MA
HEIGHT: 6′ **WEIGHT:** 175 lbs.
BATS: Left **THROWS:** Left
ACQUIRED: Second-round pick in 6/84 free-agent draft

Glavine suffered through a seven-game losing streak and an awful season record during his first full year with the Braves. He finished at 7-17, losing from June 15 through August 7 before winning again. Glavine, only 23 years old, spent three and a half seasons in the Atlanta minor league system before making a late-season debut in 1987. He went 2-4 in nine starts in '87, ending with a 5.54 ERA. He almost became a professional hockey player after high school, getting drafted by the Los Angeles Kings of the NHL. After his first-season shelling in 1988, Glavine should be ready for anything in 1989.

Glavine's 1989 cards should be a nickel or less. Until he can post a winning season in the majors, don't invest in his cards. Our pick for his best 1989 card is Donruss.

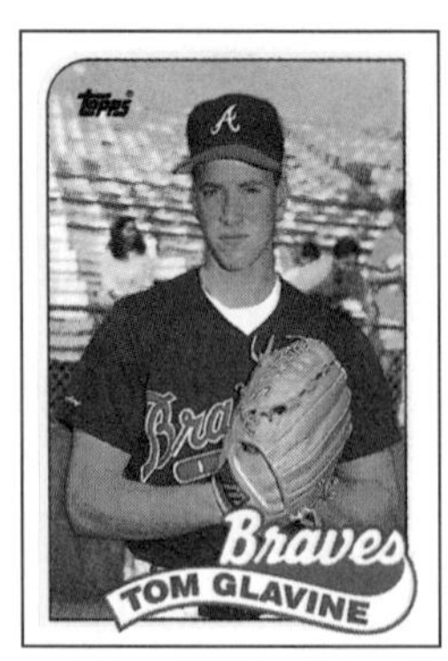

JERRY DON GLEATON

	W	L	ERA	G	SV	IP	H	R	BB	SO
1988	0	4	3.55	42	3	38.0	33	17	17	29
Life	10	18	4.66	165	11	243.1	243	142	110	135

POSITION: Pitcher
TEAM: Kansas City Royals
BORN: September 14, 1957 Brownwood, TX
HEIGHT: 6′3″ **WEIGHT:** 210 lbs.
BATS: Left **THROWS:** Left
ACQUIRED: Signed as a free agent, 11/86

Gleaton, in his second season with Kansas City, continued to serve the team as a lefthanded set-up man. He was third on the team in appearances, with 42. Often he'd be called upon only to pitch to select hitters. Gleaton did finish 20 games that he appeared in during 1987. After two mediocre seasons with the ChiSox in 1984 and 1985, he spent an entire season in the minors. The Royals signed him in 1987, and he worked in 48 games. Gleaton isn't the fanciest or most overpowering pitcher in existence, but he gets the job done when called upon.

Gleaton, at age 31, has modest career statistics. Middle relievers don't grab headlines often, so their cards have little appeal. Gleaton is no exception, and his common-priced cards aren't good investments. Our pick for his best 1989 card is Donruss.

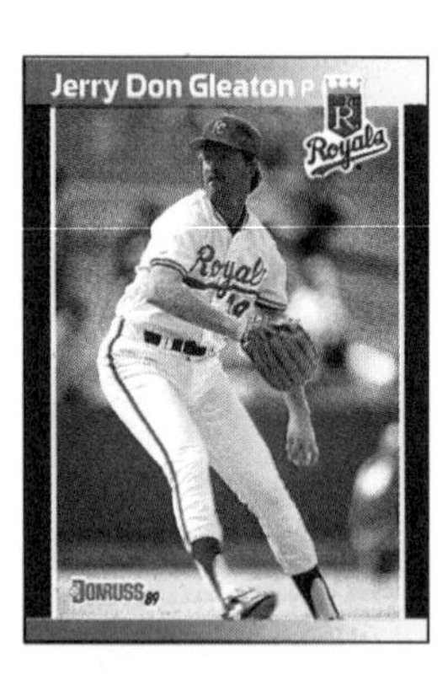

GERMAN GONZALEZ

	W	L	ERA	G	SV	IP	H	R	BB	SO
1988	0	0	3.38	16	1	21.1	20	8	8	19
Life	0	0	3.38	16	1	21.1	20	8	8	19

POSITION: Pitcher
TEAM: Minnesota Twins
BORN: October 3, 1965
Rio Caribe, Venezuela
HEIGHT: 6′ **WEIGHT:** 170 lbs.
BATS: Right **THROWS:** Right
ACQUIRED: Signed as a free agent, 1986

Gonzalez is a promising righty. After an incredibly productive year at Double-A Orlando in 1988, he received a late-season spot in the Minnesota bullpen. For Orlando, Gonzalez recorded 30 saves in 62 innings pitched, earning a 2-1 record and a microscopic 1.02 ERA. Upon joining the Twins, he limited A.L. batters to just 12 hits in his first 13 appearances and compiled a neat 0.54 ERA along the way. In 1987 at Kenosha, he was second in the Midwest League in relief points (49) and third in saves (19). Based on his past success, Gonzalez has a good shot at sticking in the Twin bullpen in 1989.

Gonzalez's 1989 cards should open in the 25-cent range. Since Jeff Reardon is the Minnesota stopper, Gonzalez will be a set-up reliever. His cards are not a solid investment at that price. Our pick for his best 1989 card is Topps.

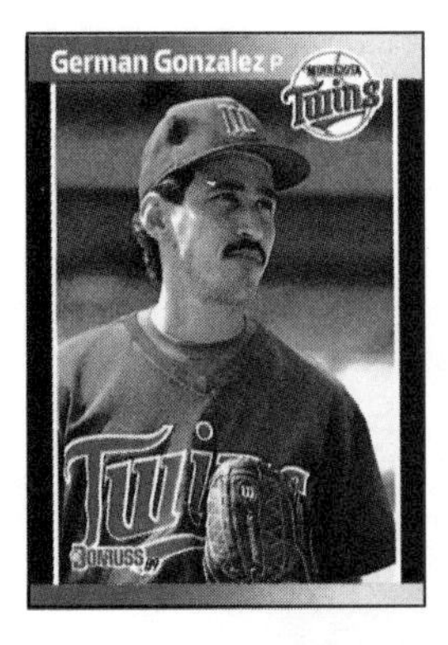

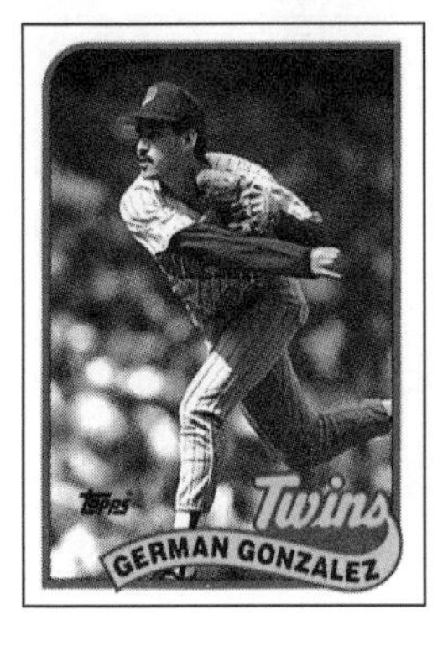

DWIGHT GOODEN

	W	L	ERA	G	CG	IP	H	R	BB	SO
1988	18	9	3.19	34	10	248.1	242	98	57	175
Life	91	35	2.62	158	52	1172.2	960	381	332	1067

POSITION: Pitcher
TEAM: New York Mets
BORN: November 16, 1964 Tampa, FL
HEIGHT: 6′3″ **WEIGHT:** 195 lbs.
BATS: Right **THROWS:** Right
ACQUIRED: First-round pick in 6/82 free-agent draft

Gooden posted yet another strong season for the Mets, finishing with an 18-9 record and a 3.19 ERA. He maintained his sparkling winning percentage and helped the Mets win their division. After five seasons, Gooden has proven that he's here to stay as a top pitcher in the National League. In 1985, his best season, he went 24-4, with a 1.53 ERA and 268 Ks in 276$\frac{2}{3}$ innings. He was 15-7 in 1987, with a 3.21 ERA. He has never won less than 15 games in a season. At age 24, Gooden has every opportunity to become one of the game's greatest pitchers. Even if he pitches only one more decade, he could reasonably reach 200 wins and 3,000 career strikeouts.

Gooden's 1989 cards should sell for as much as 75 cents. Based on his noted past and unlimited future, the price is reasonable. Our pick for his best 1989 card is Score.

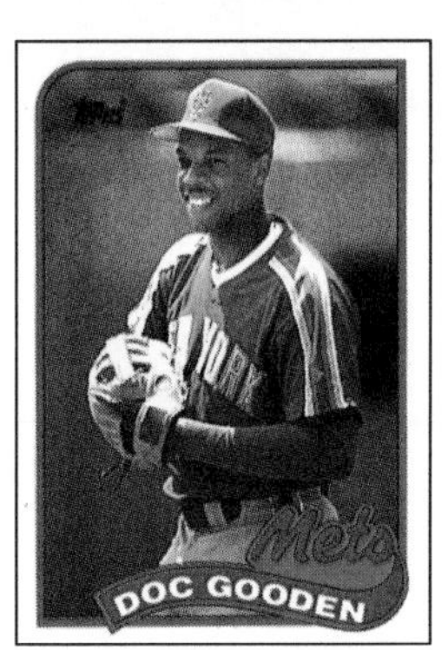

DON GORDON

	W	L	ERA	G	SV	IP	H	R	BB	SO
1988	3	4	4.40	38	1	59.1	65	33	19	20
Life	3	8	4.72	78	3	131.2	150	89	42	56

POSITION: Pitcher
TEAM: Cleveland Indians
BORN: October 10, 1959
New York, NY
HEIGHT: 6′1″ **WEIGHT:** 185 lbs.
BATS: Right **THROWS:** Right
ACQUIRED: Signed as a free agent, 8/87

Gordon got his second steady season of work with the Indians in 1988. The righthanded reliever pitched in a career-high 38 games with the Tribe last season, where he won his first three major league decisions. Gordon started his pro career in 1982 with the Tiger organization, and then moved into the Blue Jay system. He spent four seasons in the minors before getting a 1986 shot in Toronto. The Blue Jays released him in mid-1987, and the Indians gave him another chance. Gordon needs to lower his ERA if he'd like to lengthen his career.

Gordon's 1989 cards will be found in the commons box. He's an unproven 29-year-old pitcher with a lackluster past record. Avoid investing in his cards until his statistics sharpen up. Our pick for his best 1989 card is Score.

TOM GORDON

	W	L	ERA	G	CG	IP	H	R	BB	SO
1988	0	2	5.17	5	0	13.2	16	9	7	18
Life	0	2	5.17	5	0	13.2	16	9	7	18

POSITION: Pitcher
TEAM: Kansas City Royals
BORN: November 18, 1967
Avon Park, FL
HEIGHT: 5′9″ **WEIGHT:** 160 lbs.
BATS: Right **THROWS:** Right
ACQUIRED: Sixth-round pick in 6/85 free-agent draft

Gordon kept the travel agents busy in 1988, and now the Royals have all but told the righty to unpack his bags in Missouri. Gordon started the '88 season at Class-A Appleton, going 7-5 with a 2.06 ERA in 17 games. He struck out an incredible 172 batters, walking just 43 in 118 innings. Moving to Double-A Memphis, he was 6-0 in six games, with 62 Ks in 47 innings and a 0.38 ERA. His next stop was Triple-A Omaha, winning all three starts, with 29 Ks in 20 innings and a 1.33 ERA. He finally traveled to Kansas City, fanning ten in his first nine innings.

Expect Gordon's 1989 cards to open in the 35-cent range. He looks like he has a lot of Ks ahead of him, but that is a high price for investing. Our pick for his best 1989 card is Donruss.

GOOSE GOSSAGE

	W	L	ERA	G	SV	IP	H	R	BB	SO
1988	4	4	4.33	46	13	43.2	50	23	15	30
Life	110	97	2.92	811	302	1578.0	1293	572	626	1349

POSITION: Pitcher
TEAM: Chicago Cubs
BORN: July 5, 1951
Colorado Springs, CO
HEIGHT: 6′3″ **WEIGHT:** 225 lbs.
BATS: Right **THROWS:** Right
ACQUIRED: Traded from Padres with Ray Hayward for Keith Moreland and Mike Brumley, 2/88

Superstar-quality relievers like Gossage are few and far between. Traded to the Cubs by the Padres at the start of last season, Goose topped the staff in saves with 13, while going 4-4 with a 4.33 ERA in 46 outings. Prior to injuring his rib cage early in 1987, Gossage had strung together seven consecutive seasons with 20 or more saves. He has saved at least 20 games in ten different seasons. His personal high of 33 saves came in 1980 for the Yankees, when he led the A.L. in that department while going 6-2 in 64 games with a 2.27 ERA. Gossage is at the end of a Hall of Fame career.

Gossage's cards are currently holding in the 15- to 20-cent range. He's not a big ticket anymore, but his cards are still not a bad investment at 20 cents. Our pick for his best 1989 card is Topps.

JIM GOTT

	W	L	ERA	G	SV	IP	H	R	BB	SO
1988	6	6	3.49	67	34	77.1	68	30	22	76
Life	35	48	4.18	256	50	748.0	731	391	309	529

POSITION: Pitcher
TEAM: Pittsburgh Pirates
BORN: August 3, 1959 Hollywood, CA
HEIGHT: 6′4″ **WEIGHT:** 200 lbs.
BATS: Right **THROWS:** Right
ACQUIRED: Signed as a free agent, 8/87

The Bucs took the advice: If you Gott it, flaunt it. Gott, a converted starter, became the Pirates' relief ace in 1988, breaking Kent Tekulve's old team record of 31 saves. In 1987, Gott set another club mark by converting seven straight save opportunities. The righty finished that year with 13 of 16 save conversions. Beginning in 1988, Gott was the unofficial dean of the Pirates, with a team-leading six years of major league service. Gott is one of the hardest throwers in the majors, consistently throwing at about 95 mph.

Gott's 1989 cards should start in the 5- to 10-cent range. Hang on to any Gott singles you acquire in wax packs, but don't stock up on his cards until he posts another quality season. Our pick for his best 1989 card is Score.

MARK GRACE

	BA	G	AB	R	H	2B	3B	HR	RBI	SB
1988	.296	134	486	65	144	23	4	7	57	3
Life	.296	134	486	65	144	23	4	7	57	3

POSITION: First base
TEAM: Chicago Cubs
BORN: June 28, 1964
Winston-Salem, NC
HEIGHT: 6′2″ **WEIGHT:** 190 lbs.
BATS: Left **THROWS:** Left
ACQUIRED: 25th-round pick in 6/85 free-agent draft

Grace spent the first month of the 1988 season in the minors, while the Cubs made room for him. Once he joined the Cubs, he showed that he was the real item and batted close to .300. He also played first flawlessly. One of the most highly touted rookies of the season, he is seen by many as being in the class of Wally Joyner and Keith Hernandez. Grace didn't find his home-run stroke (especially in Wrigley Field), but his power stats should increase with experience. A premier player at Double-A Pittsfield in 1987, Grace batted .333, with 17 homers and 101 RBIs. In 1987, he was rated as the top Eastern League prospect by *Baseball America.*

Grace's 1989 cards will start somewhere between 75 cents and a dollar. They should be a solid long-term investment. Our pick for his best 1989 card is Donruss.

MIKE GREENWELL

	BA	G	AB	R	H	2B	3B	HR	RBI	SB
1988	.325	158	590	86	192	39	8	22	119	16
Life	.326	331	1068	168	348	73	14	45	220	22

POSITION: Outfield
TEAM: Boston Red Sox
BORN: July 18, 1963 Louisville, KY
HEIGHT: 6′ **WEIGHT:** 190 lbs.
BATS: Left **THROWS:** Right
ACQUIRED: Sixth-round pick in 6/82 free-agent draft

Greenwell firmly established himself as a solid hitter in 1988, his second full major league season. Looking in the final American League offensive stats, you'll find his name among the top five of virtually every department. You name it, he did it, including 119 RBIs, 22 home runs, and a .325 batting average, trailing only Wade Boggs and Kirby Puckett. Greenwell finished second to Boggs in most Boston offensive categories. Greenwell's stolen base total was second on the BoSox only to Ellis Burks'. Greenwell hit .328 in 1987, with 19 home runs, 89 RBIs, 71 runs scored, and 31 doubles. After two dazzling seasons, Greenwell will be shopping for an MVP award in 1989.

Be prepared to see Greenwell's 1989 card prices nearing $1. Buy early, because prices will double if he continues his hitting rampage. Our pick for his best 1989 card is Topps.

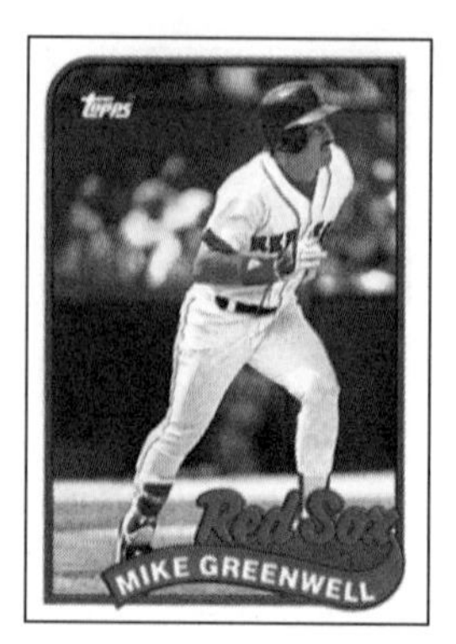

TOMMY GREGG

	BA	G	AB	R	H	2B	3B	HR	RBI	SB
1988	.295	25	44	5	13	4	0	1	7	0
Life	.288	35	52	8	15	5	0	1	7	0

POSITION: Outfield
TEAM: Atlanta Braves
BORN: July 29, 1963 Boone, NC
HEIGHT: 6′1″ **WEIGHT:** 190 lbs.
BATS: Left **THROWS:** Left
ACQUIRED: Traded from Pirates for Ken Oberkfell, 8/88

Swapped to Atlanta in the Ken Oberkfell trade, Gregg was hitting close to .300 at Triple-A Buffalo at the time of the deal. In 1987, he had a .376 average at Double-A Harrisburg. Gregg was Pittsburgh's seventh-round draft pick in June 1985 out of Wake Forest University. He saw limited action for the Pirates early in 1988, hitting .200. Gregg doesn't hit many homers, but he displays good speed and offensive versatility. The Indians drafted Gregg twice, in 1981 and 1984, but were unable to sign him. His first professional season, 1985, saw him bat .313 for Class-A Macon. The Braves may have found themselves a starting outfielder in Gregg.

Gregg's 1989 cards will be in the 10- to 15-cent category. Wait to see if he opens with Atlanta before buying at that price. Our pick for his best 1989 card is Donruss.

ALFREDO GRIFFIN

	BA	G	AB	R	H	2B	3B	HR	RBI	SB
1988	.199	95	316	39	63	8	3	1	27	7
Life	.254	1467	5218	609	1326	191	71	23	423	168

POSITION: Shortstop
TEAM: Los Angeles Dodgers
BORN: March 6, 1957 Santo Domingo, Dominican Republic
HEIGHT: 5′11″ **WEIGHT:** 165 lbs.
BATS: Both **THROWS:** Right
ACQUIRED: Traded from A's with Jay Howell and Jesse Orosco for Bob Welch, Charlie Spikes, and Jack Savage, 12/87

A broken wrist curtailed Griffin's first season with the Dodgers in 1988. He got into just 95 games, and his hitting never was the same. But Griffin gave the Dodgers their first legitimate shortstop since Bill Russell. Griffin's glovework shored up a shaky Dodgers' defense, and his speed added another facet to the team's offense. He first signed as a free agent with the Indians at age 16. He was the 1979 A.L. Rookie of the Year with Toronto. A healthy Griffin will be necessary if the Dodgers want to defend their world championship in 1989.

Griffin's 1989 cards should be a dime or less, which is a reasonable price for investors. That price will go up quickly if he plays a full season at his usual level. Our pick for his best 1989 card is Score.

GREG GROSS

	BA	G	AB	R	H	2B	3B	HR	RBI	SB
1988	.203	98	133	10	27	1	0	0	5	0
Life	.288	1749	3670	447	1058	130	46	7	304	39

POSITION: Outfield
TEAM: Philadelphia Phillies
BORN: August 1, 1952 York, PA
HEIGHT: 5′10″ **WEIGHT:** 175 lbs.
BATS: Left **THROWS:** Left
ACQUIRED: Traded from Cubs with Manny Trillo and Dave Rader for Barry Foote, Ted Sizemore, Jerry Martin, Derek Botelho, and Henry Mack, 2/79

One of the premier pinch-hitters in the history of the game, Gross has been a big leaguer for 15 seasons. He's going into the 1989 season from a year when his batting average fell to an all-time low of .203, 85 points below his lifetime average. Gross batted .314 in 156 games for the Astros in 1974, .294 for them in 1976, and .286 for them in 1977—those three years were his only ones as a starter. His top year for the Quaker City club was 1984, when he batted .322 in 112 contests. As a pinch-hitter, Gross has been one of the best in the business for a decade.

Although he is third on the all-time pinch-hitting list and can pass leader Manny Mota in 1989, his cards do not interest collectors. His 1989 cards rate in the commons box. Our pick for his best 1989 card is Topps.

KEVIN GROSS

	W	L	ERA	G	CG	IP	H	R	BB	SO
1988	12	14	3.69	33	5	231.2	209	101	89	162
Life	60	66	3.87	203	23	1104.2	1088	521	430	727

POSITION: Pitcher
TEAM: Montreal Expos
BORN: June 8, 1961 Downey, CA
HEIGHT: 6′5″ **WEIGHT:** 200 lbs.
BATS: Right **THROWS:** Right
ACQUIRED: Traded from Phillies for Floyd Youmans and Jeff Parrett, 12/88

Gross was the lone Phillies' representative on the 1988 All-Star team, and yet he finished the season with more losses (14) than wins (12). Still, his 12 wins were high for the staff, and his 162 strikeouts and 3.69 ERA were also best among all Phillies' starters. Gross won only nine games in 1987. A herniated disc got his '87 season off to a bad start, and a 10-day suspension for using sandpaper ended the year for him on a down note. Gross could be the ace of the Expo staff, and he could end 1989 as one of the N.L.'s aces as well.

Gross is still in that twilight zone between good player and star. Right now his cards are just about commons. He's still not a good investment risk. Our pick for his best 1989 card is Fleer.

KELLY GRUBER

	BA	G	AB	R	H	2B	3B	HR	RBI	SB
1988	.278	158	569	75	158	33	5	16	81	23
Life	.250	403	1082	146	270	51	9	34	135	37

POSITION: Infield
TEAM: Toronto Blue Jays
BORN: February 26, 1962 Bellaire, TX
HEIGHT: 6′ **WEIGHT:** 185 lbs.
BATS: Right **THROWS:** Right
ACQUIRED: Drafted from Indians, 12/83

Gruber proved in 1988 that he could handle third base for the Blue Jays on a full-time basis. He led the 1988 Jays in games played and was second on the team with 23 stolen bases. Settling down to one position has been an adjustment for this former utilityman. Gruber made a team-high 16 errors in 1988, some of which could be attributed to fielding on Toronto's artificial turf. His hitting was the biggest concern for the Blue Jays, and he seems to be satisfying those expectations. He hit .278 in 1988, with 16 homers and 81 RBIs. Expect Gruber to settle into his starting role in 1989 and continue to improve.

Gruber's cards sell for less than a nickel now. Watch for those prices to go up as his hitting ability blossoms. Our pick for his best 1989 card is Topps.

CECILIO GUANTE

	W	L	ERA	G	SV	IP	H	R	BB	SO
1988	5	6	2.82	63	12	79.2	67	26	26	65
Life	21	25	3.27	287	33	479.1	408	195	182	404

POSITION: Pitcher
TEAM: Texas Rangers
BORN: February 1, 1960 Jacagua, Dominican Republic
HEIGHT: 6′3″ **WEIGHT:** 185 lbs.
BATS: Right **THROWS:** Right
ACQUIRED: Traded from Yankees for Dale Mohorcic, 8/88

Guante tallied the most saves of his seven-year major league career while pitching for the 1988 Yankees. He had a subpar '87 season with the Yankees, gaining only one save and three wins in 23 appearances. The relief-poor Rangers welcomed Guante in mid-1988. He ended the season by making 63 appearances, second only to teammate Mitch Williams. Guante notched 12 saves, the most in his career. He posted a 5-6 record, with a 2.82 ERA. The Rangers had the third-lowest save total in the league (31), so they'll need another strong outing from Guante in 1989.

Guante has small totals for a seven-year reliever. That's why his cards will be available at less than a nickel for 1989. Unless Guante becomes an All-Star, there's no way his cards will see quick price escalations. Our pick for his best 1989 card is Topps.

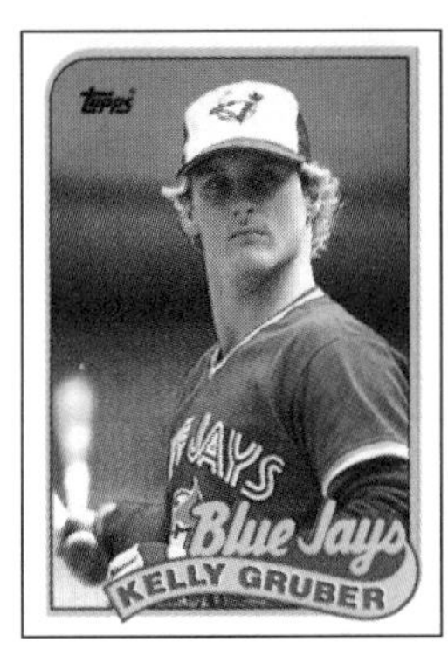

MARK GUBICZA

	W	L	ERA	G	CG	IP	H	R	BB	SO
1988	20	8	2.70	35	8	269.2	237	94	83	183
Life	69	56	3.62	163	25	1058.1	955	463	439	677

POSITION: Pitcher
TEAM: Kansas City Royals
BORN: August 14, 1962 Philadelphia, PA
HEIGHT: 6′5″ **WEIGHT:** 210 lbs.
BATS: Right **THROWS:** Right
ACQUIRED: Second-round pick in 6/81 free-agent draft

Gubicza put together his first 20-game win season in 1988. He was 20-8 with a 2.70 ERA. The 26-year-old righthander went 13-18 with a 3.98 ERA in 1987, then received extra pressure when the Royals traded away pitcher Danny Jackson. Gubicza got his 20th win the last week of the season, but it was a complete-game dandy. He stopped the Mariners, 3-0, allowing only three hits through nine innings. He has won in double figures for the Royals in each of his five seasons. Gubicza will be a regular member of the 20-game winner's circle as long as Kansas City can keep scoring runs behind him.

Gubicza's quick success may propel his 1989 cards up to a quarter. However, with only three winning seasons under his belt so far, investors would be safest to buy cards only in the 10- to 15-cent range. Our pick for his best 1989 card is Donruss.

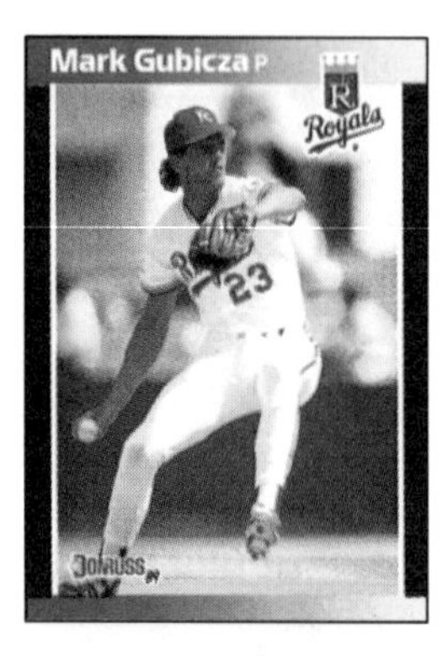

PEDRO GUERRERO

	BA	G	AB	R	H	2B	3B	HR	RBI	SB
1988	.286	103	364	40	104	14	2	10	65	4
Life	.307	1080	3751	577	1153	176	25	176	615	88

POSITION: First base
TEAM: St. Louis Cardinals
BORN: June 29, 1956 San Pedro de Macoris, Dominican Republic
HEIGHT: 5′11″ **WEIGHT:** 195 lbs.
BATS: Right **THROWS:** Right
ACQUIRED: Traded from Dodgers for John Tudor, 9/88

The Cardinals parted with John Tudor, their star pitcher, to acquire Guerrero for full-time duty at first base, hoping he might match the banner years of Jack Clark. The first half of Guerrero's 1988 season with the Dodgers was marred by injuries. However, his 1987 performance (.338, 27 homers, 89 RBIs) won him UPI Comeback Player of the Year honors. He exceeded 30 homers and 100 RBIs both in 1982 and 1983. If he can return to his 1987 form, the Cardinals may bounce back to the World Series. With some of the runnin' Redbirds hitting in front of him, Guerrero should be able to post some impressive RBI numbers.

Pick up Guerrero's 1989 cards quickly at 15 cents apiece, while doubts still linger about his health. If he helps the Cardinals regain their winning form, his card values will zoom. Our pick for his best 1989 card is Score.

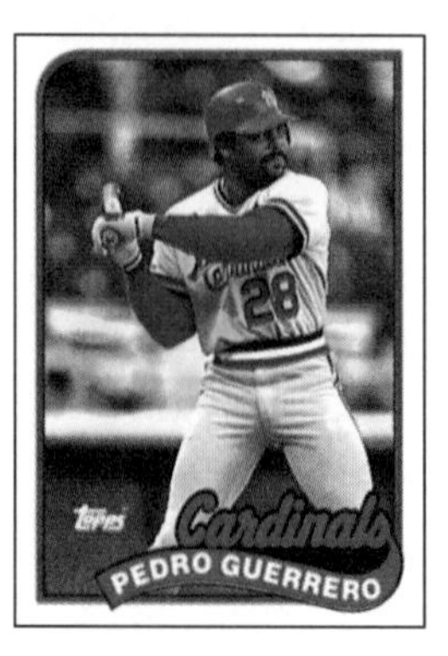

RON GUIDRY

	W	L	ERA	G	CG	IP	H	R	BB	SO
1988	2	3	4.18	12	0	56.0	57	28	15	32
Life	170	91	3.29	368	95	2393.0	2198	953	633	1778

POSITION: Pitcher
TEAM: New York Yankees
BORN: August 20, 1950 Lafayette, LA
HEIGHT: 5′11″ **WEIGHT:** 160 lbs.
BATS: Left **THROWS:** Left
ACQUIRED: Third-round pick in 6/71 free-agent draft

Guidry, once the biggest winner on the Yankees, suffered through his third straight losing season in 1988. Guidry was one of baseball's top starting hurlers in the early 1980s. However, he hasn't had a winning record since his league-leading 22-6 effort in 1985. In 1988, Guidry pitched in just 12 games and won only two. He was plagued by an uncharacteristically high ERA. Even with three straight losing years, Guidry still owns a stunning lifetime winning percentage of .651. However, it seems that Guidry's brilliant few years might quietly end after the 1989 season.

Guidry's 1989 cards will sell for 20 cents, a price that is too high. Guidry could retire after 1989 without 200 wins. He'll never get close to the Hall of Fame with those stats, and his cards won't be profitable investments. Our pick for his best 1989 card is Topps.

OZZIE GUILLEN

	BA	G	AB	R	H	2B	3B	HR	RBI	SB
1988	.261	156	566	58	148	16	7	0	39	25
Life	.266	614	2164	251	575	78	27	5	170	65

POSITION: Shortstop
TEAM: Chicago White Sox
BORN: January 20, 1964
Ocumare del Tuy, Venezuela
HEIGHT: 6′1″ **WEIGHT:** 150 lbs.
BATS: Left **THROWS:** Right
ACQUIRED: Traded from Padres with Bill Long, Luis Salazar, and Tom Lollar for LaMarr Hoyt, Todd Simmons, and Kevin Kristan, 12/84

Guillen's offense slipped somewhat from 1987, but his durability and steady defense remained for the 1988 White Sox. In 1987, he achieved career highs in hits, RBIs, and steals. Guillen, the 1985 A.L. Rookie of the Year, saw his average slip into the .260s in 1988. However, Guillen was the only ChiSox with double figures in stolen bases in 1988, ending with 25. At one time, the White Sox felt that he could be their leadoff hitter, but he has never been able to increase his on-base average. Although Guillen will never be an explosive hitter, he'll remain as a slick-fielding, contact-hitting mainstay for the Sox for many years.

Guillen's 1989 cards should sell at less than a nickel apiece. Until he hikes his batting average up, his cards won't be worth much more. Our pick for his best 1989 card is Donruss.

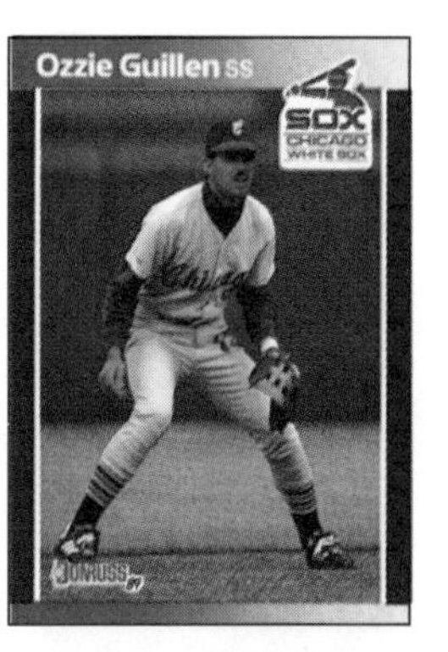

JOSE GUZMAN

	W	L	ERA	G	CG	IP	H	R	BB	SO
1988	11	13	3.70	30	6	206.2	180	99	82	157
Life	37	44	4.21	101	14	620.0	602	328	238	411

POSITION: Pitcher
TEAM: Texas Rangers
BORN: April 9, 1963
Santa Isabel, Puerto Rico
HEIGHT: 6'3" **WEIGHT:** 185 lbs.
BATS: Right **THROWS:** Right
ACQUIRED: Signed as a free agent, 2/81

Guzman's 1988 record with Texas does not indicate the small improvements he made in his performance. He lowered his ERA by nearly one entire point in 1988, and he achieved a career high in strikeouts with 157. Guzman has proved his durability to the Rangers by hurling more than 200 innings for two straight seasons. In 1987, he was 14-14, with a 4.67 ERA and 143 strikeouts in 208⅓ innings. He added his first two career shutouts and six complete games to his 1988 accomplishments. Watch for continued improvements from Guzman in 1989.

Guzman and other Texas hurlers have been ignored in the past, simply because the team has a losing record. Therefore, his cards are common-priced. Guzman has many good seasons ahead of him, and his cards seem like safe investments. Our pick for his best 1989 card is Score.

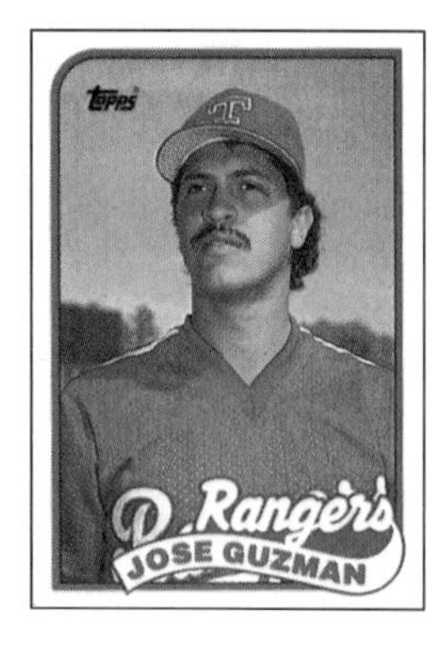

CHRIS GWYNN

	BA	G	AB	R	H	2B	3B	HR	RBI	SB
1988	.182	12	11	1	2	0	0	0	0	0
Life	.209	29	43	3	9	1	0	0	2	0

POSITION: Outfield
TEAM: Los Angeles Dodgers
BORN: October 13, 1964
Los Angeles, CA
HEIGHT: 6' **WEIGHT:** 210 lbs.
BATS: Left **THROWS:** Left
ACQUIRED: First-round pick in 6/85 free-agent draft

Chris Gwynn will probably spend his career as Tony Gwynn's "little brother," but that won't bother either Chris or the Dodgers if he can come anywhere near the numbers compiled by Tony. One of many Dodger outfield prospects, Chris hit .299 with 61 RBIs in 1988 at Triple-A Albuquerque. In 1987, he batted an anemic .219 for the Dodgers in a late-season stint, but showed promise of good things to come. Gwynn batted .279 for Albuquerque in 1987. He was the 16th member of the talented 1984 U.S. Olympic Team to make the majors. Gwynn could help the Dodgers regain their world championship in 1989.

Gwynn's 1989 cards should open in the 25- to 30-cent range. He has the talent to be in the major leagues a long time. Those prices are great for investing. Our pick for his best 1989 card is Fleer.

TONY GWYNN

	BA	G	AB	R	H	2B	3B	HR	RBI	SB
1988	.313	133	521	64	163	22	5	7	70	26
Life	.331	902	3474	535	1151	165	44	41	354	181

POSITION: Outfield
TEAM: San Diego Padres
BORN: May 9, 1960 Los Angeles, CA
HEIGHT: 5′11″ **WEIGHT:** 205 lbs.
BATS: Left **THROWS:** Left
ACQUIRED: Third-round pick in 6/81 free-agent draft

Gwynn's batting title was a major accomplishment in 1988, especially when you see how many N.L. teams didn't have a single starter hitting above .300. He hit .313 in 1988, with seven homers and 70 RBIs. In 1987, he batted .370, scored 119 runs, and had 56 stolen bases. He also won the Gold Glove award. Gwynn, at age 28, is the National League's finest hitter. He passed the 1,000-hit milestone in 1988 and swiped 26 bases. The Padres played respectably in 1988 and could contend for a pennant next year. Now that San Diego has Jack Clark hitting behind him, Gwynn could be scoring many more runs this year.

As more people discover Gwynn's talents, his card prices will rise. At 35 cents, his 1989 cards are reasonably priced. Their value could double if the Padres win their division. Our pick for his best 1989 card is Fleer.

ALBERT HALL

	BA	G	AB	R	H	2B	3B	HR	RBI	SB
1988	.247	85	231	27	57	7	1	1	15	15
Life	.254	355	772	121	196	35	7	5	52	64

POSITION: Outfield
TEAM: Atlanta Braves
BORN: March 7, 1958 Birmingham, AL
HEIGHT: 5′11″ **WEIGHT:** 158 lbs.
BATS: Both **THROWS:** Right
ACQUIRED: Sixth-round pick in 6/77 free-agent draft

Hall had the sixth-highest batting average of the 1988 Braves. He played part-time for the Braves last season, hitting .247 with one homer and 15 RBIs. Hall has appeared with the Braves for eight straight seasons, although some of that time has been spent moving between Atlanta and the minor leagues. His best year in the majors was 1987. He hit a career-high .284, with three homers and 24 RBIs. Also, he was successful in 77 percent of his stolen base attempts, swiping 33 out of 43. If Hall could hit above .300 or hit a few more homers, he'd become a star.

As it is now, Hall is struggling to be a full-time outfielder. His 1989 cards are a nickel or less. See if Hall's average and playing time go up before investing in his cards. Our pick for his best 1989 card is Topps.

DREW HALL

	W	L	ERA	G	SV	IP	H	R	BB	SO
1988	1	1	7.66	19	1	22.1	26	20	9	22
Life	3	4	6.41	45	2	78.2	90	63	33	63

POSITION: Pitcher
TEAM: Texas Rangers
BORN: March 27, 1963 Louisville, KY
HEIGHT: 6′5″ **WEIGHT:** 200 lbs.
BATS: Left **THROWS:** Left
ACQUIRED: Traded from Cubs with Rafael Palmeiro and Jamie Moyer for Mitch Williams, Paul Kilgus, Steve Wilson, Curtis Wilkerson, Luis Benitez, and Pablo Delgado, 12/88

Hall seems to be ready to make his mark as a major league relief pitcher. At Triple-A Iowa in 1988, he chalked up 19 saves in 49 outings, going 4-3 with a 2.34 ERA. In limited action for Chicago in '88, he was 1-1, but his ERA was over 7.00, much too high for the stopper role the Cubs planned for him. Hall was rated by *Baseball America* as the top pitcher in the Triple-A American Association in 1987. He went 6-3 with a 4.48 ERA in 35 games for Iowa. He also appeared in 21 games for the parent Cubs that year, finishing 1-1. If Hall is ready for the majors, he could solve the Texas bullpen woes.

Hall's 1989 cards will open in the 10- to 15-cent range. Wait to see if he becomes the Ranger stopper before investing at that price. Our pick for his best 1989 card is Fleer.

MEL HALL

	BA	G	AB	R	H	2B	3B	HR	RBI	SB
1988	.280	150	515	69	144	32	4	6	71	7
Life	.281	732	2416	336	678	138	18	71	350	27

POSITION: Outfield
TEAM: Cleveland Indians
BORN: September 16, 1960 Lyons, NY
HEIGHT: 6′1″ **WEIGHT:** 185 lbs.
BATS: Left **THROWS:** Left
ACQUIRED: Traded from Cubs with Joe Carter and Darryl Banks for Rick Sutcliffe, Ron Hassey, and George Frazier, 6/84

Hall didn't hit his usual share of round-trippers for the 1988 Indians, but he did show more overall hitting ability than ever before. He played the most games of his career (150) and had more hits than ever (144). He still drove in 71 runs and struck out just 50 times. Hall's six home runs were a surprise, considering that he had thumped 18 round-trippers both in 1986 and 1987. However, Tribe fans will gladly accept his decreased homer output in exchange for a higher average and more RBIs. Playing for several losing teams hasn't helped gain Hall much recognition. A strong 1989 campaign could change all that.

Hall's cards should be available for a dime or less in 1989. At age 28, Hall should have several strong seasons to look forward to. His cards are very good investments. Our pick for his best 1989 card is Fleer.

DARRYL HAMILTON

	BA	G	AB	R	H	2B	3B	HR	RBI	SB
1988	.184	44	103	14	19	4	0	1	11	7
Life	.184	44	103	14	19	4	0	1	11	7

POSITION: Outfield
TEAM: Milwaukee Brewers
BORN: December 3, 1964
Baton Rouge, LA
HEIGHT: 6′1″ **WEIGHT:** 180 lbs.
BATS: Left **THROWS:** Right
ACQUIRED: 11th-round pick in 6/86 free-agent draft

Hamilton made it to the majors with less than three years of experience in pro ball. In 1988 with Triple-A Denver, he batted .320, around a mid-season trip to Milwaukee. With the Brewers, Hamilton batted at about the .200 mark in limited action. While batting .328 and hitting eight home runs at Class-A Stockton in 1987, he was overshadowed by Gary Sheffield (whom he then beat to the majors). He began his career at Class-A Helena in 1986, where he terrorized pitchers by hitting .391 and 35 RBIs in just 65 games. Hamilton might be terrorizing A.L. pitchers in 1989.

One thing that should come to Hamilton with maturity will be more long-ball punch—the only ingredient he now seems to be missing. His 1989 cards will open in the 25-cent range. Our pick for his best 1989 card is Topps.

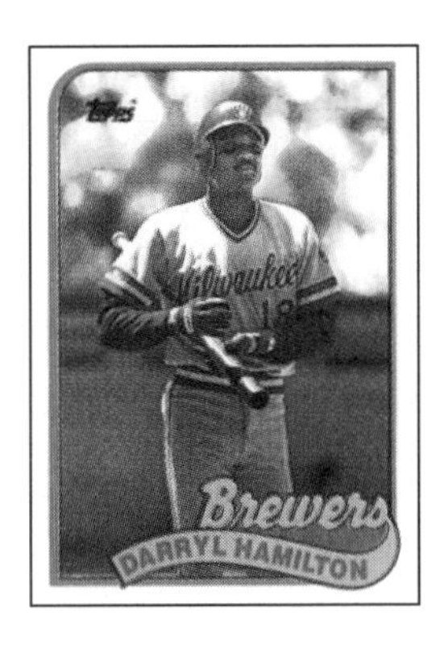

JEFF HAMILTON

	BA	G	AB	R	H	2B	3B	HR	RBI	SB
1988	.236	111	309	34	73	14	2	6	33	0
Life	.230	217	539	61	124	22	2	11	53	0

POSITION: Third base
TEAM: Los Angeles Dodgers
BORN: March 19, 1964 Flint, MI
HEIGHT: 6′3″ **WEIGHT:** 207 lbs.
BATS: Right **THROWS:** Right
ACQUIRED: 29th selection in 6/82 free-agent draft

When injuries struck the 1987 Dodgers in a big way, the team plugged rookie Hamilton right into the starting lineup. He promptly got his first major league hit, and his improvements since have been just as steady. Hamilton fuels the Dodgers with a smooth defense that's been missing from the team's infield for years. In 1988, he hit .236 for the world champions, with six homers and 33 RBIs. He hit .217 in 1987. He may not make local fans forget former third sacker Ron Cey, but Hamilton's average is sure to go up, and his experience will grow when he has the hot corner all to himself for an entire season.

Hamilton has more than a decade of continued excellence ahead, making his 1989 cards bargains at their current low price of 3 to 5 cents apiece. Our pick for his best 1989 card is Topps.

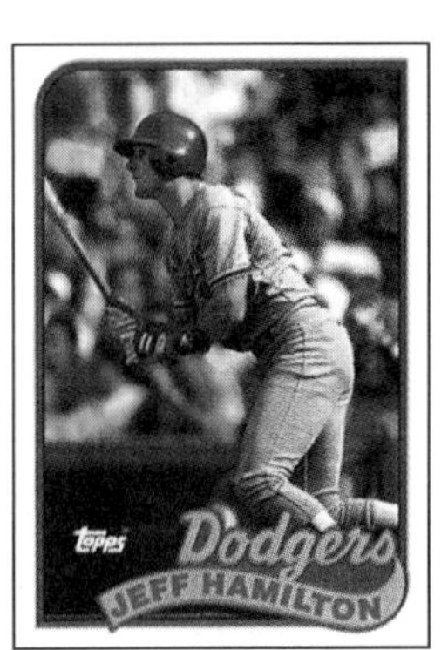

ATLEE HAMMAKER

	W	L	ERA	G	SV	IP	H	R	BB	SO
1988	9	9	3.73	43	5	144.2	136	68	41	65
Life	49	51	3.52	171	5	903.0	868	399	226	536

POSITION: Pitcher
TEAM: San Francisco Giants
BORN: January 24, 1958 Carmel, CA
HEIGHT: 6'2" **WEIGHT:** 200 lbs.
BATS: Both **THROWS:** Right
ACQUIRED: Traded from Royals with Renie Martin, Craig Chamberlain, and Brad Wellman for Vida Blue and Bob Tufts, 3/82

The often-injured Hammaker did pitch an entire season for the 1988 San Francisco Giants. He missed the entire 1986 season due to injuries, appeared in 43 games in '88, and hurled 144⅔ innings, fourth-highest on the team. Hammaker became a starter-reliever in 1988, earning his first five career saves. As a reliever, he had 11 games finished. As a starter, he earned three complete games and a shutout. Hammaker's finest season ever was in 1982, a 12-8 campaign during his first year with the Giants. Hammaker may prolong his career with the Giants, filling in both as a starter and a reliever.

Card investors seldom profit off the careers of "swing men." Hammaker's 1989 cards will be three cents or less, but they won't appreciate in value as long as Hammaker is without a specific role. Our pick for his best 1989 card is Fleer.

MIKE HARKEY

	W	L	ERA	G	CG	IP	H	R	BB	SO
1988	0	3	2.60	5	0	34.2	33	14	15	18
Life	0	3	2.60	5	0	34.2	33	14	15	18

POSITION: Pitcher
TEAM: Chicago Cubs
BORN: October 25, 1966 Diamond Bar, CA
HEIGHT: 6'5" **WEIGHT:** 210 lbs.
BATS: Right **THROWS:** Right
ACQUIRED: First-round pick in 6/87 free-agent draft

The Cubs think that Harkey is for real. He started the 1988 season in Double-A Pittsfield, going 9-2 with a 1.08 ERA in the first half of the season, while throwing his fastball consistently in the 90s. Promoted to Triple-A Iowa, he never missed a beat. In his debut he pitched a four-hitter; in his second start he pitched a one-hit 2-0 shutout. When the final stats were in, he had a 7-2 record with a 3.55 ERA and 62 strikeouts. Late in the season, he got his first taste of big league competition and kept his ERA under 3.00. The Cubs are looking for Harkey to post some big numbers.

Harkey's 1989 cards will be a bargain at 35 cents. With a 97-mph fastball, he could challenge for the league's top rookie honors. Our pick for his best 1989 card is Topps.

GREG HARRIS

	W	L	ERA	G	SV	IP	H	R	BB	SO
1988	4	6	2.36	66	1	107.0	80	34	52	71
Life	31	41	3.55	324	37	687.2	615	314	286	550

POSITION: Pitcher
TEAM: Philadelphia Phillies
BORN: November 2, 1955 Lynwood, CA
HEIGHT: 6′ **WEIGHT:** 165 lbs.
BATS: Right **THROWS:** Right
ACQUIRED: Signed as a free agent, 4/88

One of the few pleasant surprises for the Phillies in 1989 was Harris, whom they signed as a free agent at the close of spring training. He went 5-10 with a 4.86 ERA for Texas in 1987, and he didn't figure in their plans for 1988. After an impressive spring training with the Indians, Harris was not offered a contract by the Tribe and signed on with the Phils. He went 4-6 in 66 games in 1988—mostly in middle relief—and his 2.36 ERA was the best on the staff. His best season was 1986, when he won ten games in relief, with a 2.83 ERA and 20 saves. Harris should be the Philadelphia set-up man for several more years.

Harris' cards are commons. He's a solid journeyman pitcher, but not investment material. Our pick for his best 1989 card is Donruss.

GREG HARRIS

	W	L	ERA	G	CG	IP	H	R	BB	SO
1988	2	0	1.50	3	1	18.0	13	3	3	15
Life	2	0	1.50	3	1	18.0	13	3	3	15

POSITION: Pitcher
TEAM: San Diego Padres
BORN: December 1, 1963
Greensboro, NC
HEIGHT: 6′2″ **WEIGHT:** 190 lbs.
BATS: Right **THROWS:** Right
ACQUIRED: Tenth-round pick in 6/85 free-agent draft

Harris took less than four years to make it to San Diego, and the prognosis is that he'll be a big league hurler for many years to come. Recalled from Triple-A Las Vegas at the end of the 1988 season, he set the Padre record for strikeouts by a pitcher making his first big league start, when he fanned 11 Astros in September. Winner of nine games for Las Vegas in 1988, with a solid 3.55 ERA, Harris fanned 134 in 150 innings. At Double-A Wichita in 1987, he went 12-11 with 170 strikeouts. In 1986, he fanned 176 for Charleston, going 13-7 with a healthy 2.63 ERA. With his solid minor league performances, Harris has earned his shot.

Harris looks like he will find a spot on the Padres in 1989. His 1989 cards will open at the 20-cent plateau. Our pick for his best 1989 card is Donruss.

BRYAN HARVEY

	W	L	ERA	G	SV	IP	H	R	BB	SO
1988	7	5	2.13	50	17	76.0	59	22	20	67
Life	7	5	2.00	53	17	81.0	65	22	22	70

POSITION: Pitcher
TEAM: California Angels
BORN: June 2, 1963 Chattanooga, TN
HEIGHT: 6′2″ **WEIGHT:** 212 lbs.
BATS: Right **THROWS:** Right
ACQUIRED: Signed as a free agent, 6/85

Harvey emerged as the Angels' top reliever in 1988 and owned the best ERA (2.13) on the staff. He finished with a 7-5 record. He recovered from some ups and downs in 1987 that might have retarded the progress of another player. Recalled by the Angels from Double-A Midland in mid-1987, he did almost nothing—pitching but five innings. At Midland, though, he chalked up 20 saves in 43 games, going 2-2 with a 2.04 ERA. He used his 95-mph fastball and 85-mph forkball to strike out 78 in 43 innings, walking just 28. Harvey looks like he is entrenched as the California stopper, and he could help the Angels surge to the top of the A.L. West in 1989.

Harvey's 1989 cards will open in the 35- to 40-cent range. We wouldn't recommend buying in the short term until he is established. Our pick for his best 1989 card is Donruss.

RON HASSEY

	BA	G	AB	R	H	2B	3B	HR	RBI	SB
1988	.257	107	323	32	83	15	0	7	45	2
Life	.276	949	2799	296	772	145	7	60	379	12

POSITION: Catcher
TEAM: Oakland A's
BORN: February 27, 1953 Tucson, AZ
HEIGHT: 6′2″ **WEIGHT:** 195 lbs.
BATS: Left **THROWS:** Right
ACQUIRED: Signed as a free agent, 1/88

Hassey served as a key backup for injured catcher Terry Steinbach with the 1988 Oakland Athletics. Hassey's seven homers, 45 RBIs, and .257 average in 107 games were added bonuses for the team. Hassey's primary responsibility was serving as relief ace Dennis Eckersley's personal backstop. When Eckersley had his greatest season ever in 1988, (45 saves), Hassey usually entered the game with him. Hassey is a dependable glove man. He committed only three errors all season. With the White Sox in 1987, he caught only 24 games. He hit .214, with three homers in 145 at-bats. At age 36, Hassey is the league's most reliable relief catcher.

Hassey's 1989 cards are commons, sold at a nickel or less. Despite his fine career as a substitute, his cards will never have enough appeal to be good investments. Our pick for his best 1989 card is Score.

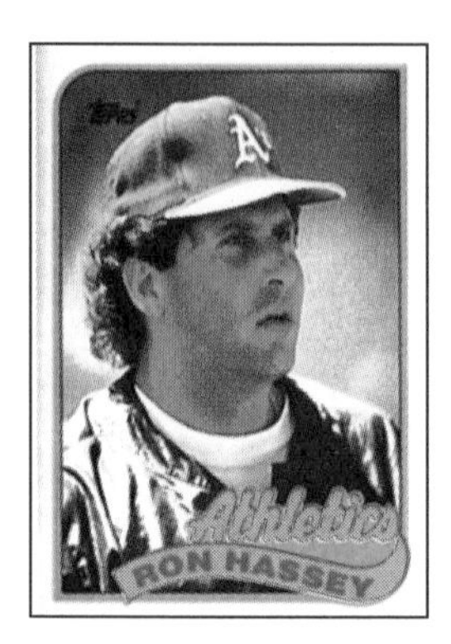

BILLY HATCHER

	BA	G	AB	R	H	2B	3B	HR	RBI	SB
1988	.268	145	530	79	142	25	4	7	52	32
Life	.272	474	1685	255	458	80	12	26	161	127

POSITION: Outfield
TEAM: Houston Astros
BORN: October 4, 1960 Williams, AZ
HEIGHT: 5′9″ **WEIGHT:** 175 lbs.
BATS: Right **THROWS:** Right
ACQUIRED: Traded from Cubs with Steve Engel for Jerry Mumphrey, 12/85

Hatcher spent his third season as a starting outfielder for the Astros in 1988. The fleet flychaser stole 32 bases, giving him 30-plus swipes for the last three seasons. He couldn't match his 1987 totals, which included 11 home runs, 63 RBIs, 53 stolen bases, and a .296 batting average. He did maintain his reputation as a fine fielder, making only five errors in 1988. Hatcher finally broke into the Chicago Cub lineup after three and a half seasons in the minors. Ever since Houston acquired him for the 1986 season, he has been a regular. Hatcher could help lead the Astros to the top of the N.L. West in 1989.

Hatcher's 1989 cards should be three cents or less from most dealers. That's a reasonable investment, considering that Hatcher's 1987 success could return in 1989. Our pick for his best 1989 card is Topps.

MICKEY HATCHER

	BA	G	AB	R	H	2B	3B	HR	RBI	SB
1988	.293	88	191	22	56	8	0	1	25	0
Life	.282	951	3021	318	852	160	17	36	337	10

POSITION: Outfield; infield
TEAM: Los Angeles Dodgers
BORN: March 15, 1955 Cleveland, OH
HEIGHT: 6′2″ **WEIGHT:** 185 lbs.
BATS: Right **THROWS:** Right
ACQUIRED: Signed as a free agent, 4/87

Hatcher became a minor celebrity during the 1988 World Series. The Dodger utilityman was thrust into a starting role when star outfielder Kirk Gibson was injured. America loved Hatcher both for his inspired play and his colorful personality off the field. In 1988, Hatcher led all Dodger hitters with a .293 average. Playing various positions, he made only three errors all season. He hit .282 in limited duty with the Dodgers in '87. Hatcher is the heart of the Dodgers' bench, and he should be a key substitute for the team in 1989.

Hatcher's 1989 cards will be a nickel or less. His wacky sense of humor could mean an entertainment career after he retires. Old baseball cards of broadcaster/comedian Bob Uecker bring big bucks; investors may want a few extras of Hatcher's issues just in case. Our pick for his best 1989 card is Topps.

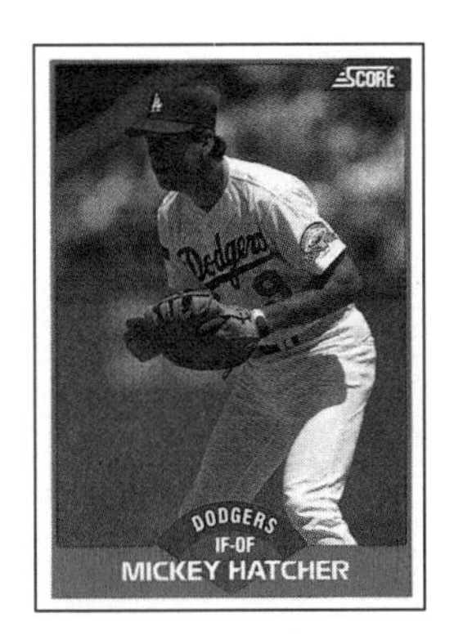

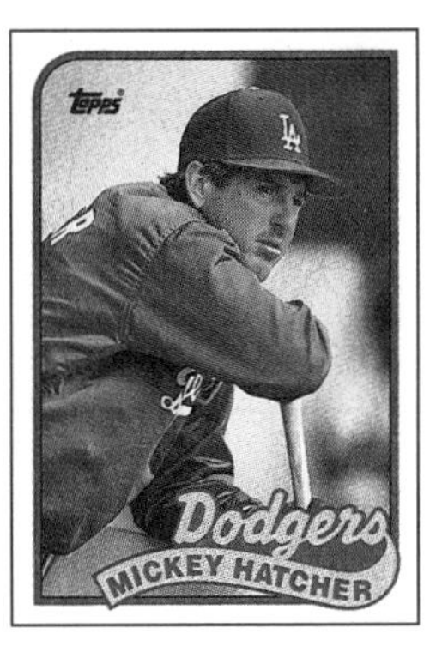

ANDY HAWKINS

	W	L	ERA	G	CG	IP	H	R	BB	SO
1988	14	11	3.35	33	4	217.2	196	88	76	91
Life	60	58	3.84	199	19	1102.2	1089	531	412	489

POSITION: Pitcher
TEAM: New York Yankees
BORN: January 21, 1960 Waco, TX
HEIGHT: 6′3″ **WEIGHT:** 215 lbs.
BATS: Right **THROWS:** Right
ACQUIRED: Signed as a free agent, 12/88

Hawkins rebounded from a horrible 1987 season to post a snappy 14-11 mark in 1988. He had the second highest innings pitched total on the Padres. He highlighted his year with four complete games and two shutouts. Hawkins first broke in with the Padres in 1982. He suffered through three straight losing seasons before winning big in 1985. He won a career-high 18 games in 1985, against eight losses. In 1986, Hawkins went 10-8, the second time he worked more than 200 innings in a season. Hawkins is a willing worker who seems to do best when he pitches often.

Hawkins' 1989 cards will sell for a nickel or less. His cards are somewhat risky investments, but he still seems to have the potential to win 20 games. As commons, Hawkins' cards are relatively safe gambles. Our pick for his best 1989 card is Donruss.

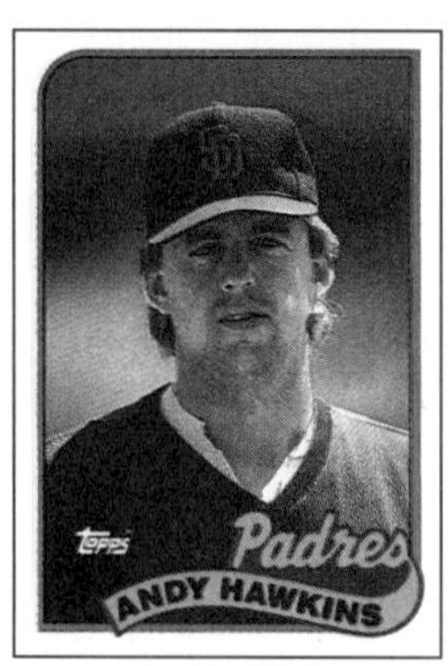

VON HAYES

	BA	G	AB	R	H	2B	3B	HR	RBI	SB
1988	.272	104	367	43	100	28	2	6	45	20
Life	.276	1041	3651	526	1007	209	29	96	495	189

POSITION: Outfield; first base
TEAM: Philadelphia Phillies
BORN: August 31, 1958 Stockton, CA
HEIGHT: 6′5″ **WEIGHT:** 195 lbs.
BATS: Left **THROWS:** Left
ACQUIRED: Traded from Indians for Julio Franco, Manny Trillo, George Vukovich, Jay Baller, and Jerry Willard, 12/82

On the injured list for six weeks in 1988, Hayes still managed to hit .272 for the Phillies, with six homers and 45 RBIs. Regarded as a blue chip player, Hayes was acquired from the Indians in December 1982, when the Phillies sent five players to the Tribe in return for him. He hit a career-high .305 in 1986, when he finished eighth in the MVP balloting. His average was down in '87 (.277), but he hit a career-high 21 homers. Ricky Jordan became the Phils' first baseman in 1988, and Hayes' future with the Phillies seems to be as an outfielder.

Hayes' 1989 cards will open in the 25- to 30-cent range. That is a high price for a player coming off an injury, but that price would double if Hayes would turn in an MVP-quality season. Our pick for his best 1989 card is Donruss.

ED HEARN

	BA	G	AB	R	H	2B	3B	HR	RBI	SB
1988	.222	7	18	1	4	2	0	0	1	0
Life	.263	62	171	19	45	9	0	4	14	0

POSITION: Catcher
TEAM: Kansas City Royals
BORN: August 23, 1960 Stuart, FL
HEIGHT: 6′3″ **WEIGHT:** 215 lbs.
BATS: Right **THROWS:** Right
ACQUIRED: Traded from Mets with Rick Anderson and Mauro Gozzo for David Cone and Chris Jelic, 3/87

Hearn hasn't been the luckiest player around. Due to assorted injuries, he has played only 13 games in the last two years. Worst of all, Royals fans have been waiting for Hearn to be as successful as pitcher David Cone has been since he moved from Kansas City to the Mets. Hearn labored for seven years in the minor leagues and spent one year on the disabled list before getting his shot with the Mets in 1986. In 49 games, he had four homers, 10 RBIs, and a .265 batting average. If Hearn can play a full season in 1989, the Royals can see whether the trade was a good deal.

Hearn is 28, has little major league experience, and hasn't been healthy recently. These negatives add up to doom for investing in Hearn's 1989 cards, priced as commons. Our pick for his best 1989 card is Topps.

MIKE HEATH

	BA	G	AB	R	H	2B	3B	HR	RBI	SB
1988	.247	86	219	24	54	7	2	5	18	1
Life	.250	1032	3307	374	828	136	22	68	376	40

POSITION: Catcher
TEAM: Detroit Tigers
BORN: February 5, 1955 Tampa, FL
HEIGHT: 5′11″ **WEIGHT:** 180 lbs.
BATS: Right **THROWS:** Right
ACQUIRED: Traded from Cardinals for Mike Laga and Ken Hill, 8/86

Heath was one of the Tigers' key substitutes in 1988, appearing in 86 games. In his 11th major league season, he served as a backup for Tigers star catcher Matt Nokes. Heath was originally an infielder in the minor leagues, but he'd been a catcher for the Yankees, A's, and Cards before joining the Tigers. Heath's best previous season was with Oakland in 1984. He played a career-high 140 games, hitting .248, with 13 home runs and 64 RBIs. In 1987, he hit .281 in limited duty. It looks like Heath might spend the rest of his career as a pinch-hitter and defensive replacement.

Heath's 1989 cards are available at three cents or less. Due to his non-starting status, it's likely that his cards will never gain in value. Our pick for his best 1989 card is Topps.

NEAL HEATON

	W	L	ERA	G	CG	IP	H	R	BB	SO
1988	3	10	4.99	32	0	97.1	98	54	43	43
Life	55	76	4.65	218	21	1076.0	1170	606	376	484

POSITION: Pitcher
TEAM: Montreal Expos
BORN: March 3, 1960 Jamaica, NY
HEIGHT: 6′2″ **WEIGHT:** 195 lbs.
BATS: Left **THROWS:** Left
ACQUIRED: Traded from Twins with Jeff Reed, Yorkis Perez, and Al Cardwood for Jeff Reardon and Tom Nieto, 2/87

Heaton had an off year in 1988, winning only 3 of 13 decisions, with two saves. Expo fans hope he'll bounce back this season to the form that made him a 13-game-winner for Montreal in 1987. He won seven of his first eight decisions for the Expos in 1987 before N.L. batters solved his pitches. Heaton ended the 1987 season at 13-10, with a high 4.52 ERA. He came to Montreal in a deal that included Jeff Reardon. Heaton, traded to Minnesota from the Tribe in mid-season 1986, finished that season 7-15. Heaton gives to Montreal an experienced lefthanded pitcher who is used in both starting and relief roles.

Heaton's 1989 cards will be commons. Unless he catches fire and becomes a big winner, their value won't noticeably appreciate. Our pick for his best 1989 card is Donruss.

DAVE HENDERSON

	BA	G	AB	R	H	2B	3B	HR	RBI	SB
1988	.304	146	507	100	154	38	1	24	94	2
Life	.262	926	2886	417	757	167	13	112	394	31

POSITION: Outfield
TEAM: Oakland A's
BORN: July 21, 1958 Dos Palos, CA
HEIGHT: 6′2″ **WEIGHT:** 210 lbs.
BATS: Right **THROWS:** Right
ACQUIRED: Signed as a free agent, 12/87

Henderson was a surprise star for the 1988 A's. He became the starting center fielder, and he had the best season of his career. He finished the year with a .304 average, 24 home runs, 94 RBIs, 38 doubles, 100 runs scored, and 154 base hits, all career highs. He accomplished all of this after having a horrible season in 1987. Henderson began that season with the Red Sox, hitting but .234 in 75 games. He was traded to San Francisco, where he hit .238 and was released at the end of the season. The Oakland management hopes that Henderson's renaissance will continue in 1989.

Henderson's 1989 cards will sell in the 5- to 10-cent range. He will need several seasons like the one he had in 1988 for his cards to remain in the premium category. Wait to see if he opens '89 well before buying. Our pick for his best 1989 card is Score.

RICKEY HENDERSON

	BA	G	AB	R	H	2B	3B	HR	RBI	SB
1988	.305	140	554	118	169	30	2	6	50	93
Life	.292	1322	4983	1058	1455	235	44	126	504	794

POSITION: Outfield
TEAM: New York Yankees
BORN: December 25, 1958 Chicago, IL
HEIGHT: 5′10″ **WEIGHT:** 195 lbs.
BATS: Right **THROWS:** Left
ACQUIRED: Traded from A's with Bert Bradley for Jose Rijo, Stan Javier, Jay Howell, Eric Plunk, and Tim Birtsas, 12/84

All it took was a full season in 1988 for Henderson to re-establish himself as one of baseball's most exciting players. Playing less than 100 games in 1987 because of injuries, he was unable to produce his usual banner statistics. His string of seven consecutive seasons leading the A.L. in stolen bases was broken in '87, when he stole just 41. But in 1988, Henderson batted .305 and had an on-base percentage near .400. His league-leading stolen base total (93) was more than double the number of any other American Leaguer's. He was third in the A.L. with 118 runs scored. If Henderson's homer totals grow in 1989, his card values will, too.

At their current prices of 35 cents or less, Henderson's 1989 cards are a good value. If the Yankees win the pennant, Henderson's card values could double. Our pick for his best 1989 card is Donruss.

TOM HENKE

	W	L	ERA	G	SV	IP	H	R	BB	SO
1988	4	4	2.91	52	25	68.0	60	23	24	66
Life	19	19	3.03	256	102	353.1	280	130	121	405

POSITION: Pitcher
TEAM: Toronto Blue Jays
BORN: December 21, 1957
Kansas City, MO
HEIGHT: 6′5″ **WEIGHT:** 215 lbs.
BATS: Right **THROWS:** Right
ACQUIRED: Selected in player compensation pool draft, 1/85

The mediocre season of the Toronto Blue Jays obscured the 1988 statistics of Henke, the team's noted closer. He reached the 25-save level in 1988, but the team's inability to stay in games during the late innings eliminated many of the righthander's chances for work. Nevertheless, he finished nearly 90 percent of the games he pitched. In 1987, when the Blue Jays battled for the A.L. East pennant, he led the American League in saves, with 34. Henke reached 100 career saves late in 1988, and should be able to keep adding to that mark for another decade.

Henke's cards are available at 5 to 10 cents each. Relief pitchers don't make good investment vehicles in many cases, because of their shaky futures and lack of acclaim. Even at those reasonable prices, Henke falls into this category. Our pick for his best 1989 card is Score.

MIKE HENNEMAN

	W	L	ERA	G	SV	IP	H	R	BB	SO
1988	9	6	1.87	65	22	91.1	72	23	24	58
Life	20	9	2.44	120	29	188.0	158	59	54	133

POSITION: Pitcher
TEAM: Detroit Tigers
BORN: December 11, 1961
St. Charles, MO
HEIGHT: 6′4″ **WEIGHT:** 195 lbs.
BATS: Right **THROWS:** Right
ACQUIRED: Third-round pick in 6/84 free-agent draft

In 1988, just his second full big-league season, Henneman became the bullpen wizard of Detroit. Although the Tigers fell a bit short in the pennant race, the righthander contributed all year long with more than 20 saves. He almost doubled the output of Guillermo Hernandez, the former stopper for the team. Henneman whittled his ERA to a league-leading 1.87, down from 2.98 in 1987. He was among league leaders in total games pitched, and his record was 9-6. In 1987, he won 11 games, all in relief, and had seven saves. With Henneman as Detroit's closer in 1989, Tiger starting pitchers can again breathe easy.

Henneman has two successful seasons under his belt, and his 1989 cards should sell for between 10 and 25 cents each. He is still unproven, so we don't advise investing at those prices. Our pick for his best 1989 card is Score.

GUILLERMO HERNANDEZ

	W	L	ERA	G	SV	IP	H	R	BB	SO
1988	6	5	3.06	63	10	67.2	50	24	31	59
Life	68	61	3.30	712	132	1013.2	916	410	333	758

POSITION: Pitcher
TEAM: Detroit Tigers
BORN: November 14, 1954
Aguada, Puerto Rico
HEIGHT: 6′2″ **WEIGHT:** 185 lbs.
BATS: Left **THROWS:** Left
ACQUIRED: Traded from Phillies with Dave Bergman for Glenn Wilson and John Wockenfuss, 3/84

Hernandez, once the Tiger relief ace, was subpar for the second straight season in 1988. He had ten saves, which would be admirable for most players. However, Hernandez was one of the premier relief specialists in the A.L. during the 1984 and '85 seasons. In 1984, Hernandez had a career-best 32 saves and nine wins, leading the Tigers to a world championship. He saved two World Series victories as well, and was named Cy Young Award winner and MVP that year. However, Hernandez's stats and saves have declined each year since, casting serious doubts about his future.

Hernandez is a classic example of the pitfalls of investing in cards of relievers. His 1989 cards will sell at a nickel or less. His shrinking stats and advancing age (34) are two main reasons not to invest. Our pick for his best 1989 card is Fleer.

KEITH HERNANDEZ

	BA	G	AB	R	H	2B	3B	HR	RBI	SB
1988	.276	95	348	43	96	16	0	11	55	2
Life	.300	1970	7025	1099	2106	416	60	157	1044	98

POSITION: First base
TEAM: New York Mets
BORN: October 20, 1953
San Francisco, CA
HEIGHT: 6′ **WEIGHT:** 195 lbs.
BATS: Left **THROWS:** Left
ACQUIRED: Traded from Cardinals for Neil Allen and Rick Ownby, 6/83

Hernandez, age 35, was hampered by injuries early in 1988, and he didn't get to play in 100 games. Still, his contributions were vital in the Mets' division title win. He collected his 1,000th career RBI in 1988, and slugged 11 home runs and 55 RBIs. In 1987, he hit .290, with 18 homers and 89 RBIs. He is widely considered the best fielding first baseman in the National League. And he is a clutch hitter. Last year, injuries seriously sidetracked his march toward the 3,000-hit mark. However, a healthy Hernandez is just the ticket the Mets need to keep their pennant in 1989.

Yes, Hernandez does have an admirable career so far, but his current numbers don't merit paying 25 cents each for his 1989 cards. If he can return to his 1987 self, then those prices will bring long-term gains. Our pick for his best 1989 card is Topps.

LARRY HERNDON

	BA	G	AB	R	H	2B	3B	HR	RBI	SB
1988	.224	76	174	16	39	5	0	4	20	0
Life	.274	1537	4877	605	1334	186	76	107	550	92

POSITION: Outfield
TEAM: Detroit Tigers
BORN: November 3, 1953 Sunflower, MS
HEIGHT: 6′3″ **WEIGHT:** 200 lbs.
BATS: Right **THROWS:** Right
ACQUIRED: Traded from Giants for Dan Schatzeder and Mike Chris, 12/81

Herndon, a former starting outfielder, got only part-time duty with the 1988 Detroit Tigers. The veteran was coming off one of his best-hitting seasons ever, a .324 outing with the Tigers in 1987. His accomplishments included nine home runs and 47 RBIs in just 89 games. The slumping Herndon was far from those stats in 1988, as he submitted one of his worst seasons since joining the Tigers in 1982. Herndon's best season as a Tiger came in 1983. In 153 games, he hit .302, with 20 homers and 92 RBIs. Now age 35, Herndon likely will be a Tigers reserve the rest of his career.

Herndon's cards will be a nickel or less in 1989. His lifetime stats are just average, not good enough to spark investment interest in his cards. Our pick for his best 1989 card is Score.

TOMMY HERR

	BA	G	AB	R	H	2B	3B	HR	RBI	SB
1988	.263	86	304	42	80	16	0	1	21	10
Life	.273	1115	4026	540	1101	195	31	20	456	162

POSITION: Second base
TEAM: Philadelphia Phillies
BORN: April 4, 1956 Lancaster, PA
HEIGHT: 6′ **WEIGHT:** 175 lbs.
BATS: Both **THROWS:** Right
ACQUIRED: Traded from Twins with Tom Nieto and Eric Bullock for Shane Rawley, 10/88

Herr returns to the N.L. East with his boyhood favorite team—the Phillies. He spent most of the 1988 season hurt and unhappy as a Twin. Herr began the 1988 season with the Cardinals, for whom he had played since 1979, and was batting .260 when he was dealt to Minnesota for Tom Brunansky. No sooner had Herr arrived in a Twins uniform than he announced that he didn't want to be there. After batting .263 for Minnesota, he was traded to the Phillies. Herr's slated to be the Phillie second baseman, with Juan Samuel moving to center field.

A good solid player, but not considered a superstar, Herr's cards routinely sell in the 10- to 15-cent range. That price is way too high for any kind of investing. Our pick for his best 1989 card is Topps.

OREL HERSHISER

	W	L	ERA	G	CG	IP	H	R	BB	SO
1988	23	8	2.26	35	15	267.0	208	73	73	178
Life	83	49	2.77	196	50	1200.1	1014	433	357	833

POSITION: Pitcher
TEAM: Los Angeles Dodgers
BORN: September 16, 1958 Buffalo, NY
HEIGHT: 6′3″ **WEIGHT:** 190 lbs.
BATS: Right **THROWS:** Right
ACQUIRED: 17th-round pick in 6/79 free-agent draft

Just goes to show you what an improved defense and a consistent offense can do for you. After two seasons of pitching .500 baseball, in 1988 Hershiser became a 20-game winner for the first time in his five-year career. Last year he also broke Don Drysdale's record of 58 consecutive scoreless innings. Hershiser was the N.L. Championship Series MVP, World Series MVP, and unanimous selection for the Cy Young Award. He even picked up a save. At 30, Hershiser could remain one of the toughest pitchers to beat for another decade.

Hershiser's strong 1988 effort for the world champions will hike up the price of his 1989 cards. He finally got the national spotlight to shine on him. Even at 15 cents each, his cards would be a strong investment. Our pick for his best 1989 card is Fleer.

JOE HESKETH

	W	L	ERA	G	SV	IP	H	R	BB	SO
1988	4	3	2.85	60	9	72.2	63	30	35	64
Life	22	15	3.07	129	11	384.1	341	152	141	307

POSITION: Pitcher
TEAM: Montreal Expos
BORN: February 16, 1958
Lackawanna, NY
HEIGHT: 6′2″ **WEIGHT:** 165 lbs.
BATS: Right **THROWS:** Left
ACQUIRED: Second-round pick in 6/80
free-agent draft

Hesketh's talents help to illustrate just how deep the Montreal bullpen staff really is. Last year he appeared in 60 games—all in relief—going 4-3 with a 2.85 ERA and nine saves in 72⅔ innings of work. Tim Burke, Andy McGaffigan, Jeff Parrett, and Hesketh are the fearsome foursome in the Expo bullpen. Hesketh pitched in 18 games in '87, keeping his ERA at 3.14. As a starter in 1985, he was 10-5 in 25 games, with a 2.49 ERA. He was injured and missed most of 1986, pitching in only 15 games. The Expos will battle for the N.L. East crown in 1989, and one of their weapons will be a strong bullpen including Hesketh.

Hesketh's inclination to be sidelined due to injuries has kept and will keep his cards as commons for the foreseeable future. Our pick for his best 1989 card is Topps.

TED HIGUERA

	W	L	ERA	G	CG	IP	H	R	BB	SO
1988	16	9	2.45	31	8	227.1	168	66	59	192
Life	69	38	3.25	132	44	949.2	816	375	283	766

POSITION: Pitcher
TEAM: Milwaukee Brewers
BORN: November 9, 1958
Los Mochis, Mexico
HEIGHT: 5′10″ **WEIGHT:** 178 lbs.
BATS: Both **THROWS:** Left
ACQUIRED: Purchased from Juarez in
Mexican League, 9/83

Higuera had his third close brush with the 20-game win echelon in 1988. He finished 16-9, with a 2.45 ERA. He struck out 192 batters and walked only 59 in 227⅓ innings. In just four seasons with the Brewers, he's averaging better than 15 wins a year. The fiery lefty topped his squad in victories, ERA, innings pitched, and strikeouts last season. In 1987, he finished third in the league in strikeouts, and was 18-10, with a 3.85 ERA. His best season was in 1986, when he went 20-11, with a 2.79 ERA. After getting his start in the Mexican League, he was 26 when he debuted with the Brewers. However, Higuera has made up for lost time with four admirable seasons.

Higuera's 1989 cards should be in the range of 10 cents. His card values will at least double when he finally gets that 20-game season. Our pick for his best 1989 card is Score.

SHAWN HILLEGAS

	W	L	ERA	G	CG	IP	H	R	BB	SO
1988	6	6	3.71	17	0	96.2	84	42	35	56
Life	10	9	3.67	29	0	154.2	136	69	66	107

POSITION: Pitcher
TEAM: Chicago White Sox
BORN: August 21, 1964 Dos Palos, CA
HEIGHT: 6′3″ **WEIGHT:** 205 lbs.
BATS: Right **THROWS:** Right
ACQUIRED: Traded from Dodgers for Ricky Horton, 8/88

The White Sox obtained Hillegas from the Dodgers late in the 1988 campaign. In 1988, he divided his time between the Dodgers and Triple-A Albuquerque, where he went 6-4 with a 3.49 ERA with 65 strikeouts in 101 innings. He was a 13-game winner for Triple-A Albuquerque in 1987 with a 3.37 ERA; he fanned 105 in 166 innings. Hillegas picked up four more wins in '87 for the Dodgers in a late-season recall. He's a big, strong hurler with a fastball consistently in the 90s, and he gets his breaking ball over for strikes. The White Sox look to Hillegas to be a member of their starting rotation this season.

Hillegas' 1989 cards will open in the 10- to 15-cent range. He could be an important part of the ChiSox youth movement. Our pick for his best 1989 card is Topps.

BRIAN HOLMAN

	W	L	ERA	G	CG	IP	H	R	BB	SO
1988	4	8	3.23	18	1	100.1	101	39	34	58
Life	4	8	3.23	18	1	100.1	101	39	34	58

POSITION: Pitcher
TEAM: Montreal Expos
BORN: January 25, 1965 Denver, CO
HEIGHT: 6′4″ **WEIGHT:** 185 lbs.
BATS: Right **THROWS:** Right
ACQUIRED: First-round pick in 6/83 free-agent draft

Holman had an outstanding record (8-1) for Triple-A Indianapolis in 1988. He had a 2.36 ERA and fanned 70 in 91 innings. Recalled to Montreal in 1988, his won-lost record was not that impressive, but he did keep his ERA right around 3.00. At Double-A Jacksonville in 1987, Holman had the best ERA in the league (2.50) and an outstanding 14-5 record. He had 115 strikeouts against only 56 walks, another important statistic. *Baseball America* rated him as having the best curveball in the Southern League and picked him as the eighth best big league prospect. Not an overpowering pitcher, Holman spots the ball well and has excellent control.

Holman's 1989 cards will open at 15 cents. Although we can't recommend investing at that price, he has a good future with the Expos if he lives up to his potential. Our pick for his best 1989 card is Fleer.

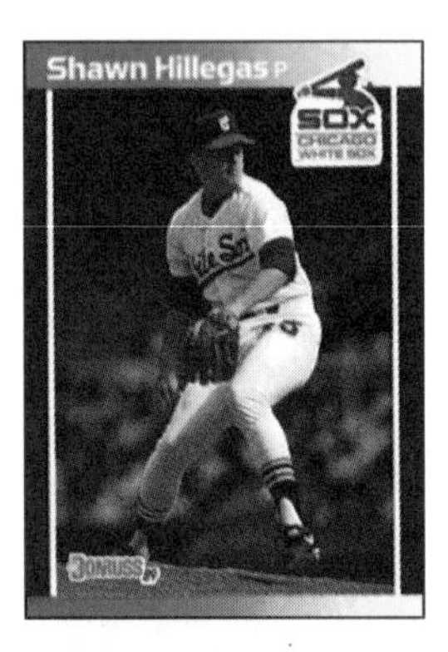

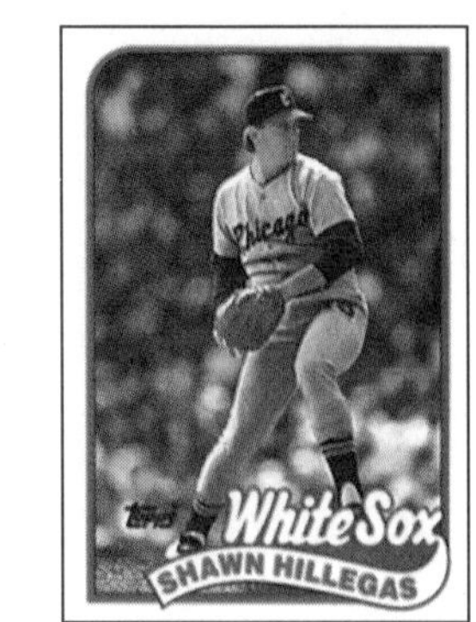

BRIAN HOLTON

	W	L	ERA	G	SV	IP	H	R	BB	SO
1988	7	3	1.70	45	1	84.2	69	19	26	49
Life	13	9	3.12	113	3	196.1	193	78	65	132

POSITION: Pitcher
TEAM: Baltimore Orioles
BORN: November 29, 1959
McKeesport, PA
HEIGHT: 6′ **WEIGHT:** 193 lbs.
BATS: Right **THROWS:** Right
ACQUIRED: Traded from Dodgers with Ken Howell and Juan Bell for Eddie Murray, 12/88

Holton will join a shaky Oriole bullpen in 1989. He had his best season ever with the 1988 Dodgers. Before the 1988 season started, he had a 6-6 lifetime mark with an unimpressive 4.19 ERA. However, in 1988, he turned his career around. Holton tallied a career-best seven wins, one more than he had scored in two previous seasons. His biggest achievement was a team-leading 1.70 ERA, nearly 2.5 points below his career total. He has the ability to start and relieve, although he spent 1988 as a vital middle reliever. He was a big part of the Dodgers' drive to their world championship. Holton will be one of the Orioles' best pitchers in 1989.

Holton's 1989 cards won't be more than a nickel. Despite his fine 1988 performance, his cards are unlikely to gain in value while he remains in the unglamorous relief role he holds. Our pick for his best 1989 card is Donruss.

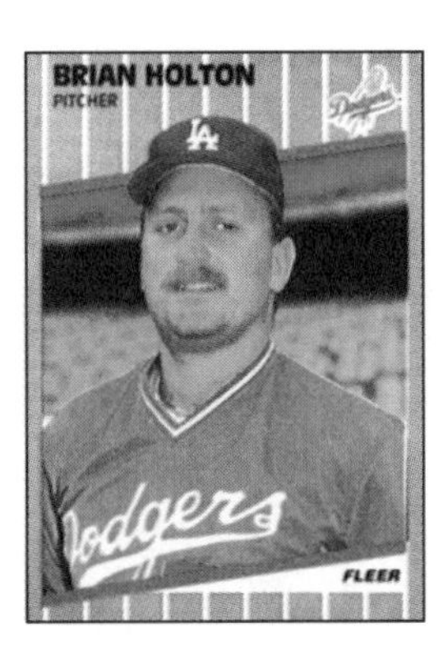

RICK HONEYCUTT

	W	L	ERA	G	SV	IP	H	R	BB	SO
1988	3	2	3.50	55	7	79.2	74	36	25	47
Life	93	123	3.82	346	8	1781.1	1850	877	532	798

POSITION: Pitcher
TEAM: Oakland A's
BORN: June 29, 1954 Chattanooga, TN
HEIGHT: 6′1″ **WEIGHT:** 190 lbs.
BATS: Left **THROWS:** Left
ACQUIRED: Traded from Dodgers for Tim Belcher, 8/87

Like teammate Dennis Eckersley, Honeycutt got a second chance with his career when he moved from the starting rotation to the bullpen. He looked washed-up after 1987, when he had a combined 3-16 and 4.72 ERA mark with the Dodgers and the A's. However, Honeycutt adapted perfectly to the role of reliever. He finished 17 games and had seven saves, second on the club to Eckersley. Honeycutt's ERA dropped more than an entire point. He had started at least 20 games for ten consecutive seasons before moving into the bullpen. Honeycutt's rebirth as a reliever should prolong his career by several seasons and could be a blessing for the A's.

Honeycutt's lifetime stats are average at best. Based on his lifetime totals, his cards seem unlikely to climb above their prices as commons. Our pick for his best 1989 card is Fleer.

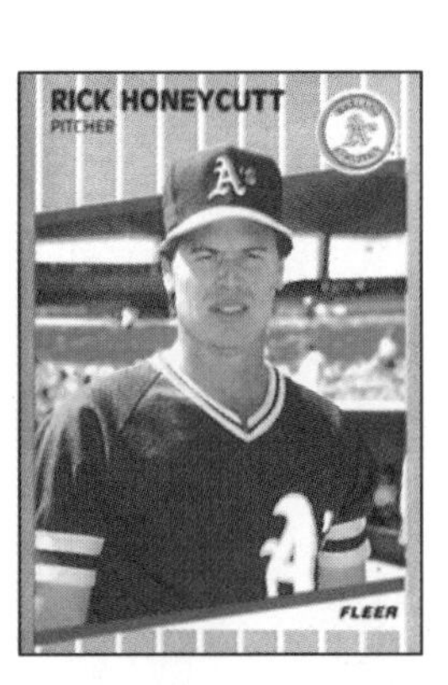

RICKY HORTON

	W	L	ERA	G	SV	IP	H	R	BB	SO
1988	7	11	4.88	64	2	118.1	131	71	38	36
Life	31	23	3.53	259	14	559.0	559	237	179	275

POSITION: Pitcher
TEAM: Los Angeles Dodgers
BORN: July 30, 1959 Poughkeepsie, NY
HEIGHT: 6'2" **WEIGHT:** 195 lbs.
BATS: Left **THROWS:** Left
ACQUIRED: Traded from White Sox for Shawn Hillegas, 8/88

Horton was the lefthanded relief pitcher the Dodgers sought to clinch their division in 1988. Pitching in just 12 games, Horton was ineffective, gaining just one win. Horton pitched as a starter/reliever for the Cardinals from 1984 through 1987 before getting traded to the Chicago White Sox prior to the 1988 season. Horton's last season with the Cardinals was his best, as he logged an 8-3 mark with seven saves. His career stats are average for a starter/reliever with five years of experience. Horton needs a solid comeback to stick with the Dodgers in 1989.

Split duties will keep Horton from accumulating the needed stats for stardom, and will keep the prices of his cards low. His 1989 cards will be three cents or less, but aren't good investment possibilities. Our pick for his best 1989 card is Donruss.

CHARLIE HOUGH

	W	L	ERA	G	CG	IP	H	R	BB	SO
1988	15	16	3.32	34	10	252.0	202	111	126	174
Life	164	144	3.55	683	88	2706.0	2278	1233	1168	1780

POSITION: Pitcher
TEAM: Texas Rangers
BORN: January 5, 1948 Honolulu, HI
HEIGHT: 6'2" **WEIGHT:** 190 lbs.
BATS: Right **THROWS:** Right
ACQUIRED: Purchased from Dodgers, 7/80

If the A.L. has an ageless wonder, it has to be Hough. At age 40, he was fourth in the league with 252 innings pitched. Last year Hough became the oldest pitcher ever to lead the league in innings pitched (283⅓) and starts (40). After years of relief work with the Dodgers, the wily knuckleballer started his career anew as a starter for Texas. His mastery of the unpredictable pitch and his effortless delivery could help him near longevity records for major league pitchers. Meanwhile, Hough gives the Rangers an experienced core to a young, talented pitching staff.

Like knuckleballer Hoyt Wilhelm, Hough may rack up some impressive numbers before he finally decides to retire. His commons cards could have long-term gains if Hough lasts another five years and keeps winning. Our pick for his best 1989 card is Score.

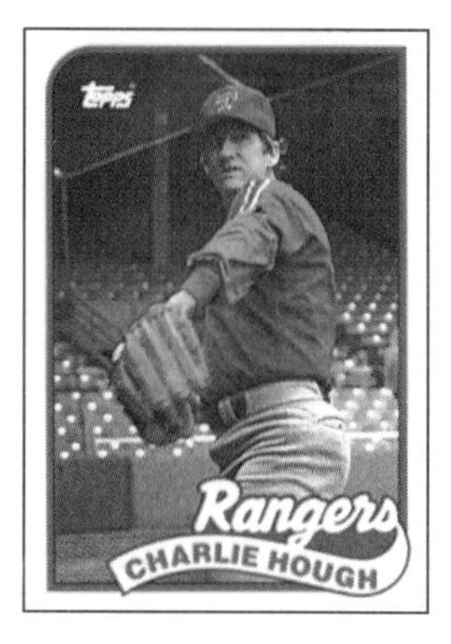

JACK HOWELL

	BA	G	AB	R	H	2B	3B	HR	RBI	SB
1988	.254	154	500	59	127	32	2	16	63	2
Life	.247	398	1237	168	305	68	9	48	166	9

POSITION: Third base
TEAM: California Angels
BORN: August 18, 1961 Tucson, AZ
HEIGHT: 6′ **WEIGHT:** 185 lbs.
BATS: Left **THROWS:** Right
ACQUIRED: Signed as a free agent, 6/83

Howell didn't duplicate his power production from 1987, but he was a significant part of the 1988 Angels offense. He played in a career-high 154 games and had the most hits of his career, 127. Howell had seven fewer homers in 1988 than he did the year before, but only one less RBI. He also increased his batting average by nine points. He inherited the full-time chores at third base from Doug DeCinces and was a steady defensive influence on the team. Howell seems capable of averaging 20 homers or more in the future, which could gain him the recognition he deserves.

Howell, at age 27, could be a slugging star for the Angels for at least another decade. His cards, at a nickel or less, would be a safe investment. Our pick for his best 1989 card is Score.

JAY HOWELL

	W	L	ERA	G	SV	IP	H	R	BB	SO
1988	5	3	2.08	50	21	65.0	44	16	21	70
Life	34	33	3.89	288	89	499.1	491	230	188	417

POSITION: Pitcher
TEAM: Philadelphia Phillies
BORN: November 26, 1955 Miami, FL
HEIGHT: 6′3″ **WEIGHT:** 205 lbs.
BATS: Right **THROWS:** Right
ACQUIRED: Traded from Orioles with Gordon Dillard for Phil Bradley, 12/88

Howell was traded twice in one week at the winter meetings—first to the Orioles, then to the Phillies. Howell lived up to everyone's expectations as the relief ace of the Dodgers. Previously, Howell had recorded 16 saves in 1987 with Oakland and was slated to become the star of the Dodger bullpen. He came through, recording the second-highest save total and the lowest ERA of his six-year big league career. Howell's best season came with the A's in 1985, when he went 9-8 with 29 saves. He has been in pro baseball since 1976, but he was a starter until 1984 with the Yankees. Howell's role will be as a second reliever in 1989.

Howell's success and notoriety mean that his 1989 cards will be fair investments at a dime or less. Our pick for his best 1989 card is Fleer.

KENT HRBEK

	BA	G	AB	R	H	2B	3B	HR	RBI	SB
1988	.312	143	510	75	159	31	0	25	76	0
Life	.292	1047	3803	565	1110	207	16	176	640	16

POSITION: First base
TEAM: Minnesota Twins
BORN: May 21, 1960 Minneapolis, MN
HEIGHT: 6′4″ **WEIGHT:** 235 lbs.
BATS: Left **THROWS:** Right
ACQUIRED: 17th-round pick in 6/78 free-agent draft

Hrbek fans got both good and bad news in his 1988 season. Although Hrbek couldn't match his 1987 totals of 34 homers and 90 RBIs, he gathered more than 20 extra hits in 1988 and saw his batting average climb more than 20 points, promising events for any power hitter. He hit .312, with 25 round-trippers and 76 RBIs in 1988. Prior to 1988, he had at least 80 RBIs in six straight years. Hrbek notched his 1,000th career hit this year, his seventh full season in the majors. He has hit 20 or more round-trippers for five consecutive seasons. If he continues his current pace, Hrbek will have 200 career home runs less than two seasons from now.

Hrbek's 1989 cards should be reasonably priced at 10 to 15 cents. That value will go up quickly if he helps the Twins repeat their 1987 World Series showing. Our pick for his best 1989 card is Donruss.

CHARLES HUDSON

	W	L	ERA	G	CG	IP	H	R	BB	SO
1988	6	6	4.49	28	1	106.1	93	53	36	58
Life	49	55	3.98	190	14	941.0	922	469	330	557

POSITION: Pitcher
TEAM: New York Yankees
BORN: March 16, 1959 Ennis, TX
HEIGHT: 6′3″ **WEIGHT:** 185 lbs.
BATS: Both **THROWS:** Right
ACQUIRED: Traded from Phillies with Jeff Knox for Mike Easler and Tom Barrett, 12/86

Hudson, shuttled between the bullpen and the starting rotation, got into just 28 games for the 1988 Yankees. His appearances were his fewest since 1983, his rookie season. The lack of work kept Hudson ineffective as a pitcher. He did have a 6-6 mark with two saves and one complete game. Hudson finished ten games, perhaps a signal that he might function best in the bullpen in the future. Hudson never lived up to expectations during four years with Philadelphia. His best outcome there was in 1983, when he went 8-8 as a starter. Hudson, just 30, isn't washed up, but he'll have to battle to get playing time in 1989.

Hudson's 1989 cards are valued at three cents each. Hudson's only had one winning season since 1983, so don't invest until he has another. Our pick for his best 1989 card is Donruss.

BRUCE HURST

	W	L	ERA	G	CG	IP	H	R	BB	SO
1988	18	6	3.66	33	7	216.2	222	98	65	166
Life	88	73	4.23	237	54	1459.1	1569	747	479	1043

POSITION: Pitcher
TEAM: Boston Red Sox
BORN: March 24, 1958 St. George, UT
HEIGHT: 6′3″ **WEIGHT:** 205 lbs.
BATS: Left **THROWS:** Left
ACQUIRED: First-round pick in 6/76 free-agent draft

Ever a competitor, Hurst was chasing 20 wins through the last week of 1988. Last season marked the lefty's sixth straight year of double-figure triumphs, ending the year at 18-6, with a 3.66 ERA. In 1987, Hurst was 15-13, with a lofty 4.41 ERA. In Boston's pennant-winning season, 1986, he was 13-8, with a 2.99 ERA. The BoSox duo of Hurst and Roger Clemens ranks as one of baseball's best pitching pairs. At age 31, Hurst has entered the halfway point of his career. If he stays healthy, he'll be a chief competitor for the Red Sox in 1989 and for years to come.

Unlike cards of Clemens, Hurst's 1989 cards will be inexpensive, 10 cents at the most. We recommend investing in his cards, because the rewards will be fast and substantial once he becomes known as a constant 20-game threat. Our pick for his best 1989 card is Score.

PETE INCAVIGLIA

	BA	G	AB	R	H	2B	3B	HR	RBI	SB
1988	.249	116	418	59	104	19	3	22	54	6
Life	.257	408	1467	226	377	66	9	79	222	18

POSITION: Designated hitter; outfield
TEAM: Texas Rangers
BORN: April 2, 1964 Pebble Beach, CA
HEIGHT: 6′1″ **WEIGHT:** 220 lbs.
BATS: Right **THROWS:** Right
ACQUIRED: Traded from Expos for Bob Sebra and Jim Anderson, 11/85

Incaviglia hit 22 homers in 1988, down from his 27-homer output in 1987. His batting average also dropped from .271 to .249. The Rangers hope that '88 was just an aberration and that he will be back on his game in 1989. In 1986, he hit a career-high 30 homers, and he led the league in strikeouts, with 185 whiffs. He has reduced the number of strikeouts ever since, indicating that Incaviglia is becoming more disciplined. Texas would probably sacrifice having him strike out a few more times for having him smash 30 homers and 100 RBIs a season. If Incaviglia gets on a tear, he could easily lead the A.L. in homers.

Incaviglia's 1989 cards will sell in the 10- to 20-cent range. He may never hit for high average, but he will always be in demand because of his slugging ability. Our pick for his best 1989 card is Donruss.

BO JACKSON

	BA	G	AB	R	H	2B	3B	HR	RBI	SB
1988	.246	124	439	63	108	16	4	25	68	27
Life	.238	265	917	118	218	35	7	49	130	40

POSITION: Outfield
TEAM: Kansas City Royals
BORN: November 30, 1962
Bessemer, AL
HEIGHT: 6′1″ **WEIGHT:** 222 lbs.
BATS: Right **THROWS:** Right
ACQUIRED: Fourth-round pick in 6/86 free-agent draft

After a seesaw rookie season and a new career as a pro football running back, Jackson caused some fans to worry that he'd leave baseball forever. But a stellar baseball season in 1988 proved that Jackson can handle full-time jobs with both the Royals and the NFL's L.A. Raiders. Jackson thumped a career-best 25 home runs and 68 RBIs last year. Unfortunately, he led the Royals with 146 strikeouts in 439 at-bats, and his average crept up to only .246. Jackson's storied speed could help him become a high-average hitter if he acquires some batting selectivity in 1989.

Jackson's 1989 cards will sell in the 25-cent range. This price isn't investment-worthy until Jackson becomes a complete player. There's also the possibility of a severe football injury that could snuff out his baseball future. Our pick for his best 1989 card is Score.

DANNY JACKSON

	W	L	ERA	G	CG	IP	H	R	BB	SO
1988	23	8	2.73	35	15	260.2	206	86	71	161
Life	60	57	3.43	154	35	973.1	921	431	376	591

POSITION: Pitcher
TEAM: Cincinnati Reds
BORN: January 5, 1962
San Antonio, TX
HEIGHT: 6′ **WEIGHT:** 190 lbs.
BATS: Right **THROWS:** Left
ACQUIRED: Traded from Royals for Kurt Stillwell, 1/88

Jackson fulfilled the expectations of fans everywhere in 1988. After an awful 9-18 year in 1987, the Royals sent him to Cincinnati, where the southpaw blossomed into one of the league's finest hurlers. Jackson topped the Reds in virtually every pitching category, going 23-8 with a 2.73 ERA. Jackson struck out 161 batters in 260⅔ innings. He also showed control, walking only 71. After floundering in the A.L. for five seasons, he has found a promising future with the Reds. The Reds, in turn, may have found in Jackson a way to wrestle the pennant away from the Dodgers.

Jackson's sterling season may lift his 1989 cards up to the 15-cent range. However, don't invest more than a nickel apiece in his cards until he shows that same form a second straight season. Our pick for his best 1989 card is Fleer.

MIKE JACKSON

	W	L	ERA	G	SV	IP	H	R	BB	SO
1988	6	5	2.63	62	4	99.1	74	37	43	76
Life	9	15	3.45	126	5	222.0	174	97	103	172

POSITION: Pitcher
TEAM: Seattle Mariners
BORN: December 22, 1964 Houston, TX
HEIGHT: 6′ **WEIGHT:** 185 lbs.
BATS: Right **THROWS:** Right
ACQUIRED: Traded from Phillies with Glenn Wilson and Dave Grundage for Phil Bradley and John Fortungo, 12/87

Jackson needed just one season to become one of the best pitchers on the Seattle staff. He had the lowest ERA of any Mariners' pitcher in 1988 (2.63). He was the only M's hurler with an ERA below 3.00. Jackson's 62 appearances led the pitching staff. He finished 29 of those appearances. He had a chance to become the Phillies' fifth starter in 1987, but his 3-10 record, 4.20 ERA didn't win him the job. However, it looks like Jackson has won a major role in Seattle's bullpen for 1989.

Jackson's 1989 cards will be three cents or less. He'll get lots of work with the Mariners, and he should enjoy continued success. His cards could be a mildly interesting investment, one which would be safest in limited quantities. Our pick for his best 1989 card is Fleer.

BROOK JACOBY

	BA	G	AB	R	H	2B	3B	HR	RBI	SB
1988	.241	152	552	59	133	25	0	9	49	2
Life	.273	767	2738	351	747	126	14	85	326	11

POSITION: Third base
TEAM: Cleveland Indians
BORN: November 23, 1959 Philadelphia, PA
HEIGHT: 5′11″ **WEIGHT:** 175 lbs.
BATS: Right **THROWS:** Right
ACQUIRED: Traded from Braves with Brett Butler and Rick Behenna for Len Barker, 8/83.

Jacoby did an adequate job for the 1988 Indians, but his final statistics were only a glimmer of his 1987 accomplishments. In 1987, he reached career highs of 32 home runs, 69 RBIs, and a .300 batting average. Jacoby's hitting suffered in 1988, but he made only ten errors at the hot corner, quite a reduction from his 22-error season in 1987. He was almost given away in a 1983 trade with Atlanta. He's been a regular for the Tribe since, and should be at third base for years to come. Jacoby has been a strong run producer for the Tribe in the past. A full recovery from his slump could give the Indians a needed lift for 1989.

Jacoby's 1989 cards should cost less than 10 cents. His power should return, and his cards should bring eventual returns. Our pick for his best 1989 card is Score.

CHRIS JAMES

	BA	G	AB	R	H	2B	3B	HR	RBI	SB
1988	.242	150	566	57	137	24	1	19	66	7
Life	.263	281	970	110	255	47	7	37	125	10

POSITION: Outfield; third base
TEAM: Philadelphia Phillies
BORN: October 4, 1962 Rusk, TX
HEIGHT: 6′1″ **WEIGHT:** 190 lbs.
BATS: Right **THROWS:** Right
ACQUIRED: Selected in 10/81 free-agent draft

While the Phillies rode out the tail end of the '88 campaign in last place, James was putting on a hitting display. In just the last month of the season, he had seven homers, 22 RBIs, and a .313 average, and finished the year with 19 homers, 66 RBIs, and a .242 mark. In 1987, his first full season in the bigs, he poked 17 homers and posted 54 RBIs. The Phils have tried James at third base; once he settles into one position, his average should climb. Being the successor to Mike Schmidt is the ultimate challenge, but it looks as though James is up to it.

At the end of the 1988 season, James' cards could be found for 5 to 10 cents each. He could lead the Phillies in homers again in 1989, so if his cards remain priced low, grab them. Our pick for his best 1989 card is Score.

DION JAMES

	BA	G	AB	R	H	2B	3B	HR	RBI	SB
1988	.256	132	386	46	99	17	5	3	30	9
Life	.284	423	1336	184	380	74	16	14	125	30

POSITION: Outfield
TEAM: Atlanta Braves
BORN: November 9, 1962 Philadelphia, PA
HEIGHT: 6′1″ **WEIGHT:** 170 lbs.
BATS: Left **THROWS:** Left
ACQUIRED: Traded from Brewers for Brad Komminsk, 1/87

James' 1988 average dropped some 56 points from last season, but he remained one of the offensive highlights of the 1988 Braves season. He hit .256, the fourth-best average on the team. His power stats dropped considerably from his 1987 accomplishments of ten homers and 61 RBIs. James was a big hit in his first season in Atlanta, when he led the team with a .312 average. His career went nowhere in Milwaukee, even though he posted a .295 average in 128 games in 1984. For the Braves, James' hitting, smooth defense, and speed make him one of the team's best.

James' 1989 cards should be a nickel or less, especially after his 1988 slump. Invest when interest in his cards is down. At age 26, he'll have a comeback in 1989. Our pick for his best 1989 card is Fleer.

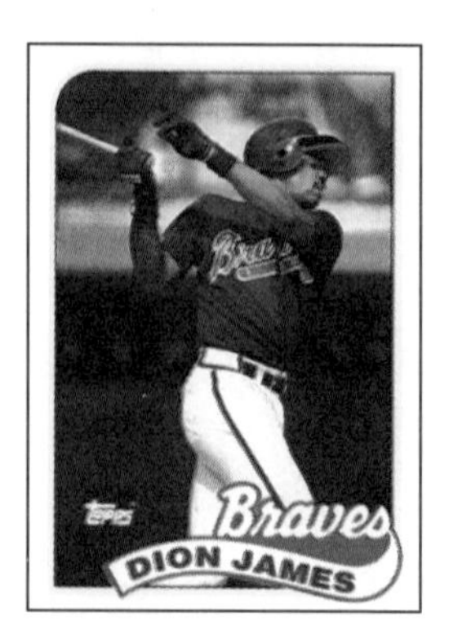

STAN JAVIER

	BA	G	AB	R	H	2B	3B	HR	RBI	SB
1988	.257	125	397	49	102	13	3	2	35	20
Life	.230	272	669	85	154	24	4	4	52	31

POSITION: Outfield
TEAM: Oakland A's
BORN: January 9, 1965 San Francisco de Macoris, Dominican Republic
HEIGHT: 6′ **WEIGHT:** 180 lbs.
BATS: Both **THROWS:** Right
ACQUIRED: Traded from Yankees with Jay Howell, Tim Birtsas, Jose Rijo, and Eric Plunk for Rickey Henderson and Bert Bradley, 12/84

Javier had the biggest hitting performance in his three-year major league career in 1988. He became the team's fourth outfielder and defensive replacement, playing in 125 games. The son of former Cardinals second baseman Julian Javier, Stan Javier was a key to the trade that sent Rickey Henderson to the Yankees. One of Javier's biggest assets is his speed. His 20 stolen bases were fourth on the team in 1988. Javier likely won't win a starting job in 1989, but he'll continue to be a vital part of the A's.

Javier is not a power hitter, a strike against him when it comes to card values. His 1989 issues will be a nickel or less. Because he sees only part-time duty, it's unlikely that his cards will gain in value soon. Our pick for his best 1989 card is Score.

GREGG JEFFERIES

	BA	G	AB	R	H	2B	3B	HR	RBI	SB
1988	.321	29	109	19	35	8	2	6	17	5
Life	.330	35	115	19	38	9	2	6	19	5

POSITION: Third base
TEAM: New York Mets
BORN: August 1, 1967
HEIGHT: 5′10″ **WEIGHT:** 170 lbs.
BATS: Both **THROWS:** Right
ACQUIRED: First-round pick in 6/85 free-agent draft

Jefferies came up to the Mets late in the 1988 season, and before you knew it, he was named N.L. Player of the Week. Scouts have pinned a "can't miss" tag on him from day one. Jefferies made the Triple-A All-Star team in 1988, after hitting .280 at Tidewater. He was twice named "Minor League Player of the Year" (1986 and '87). For Double-A Jackson in 1987, he batted .367, with 20 home runs and 101 RBIs. The Mets then gave him a late-season shot, and he was three for six with two RBIs. Originally a shortstop, he was shifted to third base in '88.

Jefferies' 1989 cards will open in the $1 range. The sky is the limit if he lives up to his potential. Our pick for his best 1989 card is Topps.

STEVE JELTZ

	BA	G	AB	R	H	2B	3B	HR	RBI	SB
1988	.187	148	379	39	71	11	4	0	27	3
Life	.208	537	1383	144	287	35	17	1	95	13

POSITION: Shortstop
TEAM: Philadelphia Phillies
BORN: May 29, 1959 Paris, France
HEIGHT: 5′11″ **WEIGHT:** 175 lbs.
BATS: Both **THROWS:** Right
ACQUIRED: Ninth-round pick in 6/80 free-agent draft

He is the defensive equal of N.L. All-Star Ozzie Smith at shortstop; however, Jeltz's futility with the bat leaves his career longevity open to serious doubt. He batted a meek .187 in 1988, coming to the plate 379 times and going without a home run for the fourth straight season. He first joined the Phillies in late-season 1983 and, in a preview of things to come, hit .125 in 13 games. He became the Phils' regular shortstop midway in the 1985 season and hit .189. In 1986, he batted .219, and in 1987 he hit a career-high .232. Jeltz is not a long-ball threat; in fact, he has failed to hit a home run in his last 1,116 plate appearances.

Jeltz's cards are commons. They always will be commons. They are not good investments. They never will be. Our pick for his best 1989 card is Donruss.

DOUG JENNINGS

	BA	G	AB	R	H	2B	3B	HR	RBI	SB
1988	.208	71	101	9	21	6	0	1	15	0
Life	.208	71	101	9	21	6	0	1	15	0

POSITION: Outfield
TEAM: Oakland A's
BORN: September 30, 1964 Atlanta, GA
HEIGHT: 5′10″ **WEIGHT:** 165 lbs.
BATS: Left **THROWS:** Left
ACQUIRED: Drafted from Angels, 12/87

Jennings got lots of playing time during his 1988 rookie season with the Athletics. He got into 71 games, mostly in substitute capacities. Jennings provided great late-inning defense, making only one error all season long. His .208 average was blighted by 28 strikeouts, approximately one for every 3.6 times to the plate. In 1987 at Double-A Midland, Jennings hit .338, with 30 homers, 106 runs scored, 33 doubles, and 104 RBIs. He hit .317 at Class-A Palm Springs in 1986. It's obvious that all the starting outfield spots are locked on the 1989 Oakland club. Jennings, however, could be a factor in A's playoff bid this year.

Jennings will debut in most 1989 sets. Based on his mediocre first-year stats, don't pay more than a nickel for his card. Our pick for his best 1989 card is Topps.

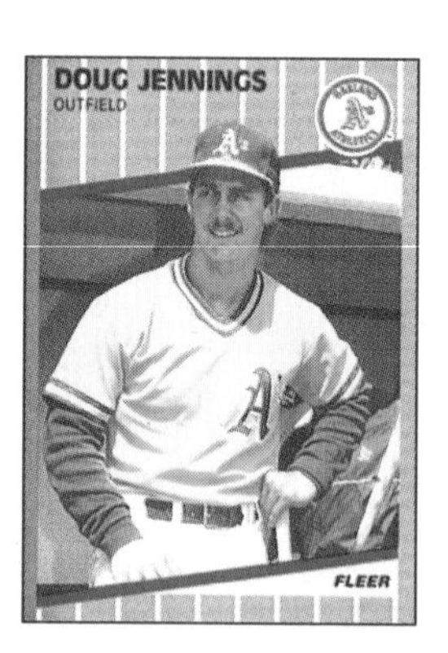

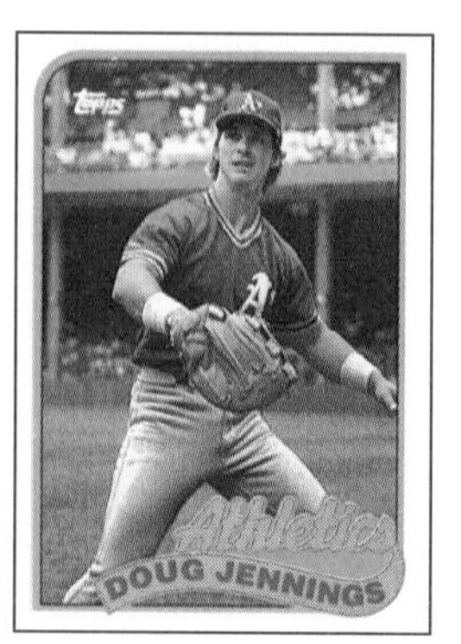

TOMMY JOHN

	W	L	ERA	G	CG	IP	H	R	BB	SO
1988	9	8	4.49	35	0	176.1	221	96	46	81
Life	286	224	3.31	750	162	4643.2	4696	1972	1237	2227

POSITION: Pitcher
TEAM: New York Yankees
BORN: May 22, 1943 Terre Haute, IN
HEIGHT: 6′3″ **WEIGHT:** 200 lbs.
BATS: Right **THROWS:** Left
ACQUIRED: Signed as a free agent, 5/86

Even at age 45, John was one of the most effective pitchers for the Yankees in 1988. He went 9-8 in both starting and relief assignments, finishing two games he relieved in. John started his career in 1963, and since then he has pitched with the Tribe, White Sox, Dodgers, Angels, and A's. A three-time winner of 20 games, he had his best year with the 1980 Yankees, going 22-9. John's career was almost ended by arm surgery in 1975. After missing the 1975 season, he has been pitching on a regular basis. Nearing 300 career wins, John could make the Hall of Fame based mostly on longevity.

John's 1989 cards will be 15 cents or less. Buy a few extras of this ageless wonder. If the 1989 cards are his last ever, they'll escalate in value once he is enshrined at Cooperstown. Our pick for his best 1989 card is Score.

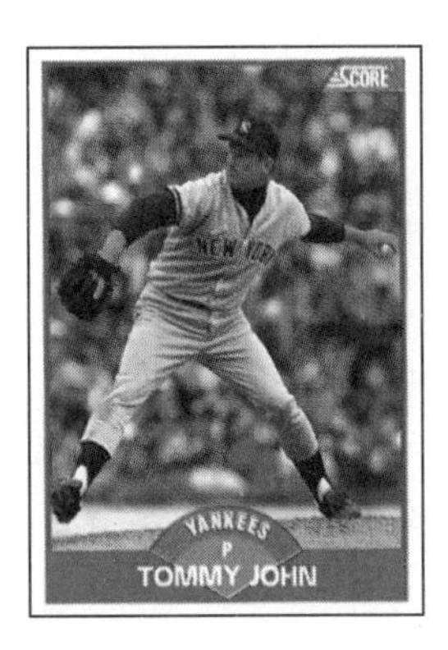

HOWARD JOHNSON

	BA	G	AB	R	H	2B	3B	HR	RBI	SB
1988	.230	148	495	85	114	21	1	24	68	23
Life	.251	716	2234	323	560	94	7	100	321	86

POSITION: Third base; shortstop
TEAM: New York Mets
BORN: November 26, 1960
Clearwater, FL
HEIGHT: 5′11″ **WEIGHT:** 175 lbs.
BATS: Both **THROWS:** Right
ACQUIRED: Traded from Tigers for Walt Terrell, 12/84

Playing both third and short last year, Johnson batted .230 for New York in 148 games. He belted 24 home runs, good for 68 RBIs, seven of them game winners. In 1987, he was a member of the 30-30 club (with 36 homers, 32 stolen bases), only the second infielder in big league history to do that. Johnson's 36 home run mark was also a new record for switch-hitters. He has his work cut out for him to keep his job, with Gregg Jefferies and Dave Magadan vying for playing time. Hojo doesn't always hit high for average, but he swings a dangerous bat, and the Mets like to keep him in the lineup as much as possible.

Johnson's 1989 cards are not highly collectible, nor are they recommended as long-term income producers. Our pick for his best 1989 card is Fleer.

LANCE JOHNSON

	BA	G	AB	R	H	2B	3B	HR	RBI	SB
1988	.185	33	124	11	23	4	1	0	6	6
Life	.197	66	183	15	36	6	2	0	13	12

POSITION: Outfield
TEAM: Chicago White Sox
BORN: July 7, 1963 Cincinnati, OH
HEIGHT: 5′11″ **WEIGHT:** 155 lbs.
BATS: Left **THROWS:** Left
ACQUIRED: Traded from Cardinals for Jose DeLeon, 4/88

Johnson has excellent speed, runs the bases well, covers all kinds of territory defensively, has a great arm, and best of all, he hits for average. Johnson started 1988 with the ChiSox, but he was disappointing, hitting only .185. He was sent to Triple-A Vancouver, where he hit .307, regaining both his batting stroke and his confidence. Louisville fans appreciated his talents in 1987, when he delivered with a .333 average, including 11 triples, five homers, and 41 stolen bases with the Triple-A club. Called to St. Louis late in the season, Johnson saw limited action and hit .220. At 25, Johnson is ready to make his mark in the majors.

Johnson's 1989 cards should be in the 10- to 15-cent range. Stock up on them at that price while you have the chance. Our pick for his best 1989 card is Topps.

RANDY JOHNSON

	W	L	ERA	G	CG	IP	H	R	BB	SO
1988	3	0	2.42	4	1	26.0	23	8	7	25
Life	3	0	2.42	4	1	26.0	23	8	7	25

POSITION: Pitcher
TEAM: Montreal Expos
BORN: September 10, 1963 Walnut Creek, CA
HEIGHT: 6′10″ **WEIGHT:** 225 lbs.
BATS: Right **THROWS:** Left
ACQUIRED: Second-round pick in 6/85 free-agent draft

Although Johnson has had control problems, he has a 93-plus-mph fastball, and Expo fans expect great things from the lefty. At Triple-A Indianapolis in 1988, Johnson had 111 strikeouts in 118 innings (against 72 walks), with an 8-7 record and 3.26 ERA. He was a late-season recall and kept his ERA under 3.00 for the Expos. Because of his numbers, the Expos project him as a starter in 1989. At Jacksonville in 1987, Johnson went 11-8 with a 3.78 ERA and led the Double-A Southern League in strikeouts with 163. But he also gave up 128 bases on balls in 140 innings, and the Montreal brass decided he needed further seasoning.

Johnson has gained some greatly needed maturity. His 1989 cards should open in the 20- to 25-cent range. That is a little high for investing. Our pick for his best 1989 card is Score.

WALLACE JOHNSON

	BA	G	AB	R	H	2B	3B	HR	RBI	SB
1988	.309	86	94	7	29	5	1	0	3	0
Life	.261	296	406	37	106	13	5	2	37	17

POSITION: Infield
TEAM: Montreal Expos
BORN: December 25, 1956 Gary, IN
HEIGHT: 6′ **WEIGHT:** 173 lbs.
BATS: Both **THROWS:** Right
ACQUIRED: Signed as a free agent, 4/84

A journeyman ballplayer who has been in and out of the Expo organization twice, Johnson had a career year for Montreal in 1988, hitting .309 in 86 games, with two game-winning RBIs in 94 at-bats. He also worked opposing hurlers for 12 walks—giving him an on-base percentage of .387, best on the club. Johnson's future was really in doubt before the start of the 1988 season, having batted .247 in 1987. He began 1983 with Montreal, but he was traded to the Giants, who released him a year later. The Expos re-signed him as a free agent in 1984. Johnson should help the Expos with pinch-hitting and experience off the bench.

Johnson's 1989 cards are commons. Although he has led the league in pinch hits, he has never generated much interest in his cards. Our pick for his best 1989 card is Fleer.

BARRY JONES

	W	L	ERA	G	CG	IP	H	R	BB	SO
1988	3	3	2.84	59	3	82.1	72	28	38	48
Life	8	11	3.59	117	7	163.0	156	78	82	105

POSITION: Pitcher
TEAM: Chicago White Sox
BORN: February 15, 1963 Centerville, IN
HEIGHT: 6′4″ **WEIGHT:** 215 lbs.
BATS: Right **THROWS:** Right
ACQUIRED: Traded from Pirates for Dave LaPoint, 8/88

Jones got another shot at the major leagues with a brief appearance with the White Sox in 1988. Jones had two chances with the 1986 and 1987 Pirates, pitching in 26 and 32 games respectively. One of his biggest problems was control. He issued more than one walk every two innings in both seasons with the Pirates, as well as in his 17-game trial with the White Sox in 1988. He was 2-2 with the ChiSox, with an impressive 2.42 ERA. Jones was a third-round draft pick in 1984, but he hasn't tapped his potential yet.

Jones' 1989 cards will be priced as commons. He simply doesn't have enough experience (not to mention control) for collectors to invest in yet. Our pick for his best 1989 card is Topps.

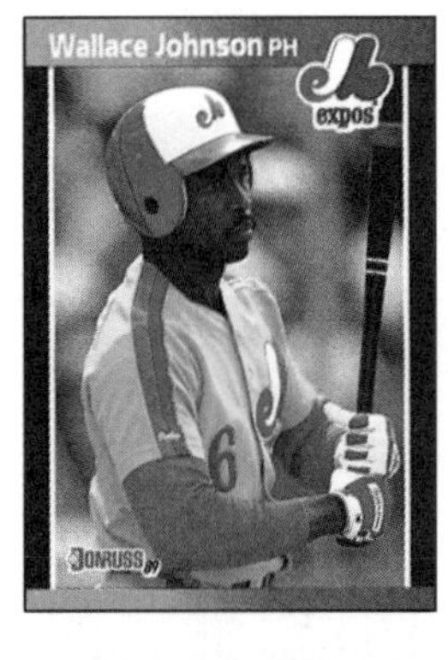

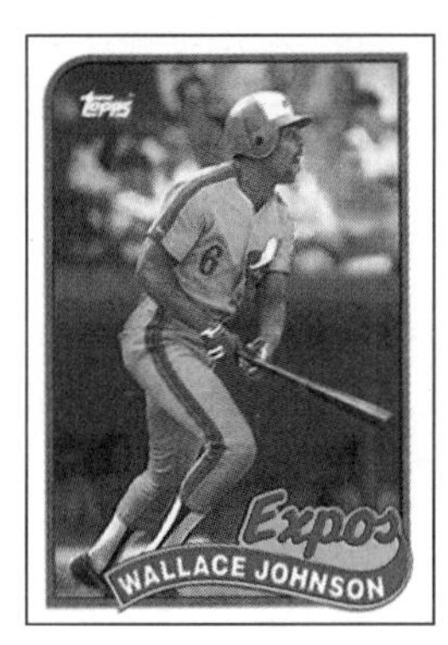

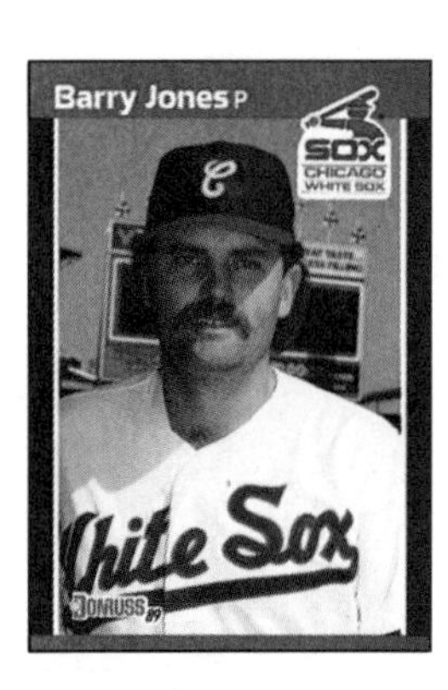

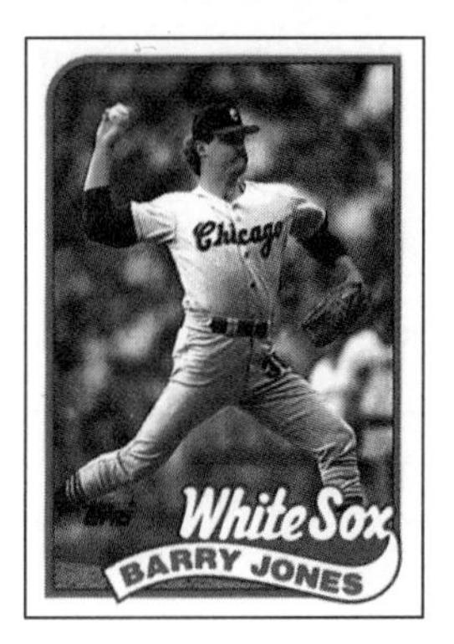

DOUG JONES

	W	L	ERA	G	SV	IP	H	R	BB	SO
1988	3	4	2.27	51	37	83.1	69	26	16	7
Life	10	9	2.81	115	46	195.1	193	79	47	17

POSITION: Pitcher
TEAM: Cleveland Indians
BORN: June 24, 1957 Covina, CA
HEIGHT: 6′2″ **WEIGHT:** 190 lbs.
BATS: Right **THROWS:** Right
ACQUIRED: Signed as a minor league free agent, 4/85

Jones easily shattered the Tribe's old season record of 23 saves in mid-1988 and didn't stop, ending with 37 saves. Although he has only had one full season with the Tribe, he has been in and out of organized baseball since 1978. Jones made a brief appearance with the 1982 Brewers. He led his 1988 club in ERA and appearances. Jones appeared in the 1988 All-Star game. He had eight saves in 1987, going 6-5 in 49 appearances, with a 3.15 ERA. If the Indians hope to improve on their record in 1989 and make a pennant run, they will need another strong performance from Jones.

Despite Jones' record-setting season of relief, his age and the possibility of overwork might prevent a long career. His 1989 cards will be priced initially at 15 to 25 cents. Resist investing in his cards. Our pick for his best 1989 card is Score.

ODELL JONES

	W	L	ERA	G	SV	IP	H	R	BB	SO
1988	5	0	4.35	28	1	80.2	75	47	29	48
Life	24	35	4.42	201	13	549.1	579	304	213	338

POSITION: Pitcher
TEAM: Milwaukee Brewers
BORN: January 13, 1953 Tulare, CA
HEIGHT: 6′3″ **WEIGHT:** 175 lbs.
BATS: Right **THROWS:** Right
ACQUIRED: Signed as a free agent

Jones put in a strong performance with the 1988 Brew Crew. He notched five victories with zero losses and one save. His ERA was 4.35, and he struck out 48 batters in 80⅔ innings, while walking only 29. Before his surprising '88 success, Jones last pitched on the major league level with the Orioles in 1986, going 2-2 with a 3.83 ERA. He helped resuscitate his career by developing a split-fingered fastball. Jones, who first saw action in the major leagues in 1975 with Pittsburgh, had his best season in 1983 with the Rangers, when he notched ten saves and a 3.09 ERA. Jones could help Milwaukee in its bid to win the American League East in 1989.

Jones doesn't have very good major league stats over his nine-year career. His 1989 cards will be in the commons box. Leave them there. Our pick for his best 1989 card is Fleer.

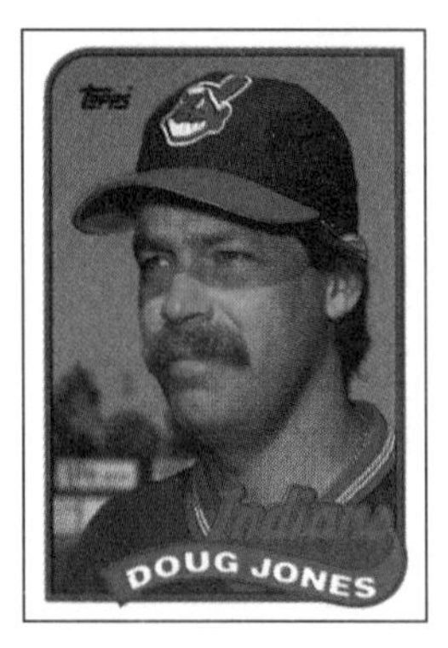

RON JONES

	BA	G	AB	R	H	2B	3B	HR	RBI	SB
1988	.290	33	124	15	36	6	1	8	26	0
Life	.290	33	124	15	36	6	1	8	26	0

POSITION: Outfield
TEAM: Philadelphia Phillies
BORN: June 11, 1964 Sanguin, TX
HEIGHT: 5'11" **WEIGHT:** 200 lbs.
BATS: Left **THROWS:** Right
ACQUIRED: Signed as a free agent, 10/84

After a couple of slow years, Jones came back into the spotlight in 1988, hitting 16 home runs, 75 RBIs, and .267 at Triple-A Maine. Those numbers got him a late-season recall to the Phillies. He displayed good long-ball power, with seven homers in his first 24 games. He made the long jump from Class-A ball to Triple-A in 1986. Jones started at Class-A Clearwater in 1986, batting .371 in 108 games. Promoted to Triple-A Portland in '86, however, he hit an embarrassing .118. That setback loused him up in 1987, when he hit .242 at Maine in 90 contests before injuries ended his season. Jones has earned a long look by the Phillie management in 1989.

Jones' 1988 cards will open in the 35- to 40-cent range. He's a prospect, but invest cautiously at that price. Our pick for his best 1989 card is Score.

TIM JONES

	BA	G	AB	R	H	2B	3B	HR	RBI	SB
1988	.269	31	52	2	14	0	0	0	3	4
Life	.269	31	52	2	14	0	0	0	3	4

POSITION: Shortstop
TEAM: St. Louis Cardinals
BORN: December 1, 1962 Sumter, SC
HEIGHT: 5'10" **WEIGHT:** 175 lbs.
BATS: Left **THROWS:** Right
ACQUIRED: Third-round pick in 6/85 free-agent draft

Jones has the Cardinals thinking the unthinkable—that the venerable Ozzie Smith might soon be expendable. Jones has shown the ability to hit and to field his position at every level of the St. Louis farm system. At Triple-A Louisville in 1988, Jones hit .257 and six homers (a career high). He was called up to the big club, where he played some second base and batted close to the .300 mark. He hit .330 for Double-A Arkansas in a half season in 1987, before being promoted to Louisville—where he hit .268. Jones is in the hunt for a starting job in the St. Louis middle infield in 1989.

Jones looks like he will make a strong bid to be a Cardinal in '89. His 1989 cards will open in the 15- to 20-cent range. Our pick for his best 1989 card is Score.

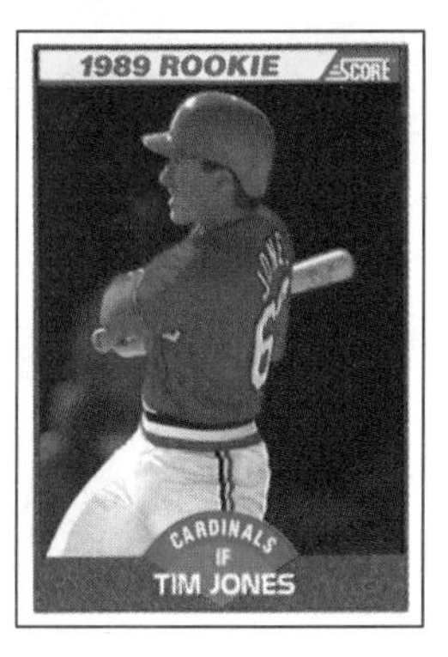

TRACY JONES

	BA	G	AB	R	H	2B	3B	HR	RBI	SB
1988	.295	90	224	29	66	6	1	3	24	18
Life	.299	253	669	98	200	26	4	15	78	56

POSITION: Outfield
TEAM: San Francisco Giants
BORN: March 31, 1961 Hawthorne, CA
HEIGHT: 6′3″ **WEIGHT:** 180 lbs.
BATS: Right **THROWS:** Right
ACQUIRED: Traded from Expos for Mike Aldrete, 12/88

Jones comes to the Giants after a good season. He hit .295 in 90 games (224 at-bats) and drove in 24 runs for the Expos. One of the most promising prospects in the Cincinnati organization, his move to the Giants may be traced to his lack of home run and RBI power. Jones hit .290, with ten homers, 44 RBIs, 53 runs scored, and 31 stolen bases for Cincinnati in 1987. He hit .349 in 46 games for the Reds in 1986, but missed almost two months on the disabled list. Jones, a fiery player, could be the driving force that the Giants need to get back on top.

Jones is still a prospect, and it wouldn't hurt to invest in and hold on to his 1989 cards. They're cheap at the moment at 5 to 10 cents, and they could suddenly leap in value. Our pick for his best 1989 card is Donruss.

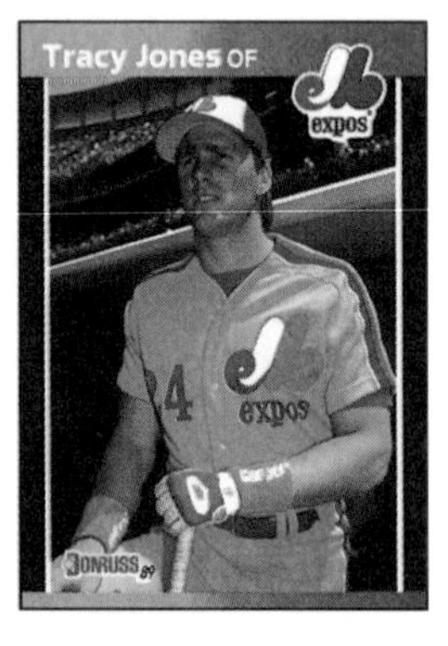

RICKY JORDAN

	BA	G	AB	R	H	2B	3B	HR	RBI	SB
1988	.308	69	273	41	84	15	1	11	43	1
Life	.308	69	273	41	84	15	1	11	43	1

POSITION: First base
TEAM: Philadelphia Phillies
BORN: May 26, 1965 Richmond, CA
HEIGHT: 6′5″ **WEIGHT:** 185 lbs.
BATS: Right **THROWS:** Right
ACQUIRED: First-round pick in 6/83 free-agent draft

Jordan was one of the few bright spots in an otherwise dismal 1988 for the Phillies. Jordan joined the team in mid-season after Von Hayes went on the disabled list. He wasted little time in endearing himself to the Philadelphia fans, showing long-ball power and batting over .300. Jordan strung together an 18-game hitting streak late in the season. At Triple-A Maine in '88, Jordan hit .308, with seven home runs, 36 RBIs, and 42 runs scored. At Double-A Reading in 1987, he hit .318, 16 homers, and 95 RBIs—all career highs. While his fielding still needs work, there's little doubt that Jordan is the Philadelphia first baseman of the future.

Jordan's 1989 cards will open at or around $1 each. They're good investments, because he will have every opportunity to succeed. Our pick for his best 1989 card is Score.

WALLY JOYNER

	BA	G	AB	R	H	2B	3B	HR	RBI	SB
1988	.295	158	597	81	176	31	2	13	85	8
Life	.290	461	1754	263	509	91	6	69	302	21

POSITION: First base
TEAM: California Angels
BORN: June 16, 1962 Atlanta, GA
HEIGHT: 6′2″ **WEIGHT:** 185 lbs.
BATS: Left **THROWS:** Left
ACQUIRED: Third-round pick in 6/83 free-agent draft

Joyner suffered a slight dropoff from his sophomore slugging during 1987, but he proved in 1988 that he's still a capable batsman. He hit .295, with 13 homers and 85 RBIs. During the 1986 and 1987 seasons, Joyner had cumulative totals of 56 home runs and 217 RBIs, so fan expectations were high last year. He finished second in the balloting for Rookie of the Year in 1986, and some felt that he had better stats than did the winner, Jose Canseco. Fans were disappointed with Joyner's power dropoff. But Joyner, with his boyish looks, has quickly cultivated mass appeal unknown to other star players. If he leads the Angels into a World Series, Joyner's card values will explode.

Currently, 1989 Joyner cards should be selling at 75 cents. That's a reasonable price that could bring quick profits if Joyner wins an MVP award. Our pick for his best 1989 card is Donruss.

ROBERTO KELLY

	BA	G	AB	R	H	2B	3B	HR	RBI	SB
1988	.247	38	77	9	19	4	1	1	7	5
Life	.256	61	129	21	33	7	1	2	14	14

POSITION: Outfield
TEAM: New York Yankees
BORN: October 1, 1964
Panama City, Panama
HEIGHT: 6′3″ **WEIGHT:** 185 lbs.
BATS: Right **THROWS:** Right
ACQUIRED: Signed as a free agent, 2/82

Kelly split the 1988 campaign between the Yankees and Triple-A Columbus, and didn't compile dazzling numbers at either location. With the '88 Yankees, he batted about .250. At Columbus, he hit .333 with 11 stolen bases. In a brief stint with the 1987 Yanks, Kelly hit .269. A classic center fielder and an outstanding base runner, he stole 51 bases at Columbus in 1987 while he was batting .278, with 13 home runs and 62 RBIs. His supporters say that he can do everything—run, hit, hit for power, field, and throw—that's necessary for major league stardom. And his stats would appear to support that contention.

The Yankees have been bringing him along patiently for years, but it appears 1989 will be the pivotal year in his career. Kelly's 1989 cards will open around 15 cents. Our pick for his best 1989 card is Topps.

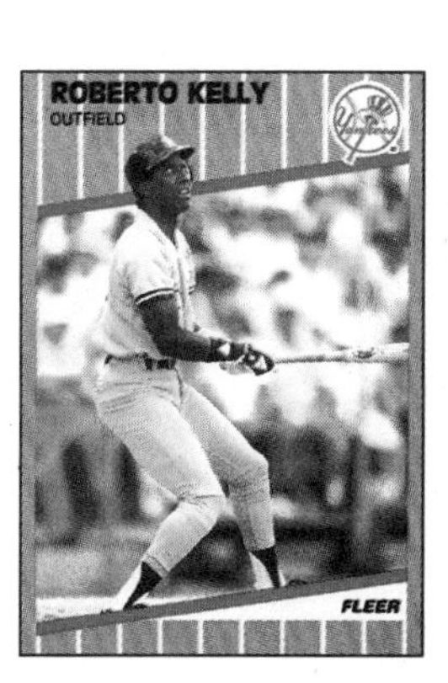

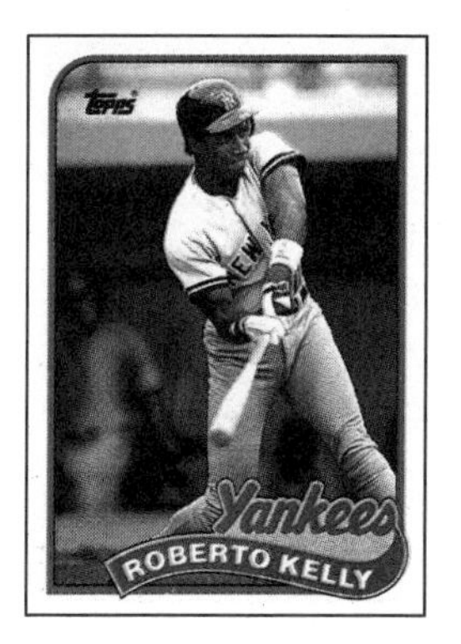

TERRY KENNEDY

	BA	G	AB	R	H	2B	3B	HR	RBI	SB
1988	.226	85	265	20	60	10	0	3	16	0
Life	.266	1190	4150	418	1104	200	11	103	555	4

POSITION: Catcher
TEAM: Baltimore Orioles
BORN: June 4, 1956 Euclid, OH
HEIGHT: 6′4″ **WEIGHT:** 230 lbs.
BATS: Left **THROWS:** Right
ACQUIRED: Traded from Padres with Mark Williamson for Storm Davis, 10/86.

Like most of his teammates, Kennedy suffered through a forgettable season in 1988. His statistics were the lowest since 1980, when he was breaking in with St. Louis. This four-time All-Star was haunted by injuries in 1988, a marked contrast from his 1987 accomplishments. In 1987, Kennedy played in 143 games. He hit .250 with 18 home runs and 62 RBIs. His career highs were with the Padres, when he had 21 homers in '82 and 98 RBIs in '83. Some skeptics may wonder if seven straight seasons of catching more than 100 games finally caught up with Kennedy in 1988. The 1989 Orioles, if they hope to escape from the cellar, need a healthy Kennedy to compete.

If his health returns this year, he has All-Star potential. His cards are good investments at prices of a nickel or less. Our pick for his best 1989 card is Topps.

JIMMY KEY

	W	L	ERA	G	CG	IP	H	R	BB	SO
1988	12	5	3.29	21	2	131.2	127	55	30	65
Life	61	35	3.23	191	17	899.0	817	360	252	496

POSITION: Pitcher
TEAM: Toronto Blue Jays
BORN: April 22, 1961 Huntsville, AL
HEIGHT: 6′1″ **WEIGHT:** 190 lbs.
BATS: Right **THROWS:** Left
ACQUIRED: Third-round pick in 6/82 free-agent draft

Injuries sidelined Key from a potentially great season in 1988. He won 12 out of 21 starts and seemed headed toward a possible 20-game winner's status. Ever since the Blue Jays converted Key from a reliever in 1984 to a starter, he's been a consistent winner. His lifetime winning percentage is .635. If he had a few more starts in 1988, the Blue Jays might have been division winners. Instead, they finished two games out. Prior to his first win in 1985, five years had passed since a lefty starter had won for Toronto. Expect Key, if healthy, to keep on winning in 1989.

Key seems to have many promising seasons ahead of him. At a nickel or less, his cards could become real prizes if he pitches the Jays to their first World Series. Our pick for his best 1989 card is Donruss.

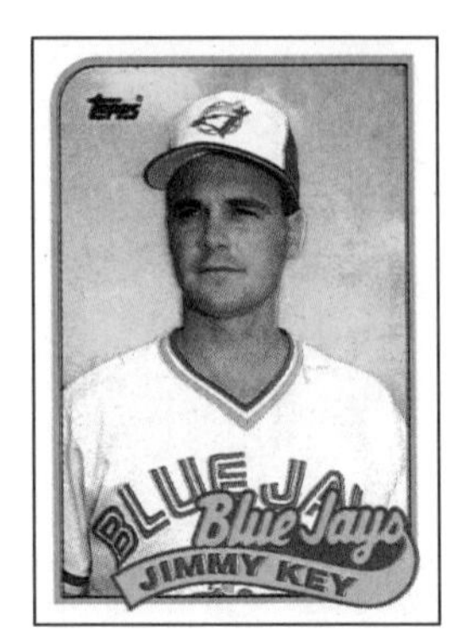

PAUL KILGUS

	W	L	ERA	G	CG	IP	H	R	BB	SO
1988	12	15	4.16	32	5	203.1	190	105	71	88
Life	14	22	4.15	57	5	292.2	285	150	102	130

POSITION: Pitcher
TEAM: Chicago Cubs
BORN: February 2, 1962
Bowling Green, KY
HEIGHT: 6′1″ **WEIGHT:** 175 lbs.
BATS: Left **THROWS:** Left
ACQUIRED: Traded from Rangers with Mitch Williams, Curtis Wilkerson, Steve Wilson, Luis Benitez, and Pablo Delgado for Rafael Palmeiro, Jamie Moyer, and Drew Hall, 12/88

Kilgus is the new lefthanded hope for the Cubs. He was full of surprises with the 1988 Rangers. His 1987 debut amounted to a dismal 2-7 record. In 1988, however, Kilgus won in double figures. He tallied more than 200 innings of work, and led the Rangers staff with three shutouts. Also, he registered the first five complete games of his career in 1988. No Ranger pitcher got tons of offensive support last season, as evidenced by the team's 31 one-run losses. Kilgus, with a different offense supporting him, should win more games in 1989 if he has a few more leads to work with.

Kilgus could become a winner for the first time in 1989. His cards could bring surprising payoffs at their current low prices of three cents or less. Our pick for his best 1989 card is Topps.

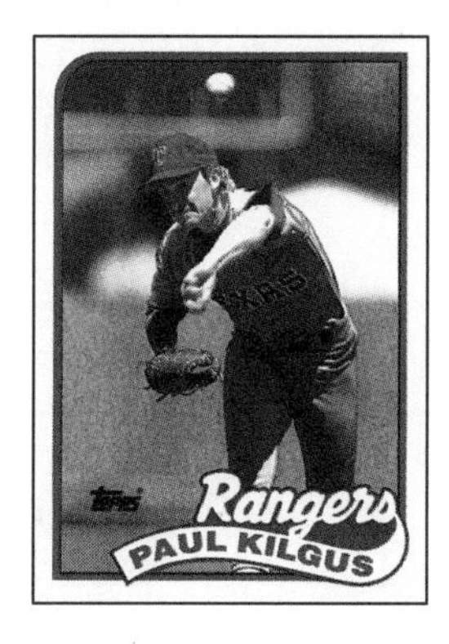

MIKE KINGERY

	BA	G	AB	R	H	2B	3B	HR	RBI	SB
1988	.203	57	123	21	25	6	0	1	9	3
Life	.259	239	686	84	178	39	9	13	75	17

POSITION: Oufield; first base
TEAM: Seattle Mariners
BORN: March 29, 1961 St. James, MN
HEIGHT: 6′ **WEIGHT:** 180 lbs.
BATS: Left **THROWS:** Left
ACQUIRED: Traded from Royals with Scott Bankhead and Steve Shields for Danny Tartabull and Rick Luecken, 12/86

Kingery suffered through the worst slump of his three-year major league career with the 1988 Mariners. After achieving a career-high .280 average as the M's fourth outfielder in 1987, he struggled to keep his average above .200, as he appeared in only 57 games in 1988. Kingery is appreciated by the Mariners both for his fielding and hitting ability. He spelled Alvin Davis at first base and filled in the outfield as well in 1988. In 1987, he led all Seattle outfielders in assists. Kingery will need a good spring training performance, however, to keep his spot on the roster in 1989.

Kingery's cards sell as commons. He'll be 28 years old when the season starts, but has never played a full big league season yet. Avoid his cards until he wins a starting role somewhere. Our pick for his best 1989 card is Topps.

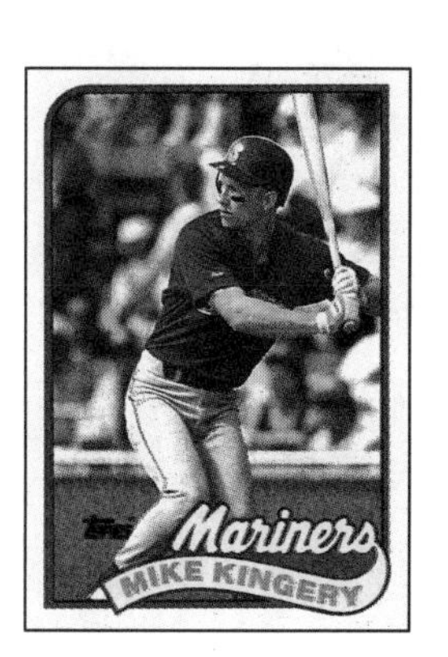

BOB KIPPER

	W	L	ERA	G	SV	IP	H	R	BB	SO
1988	2	6	3.74	50	0	65.0	54	33	26	39
Life	14	26	4.90	101	0	317.2	322	191	122	216

POSITION: Pitcher
TEAM: Pittsburgh Pirates
BORN: July 8, 1964 Aurora, IL
HEIGHT: 6′2″ **WEIGHT:** 200 lbs.
BATS: Right **THROWS:** Left
ACQUIRED: Traded from Angels with Mike Brown and Pat Clements for John Candelaria, George Hendrick, and Al Holland, 8/85

Kipper was 2-6, with a 3.74 ERA in 50 relief appearances for the Pirates in 1988. It was his first year in the bullpen. He was the Angels' first pick in the June 1982 draft. He opened the 1985 season with the Angels. After going 0-1 in two games, Kipper was sent down to the minors, then he was traded to Pittsburgh. He finished the 1985 season with the Pirates, going 1-2. He went 6-8 for the Bucs in 1986 and was 5-9 in 1987, all as a starter. Kipper is a promising pitcher who could have a great year in 1989 if he gets used to being a reliever.

Kipper's best years are still ahead of him, and his cards are worth holding on to as sheer speculation. Right now they're found in the commons box. Our pick for his best 1989 card is Topps.

RON KITTLE

	BA	G	AB	R	H	2B	3B	HR	RBI	SB
1988	.258	75	225	31	58	8	0	18	43	0
Life	.237	670	2154	290	510	74	3	145	370	16

POSITION: Designated hitter; outfield
TEAM: Chicago White Sox
BORN: January 5, 1958 Gary, IN
HEIGHT: 6′3″ **WEIGHT:** 220 lbs.
BATS: Right **THROWS:** Right
ACQUIRED: Signed as a free agent, 11/88

Kittle is expected to supply the White Sox with much-needed run production in 1989. He supplied some full-time power in part-time fashion for the 1988 Tribe. He didn't even appear in half the Tribe's games, yet he was among team leaders in homers with 18. Kittle first gained acclaim as the A.L. Rookie of the Year in 1983 with the White Sox. Kittle pounded 35 homers and 100 RBIs in his first season. He's never matched those totals since. Strikeouts have always been Kittle's biggest foe. In 1988, he whiffed 65 times, one strikeout for every 3.46 plate appearances. Nevertheless, Kittle's homer-hitting ability should keep him working for several more seasons.

A low career average and a high number of strikeouts have limited any value increases in Kittle's cards. His 1989 issues will be a nickel or less. Our pick for his best 1989 card is Donruss.

BOB KNEPPER

	W	L	ERA	G	CG	IP	H	R	BB	SO
1988	14	5	3.14	27	3	175.0	156	70	67	103
Life	136	140	3.54	398	77	2498.1	2491	1132	763	1385

POSITION: Pitcher
TEAM: Houston Astros
BORN: May 25, 1954 Akron, OH
HEIGHT: 6′2″ **WEIGHT:** 210 lbs.
BATS: Left **THROWS:** Left
ACQUIRED: Traded from Giants with Chris Bourjos for Enos Cabell, 12/80

This veteran lefty went into the 1988 season fourth in career wins among active N.L. hurlers. Knepper won 14 games in 1988. Although he had a terrible 8-17 year in 1987, Knepper won at least 15 games a year for the Astros from 1984 to 1986. His career high for victories is 17. He is a valuable commodity for the pitching-rich Astros, who served him up as a starter behind Mike Scott and Nolan Ryan. The outspoken hurler, at age 35, has hinted that he'd like to retire after 1989. Possibly a 1989 pennant could keep his durable left arm in the Astro rotation for a few more years.

Knepper's 1989 cards will sell for a nickel or less. Because of a seesaw career, Knepper's cards would be questionable investments if he announces his 1989 retirement. Our pick for his best 1989 card is Topps.

CHAD KREUTER

	BA	G	AB	R	H	2B	3B	HR	RBI	SB
1988	.275	16	51	3	14	2	1	1	5	0
Life	.275	16	51	3	14	2	1	1	5	0

POSITION: Catcher
TEAM: Texas Rangers
BORN: August 26, 1964
Marin County, CA
HEIGHT: 6′2″ **WEIGHT:** 190 lbs.
BATS: Both **THROWS:** Right
ACQUIRED: Seventh-round pick in 6/85 free-agent draft

In his big league debut, Kreuter keyed the Rangers' 9-1 win over the Oakland A's with a single and a three-run home run in the same inning. He joined the Rangers after hitting .265 with 51 RBIs for Texas League champion Tulsa. A switch-hitter, he has yet to hit for a high average, but scouts feel that his offensive skills are improving on a yearly basis. Defensively, they say, he's already a big league receiver. His '88 stats are a marked improvement from the .217 he batted at Port Charlotte in 1987 and the .220 he hit at Salem the year before. Kreuter has the talent to be a major league backstop for years.

Kreuter's 1989 cards should open for 10 to 15 cents. Watch to see if his offense improves before making an investment. Our pick for his best 1989 card is Score.

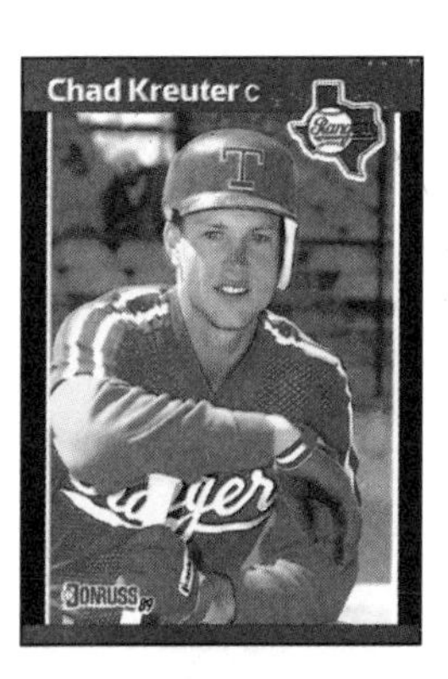

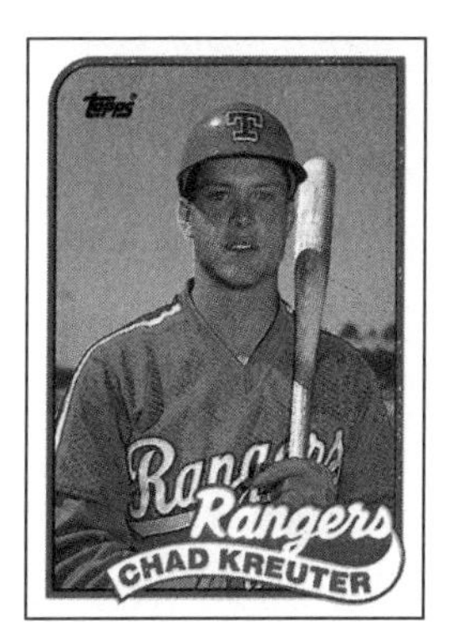

JOHN KRUK

	BA	G	AB	R	H	2B	3B	HR	RBI	SB
1988	.241	120	378	54	91	17	1	9	44	5
Life	.287	380	1103	159	317	47	5	33	173	25

POSITION: Outfield; first base
TEAM: San Diego Padres
BORN: February 9, 1961 Charleston, WV
HEIGHT: 5'10" **WEIGHT:** 190 lbs.
BATS: Left **THROWS:** Left
ACQUIRED: Third-round pick in 6/81 free-agent draft

Kruk was one of the biggest disappointments on the Padres. After his first two seasons of .300-plus hitting, everyone thought he would be the team's next Steve Garvey. However, in just 120 games, Kruk hit a career-low .241 with nine homers and 44 RBIs. Those totals might surpass those of some major leaguers, but future stars like Kruk seem beyond such a season. In 1987, he had an incredible season. He hit .313 with 20 homers, 91 RBIs, and even stole 18 bases. Kruk, only 28 years old, has lots of time left in his career and should shake his slump in 1989.

Kruk's 1989 cards should be about 15 cents each. If you spot one of his cards for a dime or less, grab it. He should be playing at his best in 1989. Get his cards while they're briefly underpriced. Our pick for his best 1989 card is Score.

MIKE KRUKOW

	W	L	ERA	G	CG	IP	H	R	BB	SO
1988	7	4	3.54	20	1	124.2	111	51	31	75
Life	120	114	3.90	361	41	2147.0	2151	1049	749	1460

POSITION: Pitcher
TEAM: San Francisco Giants
BORN: January 31, 1952 Long Beach, CA
HEIGHT: 6'4" **WEIGHT:** 205 lbs.
BATS: Right **THROWS:** Right
ACQUIRED: Traded from Phillies with Mark Davis and C. L. Penigar for Jose Morgan and Al Holland, 12/82

Krukow again failed to regain his past winning form for the 1988 San Francisco Giants. He had his biggest season ever in 1986 with the Giants. He went 20-9, with ten complete games, two shutouts, and a career-low 3.05 ERA. His success evaporated in 1987, as his record dipped to 5-6. The struggle continued in 1988, as Krukow won just seven out of 20 games. He has been in organized baseball since 1973, and had pitched with the Cubs and Phillies prior to his stay with the Giants. At age 37, Krukow faces a make-or-break season with the 1989 Giants.

Card investors may have learned a painful lesson after Krukow's brief glory in 1986. It's best to build on consistent achievements, not just selected accomplishments. Krukow's 1989 cards, priced at a nickel or less, should be avoided. Our pick for his best 1989 card is Topps.

JEFF KUNKEL

	BA	G	AB	R	H	2B	3B	HR	RBI	SB
1988	.227	55	154	14	35	9	3	2	15	0
Life	.217	130	345	32	75	11	6	7	26	4

POSITION: Infield
TEAM: Texas Rangers
BORN: March 25, 1962
West Palm Beach, FL
HEIGHT: 6′2″ **WEIGHT:** 175 lbs.
BATS: Right **THROWS:** Right
ACQUIRED: First-round pick in 6/83 free-agent draft

Kunkel had a bad year at the plate, hitting .227. He was the projected Ranger shortstop when he was drafted in 1983, but he battled injuries in his first four years in pro baseball. Kunkel was called up in 1984, and he hit .204 in 50 games. He spent the next three years trying to get his game back together. He is now a utility infielder; the Rangers, by re-signing Scott Fletcher and trading for Julio Franco, have indicated that Kunkel doesn't have a future as a starter in Texas. Kunkel is a former "can't miss" who probably will play out his career in a back-up capacity.

Kunkel's 1989 cards will be priced as commons. He is 27, so if he did turn his career around, he probably wouldn't stay around long enough to accumulate any great stats. Our pick for his best 1989 card is Fleer.

MIKE LaCOSS

	W	L	ERA	G	CG	IP	H	R	BB	SO
1988	7	7	3.62	19	1	114.1	99	55	47	70
Life	81	84	4.01	339	24	1464.1	1507	747	597	636

POSITION: Pitcher
TEAM: San Francisco Giants
BORN: May 30, 1956 Glendale, CA
HEIGHT: 6′6″ **WEIGHT:** 200 lbs.
BATS: Right **THROWS:** Right
ACQUIRED: Signed as a free agent, 3/86

LaCoss, appearing in his 11th major league season, had a mediocre season as a starter for the 1988 Giants. After 1987, he had a light year as a starter. Coming off a 13-10 season in 1987 pitching 171 innings as a starter-reliever, LaCoss saw his victories cut by nearly one half last season. He seemed reborn as a pitcher after joining the Giants in 1986. Following a 14-9 rookie season with the 1979 Cincinnati Reds (which earned him a berth on the N.L. All-Star team), he floundered with Houston and Kansas City. However, LaCoss has remained one of the Giants' most consistent hurlers.

LaCoss doesn't have a lifetime winning record. His career stats don't merit investing in his 1989 cards, which will sell at three cents or less. Our pick for his best 1989 card is Topps.

MIKE LAGA

	BA	G	AB	R	H	2B	3B	HR	RBI	SB
1988	.130	41	100	5	13	0	0	1	4	0
Life	.199	148	376	34	75	16	0	13	44	1

POSITION: First base
TEAM: St. Louis Cardinals
BORN: June 4, 1960 Ridgewood, NJ
HEIGHT: 6′3″ **WEIGHT:** 198 lbs.
BATS: Left **THROWS:** Left
ACQUIRED: Traded from Tigers with Ken Hill for Mike Heath, 8/86

Laga (.130 average, one home run in 100 at-bats) could help the Cardinals solve their lack of power problem if he could swing the bat like he did on the farm. He was once among the crown jewels of the Tigers' farm system, hitting 30-or-more home runs three different seasons (1981, 1982, and 1984) for Detroit's minor league teams. The last time the oft-injured Laga was healthy enough to play a full season for anybody was 1984, when he played in 153 games for Triple-A Evansville, had a .265 batting average, 30 home runs, and 94 runs batted in. He played in 1988 at Triple-A Louisville, where he hit .204. Laga batted .304 for Louisville in 1987, with 29 homers and 91 RBIs.

Laga's cards are commons. There is no investment potential that we can see. Our pick for his best 1989 card is Score.

DENNIS LAMP

	W	L	ERA	G	SV	IP	H	R	BB	SO
1988	7	6	3.48	46	0	82.2	92	39	19	49
Life	82	85	3.92	478	33	1493.0	1632	747	452	675

POSITION: Pitcher
TEAM: Boston Red Sox
BORN: September 23, 1952
Los Angeles, CA
HEIGHT: 6′4″ **WEIGHT:** 200 lbs.
BATS: Right **THROWS:** Right
ACQUIRED: Signed as a free agent, 1/88

Lamp signed on with the Red Sox in 1988, helping Boston to win the tough A.L. East. In 1988, he was 7-6, with a 3.48 ERA, all in relief. He struck out 49 batters and gave up just 19 bases on balls in 82⅔ innings of work. He really turned his career around. Lamp had compiled ERAs over 5.00 for two seasons in a row prior to 1988. He was 1-3 with Oakland in 1987, with a 5.08 ERA; he was 2-6 with Toronto in 1986, with a 5.05 ERA. Lamp's best season was in 1985 with Toronto. He was 11-0 with a 3.32 ERA. He compiled 15 saves in 1983. Lamp is a valuable pitcher who will help the BoSox as both a starter and a reliever.

Lamp's 1989 cards will be in the commons box. He hasn't compiled the career stats to merit investment in his cards. Our pick for his best 1989 card is Fleer.

LES LANCASTER

	W	L	ERA	G	SV	IP	H	R	BB	SO
1988	4	6	3.78	44	5	85.2	89	42	34	36
Life	12	9	4.46	71	5	218.0	227	118	85	114

POSITION: Pitcher
TEAM: Chicago Cubs
BORN: April 21, 1962 Dallas, TX
HEIGHT: 6′2″ **WEIGHT:** 205 lbs.
BATS: Right **THROWS:** Right
ACQUIRED: Signed as a free agent, 6/85

Lancaster worked his way up through the Cub farm system, and he was used mostly in relief in 1988. He ran up a 4-6 record in 44 games (three starts and one complete game), saving five and registering a 3.78 ERA. In 85⅔ innings of work, Lancaster fanned 36, walked 34, and was credited with three wild pitches. His debut in the majors in 1987 resulted in more production. Lancaster was 8-3 in 132 innings with 78 strikeouts. His ERA (4.90) was a little high, but he was usually effective. Lancaster started '87 at Triple-A Iowa, where he was 5-3 with a 3.22 ERA.

Lancaster will be 27 this season, and it's nearing crunch time in his career. His cards, at the moment, are not good investment buys. You'll find them in the commons box. Our pick for his best 1989 card is Fleer.

MARK LANGSTON

	W	L	ERA	G	CG	IP	H	R	BB	SO
1988	15	11	3.34	35	9	261.1	222	108	110	235
Life	70	62	4.03	166	39	1124.1	1008	566	556	1018

POSITION: Pitcher
TEAM: Seattle Mariners
BORN: August 20, 1960 San Diego, CA
HEIGHT: 6′2″ **WEIGHT:** 180 lbs.
BATS: Right **THROWS:** Left
ACQUIRED: Third-round pick in 6/81 free-agent draft

It's amazing that Langston even had a .500 record in 1988. He was 15-11 with a 3.34 ERA and 235 Ks. Don't think that the lefthander is untalented, because he's anything but. However, last season the Mariners pitchers got very little run-scoring support. He finished second in the strikeout race, missing his chance to lead the A.L. in that department for the fourth time. In 1987, Langston was 19-13, with a 3.84 ERA and a career-high 262 strikeouts in 272 innings. He has accumulated 70 victories in five seasons. If you look past the losses Langston will suffer in 1989 and check his ability, you'll see why he'd be a superstar with a division contender.

Langston's 1989 cards should sell at a nickel apiece. Invest heartily. If he ever pitches for a competitive team, his winning percentage will finally reflect his star abilities. Our pick for his best 1989 card is Fleer.

CARNEY LANSFORD

	BA	G	AB	R	H	2B	3B	HR	RBI	SB
1988	.279	150	556	80	155	20	2	7	57	29
Life	.290	1440	5588	803	1622	259	36	139	696	164

POSITION: Third base
TEAM: Oakland A's
BORN: February 7, 1957 San Jose, CA
HEIGHT: 6'2" **WEIGHT:** 195 lbs.
BATS: Right **THROWS:** Right
ACQUIRED: Traded from Red Sox with Gary Hancock for Jeff Newman and Tony Armas, 12/82

Lansford has given the A's the consistent third baseman they've missed since the days of Sal Bando. His homer and RBI tallies fell off dramatically in 1988, when he hit .279, with seven homers and 57 RBIs. He hit .289 in 1987, with 19 homers and 76 RBIs. Still, Lansford hit in the .270s last season and came into his own as a base bandit, swiping 29 bases. He is a get-your-uniform-dirty type of player. This one-time batting champ may not rival the hitting displays of Jose Canseco and Mark McGwire, but Lansford will be providing a veteran bat to the lineup as the A's try to defend their pennant.

Lansford's 1989 cards are safe investments at 5 to 10 cents each. If he returns to his previous form, his cards could rise to a quarter by year's end. Our pick for his best 1989 card is Fleer.

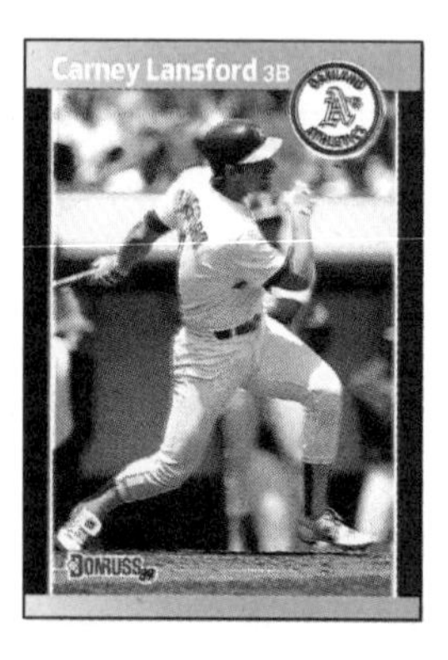

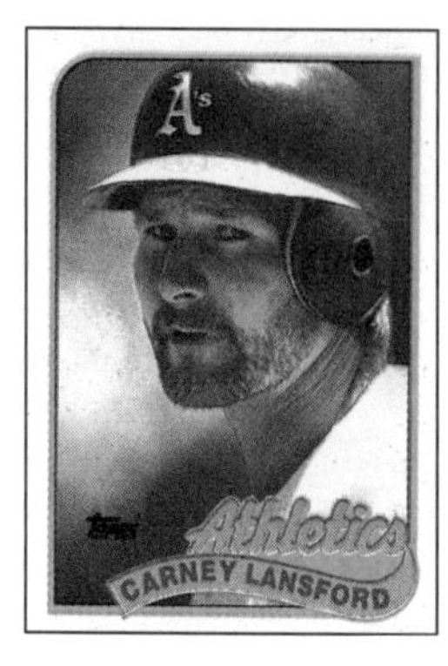

DAVE LaPOINT

	W	L	ERA	G	CG	IP	H	R	BB	SO
1988	14	13	3.25	33	2	213.1	205	87	57	98
Life	67	66	3.81	244	9	1210.2	1262	581	451	681

POSITION: Pitcher
TEAM: New York Yankees
BORN: July 29, 1959 Glens Falls, NY
HEIGHT: 6'3" **WEIGHT:** 205 lbs.
BATS: Left **THROWS:** Left
ACQUIRED: Signed as a free agent, 12/88

LaPoint signed on with the Yankees, who want him to help bring the pennant back to the Bronx. In 1988, he was 4-2 in eight starts for the Pirates and 10-11 in 25 starts with the White Sox. His 14 wins were a career high—previously he had won 12 games twice (1983 and 1984) as a member of the Cardinals. Originally signed by Milwaukee in 1977, LaPoint was with St. Louis until traded to the Giants in 1985. He has also pitched for Detroit and San Diego, both in 1986 as the result of trades. LaPoint will be looked upon as a key member of the Yankee rotation in 1989.

LaPoint, at 29, is a marginal starter. He could still attain star status with a 20-win season for the Yanks. For now, he's not a big-ticket investment for card collectors. Our pick for his best 1989 card is Fleer.

BARRY LARKIN

	BA	G	AB	R	H	2B	3B	HR	RBI	SB
1988	.296	151	588	91	174	32	5	12	56	40
Life	.275	317	1186	182	326	52	10	27	118	69

POSITION: Shortstop
TEAM: Cincinnati Reds
BORN: April 28, 1964 Cincinnati, OH
HEIGHT: 6′ **WEIGHT:** 180 lbs.
BATS: Right **THROWS:** Right
ACQUIRED: First-round pick in 6/85 free-agent draft

Last season looked like the beginning of a great career for Larkin. He registered career highs in all offensive categories in his first full year as the team's starting shortstop. Larkin hit .296 and belted 12 homers and 56 RBIs. He also stole 40 bases. He led Reds regulars in games played, hits, and stolen bases. He was selected to play in the All-Star game. In 1987, Larkin hit .244, but he belted 12 homers and won the shortstop job from Kurt Stillwell, who was traded for Danny Jackson. One of the lesser-known members of the 1984 U.S. Olympic team, Larkin is quickly becoming known as one of the most flashy and versatile shortstops in the game today.

Larkin's 1989 cards will be priced at 10 cents or less. Buy them quickly, because those values will increase steadily. Our pick for his best 1989 card is Donruss.

GENE LARKIN

	BA	G	AB	R	H	2B	3B	HR	RBI	SB
1988	.267	149	505	56	135	30	2	8	70	3
Life	.267	234	738	79	197	41	4	12	98	4

POSITION: First base; designated hitter
TEAM: Minnesota Twins
BORN: October 24, 1962 Flushing, NY
HEIGHT: 6′3″ **WEIGHT:** 195 lbs.
BATS: Both **THROWS:** Right
ACQUIRED: 20th-round pick in 6/84 free-agent draft

In his first full season with the Twins in 1988, Larkin repeated his hitting exploits of 1987. He played just part-time with the Twins during his rookie season, and he hit a tidy .266. In 1988, serving both as a designated hitter and a backup first baseman, Larkin added to his first-season feats. He registered eight homers, 70 RBIs, and a .267 average. At age 26, he has a long career to look forward to. After two and a half years of minor league fine-tuning, Larkin seems ready to become one of Minnesota's most dependable hitters in the years ahead.

Larkin's 1989 cards should start at a dime. That price is a good one for investing. When Larkin becomes a consistent .300 hitter, that price will shoot up fast. Our pick for his best 1989 card is Fleer.

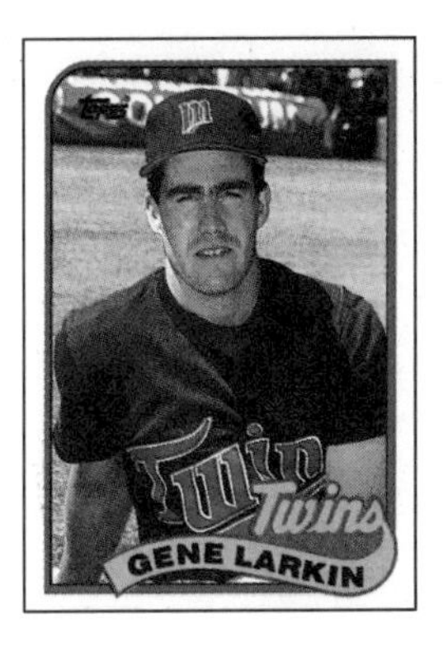

TIM LAUDNER

	BA	G	AB	R	H	2B	3B	HR	RBI	SB
1988	.251	117	375	38	94	18	1	13	54	0
Life	.225	634	1799	197	405	86	4	71	236	2

POSITION: Catcher
TEAM: Minnesota Twins
BORN: June 7, 1958 Mason City, IA
HEIGHT: 6'3" **WEIGHT:** 214 lbs.
BATS: Right **THROWS:** Right
ACQUIRED: Third-round pick in 6/79 free-agent draft

Laudner appeared in a career-high 117 games, and appeared to have firm hold on the Twins' starting catcher's job in 1988. He set several personal offensive records in 1988, including average, hits, doubles, RBIs, and runs scored. Laudner, a member of the Twins since 1981, has faced yearly battles for playing time. His defense is one of his best assets. In 1988, he committed just five errors. He'll be given the task of handling a vastly improved pitching staff. The Twins hope to recapture their past world championship in 1989. Laudner will play a large role in that quest.

Laudner's cards are commons, sold at three cents or less. His 1988 season was promising, but his career stats are lackluster. Refrain from investing until he has further success. Our pick for his best 1989 card is Fleer.

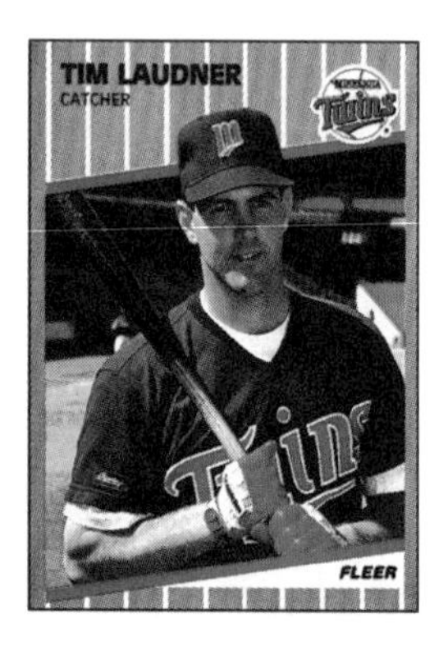

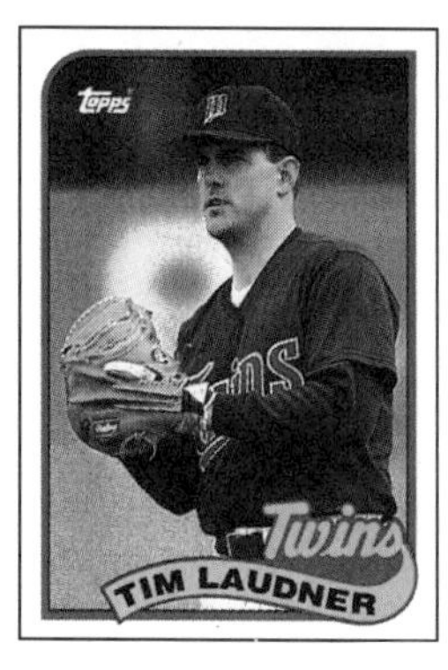

MIKE LaVALLIERE

	BA	G	AB	R	H	2B	3B	HR	RBI	SB
1988	.261	120	352	24	92	18	0	2	47	3
Life	.261	369	1036	77	270	48	2	6	119	3

POSITION: Catcher
TEAM: Pittsburgh Pirates
BORN: August 18, 1960 Charlotte, NC
HEIGHT: 5'10" **WEIGHT:** 180 lbs.
BATS: Both **THROWS:** Right
ACQUIRED: Traded from Cardinals with Andy Van Slyke and Mike Dunne for Tony Pena, 4/87

LaValliere's teammates call him a "player's player," and he earned this admiration in 1988 with another fine season, hitting .261, with two homers and 47 RBIs. Boasting only three passed balls in 1,815 innings of catching duties coming into 1988, LaValliere's consistency and hustle are obvious. A 1987 Gold Glove winner who chips away steadily at hits, LaValliere is taken for granted by the media. But the Bucs sing his praises loud and long. He has stepped from the shadow of former Pirates catcher Tony Pena to become a star in his own right, and LaValliere deserves credit for helping mold an impressive pitching staff for the 1989 season.

With near-perfect fielding and a future as a switch-hitter, LaValliere is a dependable influence on the Pirates, and his 1989 cards will be bargains at a nickel or less. Our pick for his best 1989 card is Topps.

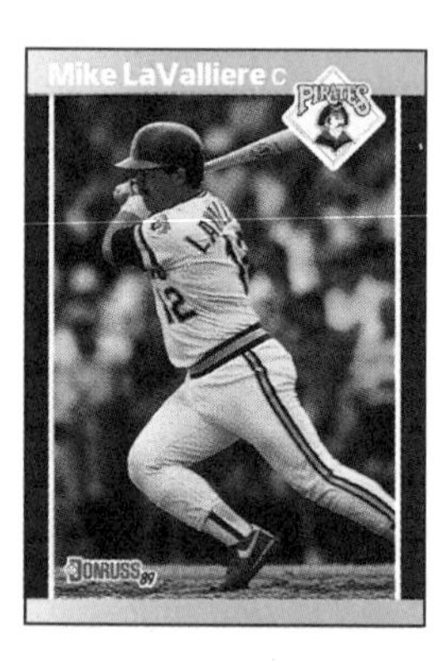

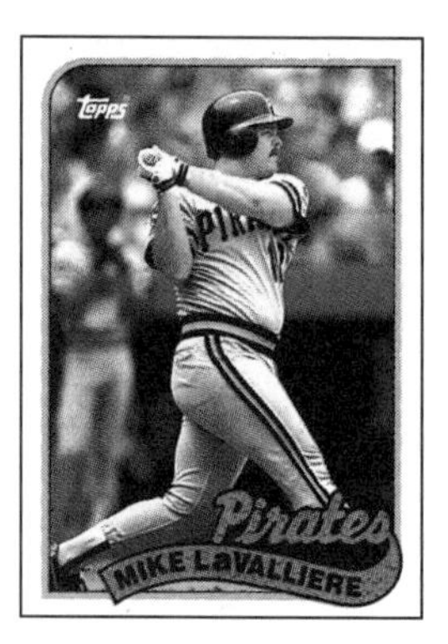

VANCE LAW

	BA	G	AB	R	H	2B	3B	HR	RBI	SB
1988	.293	151	556	73	163	29	2	11	78	1
Life	.260	1008	3260	404	848	164	22	64	391	32

POSITION: Third base
TEAM: Chicago Cubs
BORN: October 1, 1956 Boise, ID
HEIGHT: 6′1″ **WEIGHT:** 190 lbs.
BATS: Right **THROWS:** Right
ACQUIRED: Signed as a free agent, 12/87

One of the most pleasant surprises for the 1988 Cubs was new third baseman Law. Having to replace departed Cub Keith Moreland wasn't easy to begin with, but Law responded with a career-high .293 batting average, an on-base average near that of teammate Mark "Amazing" Grace, and 78 RBIs. Law has hit double figures in home runs for four of the last five years. A versatile player, Law has appeared at all three bases and on the mound. He is the son of Cy Young Award-winner Vernon Law. Vance is a solid player who is a great asset to Chicago.

Law's cards remain available for five cents or less. A winning 1989 season with the Cubs, however, would surely enhance his cards' short-term collectibility. Our pick for his best 1989 card is Topps.

CHARLIE LEA

	W	L	ERA	G	CG	IP	H	R	BB	SO
1988	7	7	4.85	24	0	130.0	156	79	50	72
Life	62	48	3.54	152	22	923.0	864	407	341	535

POSITION: Pitcher
TEAM: Minnesota Twins
BORN: December 25, 1956
Orleans, France
HEIGHT: 6′4″ **WEIGHT:** 195 lbs.
BATS: Right **THROWS:** Right
ACQUIRED: Signed as a free agent, 11/87

Lea made one of the most admirable comebacks of 1988. He had been on the disabled list for practically all of 1985 and 1986, but he came back and pitched again last seaso for Minnesota. The Expos, Lea's old team, were reluctant about re-signing him, so he found a team in need of pitching. Lea went 7-7 with Minnesota, which might seem only passable to some. For Lea, however, it's a moral victory, considering that many players would have retired when faced with such an injury. He was the N.L.'s winning pitcher in the 1984 All-Star game. Lea is a tough athlete and an inspirational player.

Lea's 1989 cards should be a nickel or less. If he leads the 1989 team in wins, his comback will make headlines. His cards' values, too, would benefit from such publicity. Our pick for his best 1989 card is Fleer.

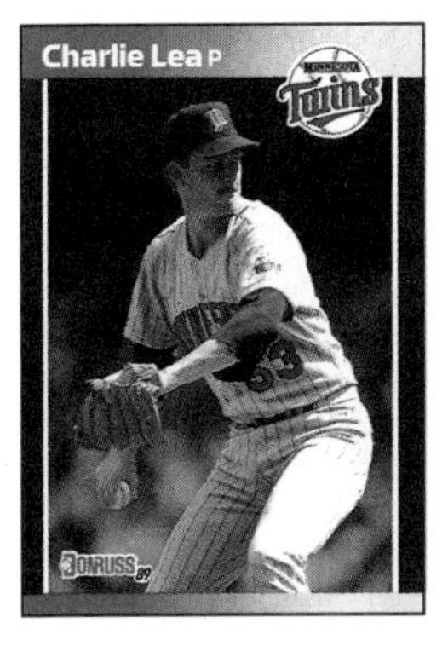

RICK LEACH

	BA	G	AB	R	H	2B	3B	HR	RBI	SB
1988	.276	87	199	21	55	13	1	0	23	0
Life	.263	611	1306	149	344	73	9	15	144	6

POSITION: Outfield; designated hitter
TEAM: Toronto Blue Jays
BORN: May 4, 1957 Ann Arbor, MI
HEIGHT: 6′ **WEIGHT:** 195 lbs.
BATS: Left **THROWS:** Left
ACQUIRED: Signed as a free agent, 4/84

Leach continued to be a key member of the Toronto bench in 1988. He pinch-hit, served as a designated hitter, and played the outfield. He had a .276 average and 23 RBIs in 199 at-bats, but he didn't hit a home run. Leach, a Michigan native, enjoyed what must have been two childhood dreams of any boy in that state. He became a star quarterback at the University of Michigan, then started a pro baseball career with the Detroit Tigers. The Tigers released Leach in 1983, and he was adopted by the Blue Jays. Toronto's gamble paid off. Four years later, Leach is one of the team's top substitutes.

Cards of Leach will be about three cents each in 1989. As a nonstarter, Leach's cards aren't good investments. Our pick for his best 1989 card is Fleer.

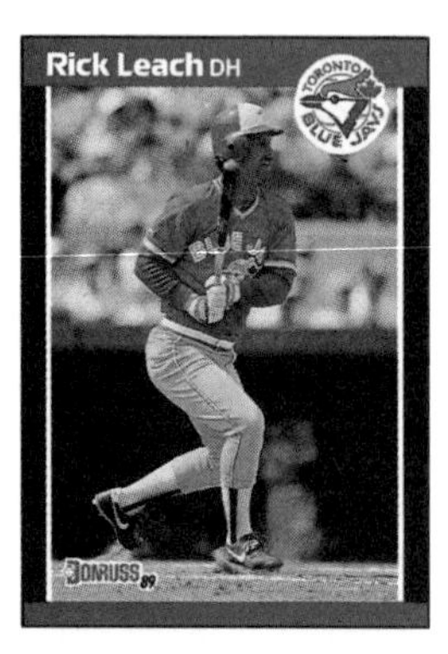

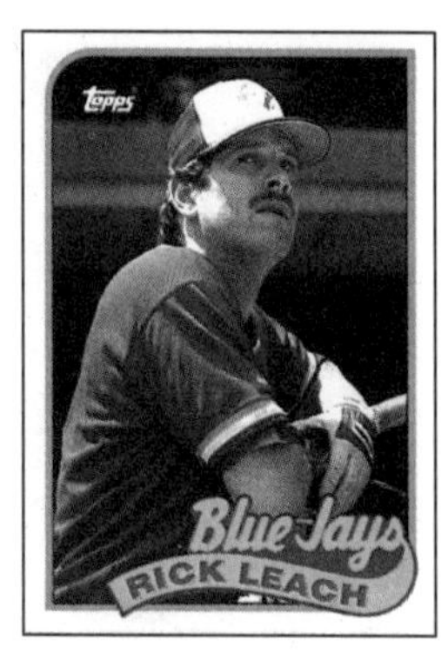

TERRY LEACH

	W	L	ERA	G	SV	IP	H	R	BB	SO
1988	7	2	2.54	52	3	92.0	95	32	24	51
Life	24	9	3.05	166	7	366.0	353	141	100	192

POSITION: Pitcher
TEAM: New York Mets
BORN: March 13, 1954 Selma, AL
HEIGHT: 6′ **WEIGHT:** 215 lbs.
BATS: Right **THROWS:** Right
ACQUIRED: Re-signed as a free agent, 4/87

Rescued from the scrap pile by the Mets in 1987, Leach rewarded their confidence with a sparkling 11-1 record in 44 games with a 3.22 ERA and 61 strikeouts in 131⅓ innings of work. To prove that 1987 was no fluke, he went 7-2 for them last year in 52 games, mostly as a long or middle reliever. Leach had only won six games in the first four years of his career. In fact, he went to spring training in 1987 as a nonroster player, and not a single one of the bubble-gum card companies issued a regular Leach card for that year. Leach is an unsung hurler on the great Mets' staff.

Leach's 1989 cards are priced as commons. Since he's a middle reliever, his cards' values will never appreciate. Our pick for his best 1989 card is Topps.

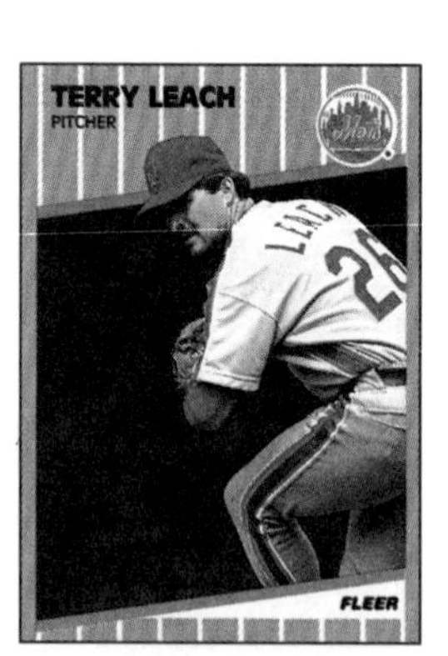

TIM LEARY

	W	L	ERA	G	CG	IP	H	R	BB	SO
1988	17	11	2.91	35	9	228.2	201	87	56	180
Life	37	42	3.78	135	13	624.1	654	302	176	421

POSITION: Pitcher
TEAM: Los Angeles Dodgers
BORN: March 21, 1958
Santa Monica, CA
HEIGHT: 6'3" **WEIGHT:** 205 lbs.
BATS: Right **THROWS:** Right
ACQUIRED: Traded from Brewers with Tim Crews for Greg Brock, 12/86

Leary, a righthander with good control, joined the Dodgers along the comeback trail. Many fans were shocked when the Dodgers traded away a first baseman like Greg Brock to obtain Leary from the Brewers. After a horrendous 3-11 season in 1987, many baseball people thought Leary was finished. However, he made an amazing comeback in 1988, flirting with the 20-game plateau. He had a good strikeout-to-walk ratio in '88. Following his 9-0 record after one season of Mexican League ball, his 1988 return to form seemed imminent. Leary should be a key starter in the Dodger rotation for a few more years.

After only one impressive season, Leary's cards should be priced as commons in 1989. Gobble them up, then cash in when he reaches the 20-win mark. Our pick for his best 1989 card is Fleer.

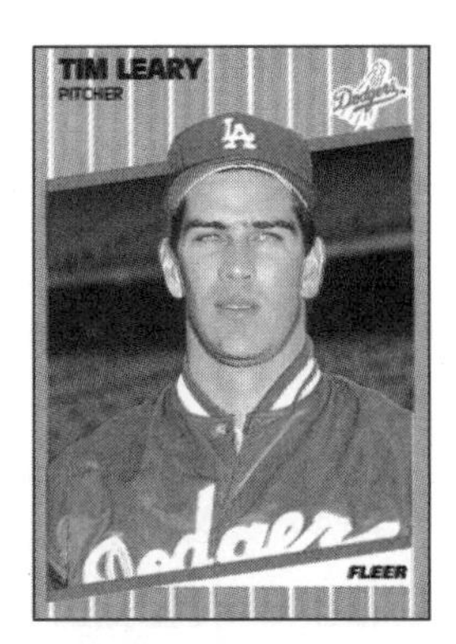

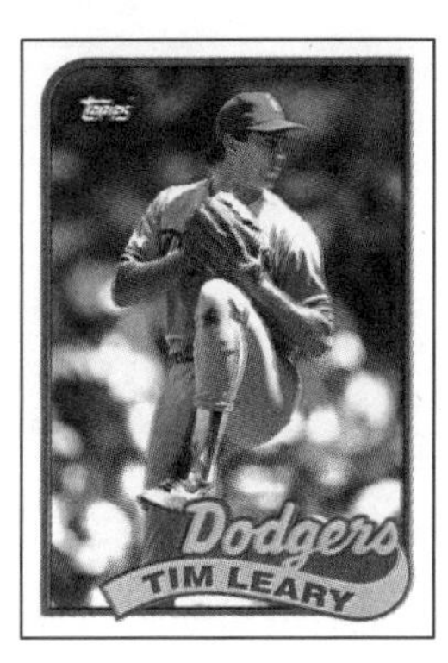

MANNY LEE

	BA	G	AB	R	H	2B	3B	HR	RBI	SB
1988	.291	116	381	38	111	16	3	2	38	3
Life	.268	271	620	69	166	18	7	4	56	6

POSITION: Outfield
TEAM: Toronto Blue Jays
BORN: June 17, 1965 San Pedro de Macoris, Dominican Republic
HEIGHT: 5'9" **WEIGHT:** 151 lbs.
BATS: Both **THROWS:** Right
ACQUIRED: Drafted from Astros, 12/84

Lee is one of many talented players the Blue Jays discovered buried in the minor league systems of other teams. He made the most of his opportunities with Toronto in 1988 by doubling most of his accomplishments of the past three seasons. Beginning in 1985, Lee received minimal playing time. However, last season was his chance to shine. His career average was .230 going into 1988, when he hit a career-best .291. He filled in ably at a number of positions, giving his Blue Jays much-needed bench strength. It's questionable whether he can break into the starting lineup for Toronto in 1989. But based on his 1988 performance, Lee certainly deserves a chance.

Lee's cards are commons. As soon as Lee can come close to duplicating his success of 1988, his cards would be considerable investments. Our pick for his best 1989 card is Fleer.

CRAIG LEFFERTS

	W	L	ERA	G	SV	IP	H	R	BB	SO
1988	3	8	2.92	64	11	92.1	74	33	23	58
Life	30	35	3.06	402	34	576.2	507	219	183	351

POSITION: Pitcher
TEAM: San Francisco Giants
BORN: September 29, 1957 Munich, West Germany
HEIGHT: 6′1″ **WEIGHT:** 210 lbs.
BATS: Left **THROWS:** Left
ACQUIRED: Traded from San Diego with Dave Dravecky and Kevin Mitchell for Chris Brown, Keith Comstock, Mark Davis, and Mark Grant, 7/87

Lefferts appeared in a personal-best 64 games for the 1988 San Francisco Giants. He outdid himself with a career high of 11 saves, one more than he earned with the 1984 division-winning San Diego Padres. He also earned a save in the Padres' losing effort against the Detroit Tigers in the World Series. Lefferts won two games in the 1984 National League Championship Series versus his original team, the Chicago Cubs. In 1987, he contributed three wins and four saves to the Giants' division title. Lefferts will be counted on in the team's 1989 pennant drive.

Lefferts has minimal stats from his six-year major league career. While he's been effective, his wins and ERA from each season are modest. These signals tell investors to steer clear of Lefferts' 1989 cards, priced at three cents. Our pick for his best 1989 card is Topps.

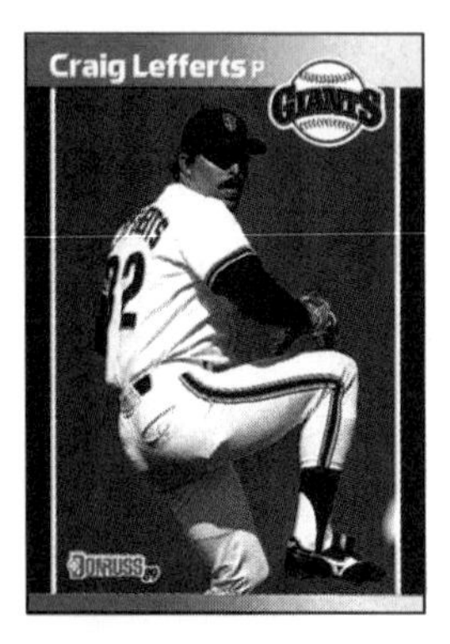

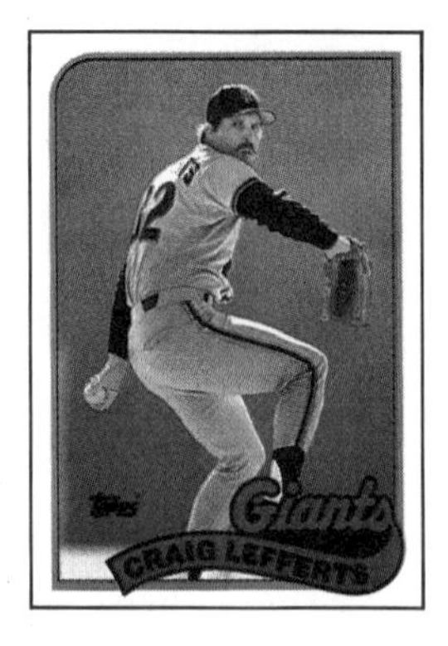

CHARLIE LEIBRANDT

	W	L	ERA	G	CG	IP	H	R	BB	SO
1988	13	12	3.19	35	7	243.0	244	98	62	125
Life	87	67	3.61	243	37	1411.2	1458	631	424	651

POSITION: Pitcher
TEAM: Kansas City Royals
BORN: October 4, 1956 Chicago, IL
HEIGHT: 6′3″ **WEIGHT:** 200 lbs.
BATS: Right **THROWS:** Left
ACQUIRED: Traded from Reds for Bob Tufts, 5/83

Leibrandt posted double-figure wins for the fifth straight season for Kansas City in 1988. He joined the Royals in 1984 after a year in the minors, and he has won ten or more games every year since 1984. In 1988, Leibrandt hurled a career-high 243 innings, which included seven complete games and two shutouts. The veteran lefty went 17-9 in 1985, helping the Royals capture a world championship. Leibrandt may never be a member of the Hall of Fame, but he continues to perform as one of the most dependable pitchers in Royals history.

Leibrandt's cards are commons, found at three cents or less. His cards will never have enormous values, but his 1989 issues could climb to a dime or more if Leibrandt hurls a no-hitter or wins 20 games. If that happens, sell fast. Our pick for his best 1989 card is Score.

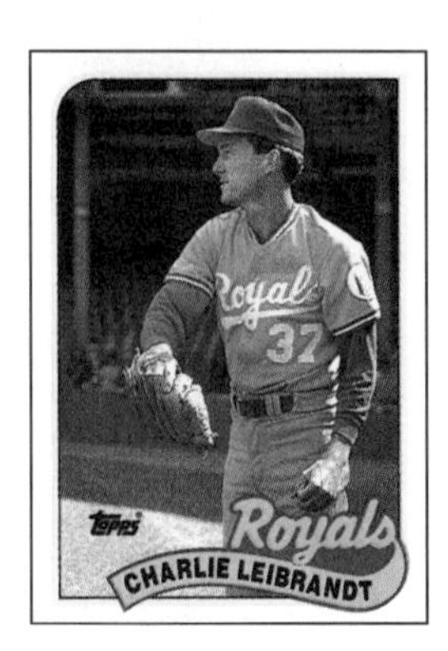

DAVE LEIPER

	W	L	ERA	G	SV	IP	H	R	BB	SO
1988	3	0	2.17	35	1	54.0	45	19	14	33
Life	9	3	3.75	133	4	161.0	150	79	60	94

POSITION: Pitcher
TEAM: San Diego Padres
BORN: June 18, 1962 Whittier, CA
HEIGHT: 5′11″ **WEIGHT:** 160 lbs.
BATS: Left **THROWS:** Left
ACQUIRED: Traded from A's for Storm Davis, 8/87

Leiper had a perfect season in 1988, at least in terms of winning percentage. He tallied three wins in three decisions, a 1.000 winning percentage. Leiper kept his ERA under 3.00, at 2.17. He had a good season in 1987, pitching for both the A's and the Padres. He was 3-1, with a 3.95 ERA. Leiper made a career-high 57 appearances in 1987, and he notched two saves. He played his college baseball at Fullerton (CA). The Padres will continue to count on Leiper for middle relief against lefthanded batters and some long-relief duty, and he could be a big part of San Diego's pennant drive in 1989.

Since middle relievers don't rack up wins or saves, they are largely ignored by collectors. Leiper's cards are commons. Our pick for his best 1989 card is Fleer.

AL LEITER

	W	L	ERA	G	CG	IP	H	R	BB	SO
1988	4	4	3.92	14	0	57.1	49	27	33	60
Life	6	6	4.61	18	0	80.0	73	43	48	88

POSITION: Pitcher
TEAM: New York Yankees
BORN: October 23, 1965
Toms River, NJ
HEIGHT: 6′2″ **WEIGHT:** 200 lbs.
BATS: Left **THROWS:** Left
ACQUIRED: Second-round pick in 6/84 free-agent draft

Leiter spent only part of his second season with the Yankees. The lefthanded starter got another brief shot at the majors in 1988, as he did in 1987. He fared well in 1988 with New York, averaging more than one strikeout per inning. At age 23, he is young enough to last many more seasons in pro baseball. The Yankees consider Leiter one of their brightest lefthanded hopes, and they'll try again in 1989 to keep him in the starting rotation.

In 1988, the Al Leiter Topps card was one of the most popular cards in baseball. Topps incorrectly put minor leaguer Steve George's picture on Leiter's card, later correcting the mistake. Leiter's 1989 cards will be selling for a quarter or slightly less. Wait and see how he does in 1989 before gambling on his cards. Our pick for his best 1989 card is Topps.

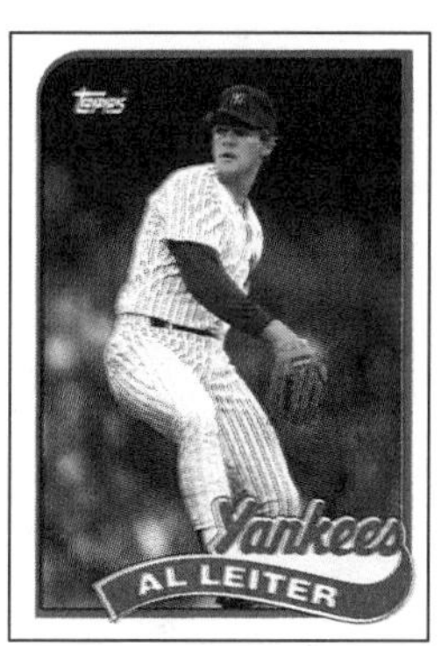

CHET LEMON

	BA	G	AB	R	H	2B	3B	HR	RBI	SB
1988	.264	144	512	67	135	29	4	17	64	1
Life	.276	1757	6132	889	1694	361	55	203	805	54

POSITION: Outfield
TEAM: Detroit Tigers
BORN: February 12, 1955 Jackson, MS
HEIGHT: 6′ **WEIGHT:** 185 lbs.
BATS: Right **THROWS:** Right
ACQUIRED: Traded from White Sox for Steve Kemp, 11/81

Lemon enjoyed another fine season for the Tigers in 1988, his seventh year with the club. He was one reason the Tigers battled for the A.L. East pennant until the last week of the season. He was third on the club in home runs, trailing only Darrell Evans and Fred Lynn. Lemon finished 1988 in a flurry, hitting three home runs during the final week of the season. Known for his fine fielding and clutch hitting, Lemon will be a key to the Tigers' pennant hopes in 1989.

Outside of Detroit, most fans overlook Lemon's past accomplishments and current talents. His cards are priced at a nickel or less. The only possible way his cards will gain short-term value is if Lemon helps the Tigers win their division this season. Our pick for his best 1989 card is Topps.

JEFF LEONARD

	BA	G	AB	R	H	2B	3B	HR	RBI	SB
1988	.242	138	534	57	129	27	1	10	64	17
Life	.269	1131	4001	506	1078	183	36	110	555	153

POSITION: Outfield
TEAM: Seattle Mariners
BORN: September 22, 1955 Philadelphia, PA
HEIGHT: 6′4″ **WEIGHT:** 210 lbs.
BATS: Right **THROWS:** Right
ACQUIRED: Signed as a free agent, 12/88

Leonard came to the Brewers to be a run producer in the early part of 1988, but he found the going a little rough. He hit only .235, with eight home runs and 44 RBIs. Leonard was the MVP of the N.L. Championship Series for the Giants, ending the seven-game series with a .417 average, four home runs, and five RBIs in a losing cause. He had been a good RBI man for the Giants in the six full years that he played with them, averaging 65 runs batted in a year. If he could continue that level for the Mariners, Leonard might be able to push them to respectability in 1989.

Leonard's 1989 cards will be found in the 5- to 10-cent range, based mainly on his MVP performance in the '87 playoffs. That is not a good investment price. Our pick for his best 1989 card is Fleer.

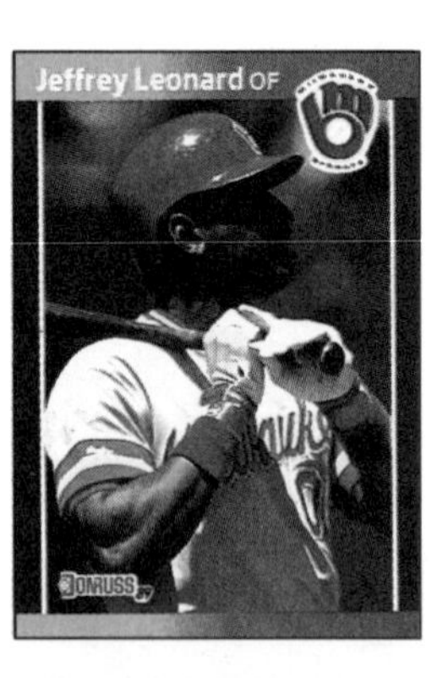

JOSE LIND

	BA	G	AB	R	H	2B	3B	HR	RBI	SB
1988	.262	154	611	82	160	24	4	2	49	15
Life	.273	189	754	103	206	32	8	2	60	17

POSITION: Second base
TEAM: Pittsburgh Pirates
BORN: May 1, 1964 Toabaja, Puerto Rico
HEIGHT: 5′11″ **WEIGHT:** 155 lbs.
BATS: Right **THROWS:** Right
ACQUIRED: Signed as a free agent, 12/82

To make way for Lind, the Pirates dealt Johnny Ray to California late in the 1987 campaign. Lind has rewarded their faith. Signed as a free agent by Pittsburgh in 1982, he is an excellent second baseman, with soft hands, outstanding range, quick feet, good instincts, good arm, and is adept at turning the double play. Though only a .260s hitter, his defense more than compensates for a lack of punch. At Triple-A Vancouver in 1987, Lind batted .268, with 31 RBIs and 21 stolen bases. When he was recalled by the Pirates last season, he amazed everyone by hitting .322— including four triples!

Lind's 1989 cards should open in the 25-cent range. Some baseball experts now call him the best at the keystone sack in the N.L. His cards are very good investments. Our pick for his best 1989 card is Topps.

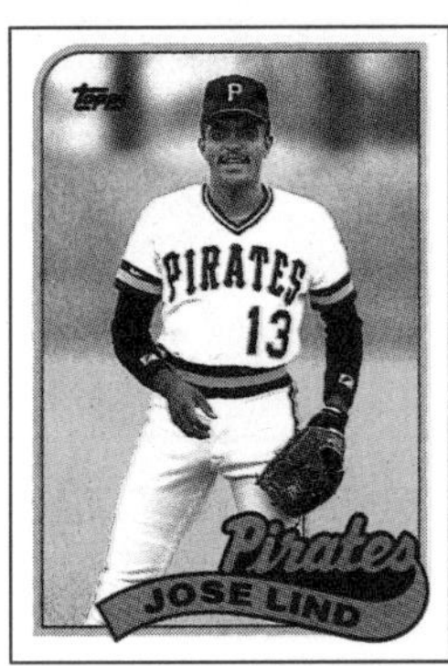

NELSON LIRIANO

	BA	G	AB	R	H	2B	3B	HR	RBI	SB
1988	.264	99	276	36	73	6	2	3	23	12
Life	.256	136	434	65	111	12	4	5	33	25

POSITION: Second base
TEAM: Toronto Blue Jays
BORN: June 3, 1964 Puerto Plata, Puerto Rico
HEIGHT: 5′10″ **WEIGHT:** 165 lbs.
BATS: Both **THROWS:** Right
ACQUIRED: Signed as a free agent, 11/82

Liriano made a strong bid for the Toronto starting second baseman's job in 1988. He increased his stats in all offensive categories in 1988, hitting .264, popping three homers, scoring 36 runs, and stealing 12 bases. After four years in the minor leagues, Liriano got his big break in 1987, playing in 37 games. He hit .241, with two homers and 10 RBIs. His speed and contact-hitting ability give the team a solid leadoff hitter. He is also a smooth fielder. Expect Liriano to be the Blue Jays' starting second baseman in 1989.

With just more than 100 games to his credit, Liriano can't be fully judged as a player. His 1989 cards will cost a nickel, but don't invest until his talents are displayed over the course of a full season. Our pick for his best 1989 card is Fleer.

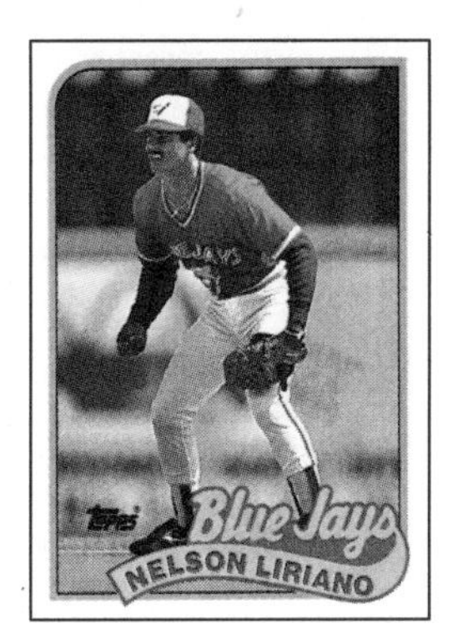

STEVE LOMBARDOZZI

	BA	G	AB	R	H	2B	3B	HR	RBI	SB
1988	.209	103	287	34	60	15	2	3	27	2
Life	.233	423	1226	148	286	58	11	19	104	13

POSITION: Second base
TEAM: Minnesota Twins
BORN: April 26, 1960 Malden, VA
HEIGHT: 6′ **WEIGHT:** 175 lbs.
BATS: Right **THROWS:** Right
ACQUIRED: Ninth-round pick in 6/81 free-agent draft

Lombardozzi almost lost his starting second baseman's job with the Minnesota Twins in 1988. In mid-season, the Twins traded popular outfielder Tom Brunansky for second baseman Tom Herr. Herr briefly held the role, but injuries to Herr put Lombardozzi back on top. Now that Herr's been traded, Lombardozzi has his job again. Never a high-average hitter in his past three seasons as a starter, Lombardozzi has been best-known for his defense. In 1988, he committed just five errors in 103 games. Lombardozzi needs to generate more offense in 1989 if he wants to keep his starting status.

Due to his low career average, Lombardozzi's cards don't seem likely to see any short-term value increases. Even at their price of three cents, his cards are risky investments. Our pick for his best 1989 card is Fleer.

BILL LONG

	W	L	ERA	G	CG	IP	H	R	BB	SO
1988	8	11	4.03	47	3	174.0	187	89	43	77
Life	16	20	4.44	80	8	357.0	391	191	76	162

POSITION: Pitcher
TEAM: Chicago White Sox
BORN: February 29, 1960 Cincinnati, OH
HEIGHT: 6′ **WEIGHT:** 185 lbs.
BATS: Right **THROWS:** Right
ACQUIRED: Traded from Padres to White Sox with Luis Salazar, Ozzie Guillen, and Tim Lollar for LaMarr Hoyt, Todd Simmons, and Kevin Kristan, 12/84

Long, in his second full season with the White Sox, served the team both in starting and relief roles. He equaled his 1987 total of eight wins again in 1988. Fourteen games finished, three complete games, and two saves were additional highlights in his season. The long ball was Long's biggest problem in 1988. He gave up 21 homers, second only to teammate Melido Perez. Long has served in a variety of assignments for the White Sox, but might distinguish himself better in one category. Until then, Long will be one of the best double-duty men the White Sox have.

Long's cards are commons, selling at less than a nickel. Until he can reverse his losing record and 4.00-plus ERA, avoid investing in his cards. Our pick for his best 1989 card is Fleer.

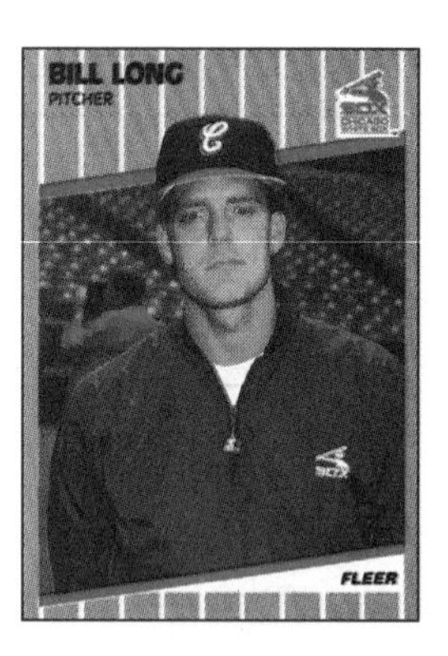

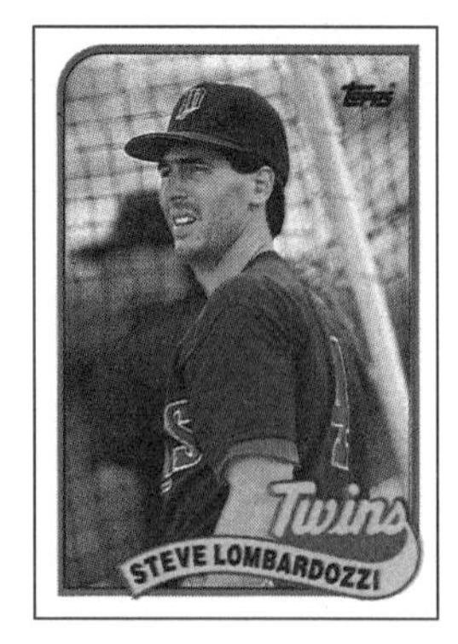

FRED LYNN

	BA	G	AB	R	H	2B	3B	HR	RBI	SB
1988	.246	114	391	46	96	14	1	25	56	2
Life	.287	1762	6376	1001	1828	374	41	289	1042	69

POSITION: Outfield
TEAM: Detroit Tigers
BORN: February 3, 1952 Chicago, IL
HEIGHT: 6′1″ **WEIGHT:** 190 lbs.
BATS: Left **THROWS:** Left
ACQUIRED: Traded from Orioles, 8/88

Lynn was picked up by the Tigers in late 1988 for aid in their run for the A.L. East pennant. The run was unsuccessful, but he did his best, sharing his season first with the Orioles and then the Tigers. Lynn blasted 25 home runs, his finest total since his 1979 season with Boston. He debuted in 1975 with Boston, winning both the MVP and Rookie of the Year awards and leading the team to the World Series. Lynn might win a starting job with the 1989 Tigers if he can stay free of injuries.

Lynn has played in only 140 or more games in four of his 15 total seasons. His 1989 cards will cost about a dime. Invest, but sell for short-term gains as soon as Lynn has one more good season. Our pick for his best 1989 card is Donruss.

STEVE LYONS

	BA	G	AB	R	H	2B	3B	HR	RBI	SB
1988	.269	146	472	59	127	28	3	5	45	1
Life	.261	456	1283	167	335	62	10	12	114	20

POSITION: Infield
TEAM: Chicago White Sox
BORN: June 3, 1960 Tacoma, WA
HEIGHT: 6′3″ **WEIGHT:** 192 lbs.
BATS: Left **THROWS:** Right
ACQUIRED: Traded from Red Sox for Tom Seaver, 6/86

Lyons played in 146 games, the most of his career, for the 1988 White Sox. He hit a respectable .269, and knocked in a career-best 45 runs. He plays third base most often, but he can fill in at any other position. Lyons has said that he wants to play all nine positions in one game in the future, a feat that would put him in the A.L. record books. Lyons is the answer to a future trivia question: "Whom did the White Sox receive when they traded away a Hall of Fame pitcher?" With Lyons' versatility, he is sure to play a role for the Sox in 1989.

Cards of Lyons will sell for a nickel or less in 1989. Don't invest in them until he wins a starting position somewhere. Our pick for his best 1989 card is Fleer.

MIKE MACFARLANE

	BA	G	AB	R	H	2B	3B	HR	RBI	SB
1988	.265	70	211	25	56	15	0	4	26	0
Life	.261	78	230	25	60	16	0	4	29	0

POSITION: Catcher
TEAM: Kansas City Royals
BORN: April 12, 1964 Stockton, CA
HEIGHT: 6′ **WEIGHT:** 200 lbs.
BATS: Right **THROWS:** Right
ACQUIRED: Fourth-round pick in 6/85 free-agent draft

Macfarlane, whom the Royals project as their "catcher of the future," split the season between Kansas City and Triple-A Omaha. He is making his way back to full capacity after rotator cuff surgery that limited his 1986 season to 40 games and his 1987 season to three-days-a-week catching duty. In a brief appearance at Kansas City in 1987, when catcher Jamie Quirk went on the 15-day disabled list, Macfarlane batted .211 in 19 at-bats. At Omaha in 1987, he batted .262 in 87 games, with 13 homers and 50 RBIs. In 1986, at Double-A Memphis, he hit 12 homers while batting .241. Macfarlane should open the 1989 season as the Royals' number two catcher.

Macfarlane's first big league cards in 1989 should open in the 10- to 15-cent range. They may be a gamble at that price. Our pick for his best 1989 card is Fleer.

GREG MADDUX

	W	L	ERA	G	CG	IP	H	R	BB	SO
1988	18	8	3.18	34	9	249.0	230	97	81	140
Life	26	26	4.21	70	11	435.2	455	228	166	261

POSITION: Pitcher
TEAM: Chicago Cubs
BORN: April 14, 1966 San Angelo, TX
HEIGHT: 6′ **WEIGHT:** 150 lbs.
BATS: Right **THROWS:** Right
ACQUIRED: Second-round pick in 6/84 free-agent draft

Few fans imagined that a pitcher with a lifetime 8-18 record would become the mound ace of the 1988 Cubs. But Maddux did just that, earning a spot on the N.L. All-Star staff and leading the Cubs in wins. The righthander was 18-8, with a 3.18 ERA. Maddux suffered through a 6-14 season in 1987. Previously, his biggest accomplishment had been a 10-1 performance with Triple-A Iowa in 1986. His brother, Mike, is a starting pitcher for Philadelphia. Greg has become, with Rick Sutcliffe, a one-two punch that the Cubs are counting on to bring them to the top in 1989.

Maddux may have a bright future, and his 1989 cards will approach 20 cents. But based on his second-half slump in 1988, doubts still remain. Don't gamble more than a nickel each investing in his cards right now. Our pick for his best 1989 card is Fleer.

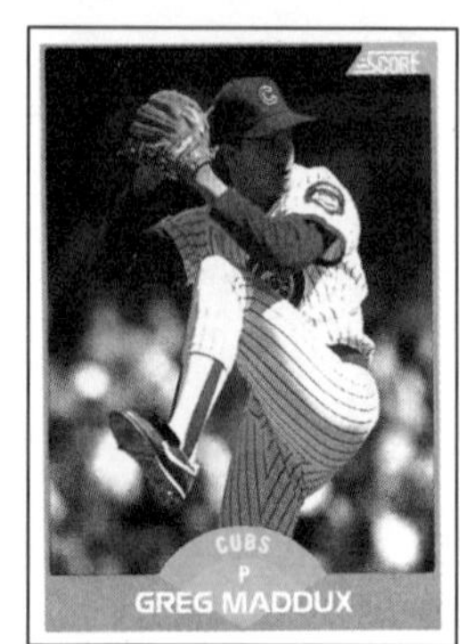

MIKE MADDUX

	W	L	ERA	G	SV	IP	H	R	BB	SO
1988	4	3	3.76	25	0	88.2	91	41	34	59
Life	9	10	4.36	48	0	183.2	196	102	73	118

POSITION: Pitcher
TEAM: Philadelphia Phillies
BORN: August 27, 1961 Dayton, OH
HEIGHT: 6′2″ **WEIGHT:** 180 lbs.
BATS: Right **THROWS:** Right
ACQUIRED: Fifth-round pick in 6/82 free-agent draft

Maddux showed flashes of brilliance in 1988, though he spent an extended tour on the disabled list. When not ailing, he appeared in 25 games for the Phils, 11 as a starter, and compiled a 4-3 record and a 3.76 ERA. He was 6-6 for Triple-A Maine and 2-0 for the Phillies in 1987. At Triple-A Portland in 1986, he was 5-2 with a 2.36 ERA. Maddux was brought up to Philadelphia, where he beat the Pirates on August 15 for his first big league win, and finished the year at 3-7. Younger brother Greg pitches for the Cubs, and they are 1-1 in head-to-head competition. Mike Maddux should be an important part of the Phillies' drive to respectability in 1989.

Maddux's 1989 cards will be in the commons box. He appears destined for a career that will keep his cards there. Our pick for his best 1989 card is Topps.

DAVE MAGADAN

	BA	G	AB	R	H	2B	3B	HR	RBI	SB
1988	.277	112	314	39	87	15	0	1	35	0
Life	.298	207	524	63	156	28	1	4	62	0

POSITION: Third base; first base
TEAM: New York Mets
BORN: September 30, 1962 Tampa, FL
HEIGHT: 6′3″ **WEIGHT:** 190 lbs.
BATS: Left **THROWS:** Right
ACQUIRED: Fourth-round pick in 6/83 free-agent draft

Magadan is a hitter, there's no doubt about that. What troubles the Mets is that they have no place to play him. What has kept him from dislodging any of New York's starters is his lack of long-ball power. Magadan has hit only eight home runs in his entire pro career—including four in the minor leagues between 1983 and 1986. Magadan's .277 average in 1988 was a career low, but he had five game-winning RBIs in 112 games. Magadan hit .318 for the 1987 Mets and had a career-high three homers. Magadan is too talented not to be an important member of the Mets in 1989.

The only way Magadan's 1989 cards will appreciate in value is if he becomes an N.L. batting champion some time in the future. Hold on to the Magadan cards you have. Our pick for his best 1989 card is Fleer.

JOE MAGRANE

	W	L	ERA	G	CG	IP	H	R	BB	SO
1988	5	9	2.18	24	4	165.1	133	57	51	100
Life	14	16	2.87	51	8	335.2	290	132	111	201

POSITION: Pitcher
TEAM: St. Louis Cardinals
BORN: July 2, 1964 Des Moines, IA
HEIGHT: 6′6″ **WEIGHT:** 225 lbs.
BATS: Right **THROWS:** Left
ACQUIRED: First-round pick in 6/85 free-agent draft

Magrane was injured for part of the 1988 season, and he even spent some time at Triple-A Louisville. He was 5-9 with St. Louis in '88, but his 2.18 ERA was second only to John Costello's on the staff. Magrane had four complete games in his 24 starts and struck out an even 100 in his 165⅓ innings. At Louisville for rehabilitation, he was 2-1 in four games with 28 strikeouts in 20 innings. The lefthander first joined St. Louis in April 1987 and finished the year with a 9-7 record, 101 strikeouts, and a 3.54 ERA. All the projections say that Magrane will be one of the N.L.'s top hurlers for years to come.

Magrane's cards cost about 30 cents at the moment. They are worth holding for potential investor appreciation. Our pick for his best 1989 card is Score.

RICK MAHLER

	W	L	ERA	G	CG	IP	H	R	BB	SO
1988	9	16	3.69	39	5	249.0	279	125	42	131
Life	78	88	3.97	294	36	1530.0	1623	755	488	755

POSITION: Pitcher
TEAM: Cincinnati Reds
BORN: August 5, 1953 Austin, TX
HEIGHT: 6′1″ **WEIGHT:** 202 lbs.
BATS: Right **THROWS:** Right
ACQUIRED: Signed as a free agent, 12/88

Mahler joins the Reds as a veteran pitcher who could help lead them to the playoffs. His 9-16 losing record was the best on the 1988 Braves. He tied Pete Smith for most complete games (five). Mahler even worked a bit of relief in his 249 innings, his highest total in the last three seasons. His best season with the Braves was in 1985. Mahler's 17-15 mark helped the Braves capture their division. He spent ten years with the Braves. Mahler should rack up more wins in 1989, since he is working with a much better offensive team.

Mahler's career losing record and high ERA might discourage collectors from investing in his 1989 cards, priced at 3 cents. If he racks up 15 or more wins and the Reds capture the division, sell quickly. Our pick for his best 1989 card is Fleer.

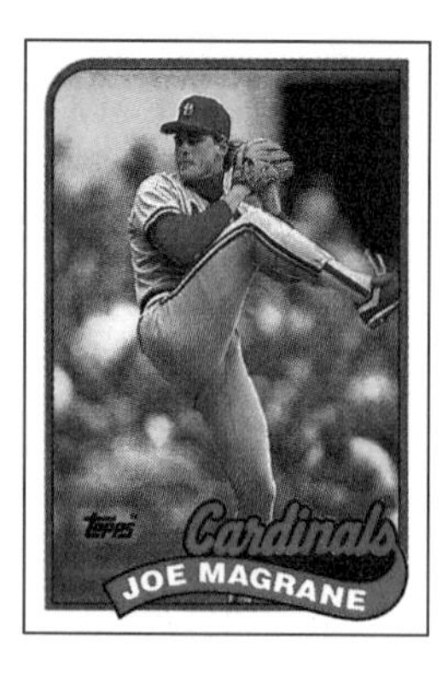

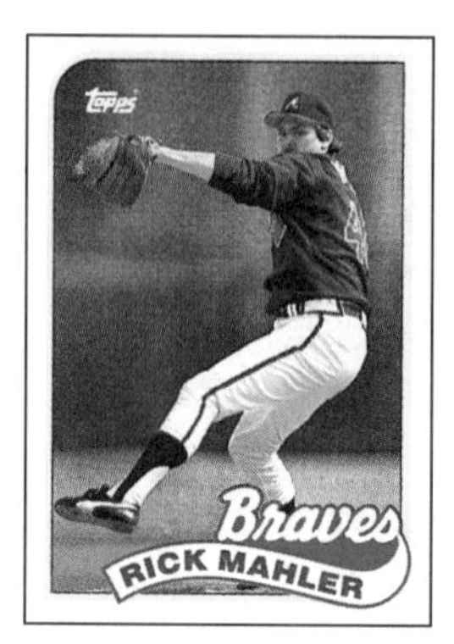

CANDY MALDONADO

	BA	G	AB	R	H	2B	3B	HR	RBI	SB
1988	.255	142	499	53	127	23	1	12	68	6
Life	.258	689	1891	221	487	104	10	61	291	19

POSITION: Outfield
TEAM: San Francisco Giants
BORN: September 5, 1960 Humacao, Puerto Rico
HEIGHT: 6′ **WEIGHT:** 190 lbs.
BATS: Right **THROWS:** Right
ACQUIRED: Traded from Dodgers for Alex Trevino, 12/85

Maldonado did not have as good a season in 1988 as he had in 1987, but he did contribute. He hit .255 in 1988, with 12 home runs and 68 RBIs. In 1987, he helped the Giants win the N.L. West by hitting 20 homers, 85 RBIs, and a .292 average. Maldonado has slugged 50 home runs in three years since coming to the Giants. In 1986, he led the N.L. in pinch hitting, going 17 for 40 for a .425 average and four homers. He finished the season at .252, 18 homers, and 85 RBIs. If the Giants hope to repeat their 1987 success, they will need Maldonado to return to his '87 form.

Maldonado's 1989 cards will be available for 5 or 10 cents each. Since he has only hit 61 career home runs, his cards are not good long-term investments. Our pick for his best 1989 card is Topps.

FRED MANRIQUE

	BA	G	AB	R	H	2B	3B	HR	RBI	SB
1988	.235	140	345	43	81	10	6	5	37	6
Life	.242	301	710	81	172	24	10	11	70	12

POSITION: Second base
TEAM: Chicago White Sox
BORN: November 5, 1961 Bolivar, Venezuela
HEIGHT: 6′1″ **WEIGHT:** 175 lbs.
BATS: Right **THROWS:** Right
ACQUIRED: Traded from Cardinals for Bill Dawley, 12/86

Manrique got his first year-long shot at a starting role with the 1988 White Sox, and he responded with one of the best seasons in his career. He tallied several career highs, including games, hits, triples, homers, runs scored, and RBIs. He became the starting second baseman near the end of the 1987 season, when he hit .258 in 115 games. Manrique is a defensive standout on the Chicago club. Manrique has waited a long time for his opportunity for success. Before he became a White Sox, Manrique played in the Blue Jays, Expos, and Cardinals systems.

Manrique, at age 27, has gotten a late start in the majors. His cards, even at common prices, aren't currently considered good investments. If he can raise his average in 1989, things could change. Our pick for his best 1989 card is Score.

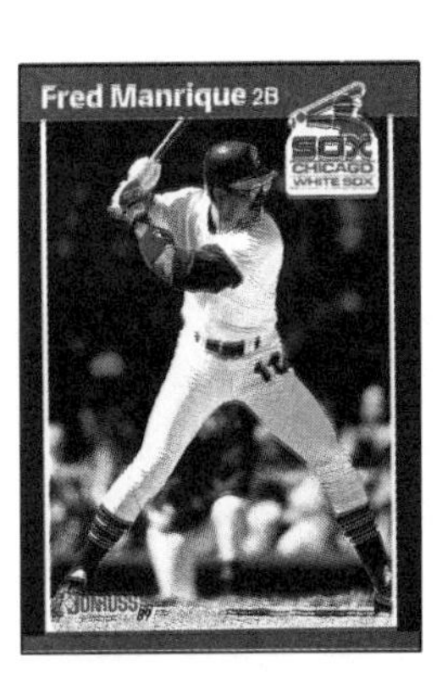

KIRT MANWARING

	BA	G	AB	R	H	2B	3B	HR	RBI	SB
1988	.250	40	116	12	29	7	0	1	15	0
Life	.244	46	123	12	30	7	0	1	15	0

POSITION: Catcher
TEAM: San Francisco Giants
BORN: July 15, 1965 Elmira, NY
HEIGHT: 5′11″ **WEIGHT:** 185 lbs.
BATS: Right **THROWS:** Right
ACQUIRED: Second-round pick in 6/86 free-agent draft

Most baseball insiders look at Manwaring as the Giant catcher of the future. Manwaring divided his 1988 playing time between Triple-A Phoenix (hitting .282) and San Francisco, where he hit at the .250-mark. He has a strong arm, calls a good game, and blocks the plate well. His skill at handling pitchers has improved markedly over the past two seasons. At Shreveport in the Texas League in 1987, Manwaring batted .267 and showed some power, with 17 extra base hits among his total of 82. In 1986, he hit .245 in 49 games at Clinton. Manwaring should have a good shot at the Giants' catcher job, at least on a part-time basis.

Manwaring's 1989 cards should open at the 40- to 50-cent range. Although priced high for the short term, they are good investments for the long term. Our pick for his best 1989 card is Topps.

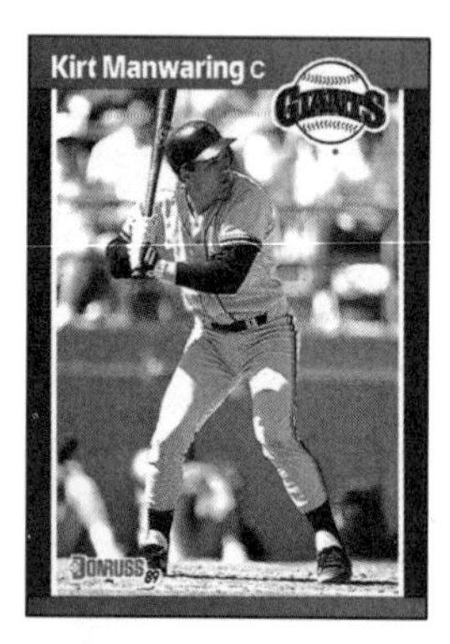

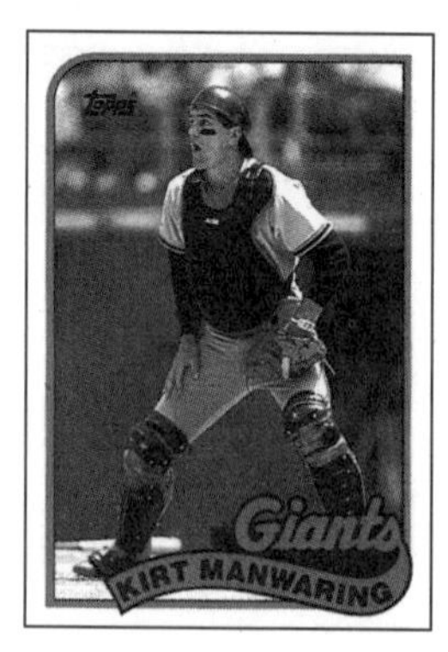

MIKE MARSHALL

	BA	G	AB	R	H	2B	3B	HR	RBI	SB
1988	.277	144	542	63	150	27	2	20	82	4
Life	.273	823	2872	354	784	134	5	126	422	24

POSITION: Outfield
TEAM: Los Angeles Dodgers
BORN: January 12, 1960 Libertyville, IL
HEIGHT: 6′5″ **WEIGHT:** 215 lbs.
BATS: Right **THROWS:** Right
ACQUIRED: Sixth-round pick in 6/78 free-agent draft

Marshall was the second-leading home run hitter on the 1988 Dodgers, playing in a career-high 144 games. He has been tormented by injuries since 1983, and a bad back stopped Marshall from playing in all five World Series games. He hit 20 homers and 82 RBIs in '88, finishing with a .277 average. Marshall's best season ever was in 1985, when he hit .293, with 28 homers and 95 RBIs. In 1981, he was named Minor League Player of the Year after winning the triple crown. He has shown that he is one of the premier players in the league. Marshall may win a couple of MVP awards before his career is over.

Marshall's 1989 cards will cost about a dime, a good price for investors. If he leads the Dodgers back to the World Series, that price will soar. Our pick for his best 1989 card is Fleer.

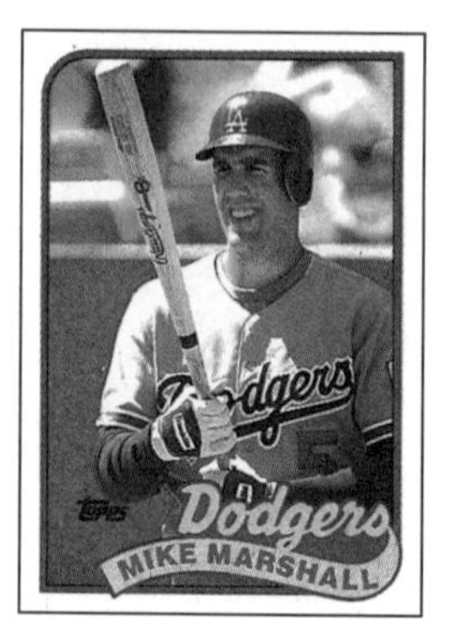

CARMELO MARTINEZ

	BA	G	AB	R	H	2B	3B	HR	RBI	SB
1988	.236	121	365	48	86	12	0	18	65	1
Life	.252	701	2147	271	541	102	5	82	314	8

POSITION: Outfield
TEAM: San Diego Padres
BORN: July 28, 1960
Dorado, Puerto Rico
HEIGHT: 6'2" **WEIGHT:** 220 lbs.
BATS: Right **THROWS:** Right
ACQUIRED: Traded from Cubs with Craig Lefferts and Fritz Connally for Scott Sanderson, 12/83

Martinez belted 18 homers for the 1988 Padres, the most he's hit since 1985. He batted only .236 but had 65 RBIs. His 1987 totals were 15 homers, 70 RBIs, and a .273 average. Martinez, a natural first baseman, couldn't crack the Cubs starting lineup for years. Finally, Chicago traded him in 1983. His presence helped San Diego to the 1984 World Series. Martinez hit six home runs during the last two months of 1988. If he can keep his average up, Martinez might become one of the league's most respected power hitters.

Expect the 1989 cards of Martinez to be three cents or less. Because Martinez is just 28, he still seems to have the potential to become a 25-homer man. Invest in his cards, but sell as soon as he has one profitable season. Our pick for his best 1989 card is Fleer.

DAVE MARTINEZ

	BA	G	AB	R	H	2B	3B	HR	RBI	SB
1988	.255	138	447	51	114	13	6	6	46	23
Life	.259	333	1014	134	263	32	15	15	89	43

POSITION: Outfield
TEAM: Montreal Expos
BORN: September 26, 1964
New York, NY
HEIGHT: 5'10" **WEIGHT:** 160 lbs.
BATS: Left **THROWS:** Left
ACQUIRED: Traded from Cubs for Mitch Webster, 7/88

Martinez came to the Expos in mid-1988 and immediately took over the center field post. He played 63 games for Montreal, and he had a .257 average, two homers, 24 runs scored, and 12 RBIs. He ended the season with 23 stolen bases. Martinez had a great season in 1987, his first full year in the major leagues. He hit .292, with 71 runs scored, eight home runs, and 36 RBIs. At Triple-A Iowa in '86, he was impressive, ending with a .289 average, 42 stolen bases, 52 runs scored, and 32 RBIs in 83 games. The Expos think that Martinez will be a leadoff man and spark plug in center for years to come.

Martinez's 1989 cards will be in the 5- to 10-cent range. He should continue to develop, and his cards are good buys at that price. Our pick for his best 1989 card is Donruss.

DENNIS MARTINEZ

	W	L	ERA	G	CG	IP	H	R	BB	SO
1988	15	13	2.72	34	9	235.1	215	94	55	120
Life	137	116	3.97	394	81	2253.1	2273	1104	706	1125

POSITION: Pitcher
TEAM: Montreal Expos
BORN: May 14, 1955 Granada, Nicaragua
HEIGHT: 6'1" **WEIGHT:** 183 lbs.
BATS: Right **THROWS:** Right
ACQUIRED: Traded from Orioles for Rene Gonzales, 6/86

Martinez proved in 1988 that he's firmly back on the winning track. The righty suffered through three rocky seasons with Baltimore before being traded to Montreal early in 1986. Martinez had an ERA above or near 5.00 each season before 1987, when he went 11-4 with a 3.30 ERA. In 1988, Martinez proved that he can win in the N.L., going 15-13 with a 2.72 ERA. He led the Expos in complete games and innings pitched. Martinez led the A.L. in wins in 1981, with 14. He exceeded 10 wins six times for the Orioles. Martinez just may top 20 wins for the Expos in the near future.

After two years, it appears that Martinez has made more than a temporary comeback. His 1989 cards will sell at a nickel apiece. Risk a dollar and you may quadruple your investment if Martinez wins 20 games. Our pick for his best 1989 card is Donruss.

EDGAR MARTINEZ

	BA	G	AB	R	H	2B	3B	HR	RBI	SB
1988	.281	14	32	0	9	4	0	0	5	0
Life	.333	27	75	6	25	9	2	0	10	0

POSITION: Third base
TEAM: Seattle Mariners
BORN: January 2, 1963 New York, NY
HEIGHT: 5'11" **WEIGHT:** 175 lbs.
BATS: Right **THROWS:** Right
ACQUIRED: Signed as a free agent, 12/82

The Pacific Coast League's batting champion for 1988, Martinez looms large in the plans of the rebuilding Mariners in 1989. He batted .363 for Calgary last season, with eight home runs and 64 RBIs. Recalled to the parent club late in '88, he hit about .300. In a cameo appearance with the M's in 1987, Martinez slugged .372 in 13 contests. His first full year in Triple-A, 1987, Martinez batted .329 for Calgary. At Class-A Wasau in 1984, Martinez hit .303 in 126 games with a career-high 15 homers. He moved up to Double-A Chattanooga in 1985, where he batted .258 that year and .264 the following season. Martinez should find a spot on the '89 Mariners.

Martinez's 1989 cards will open at a bargain-rate 20 cents. If he produces for the M's, his card values will soar. Our pick for his best 1989 card is Fleer.

RAMON MARTINEZ

	W	L	ERA	G	CG	IP	H	R	BB	SO
1988	1	3	3.79	9	0	35.2	27	17	22	23
Life	1	3	3.79	9	0	35.2	27	17	22	23

POSITION: Pitcher
TEAM: Los Angeles Dodgers
BORN: March 22, 1968 Santo Domingo, Dominican Republic
HEIGHT: 6′4″ **WEIGHT:** 185 lbs.
BATS: Right **THROWS:** Right
ACQUIRED: Signed as a free agent, 9/84

The ace of the San Antonio pitching staff during the 1988 season, Martinez was recalled by the parent Los Angeles Dodgers in late summer and impressed N.L. observers with his performance. At San Antonio in 1988, Martinez went 8-4 with a 2.46 ERA and 89 strikeouts in 95 innings. He broke into pro ball three years ago at Bakersfield, going 4-8 with a 4.75 ERA. The following year, he was a 16-game winner (against only 5 losses) at Class-A Vero Beach. A Florida State League All-Star that year, he was the choice of rival managers as the league's best prospect. Martinez has a good shot to crack the tough Dodger rotation in 1989.

His 1989 cards will open in the 25- to 30-cent range. Considering his youth, those prices could be cheap. Our pick for his best 1989 card is Topps.

GREG MATHEWS

	W	L	ERA	G	CG	IP	H	R	BB	SO
1988	4	6	4.24	13	1	68.0	61	34	33	31
Life	26	25	3.79	68	4	411.0	384	182	148	206

POSITION: Pitcher
TEAM: St. Louis Cardinals
BORN: May 17, 1962 Harbor City, CA
HEIGHT: 6′2″ **WEIGHT:** 180 lbs.
BATS: Both **THROWS:** Left
ACQUIRED: Tenth-round pick in 6/84 free-agent draft

Mathews was out of action for much of the 1988 season, and he was unable to match the 11-win seasons he had in both 1986 and 1987. Limited to just 13 starts last year, the lefty went 4-6 with a 4.24 ERA and just one complete game. In his 1986 rookie season, Mathews was 11-8 in 23 outings. He was 3-3 in seven games for Triple-A Louisville. In 1987, Mathews again started out in Triple-A, where he was 3-0 for Louisville, before traveling to St. Louis for an 11-11 record, with a 3.73 ERA. Mathews should be the Cards' number two or three starter this year and is expected to get back on the winning track.

His cards are sold as commons. He is still young enough for collectors to hold on to his cards for long-term investment potential. Our pick for his best 1989 card is Fleer.

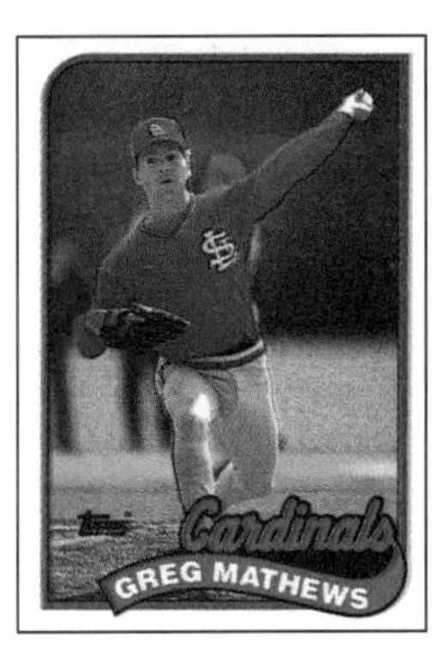

DON MATTINGLY

	BA	G	AB	R	H	2B	3B	HR	RBI	SB
1988	.311	144	599	94	186	37	0	18	88	1
Life	.327	857	3391	536	1109	235	13	141	604	5

POSITION: First base
TEAM: New York Yankees
BORN: April 20, 1961 Evansville, IN
HEIGHT: 5′11″ **WEIGHT:** 185 lbs.
BATS: Left **THROWS:** Left
ACQUIRED: 19th-round pick in 6/79 free-agent draft

Mattingly's power stats suffered a bit of a letdown from his 1987 accomplishments, but fans still regard him as one of baseball's best hitters. Teammate Dave Winfield actually edged Mattingly in several offensive departments in 1988, but Mattingly hit .311, with 18 homers and 88 RBIs. In 1987, he hit .327, with 30 home runs and 115 RBIs. He has led the A.L. in batting average, hits, doubles, RBIs, and slugging percentage. It's easy to project that Mattingly, with five major league seasons behind him, will reach 3,000 hits in another decade. There's no limit to what one of baseball's youngest superstars could do in the 1990s.

Because Mattingly suffered a temporary slip in power production, expect a small decrease in the price of Mattingly cards. If his 1989 cards go below their current asking price of $1.50, buy immediately. Our pick for his best 1989 card is Fleer.

LEE MAZZILLI

	BA	G	AB	R	H	2B	3B	HR	RBI	SB
1988	.147	68	116	9	17	2	0	0	12	4
Life	.261	1399	3998	549	1042	186	24	87	442	192

POSITION: Outfield; first base
TEAM: New York Mets
BORN: March 25, 1955 New York, NY
HEIGHT: 6′1″ **WEIGHT:** 180 lbs.
BATS: Both **THROWS:** Right
ACQUIRED: Signed as a free agent, 8/86

Mazzilli played a valuable role on the 1988 pennant-winning Mets. He served as a pinch hitter and backup outfielder and first baseman, and he was a veteran influence during their pennant drive. He is an especially valuable pinch hitter because he's a switch-hitter. Mazzilli is a fan favorite at Shea Stadium, having been an All-Star in 1979. That year, he hit .303, with 15 home runs and 79 RBIs. He hit 16 home runs in 1978 and '80, his career high. In 1987, he led the N.L. with 17 pinch hits. Mazzilli is a useful role player for the Mets.

Mazzilli's 1989 cards will be in the commons box. If he would help the Mets win the world championship, his cards might rise slightly. But they are not good investments. Our pick for his best 1989 card is Score.

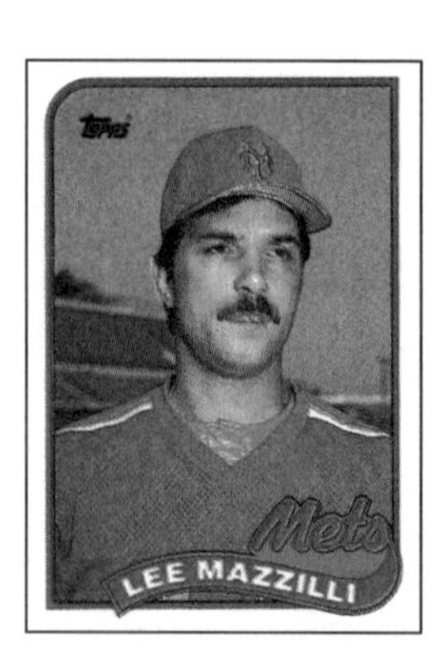

KIRK McCASKILL

	W	L	ERA	G	CG	IP	H	R	BB	SO
1988	8	6	4.31	23	4	146.1	155	78	61	98
Life	41	34	4.22	101	21	657.0	635	333	251	458

POSITION: Pitcher
TEAM: California Angels
BORN: April 9, 1961
Kapukasing, Ontario
HEIGHT: 6′1″ **WEIGHT:** 190 lbs.
BATS: Right **THROWS:** Right
ACQUIRED: Fourth-round pick in 6/82 free-agent draft

McCaskill didn't seem at full strength when pitching for the 1988 Angels. He was disabled during most of the 1987 season with elbow surgery. Although he did pitch in 146⅓ innings in 1988, winning eight of 14 decisions, his sharpness wasn't there. McCaskill, prior to surgery, had a stunning season in 1986. He went 17-10 with a 3.36 ERA, ten complete games, and two shutouts. The native Canadian struck out 202 in 246 innings in 1986. In 1987, he pitched in only 14 games, with a 4-6 record and 5.67 ERA. Contingent upon his health, McCaskill could be one of California's biggest winners in 1989.

McCaskill's 1989 cards will be commons, available at three cents or less. Until he proves he has the ability to pitch a full season again and to win consistently, don't risk investing in McCaskill's cards. Our pick for his best 1989 card is Score.

BOB McCLURE

	W	L	ERA	G	SV	IP	H	R	BB	SO
1988	2	3	5.40	33	3	30.0	35	18	8	19
Life	56	52	3.88	509	49	1006.1	977	486	436	609

POSITION: Pitcher
TEAM: New York Mets
BORN: April 29, 1952 Oakland, CA
HEIGHT: 5′11″ **WEIGHT:** 175 lbs.
BATS: Both **THROWS:** Left
ACQUIRED: Signed as a free agent, 7/88

McClure signed on to the Mets for the pennant drive in 1988. He had three saves in '88 in 33 games, notching a 5.40 ERA. He also had twice as many strikeouts (19) as bases on balls (8). McClure pitched for the Brewers from 1977 until 1986. His best season as a starter for Milwaukee was 1982, when he was 12-7, with a 4.22 ERA, five complete games, 99 strikeouts, and 74 walks in 172⅔ innings of work. He pitched in 52 games with Montreal in 1987, ending with a 6-1 record, a 3.44 ERA, and five saves. He was released by the Expos in mid-1988 before he was picked up by the Mets. McClure figures to continue to see action with New York in 1989.

McClure's 1989 cards are commons, and they will remain so. Although he's had a 14-year career, he has not compiled the stats that interest collectors. Our pick for his best 1989 card is Fleer.

LANCE McCULLERS

	W	L	ERA	G	SV	IP	H	R	BB	SO
1988	3	6	2.49	60	10	97.2	70	29	55	81
Life	21	28	2.96	229	36	392.0	311	150	188	326

POSITION: Pitcher
TEAM: New York Yankees
BORN: March 8, 1964 Tampa, FL
HEIGHT: 6′1″ **WEIGHT:** 215 lbs.
BATS: Both **THROWS:** Right
ACQUIRED: Traded from Padres with Jimmy Jones and Stan Jefferson for Jack Clark and Pat Clements, 10/88

The Yankees were willing to give up their top home run hitter of 1988 to obtain McCullers. The Padres parted with McCullers, who was second on San Diego in saves (ten) and fourth in ERA (2.49). He came up in the Phillie system, but was obtained in 1983 by San Diego. McCullers had 70 and 78 appearances with the Padres in 1986 and 1987. His 1986 record was 10-10 with five saves and a 2.78 ERA. In 1987, he earned 16 saves and struck out 126 men in 123 innings. The addition of McCullers should take some heat off Yankee bullpen ace Dave Righetti.

Expect the 1989 cards of McCullers to sell for a nickel apiece. Buy them fast. He should have good luck in a new league, and he'll get lots of acclaim for his accomplishments in a media outlet like New York. Our pick for his best 1989 card is Donruss.

JACK McDOWELL

	W	L	ERA	G	CG	IP	H	R	BB	SO
1988	5	10	3.97	26	1	158.2	147	85	68	84
Life	8	10	3.66	30	1	186.2	163	91	74	99

POSITION: Pitcher
TEAM: Chicago White Sox
BORN: January 16, 1966 Van Nuys, CA
HEIGHT: 6′5″ **WEIGHT:** 185 lbs.
BATS: Right **THROWS:** Right
ACQUIRED: First-round pick in 6/87 free-agent draft

In 1988, McDowell didn't match the level of excitement he created during his 1987 debut. He won only a third of his games and had an average ERA for the 1988 White Sox. In McDowell's defense, he had less than a half-season's worth of professional experience before getting called up to the White Sox in late 1987. During that four-game test, McDowell submitted a sparkling 3-0 record and a 1.93 ERA. The lanky righthander got his first taste of an entire professional season in 1988. He was only 5-10, but he had a pretty fair 3.97 ERA. More seasoning should help McDowell become a more complete pitcher.

McDowell's 1989 cards will sell for as much as a quarter. At those prices, it's best to wait until McDowell can fully prove himself before investing. Our pick for his best 1989 card is Fleer.

ODDIBE McDOWELL

	BA	G	AB	R	H	2B	3B	HR	RBI	SB
1988	.247	120	437	55	108	19	5	6	37	33
Life	.250	513	1822	288	455	83	21	56	180	115

POSITION: Outfield
TEAM: Cleveland Indians
BORN: August 25, 1962 Hollywood, FL
HEIGHT: 5′9″ **WEIGHT:** 160 lbs.
BATS: Left **THROWS:** Left
ACQUIRED: Traded from Rangers with Pete O'Brien and Jerry Browne for Julio Franco, 12/88

McDowell now figures in the Tribe's long-term plans. He missed roughly a fourth of his 1988 season, but he still provided the Rangers with his trademarks, speed and defense. McDowell's 33 stolen bases tied him for the team lead. His outfield play consisted of only three errors in 120 games. His power totals weren't close to matching his output for his first three seasons with Texas. Prior to the start of the 1988 season, McDowell never hit less than 14 homers in a year. His 89 strikeouts were his offensive downfall. With a little more selectivity at the plate, McDowell could be regarded as one of the league's best sluggers.

McDowell's 1989 cards are priced as commons. Invest in these bargains. If he can cut down on the Ks, he could become a home run threat. Our pick for his best 1989 card is Fleer.

ROGER McDOWELL

	W	L	ERA	G	SV	IP	H	R	BB	SO
1988	5	5	2.63	62	16	89.0	80	31	31	46
Life	32	24	3.12	255	80	433.0	390	163	138	213

POSITION: Pitcher
TEAM: New York Mets
BORN: December 21, 1960 Cincinnati, OH
HEIGHT: 6′1″ **WEIGHT:** 175 lbs.
BATS: Right **THROWS:** Right
ACQUIRED: Third-round pick in 6/83 free-agent draft

McDowell was second on the Mets in saves last season with 16, and he appeared in more games (62) than any other member of the staff. He fashioned a 5-5 record and an impressive 2.63 ERA for New York last year. In 1986, McDowell saved 22 and had a 14-9 record in 70 games. He has overcome a number of nagging injuries over the past two seasons. He came up with the Mets in 1985 and recorded 17 saves in 62 games. He comes at opponents with superb control and a hard sinker. McDowell joins with Randy Myers to give the N.L. East champion Mets a solid righty-lefty bullpen duo.

One of the N.L.'s best relievers, McDowell's cards don't excite collectors all that much. Consequently we can't suggest them for any kind of short-term or long-term profitability. Our pick for his best 1989 card is Fleer.

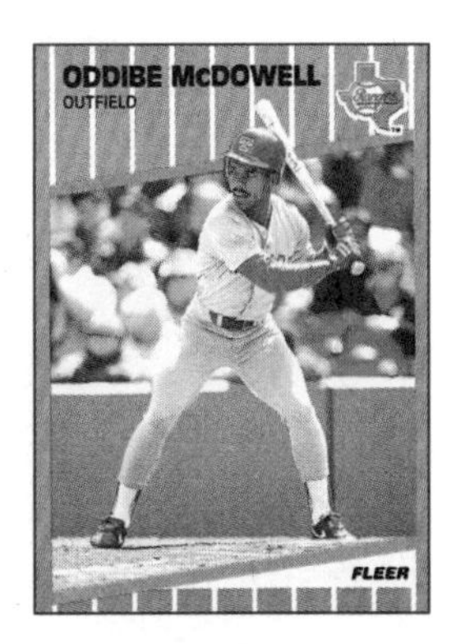

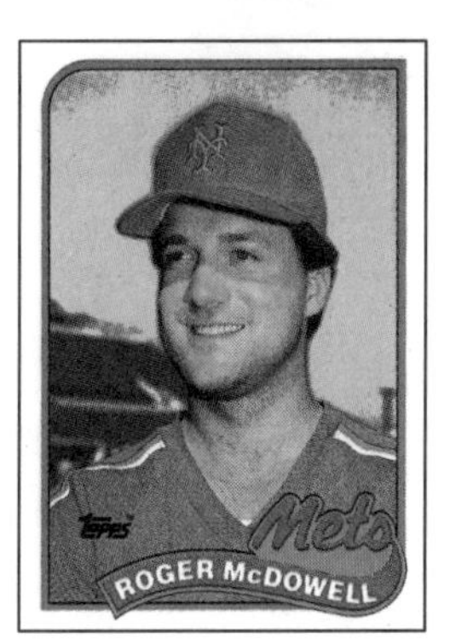

ANDY McGAFFIGAN

	W	L	ERA	G	SV	IP	H	R	BB	SO
1988	6	0	2.76	63	4	91.1	81	31	37	71
Life	31	25	3.16	274	21	667.0	589	257	230	514

POSITION: Pitcher
TEAM: Montreal Expos
BORN: October 25, 1956
West Palm Beach, FL
HEIGHT: 6′3″ **WEIGHT:** 185 lbs.
BATS: Right **THROWS:** Right
ACQUIRED: Traded from Reds with Jay Tibbs, Dann Bilardello, and John Stuper for Bill Gullickson and Sal Butera, 12/85

McGaffigan had a great campaign for Montreal in 1988, and he was flawless in one regard. He was a perfect 6-0 last season for the Expos, appearing in relief in 63 games. His 2.76 ERA was among the best on the staff, and he fanned 71 in $91\frac{1}{3}$ innings of work. He also had four saves. In 1987, McGaffigan had an equally strong year, going 5-2 in 120 innings of work and striking out 100 batters. He was 10-5 in 1986, starting 14 games and appearing in 48. He had a 2.65 ERA that year. McGaffigan is a fine middle reliever who will aid in the Expo drive for the pennant in 1989.

McGaffigan's cards are generally considered commons. While he is a good, steady reliever, there is little investment potential in that type of player. Our pick for his best 1989 card is Fleer.

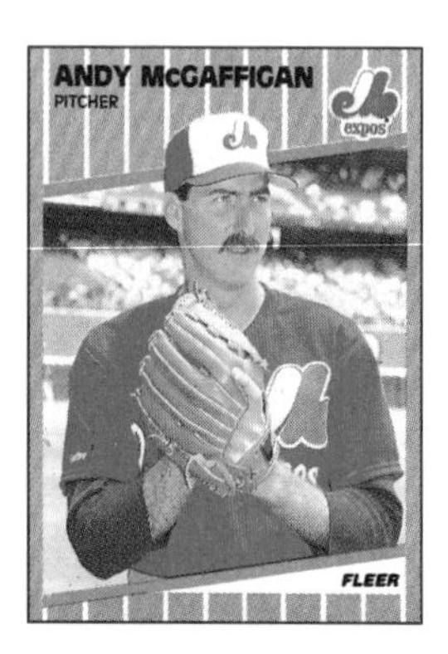

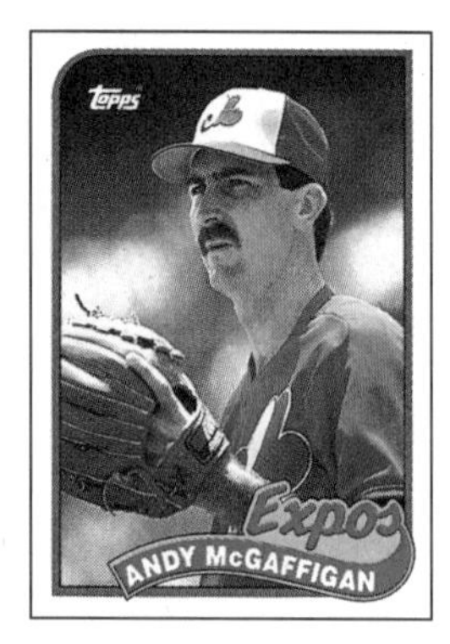

WILLIE McGEE

	BA	G	AB	R	H	2B	3B	HR	RBI	SB
1988	.292	137	562	73	164	24	6	3	50	41
Life	.295	981	3885	528	1147	162	69	46	466	238

POSITION: Outfield
TEAM: St. Louis Cardinals
BORN: November 2, 1958
San Francisco, CA
HEIGHT: 6′1″ **WEIGHT:** 176 lbs.
BATS: Both **THROWS:** Right
ACQUIRED: Traded from Yankees for Bob Sykes, 10/81

McGee and the Cardinals seem to have great seasons every other year, so 1989 should be a productive season for both. Injuries and extended slumps didn't show the public McGee's true abilities in 1988. In 1987, he set personal highs with 11 homers and 105 RBIs. His greatest season so far was in 1985, when he led the league with a .353 average, 216 hits, and 18 triples, winning the N.L. MVP award. A veteran of three World Series, McGee has a composite Series average of .291 with three homers and 11 RBIs. He spent five years struggling through the Yankee system before becoming a Redbird. McGee is the prototype Cardinal, a switch-hitter with plenty of speed.

McGee's poor showing in 1988 should keep his new cards at 10 cents or less. Such a buy would be worthwhile. Our pick for his best 1989 card is Fleer.

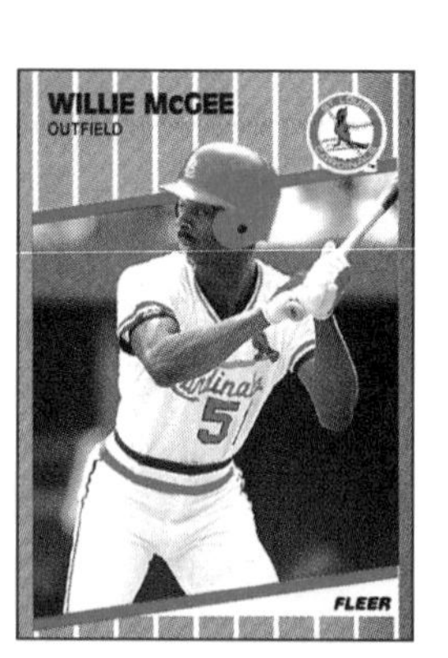

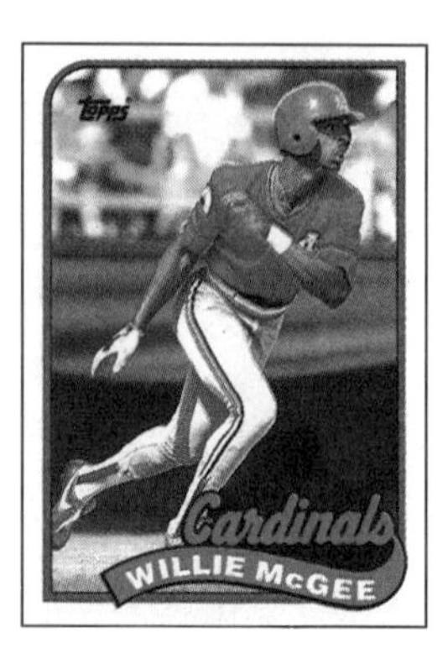

FRED McGRIFF

	BA	G	AB	R	H	2B	3B	HR	RBI	SB
1988	.282	154	536	100	151	35	4	34	82	6
Life	.269	264	836	159	225	51	4	54	125	9

POSITION: First base; designated hitter
TEAM: Toronto Blue Jays
BORN: October 31, 1963 Tampa, FL
HEIGHT: 6′3″ **WEIGHT:** 215 lbs.
BATS: Left **THROWS:** Left
ACQUIRED: Traded from Yankees with Dave Collins and Mike Morgan for Dale Murray and Tom Dodd, 12/82

McGriff's continued fine play in 1988 won him the starting first baseman's job for the Toronto Blue Jays. He belted 34 home runs and had 82 RBIs for Toronto, and lifted his average nearly 40 points from 1987's mark of .247. He also scored 100 runs and slugged 35 doubles. In 1987, McGriff, then a designated hitter, set a team record for most home runs by a rookie, with 20 round-trippers. He also scored 58 runs and drove in 43 base runners. This 25-year-old power hitter will be in the Toronto starting lineup for a long while if he keeps belting homers at his current pace.

McGriff's emerging power could bring him a few home run titles in the coming seasons. His 1989 cards should sell at 10 cents or less. The cards are worth investing in for the long term. Our pick for his best 1989 card is Topps.

MARK McGWIRE

	BA	G	AB	R	H	2B	3B	HR	RBI	SB
1988	.260	155	550	87	143	22	1	32	99	0
Life	.271	324	1160	194	314	51	5	84	226	1

POSITION: First base
TEAM: Oakland A's
BORN: October 1, 1963 Pomona, CA
HEIGHT: 6′5″ **WEIGHT:** 225 lbs.
BATS: Right **THROWS:** Right
ACQUIRED: First-round pick in 6/84 free-agent draft

McGwire proved he's a legitimate major league slugger with his 1988 accomplishments. He smashed 32 homers and was second on the A's (only to league-leading teammate Jose Canseco) in RBIs, with 99. McGwire's batting average dropped nearly 30 points in 1988 to .260, but he demonstrated that he can continue as one of the league's dominant power hitters. He broke the rookie record for home runs in 1987 with 49, driving in 118 runs. He won the A.L. Rookie of the Year award that year. After a second strong season, McGwire has convinced even more fans that he's planning a long career in the majors.

McGwire's 1989 cards will cost at least $1, which is too high, considering McGwire's drop in average and power from his incredible rookie season. Keep all the McGwire cards you find in wax packs, though. Our pick for his best 1989 card is Topps.

MARK McLEMORE

	BA	G	AB	R	H	2B	3B	HR	RBI	SB
1988	.240	77	233	38	56	11	2	2	16	13
Life	.236	220	670	99	158	24	5	5	57	38

POSITION: Second base
TEAM: California Angels
BORN: October 4, 1964 San Diego, CA
HEIGHT: 5′11″ **WEIGHT:** 175 lbs.
BATS: Both **THROWS:** Right
ACQUIRED: Ninth-round pick in 6/82 free-agent draft

McLemore, once viewed as the Angels' second baseman of the future, had to battle for playing time in 1988. With the success of second baseman Johnny Ray and shortstop Dick Schofield, McLemore was able to see action in only 77 games. He hit a career-best .240, and was third on the Angels in stolen bases with 13. His speed is his best-known asset. He stole 67 bases with two minor league teams in 1986. He has more fielding ability than Ray, but McLemore will have to raise his batting average before he can reclaim second base as his own.

McLemore has definite potential, but most of it has remained untapped in two full seasons with the Angels. Based on his career statistics, his common-priced cards don't have much appeal as investments yet. Our pick for his best 1989 card is Donruss.

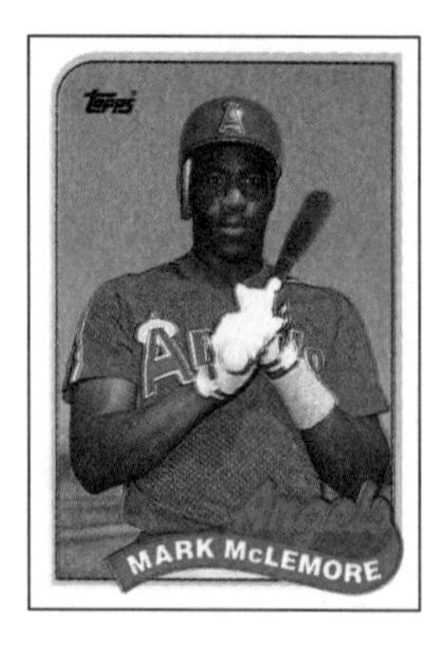

KEVIN McREYNOLDS

	BA	G	AB	R	H	2B	3B	HR	RBI	SB
1988	.288	147	552	82	159	30	2	27	99	21
Life	.270	794	2931	401	792	146	24	121	454	52

POSITION: Outfield
TEAM: New York Mets
BORN: October 16, 1959 Little Rock, AR
HEIGHT: 6′1″ **WEIGHT:** 205 lbs.
BATS: Right **THROWS:** Right
ACQUIRED: Traded from Padres with Gene Walter for Shawn Abner, Stanley Jefferson, Kevin Mitchell, Kevin Armstrong, and Kevin Brown, 12/86

Playing beside superstar Darryl Strawberry on a regular basis has obscured the success of McReynolds. He pushed his batting average to .288 in 1988, as he finished the year with 99 RBIs. He surpassed 25 homers for the third straight season, slugging 27; he surpassed 90 RBIs three seasons in a row. McReynolds claimed a career best for stolen bases, illustrating another role he plays in the potent Met offense. In '87, he hit .276, with 29 home runs and 95 RBIs. He has reached the 100-homer mark in only five full seasons. After only two seasons with New York, McReynolds may join other Mets players in receiving due credit for their talent.

Until then, McReynolds' 1989 cards will sell for 15 cents or less. These cards are good investments that will rise quickly if he wins any batting awards. Our pick for his best 1989 card is Score.

LOUIE MEADOWS

	BA	G	AB	R	H	2B	3B	HR	RBI	SB
1988	.190	35	42	5	8	0	1	2	3	4
Life	.208	41	48	6	10	0	1	2	3	5

POSITION: Outfield
TEAM: Houston Astros
BORN: April 29, 1961 Maysville, NC
HEIGHT: 5′11″ **WEIGHT:** 190 lbs.
BATS: Left **THROWS:** Left
ACQUIRED: Second-round pick in 6/82 free-agent draft

Meadows appears ready to find a spot on the Houston roster in 1989. In 1988 at Triple-A Tucson, he batted .254 and stole 20 bases. He did have a brief tour in the National League last summer. Though Meadows batted only .190, he did hit a couple of home runs and displayed the kind of defensive skills needed in the Astrodome. He batted .333 in a brief six-game stint with Houston in 1986. He possesses power and speed, but he has not put together the kind of season to keep him in the majors. Meadows, though, has a good shot at being the Astros' fourth outfielder in 1989.

Meadows' 1989 cards should open in the 10- to 15-cent range. If he lives up to his potential, his cards could gain in value. Our pick for his best 1989 card is Topps.

LUIS MEDINA

	BA	G	AB	R	H	2B	3B	HR	RBI	SB
1988	.255	16	51	10	13	0	0	6	8	0
Life	.255	16	51	10	13	0	0	6	8	0

POSITION: Outfield
TEAM: Cleveland Indians
BORN: March 26, 1963 Downy, CA
HEIGHT: 6′3″ **WEIGHT:** 190 lbs.
BATS: Right **THROWS:** Left
ACQUIRED: Ninth-round pick in 6/85 free-agent draft

This could be the year when fans recognize just how good Medina is. At Triple-A Colorado Springs in 1988, Medina batted .310, with 28 home runs and 81 RBIs. He got a late-season call to Cleveland, and the hits just kept coming. Medina's 1987 season came to an end in August due to elbow surgery. While he was playing at Double-A Williamsport, he hit .320, 16 homers, and 68 RBIs. Defense is not his strong suit, but he can be a competent major league left fielder. His best spot might be as a designated hitter, where he can't do damage in the field.

Medina should give the Tribe a good stick for years to come. Look for his 1989 cards to open in the 25- to 30-cent range. Our pick for his best 1989 card is Donruss.

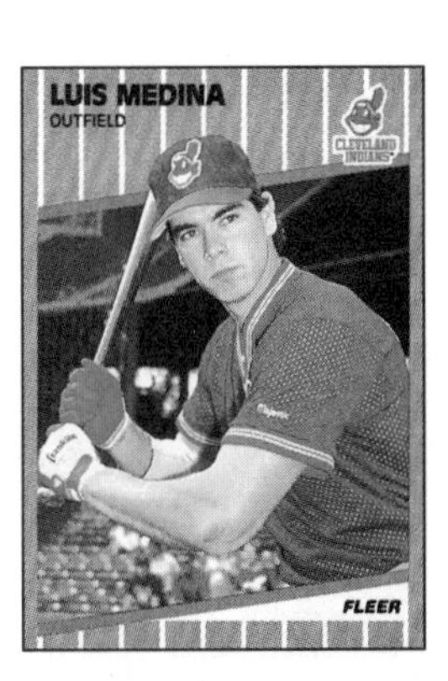

BOB MELVIN

	BA	G	AB	R	H	2B	3B	HR	RBI	SB
1988	.234	92	273	23	64	13	1	8	27	0
Life	.220	306	869	88	191	39	4	24	87	3

POSITION: Catcher
TEAM: San Francisco Giants
BORN: October 28, 1961 Palo Alto, CA
HEIGHT: 6′4″ **WEIGHT:** 205 lbs.
BATS: Right **THROWS:** Right
ACQUIRED: Traded from Tigers with Juan Berenguer and Scott Medvin for Dave LaPoint, Eric King, and Matt Nokes, 10/85

Melvin seems ready to take over full-time catching duties for the Giants. In 1988, he hit only .234, but fellow backstop Bob Brenly ended with only a .189 average. Melvin was acquired in the Matt Nokes deal. Some wonder whether Nokes is a better catcher. But Melvin is excellent defensively, and he seems to be improving at the plate. He also managed eight home runs and 27 RBIs in 1988. In the Giants' pennant-winning season, 1987, he had a paltry .199 average in the regular season, but he hit .429 in three games during the National League Championship Series. Melvin will become a better hitter with more experience.

Melvin's 1989 cards will be priced as commons. Smart investors will put a few dollars in his cards and sock them away until he becomes an All-Star. Our pick for his best 1989 card is Score.

JOEY MEYER

	BA	G	AB	R	H	2B	3B	HR	RBI	SB
1988	.263	103	327	22	86	18	0	11	45	0
Life	.263	103	327	22	86	18	0	11	45	0

POSITION: First base; designated hitter
TEAM: Milwaukee Brewers
BORN: May 10, 1962 Honolulu, HI
HEIGHT: 6′3″ **WEIGHT:** 260 lbs.
BATS: Right **THROWS:** Right
ACQUIRED: Fifth-round pick in 6/83 free-agent draft

Meyer arrived in Milwaukee to stay in 1988, batting close to .270. And while he didn't tear up the A.L., he did show promise. Three years ago, he so terrorized the Double-A Texas League with El Paso that he earned his first shot with the Brewers. Nothing much happened, though, and he spent another year, 1987, in the minor leagues at Triple-A Denver. There he hit .311 with 29 home runs and 92 RBIs. Six seats in the upper deck at Denver's Mile High Stadium are painted to signify the landing area of Meyer's most prodigious home runs—approximately 583 feet from home plate!

His 1989 cards will sell for 20 to 25 cents until he begins to emerge as a consistent A.L. home run threat. Our pick for his best 1989 card is Fleer.

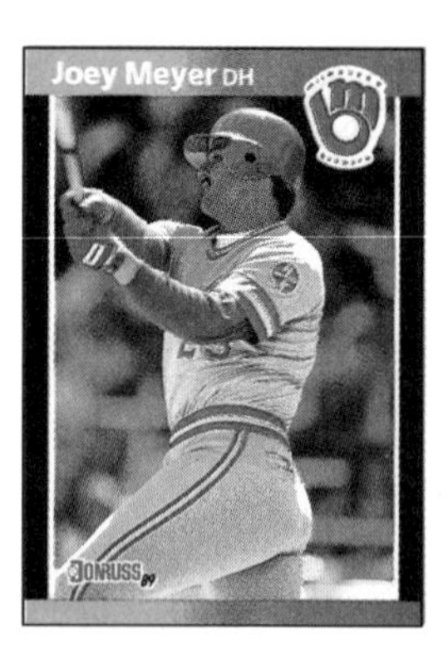

KEITH MILLER

	BA	G	AB	R	H	2B	3B	HR	RBI	SB
1988	.214	40	70	9	15	1	1	1	5	0
Life	.281	65	121	23	34	3	3	1	6	8

POSITION: Infield
TEAM: New York Mets
BORN: June 12, 1963 Midland, TX
HEIGHT: 5′11″ **WEIGHT:** 175 lbs.
BATS: Right **THROWS:** Right
ACQUIRED: Signed as a free agent, 9/84

Miller had a good season at Triple-A Tidewater, and it looks like he'll start the season at Shea Stadium. At Tidewater in 1988, he hit .281, with one homer, 15 RBIs, and 23 runs in 171 at-bats. In 1987, he batted .378 in 51 at-bats for the Mets before being injured and ultimately farmed out to Tidewater. In 1986, Miller paced the Double-A Texas League in triples with eight, stole 25 bases, and batted .329—third best in the loop. He is one of two Keith Millers headed for the majors in 1989. This Miller seems destined for a utility role behind such people as Kevin Elster and Gregg Jefferies. On another club, Miller would probably figure in a starting role.

Miller's 1989 cards will open in the commons box. Don't invest in his cards until he wins a starting job. Our pick for his best 1989 card is Topps.

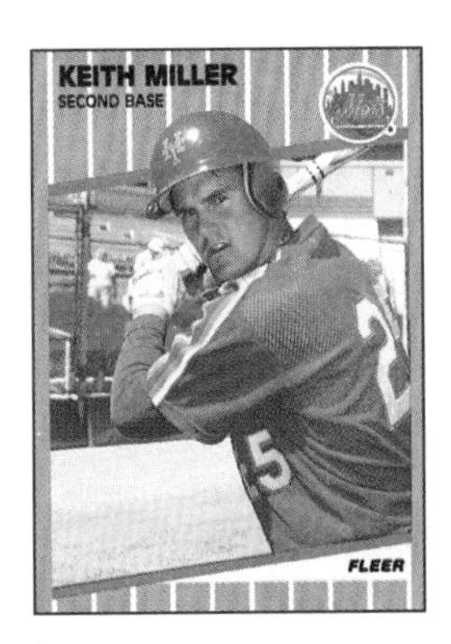

GREG MINTON

	W	L	ERA	G	SV	IP	H	R	BB	SO
1988	4	5	2.85	44	7	79.0	67	37	34	46
Life	54	61	3.19	637	142	1025.2	995	426	439	433

POSITION: Pitcher
TEAM: California Angels
BORN: July 29, 1951 Lubbock, TX
HEIGHT: 6′2″ **WEIGHT:** 190 lbs.
BATS: Both **THROWS:** Right
ACQUIRED: Signed as a free agent, 6/87

Minton proved that he's still an effective reliever in 1988. He appeared in 44 games and finished the year with four wins, seven saves, and a sharp 2.85 ERA. Minton had been a member of the Giants since 1975, before being released in mid-1987. The Angels snapped up the veteran relief ace. Minton's 1987 totals were six wins, 11 saves, and a 3.17 ERA that was tops on the club. If his wins are added to his saves, Minton has been responsible for more than 200 victories. However, the Hall of Fame will have a glut of relievers up for election in the next ten years. Minton will have to shine for three more years to have a chance.

Minton has an uncertain future. His 1989 cards are risky investments, even at their current value of three cents or less. Our pick for his best 1989 card is Fleer.

PAUL MIRABELLA

	W	L	ERA	G	SV	IP	H	R	BB	SO
1988	2	2	1.65	38	4	60.0	44	12	21	33
Life	15	27	4.40	241	13	425.2	442	238	205	224

POSITION: Pitcher
TEAM: Milwaukee Brewers
BORN: March 20, 1954 Belleville, NJ
HEIGHT: 6′1″ **WEIGHT:** 180 lbs.
BATS: Both **THROWS:** Left
ACQUIRED: Signed as a free agent, 2/87

Mirabella broke out and had a great season in 1988, becoming a principal set-up man for the Brewers. He appeared in 38 games, compiling a scanty 1.65 ERA, two wins, four saves, and 33 strikeouts in 60 innings of work. He worked to batters before relief ace Dan Plesac came in. Mirabella's '88 stats show a marked improvement over his 1987 numbers. He was 2-1, with a 4.91 ERA in 29 appearances. He has bounced around the A.L. in his 11 years in the majors, playing for Texas (twice), the Yankees, Toronto, Baltimore, Seattle, and the Brewers. Mirabella has finally found a home in Milwaukee.

Mirabella's 1989 cards will be priced as commons. Even though he had a good season in 1988, his cards probably will never be worth much more. Our pick for his best 1989 card is Score.

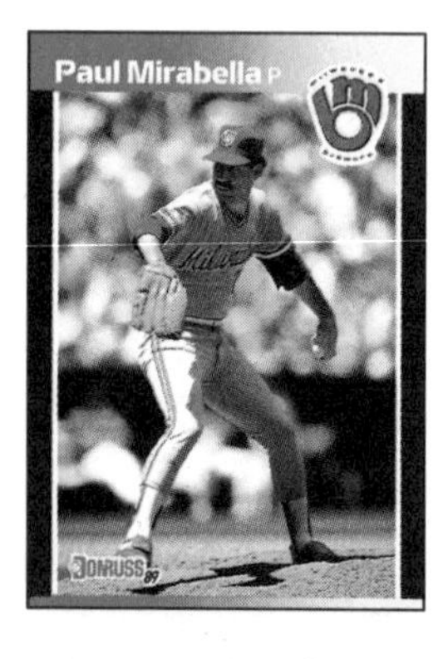

KEVIN MITCHELL

	BA	G	AB	R	H	2B	3B	HR	RBI	SB
1988	.251	148	505	60	127	25	7	19	80	5
Life	.268	394	1311	179	351	67	11	53	194	17

POSITION: Third base
TEAM: San Francisco Giants
BORN: January 13, 1962 San Diego, CA
HEIGHT: 5′11″ **WEIGHT:** 210 lbs.
BATS: Right **THROWS:** Right
ACQUIRED: Traded from San Diego with Dave Dravecky and Craig Lefferts for Chris Brown, Keith Comstock, Mark Davis, and Mark Grant, 7/87

Mitchell played as if he had been the Giants' starting third baseman forever during his 1988 season. He joined the team in July 1987 and laid claim to the starting job early in 1988. Mitchell had career highs in doubles (25), triples (seven), and RBIs (80) last season. In 1987, he was a motivating force behind the Giants' pennant acquisition. After moving to the Giants, he hit .306 with 15 homers and 44 RBIs in just 69 games. He played seven positions for the 1986 New York Mets, and hit .250 in the 1986 World Series against Boston. Mitchell should be an offensive force for the Giants in 1989.

Mitchell is for real, and he'll keep getting better with time. If you spot his 1989 cards for a nickel or less, buy them. At age 27, this player seems destined for stardom. Our pick for his best 1989 card is Topps.

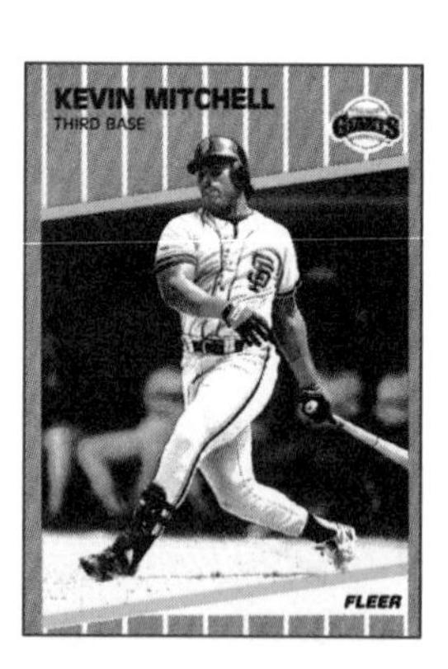

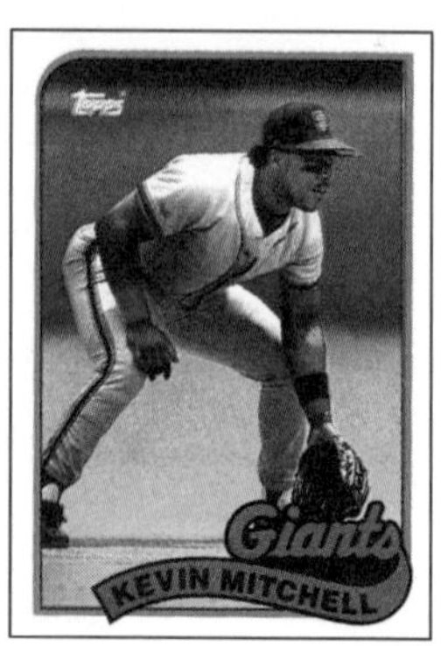

DALE MOHORCIC

	W	L	ERA	G	SV	IP	H	R	BB	SO
1988	4	8	4.22	56	6	74.2	83	42	29	44
Life	13	18	3.20	188	29	253.0	257	101	63	121

POSITION: Pitcher
TEAM: New York Yankees
BORN: January 25, 1956 Cleveland, OH
HEIGHT: 6′3″ **WEIGHT:** 230 lbs.
BATS: Right **THROWS:** Right
ACQUIRED: Traded from Rangers for Cecilio Guante, 8/88

Mohorcic is an ironman when it comes to appearances. He pitched in 56 games in 1988, which was second on the Yankees to Dave Righetti. Mohorcic pitched in 74 games with the 1987 Rangers, and he kept his ERA to just below 3.00. He also pitched in 58 games for the '86 Rangers (with a 2.51 ERA). His record in '88 was 4-8, with a 4.22 ERA, six saves, and 44 strikeouts in 74⅔ innings. Mohorcic set a Ranger record in 1986 as their oldest rookie (30 years old). He also set a record that year for most consecutive relief appearances, with 13. Mohorcic can make up for lost time for the Yankees by continuing to be a durable middle reliever.

Mohorcic's 1989 cards will be in the commons box. Middle relievers, even those as sturdy as Mohorcic, seldom generate much collector interest. Our pick for his best 1989 card is Donruss.

PAUL MOLITOR

	BA	G	AB	R	H	2B	3B	HR	RBI	SB
1988	.312	154	609	115	190	34	6	13	60	41
Life	.299	1282	5213	905	1557	275	56	108	525	317

POSITION: Third base; designated hitter
TEAM: Milwaukee Brewers
BORN: August 22, 1956 St. Paul, MN
HEIGHT: 6′ **WEIGHT:** 175 lbs.
BATS: Right **THROWS:** Right
ACQUIRED: First-round pick in 6/77 free-agent draft

Although Molitor avoided injury in 1988, he had trouble topping 1987's 39-game hitting streak (who wouldn't?). That streak, fourth longest in baseball history, helped him gain national recognition. Still, Molitor had a good season last year, hitting .312, scoring 115 runs, stealing 41 bases, and driving in 60 runs. In 1987, he led the A.L. with 41 doubles and 114 runs scored, while he hit .353. In 1981, he scored a career-high 136 runs. With the emergence of rookie Gary Sheffield as the Brewer infield star of the future, Molitor could become a full-time designated hitter and prolong his injury-filled career.

Molitor's 1989 cards will be sold at a dime or less by most dealers. His cards remain one of the best bargains for collectors. If the Brewers win a division crown, those prices could easily triple. Our pick for his best 1989 card is Topps.

JEFF MONTGOMERY

	W	L	ERA	G	SV	IP	H	R	BB	SO
1988	7	2	3.45	45	1	62.2	54	25	30	47
Life	9	4	4.17	59	1	82.0	79	40	39	60

POSITION: Pitcher
TEAM: Kansas City Royals
BORN: January 7, 1962 Wellston, OH
HEIGHT: 5′11″ **WEIGHT:** 170 lbs.
BATS: Right **THROWS:** Right
ACQUIRED: Traded from Reds for Van Snider, 2/88

Montgomery had the best season of his short career with the 1988 Royals. The righty reliever finished 13 games he appeared in, tallying the fifth best win and ERA totals on the squad. He won a total of seven games, and he notched one save. Montgomery spent four years in the Reds' minor league system before getting a late-season test in Cincinnati in 1987. His success was inconclusive, although his ERA was a high 6.52. Montgomery has helped fill a void in the Royals' bullpen, and he'll get more opportunities to perform in 1989.

Montgomery's cards will be about a nickel in 1989. Proceed slowly when investing here. Cards for most relievers just don't gain in value, and Montgomery hasn't really proved himself yet. Our pick for his best 1989 card is Fleer.

MIKE MOORE

	W	L	ERA	G	CG	IP	H	R	BB	SO
1988	9	15	3.78	37	9	228.2	196	104	63	182
Life	66	96	4.38	227	56	1457.0	1498	783	535	937

POSITION: Pitcher
TEAM: Oakland A's
BORN: November 26, 1959 Eakly, OK
HEIGHT: 6′4″ **WEIGHT:** 205 lbs.
BATS: Right **THROWS:** Right
ACQUIRED: Signed as a free agent, 11/88

Moore should find new life with the A's. He wasn't able to shake his losing woes in 1988. As a Mariner in '88, he went 9-15, which followed his 9-19 record in 1987. Moore wasn't as bad as his record might indicate. He was one of the top pitchers of the last two months of the season, amassing a 2.34 ERA for that period. He did have one winning season in 1983, a 17-10 effort. Now that he has the extremely powerful Oakland offense behind him, Moore's record should improve as well.

Moore has a pretty bad lifetime win-loss mark. He'll be lucky to even his record at .500 within the next five seasons. Only the most daring investor would gamble on this player's cards, priced at three cents or less 1989. Our pick for his best 1989 card is Donruss.

KEITH MORELAND

	BA	G	AB	R	H	2B	3B	HR	RBI	SB
1988	.256	143	511	40	131	23	0	5	64	2
Life	.279	1183	4156	466	1161	194	14	115	629	25

POSITION: First base; third base
TEAM: Detroit Tigers
BORN: May 2, 1954 Dallas, TX
HEIGHT: 6′ **WEIGHT:** 200 lbs.
BATS: Right **THROWS:** Right
ACQUIRED: Traded from Padres with Chris Brown for Walt Terrell, 10/88

Moreland could serve his newest team, the Tigers, in many ways. He has played first base, third base, outfield, and catcher in his long career, which began in 1978 with Philadelphia. His 1988 season, spent with San Diego, saw him hit .256 with five homers and 64 RBIs. Only a year before, Moreland pounded out 27 homers and 88 RBIs for the 1987 Cubs. He has managed at least 10 homers and 60 RBIs a year since 1982, a hopeful sign for the Tigers. Moreland could help the Tigers regain the A.L. East championship in 1989.

Moreland's 1989 cards could be a great investment at a nickel or less. The Tigers should provide Moreland with full-time work somewhere, and the change of scenery might do his career good. He should be one of the team's best power hitters. Our pick for his best 1989 card is Fleer.

MIKE MORGAN

	W	L	ERA	G	CG	IP	H	R	BB	SO
1988	1	6	5.43	22	2	71.1	70	45	23	29
Life	34	68	4.90	157	24	785.1	905	464	313	342

POSITION: Pitcher
TEAM: Baltimore Orioles
BORN: October 8, 1959 Tulare, CA
HEIGHT: 6′2″ **WEIGHT:** 195 lbs.
BATS: Right **THROWS:** Right
ACQUIRED: Traded from Mariners for Ken Dixon, 12/87

Morgan's hard luck continued in his first season with the Orioles. He came to the Orioles, his fifth American League team, via the Mariners. Unfortunately, his losing record followed him to Baltimore. Used both in starting and relief roles, Morgan did hurl two complete games and finish six others in relief. Signed straight out of high school by then-Oakland A's owner Charlie Finley, Morgan made his major league debut just one week after graduating from high school. Morgan has never posted a winning record, and that trend may continue in 1989.

Some may wonder what Morgan could do with a winning team. Until then, he'll continue to be one of the A.L.'s biggest mysteries. Don't bother investing in his cards, even at their common prices. Our pick for his best 1989 card is Donruss.

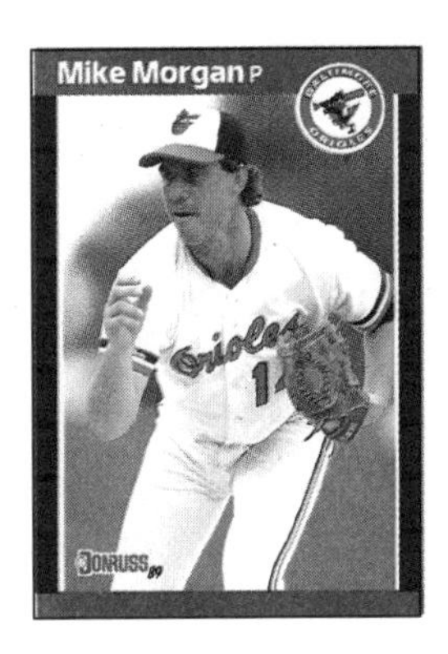

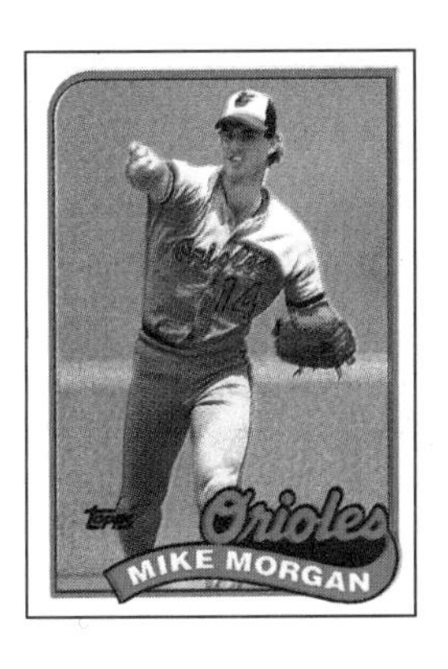

HAL MORRIS

	BA	G	AB	R	H	2B	3B	HR	RBI	SB
1988	.100	15	20	2	1	0	0	0	0	0
Life	.100	15	20	2	1	0	0	0	0	0

POSITION: Outfield
TEAM: New York Yankees
BORN: April 9, 1965 Munster, IN
HEIGHT: 6'3" **WEIGHT:** 200 lbs.
BATS: Left **THROWS:** Left
ACQUIRED: Seventh-round pick in 6/86 free-agent draft

Morris batted .296 at 1988 Triple-A Columbus, leading the team in base hits (134), as well as racking up three homers and 38 RBIs. He broke in with Oneonta in the New York-Penn league in 1986, hitting .378 in 36 games. A manpower shortage at Double-A Albany that year caused the Bronx Bombers to rush Morris up two classifications to Albany. The move didn't do much for him: He hit a meager .215 in 25 contests. In 1987 at Albany, however, Morris felt right at home and batted .326 in 135 games, accounting for 73 RBIs and 173 base hits. Morris is a great hitter, and he should improve his power stats as he gets more experience at the plate.

Morris should challenge for a spot on the Yankee roster this spring. His 1989 cards should open in the 20- to 25-cent range. Our pick for his best 1989 card is Donruss.

JACK MORRIS

	W	L	ERA	G	CG	IP	H	R	BB	SO
1988	15	13	3.94	34	10	235.0	225	115	83	168
Life	177	118	3.59	370	133	2623.1	2347	1136	930	1703

POSITION: Pitcher
TEAM: Detroit Tigers
BORN: May 16, 1956 St. Paul, MN
HEIGHT: 6'3" **WEIGHT:** 200 lbs.
BATS: Right **THROWS:** Right
ACQUIRED: Re-signed as a free agent, 12/87

Morris remained the top winner of the 1980s with another strong performance for the 1988 Tigers. The veteran hurler led his team in wins, strikeouts, and innings pitched. Morris' success in 1988 was earned. He completed ten games and threw two shutouts. Morris, at age 33, shows no signs of slowing down. He's been active with Detroit since 1977, and twice has won 20 games a season. The last time he won fewer than 15 games was during the strike-shortened season of 1981. Morris should top 200 wins by early 1990, which will put him one step closer to the Hall of Fame.

Expect 1989 cards of Morris to sell for the bargain price of 20 cents or less. Barring an injury, Morris could pitch his way to Cooperstown. Save his cards for a long-term rise in value once he's enshrined. Our pick for his best 1989 card is Topps.

LLOYD MOSEBY

	BA	G	AB	R	H	2B	3B	HR	RBI	SB
1988	.239	128	472	77	113	17	7	10	42	31
Life	.261	1257	4622	696	1208	217	57	138	608	231

POSITION: Outfield
TEAM: Toronto Blue Jays
BORN: November 5, 1959 Portland, OR
HEIGHT: 6'3" **WEIGHT:** 200 lbs.
BATS: Left **THROWS:** Right
ACQUIRED: First-round pick in 6/78 free-agent draft

Moseby couldn't duplicate the super season he enjoyed in 1987 again in 1988 for the Blue Jays. In 1987, Moseby clobbered 26 homers and 96 RBIs while batting .282. Last season, however, Moseby struggled and played in nearly 30 fewer games. His average sank to an undistinguished .239, and his power stats dropped to ten homers and 42 RBIs. His 93 strikeouts derailed much of his season, as he struck out once for nearly every six at-bats. Don't think his slump is permanent, however. Moseby should be back at full force in 1989.

Slumps seldom help players, but they sometimes level off cards with rising values. Moseby's troubles should take his 1989 cards down to a value of 10 cents. That's an inviting price for investors who are prepared for a Moseby comeback this season. Our pick for his best 1989 card is Topps.

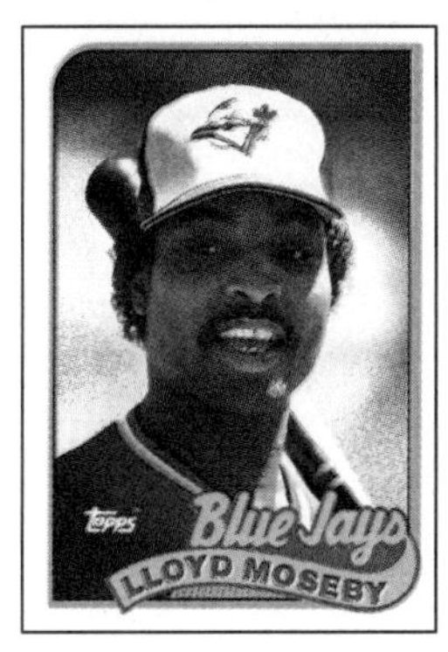

JOHN MOSES

	BA	G	AB	R	H	2B	3B	HR	RBI	SB
1988	.316	105	206	33	65	10	3	2	12	11
Life	.259	491	1266	180	328	52	13	9	98	81

POSITION: Outfield
TEAM: Minnesota Twins
BORN: August 9, 1957 Los Angeles, CA
HEIGHT: 5'10" **WEIGHT:** 170 lbs.
BATS: Both **THROWS:** Right
ACQUIRED: Signed as a free agent, 4/88

Moses truly outdid himself for the 1988 Twins. He was a lifetime .248 hitter going into last season. However, in his first year with Minnesota, Moses hit a career high of .316. He was a defensive gem for the Twins, going without an error all season. His 11 stolen bases highlighted his 1988 accomplishments. Moses never did nail down a starting spot, mostly because he isn't the typical power-hitting outfielder. However, following his 1988 success, he'll be a real contender for a starting spot in 1989.

Why shouldn't Moses' cards be good investments at their prices of three cents or less? One good season does not a star make. If Moses can play a full season and hit .300, investors may reconsider. Our pick for his best 1989 card is Donruss.

JAMIE MOYER

	W	L	ERA	G	CG	IP	H	R	BB	SO
1988	9	15	3.48	34	3	202.0	212	84	55	121
Life	28	34	4.42	85	5	490.1	529	263	194	313

POSITION: Pitcher
TEAM: Texas Rangers
BORN: November 11, 1962
Sellersville, PA
HEIGHT: 6′ **WEIGHT:** 170 lbs.
BATS: Left **THROWS:** Left
ACQUIRED: Traded from Cubs with Rafael Palmeiro and Drew Hall for Mitch Williams, Paul Kilgus, Steve Wilson, Curtis Wilkerson, Luis Benitez, and Pablo Delgado, 12/88

The Rangers traded for Moyer, hoping that he could be their lefthanded starting ace. He has all the tools to be a big and consistent winner in the majors. In 1988, he won nine games for the Cubs (against 15 losses), with a 3.48 ERA and three complete games in 34 outings. Like many lefties, his tendency toward wildness has hurt him. His first big league win was against his boyhood favorite team, the Phillies, and the pitcher he idolized as a youngster, Steve Carlton. If Moyer could enjoy a little of Carlton's success, Texas would be a very happy organization.

Moyer's card status is still one of speculation. Be conservative in your acquisitions, but buy his 1989 cards for a nickel or so, if you can. Our pick for his best 1989 card is Score.

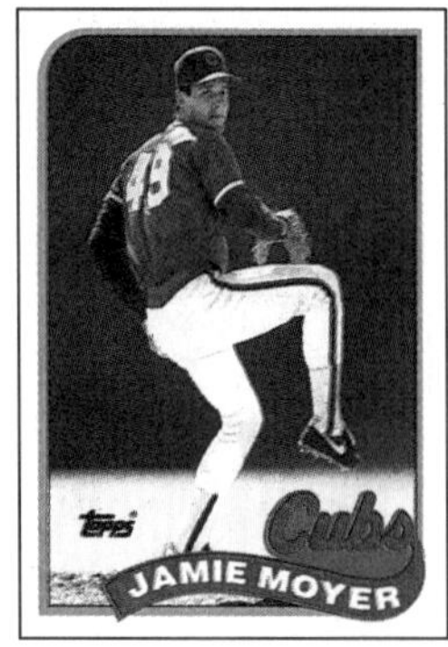

RANCE MULLINIKS

	BA	G	AB	R	H	2B	3B	HR	RBI	SB
1988	.300	119	337	49	101	21	1	12	48	1
Life	.277	1065	2957	381	818	199	14	66	366	13

POSITION: Third base; designated hitter
TEAM: Toronto Blue Jays
BORN: January 15, 1956 Tulare, CA
HEIGHT: 5′11″ **WEIGHT:** 175 lbs.
BATS: Left **THROWS:** Right
ACQUIRED: Traded from Royals for Phil Huffman, 3/82

Mulliniks turned in another workmanlike performance for the Blue Jays in 1988. He hit .300, with a career-high 12 home runs, 21 doubles, and 48 RBIs (ten game winners). He has been a consistent offensive player for Toronto, hitting double figures in round-trippers and the mid-40s in ribbies a year. In 1987, he hit .310, with 11 home runs and 44 RBIs. He has been the lefthanded-hitting half of the Blue Jay platoon at third base since 1982. Toronto has counted on Mulliniks to produce for years, and there is no reason to think that he will disappoint in 1989.

Since Mulliniks is not a full-time player, his cards have never been in demand. His 1989 cards will open as commons. He probably will not be an every-day player in '89, and his cards should remain cheap. Our pick for his best 1989 card is Fleer.

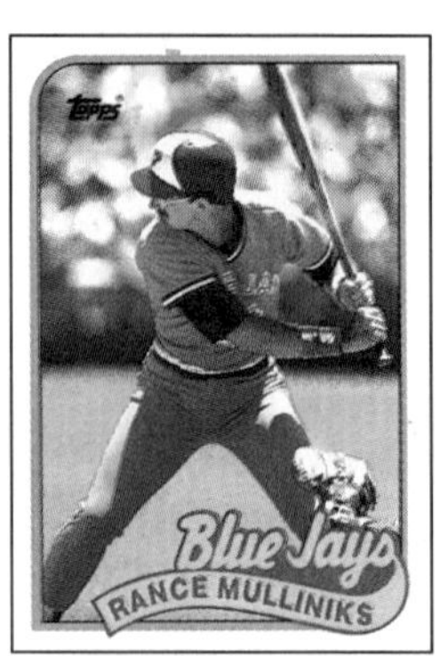

DALE MURPHY

	BA	G	AB	R	H	2B	3B	HR	RBI	SB
1988	.226	156	592	77	134	35	4	24	77	3
Life	.274	1675	6175	1005	1689	276	37	334	1004	148

POSITION: Outfield
TEAM: Atlanta Braves
BORN: March 12, 1956 Portland, OR
HEIGHT: 6′5″ **WEIGHT:** 215 lbs.
BATS: Right **THROWS:** Right
ACQUIRED: First-round pick in 6/74 free-agent draft

A horrible first-half slump in 1988 forced Murphy's offensive stats to their lowest in the 1980s. Still, he hit 24 home runs and collected his 1,000th career RBI last season. He was only the fourth player in history to win back-to-back MVP awards (in 1982 and 1983). He also has the second highest home run total of the 1980s, trailing only Mike Schmidt. Starting the '88 season, Murphy had played in 740 consecutive games. He had a great season in 1987, slugging a career-high 44 homers while collecting 115 runs and 105 RBIs. If the Braves contend for a pennant, you'll know that "Murph" will be leading the way.

Murphy's 1988 slump should reduce interest in his 1989 cards somewhat. Buy them fast at their 35-cent value. When he's elected to the Hall of Fame, you'll be glad you did. Our pick for his best 1989 card is Fleer.

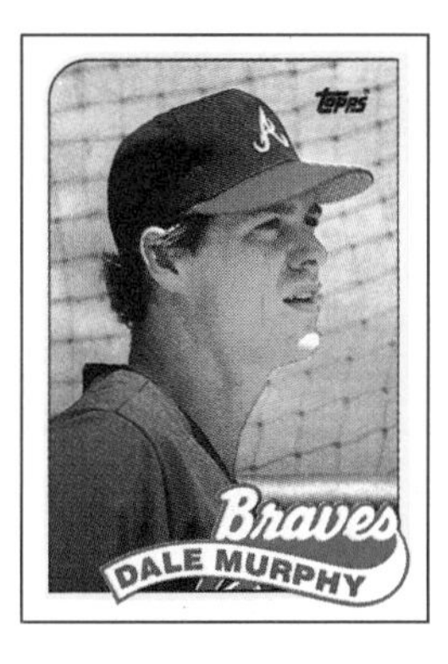

ROB MURPHY

	W	L	ERA	G	SV	IP	H	R	BB	SO
1988	0	6	3.08	76	3	84.2	69	31	38	74
Life	14	11	2.60	199	7	238.2	188	74	93	210

POSITION: Pitcher
TEAM: Cincinnati Reds
BORN: May 26, 1960 Miami, FL
HEIGHT: 6′2″ **WEIGHT:** 205 lbs.
BATS: Left **THROWS:** Left
ACQUIRED: First-round pick in 1/81 free-agent draft

Murphy didn't have the best of luck with the 1988 Cincinnati Reds. He led National League pitchers in appearances with 76. However, he carried a six-game losing streak with him through the end of the season. Prior to 1988, Murphy had a career record of 14-5. Murphy is one of baseball's most durable pitchers. In 1987, he set a major league record for lefty relievers by appearing in 87 games. He may never become famous stuck in the unglamorous role of middle relief. However, Murphy could become known as one of baseball's ironmen if he continues to work at this pace.

Murphy's 1988 cards should be three cents or less. Regardless of the talent Murphy has for middle relief, his cards won't be good investments. Collectors prefer cards of home run hitters, strikeout artists, and bullpen aces. Our pick for his best 1989 card is Topps.

EDDIE MURRAY

	BA	G	AB	R	H	2B	3B	HR	RBI	SB
1988	.284	161	603	75	171	27	2	28	84	5
Life	.295	1820	6845	1048	2021	351	25	333	1190	61

POSITION: First base
TEAM: Los Angeles Dodgers
BORN: February 24, 1956
Los Angeles, CA
HEIGHT: 6′2″ **WEIGHT:** 205 lbs.
BATS: Both **THROWS:** Right
ACQUIRED: Traded from Orioles for Brian Holton, Ken Howell, and Juan Bell, 12/88

In 1988, Murray reached two more milestones on his way to the Hall of Fame. He scored his 1,000th career run and got his 2,000th career hit. He is in third place among home run hitters in the 1980s, trailing Mike Schmidt and Dale Murphy. Murray will try to help the Dodgers repeat as world champions. He hit .284 in 1988 with the Orioles, with 28 homers and 84 RBIs. Except for the strike-shortened 1981 season (when he led the A.L. in RBIs with 78), he has at least 84 ribbies for 11 consecutive years. His consistent excellence has silenced many of his critics. Murray's play showed why he's one of today's superstars.

Murray's 1989 cards are good investments at a quarter or less. Even after 12 seasons, he's still going strong; his cards should continue that way, too. Our pick for his best 1989 card is Topps.

JEFF MUSSELMAN

	W	L	ERA	G	CG	IP	H	R	BB	SO
1988	8	5	3.18	15	0	85.0	80	34	30	39
Life	20	10	3.86	89	0	179.1	163	84	89	97

POSITION: Pitcher
TEAM: Toronto Blue Jays
BORN: June 21, 1963 Doylestown, PA
HEIGHT: 6′ **WEIGHT:** 180 lbs.
BATS: Left **THROWS:** Left
ACQUIRED: Sixth-round pick in 6/85 free-agent draft

Injuries stopped Musselman from building on his successful 1987 rookie season in '88. While he made 68 appearances in 1987, he got into just 15 games in 1988. Despite his shortened season, Musselman still won eight games and posted an admirable 3.18 ERA. He became a full-time starter in 1988 also. In 1987, he was 12-5, with a 4.15 ERA and three saves. With the success he has enjoyed in his first two seasons, it's amazing to discover that his minor league career consisted of just two seasons. Musselman, if healthy, could resume his winning ways in 1989.

Musselman's 1989 cards, at a nickel or less, could be tempting investments. Cautious speculators will want to wait to invest until Musselman's stamina, since he's coming back from assorted hurts, isn't a factor. Our pick for his best 1989 card is Topps.

RANDY MYERS

	W	L	ERA	G	SV	IP	H	R	BB	SO
1988	7	3	1.72	55	26	68.0	45	15	17	69
Life	10	9	2.95	120	32	155.2	117	56	57	176

POSITION: Pitcher
TEAM: New York Mets
BORN: September 19, 1962
Vancouver, WA
HEIGHT: 6′1″ **WEIGHT:** 190 lbs.
BATS: Left **THROWS:** Left
ACQUIRED: First-round pick in 6/82 free-agent draft

Myers' team-leading 26 saves for the 1988 Mets set a club record for a lefthander. He appeared in 55 games, fashioned a 7-3 record, and had a classy 1.72 ERA in 68 innings of work. He had 69 strikeouts and walked only 17. When Myers throws baseballs, they look like aspirin tablets. In 1987, his first real big league season, he went 3-6 in 54 games, earning six saves and fanning 92 in 75 innings. At Triple-A Tidewater in 1986, he saved 12 games for the Tides, and he had a late-season ten-game look with the Mets. Myers should be saving many games for the Mets' great starting rotation in 1989.

Myers is considered a potential superstar. Buy his 1989 cards at about a dime, and hold on to them for potential profits over the years. Our pick for his best 1989 card is Fleer.

GENE NELSON

	W	L	ERA	G	SV	IP	H	R	BB	SO
1988	9	6	3.06	54	3	111.2	93	42	38	67
Life	43	45	4.23	268	15	764.0	758	387	302	466

POSITION: Pitcher
TEAM: Oakland A's
BORN: December 3, 1960 Tampa, FL
HEIGHT: 6′ **WEIGHT:** 175 lbs.
BATS: Right **THROWS:** Right
ACQUIRED: Traded from White Sox with Bruce Tanner for Donnie Hill, 12/86

Nelson had one of his best seasons with the 1988 Athletics. He went 9-6, with 20 games finished and three saves in 1988. Nelson's ERA was 3.06, his finest ever in eight major league seasons. He began his career in 1981 with the Yankees. In 1987, he was 6-5, with 54 appearances, a 3.93 ERA, three saves, and 94 strikeouts in 123⅔ innings. He won his most games ever (ten) pitching in 1985 for the White Sox and then-manager Tony LaRussa. LaRussa wanted Nelson back when he took Oakland's managing job. Nelson was one of Oakland's best pitchers in the 1988 World Series.

Despite his success, Nelson still has a lifetime losing record and a career ERA above 4.00. See if he and his Oakland teammates have another successful season before investing in his cards. Our pick for his best 1989 card is Fleer.

AL NEWMAN

	BA	G	AB	R	H	2B	3B	HR	RBI	SB
1988	.223	105	260	58	35	7	0	0	19	12
Life	.215	335	781	168	109	26	5	1	57	40

POSITION: Infield
TEAM: Minnesota Twins
BORN: June 30, 1960 Kansas City, MO
HEIGHT: 5′8″ **WEIGHT:** 175 lbs.
BATS: Both **THROWS:** Right
ACQUIRED: Traded from Expos for Mike Shade, 2/87

Newman continued to fill in wherever needed for the 1988 Twins. The switch-hitting utilityman shuttled between second base, shortstop, and third base during his second season in Minnesota. His average remained low, but he made only six errors in 105 games. Newman's speed is another of his assets. He stole 12 bases in 15 attempts in 1988. He drove in a career-high 29 runs in 1987, playing an important role in the Twins' world championship. He hit .221 that year. Newman will continue to be a key member of the Twins' bench in 1989.

Newman's average is too low to earn any starting position. His cards are common-priced, but aren't suitable investments. His part-time status would eliminate any real demand for his cards. Our pick for his best 1989 card is Fleer.

TOM NIEDENFUER

	W	L	ERA	G	SV	IP	H	R	BB	SO
1988	3	4	3.51	52	18	59.0	59	23	19	40
Life	36	37	3.05	407	95	552.0	489	196	186	427

POSITION: Pitcher
TEAM: Seattle Mariners
BORN: August 13, 1959
St. Louis Park, MN
HEIGHT: 6′5″ **WEIGHT:** 227 lbs.
BATS: Right **THROWS:** Right
ACQUIRED: Signed as a free agent, 12/88

If the Mariners thought they had problems in their bullpen, they can point to relief artist Niedenfuer as an answer this season. He posted 18 saves for the last-place Orioles and finished an amazing 42 of 52 games in which he appeared. In all, he was responsible for more than one-third of the Orioles' total victories, either by way of save or victory. Baptized under fire with a 1981 first-season appearance for the Dodgers in the World Series, Niedenfuer has gone on to become one of five major leaguers with at least ten saves for five consecutive seasons.

So far, Niedenfuer's only high-priced card is due to an error on the 1988 Score issue that misspells his name "Neidenfuer." His 1989 cards will cost 5 cents each, a price that's sure to rise. Our pick for his best 1989 card is Topps.

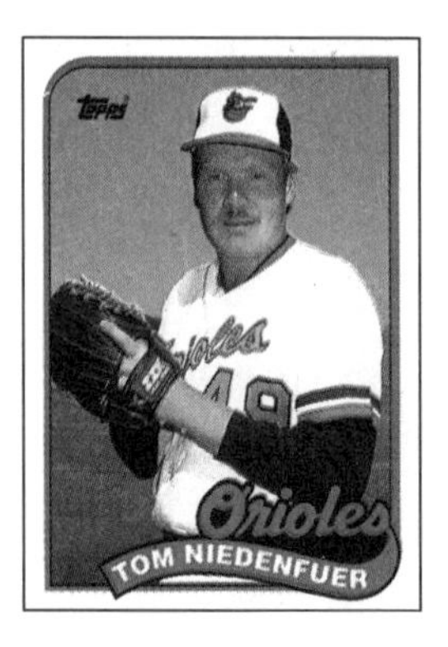

JUAN NIEVES

	W	L	ERA	G	CG	IP	H	R	BB	SO
1988	7	5	4.08	25	1	110.1	84	53	50	73
Life	32	25	4.71	94	8	490.2	507	289	227	352

POSITION: Pitcher
TEAM: Milwaukee Brewers
BORN: January 5, 1965 Santurce, Puerto Rico
HEIGHT: 6'3" **WEIGHT:** 190 lbs.
BATS: Left **THROWS:** Left
ACQUIRED: Signed as a free agent, 7/83

It took the "sophomore jinx" an extra year to catch up with Nieves. He seemed on the verge of success after going 14-8 in 1987. As a preview to the upcoming season, the lefty hurled an April 1987 no-hitter against the Orioles. Nieves couldn't find that magic again in 1988, when he was banished to the bullpen temporarily to regain his form. Even there, he finished four games and earned his first major league save. It's certain that the Brewers need a comeback from Nieves in 1989 to remain competitive in the strong A.L. East.

In three major league seasons, Nieves' ERA has never been below 4.00. He may need only seasoning to become a big winner. However, avoid investing in his common-priced cards until he puts together a big year. Our pick for his best 1989 card is Score.

AL NIPPER

	W	L	ERA	G	CG	IP	H	R	BB	SO
1988	2	4	3.04	22	0	80.0	72	37	34	27
Life	44	47	4.46	135	21	773.2	811	433	284	369

POSITION: Pitcher
TEAM: Chicago Cubs
BORN: April 2, 1959 San Diego, CA
HEIGHT: 6' **WEIGHT:** 188 lbs.
BATS: Right **THROWS:** Right
ACQUIRED: Traded from Red Sox with Calvin Schiraldi for Lee Smith, 12/87

Nipper was the low man on the Cubs ERA list with a 3.04 mark, but he saw only limited action in 22 games (12 starts). He ended the year with a disappointing 2-4 record. He was one of the two players in the trade that sent Lee Smith to the Red Sox before the 1988 season. For Boston in 1987, Nipper had a 5.43 ERA and 89 strikeouts in 174 innings, going 11-12—matching his career-high victory total. In 1984, he was 11-6 for the BoSox, with a 3.89 ERA. A steady, solid hurler for the Red Sox in the past, the Cubs have high hopes that Nipper will solidify the starting rotation in 1989.

Nipper's cards are not high demand items and not recommended for the investor. They will be priced as commons. Our pick for his best 1989 card is Topps.

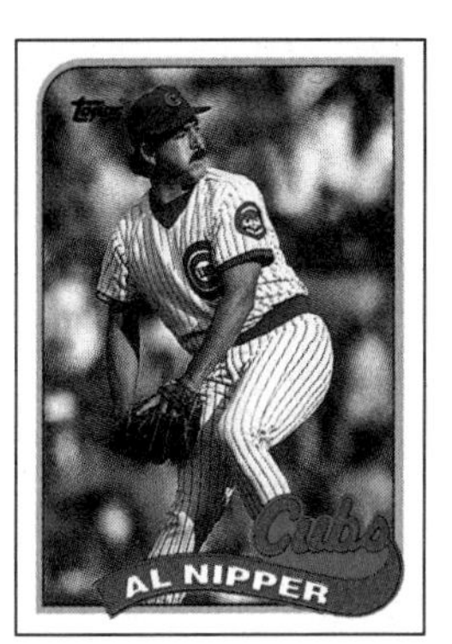

DONELL NIXON

	BA	G	AB	R	H	2B	3B	HR	RBI	SB
1988	.346	59	78	15	27	3	0	0	6	11
Life	.286	105	210	32	60	7	0	3	18	32

POSITION: Outfield
TEAM: San Francisco Giants
BORN: December 31, 1961
Evergreen, NC
HEIGHT: 6′1″ **WEIGHT:** 185 lbs.
BATS: Right **THROWS:** Right
ACQUIRED: Traded from Mariners for Rod Scurry, 6/88

Nixon ended the 1988 season with the best batting average (.346) on the Giants. He hit .281 in '88 at Triple-A Calgary before being traded to the Giants. Nixon dazzled the baseball world in 1983, when he stole 144 bases for Class-A Bakersfield. But in 1984, he ran full tilt into a cinder-block wall, suffering a serious fracture of his left leg. He missed the next two seasons as a result. Nixon started 1987 in Triple-A and found that all the pieces fit again, hitting .323 with five homers and 52 RBIs. He also recovered his speed and stole 46 bases. An exciting player with crowd appeal potential, Nixon could become a fan favorite in San Francisco.

Nixon's 1989 cards will open in the 20-cent range, a good price for investing. Our pick for his best 1989 card is Fleer.

OTIS NIXON

	BA	G	AB	R	H	2B	3B	HR	RBI	SB
1988	.244	90	271	47	66	8	2	0	15	46
Life	.225	380	650	134	146	16	3	3	34	105

POSITION: Outfield
TEAM: Montreal Expos
BORN: January 9, 1959 Evergreen, NC
HEIGHT: 6′2″ **WEIGHT:** 175 lbs.
BATS: Both **THROWS:** Right
ACQUIRED: Signed as a free agent, 3/88

The Expos rescued Nixon from the baseball scrap heap in 1988 and gave him a new lease on his baseball life. In 90 games for Montreal, he batted .244, but his 46 stolen bases tied him for fourth place in the N.L. Nixon started the 1988 campaign at Triple-A Indianapolis and was batting .285 with 40 stolen bases when he was recalled. His career seemed to be over in 1987, when the Tribe released him after he hit just .059 in 19 games. Nixon now has the inside shot at the starting center fielder job for the Expos.

Nixon's 1989 cards will be found in the commons box. They probably will not appreciate unless he steals 100 bases some year. He would have to have a much better on-base average for that to happen. Our pick for his best 1989 card is Fleer.

MATT NOKES

	BA	G	AB	R	H	2B	3B	HR	RBI	SB
1988	.251	122	382	53	96	18	0	16	53	0
Life	.270	283	920	127	248	35	2	51	147	2

POSITION: Catcher
TEAM: Detroit Tigers
BORN: October 31, 1963 San Diego, CA
HEIGHT: 6′1″ **WEIGHT:** 185 lbs.
BATS: Left **THROWS:** Right
ACQUIRED: Traded from Giants with Dave LaPoint and Eric King for Juan Berenguer, Bob Melvin, and Scott Medvin, 10/85

An injured Nokes missed 40 games during 1988, and saw his superb 1987 statistics nearly chopped in half. He belted only 16 homers last year, down from 32 in 1987. His average fell nearly 40 points, and he drove in 44 fewer runs. His strong fielding continued, however, as he proved to be one of the slickest Detroit backstops since Lance Parrish. There's no doubt that a healthy Nokes might have helped make up the one-game difference in the final divisional standings between the first-place Red Sox and the second-place Tigers. Nokes, back at full strength in 1989, can make Detroit a contender again.

Nokes' 1989 cards may bring a dollar or more. Pass at those prices, until Nokes proves he's fully recovered and ready to return to his 1987 potential. Our pick for his best 1989 card is Topps.

KEN OBERKFELL

	BA	G	AB	R	H	2B	3B	HR	RBI	SB
1988	.271	140	476	49	129	22	4	3	42	4
Life	.282	1334	4407	516	1241	220	42	26	393	61

POSITION: Infield
TEAM: Pittsburgh Pirates
BORN: May 4, 1956 Maryville, IL
HEIGHT: 6′ **WEIGHT:** 175 lbs.
BATS: Left **THROWS:** Right
ACQUIRED: Traded from Braves for Tommy Gregg, 8/88

Oberkfell was acquired from Atlanta last August, and the versatile veteran played all four infield positions for the 1988 Pirates during their late-season pennant run. He finished the season batting .271, with three homers and 42 RBIs. Oberkfell's remaining years will be spent as a utilityman. He spent five seasons as a solid third baseman for St. Louis; he capped his career by hitting .292 for them in the 1982 World Series. He hit .280 in 1987 for the Braves, with three homers and 48 RBIs. In 1986, he batted .270, with five home runs and 48 RBIs. Oberkfell will be an experienced hand for the Pirates during their 1989 run for the pennant.

Oberkfell has had a solid big league career, but his cards do not captivate collectors. His 1989 cards will be located in the commons box. Our pick for his best 1989 card is Donruss.

CHARLIE O'BRIEN

	BA	G	AB	R	H	2B	3B	HR	RBI	SB
1988	.220	40	118	12	26	6	0	2	9	0
Life	.220	66	164	17	36	10	1	2	10	0

POSITION: Catcher
TEAM: Milwaukee Brewers
BORN: May 1, 1961 Tulsa, OK
HEIGHT: 6′2″ **WEIGHT:** 190 lbs.
BATS: Right **THROWS:** Right
ACQUIRED: Traded from A's with Steve Kiefer for Moose Haas, 3/86

O'Brien was one of the few healthy catchers on the Brewers in 1988. His 40-game stint with the Brewers was the longest of his brief major league career. Although he had just ten hits prior to '88, half were for extra bases. His 1988 accomplishments may give backup catcher Bill Schroeder a battle for a job in 1989. O'Brien won't see a lot of playing time as long as young starting catcher B.J. Surhoff remains healthy. O'Brien, originally a member of the Athletic organization, began his pro career in 1982. His presence gives the Brewers added bench strength and a dependable glove.

Because he is confined to substitute status, O'Brien's cards probably won't move beyond their prices as commons as long as he stays with the Brewers. Our pick for his best 1989 card is Fleer.

PETE O'BRIEN

	BA	G	AB	R	H	2B	3B	HR	RBI	SB
1988	.272	156	547	57	149	24	1	16	71	1
Life	.273	946	3351	419	914	161	16	114	487	19

POSITION: First base
TEAM: Cleveland Indians
BORN: February 9, 1958 Santa Monica, CA
HEIGHT: 6′1″ **WEIGHT:** 197 lbs.
BATS: Left **THROWS:** Left
ACQUIRED: Traded from Rangers with Oddibe McDowell and Jerry Browne for Julio Franco, 12/88

O'Brien has been one of the most consistent home run hitters in the American League during the past five seasons. The first baseman hit 16 home runs for the Rangers, the fewest since his rookie season of 1983. O'Brien's career-high for round-trippers is 23, which he reached both in 1986 and 1987. In 1985, he drove in a personal best 92 runs. Also, he's one of the better-fielding first basemen in the league. At age 31, O'Brien could become one of the American League's finest first basemen of the next decade.

For years, stars like Don Mattingly and Eddie Murray have cornered all the attention devoted to first basemen. O'Brien hasn't gotten his due. His cards, sold for less than a nickel, could bring short-term gains if the Tribe become contenders. Our pick for his best 1989 card is Donruss.

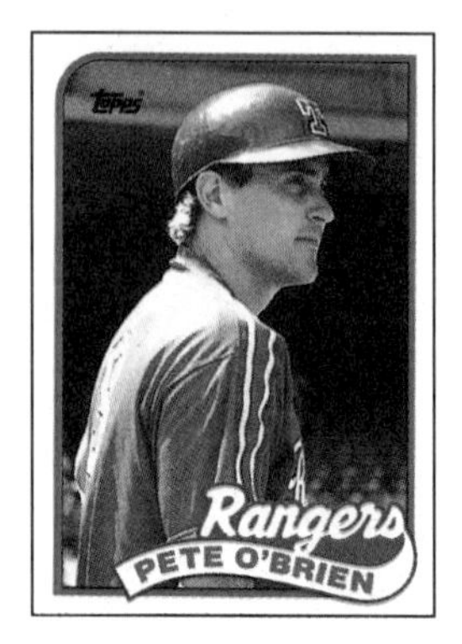

RON OESTER

	BA	G	AB	R	H	2B	3B	HR	RBI	SB
1988	.280	54	150	20	42	7	0	0	10	0
Life	.266	1103	3755	425	997	165	32	41	317	38

POSITION: Second base
TEAM: Cincinnati Reds
BORN: May 5, 1956 Cincinnati, OH
HEIGHT: 6'2" **WEIGHT:** 195 lbs.
BATS: Both **THROWS:** Right
ACQUIRED: Ninth-round selection in 6/74 free-agent draft

Oester, because of a bad knee, appeared in just 54 games for the 1988 Reds, the least action he's seen in the last eight seasons. Once the full-time second baseman for the Reds, he played in at least 150 games from 1982 through 1986. He still participated in 69 contests in 1987. This year, he hit an admirable .280. Oester has always been a slick fielder, too. He made just one error all season in 1988. Competition from young Jeff Treadway may keep Oester's playing time to a minimum in 1989. However, at age 32, he doesn't seem washed up yet. Oester will be a stabilizing force on the young Red squad.

Oester's 1989 cards will be a nickel or less. His lifetime stats are average but don't justify investment in his cards. Our pick for his best 1989 card is Score.

BOB OJEDA

	W	L	ERA	G	CG	IP	H	R	BB	SO
1988	10	13	2.88	29	5	190.1	158	74	33	133
Life	75	62	3.68	211	32	1172.1	1122	532	380	727

POSITION: Pitcher
TEAM: New York Mets
BORN: December 17, 1957 Los Angeles, CA
HEIGHT: 6'1" **WEIGHT:** 185 lbs.
BATS: Left **THROWS:** Left
ACQUIRED: Traded from Red Sox with John Mitchell, Tom McCarthy, and Chris Bayer for Calvin Schiraldi, Wes Gardner, John Christensen, and LaSchelle Tarver, 11/85

Ojeda's future rests upon his ability to bounce back from a freak accident. He severed the top of the middle finger on his left hand in late September, and he has gone through therapy. Before he was injured, Ojeda fashioned a 10-13 record for the Mets, appearing in 29 games, with five shutouts—all of them complete games. He had a 2.88 ERA and fanned 133 in $190\frac{1}{3}$ innings. In 1986, Ojeda was an 18-game winner for the Mets, and his winning percentage of .783 was best in the N.L. In 1987, he had elbow trouble, and was only 3-5, with a 3.88 ERA. He will have to overcome adversity again, but if anyone can persevere, Ojeda can.

Ojeda should still have several good years ahead, but collectors have taken a cautious stance toward his common-priced cards. Our pick for his best 1989 card is Score.

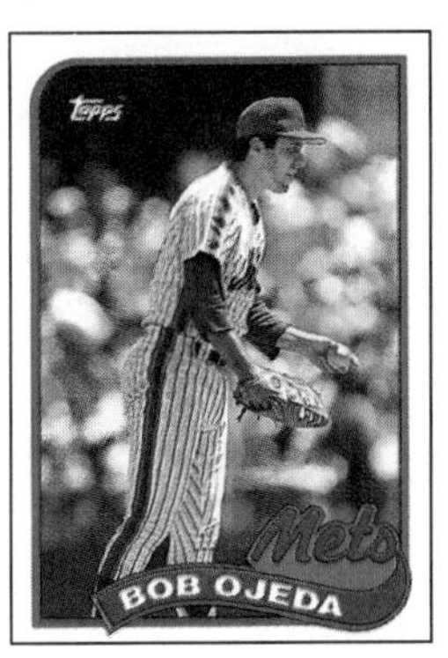

PAUL O'NEILL

	BA	G	AB	R	H	2B	3B	HR	RBI	SB
1988	.252	145	485	58	122	25	3	16	73	8
Life	.253	237	659	83	167	40	4	23	102	10

POSITION: Outfield
TEAM: Cincinnati Reds
BORN: February 25, 1963 Columbus, OH
HEIGHT: 6'4" **WEIGHT:** 205 lbs.
BATS: Left **THROWS:** Left
ACQUIRED: Fourth-round pick in 6/81 free-agent draft

O'Neill honed in on a starting outfield position with the 1988 Reds, putting together his finest season ever. He played in 145 games, second only to Barry Larkin, in compiling his impressive stats. O'Neill set career highs in almost all offensive categories. He was third on the team in home runs (16) and second on the Reds in RBIs (73) in 1988. O'Neill did a good job defensively, making just six miscues all season. The 26-year-old outfielder hit .256 in 1987, his first full year with the Reds, smashing seven home runs in just 160 at-bats. Watch for more achievements from O'Neill in 1989.

Playing beside Eric Davis and Kal Daniels has overshadowed O'Neill's talents. However, his 1988 stats should change that. His 1989 cards will be a good investment at 10 cents or less. Our pick for his best 1989 card is Topps.

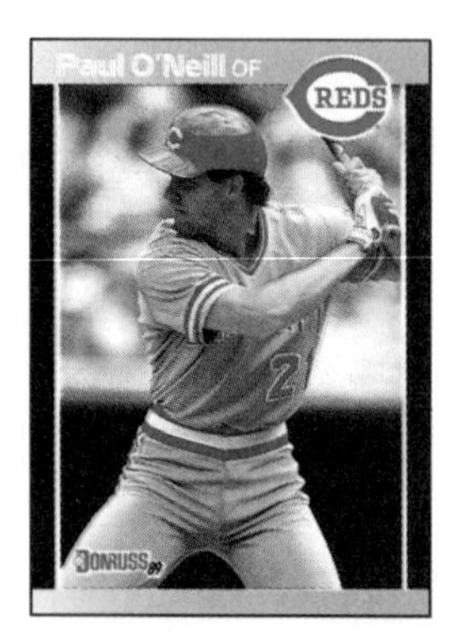

STEVE ONTIVEROS

	W	L	ERA	G	SV	IP	H	R	BB	SO
1988	3	4	4.61	10	0	54.2	57	32	21	30
Life	16	17	3.80	130	19	352.2	315	167	115	217

POSITION: Pitcher
TEAM: Oakland A's
BORN: March 5, 1961 Tularosa, NM
HEIGHT: 6' **WEIGHT:** 180 lbs.
BATS: Right **THROWS:** Right
ACQUIRED: Second-round pick in 6/82 free-agent draft

Ontiveros appeared in only ten games in 1988, and didn't display the ability that made him one of 1985's top rookies. Three wins last season were his main accomplishments. In 1987, Ontiveros won ten games in 35 appearances for the A's as both a starter and reliever. His best season ever was his 1985 debut. He gained eight saves and one victory in 39 appearances, topped off by a dazzling 1.93 ERA. His highest total for saves was ten in 1986. The biggest challenge for Ontiveros in 1989 will be staying healthy so he can pitch a whole season.

See how well Ontiveros does in 1989 before considering investing in his cards. With so many arm problems, his career could end at any time. His cards will be priced as commons this season. Our pick for his best 1989 card is Topps.

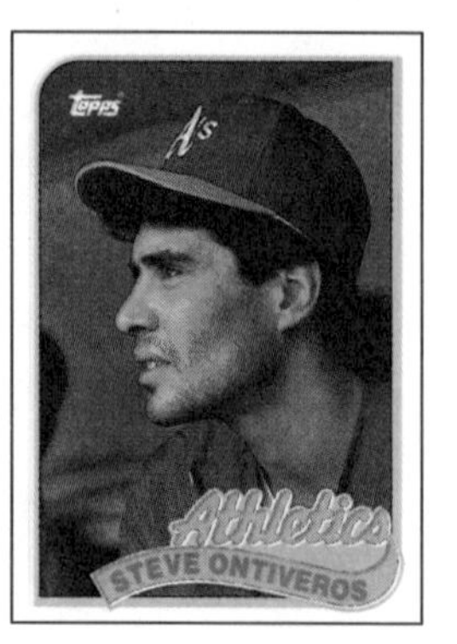

JOSE OQUENDO

	BA	G	AB	R	H	2B	3B	HR	RBI	SB
1988	.277	148	451	36	125	10	1	7	46	4
Life	.258	541	1354	151	349	35	2	9	110	28

POSITION: Infield
TEAM: St. Louis Cardinals
BORN: July 4, 1963 Rio Piedras, Puerto Rico
HEIGHT: 5′10″ **WEIGHT:** 160 lbs.
BATS: Both **THROWS:** Right
ACQUIRED: Traded from Mets with Mark Davis for Angel Salazar and John Young, 4/85

Oquendo has the bad fortune to be a good shortstop on the same team as Ozzie Smith, the best shortstop in baseball. Many teams would be very comfortable with Oquendo in that spot. He can play just about anywhere in the infield or outfield, and his versatility makes him most valuable to the Cardinals. Oquendo saw action in 148 games for the Cards last season, batting a solid .277—and outhitting Smith by seven percentage points. Oquendo's stats also included seven home runs and 46 RBIs. He was originally signed by the Mets as a 16-year-old in 1979. Oquendo will continue to be the definitive jack-of-all-trades for the Cards in 1989.

Oquendo's cards still have to be discovered by collectors. His 1989 cards will be commons. Our pick for his best 1989 card is Fleer.

JESSE OROSCO

	W	L	ERA	G	SV	IP	H	R	BB	SO
1988	3	2	2.72	55	9	53.0	41	18	30	43
Life	50	49	2.73	427	116	648.1	521	225	270	549

POSITION: Pitcher
TEAM: Cleveland Indians
BORN: April 21, 1957
HEIGHT: 6′2″ **WEIGHT:** 175 lbs.
BATS: Right **THROWS:** Left
ACQUIRED: Signed as a free agent, 12/88

Orosco comes to the Tribe to be their lefthanded short relief man. In 1988, he didn't become the stopper that the Dodgers thought they were getting. He had a good year, though, saving nine games, with a 3-2 record and an ERA under 3.00. Orosco pitched full-time for six seasons for the Mets, from 1982 to '87. His two best seasons for New York were 1983 and 1984. In '83, he was 13-7, with a 1.47 ERA and 17 saves. He racked up 31 saves in 1984, finishing with a 10-6 record and a 2.59 ERA. With righthander Doug Jones, Orosco could give the Tribe a one-two stopper combination out of the bullpen.

Orosco's 1989 cards will sell for 5 cents apiece. Investors could see some dividends if he finishes in the A.L.'s top bracket in saves in '89. Our pick for his best 1989 card is Fleer.

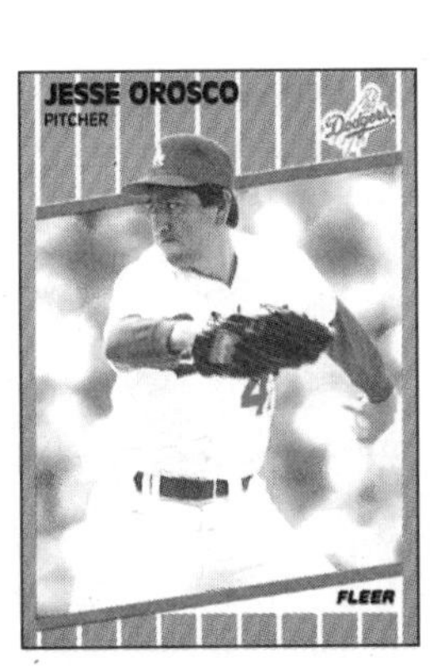

JOE ORSULAK

	BA	G	AB	R	H	2B	3B	HR	RBI	SB
1988	.288	125	379	48	109	21	3	8	27	9
Life	.276	423	1255	174	347	55	17	10	71	60

POSITION: Outfield
TEAM: Baltimore Orioles
BORN: May 31, 1962 Glen Ridge, NJ
HEIGHT: 6′1″ **WEIGHT:** 185 lbs.
BATS: Left **THROWS:** Left
ACQUIRED: Traded from Pirates for Terry Crowley and Rico Rossy, 11/87

Orsulak came back from being injured all of 1987 to find a home in Baltimore. He led the 1988 Orioles in batting, hitting .288. He also found some power, hitting eight homers and 27 RBIs in 379 at-bats. Orsulak played two full seasons for the Pirates in 1986 and 1987 before being injured. He stole 24 bases each of those seasons for the Bucs, and he led the Pittsburgh outfielders with assists both in 1985 and '86. He was drafted by the Pirates in the ninth round of the June 1980 draft. Orsulak is one of the good young players that Baltimore fans hope will get the Orioles back on track in 1989.

Orsulak's 1989 cards will be commons. Wait to see if he can improve his power stats before investing in his cards. Our pick for his best 1989 card is Fleer.

JUNIOR ORTIZ

	BA	G	AB	R	H	2B	3B	HR	RBI	SB
1988	.280	49	118	8	33	6	0	2	18	1
Life	.268	316	791	57	212	31	1	4	82	4

POSITION: Catcher
TEAM: Pittsburgh Pirates
BORN: October 24, 1959 Humacao, Puerto Rico
HEIGHT: 5′11″ **WEIGHT:** 175 lbs.
BATS: Right **THROWS:** Right
ACQUIRED: Drafted from Mets, 12/84

Ortiz played only part of the 1988 season, but he had a good season. He batted .280, with two home runs and 18 RBIs as backup to Mike LaValliere. Ortiz missed almost two months of 1988 with a broken collarbone, which he sustained in a game with the Cardinals in July, and he didn't play again until mid-September. Ortiz caught in 72 games in 1987, and he had one homer and 22 RBIs, ending with a .271 average. He hit .336 in limited action in 1986. He was originally signed by the Bucs as a non-drafted free agent in 1977. Ortiz will be an experienced number-two catcher for the Pirates in 1989.

Ortiz is a reserve catcher, and there is little collector interest in such players. His cards are all in the commons box. Our pick for his best 1989 card is Score.

SPIKE OWEN

	BA	G	AB	R	H	2B	3B	HR	RBI	SB
1988	.249	89	257	40	64	14	1	5	18	0
Life	.241	725	2410	301	580	94	32	19	212	52

POSITION: Shortstop
TEAM: Montreal Expos
BORN: April 19, 1961 Cleburne, TX
HEIGHT: 5'10" **WEIGHT:** 170 lbs.
BATS: Both **THROWS:** Right
ACQUIRED: Traded from Red Sox with Dan Gakeler for John Dopson and Luis Rivera, 12/88

Owen may be the answer to middle infield problems on the Expos. He only played part-time for the 1988 Red Sox, because it appeared that rookie Jody Reed beat him out of a job. Owen played in just 89 games, finishing with five homers, 18 RBIs, and a .249 average. He first joined the Red Sox in late 1986, giving them the insurance they needed to clinch their division and move to the World Series versus the Mets. He is far from washed up, being only 27 years old. Owen could help Montreal become a solid contender for the N.L. East pennant in 1989.

Owen's 1989 cards will be three cents or less. His career stats don't justify investing, especially since his career batting average is in the .240s. Our pick for his best 1989 card is Topps.

MIKE PAGLIARULO

	BA	G	AB	R	H	2B	3B	HR	RBI	SB
1988	.216	125	444	46	96	20	1	15	67	1
Life	.233	629	2051	272	477	101	12	101	321	6

POSITION: Third base
TEAM: New York Yankees
BORN: March 15, 1960 Medford, MA
HEIGHT: 6'2" **WEIGHT:** 195 lbs.
BATS: Left **THROWS:** Right
ACQUIRED: Sixth-round pick in 6/81 free-agent draft

A shortened season caused a slight power outage in Pagliarulo's 1988 slugging. The homer-hitting third baseman banged only 15 round-trippers last season in 125 games. His average has never been above .239 in four full major league seasons with the Yankees. Pagliarulo's above-average homer and RBI totals dipped below his career-high 1987 efforts of 32 homers and 87 RBIs. He had 28 homers and 71 RBIs in 1986. He could have some serious competition for his starting job from rookie Hensley Meulens, a young slugger in Pagliarulo's mold. If Pagliarulo could cut his strikeout total below 100, his hitting would improve considerably.

Pagliarulo's 1989 cards will sell as commons away from New York. Until his average climbs drastically, his cards aren't very good investments. If his average does climb, however, his card values will too. Our pick for his best 1989 card is Topps.

TOM PAGNOZZI

	BA	G	AB	R	H	2B	3B	HR	RBI	SB
1988	.282	81	195	17	55	9	0	0	15	0
Life	.263	108	243	25	64	10	0	2	24	1

POSITION: Catcher
TEAM: St. Louis Cardinals
BORN: July 30, 1962 Tucson, AZ
HEIGHT: 6′1″ **WEIGHT:** 190 lbs.
BATS: Right **THROWS:** Right
ACQUIRED: Eighth-round pick in 6/83 free-agent draft

Pagnozzi served in a backup role for the 1988 Cardinals, and he could find himself with more playing time in 1989. He batted an impressive .282 with 15 RBIs as an understudy to Tony Pena. Pagnozzi showed he was ready for the big time when he batted .313 for Triple-A Louisville in 1987. He did spend some time in St. Louis that season when Pena was hurt, but failed to hit big league pitching, producing only a .188 mark in 48 at-bats. He was an All-Southwest Conference choice as a catcher at the University of Arkansas. Pagnozzi's future is bright, and he looks like the St. Louis catcher of the future.

Pagnozzi's 1989 cards should open among the commons until he achieves first-string big league status. Our pick for his best 1989 card is Topps.

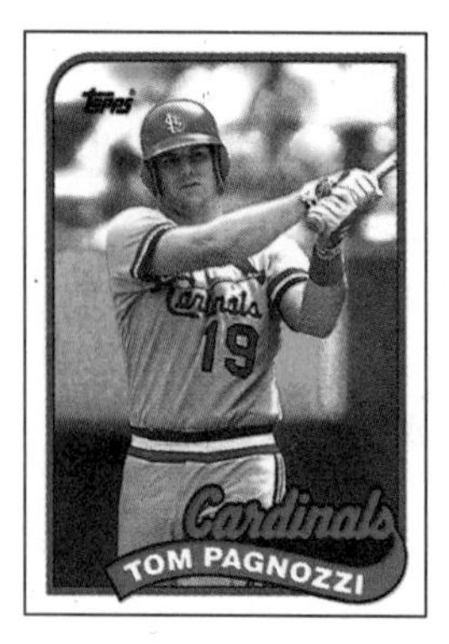

RAFAEL PALMEIRO

	BA	G	AB	R	H	2B	3B	HR	RBI	SB
1988	.307	152	580	75	178	41	5	8	53	12
Life	.294	258	874	116	257	60	6	25	95	15

POSITION: First base; outfield
TEAM: Texas Rangers
BORN: September 24, 1964 Havana, Cuba
HEIGHT: 6′ **WEIGHT:** 175 lbs.
BATS: Left **THROWS:** Left
ACQUIRED: Traded from Cubs with Drew Hall and Jamie Moyer for Mitch Williams, Paul Kilgus, Steve Wilson, Curtis Wilkerson, Luis Benitez, and Pablo Delgado, 12/88

Palmeiro, the N.L.'s second leading hitter last season, is being counted on to put up some good numbers for the Rangers. He hit .307 in 152 games for the Cubs. Palmeiro was third in the league in hits (178) and second in doubles (41). He didn't have a single game-winning RBI among his 53 ribbies. Palmeiro joined the Cubs in 1987, batting .276 in 84 games, with 14 home runs and 30 RBIs. In 1988, Palmeiro's homer production dropped off to just eight. He also saw action in 1987 at Triple-A Iowa, batting .299, with 11 home runs and 41 RBIs. The Rangers hope that Palmeiro's offensive production can lead them to a winning mark in 1989.

Palmeiro's 1989 cards are savers at between 5 and 10 cents. He has long-term batting championship potential. Collecting his cards might yield long-term investment returns. Our pick for his best 1989 card is Topps.

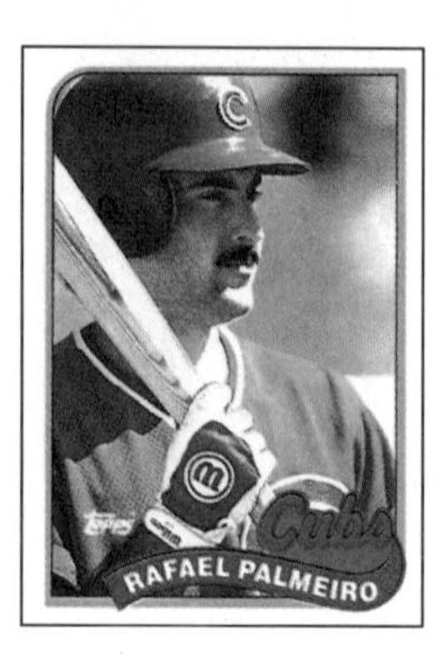

DAVID PALMER

	W	L	ERA	G	CG	IP	H	R	BB	SO
1988	7	9	4.47	22	1	129.0	129	67	48	85
Life	64	56	3.71	207	10	1068.2	1011	496	423	736

POSITION: Pitcher
TEAM: Philadelphia Phillies
BORN: October 19, 1957
Glens Falls, NY
HEIGHT: 6′1″ **WEIGHT:** 195 lbs.
BATS: Right **THROWS:** Right
ACQUIRED: Signed as a free agent, 12/87

Palmer had injury problems in 1988, and when he did pitch, he wasn't as effective as he had been in the past. He was 7-9 in '88, with a 4.47 ERA and 85 Ks in 129 innings. He missed a month with a bad elbow, but he still started 22 games. Palmer started 28 games for the 1987 Braves, going 8-11 and ending with a 4.90 ERA. His best season was in 1979 with Montreal. He won ten games and lost only two, with a 2.63 ERA and two saves. In 1986, he was 11-10, with a 3.65 ERA, $209\frac{2}{3}$ innings pitched, and 170 Ks. Philadelphia will need a healthy Palmer to contend for a pennant in 1989.

Palmer's 1989 cards will be commons. Investing in his cards would be risky, especially since he is coming off an injury. Our pick for his best 1989 card is Topps.

JIM PANKOVITS

	BA	G	AB	R	H	2B	3B	HR	RBI	SB
1988	.221	68	140	13	31	7	1	2	12	2
Life	.250	316	567	62	142	25	2	9	55	8

POSITION: Infield
TEAM: Houston Astros
BORN: August 5, 1955
Pennington Gap, VA
HEIGHT: 5′10″ **WEIGHT:** 175 lbs.
BATS: Right **THROWS:** Right
ACQUIRED: Signed as a free agent, 1/83

Pankovits spent his fourth season as a member of the Astro reserve corps. He has played second base, shortstop, third base, and outfield in his career. He had a long wait until he made the Astros first in 1984. Pankovits spent more than eight seasons in the minor leagues, beginning in 1976, before he got his big break. He hit .221 in 68 games in 1988, with two homers and 12 RBIs. The Astros traded him to the San Diego Padres in 1982, but he was granted free agency later that year and re-signed with the Astros. He eventually became a regular substitute in Houston. Pankovits is a valuable hand for the Astros.

Pankovits is not a likely candidate for a starting job in 1989. There is little interest in his common-priced baseball cards. Our pick for his best 1989 card is Topps.

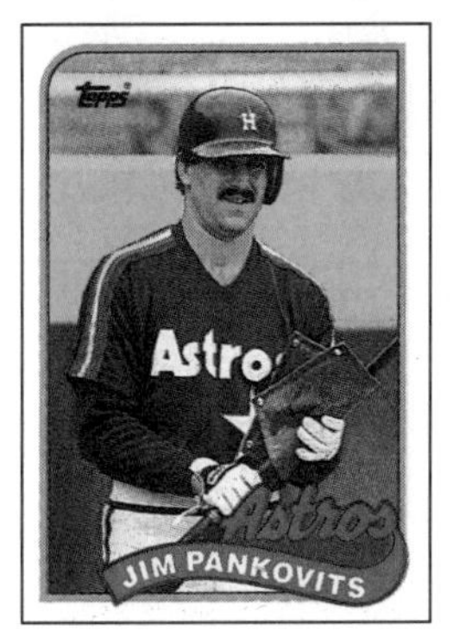

JOHNNY PAREDES

	BA	G	AB	R	H	2B	3B	HR	RBI	SB
1988	.187	35	91	17	6	2	0	1	10	5
Life	.187	35	91	17	6	2	0	1	10	5

POSITION: Second base
TEAM: Montreal Expos
BORN: September 2, 1962 Caracas, Venezuela
HEIGHT: 5'11" **WEIGHT:** 165 lbs.
BATS: Right **THROWS:** Right
ACQUIRED: Signed as a free agent, 1/84

Among the leading hitters in the Triple-A American Association for the past two seasons, Paredes hit .295 in 1988 and .312 in '87. He has also shown some speed, stealing over 30 bases two straight years for Indianapolis. There's little doubt that his potent bat and solid defensive skills can fit nicely into the Expo lineup this season. His first two years in pro ball were spent in the Phillie organization. After batting only .238 at Spartanburg in 1983, he was released. Quickly signed by the Expos, he spent the next two years at West Palm Beach. Paredes has the tools to be a starter in the majors.

Paredes' first big league cards should be in the 15- to 20-cent range. His time is now to become the starting second baseman in Montreal. Our pick for his best 1989 card is Topps.

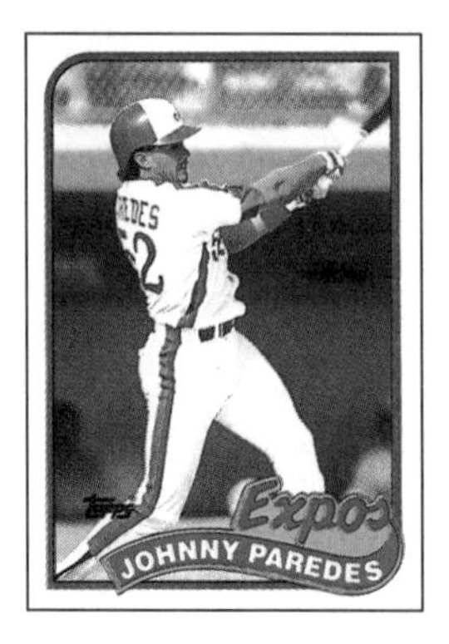

DAVE PARKER

	BA	G	AB	R	H	2B	3B	HR	RBI	SB
1988	.257	101	377	43	97	18	1	12	55	0
Life	.295	2033	7693	1098	2270	443	70	285	1245	147

POSITION: Outfield; designated hitter
TEAM: Oakland A's
BORN: June 9, 1951 Cincinnati, OH
HEIGHT: 6'5" **WEIGHT:** 230 lbs.
BATS: Left **THROWS:** Right
ACQUIRED: Traded from Reds for Jose Rijo and Tim Birtsas, 12/87

Parker brought some much-needed experience to the young Athletics. He only got to play in 101 games, but he hit 12 homers, the 12th time in his career he's hit in double figures. His shortened season was a letdown from his 1987 accomplishments with the Reds. Parker smashed 26 homers and 97 RBIs in his last N.L. season. He first came up with the 1973 Pirates, and he won a starting job by 1975. Parker's best season ever came in 1985 with the Reds, consisting of 34 homers, a league-leading 125 RBIs, and a .312 average.

Parker should be adjusted to A.L. pitching in 1989. His 1989 cards will be 10 to 15 cents each, a good investing price for a powerhouse. He could have an MVP-quality season at the plate again. Our pick for his best 1989 card is Topps.

JEFF PARRETT

	W	L	ERA	G	SV	IP	H	R	BB	SO
1988	12	4	2.65	61	6	91.2	66	29	45	62
Life	19	11	3.47	118	12	174.0	138	73	88	139

POSITION: Pitcher
TEAM: Philadelphia Phillies
BORN: August 26, 1961
Indianapolis, IN
HEIGHT: 6′4″ **WEIGHT:** 190 lbs.
BATS: Right **THROWS:** Right
ACQUIRED: Traded by Expos with Floyd Youmans for Kevin Gross, 12/88

Parrett moves into the Phillie bullpen after a great season with Montreal. He was 12-4 for the Expos in 1988, with a 2.65 ERA and six saves in 61 games. He struck out 62 batters while walking 45. In 1987, Parrett was 7-6 in 45 games for Montreal after starting the year at Triple-A with Indianapolis. He struck out 56 batters for the '87 Expos in 62 innings. He was drafted in the ninth round by the Brewers in June 1983, out of the University of Kentucky. The Phillies hope that he will solidify their bullpen in 1989. Parrett will be the set-up pitcher for stopper Steve Bedrosian.

Parrett's cards are still found mostly in the commons box, but they're worth holding on to in the event he continues to be a dominant reliever in the N.L. Our pick for his best 1989 card is Topps.

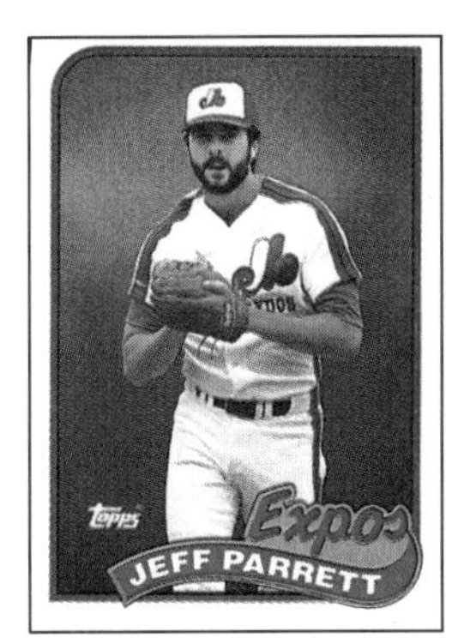

LANCE PARRISH

	BA	G	AB	R	H	2B	3B	HR	RBI	SB
1988	.215	123	424	44	91	17	2	15	60	0
Life	.257	1399	5163	663	1328	239	25	244	827	22

POSITION: Catcher
TEAM: California Angels
BORN: June 15, 1956 Clairton, PA
HEIGHT: 6′3″ **WEIGHT:** 210 lbs.
BATS: Right **THROWS:** Right
ACQUIRED: Traded from Phillies for David Holdridge, 10/88

California traded for Parrish to replace the Angels' longtime catcher, Bob Boone. Parrish never fulfilled the high expectations that the Phillies placed on him. In 1988, he hit only .215, with 15 homers and 60 RBIs. He hit .245 in 1987, with 17 homers and 67 RBIs. Those numbers are down from Parrish's great seasons in Detroit. From 1982 to '86 for the Tigers, he drove in 87, 114, 98, and 98 runs. He has also been an outstanding defensive catcher for years. The Angels hope that the move back to the A.L. will help Parrish become an elite catcher and offensive force once again.

You'll find Parrish's 1989 cards for 5 to 10 cents each. That price is worthy of a small investment, since he could regain some of his power. But some catchers wear out quickly. Our pick for his best 1989 card is Donruss.

DAN PASQUA

	BA	G	AB	R	H	2B	3B	HR	RBI	SB
1988	.227	129	422	48	96	16	2	20	50	1
Life	.242	404	1168	151	283	43	4	62	162	3

POSITION: Outfield; first base
TEAM: Chicago White Sox
BORN: October 17, 1961 Yonkers, NY
HEIGHT: 6′ **WEIGHT:** 205 lbs.
BATS: Left **THROWS:** Left
ACQUIRED: Traded from Yankees with Mark Salas and Steve Rosenberg for Richard Dotson and Scott Nielsen, 11/87

Pasqua played in only 129 games, but he led the 1988 White Sox with 20 home runs. He had played more than two seasons for the Yankees, starting in 1985, with mild success. After hitting 16 and 17 home runs in two consecutive seasons, Pasqua looked like just the power hitter the White Sox dreamed of having. He made those dreams come true with his 1988 performance. He must cut down on strikeouts in 1989 to be an effective slugger. He fanned 100 times in 422 at-bats in 1988. If Pasqua becomes a better all-around player while keeping his power, he could become one of the elite A.L. outfielders.

Pasqua's 1989 cards should be less than a nickel. If Pasqua breaks the 30-homer barrier in 1989, those prices would go up. His cards are a reasonable investment in small quantities. Our pick for his best 1989 card is Fleer.

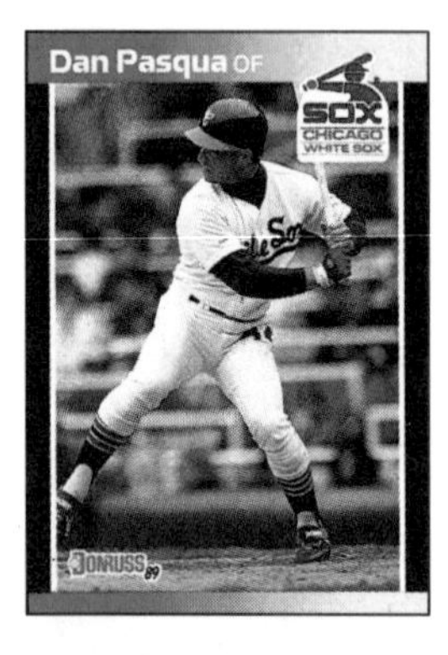

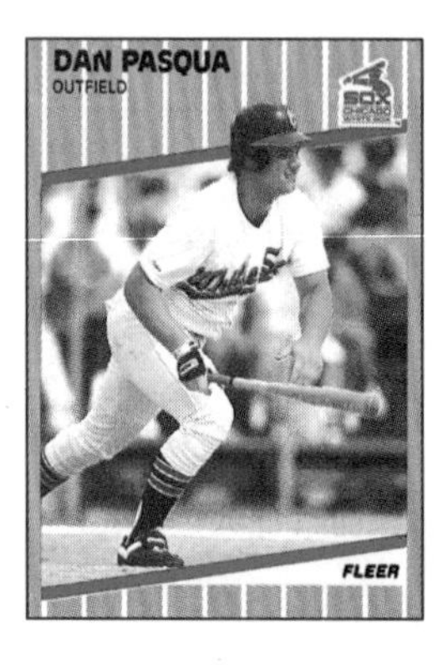

KEN PATTERSON

	W	L	ERA	G	SV	IP	H	R	BB	SO
1988	0	2	4.79	9	1	20.2	25	11	7	8
Life	0	2	4.79	9	1	20.2	25	11	7	8

POSITION: Pitcher
TEAM: Chicago White Sox
BORN: July 8, 1964
Costa Mesa, CA
HEIGHT: 6′4″ **WEIGHT:** 190 lbs.
BATS: Left **THROWS:** Left
ACQUIRED: Traded from Yankees, 1987

The ace reliever of Triple-A Vancouver in 1988, Patterson seems destined for a key role in the rebuilding phase of the White Sox in 1989. A lefthander, Patterson notched 12 saves with a 6-5 record and a 3.23 ERA at Vancouver, fanning 89 in 86 innings and walking only 36 batters. He was called up to Chicago for the final month of the season. Patterson began his pro career at Class-A Oneonta in 1985 and went 2-2 for them. In 1986 for Oneonta, he was 9-3 with a 1.35 ERA, clearly overmatching the opposition. Patterson changed from a starter to a reliever in 1987, a move that could benefit the Sox in 1989.

Patterson's 1989 cards will open in the 10- to 15-cent range. His card values will rise if he strengthens the ChiSox bullpen. Our pick for his best 1989 card is Fleer.

BILL PECOTA

	BA	G	AB	R	H	2B	3B	HR	RBI	SB
1988	.208	90	178	25	37	3	3	1	15	7
Life	.237	168	363	50	86	10	4	4	31	12

POSITION: Infield
TEAM: Kansas City Royals
BORN: February 16, 1960
Redwood City, CA
HEIGHT: 6′2″ **WEIGHT:** 195 lbs.
BATS: Right **THROWS:** Right
ACQUIRED: Tenth-round pick in 6/81 free-agent draft

Pecota played in 90 games for the 1988 Royals, more games than his entire previous major league experience. He filled in at any position for the Royals, displaying strong defense and lots of hustle. He hit .208, with one homer and 15 RBIs. Pecota's low average might be partly due to the pressure of playing a different position every day. In 1987, he hit a career-best .276 in 66 games. His versatility will get him the chance for lots more playing time with the 1989 Royals. Pecota will have to raise his average substantially in order to find a full-time job.

Pecota, at age 29, got a late start in the majors. He seems destined as a future utilityman, which kills any investment possibilities in his common-priced cards. Our pick for his best 1989 card is Fleer.

ALEJANDRO PENA

	W	L	ERA	G	SV	IP	H	R	BB	SO
1988	6	7	1.91	60	12	94.1	75	29	27	83
Life	34	35	3.01	228	27	693.0	631	281	226	496

POSITION: Pitcher
TEAM: Los Angeles Dodgers
BORN: September 25, 1959
Cambiaso, Puerto Plata,
Dominican Republic
HEIGHT: 6′1″ **WEIGHT:** 203 lbs.
BATS: Right **THROWS:** Right
ACQUIRED: Purchased from Dominican League, 10/78

Pena had his healthiest, most productive season ever in 1988 with the Dodgers. He always has displayed talent and promise, but injuries have stopped him from having back-to-back successful seasons. That wasn't the case in 1988. Pena led the Dodgers with a career high in appearances (60) and was second on the team in ERA (1.91). He was 6-7, with 83 strikeouts in 94⅓ innings. He won 12 games both in 1983 and 1984 with the Dodgers, but he began working part-time in the bullpen following shoulder surgery in 1985. Pena will be a leading player in the 1989 Dodger bullpen.

Pena was second on the Dodgers in saves in 1988, and should get more in 1989. His 1989 cards, priced at a nickel or less, may turn out to be sound investments. Our pick for his best 1989 card is Topps.

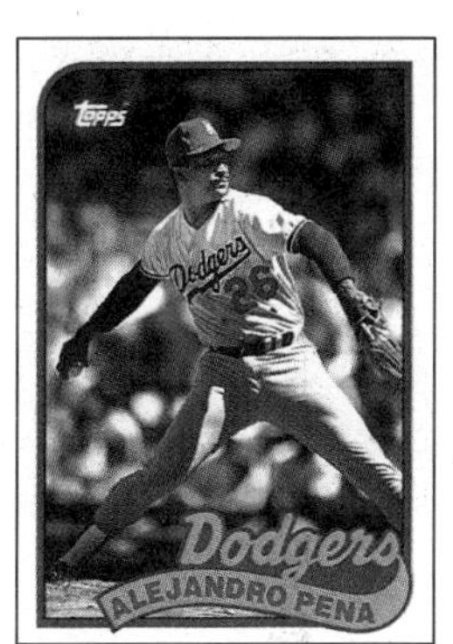

HIPOLITO PENA

	W	L	ERA	G	SV	IP	H	R	BB	SO
1988	1	1	2.51	16	0	14.1	10	8	9	10
Life	1	7	4.84	42	2	48.1	33	32	38	32

POSITION: Pitcher
TEAM: New York Yankees
BORN: January 30, 1964 Fantino, Dominican Republic
HEIGHT: 6′3″ **WEIGHT:** 175 lbs.
BATS: Left **THROWS:** Left
ACQUIRED: Traded from Pirates for Orestes Destrade, 4/88

Pena spent most of 1988 at Triple-A Columbus, finishing with a 7-6 record and a 3.87 ERA in 50 games (47 of them as a reliever). In a brief tour with the Yankees late in the season, he went 1-1 and finished with the best ERA on the staff, 2.51. The lefthander went 0-3 in 1987 with the Pirates, pitching in 16 games and getting a 4.56 ERA. In 1987 at Triple-A Vancouver, Pena was 5-6. He was 0-3 with the Pirates in '86, with a high 8.64 ERA. He was 7-4 with Vancouver in 1986. At 25 years old, he is young enough to develop slowly. Pena is talented enough to make a big difference for the 1989 Yankees.

Pena's 1989 cards will open at 15 to 20 cents. As he becomes a factor in the Yankee bullpen, his cards should be good long-term investments. Our pick for his best 1989 card is Fleer.

TONY PENA

	BA	G	AB	R	H	2B	3B	HR	RBI	SB
1988	.263	149	505	55	133	23	1	10	51	6
Life	.275	1066	3761	402	1036	176	20	78	435	54

POSITION: Catcher
TEAM: St. Louis Cardinals
BORN: June 4, 1957 Monte Cristi, Dominican Republic
HEIGHT: 6′ **WEIGHT:** 175 lbs.
BATS: Right **THROWS:** Right
ACQUIRED: Traded from Pirates for Andy Van Slyke, Mike LaValliere, and Mike Dunne, 4/87

Pena rebounded somewhat in 1988. He hit .263 in 149 games and began to reflect some of the skills he had shown with the Bucs. At one time, Pena was the one true shining light in the Pirate organization. It was assumed that wonderful things would happen to his career if he was traded to a winner. He was hurt when the Cardinals got him in early 1987, and it was mid-season before he got into the lineup. The end result was a .214 batting average and just five home runs. He has been on numerous N.L. All-Star teams as a catcher. If completely healthy, Pena could have another All-Star-quality season in 1989.

Pena's 1989 cards, which will open at 5 to 15 cents, are a tough call. Be careful in stockpiling them. Our pick for his best 1989 card is Topps.

TERRY PENDLETON

	BA	G	AB	R	H	2B	3B	HR	RBI	SB
1988	.253	110	391	44	99	20	2	6	53	3
Life	.263	644	2373	275	623	107	17	25	310	83

POSITION: Third base
TEAM: St. Louis Cardinals
BORN: July 16, 1960 Los Angeles, CA
HEIGHT: 5′9″ **WEIGHT:** 185 lbs.
BATS: Both **THROWS:** Right
ACQUIRED: Seventh-round pick in 6/82

Pendleton had a down year in 1988. He batted .253 in 110 games, with six home runs and 53 RBIs. He had a great season during the St. Louis pennant-winning year. He had a .286 batting average, a career-high 12 home runs, and 96 RBIs. That season ended on a down note for Pendleton, as he was relegated to a part-time role during the World Series due to a pulled muscle in his rib cage. He burst on to the big league scene in mid-season 1984 and batted .324 in 67 games. Pendleton has been an up-and-down player since 1984, but he still ranks as one of the National League's better third basemen.

Pendleton is a middle-range star-potential player whose cards are still priced low at 10 cents, but they may appreciate in the years to come. Our pick for his best 1989 card is Fleer.

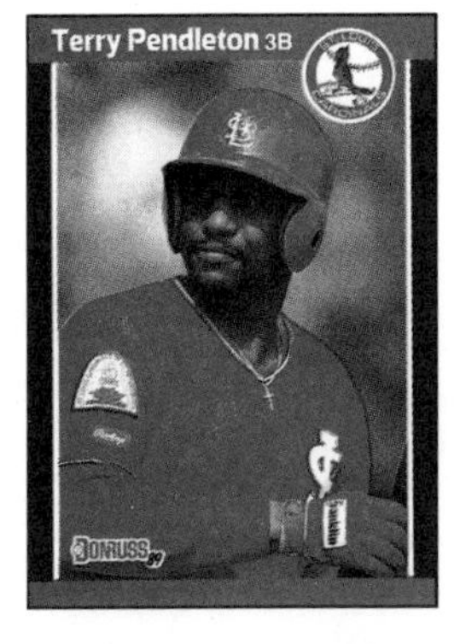

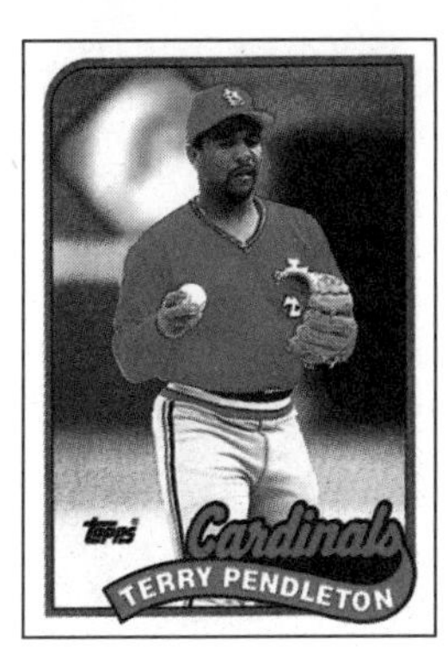

OSWALD PERAZA

	W	L	ERA	G	CG	IP	H	R	BB	SO
1988	5	7	5.55	19	1	86.0	98	62	37	61
Life	5	7	5.55	19	1	86.0	98	62	37	61

POSITION: Pitcher
TEAM: Baltimore Orioles
BORN: October 19, 1962 Puerto Cabello, Venezuela
HEIGHT: 6′4″ **WEIGHT:** 175 lbs.
BATS: Right **THROWS:** Right
ACQUIRED: Traded from Blue Jays with Jose Mesa for Mike Flanagan, 8/87

Peraza didn't have a great rookie year with the 1988 Orioles, but who did? He won five games in just 19 appearances, which amounted to nine percent of Baltimore's total wins. The Orioles gave up Mike Flanagan, their fourth-winningest pitcher of all time, to get Peraza in trade from the Blue Jays' farm system. The lanky righthander has mastery of four pitches: a fastball, slider, forkball, and changeup. After being converted from catcher, his combined record in five minor league seasons was 36-31 with a 3.58 ERA. Peraza is one of the many mound hopefuls the Orioles are testing.

After only one subpar season, Peraza's cards will be priced as commons. Don't invest heavily in his cards until he gives some definite signs that he can win in the big leagues. Our pick for his best 1989 card is Score.

MELIDO PEREZ

	W	L	ERA	G	CG	IP	H	R	BB	SO
1988	12	10	3.79	32	3	197.0	186	105	72	138
Life	13	11	3.99	35	3	207.1	204	117	77	143

POSITION: Pitcher
TEAM: Chicago White Sox
BORN: February 15, 1966 San Cristobal, Dominican Republic
HEIGHT: 6'4" **WEIGHT:** 180 lbs.
BATS: Right **THROWS:** Right
ACQUIRED: Traded from Royals with John Davis, Chuck Mount, and Greg Hibbard for Floyd Bannister and Dave Cochrane, 12/87

Perez was one of the biggest surprises for the 1988 White Sox. Everyone knew that the younger brother of Expo hurler Pascual Perez was a highly rated prospect with the Royals. When Melido came to the White Sox, however, he had just three games of major league experience. Perez didn't disappoint anyone in 1988, though. His 12 wins trailed only Jerry Reuss on the team. Perez was one of the team's most tireless performers, working nearly 200 innings. At Double-A Memphis in '87, he was 8-5, with a 3.53 ERA and 126 Ks. Perez is only 23, and should be one of Chicago's future pitching stars.

Expect Perez's 1989 cards to go for 10 to 15 cents. That's a good price and a good investment. The White Sox need pitching, and Perez seems to be a solution. Our pick for his best 1989 card is Topps.

PASCUAL PEREZ

	W	L	ERA	G	CG	IP	H	R	BB	SO
1988	12	8	2.44	27	4	188.0	133	59	44	131
Life	55	49	3.51	157	19	958.0	913	427	272	617

POSITION: Pitcher
TEAM: Montreal Expos
BORN: May 17, 1957 Haina, Dominican Republic
HEIGHT: 6'2" **WEIGHT:** 170 lbs.
BATS: Right **THROWS:** Right
ACQUIRED: Signed as a free agent, 2/87

Perez seems to have put his career back in the correct lane. He started 27 games and was 12-8 in 1988. His 2.44 ERA was the sixth best in the N.L. In 1987, his first year with the Expos, Perez went 7-0 with a 2.30 ERA. Perez once got lost on the expressway in Atlanta on the way to a game, the stuff legends are made of. He was a 15-game winner for the Braves in 1983 and a 14-game winner in 1984. He was an awful 1-13 for Atlanta in 1985. The Expos think that Perez will find his way to many more wins in 1989.

Perez is an enigma. He has the potential to be a superstar, but collectors don't stockpile his 1989 cards (at 5 cents apiece) for fear he'll disappear again. Our pick for his best 1989 card is Topps.

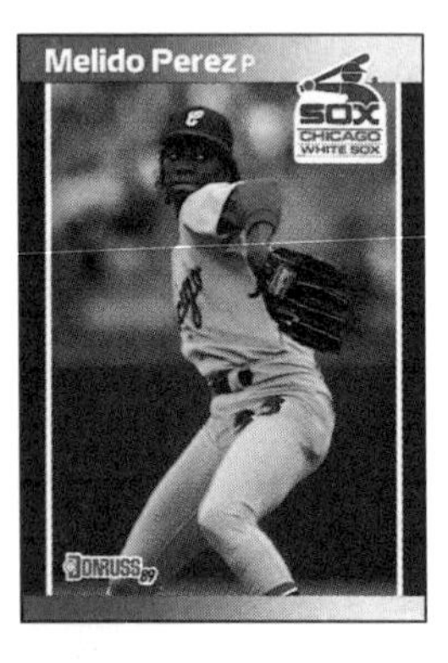

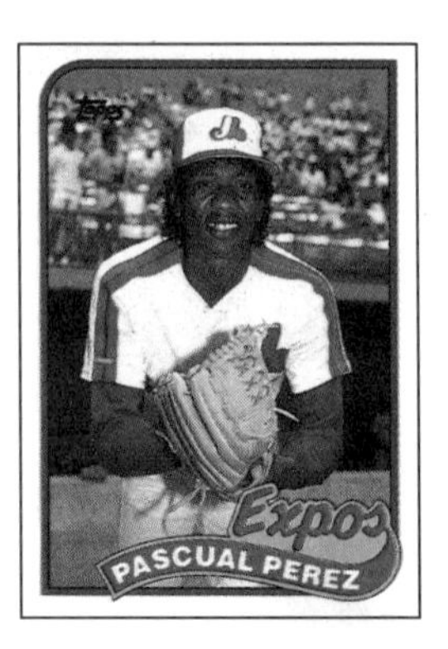

GERALD PERRY

	BA	G	AB	R	H	2B	3B	HR	RBI	SB
1988	.300	141	547	61	164	29	1	8	74	29
Life	.273	571	1774	223	484	85	5	33	225	95

POSITION: First base
TEAM: Atlanta Braves
BORN: October 30, 1960 Savannah, GA
HEIGHT: 6′ **WEIGHT:** 190 lbs.
BATS: Left **THROWS:** Right
ACQUIRED: 11th-round pick in 6/78 free-agent draft

A late-season slump stopped Perry from winning his first-ever league batting title in 1988. He owned Atlanta's first base job for the second year in '88, and he responded in fine fashion. Perry started to come into his own. He settled down as a hitter, with a .300 average and 164 base hits. He trades home runs for a first-class batting average and a respectable on-base average (.338). In 1987, he hit .270, with 12 homers, 35 doubles, and 74 RBIs. Prior to '88, it seemed that he would be a lifetime .270s type of hitter. Now, however, Perry could become one of the league's best batsmen.

Perry's 1989 cards will sell for a nickel or less, a good price to gamble on. His cards could reach a quarter with an MVP-quality outing in 1989. Our pick for his best 1989 card is Topps.

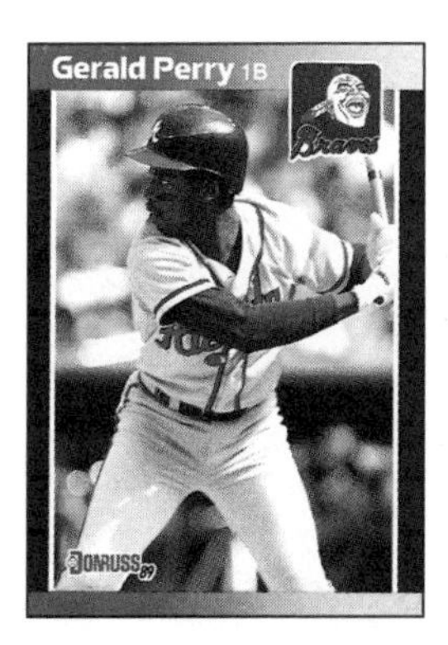

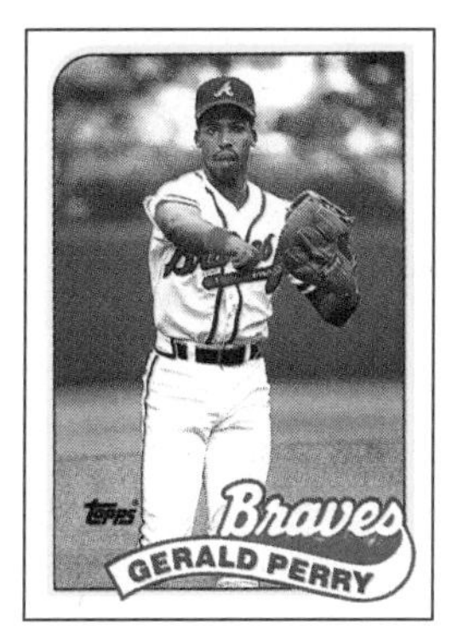

PAT PERRY

	W	L	ERA	G	SV	IP	H	R	BB	SO
1988	4	4	4.14	47	1	58.2	61	32	16	35
Life	12	9	3.59	156	5	220.2	183	97	78	109

POSITION: Pitcher
TEAM: Chicago Cubs
BORN: February 4, 1959 Taylorville, IL
HEIGHT: 6′1″ **WEIGHT:** 170 lbs.
BATS: Left **THROWS:** Left
ACQUIRED: Traded from Reds for Leon Durham, 5/88

Perry contributed a lot more to the Cubs than Leon Durham did to the Reds. Perry finished second on the team in appearances, with 47. He ended the season with a 4-4 record, a 4.14 ERA, and one save. His best season came in 1987, playing for both the Cardinals and the Reds. Perry appeared in 57 games, finishing with a 5-2 record, two saves, and a 3.56 ERA. In 1986 at St. Louis, he was 2-3 with a 3.80 ERA in 47 games and two saves. Perry is a control pitcher who could go a long way to steady the wobbly Cub bullpen.

Perry's 1989 cards are located in the commons box. Collectors are seldom interested in middle relief pitchers. He would have to get a starting job or become the Cub stopper for his card values to rise. Our pick for his best 1989 card is Fleer.

STEVE PETERS

	W	L	ERA	G	SV	IP	H	R	BB	SO
1988	3	3	6.40	44	0	45.0	57	34	22	30
Life	3	3	5.25	56	1	60.0	74	37	20	41

POSITION: Pitcher
TEAM: St. Louis Cardinals
BORN: November 14, 1962
Oklahoma City, OK
HEIGHT: 5′11″ **WEIGHT:** 175 lbs.
BATS: Left **THROWS:** Left
ACQUIRED: Sixth-round pick in 6/85 free-agent draft

Peters was the best reliever in the Double-A Texas League in 1987, picking up 23 saves in 47 games at Arkansas. Splitting eight decisions, he struck out 78, walked only 24 in 74 innings, and finished with a 1.57 ERA. Peters was promoted to Triple-A Louisville in '87, where he went 2-0 with six saves and a 0.95 ERA. A late-season promotion to the Cards that year resulted in one save and a 1.80 ERA in 12 games. He started the 1988 season back at Louisville, due to an injury that kept him out of spring training. After 22 outings, a 1-1 record, and a 3.67 ERA, Peters returned to St. Louis, where he became a fixture in the bullpen.

Peters' 1989 cards should open in the 15- to 20-cent range. Relievers are always shaky investment commodities, so you should invest accordingly. Our pick for his best 1989 card is Topps.

GENO PETRALLI

	BA	G	AB	R	H	2B	3B	HR	RBI	SB
1988	.282	129	351	35	99	14	2	7	36	0
Life	.283	366	841	90	238	38	7	16	97	4

POSITION: Catcher
TEAM: Texas Rangers
BORN: September 25, 1959
Sacramento, CA
HEIGHT: 6′1″ **WEIGHT:** 180 lbs.
BATS: Both **THROWS:** Right
ACQUIRED: Signed as a free agent, 5/85

Petralli appeared in more games in 1988 than any previous season with the Rangers. The veteran switch-hitter, previously used in a variety of positions, seemed most comfortable as the team's starting catcher. Petralli had a career best 99 hits and 36 RBIs. Both the Blue Jays' and Indians' organizations had given up on Petralli before he got another chance with Texas. He hit .270 in his first season with the team, 1985. Petralli might never become a feared home run hitter, but he consistently makes contact and might hit .300 regularly.

Petralli's 1989 cards will be readily available at about three cents each. However, because 1988 was Petralli's first full season, he isn't a proven commodity yet. Refrain from investing until Petralli can repeat his success in 1989. Our pick for his best 1989 card is Donruss.

DAN PETRY

	W	L	ERA	G	CG	IP	H	R	BB	SO
1988	3	9	4.38	22	4	139.2	139	70	59	64
Life	110	90	3.80	279	51	1778.2	1667	846	707	930

POSITION: Pitcher
TEAM: California Angels
BORN: November 13, 1958 Palo Alto, CA
HEIGHT: 6′4″ **WEIGHT:** 195 lbs.
BATS: Right **THROWS:** Right
ACQUIRED: Traded from Tigers for Gary Pettis, 12/87

A former mainstay of the Detroit starting rotation, Petry had an off season in 1988 for the Angels. He was 3-9, with a lofty 4.38 ERA in 22 starts. He missed a large chunk of the season with a leg injury. Petry won in double figures for the Tigers each year from 1980 to 1985, keeping his ERA under 4.00. His two best seasons for Detroit were in 1983 and '84. He was 19-11 in 1983, with a 3.92 ERA and a league-leading 38 starts. He was 18-8 in 1984, with a 3.24 ERA. The Angels are banking on a healthy Petry finding his old stride in 1989.

You can find 1989 cards of Petry for 5 cents or less. He has never been a 20-game winner. Investing in Petry's cards at this point in his career would be unwise. Our pick for his best 1989 card is Fleer.

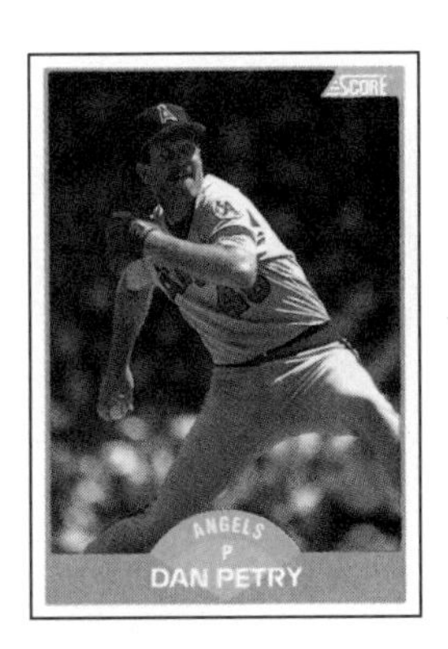

GARY PETTIS

	BA	G	AB	R	H	2B	3B	HR	RBI	SB
1988	.210	129	458	65	96	14	4	3	36	44
Life	.236	713	2321	361	547	73	27	16	179	230

POSITION: Outfield
TEAM: Detroit Tigers
BORN: April 3, 1958 Oakland, CA
HEIGHT: 6′1″ **WEIGHT:** 180 lbs.
BATS: Both **THROWS:** Right
ACQUIRED: Traded from Angels for Dan Petry, 12/87

Pettis provided some much-needed speed and defense to the Tigers outfield lineup. He swiped a team-high 44 bases and committed only five errors all season long. However, he continued to struggle with his batting average. After hitting a career-low .208 in 1987, Pettis had only a minimal improvement in 1988. His 85 strikeouts were only four less than slugger Darrell Evans' totals. Evans, however, hit 22 home runs. Pettis has true abilities, but he'll never become a full-fledged star until he can make more contact at the plate and raise his anemic batting average.

Pettis' 1989 cards are priced at a nickel or less. His average stops his cards from becoming valuable. Good fielders with lots of stolen bases and little else don't make good investments. Our pick for his best 1989 card is Topps.

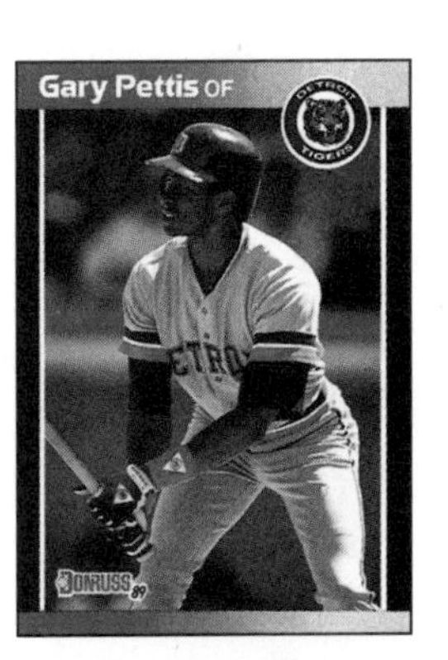

KEN PHELPS

	BA	G	AB	R	H	2B	3B	HR	RBI	SB
1988	.263	117	297	54	78	13	0	24	54	1
Life	.245	608	1540	272	378	58	7	115	278	9

POSITION: Designated hitter
TEAM: New York Yankees
BORN: August 6, 1954 Seattle, WA
HEIGHT: 6'1" **WEIGHT:** 200 lbs.
BATS: Left **THROWS:** Left
ACQUIRED: Traded from Mariners for Jay Buhner and Rick Balabon, 7/88

When Phelps hits 'em, they go forever. He stepped up to the plate 297 times in 1988, and he slugged 24 homers and 54 RBIs. He ended the season with a .263 average, which is respectable for a power hitter. His best season was in 1987 for the Mariners, when he hit 27 homers in 332 at-bats, with 68 RBIs and a .259 average. In 1986, Phelps had 24 homers and 64 RBIs, hitting .247. He has improved his batting average while maintaining his power. The Yankees hope that he continues to increase his average, but they will settle for Phelps winning a few A.L. homer crowns.

With Phelps popping round-trippers for the Yankees instead of the M's, expect his 1989 cards to be in the 5- to 10-cent range. If he wins a power award as a Yankee, that value will shoot up. Our pick for his best 1989 card is Fleer.

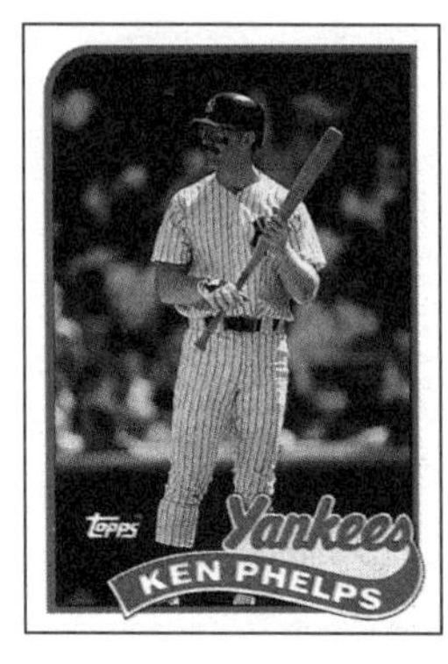

TONY PHILLIPS

	BA	G	AB	R	H	2B	3B	HR	RBI	SB
1988	.203	79	212	32	43	8	4	2	17	0
Life	.248	692	2137	306	531	92	19	29	212	53

POSITION: Infield
TEAM: Oakland A's
BORN: April 25, 1959 Atlanta, GA
HEIGHT: 5'10" **WEIGHT:** 175 lbs.
BATS: Both **THROWS:** Right
ACQUIRED: Traded from Padres with Kevin Bell for Bob Lacey and Roy Merretti, 3/81

As is the case with most players, Phillips is a better starter than role player. He played only a part-time role in the 1988 Oakland A.L. championship. He appeared in just 79 games, hitting a career-low .203. The speedy switch-hitter had more success in 1987. He amassed ten homers, 46 RBIs, and a .240 average in 111 games. In 1986, he hit .256, with 76 runs scored and 52 RBIs. Originally a Padres' organization member, he had been a regular second baseman before Glen Hubbard was acquired. However, with Hubbard's departure, Phillips might be able to earn his job back in 1989.

Phillips' new cards should be commons, priced at a nickel or less. Due to his recent slump, see if he wins a starting position before investing. Our pick for his best 1989 card is Topps.

JEFF PICO

	W	L	ERA	G	CG	IP	H	R	BB	SO
1988	6	7	4.15	29	3	112.2	108	57	37	57
Life	6	7	4.15	29	3	112.2	108	57	37	57

POSITION: Pitcher
TEAM: Chicago Cubs
BORN: February 12, 1966 Antioch, CA
HEIGHT: 6'2" **WEIGHT:** 170 lbs.
BATS: Right **THROWS:** Right
ACQUIRED: 13th-round pick in 6/84 free-agent draft

Pico pitched a shutout during his big league debut in May 1988; he was the first Cub hurler to do that in 79 years. He pitched in 29 games for Chicago in 1988, ending with a 6-7 record, one save, 13 starts, and a 4.15 ERA. He started the '88 season at Triple-A Iowa, going 5-2 in ten starts before being summoned to Wrigley Field. Pico divided the 1987 season between Double-A Pittsfield, where he went 4-4, and Triple-A Iowa, where he won six and lost five. He notched 12 victories for Class-A Winston-Salem in 1986. Pico should eventually move into the Chicago starting rotation, ending up as the third or fourth starter.

Pico's 1989 cards will open around a dime. He could be an impressive pitcher with a long career, if the indications we see are true. Our pick for his best 1989 card is Score.

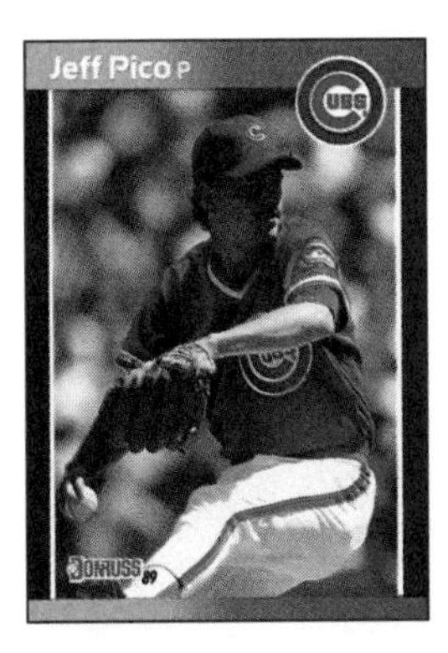

DAN PLESAC

	W	L	ERA	G	SV	IP	H	R	BB	SO
1988	1	2	2.41	50	30	52.1	46	14	12	52
Life	16	15	2.71	158	67	222.2	190	78	64	216

POSITION: Pitcher
TEAM: Milwaukee Brewers
BORN: February 4, 1962 Gary, IN
HEIGHT: 6'5" **WEIGHT:** 210 lbs.
BATS: Left **THROWS:** Left
ACQUIRED: First-round pick in 6/83 free-agent draft

It took only three seasons for Plesac to become one of the top relievers in the American League. In 1988, he achieved career bests in saves (30) and ERA (2.41). He saved 23 games in 1987, with a 2.61 ERA. In 1986, he won 10 games in relief and maintained an ERA under 3.00, while picking up 14 saves. Plesac was a starter in the minor leagues, but he has been used exclusively in relief with Milwaukee. He is a top-quality closer, an entity that the Brew Crew has missed since Rollie Fingers helped the '82 Brewers to a league championship. Plesac's similar talent could help make Milwaukee a champion again.

Plesac's 1989 cards are priced at a nickel apiece. Investors can't go wrong socking a few bucks into his cards. Now 27, Plesac could be a bullpen baron for another decade. Our pick for his best 1989 card is Topps.

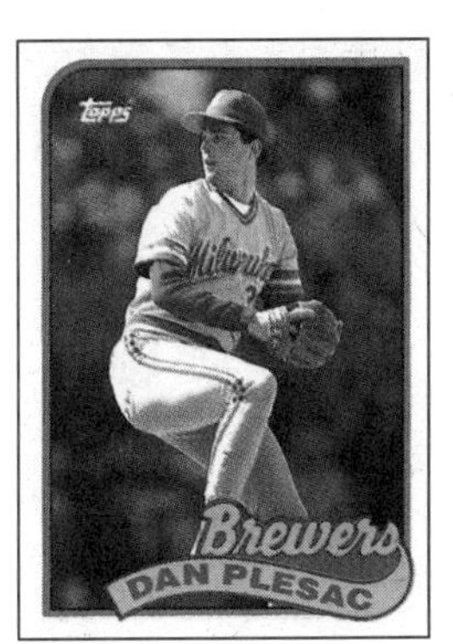

ERIC PLUNK

	W	L	ERA	G	SV	IP	H	R	BB	SO
1988	7	2	3.00	49	5	78.0	62	27	39	79
Life	15	15	4.51	107	7	293.1	244	155	203	267

POSITION: Pitcher
TEAM: Oakland A's
BORN: September 3, 1963
Wilmington, CA
HEIGHT: 6'5" **WEIGHT:** 210 lbs.
BATS: Right **THROWS:** Right
ACQUIRED: Traded from Yankees with Jose Rijo, Jay Howell, Tim Birtsas, and Stan Javier for Rickey Henderson and Bert Bradley, 12/84

Overshadowed by fellow reliever Dennis Eckersley's sterling season, Plunk's 1988 efforts didn't get the credit they deserved. After two average seasons with the A's as both a starter and reliever, he settled into the bullpen for his finest campaign ever. He set career bests in appearances, wins, saves, and ERA. His strikeout total exceeded one per inning pitched and surpassed the number of hits he allowed. Plunk was one of the few bright spots for the A's in their unsuccessful World Series bid. Expect more improvement and more success from this huge flamethrower in 1989.

Plunk, at age 25, could be a perennial All-Star if his accomplishments continue. His cards are priced as commons, and could show short-term gains if the A's and Plunk repeat their glory in 1989. Our pick for his best 1989 card is Donruss.

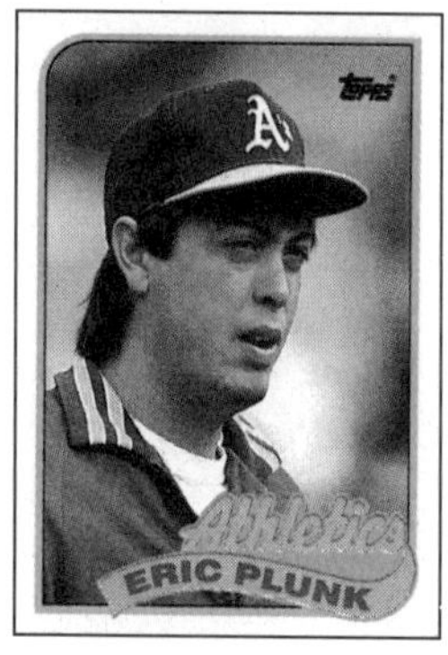

LUIS POLONIA

	BA	G	AB	R	H	2B	3B	HR	RBI	SB
1988	.292	84	288	51	84	11	4	2	27	24
Life	.289	209	723	129	209	27	14	6	76	53

POSITION: Outfield
TEAM: Oakland A's
BORN: December 12, 1964 Santiago, Dominican Republic
HEIGHT: 5'8" **WEIGHT:** 155 lbs.
BATS: Both **THROWS:** Left
ACQUIRED: Signed as a free agent, 1/84

Polonia was a big contributor to the A's 1988 championship effort. He hit .292, with 51 runs scored, 24 stolen bases, and 27 RBIs in 84 games. He is a quick flychaser who can run the basepaths and score runs, a needed commodity on the power-laden Oakland squad. In his rookie year, Polonia scored 78 runs, hitting .287 and swiping 29 bases. He also contributed four home runs. If he could increase his playing time and on-base average (.338 in 1988), he could challenge for the A.L. lead in runs scored for seasons to come. He may not have the power of teammates Jose Canseco and Mark McGwire, but Polonia provides the A's with speed and run-scoring ability.

Polonia's 1989 cards will be commons. Investing in his cards could be risky, since he isn't a full-time player. Our pick for his best 1989 card is Topps.

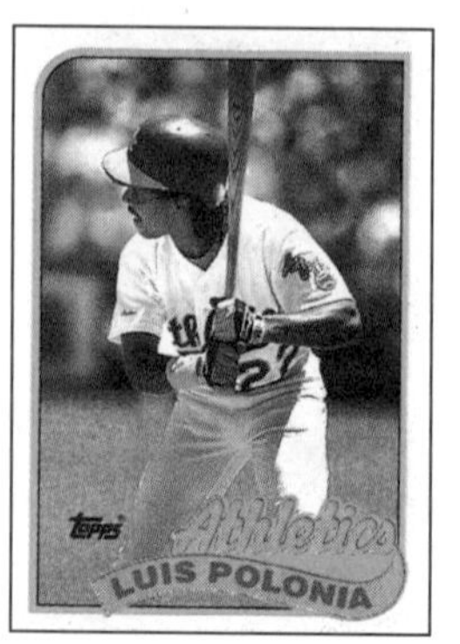

MARK PORTUGAL

	W	L	ERA	G	SV	IP	H	R	BB	SO
1988	3	3	4.53	26	3	57.2	60	30	17	31
Life	11	19	5.13	72	4	238.2	254	142	105	138

POSITION: Pitcher
TEAM: Houston Astros
BORN: October 30, 1962
Los Angeles, CA
HEIGHT: 6′ **WEIGHT:** 190 lbs.
BATS: Right **THROWS:** Right
ACQUIRED: Traded from Twins for Todd McClure, 12/88

Portugal was squeezed out of the talented Minnesota bullpen, and he goes to an Astro team in need of a middle reliever. He appeared in 26 games for the '88 Twins, winning three and saving three. He finished nine of the games he appeared in. Previously, Portugal had just one save during his entire career with the Twins. In 1987, he appeared in 13 games, finishing with a 1-3 record and a bad 7.77 ERA. He was 6-10 in 27 appearances in 1986, with 15 games started and a 4.31 ERA. If Portugal keeps lowering his ERA in 1989, he could get lots more assignments from the Astros.

Portugal's 1989 cards will be commons, priced at three cents or less. Until Portugal can clean up his weak lifetime statistics, investing in his cards would be a long shot. Our pick for his best 1989 card is Topps.

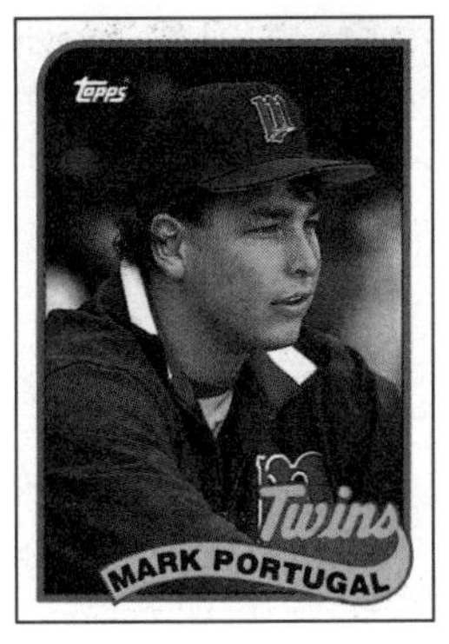

TED POWER

	W	L	ERA	G	CG	IP	H	R	BB	SO
1988	6	7	5.91	26	2	99.0	121	67	38	57
Life	50	49	4.20	324	5	779.1	781	400	331	487

POSITION: Pitcher
TEAM: Detroit Tigers
BORN: January 31, 1955 Guthrie, OK
HEIGHT: 6′4″ **WEIGHT:** 225 lbs.
BATS: Right **THROWS:** Right
ACQUIRED: Traded from Royals for Rey Palacios and Mark Lee, 8/88

Power was another late-season acquisition by the 1988 Detroit Tigers. Teams in a real battle for a pennant often go after veteran performers solely in hopes of getting clutch performances from them when it's most needed. Power had spent most of 1988 with the Royals, and gave minor aid to the Tigers. He went 6-7, only the third of eight seasons in which he had a losing mark. His ERA was the highest of his career at 5.91. Power should be adjusted to the American League strike zone in 1989, and his career should get back on track.

Power is an above-average reliever, but his records aren't stunning. His 1989 cards will be priced at three cents or less, but their investment value is limited because of Power's lifetime stats. Our pick for his best 1989 card is Donruss.

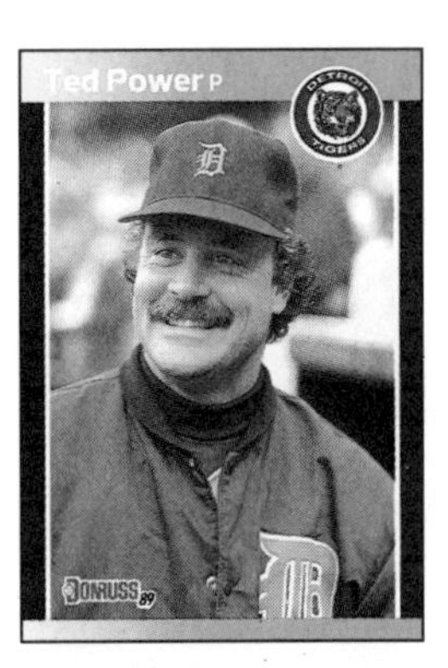

JIM PRESLEY

	BA	G	AB	R	H	2B	3B	HR	RBI	SB
1988	.230	150	544	50	125	26	0	14	62	3
Life	.252	682	2556	309	644	127	12	103	377	8

POSITION: Third base
TEAM: Seattle Mariners
BORN: October 23, 1961 Pensacola, FL
HEIGHT: 6′1″ **WEIGHT:** 195 lbs.
BATS: Right **THROWS:** Right
ACQUIRED: Fourth-round pick in 6/79 free-agent draft

Presley, in his fourth straight season as the Seattle third baseman, suffered through a lackluster year. His homers and RBIs were the lowest since 1984, when he first joined the M's. Presley's .230 average was a stark contrast to his 1987 performance of 24 homers, 88 RBIs, and a .247 average. He had a woeful time in the field, also. His 22 errors trailed only Kevin Seitzer's 26 in the A.L. miscue department. Presley has hit as many as 28 homers and 107 RBIs in a single season, so his 1988 numbers were disappointing by comparison. Presley will have a battle to keep his job in the M's infield in 1989.

Presley's 1989 cards should be in the 3-cent range. Don't give up on Presley. If he can drive in 100 runs again, his cards would sell quickly at a dime or more. Our pick for his best 1989 card is Fleer.

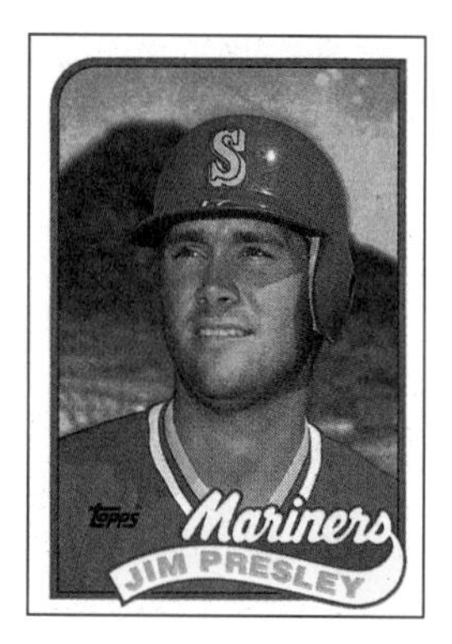

JOE PRICE

	W	L	ERA	G	SV	IP	H	R	BB	SO
1988	1	6	3.94	38	4	61.2	59	33	27	49
Life	39	39	3.55	284	13	756.1	690	335	279	541

POSITION: Pitcher
TEAM: San Francisco Giants
BORN: November 29, 1956
Inglewood, CA
HEIGHT: 6′4″ **WEIGHT:** 220 lbs.
BATS: Right **THROWS:** Left
ACQUIRED: Signed as a free agent, 2/87

Price has come back from an elbow injury to find a place in the San Francisco bullpen. In 1988, he was 1-6, but he had an acceptable 3.94 ERA in his 38 appearances, and he notched four saves. He was signed as a free agent by the Giants for their pennant-winning year, and Price contributed by going 2-2 in '87, with a 2.57 ERA and one save. The former Cincinnati starter had his best season in 1983 for the Reds, when he was 10-6, with a 2.88 ERA in 144 innings pitched. Price is a veteran hurler in the Giant bullpen, and he should continue to get more work in 1989.

Price's 1989 cards are in the commons bin. His slowdown in the years previous to 1988 has taken any collector interest in his cards away. Our pick for his best 1989 card is Topps.

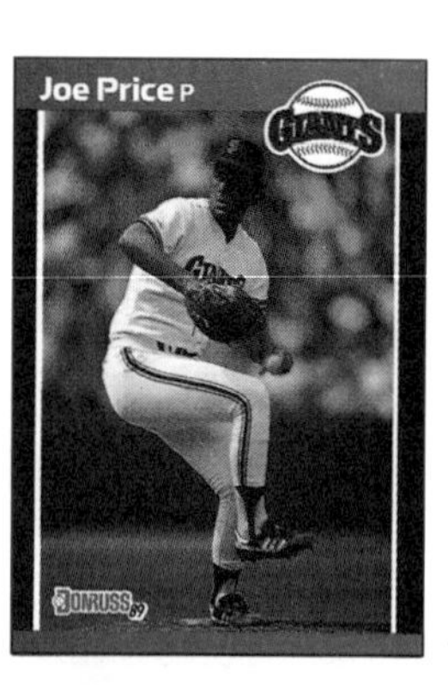

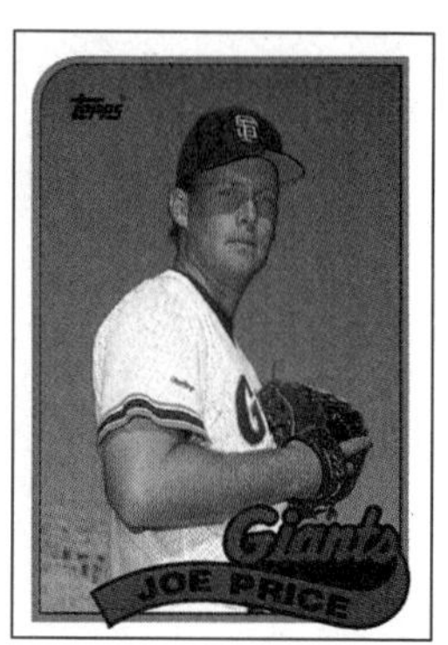

TOM PRINCE

	BA	G	AB	R	H	2B	3B	HR	RBI	SB
1988	.176	29	74	3	13	2	0	0	6	0
Life	.181	33	83	4	15	3	0	1	8	0

POSITION: Catcher
TEAM: Pittsburgh Pirates
BORN: August 13, 1964 Kankakee, IL
HEIGHT: 5′11″ **WEIGHT:** 185 lbs.
BATS: Right **THROWS:** Right
ACQUIRED: Fourth-round pick in 1/84 free-agent draft

Prince was rated among the Triple-A American Association's top ten prospects in 1988. He earned raves in Triple-A last year for his defensive prowess. Prince also was called the best defensive backstop, and the catcher with the best arm in the Eastern League (Double-A) in 1987. Prince is at the big league level in calling a game, handling pitchers, releasing the ball quickly, and throwing with accuracy. People often talk about his defense, but it should be noted that he does have some power, hitting 14 home runs at Buffalo in 1988. Prince's offense will only get better with experience, and he should open the 1989 season as the number-two catcher for the Pirates.

Prince's 1989 cards should open in the 15- to 25-cent range. At those prices, his cards are solid investments. Our pick for his best 1989 card is Score.

KIRBY PUCKETT

	BA	G	AB	R	H	2B	3B	HR	RBI	SB
1988	.356	158	657	109	234	42	5	24	121	6
Life	.320	765	3209	467	1028	152	34	87	421	73

POSITION: Outfield
TEAM: Minnesota Twins
BORN: March 14, 1961 Chicago, IL
HEIGHT: 5′8″ **WEIGHT:** 185 lbs.
BATS: Right **THROWS:** Right
ACQUIRED: First-round pick in 1/82 free-agent draft

After the Twins were eliminated from the divisional pennant race in mid-September 1988, Puckett pursued his own chase. He battled Wade Boggs for the A.L. batting crown all season long, coming in second with a .356 average. Puckett led the majors with 234 hits and wound up with the highest batting average for an A.L. right-handed hitter since Joe DiMaggio hit .381 in 1939. Puckett had career highs in doubles (42) and RBIs (121). In 1987, he led the A.L. in hits, with 207, while batting .332, with 28 homers, and 99 RBIs. Speed, power, a high batting average, and spotless fielding are the ingredients that make Puckett a complete ballplayer.

Puckett's 1989 cards should start at 25 cents, which is a great buy. The Twins' sparkplug can do it all, a fact that will reflect in his future card values. Our pick for his best 1989 card is Score.

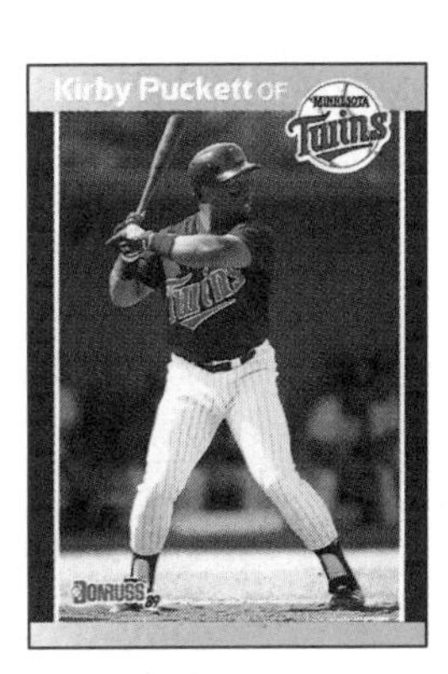

TERRY PUHL

	BA	G	AB	R	H	2B	3B	HR	RBI	SB
1988	.303	113	234	42	71	7	2	3	19	22
Life	.281	1358	4442	630	1249	200	52	62	397	207

POSITION: Outfield
TEAM: Houston Astros
BORN: July 8, 1956
Melville, Saskatchewan
HEIGHT: 6′2″ **WEIGHT:** 195 lbs.
BATS: Left **THROWS:** Right
ACQUIRED: Signed as a free agent, 9/73

Puhl ended the 1988 season as the leading Astro hitter. He hit a career-high average of .303 in 113 games, with three homers and 19 RBIs. He swiped 22 out of 26 bases in 1988, one of the best success ratios on the team. He rebounded from two down years in 1986 and '87. In '86, Puhl played in 81 games and ended with a .244 average. He hit only .230 (his lowest ever) in 1987. He was a starter from 1978 to 1984, and he consistently hit in the .280s. Although not a power hitter, he did manage 13 homers and 55 RBIs in 1980. The Astros can count on bench strength from Puhl during their pennant run in 1989.

Puhl's 1989 cards will be available for 3 cents. Although he was a starter, his career stats are not good enough to generate much interest outside of the Houston area. Our pick for his best 1989 card is Donruss.

CHARLIE PULEO

	W	L	ERA	G	CG	IP	H	R	BB	SO
1988	5	5	3.47	53	0	106.1	101	46	47	70
Life	28	38	4.23	165	3	603.2	595	320	303	370

POSITION: Pitcher
TEAM: Atlanta Braves
BORN: February 7, 1955 Glen Ridge, NJ
HEIGHT: 6′4″ **WEIGHT:** 200 lbs.
BATS: Right **THROWS:** Right
ACQUIRED: Purchased from Reds, 6/85

Puleo was one of only two Atlanta pitchers to escape the 1988 season without a losing record. He was third on the team in games pitched and had the second lowest ERA at 3.47. The Braves converted Puleo to relief after he had spent the first seven years of his pro career as a starter. He stayed the whole season with the 1987 Braves, going 6-8 in 16 starts and 19 relief appearances. It was the first time he spent an entire year in the majors since 1983. At age 34, Puleo could be in the Braves' bullpen for several more seasons.

Puleo cards won't ever be popular if he is both a starter and a reliever. His 1989 issues, at 3 cents each, aren't appealing because of his lifetime losing record. Our pick for his best 1989 card is Score.

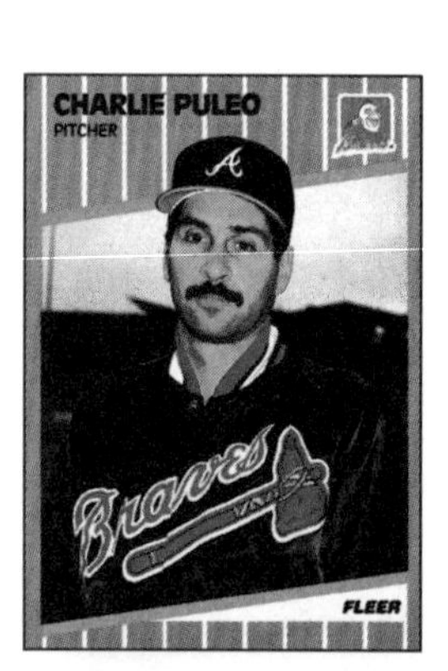

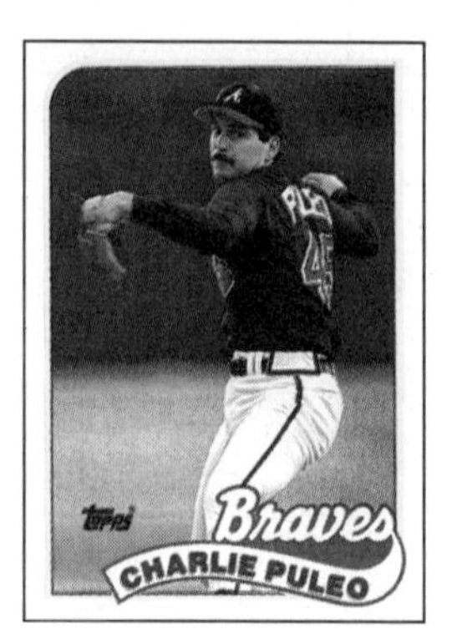

REY QUINONES

	BA	G	AB	R	H	2B	3B	HR	RBI	SB
1988	.248	140	499	63	124	30	3	12	52	0
Life	.251	373	1289	150	324	64	6	26	130	5

POSITION: Shortstop
TEAM: Seattle Mariners
BORN: November 11, 1963 Rio Piedras, Puerto Rico
HEIGHT: 5′11″ **WEIGHT:** 185 lbs.
BATS: Right **THROWS:** Right
ACQUIRED: Traded from Red Sox with John Christensen, Mike Brown, and Mike Truijillo for Spike Owen and Dave Henderson, 8/86

In his second full season as Seattle's starting shortstop, Quinones proved to be a vital ingredient in the Mariner lineup. He hit 12 home runs for the second straight season. His homer total was third among American League shortstops, trailing only Cal Ripken, Jr., and Alan Trammell. Quinones' fielding was less than spectacular, as he led the Mariners team with 23 errors. He also had some problems with strikeouts in 1988. He whiffed 71 times, roughly once in every seven at-bats. Quinones and his bat, if it keeps improving, could lead the M's to a winning record in 1989.

For now, cards of Quinones sell for a nickel or less. Until he hits .300 or the Mariners develop a winning record, his cards won't be appealing investments. Our pick for his best 1989 card is Score.

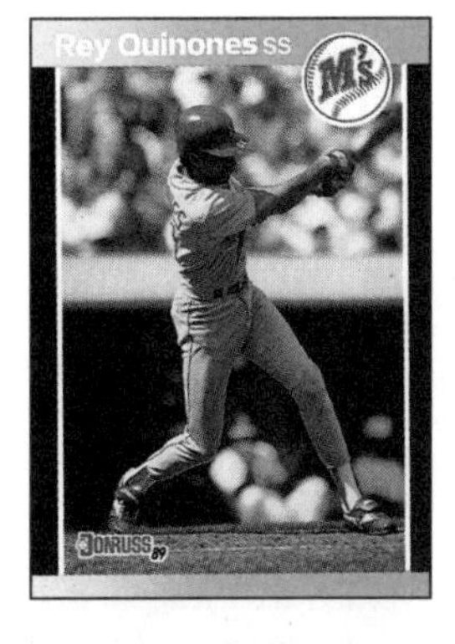

CARLOS QUINTANA

	BA	G	AB	R	H	2B	3B	HR	RBI	SB
1988	.333	5	6	1	2	0	0	0	2	0
Life	.333	5	6	1	2	0	0	0	2	0

POSITION: Outfield
TEAM: Boston Red Sox
BORN: August 26, 1965 Estado Miranda, Venezuela
HEIGHT: 6′ **WEIGHT:** 175 lbs.
BATS: Right **THROWS:** Right
ACQUIRED: Signed as a free agent, 11/84

It's uncanny how the Red Sox farm system keeps producing good young outfielders, and Quintana is just the latest example. At Triple-A Pawtucket in 1988, Quintana hit .285, with 16 homers and 66 RBIs. His 134 hits were a club high. In 1987, he batted .311 in 56 games at Double-A New Britain, missing half the season with injuries. Signed as a free agent in November 1984, Quintana played his first year of pro ball with Elmira in 1985, batting .277 in 65 games. Promoted to Class-A Greensboro in 1986, he batted .325 and drove in 81 runs with 11 homers. Quintana could challenge for a starting role on the Red Sox in 1989.

Quintana has a good chance to join the talented BoSox outfield corps this spring. His 1989 cards should open in the 30-cent range. Our pick for his best 1989 card is Score.

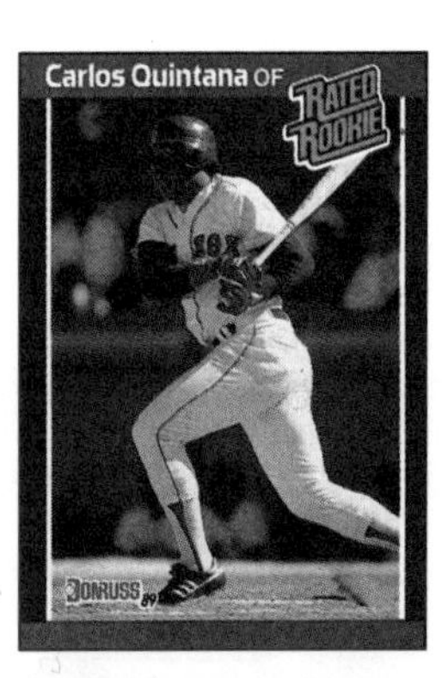

TIM RAINES

	BA	G	AB	R	H	2B	3B	HR	RBI	SB
1988	.270	109	429	66	166	19	7	12	48	33
Life	.305	1130	4331	793	1369	233	70	78	430	544

POSITION: Outfield
TEAM: Montreal Expos
BORN: September 16, 1959 Sanford, FL
HEIGHT: 5′8″ **WEIGHT:** 170 lbs.
BATS: Both **THROWS:** Right
ACQUIRED: Fifth-round pick in 6/77 free-agent draft

The 1988 accomplishments of Raines were a letdown from his excellent 1987 season, mostly due to injuries that kept him out of almost 50 games. He saw his average plummet nearly 60 points to .270. He did reach double figures in home runs and had a near-spotless season fielding. Raines stole 33 bases in '88. He led the N.L. in stolen bases from 1981 to 1984 (when Vince Coleman came into the league). Raines led the N.L. in runs scored (123) in 1987 and batting average (.334) in 1986. When the Expos have the use of Raines for an entire season and he responds with his usual star potential, the team will be a solid contender.

A disappointing 1988 season could drop Raines' 1989 cards below 25 cents. That's a worthwhile purchase, because he is bound to make a comeback. Our pick for his best 1989 card is Topps.

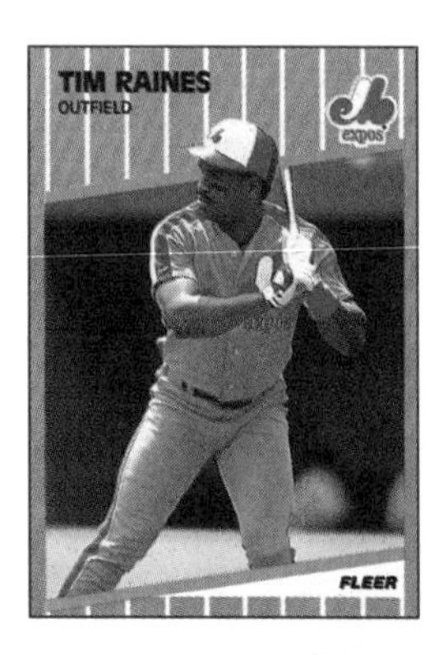

RAFAEL RAMIREZ

	BA	G	AB	R	H	2B	3B	HR	RBI	SB
1988	.276	155	566	51	156	30	5	6	59	3
Life	.264	1082	4103	438	1085	169	26	43	360	96

POSITION: Shortstop
TEAM: Houston Astros
BORN: February 18, 1959 San Pedro de Macoris, Dominican Republic
HEIGHT: 5′11″ **WEIGHT:** 190 lbs.
BATS: Right **THROWS:** Right
ACQUIRED: Traded from Braves for Mike Stoker and Ed Whited, 12/87

Ramirez adapted quickly to his new job with the 1988 Astros, putting together one of the finest seasons of his career. He hit .276, with six homers and a career-high in RBIs (59) last season. He played over seven seasons with the Braves, beginning in 1980. His previous career highs with the Braves include ten homers, 58 RBIs, and a .297 average. Ramirez was a member of the National League All-Star team in 1984. Andres Thomas beat him out of a job with the Braves. It looks as though Ramirez's fine 1988 performance will assure him that he is the starting shortstop for the Astros.

Ramirez's 1989 cards will be a nickel or less. Based on his 1988 accomplishments, his cards are a relatively safe investment with some chance of value appreciation. Our pick for his best 1989 card is Score.

WILLIE RANDOLPH

	BA	G	AB	R	H	2B	3B	HR	RBI	SB
1988	.230	110	404	43	93	20	1	2	34	8
Life	.274	1724	6364	1036	1741	260	58	48	552	252

POSITION: Second base
TEAM: Los Angeles Dodgers
BORN: July 6, 1954 Holly Hill, SC
HEIGHT: 5′11″ **WEIGHT:** 170 lbs.
BATS: Right **THROWS:** Right
ACQUIRED: Signed as a free agent, 12/88

Randolph fills a void at second base for the Dodgers, created when Steve Sax signed with the Yankees. Randolph endured a second straight season blighted by injuries in 1988. He missed 52 games, and his statistics reflect this. However, even with a shortened season, Randolph continued to etch his name deeper into the Yankee record books. He finished seventh on the team for career runs scored, just behind Yogi Berra at 1,175. At age 34, Randolph could assemble some impressive statistics and gain a reputation as one of the greatest second basemen ever. However, the current question would be Randolph's health for the 1989 season.

Randolph is a five-time All-Star with several years remaining in his career. Currently, Randolph's cards are a dime or less, which are good prices for investors. Our pick for his best 1989 card is Score.

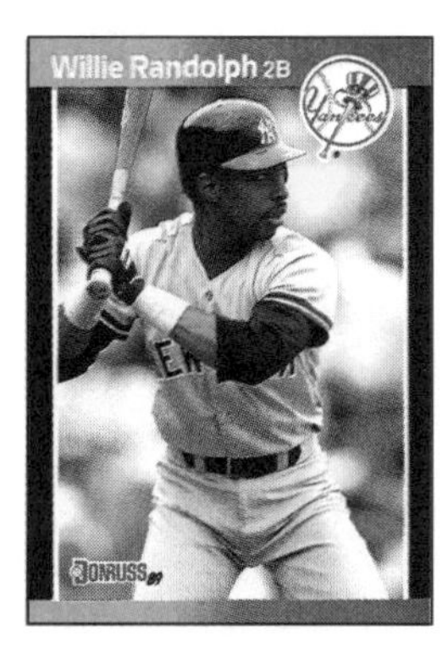

DENNIS RASMUSSEN

	W	L	ERA	G	CG	IP	H	R	BB	SO
1988	16	10	3.43	31	7	204.2	199	84	58	112
Life	59	35	4.02	145	15	861.0	777	415	309	557

POSITION: Pitcher
TEAM: San Diego Padres
BORN: April 18, 1959 Los Angeles, CA
HEIGHT: 6′7″ **WEIGHT:** 225 lbs.
BATS: Left **THROWS:** Left
ACQUIRED: Traded from Reds for Candy Sierra, 6/88

Rasmussen, a mid-season acquisition from the Reds, provided a much-needed spark for the 1988 San Diego pitching staff. He wound up tied with Eric Show for team wins with 16. Seven complete games (a career record) and a shutout highlighted Rasmussen's season, his winningest in the National League. Previously, Rasmussen's best season was in 1986 with the New York Yankees, when he logged an 18-6 mark. He broke into the majors in 1983 with the Padres, where he pitched four games. Rasmussen, age 29, could pitch for the Padres for at least another decade and could rack up some impressive career stats in the process.

Rasmussen's 1989 cards might be a long shot investment at their current prices of a nickel or less. However, those prices could triple if Rasmussen wins 20 in 1989. Our pick for his best 1989 card is Donruss.

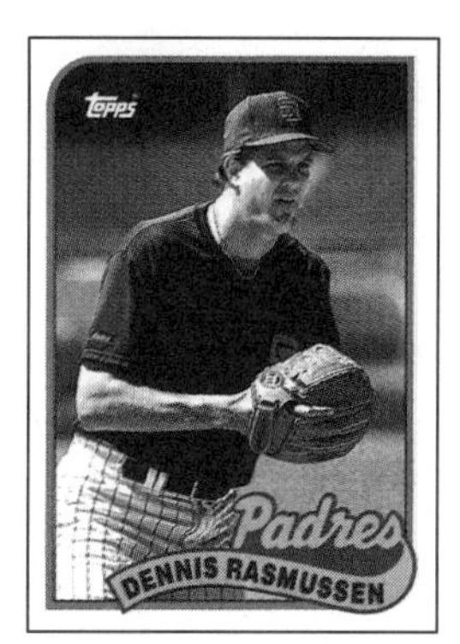

SHANE RAWLEY

	W	L	ERA	G	CG	IP	H	R	BB	SO
1988	8	16	4.18	32	4	198.0	220	111	78	87
Life	106	106	3.92	442	40	1725.2	1767	828	674	923

POSITION: Pitcher
TEAM: Minnesota Twins
BORN: July 27, 1955 Racine, WI
HEIGHT: 6′ **WEIGHT:** 185 lbs.
BATS: Right **THROWS:** Left
ACQUIRED: Traded from Phillies for Tom Herr, 11/88

Rawley is seeking a turnaround with the Twins in 1989. His career took a nosedive during the 1988 season. Coming off a 17-11 performance with the 1987 Phillies, he saw his winning streak evaporate in 1988. Rawley went 8-16 in 1988, his worst season ever as a starter. He broke in with the Mariners in 1976, and spent four seasons there as a reliever. During his three seasons with the Yankees, he was converted to a starter. Rawley will be an unknown quantity to many American League hitters in 1989, which should benefit the veteran lefty.

Rawley's 1989 cards should be a nickel or less. The 33-year-old hurler is capable of winning 20 games, which could be a jackpot for investors smart enough to stock up on his cards. Our pick for his best 1989 card is Topps.

JOHNNY RAY

	BA	G	AB	R	H	2B	3B	HR	RBI	SB
1988	.306	153	602	75	184	42	7	6	83	4
Life	.291	1114	4254	505	1237	255	33	43	489	72

POSITION: Second base
TEAM: California Angels
BORN: March 1, 1957 Chouteau, OK
HEIGHT: 5′11″ **WEIGHT:** 185 lbs.
BATS: Both **THROWS:** Right
ACQUIRED: Traded from Pirates for Bill Merrifield, 8/87

In 1988, his first full season with the Angels, Ray became one of the team's hottest hitters. Ray batted .306, with 83 RBIs and 75 runs scored. He led California in hits (184), doubles (42), and triples (seven). Ray began his career with the Pirates in 1981, and quickly developed a reputation as a tough contact hitter. While with the Pirates, he hit 30 or more doubles five straight seasons. When he was traded in the Pirate youth movement, he found a home in Anaheim. Besides being a tough out, Ray gives the Angels a scrappy veteran in the lineup.

Ray has quietly done a fine job in the majors for nearly a decade now, but his card prices don't reflect that consistency. His 1989 cards are available for a nickel; they don't represent good investments, based on his limited fame. Our pick for his best 1989 card is Fleer.

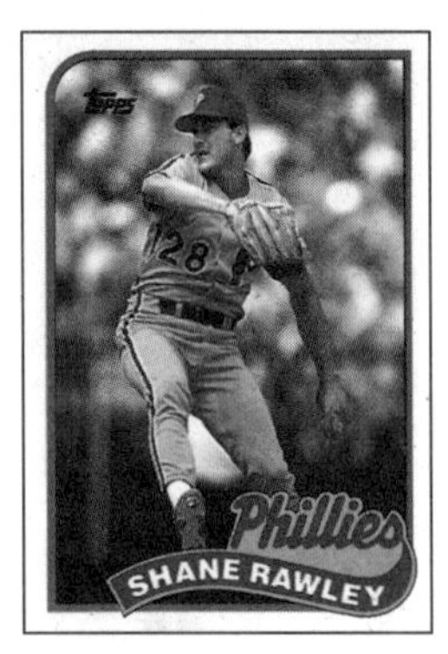

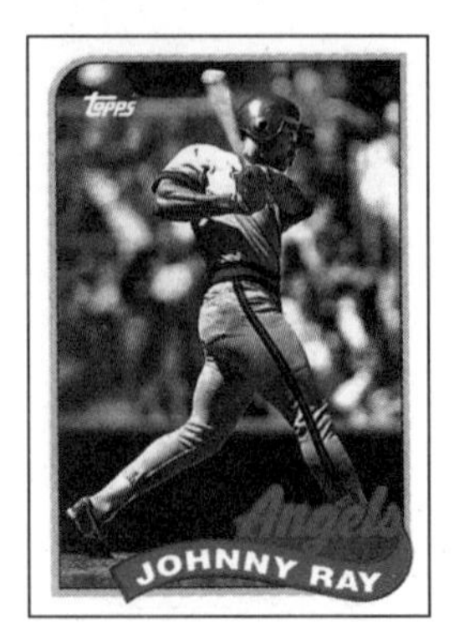

RANDY READY

	BA	G	AB	R	H	2B	3B	HR	RBI	SB
1988	.266	114	331	43	88	16	2	7	39	6
Life	.269	359	1104	170	297	64	16	25	137	15

POSITION: Infield
TEAM: San Diego Padres
BORN: January 8, 1960 San Mateo, CA
HEIGHT: 5′11″ **WEIGHT:** 180 lbs.
BATS: Right **THROWS:** Right
ACQUIRED: Traded from Brewers for Tim Pyznarski, 6/86

In 1988, Ready failed to match his exciting 1987 season with the Padres. The veteran utility infielder joined the Padres in 1986 from the Brewers, where he began in 1983. His 1987 season was divided between second base and third base, where he hit .309, with 12 homers and 54 RBIs in 124 games. Ready's average fell to .266 in 1988, and his homer level sank to seven. With more at-bats, he probably could have brought both numbers up. He is a versatile performer and able fielder. Ready seems too valuable to the Padres as a jack-of-all-trades to lock down into one starting position.

Ready is a capable utilityman, but his cards will never gain value until he becomes a starter. Bypass his 1989 cards, which will be three cents or less. Our pick for his best 1989 card is Fleer.

JEFF REARDON

	W	L	ERA	G	SV	IP	H	R	BB	SO
1988	2	4	2.47	63	42	73.0	68	21	15	56
Life	52	58	2.93	582	235	819.0	689	288	289	676

POSITION: Pitcher
TEAM: Minnesota Twins
BORN: October 1, 1955 Dalton, MA
HEIGHT: 6′1″ **WEIGHT:** 200 lbs.
BATS: Right **THROWS:** Right
ACQUIRED: Traded from Expos with Tom Neito for Jeff Reed, Neal Heaton, and Yorkis Perez, 2/87

Reardon was in top form in 1988, vaulting the 40-save mark. The Twins acquired Reardon before the 1987 season, and his eight-win, 31-save presence helped the team to a world championship. Reardon kept his ERA under 3.00 in 1988, which explains his increased success. He has saved at least 20 games in seven consecutive seasons. In three more seasons, he will have more than 300 saves to his credit if he performs at the same level. That would give him merit as a Hall of Fame candidate. Meanwhile, the Twins need Reardon's pitching magic to continue to regain their hold on the A.L. West.

Reardon's cards are bargains at 10 cents or less. Barring a career-ending injury, his cards could double in value if the Twins return to the World Series. Our pick for his best 1989 card is Score.

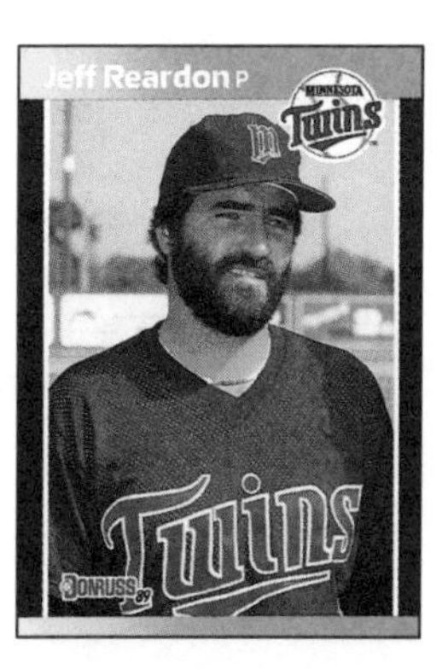

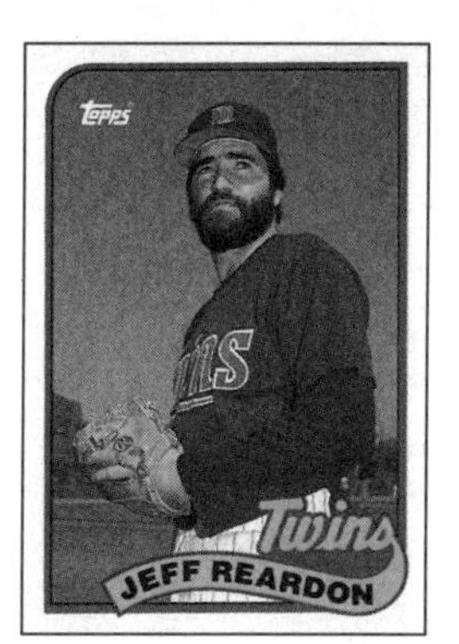

GARY REDUS

	BA	G	AB	R	H	2B	3B	HR	RBI	SB
1988	.249	107	333	54	83	12	4	8	38	31
Life	.246	696	2324	416	571	118	32	62	227	254

POSITION: Outfield
TEAM: Pittsburgh Pirates
BORN: November 1, 1956 Tanner, AL
HEIGHT: 6'1" **WEIGHT:** 185 lbs.
BATS: Right **THROWS:** Right
ACQUIRED: Traded from White Sox for Mike Diaz, 8/88

Redus came aboard the Pirates during their unsuccessful pennant run in August. He gives to the Pirates a seasoned bat and some speed. He finished the '88 season hitting only .197 for the Pirates, but his on-base average was a fair .341. In 1987, he hit .236 for the White Sox (with a .392 on-base average), slugged 12 homers, and swiped a career-high 52 bases. Redus hit 17 homers in 1983 for the Reds, ending that season with 51 RBIs and 90 runs scored. But he has never hit above .252 for a single season. Redus will be a fourth outfielder and pinch-hitter for the Pirates, who hope that he returns to his '87 form.

Redus' 1989 cards will cost 3 cents or less. With a low career batting average and little power, his cards are not high-demand items. Our pick for his best 1989 card is Score.

JEFF REED

	BA	G	AB	R	H	2B	3B	HR	RBI	SB
1988	.226	92	265	20	60	9	2	1	16	1
Life	.222	260	668	53	148	29	3	4	47	2

POSITION: Catcher
TEAM: Cincinnati Reds
BORN: November 12, 1962 Joliet, IL
HEIGHT: 6'2" **WEIGHT:** 190 lbs.
BATS: Left **THROWS:** Right
ACQUIRED: Traded from Expos with Herm Winningham and Randy St. Claire for Tracy Jones and Pat Pacillo, 7/88

Reed was the key player whom the Reds traded for in the mid-season swap that brought Tracy Jones to Montreal. Reed performed ably as the lefthanded-hitting catcher for the Reds in 1988. He hit .226, with one home run and 16 RBIs in 265 at-bats. He also played well behind the plate. In 1987 with the Expos, Reed hit .213 in 75 games, with one home run in 207 at-bats. He started his career with the Twins, and he hit .236 for them in 1986. With Bo Diaz aging, Reed should get much more work with Cincinnati in 1989.

Reed's 1989 cards will be commons. He is not seen as the Cincinnati catcher of the future and will probably be a part-timer for the rest of his career. So investing in his cards is not recommended. Our pick for his best 1989 card is Topps.

JODY REED

	BA	G	AB	R	H	2B	3B	HR	RBI	SB
1988	.293	109	338	60	99	23	1	1	28	1
Life	.293	118	368	64	108	24	2	1	36	2

POSITION: Shortstop
TEAM: Boston Red Sox
BORN: July 26, 1962 Tampa, FL
HEIGHT: 5′9″ **WEIGHT:** 160 lbs.
BATS: Right **THROWS:** Right
ACQUIRED: Eighth-round pick in 6/83 free-agent draft

Though Reed doesn't dazzle you, he plays with such an aggressive style that fans in Fenway Park have really taken a shine to him. He does have good range and a great arm, and is absolutely fearless on the double-play pivot. Reed is a relentless singles hitter who also bunts well and hits behind the runner. He has ample speed and thereby creates havoc on the base paths. While not a full-time performer for the Red Sox in 1988, he did hit .293. At Triple-A Pawtucket in 1987, Reed hit .296 with seven homers and 51 RBIs. Reed is a consistent performer for the pennant-winning BoSox.

Reed's 1989 cards will open in the 15- to 20-cent range. His cards' value should continue to improve at a steady rate. Our pick for his best 1989 card is Score.

RICK REUSCHEL

	W	L	ERA	G	CG	IP	H	R	BB	SO
1988	19	11	3.12	36	7	245.0	242	88	42	92
Life	194	175	3.38	506	100	3243.2	3274	1374	843	1851

POSITION: Pitcher
TEAM: San Francisco Giants
BORN: May 16, 1949 Quincy, IL
HEIGHT: 6′3″ **WEIGHT:** 240 lbs.
BATS: Right **THROWS:** Right
ACQUIRED: Traded from Pirates for Jeff Robinson and Scott Medvin, 6/87

Reuschel had his most productive season in a decade. He led the 1988 Giants both in wins and complete games. Prior to 1988, his best season was as a Cub in '77, when he went 20-10. Reuschel joined the Giants in late 1987 and helped them secure the pennant. He won his second Gold Glove in 1987, and he led the National League hurlers in complete games, with 12. Reuschel worked his way back to the majors after spending 1982 on the disabled list. He pitched in the minors in 1983 and 1984 before winning a regular spot with the Pirates. In 1989, he'll be counted upon to pitch the Giants back into contention.

Reuschel's cards will sell for a nickel or less in 1989. Due to his advanced age, his cards are risky investments at even a nickel. Our pick for his best 1989 card is Score.

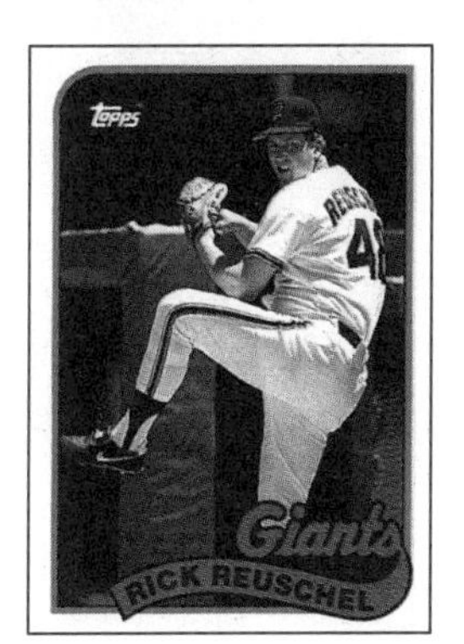

JERRY REUSS

	W	L	ERA	G	CG	IP	H	R	BB	SO
1988	13	9	3.44	32	2	183.0	183	79	43	73
Life	211	182	3.58	594	126	3520.2	3555	1609	1090	1866

POSITION: Pitcher
TEAM: Chicago White Sox
BORN: June 19, 1949 St. Louis, MO
HEIGHT: 6'5" **WEIGHT:** 225 lbs.
BATS: Left **THROWS:** Left
ACQUIRED: Signed as a free agent, 2/88

Reuss looked like his old self pitching for the White Sox in 1988. Skeptics claimed that the veteran lefty's career was over after he went 4-5 with three different teams in 1987. However, Reuss hooked up with the White Sox in 1988, and proved he could still pitch. His 13 wins and 3.44 ERA were highs on the team, and his win totals were the best since his 14-10 effort with the Dodgers in 1985. Reuss will turn 40 next season, but he should have the ability to win for at least one more year.

Reuss' 1989 cards will cost a dime or more. That price is too high, considering that he could retire at any time, and that a long line of 200-game winners are waiting to enter the Hall of Fame. Our pick for his best 1989 card is Fleer.

CRAIG REYNOLDS

	BA	G	AB	R	H	2B	3B	HR	RBI	SB
1988	.255	78	161	20	41	7	0	1	14	3
Life	.258	1390	4277	464	1104	139	65	40	363	57

POSITION: Infield
TEAM: Houston Astros
BORN: December 27, 1952 Houston, TX
HEIGHT: 6'1" **WEIGHT:** 175 lbs.
BATS: Left **THROWS:** Right
ACQUIRED: Traded from Mariners for Floyd Bannister, 12/78

With the arrival of new shortstop Rafael Ramirez, Reynolds saw a reduction of playing time with the 1988 Astros. He appeared in only 78 games, but he kept his batting average at its usual level in the .250s. Reynolds was the starting shortstop for the Astros in 1984 when Dickie Thon was injured. In 146 games that year, Reynolds hit career highs of six homers and 60 RBIs, while batting .260. Reynolds was named an All-Star in 1979, his second season with the Seattle Mariners. He joined the N.L. All-Star team in 1980, when he debuted with the Astros. It's likely that, at age 36, Reynolds will wind up his career as a backup infielder.

Because collectors have an aversion to substitutes, 1989 cards of Reynolds aren't worth investing in, even at 3 cents or less. Our pick for his best 1989 card is Topps.

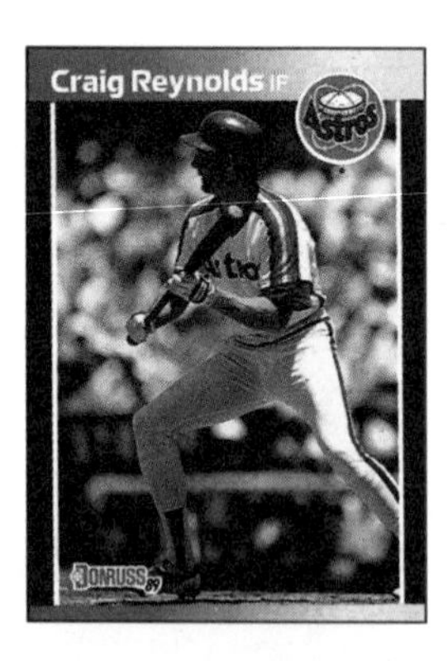

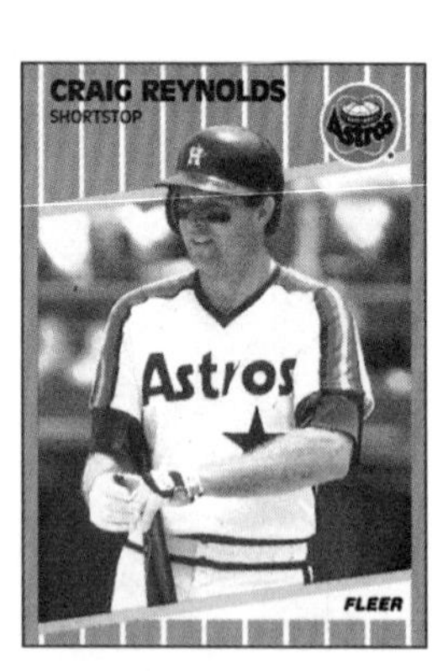

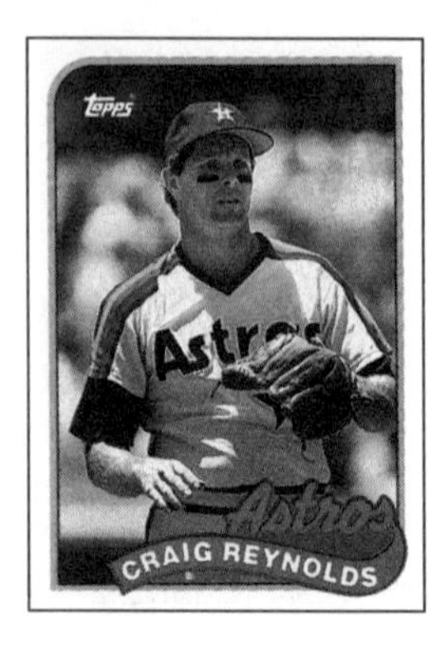

HAROLD REYNOLDS

	BA	G	AB	R	H	2B	3B	HR	RBI	SB
1988	.283	158	598	61	169	26	11	4	41	35
Life	.254	540	1746	206	444	83	25	6	107	129

POSITION: Second base
TEAM: Seattle Mariners
BORN: November 26, 1960 Eugene, OR
HEIGHT: 5′11″ **WEIGHT:** 165 lbs.
BATS: Both **THROWS:** Right
ACQUIRED: First-round pick in 6/80 free-agent draft

Although Reynolds didn't come close to matching his team record of 60 stolen bases during the 1987 season, 1988 marked the finest hitting year of his young career. He had better success in various offensive departments. His average climbed to .283. He accumulated more hits, walks, triples, and homers in 1988. He hit .275 for the M's in 1987, with 73 runs and 146 hits. Reynolds is also a wiz in the field. He tied a major league record in 1985, with 12 assists in a single game. With his fine speed and increased selectivity at the plate, Reynolds can become one of Seattle's most lethal offensive weapons in the future.

For the 1989 season, expect to find Reynolds' cards priced at 5 cents and less. His cards won't gain any value until he hits at least .300 and his stolen base totals grow. Our pick for his best 1989 card is Topps.

R.J. REYNOLDS

	BA	G	AB	R	H	2B	3B	HR	RBI	SB
1988	.248	130	323	35	80	14	2	6	51	15
Life	.263	566	1692	218	445	95	14	29	227	75

POSITION: Outfield
TEAM: Pittsburgh Pirates
BORN: April 19, 1959 Sacramento, CA
HEIGHT: 6′ **WEIGHT:** 180 lbs.
BATS: Both **THROWS:** Right
ACQUIRED: Traded from Dodgers with Sid Bream and Cecil Espy for Bill Madlock, 8/85

Reynolds had his worst batting average in the major leagues in 1988. He hit only .248 for the Pirates, but he had six homers and a career-high 51 RBIs. He also had 51 RBIs in 1987, while hitting .260 and seven homers. He is also valuable as a pinch-hitter. Reynolds had 11 pinch-hit RBIs in 1988, tying him for second in the N.L. The Pirates don't think he is the answer in right field, and they've added Glenn Wilson and Gary Redus. But if Reynolds hikes his average up and keeps coming through in the clutch, he could wind up as the starter.

Reynolds is a fourth outfielder and a commons card in everyone's box. There isn't much investment potential in his cards, unless he can convince the Pirates that he's their right fielder. Our pick for his best 1989 card is Score.

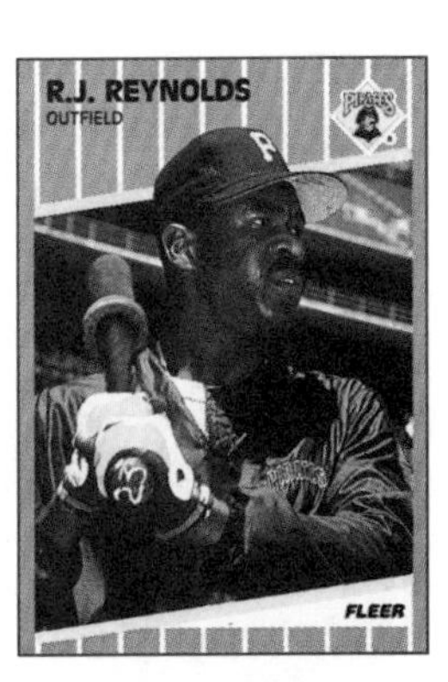

RICK RHODEN

	W	L	ERA	G	CG	IP	H	R	BB	SO
1988	12	12	4.20	30	5	197.0	206	107	56	94
Life	149	119	3.56	393	69	2496.2	2498	1094	760	1378

POSITION: Pitcher
TEAM: New York Yankees
BORN: May 16, 1953 Boynton Beach, FL
HEIGHT: 6′4″ **WEIGHT:** 202 lbs.
BATS: Right **THROWS:** Right
ACQUIRED: Traded from Pirates with Pat Clements and Cecilio Guante for Logan Easley, Brian Fisher, and Doug Drabek, 11/86

Rhoden's second year with the Yankees wasn't as impressive as the first, but he still came in second on the team in wins in 1988. His 12-12 record tied Richard Dotson for second in club victories, closely behind John Candelaria's 13. Rhoden, who joined the Yankees before the 1987 season started, led the team with a 16-10 mark in 1987. He is always good for at least ten wins per season, and he's durable, too. He usually averages 200 innings per season, and has 69 career complete games. The 1989 Yankees may have many uncertainties, but Rhoden isn't one of them.

Rhoden is capable of winning 20 games in 1989. His cards would be a great investment at a nickel or less. Don't hold on to them too long if the price starts climbing. Rhoden is age 35, and won't pitch forever. Our pick for his best 1989 card is Fleer.

JIM RICE

	BA	G	AB	R	H	2B	3B	HR	RBI	SB
1988	.264	135	485	57	128	18	3	15	72	1
Life	.300	2033	8016	1227	2403	363	77	379	1423	57

POSITION: Outfield; designated hitter
TEAM: Boston Red Sox
BORN: March 8, 1953 Anderson, SC
HEIGHT: 6′2″ **WEIGHT:** 205 lbs.
BATS: Right **THROWS:** Right
ACQUIRED: First-round pick in 6/71 free-agent draft

Although Rice may have only seemed a shadow of his former self in 1988, his contributions helped secure Boston's pennant. Now used mainly as a designated hitter, Rice whacked 15 homers and 72 RBIs in 1988. However, this career .300 hitter posted an all-time worst batting average, .264 in 135 games. Some might argue that, after two so-so seasons and at age 36, he may be looking at a fading career. But if Rice can find sufficient playing time in 1989, he'll be able to prove to the world that he can match his past performance.

Rice's 1989 cards will sell for 20 cents, a price that could be risky unless he rebounds from his two-year slide. If not, his march to Cooperstown will be halted, and his cards will never gain the great values once expected. Our pick for his best 1989 card is Topps.

DAVE RIGHETTI

	W	L	ERA	G	SV	IP	H	R	BB	SO
1988	5	4	3.52	60	25	87.0	86	35	37	70
Life	71	54	3.10	414	163	1014.0	878	392	421	846

POSITION: Pitcher
TEAM: New York Yankees
BORN: November 28, 1958 San Jose, CA
HEIGHT: 6'3" **WEIGHT:** 195 lbs.
BATS: Left **THROWS:** Left
ACQUIRED: Traded from Rangers with Mike Griffin, Paul Mirabella, and Juan Beniquez for Sparky Lyle, Larry McCall, Dave Rajsich, Mike Heath, and Domingo Ramos, 11/78

Righetti continued to be the Yankee relief ace in 1988. The lefty surpassed the 20-save mark and led the Yanks in appearances and games finished. The Yankees converted Righetti to a reliever in 1984, after he had three good seasons as a starter. "Rags" responded with a record-setting 46 saves in 1986. The Yankees grew thin on pitching in 1988, and fans have wondered if he might be moved back into the starting rotation in 1989. Some feel that he is more valuable as a stopper. A move back to starter, however, would garner Righetti more national recognition and thus help increase his cards' value.

Because relievers' cards are priced low, here's the chance to prepare for Righetti's possible return to starting duty. His cards, at 15 cents, could be a bargain for a possible 20-game winner. Our pick for his best 1989 card is Score.

JOSE RIJO

	W	L	ERA	G	CG	IP	H	R	BB	SO
1988	13	8	2.39	49	0	162.0	120	47	63	160
Life	32	38	4.07	145	5	564.0	529	296	273	515

POSITION: Pitcher
TEAM: Cincinnati Reds
BORN: May 13, 1965 San Cristobal, Dominican Republic
HEIGHT: 6'2" **WEIGHT:** 185 lbs.
BATS: Right **THROWS:** Right
ACQUIRED: Traded from A's with Tim Birtsas for Dave Parker, 12/87

Rijo had the best season of his five-year career with the 1988 Reds. Only 23 years old, he has pitched in the majors since 1984. In 1988, he set career highs with 13 wins and a 2.39 ERA. Rijo finished 12 of the games he relieved in. His 160 strikeouts were his second highest total ever. Rijo was 2-7 for the 1987 A's, with a 5.90 ERA and 67 strikeouts in 82⅓ innings of work. In 1986, he struck out 176 for the A's while compiling a 9-11 record. His career began with the Yankees, then he spent 1985 to '87 in Oakland. Rijo, one of baseball's brightest pitching prospects, should be with the Reds for a long time.

Rijo is young, experienced, and talented, a winning combination for any player. Buy his 1989 cards at their current prices of a nickel or less. Our pick for his best 1989 card is Score.

ERNEST RILES

	BA	G	AB	R	H	2B	3B	HR	RBI	SB
1988	.277	120	314	33	87	13	3	4	37	3
Life	.268	464	1562	194	419	60	13	22	167	15

POSITION: Infielder
TEAM: San Francisco Giants
BORN: October 2, 1960 Bainbridge, GA
HEIGHT: 6′1″ **WEIGHT:** 180 lbs.
BATS: Left **THROWS:** Right
ACQUIRED: Traded from Brewers for Jeffrey Leonard, 6/88

Riles didn't take long to adjust to a new league. He joined the Giants in mid-season in the trade that sent Jeffrey Leonard to the Brewers. Riles responded to the pressure and hit a career-best .294, the second-best average on the team. He filled in as a utility infielder in 79 games, and made only three errors all season. Riles had played just three seasons with the Brewers before joining the Giants. His best year was 1986, his second year in the majors. In 145 games, he hit .252 with nine homers and 47 RBIs. Riles won't be a starter in 1988, but he'll be an important player on the Giant bench.

Riles' 1989 cards, at 3 cents, will never be in demand if he's only a utility infielder. Our pick for his best 1989 card is Donruss.

BILLY RIPKEN

	BA	G	AB	R	H	2B	3B	HR	RBI	SB
1988	.207	150	512	52	106	18	1	2	34	8
Life	.239	208	746	79	178	27	1	4	54	12

POSITION: Second base
TEAM: Baltimore Orioles
BORN: December 16, 1964 Havre de Grace, MD
HEIGHT: 6′1″ **WEIGHT:** 180 lbs.
BATS: Right **THROWS:** Right
ACQUIRED: 11th-round pick in 6/82 free-agent draft

Ripken struggled with the rest of the Orioles during the dismal 1988 season. In 1987, he enjoyed a spectacular debut. However, he saw his average drop more than 100 points in his first full-time season with the O's. Ripken did manage more than 100 hits and increased his RBI totals in his second big league campaign. He played in 150 games. A strong rebound in 1989 will be needed by Ripken to keep his starting position and fulfill the high expectations fans still have of this promising youngster.

The firing of his father, manager Cal Ripken, Sr., could have prolonged Billy's slump. His 1989 cards will be a nickel or less. They should climb in price; buy them at current low prices while doubts still exist. Our pick for his best 1989 card is Fleer.

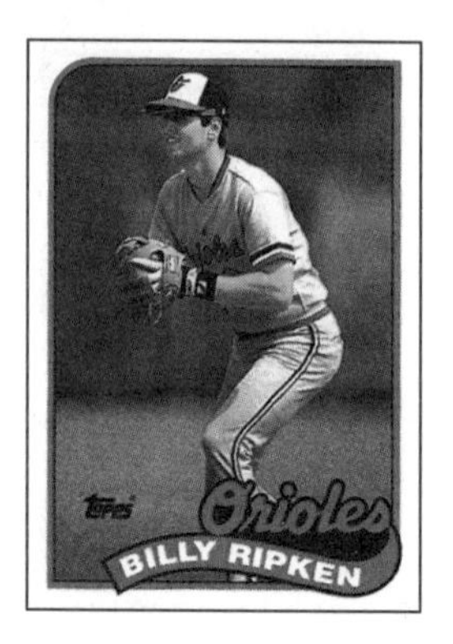

CAL RIPKEN, JR.

	BA	G	AB	R	H	2B	3B	HR	RBI	SB
1988	.264	161	575	87	152	25	1	23	81	2
Life	.280	1153	4409	713	1236	236	24	183	651	16

POSITION: Shortstop
TEAM: Baltimore Orioles
BORN: August 24, 1960 Havre de Grace, MD
HEIGHT: 6′4″ **WEIGHT:** 200 lbs.
BATS: Right **THROWS:** Right
ACQUIRED: Second-round pick in 6/78 free-agent draft

The Orioles' last-place finish masked Ripken's 1988 hitting feats. The Oriole ironman shortstop delivered with power at the plate, surpassing 20 homers and 80 RBIs for the seventh straight season, while hitting .264. He is also a dependable, steady fielder. Ripken beat out Kent Hrbek for A.L. Rookie of the Year honors in 1982 with a 28-homer, 93-RBI effort. The following year, he won the league MVP award as the Orioles entered the World Series. At 6′4″, he is the tallest full-time shortstop in major league history. Any Baltimore renaissance will include Ripken's steady leadership.

Power-hitting shortstops like Ripken are rare. His 1989 cards are a good investment at current price tags of 35 cents or less. Ripken's Hall of Fame potential will merit long-range returns for investors. Our pick for his best 1989 card is Donruss.

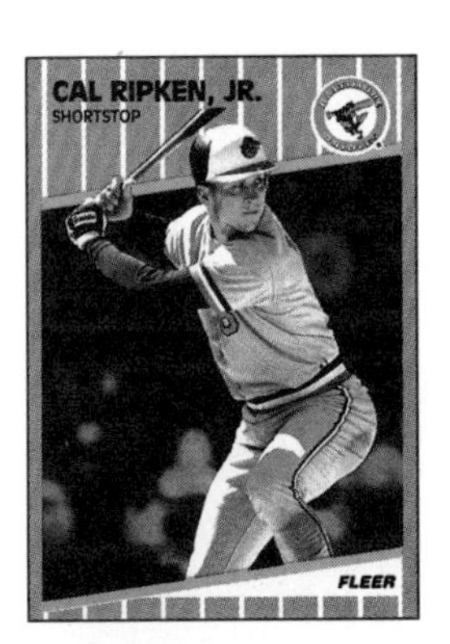

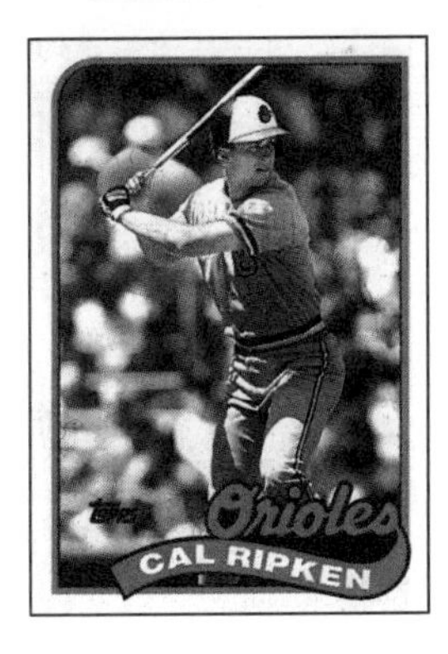

LUIS RIVERA

	BA	G	AB	R	H	2B	3B	HR	RBI	SB
1988	.224	123	371	35	83	17	3	4	30	3
Life	.214	196	569	55	122	30	4	4	44	4

POSITION: Infield
TEAM: Boston Red Sox
BORN: January 3, 1964 Cidra, Puerto Rico
HEIGHT: 5′11″ **WEIGHT:** 165 lbs.
BATS: Right **THROWS:** Right
ACQUIRED: Traded from Expos with John Dopson for Spike Owen and Dan Gakeler, 12/88

After a good season with the Expos, Rivera finds himself in Boston. Dividing the shortstop duties for Montreal, he batted .224 in 371 trips to the plate. He also showed some punch with 17 doubles, three triples, and four home runs. At Triple-A Indianapolis in 1987, Rivera was impressive, with a .312 batting mark, showed some power by hitting eight home runs, and displayed good base-running style in stealing 24. In 1987 at Montreal, he hit only .156 in 32 trips to the plate. Rivera has a solid future either as a starter or a versatile utilityman.

Rivera's 1989 cards are commons, and there's little market for them. There's always the chance that he'll become a better hitter as he matures, and you should hold his cards as a long-term investment opportunity. Our pick for his best 1989 card is Topps.

DON ROBINSON

	W	L	ERA	G	SV	IP	H	R	BB	SO
1988	10	5	2.45	51	6	176.2	152	63	49	122
Life	80	75	3.65	419	56	1421.2	1346	643	508	973

POSITION: Pitcher
TEAM: San Francisco Giants
BORN: June 8, 1957 Ashland, KY
HEIGHT: 6′4″ **WEIGHT:** 235 lbs.
BATS: Right **THROWS:** Right
ACQUIRED: Traded from Pittsburgh for Mackey Sasser, 7/87

Robinson, one of the key acquisitions that gained the Giants their 1987 title, enjoyed more success with the team in 1988. He led all San Francisco pitchers with a 2.45 ERA. He went 5-1 with seven saves over the last three months of the 1987 season for the Giants. Robinson hit a crucial home run and hurled five innings of relief to clinch the 1987 pennant. He has more than 100 career hits as a batter, and had a league-best .265 career average before starting the 1988 season. Robinson is a versatile pitcher who could put the Giants back on top in 1989.

Robinson's 1989 cards will be a nickel or less. Because he is used as a starter and reliever, his stats suffer. His lifetime marks aren't compelling enough to persuade investors to purchase his cards. Our pick for his best 1989 card is Topps.

JEFF ROBINSON

	W	L	ERA	G	SV	IP	H	R	BB	SO
1988	11	5	3.03	75	9	124.2	113	44	39	87
Life	32	32	3.59	262	31	536.1	505	243	187	388

POSITION: Pitcher
TEAM: Pittsburgh Pirates
BORN: December 13, 1960
Santa Ana, CA
HEIGHT: 6′4″ **WEIGHT:** 195 lbs.
BATS: Right **THROWS:** Right
ACQUIRED: Traded from Giants with Scott Medvin for Rick Reuschel, 8/87

Robinson is a top middle relief pitcher, and he had plenty of opportunities to show that in 1988. He was second in the National League in appearances (75), the most for a Pirate hurler since Kent Tekulve had 76 appearances in 1983. Robinson was 11-5 (all in relief) with nine saves and a 3.03 ERA. His 11 relief wins were second in the N.L. Acquired from the Giants in August 1987, he was a combined 10-10 that year (2-1 for Pittsburgh) and picked up 14 saves. Robinson is in the upper echelon of N.L. middle relievers.

Robinson's 1989 cards will sell in the 10-cent range. Being a middle reliever, he will rack up neither a lot of wins nor saves, and his cards are not going to appreciate very much in the near future. Our pick for his best 1989 card is Donruss.

JEFF ROBINSON

	W	L	ERA	G	CG	IP	H	R	BB	SO
1988	13	6	2.98	24	6	172.0	121	61	72	114
Life	22	12	4.00	53	8	299.1	253	147	126	212

POSITION: Pitcher
TEAM: Detroit Tigers
BORN: December 14, 1961 Ventura, CA
HEIGHT: 6′6″ **WEIGHT:** 210 lbs.
BATS: Right **THROWS:** Right
ACQUIRED: Third-round pick in 6/83 free-agent draft

Robinson reached the double-digit level in wins (13) for the first time in 1988, his second full year in the majors. Although he's one of two pitchers named Jeff Robinson in the majors (the other hurls for the Pirates), opposing hitters will remember this Robinson after his 1988 performance. He kept his ERA under 3.00 nearly all season long, and was among the team leaders in shutouts and complete games. In 1987, he was 9-6, with a 5.37 ERA and 98 strikeouts in $127\frac{1}{3}$ innings pitched. When people think of Tigers pitching, they think of Jack Morris or Doyle Alexander. After 1988, Robinson's name belongs there, too.

Robinson's 1989 cards will sell for less than a nickel. That's a safe investment price. His cards would climb to a quarter if he wins 20 games. Our pick for his best 1989 card is Fleer.

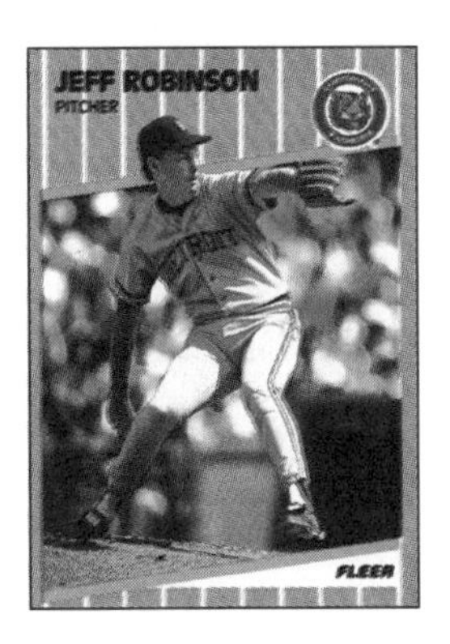

RON ROBINSON

	W	L	ERA	G	CG	IP	H	R	BB	SO
1988	3	7	4.12	17	0	78.2	88	47	26	38
Life	28	24	3.64	180	1	497.1	488	233	157	354

POSITION: Pitcher
TEAM: Cincinnati Reds
BORN: March 24, 1962 Woodlake, CA
HEIGHT: 6′4″ **WEIGHT:** 225 lbs.
BATS: Right **THROWS:** Right
ACQUIRED: First-round pick in 6/80 free-agent draft

Robinson's 1988 season with the Reds was filled with injury and disappointment. He got into just 17 games and compiled a so-so 3-7 record. The big righty had his best season in 1986. He set career highs for himself in saves (14), wins (ten), and appearances (70). He lost just three games and had 117 strikeouts in $116\frac{2}{3}$ innings of work. In 1987, he was 7-5 in 48 games, with a 3.68 ERA and four saves. After nearly four years of minor league service, he got his big break with Cincinnati in 1984. If he's healthy in 1989, the Reds bullpen should be back at full strength with Robinson present.

Robinson's 1989 cards will be three cents or less. Due to his 1988 misfortunes, his cards should be plentiful. Wait for Robinson to regain his ability before investing in his cards. Our pick for his best 1989 card is Fleer.

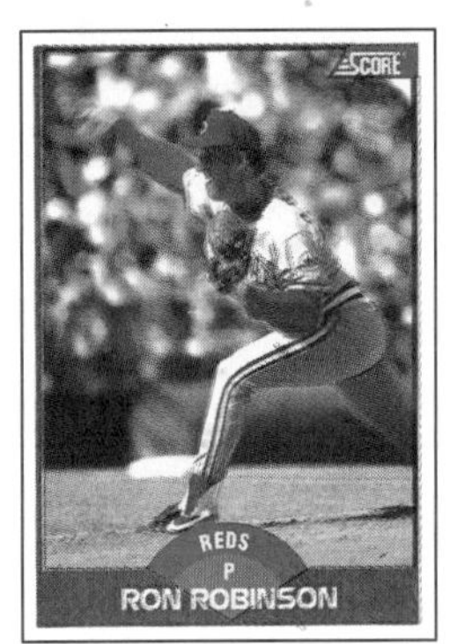

BRUCE RUFFIN

	W	L	ERA	G	CG	IP	H	R	BB	SO
1988	6	10	4.43	55	3	144.1	151	86	80	82
Life	26	28	3.82	111	12	495.1	525	257	197	245

POSITION: Pitcher
TEAM: Philadelphia Phillies
BORN: October 4, 1963 Lubbock, TX
HEIGHT: 6′3″ **WEIGHT:** 200 lbs.
BATS: Left **THROWS:** Left
ACQUIRED: Second-round pick in 6/85 free-agent draft

The Phillies were unable to decide whether they wanted Ruffin to be a starter or a reliever during 1988. He appeared in 55 games, 15 as a starter, and ended with a 6-10 record, a 4.43 ERA, and three saves. At one point it seemed that he found it almost impossible to throw any pitch in the strike zone. In 1987, Ruffin went 11-14 for the Phillies and fanned 93 batters. He was 9-4 in 1986. He was drafted out of the University of Texas, whose roster included Roger Clemens, Calvin Schiraldi, and Greg Swindell. Ruffin will probably have a starting role for years to come in the Phillies' future.

Ruffin's 1989 cards are commons, but they are good investment material. If he has the same success as his college teammates, the Phils have found a winner. Our pick for his best 1989 card is Topps.

JEFF RUSSELL

	W	L	ERA	G	CG	IP	H	R	BB	SO
1988	10	9	3.82	34	5	188.2	183	86	66	88
Life	22	44	4.24	179	10	680.0	695	364	263	383

POSITION: Pitcher
TEAM: Texas Rangers
BORN: September 2, 1961 Cincinnati, OH
HEIGHT: 6′4″ **WEIGHT:** 210 lbs.
BATS: Right **THROWS:** Right
ACQUIRED: Traded from Reds with Duane Walker for Buddy Bell, 7/85

After two previous years of being in and out of the Texas bullpen, Russell looked like a full-time starter with the 1988 Rangers. He won a career-high 10 games and notched five complete games. During 1987, Russell pitched in 52 contests with only three saves. He ended with five wins, three losses, and a 4.44 ERA. A Cincinnati native, he began his major league career in 1983 with his hometown Reds as a starter. Texas gave up star third baseman Buddy Bell to obtain Russell. Russell, given a full year in the Texas starting rotation, could be a big boost to the Rangers.

Russell has a lifetime losing record after six major league seasons. See if Russell can repeat his winning ways of 1988 before investing in his common-priced cards. Our pick for his best 1989 card is Topps.

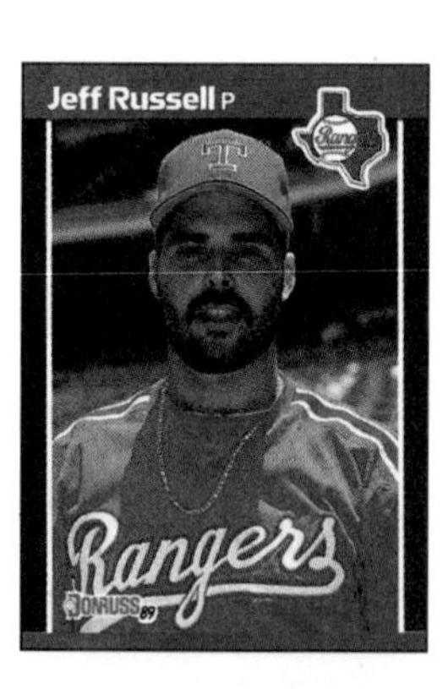

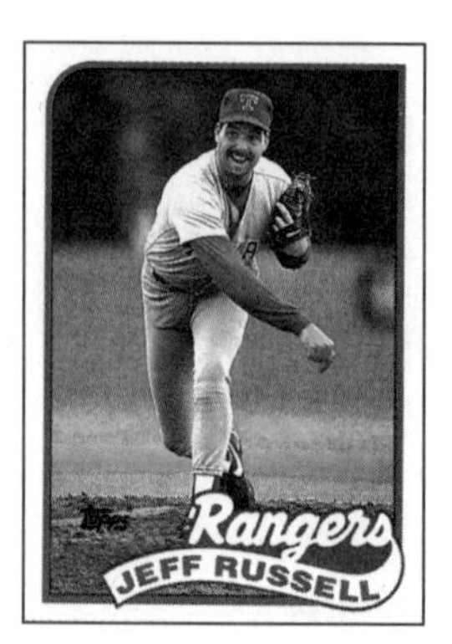

NOLAN RYAN

	W	L	ERA	G	CG	IP	H	R	BB	SO
1988	12	11	3.52	33	4	220.0	186	98	87	228
Life	273	253	3.15	678	207	4547.0	3330	1816	2442	4775

POSITION: Pitcher
TEAM: Texas Rangers
BORN: January 31, 1947 Refugio, TX
HEIGHT: 6′2″ **WEIGHT:** 190 lbs.
BATS: Right **THROWS:** Right
ACQUIRED: Signed as a free agent, 12/88

Ryan is timeless. At age 41, in his 21st major league season, the future Hall of Famer continued to fan opposing hitters (some just about half his age) by the handful. He carved out a winning record for a team that provided him little offensive support on many occasions. Baseball's all-time strikeout king held or tied a total of 38 major league records going into the 1988 season. He led the N.L. in strikeouts in 1988, the ninth time he has led his league in Ks. Ryan has been the archetypal fireballing righty for two decades.

Because 1989 could be Ryan's last year, his newest cards would take on even more meaning. Grab them now at 35 cents. When he reaches the Hall of Fame, the value of his cards will skyrocket. Our pick for his best 1989 card is Donruss.

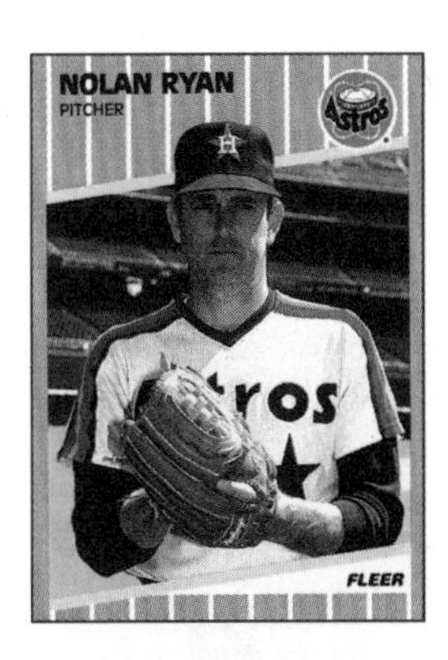

BRET SABERHAGEN

	W	L	ERA	G	CG	IP	H	R	BB	SO
1988	14	16	3.80	35	9	260.2	271	122	59	171
Life	69	55	3.49	168	40	1066.2	1031	448	215	677

POSITION: Pitcher
TEAM: Kansas City Royals
BORN: April 13, 1964
Chicago Heights, IL
HEIGHT: 6′1″ **WEIGHT:** 160 lbs.
BATS: Right **THROWS:** Right
ACQUIRED: 19th-round pick in 6/82 free-agent draft

Saberhagen's biyearly slump reappeared in 1988, throwing the thin righthander's career into another tailspin. He was coming off an 18-10 season in 1987, which included 15 complete games and four shutouts. His success evaporated in 1988, when his record fell to 14-16. He finished the year with a 3.80 ERA and 260⅔ innings pitched. Saberhagen's slump duplicated his problems from 1986. He won the A.L. Cy Young Award in 1985 with a 20-7 record. The next year, a sore shoulder limited his record to 7-12. If the pattern of highs and lows continues, Saberhagen is due for a banner season in 1989.

Saberhagen's 1989 cards should be in the 15- to 25-cent range. The prices may slip somewhat because he lapsed in 1988. Invest in his cards now, before he rebounds with another superb effort. Our pick for his best 1989 card is Donruss.

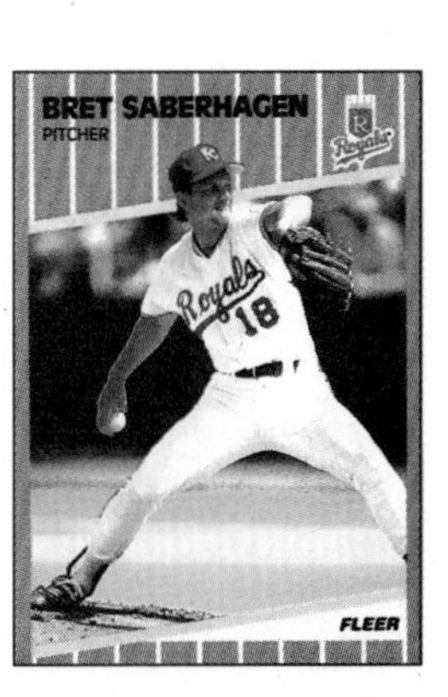

CHRIS SABO

	BA	G	AB	R	H	2B	3B	HR	RBI	SB
1988	.271	137	538	74	146	40	2	11	44	46
Life	.271	137	538	74	146	40	2	11	44	46

POSITION: Third base
TEAM: Cincinnati Reds
BORN: January 19, 1962 Detroit, MI
HEIGHT: 6′ **WEIGHT:** 185 lbs.
BATS: Right **THROWS:** Right
ACQUIRED: Second-round pick in 6/83 free-agent draft

A Pete Rose clone if there ever was one, Sabo burst on to the big league scene in 1988. An N.L. All-Star Game selection, Sabo was the darling of the Cincy fans. The N.L. Rookie of the Year batted close to .280 with the Reds in 1988, and showed some extra-base pop in his bat. He also stole 46 bases. Sabo hit .292 at Triple-A Nashville in 1987, and was named the team MVP, even though he missed one-third of the season due to injuries. Sabo is a tough, lunch-pail ballplayer who should continue to improve.

Sabo's 1989 cards should open in the 75- to 80-cent range. At that price, wait to see if he starts 1989 with some solid numbers. Our pick for his best 1989 card is Topps.

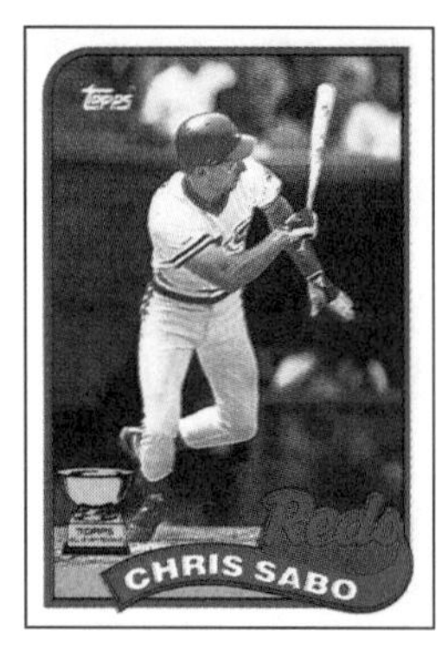

MARK SALAS

	BA	G	AB	R	H	2B	3B	HR	RBI	SB
1988	.250	75	196	17	49	7	0	3	9	0
Life	.261	372	994	118	259	41	9	26	105	3

POSITION: Catcher
TEAM: Chicago White Sox
BORN: March 8, 1961 Montebello, CA
HEIGHT: 6′ **WEIGHT:** 180 lbs.
BATS: Left **THROWS:** Right
ACQUIRED: Traded from Yankees with Dan Pasqua and Steve Rosenberg for Richard Dotson and Scott Nielsen, 11/87

Salas helped fill in for the injured Carlton Fisk for the 1988 White Sox. Salas played in 75 games for Chicago, his fourth major league team in five seasons. He hit .250, the fifth-highest average on the club. He also had three homers and only nine RBIs. Salas started his professional career in 1977, but he didn't get his first major league exposure until 1984. His most productive season was in 1985 with the Twins. He played in 120 games, hitting .300, with nine homers and 41 RBIs. Because healthy catchers are always in short supply, Salas should always have a job somewhere.

It seems that Salas may play the rest of his career as a backup catcher. Substitutes aren't good targets for card investment, so his 1989 commons cards should be avoided. Our pick for his best 1989 card is Score.

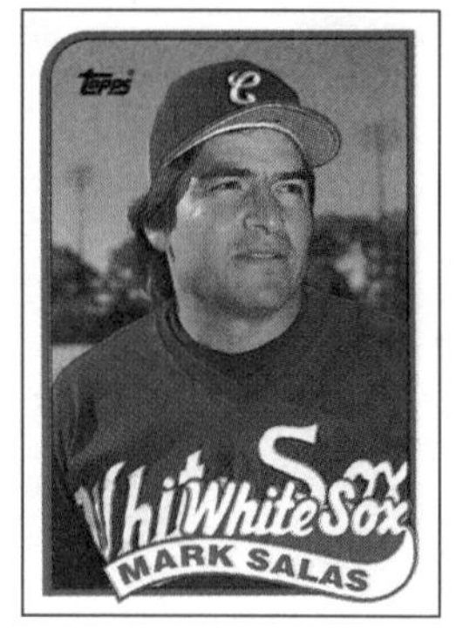

LUIS SALAZAR

	BA	G	AB	R	H	2B	3B	HR	RBI	SB
1988	.270	130	452	61	122	14	1	12	62	6
Life	.265	865	2777	306	735	98	25	54	311	112

POSITION: Infield
TEAM: Detroit Tigers
BORN: May 19, 1956
Barcelona, Venezuela
HEIGHT: 6′ **WEIGHT:** 185 lbs.
BATS: Right **THROWS:** Right
ACQUIRED: Signed as a free agent, 1/88

Salazar was the Tigers' top utility player in 1988, seeing action in 130 games. He tied his career high in RBIs with 62, and his 12 home runs ranked sixth on the team. He ended the year with a .270 average and six stolen bases. Salazar's professional career began in 1974, but he didn't get his first shot at the majors until mid-1980 with the Padres. He lasted six years with San Diego and one with the White Sox before joining Detroit. Third base might be up for grabs with the 1989 club, but it's likely that the Tigers don't want to pin Salazar down to one spot.

Being a part-timer doesn't help interest in Salazar's cards. His 1989 issues won't bring more than a nickel, and investors wouldn't profit here. Our pick for his best 1989 card is Topps.

JUAN SAMUEL

	BA	G	AB	R	H	2B	3B	HR	RBI	SB
1988	.243	157	629	68	153	32	9	12	67	33
Life	.264	801	3304	491	872	173	70	92	393	238

POSITION: Outfield
TEAM: Philadelphia Phillies
BORN: December 9, 1960 San Pedro de Macoris, Dominican Republic
HEIGHT: 5′11″ **WEIGHT:** 165 lbs.
BATS: Right **THROWS:** Right
ACQUIRED: Signed as a free agent, 4/80

Although Samuel reached double-digits for homers, along with more than 60 RBIs and 30 stolen bases in 1988, his stats fell from his sterling 1987 season. His average dived some 30 points, and his fielding was just fair. In '87, he hit .272, 28 home runs, a league-leading 15 triples, and 100 RBIs. He is also an accomplished base stealer. In late 1988, Samuel indicated a willingness to become an outfielder in 1989. The change could restore his batting prowess, and he was not one of the N.L.'s top fielding second basemen. Despite his year-long slump, Samuel remains a multi-faceted offensive threat in the team's hopes for 1989.

Samuel could find a new life in the Philadelphia outfield. His talents merit investment in his 1989 cards, which should be priced at 10 cents or less. Our pick for his best 1989 card is Topps.

ISRAEL SANCHEZ

	W	L	ERA	G	SV	IP	H	R	BB	SO
1988	3	2	4.54	19	1	35.2	36	20	18	14
Life	3	2	4.54	19	1	35.2	36	20	18	14

POSITION: Pitcher
TEAM: Kansas City Royals
BORN: August 20, 1963
Falcon Lasvias, Cuba
HEIGHT: 5′9″ **WEIGHT:** 165 lbs.
BATS: Left **THROWS:** Left
ACQUIRED: Ninth-round pick in free-agent draft, 6/82

Sanchez parlayed a 7-4 record at Triple-A Omaha in 1988 into a late-season recall to Kansas City. With the Royals, he went 3-2, with a 4.54 ERA and one save in 19 appearances. At Omaha last season, Sanchez had a 2.91 ERA and fanned 85 in 102 innings. Highly regarded in the Royal organization, he had a so-so year in 1987 at Omaha, and he had to finish strong just to be 5-12. He did have a promising overall record, though, and in 125 innings of work, he struck out 74 and walked only 46. In 1986 at Double-A Memphis, he went 13-7, notching 141 strikeouts in 190 innings.

Sanchez's 1989 cards should open in the 15- to 20-cent range. Wait to see if he wins a spot in the Royal starting rotation before investing at that price. Our pick for his best 1989 card is Topps.

RYNE SANDBERG

	BA	G	AB	R	H	2B	3B	HR	RBI	SB
1988	.264	155	618	77	163	23	8	19	69	25
Life	.284	1077	4287	652	1219	201	49	109	473	235

POSITION: Second base
TEAM: Chicago Cubs
BORN: September 18, 1959 Spokane, WA
HEIGHT: 6′2″ **WEIGHT:** 180 lbs.
BATS: Right **THROWS:** Right
ACQUIRED: Traded from Phillies with Larry Bowa for Ivan DeJesus, 1/82

After seven seasons as the starting second baseman for the Cubs, "Ryno" is touted as a Hall of Fame candidate. Sandberg, a converted shortstop, came into the 1988 season having won five consecutive Gold Gloves. He was the first player in N.L. history to win the award after only one year at a new position. Sandberg hits for power and average, too. He's hit at least 14 homers the last five seasons. In 1988, Sandberg hit .264, with 19 home runs, 69 RBIs, and 25 stolen bases. He won the league MVP award in 1984, hitting .314 with a league-leading 114 runs scored. Sandberg is the cornerstone of the Cubs.

Sandberg's cards are a bargain at 20 cents apiece or less. He'll be remembered as one of Chicago's finest second basemen, and his card values will reflect that. Our pick for his best 1989 card is Topps.

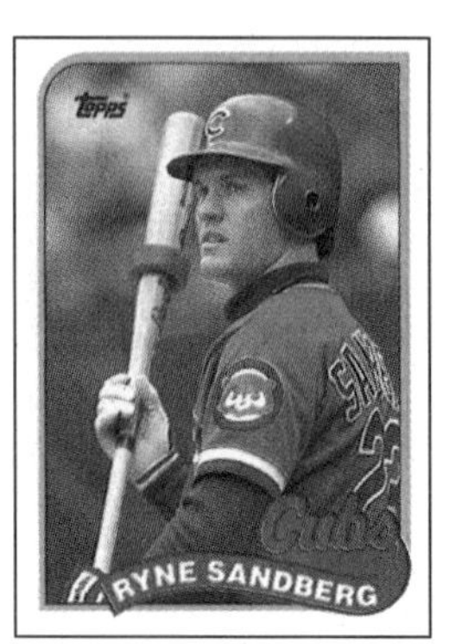

RAFAEL SANTANA

	BA	G	AB	R	H	2B	3B	HR	RBI	SB
1988	.240	148	480	50	115	12	1	4	38	1
Life	.246	661	2008	185	494	74	5	12	153	3

POSITION: Shortstop
TEAM: New York Yankees
BORN: January 31, 1958 La Romana, Dominican Republic
HEIGHT: 6′1″ **WEIGHT:** 160 lbs.
BATS: Right **THROWS:** Right
ACQUIRED: Traded from Mets for Victor Garcia, Phil Lombardi, Darren Reed, and Steve Frey, 12/87

Santana was one of the most scrutinized players on the 1988 Yankees. He was the first major leaguer ever traded between the crosstown rival New York Mets and Yankees. His season began with public criticism from then-manager Billy Martin. Santana had trouble satisfying so many expectations. His 22 errors were the third-worst in the American League. His hitting was better, as he drove in 38 runs, the second-highest total of his career. In 1987, he had 44 RBIs, five homers, and a .255 average. If Santana can withstand the pressure of playing with the turbulent Yankees, he surely should improve in 1989.

Santana's cards aren't in high demand, mostly because he's a typical low-average hitter. His 1989 cards will be a nickel or less, but they don't look like promising investments. Our pick for his best 1989 card is Donruss.

BENITO SANTIAGO

	BA	G	AB	R	H	2B	3B	HR	RBI	SB
1988	.248	139	492	49	122	22	2	10	46	15
Life	.276	302	1100	123	304	57	4	31	131	36

POSITION: Catcher
TEAM: San Diego Padres
BORN: September 3, 1965 Ponce, Puerto Rico
HEIGHT: 6′1″ **WEIGHT:** 180 lbs.
BATS: Right **THROWS:** Right
ACQUIRED: Signed as a free agent, 9/82

Santiago, the 1987 N.L. Rookie of the Year, was haunted by the "sophomore jinx" last year. In 1988, his average slipped over 50 points to .248, and he came up short in almost all other offensive categories, too. Still, he reached double figures in home runs and was among team leaders in doubles and stolen bases throughout 1988. He burst on the scene in 1987, hitting .300, with 18 homers, 79 RBIs, 64 runs, and 21 stolen bases. He also had a late-season 34-game hitting streak in '87. Santiago still has enormous potential and in 1989 could regain his rookie-year success. With Jack Clark now a Padre, Santiago could be part of a pennant-winning San Diego team in 1989.

Santiago's 1989 cards should be selling anywhere from 50 to 75 cents. Last year's slump makes speculating on Santiago's cards very risky at this time. Our pick for his best 1989 card is Topps.

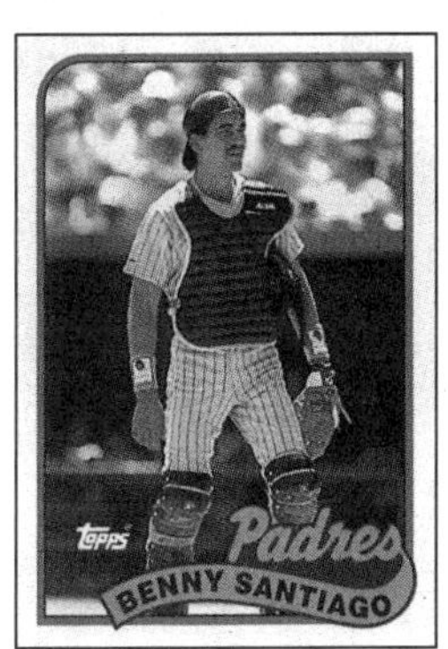

NELSON SANTOVENIA

	BA	G	AB	R	H	2B	3B	HR	RBI	SB
1988	.236	92	309	26	73	20	2	8	41	2
Life	.235	94	310	26	73	20	2	8	41	2

POSITION: Catcher
TEAM: Montreal Expos
BORN: July 27, 1961
Pinar de Rio, Cuba
HEIGHT: 6′3″ **WEIGHT:** 195 lbs.
BATS: Right **THROWS:** Right
ACQUIRED: First pick in the secondary phase of 6/82 free-agent draft

Santovenia caught more than half of the Expos games in 1988 and batted in the .240 range. Montreal Manager Buck Rodgers sees Santovenia as the number-one backstop in 1989. His best year in the minors was 1987, when he hit .279 with 19 home runs at Double-A Jacksonville. He spent a brief period with the Expos in late 1987. Santovenia has been slowly but surely making his way through the Expo farm system ever since 1982. With Double-A Memphis in 1983, he batted .242 with three homers and 44 RBIs. He spent all or parts of five seasons in Double-A waiting for opportunity to knock.

His 1989 cards will open between 15 and 20 cents. Wait to see if he can improve his hitting before buying at those prices. Our pick for his best 1989 card is Topps.

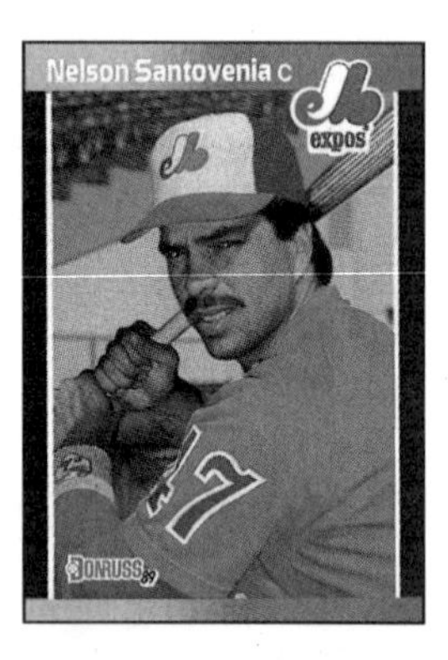

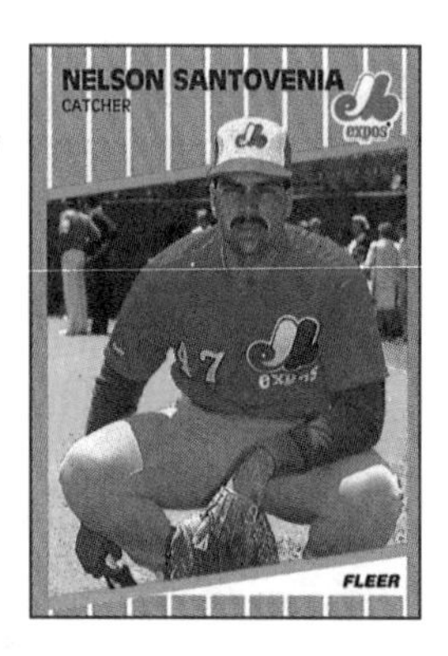

MACKEY SASSER

	BA	G	AB	R	H	2B	3B	HR	RBI	SB
1988	.285	60	123	9	35	10	1	1	17	0
Life	.267	74	150	11	40	10	1	1	19	0

POSITION: Catcher
TEAM: New York Mets
BORN: August 3, 1962 Ft. Gaines, GA
HEIGHT: 6′1″ **WEIGHT:** 190 lbs.
BATS: Left **THROWS:** Right
ACQUIRED: Traded from Pirates with Tim Drummond for Randy Milligan and Scott Henioa, 3/88

Dealt to the Mets in the Randy Milligan trade, Sasser played a valuable role for the 1988 Mets. He spelled Gary Carter, and hit over .280. Catchers who can hit are in heavy demand, and that should keep Sasser employed. The Pirates obtained Sasser from the Giants in 1987, and he batted .318 at Triple-A Vancouver with 56 RBIs. Recalled to Pittsburgh late in the year, he hit .185, but Sasser's track record as a hitter is impressive. In 1986 at Double-A Shreveport, he batted .293 with 72 RBIs. In 1984 at Clinton, he hit .292 with 65 RBIs. Sasser looks like the catcher of tomorrow for the Mets.

Some feel Sasser may succeed Carter behind the plate in 1989, allowing Carter to play a less demanding position. Sasser's 1989 cards will open at about 15 cents. Our pick for his best 1989 card is Topps.

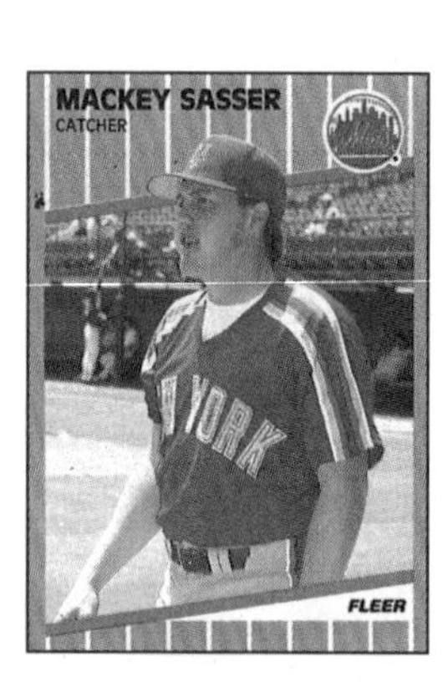

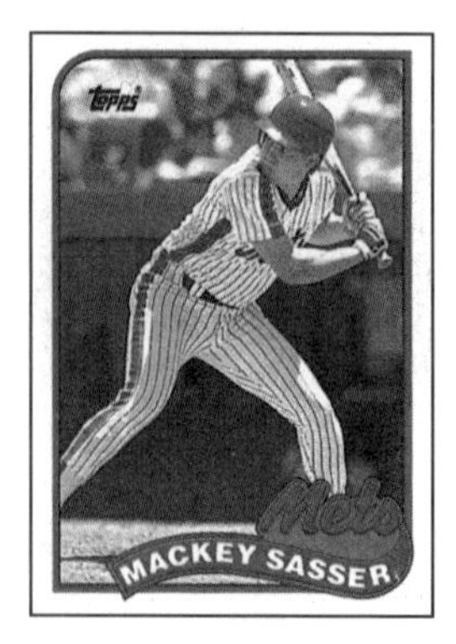

STEVE SAX

	BA	G	AB	R	H	2B	3B	HR	RBI	SB
1988	.277	160	632	70	175	19	4	5	57	42
Life	.282	1091	4312	574	1218	159	35	30	333	290

POSITION: Second base
TEAM: New York Yankees
BORN: January 29, 1960 Sacramento, CA
HEIGHT: 5′11″ **WEIGHT:** 180 lbs.
BATS: Right **THROWS:** Right
ACQUIRED: Signed as a free agent, 11/88

Sax, the new Yankee second sacker, logged his seventh full season as the Dodger second baseman in 1988 and was an active participant in the team's world championship. His output dipped a bit from his offensive totals during the past two seasons, though he maintained more than 50 RBIs and 40 stolen bases. In 1987, he posted his 1,000th career hit. Sax won the N.L. batting title by only two points in 1986, hitting a career best .332. He is one of the better-hitting second basemen around. If the Yankees hope to win the A.L. East in 1989, they will lean heavily on Sax to post big numbers.

Expect Sax's 1989 cards to sell for 10 to 15 cents in 1989. His unrealized potential makes it worthwhile to pick his cards up at 5 to 10 cents each. Our pick for his best 1989 card is Topps.

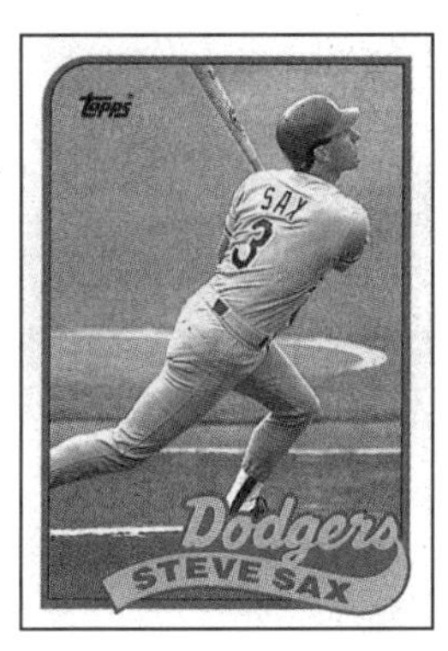

CALVIN SCHIRALDI

	W	L	ERA	G	CG	IP	H	R	BB	SO
1988	9	13	4.38	29	2	166.1	166	87	63	140
Life	23	23	4.36	131	2	344.2	340	180	139	325

POSITION: Pitcher
TEAM: Chicago Cubs
BORN: June 16, 1962 Houston, TX
HEIGHT: 6′4″ **WEIGHT:** 200 lbs.
BATS: Right **THROWS:** Right
ACQUIRED: Traded from Red Sox with Al Nipper for Lee Smith, 12/87

Schiraldi was used mainly as a starter for the 1988 Cubs, and he was 9-13 with a 4.38 ERA. He did relieve in two of his 29 appearances and earned a save. With the BoSox in 1987, he stayed in the bullpen, getting just one start. He was 14-11 in a combination of roles that saw him save six games. Once one of the top pitching prospects in the Mets' farm system, Schiraldi is now with his third big league club; no one has ever been able to quite pinpoint a role for him—starter or reliever. If he's put in one role, Schiraldi could make the Cubs winners in 1989.

Schiraldi, at 26, may still become a dominant big league hurler. Collectors, however, should be wary of stockpiling too many of his cards. Our pick for his best 1989 card is Topps.

DAVE SCHMIDT

	W	L	ERA	G	SV	IP	H	R	BB	SO
1988	8	5	3.40	41	2	129.2	129	58	38	67
Life	41	38	3.33	297	37	690.0	692	294	183	407

POSITION: Pitcher
TEAM: Baltimore Orioles
BORN: April 22, 1957 Niles, MI
HEIGHT: 6′1″ **WEIGHT:** 188 lbs.
BATS: Right **THROWS:** Right
ACQUIRED: Signed as a free agent, 1/87

Schmidt was a double-barreled asset for the 1988 Orioles, serving well as both a starter and reliever. He didn't have a banner year, but he tied for the team lead in wins with eight. His eight wins amounted to 15 percent of the team's victories. Schmidt led the O's in ERA as well. He has pitched well on offensively poor teams. He could blossom if the O's provide him with some consistent leads to work with. Schmidt's willingness to pitch in any capacity is to be admired. However, fans have to wonder what he could accomplish if the team could better define his role.

Schmidt will be in the forefront if the team makes a major comeback in 1989. His common-priced cards are decent investments. Our pick for his best 1989 card is Topps.

MIKE SCHMIDT

	BA	G	AB	R	H	2B	3B	HR	RBI	SB
1988	.249	108	390	52	97	21	2	12	62	3
Life	.269	2362	8204	1487	2204	401	59	542	1567	174

POSITION: Infield
TEAM: Philadelphia Phillies
BORN: September 27, 1949 Dayton, OH
HEIGHT: 6′2″ **WEIGHT:** 203 lbs.
BATS: Right **THROWS:** Right
ACQUIRED: Second-round pick in 6/71 free-agent draft

Recurring shoulder problems kept Schmidt's 1988 season to just over 100 games, but he still responded with first-class numbers. He advanced a few rungs on the all-time home run ladder to seventh, as he posted 12 homers in 1988. Every Schmidt hit in 1988 assured him a larger place in baseball history, and a quicker election to the Hall of Fame. Many have called him the greatest third baseman to ever play the game. He is a three-time winner of the N.L. MVP award. This could be Schmidt's final season. If his shoulder holds out, he might make his last year one to remember.

Schmidt's injury-shortened season should keep his 1989 card prices at the 35-cent level. Investing at that price will bring large bonuses when he enters the Hall of Fame. Our pick for his best 1989 card is Topps.

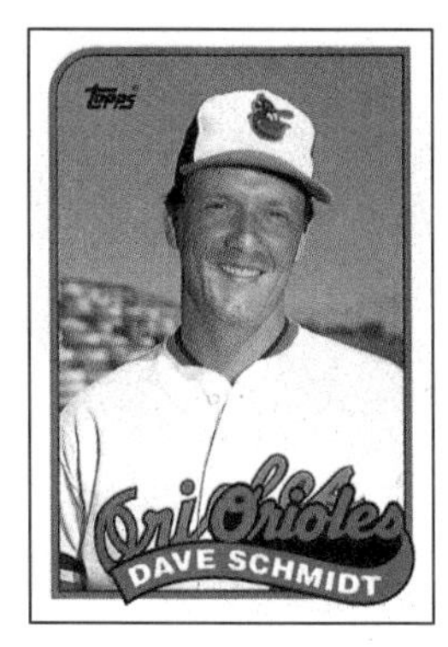

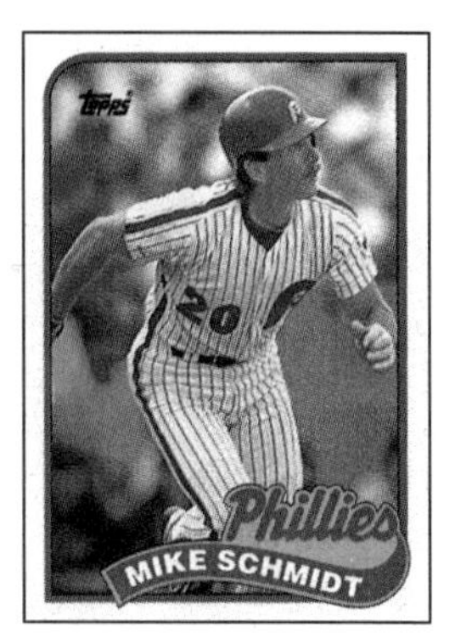

DICK SCHOFIELD

	BA	G	AB	R	H	2B	3B	HR	RBI	SB
1988	.239	155	527	61	126	11	6	6	34	20
Life	.231	736	2356	273	544	76	21	43	203	78

POSITION: Shortstop
TEAM: California Angels
BORN: November 21, 1962 Springfield, IL
HEIGHT: 5'10" **WEIGHT:** 175 lbs.
BATS: Right **THROWS:** Right
ACQUIRED: First-round pick in 6/81 free-agent draft

Schofield slumped from his previous-season performance with the 1988 Angels, but he continued to be one of California's best competitors. Only Chili Davis and Wally Joyner bettered Schofield's 155 games. Schofield, whose father was a major league shortstop during the 1960s, was one of the Angels' top fielders. He made only 13 errors all season. He has been the team's starting shortstop since 1984, and he had his best offensive season in 1986. He hit .249 with 13 homers and 57 RBIs that year. Schofield is one of the most underrated players in the A.L., but he should start to get some recognition in 1989.

Schofield's 1989 cards will be selling at a nickel or less. His career statistics can't justify any investment in his cards. Our pick for his best 1989 card is Donruss.

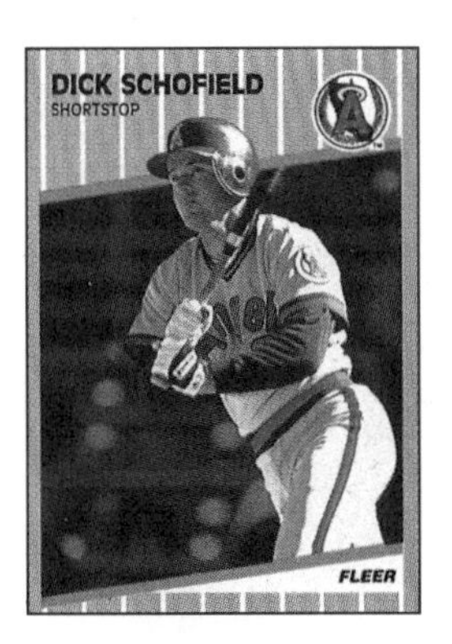

MIKE SCHOOLER

	W	L	ERA	G	SV	IP	H	R	BB	SO
1988	5	8	3.54	40	15	48.1	45	21	24	54
Life	5	8	3.54	40	15	48.1	45	21	24	54

POSITION: Pitcher
TEAM: Seattle Mariners
BORN: August 10, 1962 Anaheim, CA
HEIGHT: 6'3" **WEIGHT:** 220 lbs.
BATS: Right **THROWS:** Right
ACQUIRED: Second-round pick in 6/85 free-agent draft

The Mariners made a career decision for Schooler at the close of the 1987 season. They decided that he had a better future as a reliever than as a starter, and the decision seems to be paying off. Less than a season later, he was working out of the Seattle bullpen, leading the M's in saves, surpassing the ten-save mark. A 13-game winner as a starter at Chattanooga in 1987, he racked up eight saves in his first 28 games in Triple-A in 1988. Schooler has all the tools to challenge as one of the best relievers in the American League.

Schooler appears to be set as the team's ace stopper in 1989. His 1989 cards will begin in the 35-cent range. Beware of spending too much money on hard-throwing relievers. Our pick for his best 1989 card is Score.

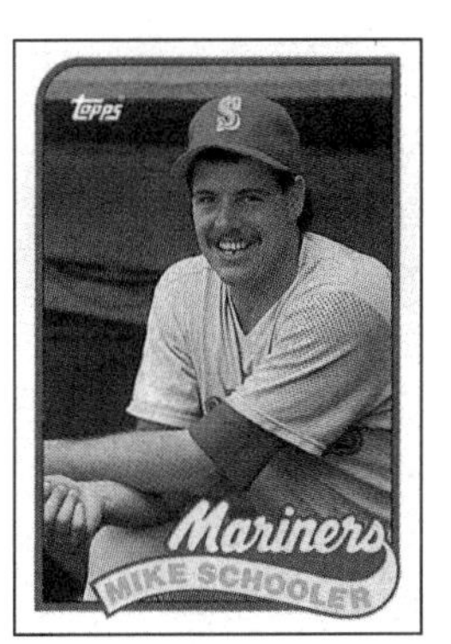

RICK SCHU

	BA	G	AB	R	H	2B	3B	HR	RBI	SB
1988	.256	89	270	22	69	9	4	4	20	6
Life	.255	402	1119	144	285	48	13	28	97	16

POSITION: Infield
TEAM: Baltimore Orioles
BORN: January 26, 1962 Philadelphia, PA
HEIGHT: 6′ **WEIGHT:** 170 lbs.
BATS: Right **THROWS:** Right
ACQUIRED: Traded from Phillies for Jeff Stone, Mike Young, and Keith Hughes, 3/88

Schu was acquired by the Orioles to fill their long-standing need for a third baseman. In 1988, he didn't nail down the starting job like everyone expected. He did appear in 89 games and wound up with a .256 batting average. Schu's best season as a hitter came in 1986 with the Phillies. In 92 games, he batted .274, with eight homers and 25 RBIs. The Phillies wanted him to become their third baseman of the future, able to eventually replace an aging Mike Schmidt. Schu is capable of playing all four infield positions, so there's no telling where he might end up with the Orioles in 1989.

Until Schu gets a starting job with the O's (or any other team), his 1989 cards will never be worth more than their common prices of three cents or less. Our pick for his best 1989 card is Topps.

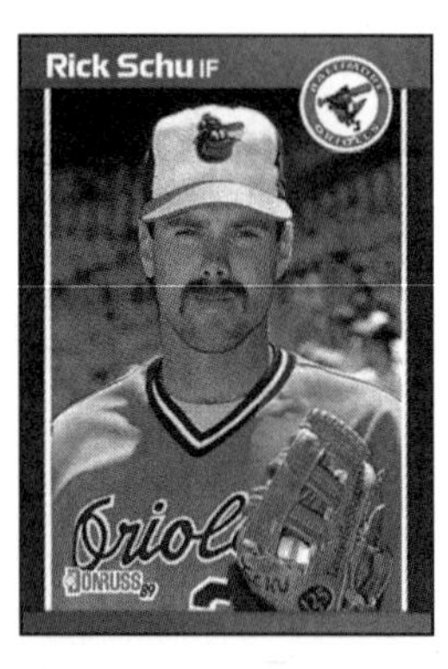

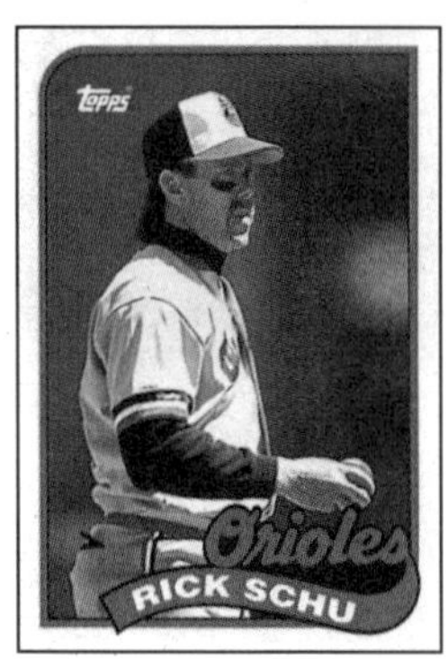

MIKE SCIOSCIA

	BA	G	AB	R	H	2B	3B	HR	RBI	SB
1988	.257	130	408	29	105	18	0	3	35	0
Life	.263	937	2837	254	746	135	7	35	272	18

POSITION: Catcher
TEAM: Los Angeles Dodgers
BORN: November 27, 1958 Darby, PA
HEIGHT: 6′2″ **WEIGHT:** 200 lbs.
BATS: Left **THROWS:** Right
ACQUIRED: First-round pick in 6/76 free-agent draft

Scioscia played in 130 games for the 1988 Los Angeles Dodgers, the third-best total for National League catchers. Only Tony Pena and Benito Santiago played in more games. Scioscia topped 100 hits for only the third time in his nine seasons with the Dodgers. Most importantly, he remained as one of the league's best defensive backstops. He's regarded as one of the best in the business when it comes to blocking the plate. When people praise the Dodger pitching staff, credit must be given to Scioscia, who's often behind the plate calling the pitches.

Scioscia's 1989 cards shouldn't be more than a nickel. Great defense doesn't impress many card investors. His offensive totals are passable, but not enough to promise any short-term gains in his card values. Our pick for his best 1989 card is Topps.

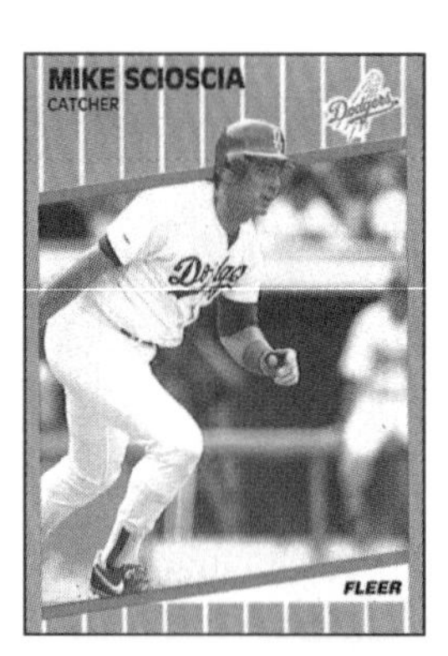

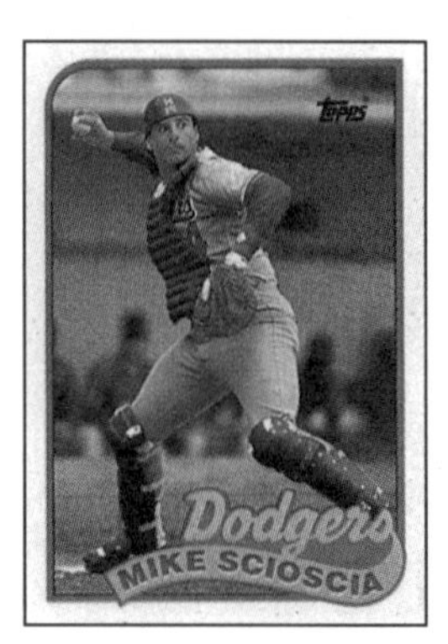

MIKE SCOTT

	W	L	ERA	G	CG	IP	H	R	BB	SO
1988	14	8	2.92	32	8	218.2	162	74	53	190
Life	95	83	3.53	280	32	1626.1	1473	709	38	1173

POSITION: Pitcher
TEAM: Houston Astros
BORN: April 26, 1955
Santa Monica, CA
HEIGHT: 6′3″ **WEIGHT:** 215 lbs.
BATS: Right **THROWS:** Right
ACQUIRED: Traded from Mets for Danny Heep, 12/82

A master of the split-fingered fastball, Scott led the 1988 Astros both in complete games and innings pitched. His respectable season still proved to be a letdown from his storybook years in 1986 and 1987. In 1986, Scott won the N.L. Championship Series MVP and Cy Young awards, as he led the league in strikeouts with 306 and tossed a no-hitter. In 1987, he made his second consecutive All-Star game appearance by starting the mid-season classic. For five seasons, Scott has been one of the most effective pitchers in the N.L.

At age 33, he hasn't won 100 games yet. A couple of sterling seasons don't make good card-investment material. His cards should open at the 10- to 20-cent range. Keep any wax-pack cards of Scott, but don't buy large numbers. Our pick for his best 1989 card is Donruss.

STEVE SEARCY

	W	L	ERA	G	CG	IP	H	R	BB	SO
1988	0	2	5.63	2	0	8	8	6	4	5
Life	0	2	5.63	2	0	8	8	6	4	5

POSITION: Pitcher
TEAM: Detroit Tigers
BORN: June 4, 1964 Knoxville, TN
HEIGHT: 6′1″ **WEIGHT:** 185 lbs.
BATS: Left **THROWS:** Left
ACQUIRED: Third-round pick in 6/85 free-agent draft

In 1988, Searcy was something of a mystery man, coming off a broken kneecap in 1987. Before being hurt, he appeared in only ten games for Triple-A Toledo and managed a 3-4 record. In 1988, however, he was the International League's strikeout king, averaging better than one strikeout per inning (176 Ks in 170 frames). The fireballing lefty was rated the second-best prospect in that league last year. He had an 11-6 record at Glens Falls in 1986, which included a 3.30 ERA and 139 strikeouts in 172 innings of work. Searcy looks like he will be striking out batters for years to come.

Searcy will come to the Detroit Tigers camp this spring with a legitimate shot at making the starting rotation. His 1989 major league cards will probably open in the 15- to 25-cent range. Our pick for his best 1989 card is Topps.

KEVIN SEITZER

	BA	G	AB	R	H	2B	3B	HR	RBI	SB
1988	.304	149	559	90	170	32	5	5	60	10
Life	.315	338	1296	211	408	69	14	22	154	22

POSITION: Third base
TEAM: Kansas City Royals
BORN: March 26, 1962 Springfield, IL
HEIGHT: 5′11″ **WEIGHT:** 180 lbs.
BATS: Right **THROWS:** Right
ACQUIRED: 11th-round pick in 6/83 free-agent draft

Seitzer's second big league season proved that his 1987 debut wasn't a fluke. In 1988, he hit .304. Seitzer's on-base percentage was one of the best in the league. However, some sophomore letdown seems natural, considering that he led the American League with 207 hits in 1987. Although he did not burn up the league in 1988, his stats and future ability rival that of any A.L. third baseman. The Royals have so much faith in him that they moved George Brett, their star third baseman, permanently to first base. Kansas City fans hope that Seitzer will lead the Royals to a few championships in the future.

Seitzer's 1989 cards should open at a dollar due to his slump. Pick them up before Seitzer rebounds in 1989. When his bat heats up this year, his cards will, too. Our pick for his best 1989 card is Topps.

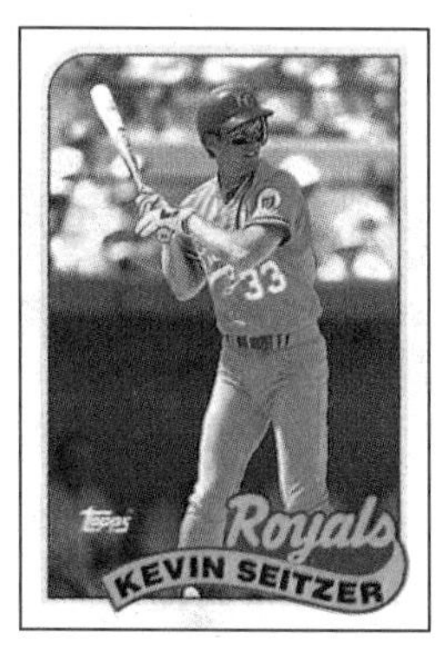

JEFF SELLERS

	W	L	ERA	G	CG	IP	H	R	BB	SO
1988	1	7	4.83	18	1	85.2	89	49	56	70
Life	13	22	4.97	61	7	329.2	364	200	164	226

POSITION: Pitcher
TEAM: Boston Red Sox
BORN: May 11, 1964 Compton, CA
HEIGHT: 6′ **WEIGHT:** 180 lbs.
BATS: Right **THROWS:** Right
ACQUIRED: Eighth-round pick in 6/82 free-agent draft

Sellers didn't share the good fortune of the rest of the 1988 pennant-winning Red Sox. He won only one out of eight decisions in 1988, and he had another fat ERA for his third straight season. Sellers has yielded an average of one walk every two innings during his four years with Boston. Good luck seemed to be coming his way in 1987. He had a 7-8 record, but he recorded four complete games and two shutouts in the process. He has been given ample opportunity to prove himself with Boston. Sellers may have to struggle for a roster spot in 1989.

Don't bother investing in the 1989 cards of Sellers, which will sell for three cents or less. Until he has one memorable season, his cards will be an investment hazard. Our pick for his best 1989 card is Donruss.

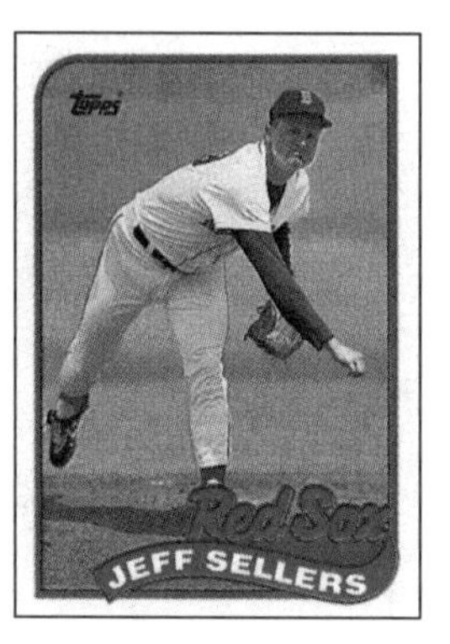

MIKE SHARPERSON

	BA	G	AB	R	H	2B	3B	HR	RBI	SB
1988	.271	46	59	8	16	1	0	0	4	0
Life	.239	88	188	19	45	7	1	0	14	2

POSITION: Infield
TEAM: Los Angeles Dodgers
BORN: October 4, 1960 Orangeburg, SC
HEIGHT: 6'3" **WEIGHT:** 185 lbs.
BATS: Right **THROWS:** Right
ACQUIRED: Traded from Blue Jays, 9/87

Sharperson was good insurance for the Dodger infield in 1988. He played good defense, and he had a good year at the plate. He hit .271 in 59 at-bats, with four RBIs. He played both second base and third base. At Triple-A Albuquerque in 1988, Sharperson hit .319, with ten doubles, 19 stolen bases, 30 RBIs, and 55 runs scored. He has a good bat, as evidenced by the two years (1985 and '86) that he led the Triple-A International League in hits. Sharperson should see more playing time in 1989, occasionally filling in for Willie Randolph at second base.

Sharperson's 1989 cards will cost a nickel or less, a good price for investing a few bucks. If he gets more playing time in 1989, Sharperson may win the second base job for good and turn a few heads. Our pick for his best 1989 card is Fleer.

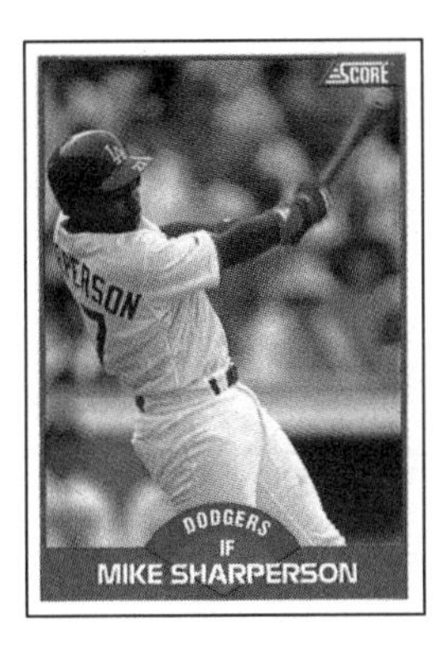

LARRY SHEETS

	BA	G	AB	R	H	2B	3B	HR	RBI	SB
1988	.230	136	452	38	104	19	1	10	47	1
Life	.273	504	1603	200	437	68	2	77	253	4

POSITION: Designated hitter; outfield
TEAM: Baltimore Orioles
BORN: December 6, 1959 Staunton, VA
HEIGHT: 6'3" **WEIGHT:** 210 lbs.
BATS: Left **THROWS:** Right
ACQUIRED: Second-round pick in 6/78 free-agent draft

Sheets wasn't immune to the slumps that plagued the entire Baltimore team throughout 1988. He had come off the finest season of his career in 1987, with 31 home runs, 94 RBIs, and a .316 average. In 1988, Sheets saw his average slump some 85 points in the same number of games, and his homer total was cut by two-thirds. Unfortunately, his 73 strikeouts ranked second on the team. Sheets could be a regular on the A.L. All-Star team if he can recapture his 1987 glory.

Sheets, at age 29, is getting a late start on stardom. He might be one of the league's best sluggers for the next few years, but any more slumps like 1988 will remove all interest in his cards. His 1989 cards sell as commons. Our pick for his best 1989 card is Donruss.

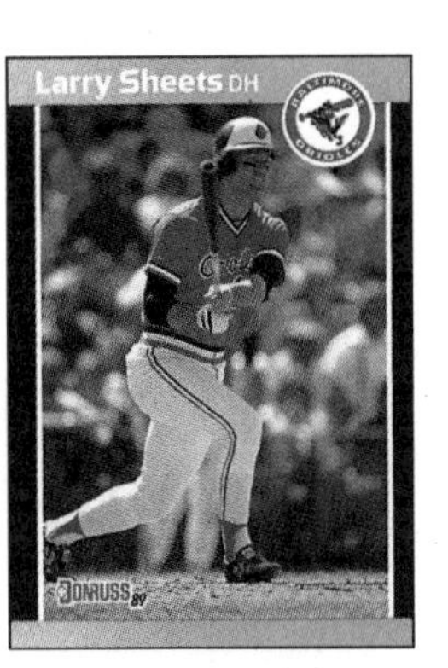

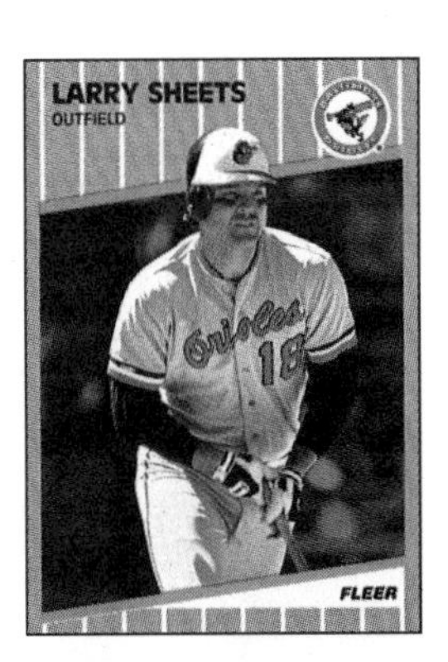

GARY SHEFFIELD

	BA	G	AB	R	H	2B	3B	HR	RBI	SB
1988	.238	24	80	12	19	1	0	4	12	3
Life	.238	24	80	12	19	1	0	4	12	3

POSITION: Shortstop
TEAM: Milwaukee Brewers
BORN: November 18, 1968 Tampa, FL
HEIGHT: 5′11″ **WEIGHT:** 190 lbs.
BATS: Right **THROWS:** Right
ACQUIRED: First-round pick in 6/86 free-agent draft

Sheffield is just 20 years old and is rated as one of the best prospects in all of organized baseball. He arrived in the majors last fall—hitting at the .250 mark—after dividing the 1988 campaign between Double-A El Paso and Triple-A Denver. He compiled impressive stats at Denver: .344 average, nine homers, and 54 RBIs in 57 games. In 77 games at El Paso, he hit .314, 19 round-trippers, and 65 RBIs. In 1987 with Class-A Stockton, Sheffield hit 17 home runs and 103 RBIs, and he stole 25 bases. With Helena in 1986, he posted a .365 batting average, including 15 homers and 71 RBIs—in just 57 contests. Sheffield is one of the most exciting young players in baseball.

His 1989 cards should start out in the 50- to 75-cent range. Buy them early before the price starts to zoom upward. Our pick for his best 1989 card is Topps.

JOHN SHELBY

	BA	G	AB	R	H	2B	3B	HR	RBI	SB
1988	.263	140	494	65	130	23	6	10	64	16
Life	.252	772	2356	318	593	99	19	62	271	84

POSITION: Outfield
TEAM: Los Angeles Dodgers
BORN: February 23, 1958 Lexington, KY
HEIGHT: 6′1″ **WEIGHT:** 175 lbs.
BATS: Both **THROWS:** Right
ACQUIRED: Traded from Orioles with Brad Havens for Tom Niedenfuer, 5/87

Although he missed 20 games in 1988—his first full season as a Dodger—"T-Bone" Shelby continued to be one of the National League's most gifted center fielders. He didn't match his 1987 power output (22 homers and 69 RBIs), but he did continue to give the Dodger lineup solid defensive play. In 1988, he popped ten homers and 64 RBIs, while hitting .263. Shelby also had 23 doubles and scored 65 runs. He matched his 1987 stolen-base mark with 16. Shelby's talent and determination have brought him continued success in all phases of the game, and made him one of the finest outfielders in the National League.

Shelby's 1989 cards should go for a nickel or less. They're good investments at that price level, especially if he helps the Dodgers to another pennant in 1989. Our pick for his best 1989 card is Donruss.

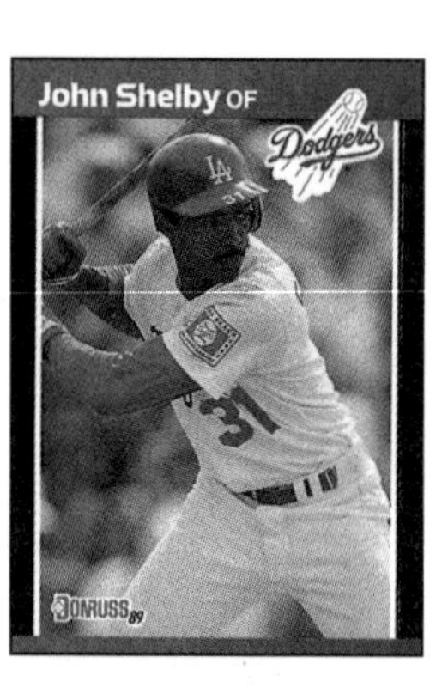

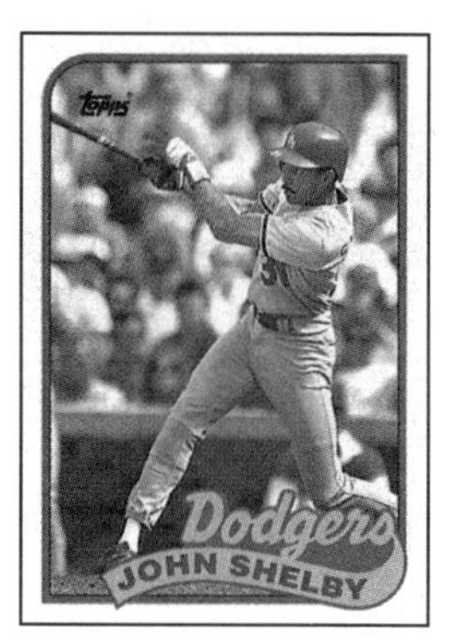

PAT SHERIDAN

	BA	G	AB	R	H	2B	3B	HR	RBI	SB
1988	.254	127	347	47	88	9	5	11	47	8
Life	.260	694	2025	270	526	82	17	41	221	77

POSITION: Outfield
TEAM: Detroit Tigers
BORN: December 4, 1957 Ann Arbor, MI
HEIGHT: 6′3″ **WEIGHT:** 195 lbs.
BATS: Left **THROWS:** Right
ACQUIRED: Signed as a free agent, 4/86

Sheridan, playing only part-time, still managed to be a big influence on the success of the 1988 Tigers. He was one of eight Tigers to hit at least ten home runs, and his eight stolen bases were third highest on the team. He remained one of the best fielders on the Tigers' team, committing just four errors all season. Sheridan was released by Kansas City after he was one of their hitting stars in the 1985 World Series. The Tigers gave him another chance to play in 1986, and Sheridan just keeps getting better.

Sheridan might be a surprise if he could play a full season. Until he gets that chance, his cards will be risky investments at their current prices of 3 cents or less. Our pick for his best 1989 card is Fleer.

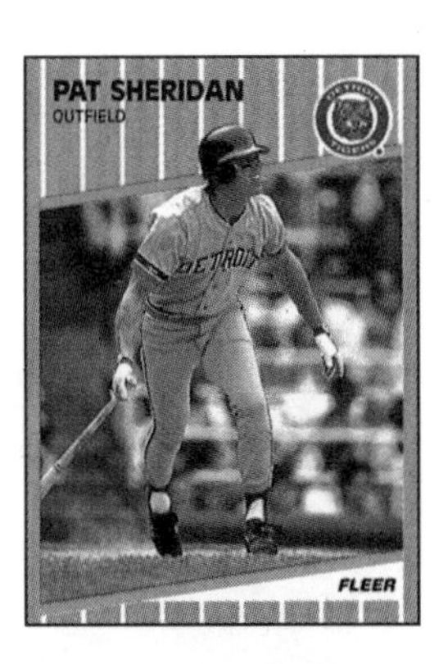

ERIC SHOW

	W	L	ERA	G	CG	IP	H	R	BB	SO
1988	16	11	3.26	32	13	234.2	201	86	53	144
Life	86	73	3.37	254	34	1390.2	1220	570	513	830

POSITION: Pitcher
TEAM: San Diego Padres
BORN: May 19, 1956 Riverside, CA
HEIGHT: 6′1″ **WEIGHT:** 190 lbs.
BATS: Right **THROWS:** Right
ACQUIRED: 18th-round pick in 6/78 free-agent draft

Show had his best season ever as a Padre starter. In 1988, he tied for the team lead in wins with a career-high 16 triumphs. Show was a tireless worker for the Padres, submitting 13 complete games and one shutout in 234⅔ innings of work last season. He had a 3.26 ERA and 144 strikeouts in '88. He switched from relieving to starting in mid-1982. Show won 15, 15, and 12 games during the next three seasons. He slumped to an all-time worst of 8-16 in 1987. Show's 1988 turnaround proves that he still is a top-notch N.L. pitcher.

Show's 1989 cards should be found at a nickel or less. He could win 20 games in 1989, which would send his card values soaring. Invest while you can at affordable levels. Our pick for his best 1989 card is Donruss.

RUBEN SIERRA

	BA	G	AB	R	H	2B	3B	HR	RBI	SB
1988	.254	156	615	77	156	32	2	23	91	18
Life	.260	427	1640	224	426	80	16	69	255	41

POSITION: Outfield
TEAM: Texas Rangers
BORN: October 6, 1965 Rio Piedras, Puerto Rico
HEIGHT: 6'1" **WEIGHT:** 175 lbs.
BATS: Both **THROWS:** Right
ACQUIRED: Signed as an undrafted free agent, 11/82

Sierra, in only his third major league season, continued to shine as one of the Rangers' brightest stars. In 1988, he did not match his best-ever marks of 30 homers and 109 RBIs, achieved in 1987. However, he did continue to lead the Rangers both in home runs and RBIs. He struck out less than 100 times in 1988, a sign that he's gaining more control at the plate. Sierra, at age 23, is the nucleus of a young Ranger club. His switch-hitting, power, and speed are talents that could carry the Rangers over the .500 hump soon.

Sierra's 1989 cards will sell from 25 to 30 cents. That price may seem steep, but he has proven that he's a future star. Those prices will go up as soon as he wins any awards or the Rangers start to win. Our pick for his best 1989 card is Fleer.

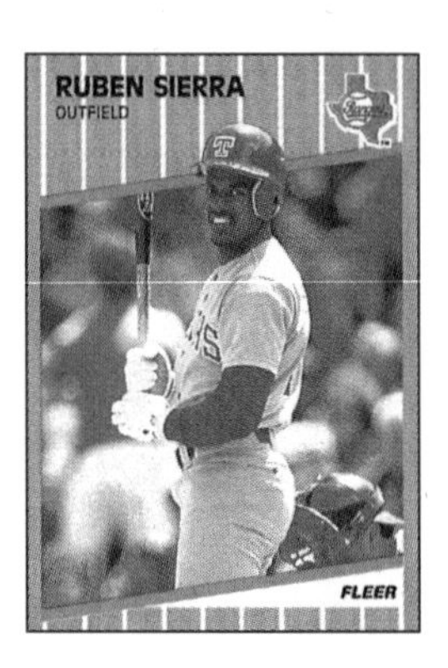

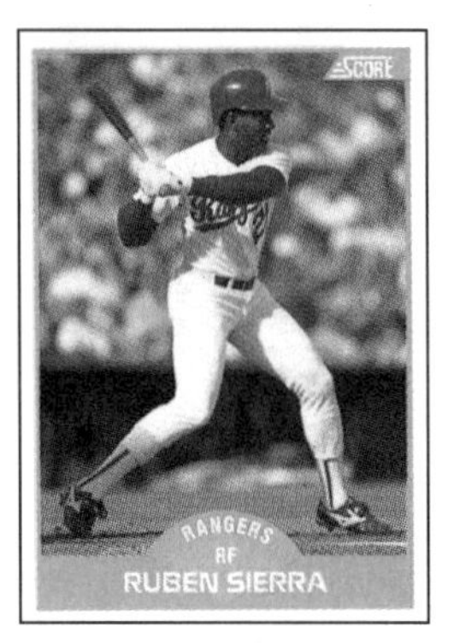

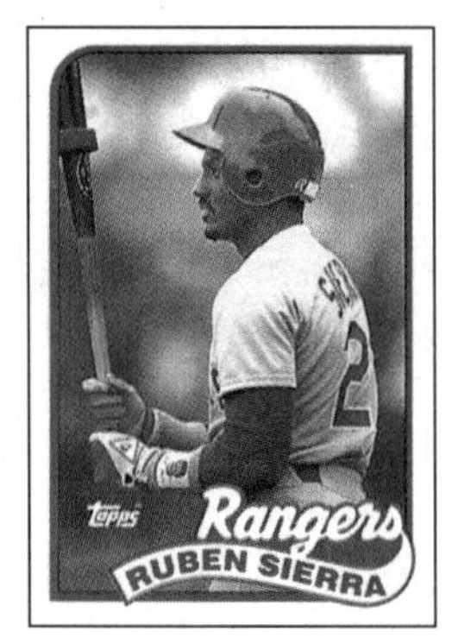

DOUG SISK

	W	L	ERA	G	SV	IP	H	R	BB	SO
1988	3	3	3.72	52	0	94.1	109	43	45	26
Life	20	19	3.22	315	33	506.2	505	223	255	189

POSITION: Pitcher
TEAM: Baltimore Orioles
BORN: September 26, 1957 Renton, WA
HEIGHT: 6'2" **WEIGHT:** 210 lbs.
BATS: Right **THROWS:** Right
ACQUIRED: Traded from Mets for Blaine Beatty and Greg Talmantez, 12/87

Sisk turned in another fine season in 1988. He finished with a 3.72 ERA for the Orioles, appearing in 52 games. He is a sinkerball pitcher, and batters usually ground out when they face him. In 1987 for the Mets, Sisk was 3-1, with a 3.46 ERA, 78 innings of work, and three saves. He saved 15 games for the 1984 Mets. His best season in the majors was in 1983; he was 5-4, with a 2.24 ERA, 11 saves, 67 appearances, and 104⅓ innings pitched. If Sisk could return to that form for the 1989 Orioles, it would go a long way toward solving their bullpen problems.

Sisk's 1989 cards will be in the commons box. Although he is a good pitcher with a fine career ERA, he will never post big enough numbers to generate much interest in his cards. Our pick for his best 1989 card is Fleer.

JOEL SKINNER

	BA	G	AB	R	H	2B	3B	HR	RBI	SB
1988	.227	88	251	23	57	15	0	4	23	0
Life	.219	337	840	70	184	34	2	13	83	2

POSITION: Catcher
TEAM: New York Yankees
BORN: February 21, 1961 La Jolla, CA
HEIGHT: 6′4″ **WEIGHT:** 205 lbs.
BATS: Right **THROWS:** Right
ACQUIRED: Traded from White Sox with Ron Kittle and Wayne Tolleson for Ron Hassey, Bill Lindsey, and Carlos Martinez, 7/86

Skinner shared the catching duties for the 1988 Yankees with Don Slaught. The move to New York in 1986 meant freedom for Skinner, who got virtually no playing time behind ironman Carlton Fisk in Chicago. However, Skinner has seen considerable action for the Yankees. While his offense was less than spectacular last season, Skinner gave the Yanks some solid defensive support behind the plate. He was charged for only four errors in 88 games. He has spent the last six seasons as a substitute, and will likely stay in that role due to his hitting. However, a team always needs a sure-handed catcher, so Skinner will always be able to find work.

Skinner's 1989 cards will sell as commons. Because he seems to be destined for second-string status, his cards aren't good investment choices. Our pick for his best 1989 card is Score.

DON SLAUGHT

	BA	G	AB	R	H	2B	3B	HR	RBI	SB
1988	.283	97	322	22	91	25	1	9	43	1
Life	.272	639	2016	214	549	120	16	45	218	12

POSITION: Catcher
TEAM: New York Yankees
BORN: September 11, 1958 Long Beach, CA
HEIGHT: 6′1″ **WEIGHT:** 190 lbs.
BATS: Right **THROWS:** Right
ACQUIRED: Traded from Texas for Brad Arnsberg, 11/87

Slaught wound up sharing the catching duties with Joel Skinner for the 1988 Yankees. In his first season in New York, Slaught hit .283 in 97 games. He also contributed nine home runs and 43 RBIs. In 1987, he hit .224 for the Rangers, with eight homers and only 16 RBIs. Power-wise, his best season ever was in 1986 with the Rangers. Slaught hit 13 homers and 46 RBIs in just 95 games. The veteran catcher first came up with the Royals in 1982, where he spent three seasons. He has never played more than 124 games in any major league season. One wonders what Slaught could do in a whole year.

Slaught could be platooned again in 1989. His lifetime hitting totals aren't spectacular. Until they improve, pass on investing in his common-priced 1989 cards. Our pick for his best 1989 card is Fleer.

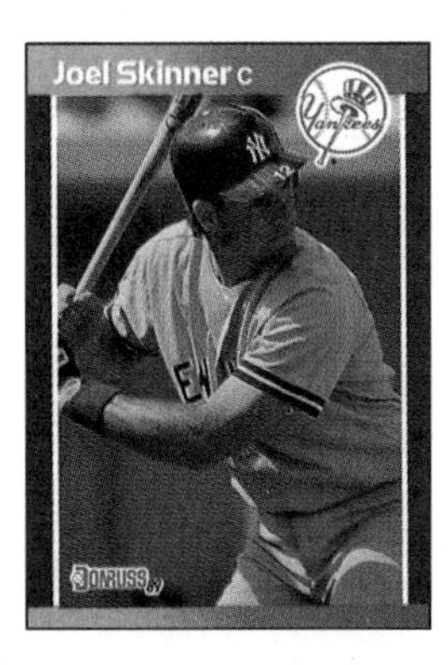

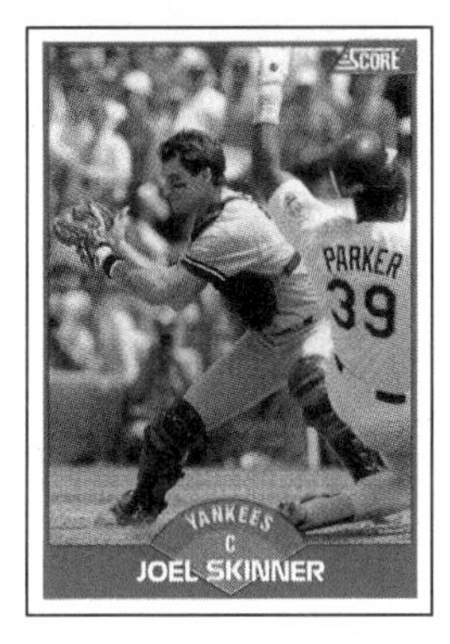

JOHN SMILEY

	W	L	ERA	G	CG	IP	H	R	BB	SO
1988	13	11	3.25	34	5	205.0	185	81	46	129
Life	19	16	3.92	109	5	291.2	258	136	100	196

POSITION: Pitcher
TEAM: Pittsburgh Pirates
BORN: March 17, 1965 Phoenixville, PA
HEIGHT: 6'4" **WEIGHT:** 180 lbs.
BATS: Left **THROWS:** Left
ACQUIRED: 12th-round pick in 6/83 free-agent draft

Smiley made the jump from Class-A to the majors in 1986 and has been a successful major league hurler since. He was converted to a starter in 1988, and the lefty thrived on the challenge. Smiley went 13-11 with a 3.25 ERA in 34 games. He pitched a one-hitter against the Expos last June and threw a two-hitter at the Cardinals last December. He was 5-5 for the 1987 Pirates in 63 relief outings. At Class-A Prince William in 1986, he appeared in 48 games. He finished with 14 saves and a 3.10 ERA. Summoned to Pittsburgh, he went 1-0 in 12 games. Smiley looks like he will be in the Pirates' starting rotation in 1989.

Smiley's 1989 cards should be savers. He has the tools to be a steady winner. Right now they're good investments in the 10-cent range. Our pick for his best 1989 card is Topps.

BRYN SMITH

	W	L	ERA	G	CG	IP	H	R	BB	SO
1988	12	10	3.00	32	1	198.0	179	79	32	122
Life	71	60	3.37	251	17	1184.2	1133	516	287	709

POSITION: Pitcher
TEAM: Montreal Expos
BORN: August 11, 1955 Marietta, GA
HEIGHT: 6'2" **WEIGHT:** 200 lbs.
BATS: Right **THROWS:** Right
ACQUIRED: Traded from Orioles with Rudy May and Randy Miller for Don Stanhouse, Joe Kerrigan, and Gary Roenicke, 12/77

Smith has been among the most reliable Montreal pitchers since joining the team back in 1981. In 1988, he was 12-10, with a 3.00 ERA and 122 strikeouts in 198 innings. Ironically, it was just two years ago that a serious shoulder problem threatened to end his career. But Smith came back in 1987, and went 10-9 in 26 outings, with a 4.37 ERA and 94 strikeouts in 150⅓ innings. He has pitched at least 150 innings for six consecutive seasons. Originally the Cardinals' 49th pick in the June 1973 draft, he had his best big league season in 1985, when he went 18-5, with a 2.91 ERA and a career-high 127 strikeouts. Smith gives to the Expos a reliable, experienced arm.

Smith's 1989 cards sell in the 5- to 10-cent range. Considering his career stats, they probably will never appreciate much beyond that number. Our pick for his best 1989 card is Topps.

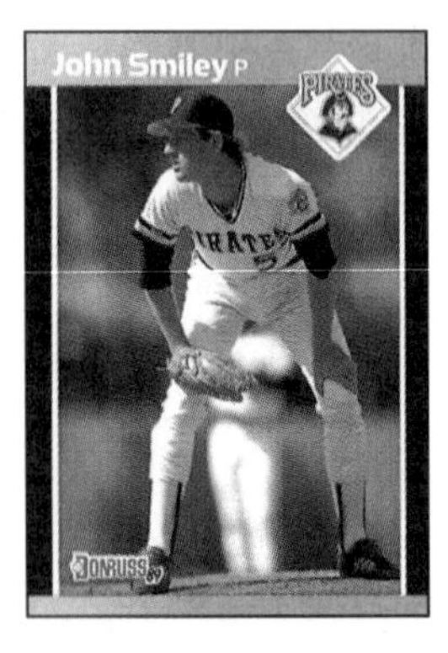

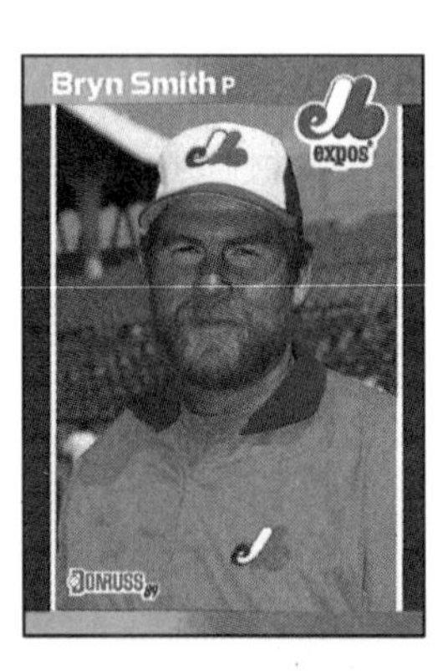

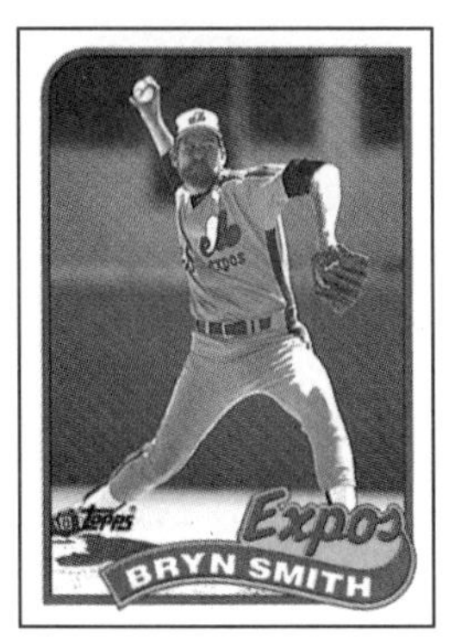

DAVE SMITH

	W	L	ERA	G	SV	IP	H	R	BB	SO
1988	4	5	2.67	51	27	57.1	60	26	19	38
Life	44	37	2.53	462	151	644.0	552	216	221	448

POSITION: Pitcher
TEAM: Houston Astros
BORN: January 21, 1955
San Francisco, CA
HEIGHT: 6′1″ **WEIGHT:** 195 lbs.
BATS: Right **THROWS:** Right
ACQUIRED: Sixth-round pick in 6/76 free-agent draft

Smith proved again in 1988 that he might be one of the greatest unknown relievers in baseball today. He reeled off his fourth-straight season of 20 or more saves in 1988. He entered the 1988 season with the lowest ERA of any reliever with at least five years of major league experience. Smith spent three frustrating seasons in the minor leagues before making the conversion to a reliever in 1979. He first starred with the Astros only one year later, when he went 7-5 with ten saves and a sparkling 1.82 ERA in 57 games. Smith's total saves rank ninth among active relievers.

Smith is simply one of baseball's best relief artists. His 1989 cards will be mistaken as commons by many uninformed dealers. At a nickel or less, you'll be getting a great investment. Our pick for his best 1989 card is Score.

LEE SMITH

	W	L	ERA	G	SV	IP	H	R	BB	SO
1988	4	5	2.80	64	29	83.2	72	34	37	96
Life	44	56	2.90	522	209	765.2	663	274	301	740

POSITION: Pitcher
TEAM: Boston Red Sox
BORN: December 4, 1957
Jamestown, LA
HEIGHT: 6′6″ **WEIGHT:** 235 lbs.
BATS: Right **THROWS:** Right
ACQUIRED: Traded from Cubs for Al Nipper and Calvin Schiraldi, 12/87

Smith made his first season in the American League a memorable one in 1988. The Red Sox eagerly pursued Smith as the stopper they'd been craving for years. The righthander fulfilled all hopes in 1988. He was among the league leaders in saves, with 29. He surpassed 200 saves for his eight-year career. Smith averaged better than one strikeout per inning again in 1988, and he kept his ERA under 3.00. He has had at least 29 saves for six consecutive seasons. Red Sox starting pitchers seem to have a bright future, as long as a reliable closer like Smith is available.

Smith will get lots of credit for Boston's strong 1988 finish, and the applause should boost his 1989 cards to 10 cents apiece. Stock up. Smith may end up as one of baseball's finest relievers ever. Our pick for his best 1989 card is Score.

OZZIE SMITH

	BA	G	AB	R	H	2B	3B	HR	RBI	SB
1988	.270	153	575	80	155	27	1	3	51	57
Life	.255	1628	5914	767	1506	246	43	16	500	403

POSITION: Shortstop
TEAM: St. Louis Cardinals
BORN: December 26, 1954 Mobile, AL
HEIGHT: 5'10" **WEIGHT:** 150 lbs.
BATS: Both **THROWS:** Right
ACQUIRED: Traded from Padres for Garry Templeton, 2/82

Like the rest of the 1988 Cardinals, Smith battled slumps all year long. Known as the "Wizard of Oz" for his legendary fielding, Smith committed more than 20 errors in 1988, his highest total in five years. Still, he managed to lead the team in doubles, with 27, while batting .270. In 1987, Smith topped .300, with 104 runs, 75 RBIs, and 43 stolen bases. He finished second in MVP voting. Going into the 1988 season, he had won eight straight Gold Gloves. While not known as an offensive powerhouse, he has hit at least .270 for four straight years. Smart fans feel Smith's slump is temporary.

The poor 1988 season by Smith will drop his card prices. His 1989 cards will be at the 15- to 25-cent level. They may be bargains, because Smith might field himself into the Hall of Fame some day. Our pick for his best 1989 card is Fleer.

PETE SMITH

	W	L	ERA	G	CG	IP	H	R	BB	SO
1988	7	15	3.69	32	5	195.1	183	89	88	124
Life	8	17	3.85	38	5	227.0	222	110	102	135

POSITION: Pitcher
TEAM: Atlanta Braves
BORN: February 27, 1966 Abington, MA
HEIGHT: 6'2" **WEIGHT:** 183 lbs.
BATS: Right **THROWS:** Right
ACQUIRED: Traded from Phillies with Ozzie Virgil for Steve Bedrosian and Milt Thompson, 12/85

Though he lost twice as many games as he won for the 1988 season (7-15), Smith was a strong member of Russ Nixon's mound corps in 1988. Smith kept his ERA at 3.69 in '88. He pitched at the Double-A level in 1987, going 9-9 with a 3.35 ERA and 119 strikeouts in 177 innings. For this effort, the Braves rewarded the righthander by bringing him up to the parent club late in the 1987 season, where he went 1-2 in six appearances, all as a starter. He was acquired from the Phillies in the Steve Bedrosian deal. At Greenville in '86, he went 1-8 with a 5.85 ERA. The Braves have some good young pitchers, and Smith is one of the most impressive.

Smith's 1989 cards will go for about 20 cents. If Atlanta's offensive production improves, his win total in 1989 could multiply. Our pick for his best 1989 card is Fleer.

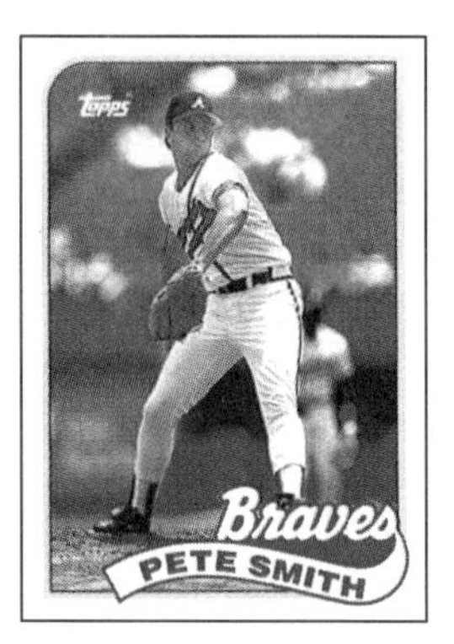

ZANE SMITH

	W	L	ERA	G	CG	IP	H	R	BB	SO
1988	5	10	4.30	23	3	140.1	159	72	44	59
Life	38	46	4.01	142	17	154.0	764	388	333	429

POSITION: Pitcher
TEAM: Atlanta Braves
BORN: December 28, 1960 Madison, WI
HEIGHT: 6′2″ **WEIGHT:** 195 lbs.
BATS: Left **THROWS:** Left
ACQUIRED: Third-round pick in 6/82 free-agent draft

Smith's 1988 record may look awful, but he tied for fourth in wins on the 1988 Braves. He didn't have much luck in 1988, which was a marked contrast from his success in 1987. He was 5-10 in '88, with a 4.30 ERA. Smith spun a 15-10 record in 1987, which was a single-season record for any Atlanta Brave lefthander. He earned three shutouts and nine complete games in 242 innings of work. In 1986, he was 8-16, with a 4.05 ERA and a career-high 139 strikeouts. A fine fielder, he went without a single error in 58 total chances in 1987. Smith could repeat that success in 1989 if the Braves score some runs for him.

Smith's 1989 cards should be three cents or less. Until the Brave offense improves, no cards of any Atlanta pitcher will increase in value. Our pick for his best 1989 card is Topps.

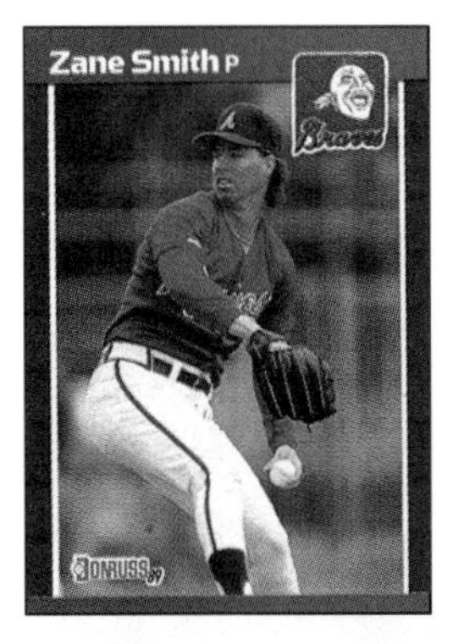

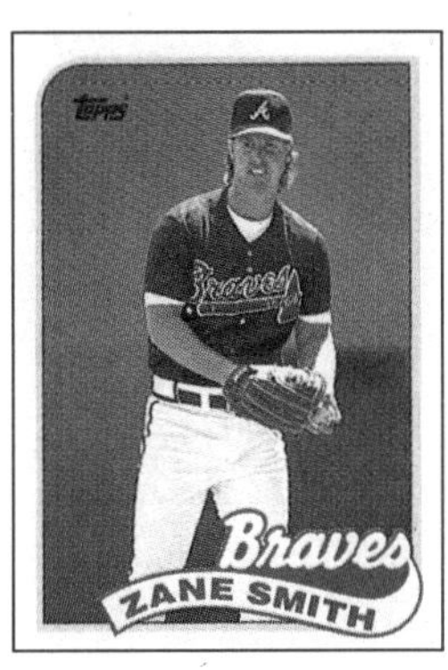

MIKE SMITHSON

	W	L	ERA	G	CG	IP	H	R	BB	SO
1988	9	6	5.97	31	1	126.2	149	87	37	73
Life	69	72	4.53	200	40	1212.2	1303	661	348	670

POSITION: Pitcher
TEAM: Boston Red Sox
BORN: January 21, 1955 Centerville, TN
HEIGHT: 6′8″ **WEIGHT:** 215 lbs.
BATS: Left **THROWS:** Right
ACQUIRED: Signed as a free agent, 1/88

Smithson made a tremendous comeback in 1988. He was released by Minnesota, and it looked as though his career was over. But the Red Sox signed him, and he came through with a 9-6 record. He had a high ERA, 5.97, but he struck out twice as many batters as he walked. In 1987 for the Twins, Smithson was 4-7, with a 5.94 ERA and only 53 strikeouts in 109 innings. He has pitched ten complete games during two seasons in his career. His best season in the majors was 1985, when he was 15-13, with a 3.68 ERA, ten complete games, and 144 Ks in 252 innings. Smithson should pitch well for the 1989 Red Sox.

Smithson's 1989 cards sell for less than 5 cents. It is unlikely that his cards will gain much value. Our pick for his best 1989 card is Fleer.

JOHN SMOLTZ

	W	L	ERA	G	CG	IP	H	R	BB	SO
1988	2	7	5.48	12	0	64.0	74	40	33	37
Life	2	7	5.48	12	0	64.0	74	40	33	37

POSITION: Pitcher
TEAM: Atlanta Braves
BORN: May 15, 1967 Detroit, MI
HEIGHT: 6′3″ **WEIGHT:** 185 lbs.
BATS: Right **THROWS:** Right
ACQUIRED: Traded from Tigers for Doyle Alexander, 8/87

Smoltz had a fine season at Triple-A Richmond in 1988, going 10-5 with a 2.79 ERA. Only 21 years old, he is one of the most highly regarded pitching prospects in baseball. He was traded to the Braves in 1987 in the deal that sent Doyle Alexander to Detroit. Smoltz's numbers in 1987 at Double-A Glens Falls were not impressive—4-10, 5.68 ERA, 88 strikeouts, 81 walks—but baseball scouts agree that he was the best pitching prospect in the Tiger system. He was picked low in the 1985 draft (23rd round). Smoltz has a blazing fastball and a great arm, but his control needs improving before he becomes a superstar.

Smoltz's 1989 cards will open in the 20-cent range. That is a great price for the speculative investor. Our pick for his best 1989 card is Score.

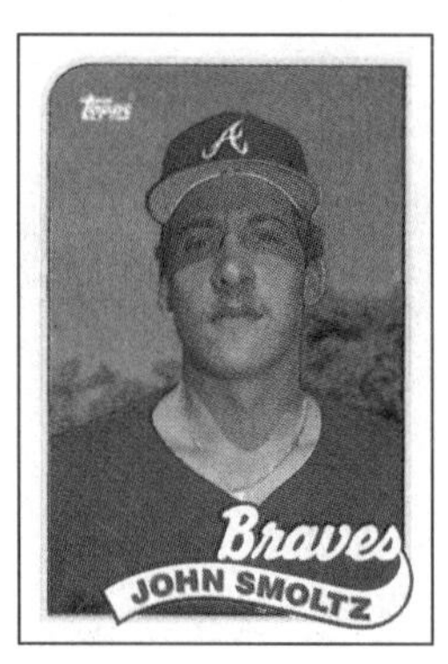

VAN SNIDER

	BA	G	AB	R	H	2B	3B	HR	RBI	SB
1988	.214	11	28	4	6	1	0	1	6	0
Life	.214	11	28	4	6	1	0	1	6	0

POSITION: Outfield
TEAM: Cincinnati Reds
BORN: August 11, 1963 Birmingham, AL
HEIGHT: 6′3″ **WEIGHT:** 180 lbs.
BATS: Left **THROWS:** Right
ACQUIRED: Traded from Royals for Jeff Montgomery, 2/88

Snider looks like a good bet to be an extra Red outfielder in 1989. His 1988 numbers were impressive—he hit .290, 23 homers, and 73 RBIs at Triple-A Nashville. He finished in the American Association top ten in average, homers, and RBIs in '88. He failed to impress the Royals at Triple-A Omaha in 1987 and was traded to the Reds. At Double-A Memphis in 1987, Snider hit .328, with nine homers and 40 RBIs. He got kind of stuck in Memphis, joining the Chicks in 1984 and playing with them all of 1985 and parts of 1986 and 1987. In 1983 at Charleston, he belted 20 home runs, batted .291, and had 94 RBIs. Snider has the tools to be an every-day player in the major leagues.

Snider appears to have a solid future. His 1989 cards will open in the 15- to 20-cent range. Our pick for his best 1989 card is Score.

CORY SNYDER

	BA	G	AB	R	H	2B	3B	HR	RBI	SB
1988	.272	142	511	71	139	24	3	26	75	5
Life	.258	402	1504	203	388	69	6	83	226	12

POSITION: Outfield
TEAM: Cleveland Indians
BORN: November 11, 1962
Inglewood, CA
HEIGHT: 6′3″ **WEIGHT:** 175 lbs.
BATS: Right **THROWS:** Right
ACQUIRED: First-round pick in 6/84 free-agent draft

Snyder continued to get his share of extra-base hits for the 1988 Indians. His homer and RBI totals dipped to 26 homers and 75 RBIs, down from 1987's 33-homer, 82-RBI output. However, he became more selective at the plate in 1988. His average soared nearly 40 points to .272, and he had 65 fewer strikeouts. Being able to play consistently in one position helped him become a more stable player in 1988. Snyder, a 1984 U.S. Olympic baseball star, will become one of the league's greatest hitting stars if he continues to polish his batting selectivity. The coming season might be a coming of age for the young Indian slugger.

Snyder's 1989 cards will be priced at a quarter or less. Gamblers may want to take a chance now, because Snyder's constant improvement should drive his card prices up fast. Our pick for his best 1989 card is Fleer.

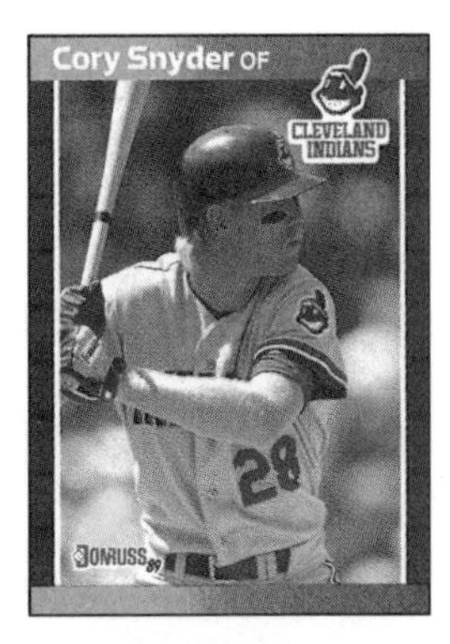

CHRIS SPEIER

	BA	G	AB	R	H	2B	3B	HR	RBI	SB
1988	.216	82	171	26	37	9	1	3	18	3
Life	.246	2232	7119	763	1750	298	50	112	718	42

POSITION: Infield
TEAM: San Francisco Giants
BORN: June 28, 1950 Alameda, CA
HEIGHT: 6′1″ **WEIGHT:** 180 lbs.
BATS: Right **THROWS:** Right
ACQUIRED: Signed as a free agent, 12/86

Speier played his 18th major league year with the club where he started, the Giants. He was the team's chief utilityman in 1988, playing any infield position. Speier, always a slick fielder, continued his defensive grace in 1988 with only three errors. When he signed with the Giants in 1987, he was rejoining the team where his career started in 1971, after only one minor league season. Speier played in San Francisco for more than six seasons and was named to three All-Star teams. Before coming back to the team by the bay, he played for the Expos, Cardinals, Twins, and Cubs. Quite likely, he'll end his career as a San Francisco backup infielder.

Substitute players don't make good card investments. Speier's 1989 cards, priced at three cents or less, should be bypassed for this reason. Our pick for his best 1989 card is Score.

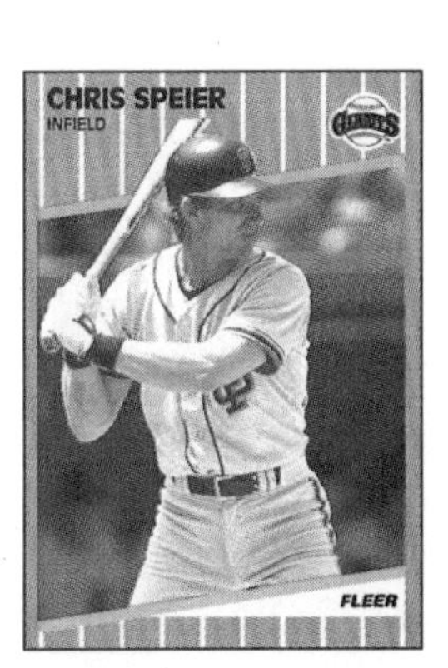

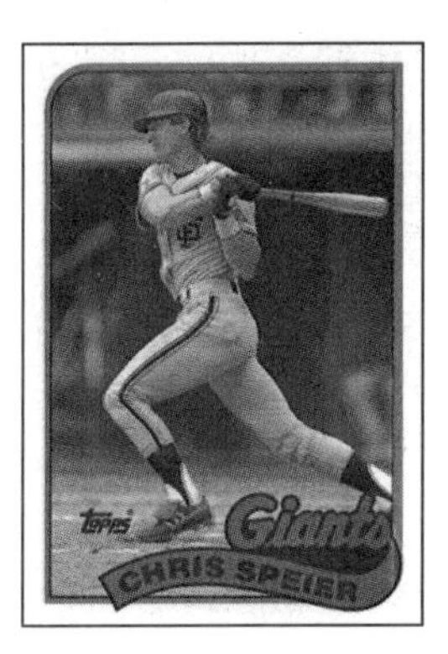

PETE STANICEK

	BA	G	AB	R	H	2B	3B	HR	RBI	SB
1988	.230	83	261	29	60	7	1	4	17	12
Life	.243	113	374	38	91	10	1	4	26	20

POSITION: Third base; second base
TEAM: Baltimore Orioles
BORN: April 18, 1963 Harvey, IL
HEIGHT: 5'11" **WEIGHT:** 185 lbs.
BATS: Both **THROWS:** Right
ACQUIRED: Sixth-round pick in 6/85 free-agent draft

In his first full season with the Orioles, Stanicek proved his worth at two infield positions. During his 34-day debut in 1987, he filled in for injured second baseman Billy Ripken. In 1988, he spelled third baseman Rick Schu. In 1989, he could battle for a starting spot at either base. Stanicek is one of the finest fielders with the O's, as he committed only four errors in 83 games last season. He led the team with 12 stolen bases out of 18 attempts last season. The young switch-hitter could nail down a full-time job in Baltimore if he can repeat his .274 batting average of 1987.

Expect Stanicek to get better with age and experience. His 1989 cards will be nice investments at five cents or less. Our pick for his best 1989 card is Fleer.

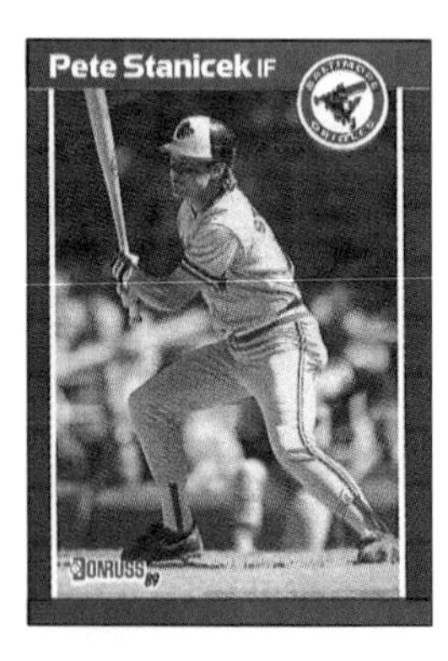

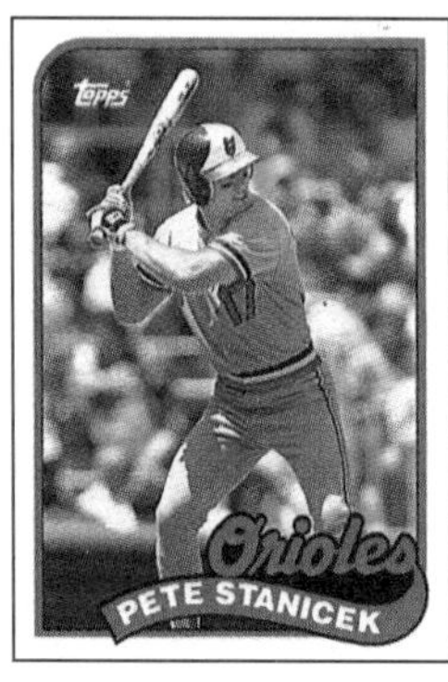

BOB STANLEY

	W	L	ERA	G	SV	IP	H	R	BB	SO
1988	6	4	3.19	57	5	101.2	90	41	29	57
Life	110	95	3.58	594	128	1628.2	1756	743	445	661

POSITION: Pitcher
TEAM: Boston Red Sox
BORN: November 10, 1954 Portland, ME
HEIGHT: 6'4" **WEIGHT:** 220 lbs.
BATS: Right **THROWS:** Right
ACQUIRED: First-round pick in 1/74 free-agent draft

Stanley, one of the best relief men in Boston history, submitted another fine effort for the club in 1988. Last season, his 12th with the team, he made 57 appearances. His six wins, five saves, and 3.19 ERA were respectable, but they barely rival Stanley's past achievements. In 1978, he tallied a 15-2 mark with 10 saves. The following year, he went 16-12 in starting and relief assignments. Some skeptics thought that his career might have been finished after he suffered through a horrible 4-15, 5.01 ERA season in 1987. Stanley's comeback needs to continue through 1989 if the Red Sox want to keep their divisional title.

Even successful relief pitchers like Stanley seldom make good card investments, because their careers are often unpredictable. His 1989 cards will be selling at a nickel or less, but should be bypassed. Our pick for his best 1989 card is Topps.

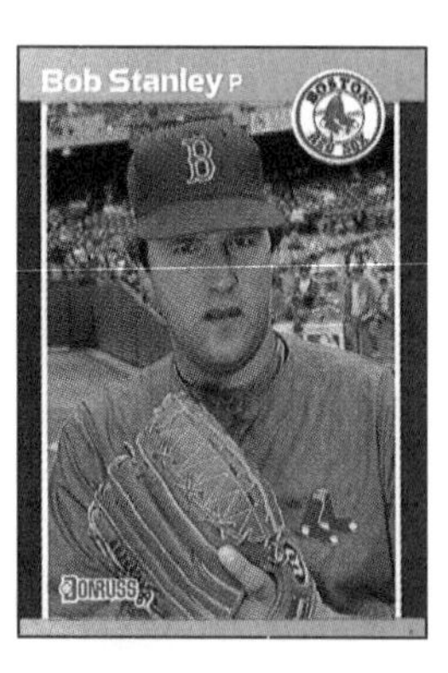

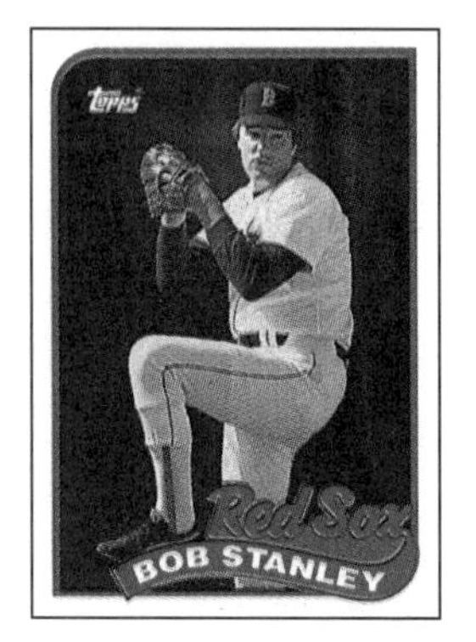

MIKE STANLEY

	BA	G	AB	R	H	2B	3B	HR	RBI	SB
1988	.229	94	249	21	57	8	0	3	27	0
Life	.255	187	495	59	126	19	1	10	65	4

POSITION: Catcher
TEAM: Texas Rangers
BORN: June 25, 1963
Fort Lauderdale, FL
HEIGHT: 6′1″ **WEIGHT:** 185 lbs.
BATS: Right **THROWS:** Right
ACQUIRED: 16th-round pick in 6/85 free-agent draft

Stanley served as the platoon catcher for the 1988 Texas Rangers in 1988, sharing the duties with incumbent Geno Petralli. Petralli played a bit more than Stanley did, but Stanley's defense seemed to be the best of the pair. Stanley only committed four errors in 94 games. Stanley won the starting catcher's job near the end of the 1987 season, hitting .273 with six homers and 37 RBIs in 78 games. Petralli had one of the best offensive seasons of his career in 1988, which will make things tougher for Stanley during his quest for more playing time.

Stanley's cards will be selling as commons in 1989. His cards aren't investment-worthy right now. However, if Stanley gets more playing time and hits like he did in 1987, things could change quickly. Our pick for his best 1989 card is Topps.

DAVE STAPLETON

	W	L	ERA	G	SV	IP	H	R	BB	SO
1988	0	0	5.93	6	0	13.2	20	9	9	6
Life	2	0	3.81	10	0	28.1	33	12	12	20

POSITION: Pitcher
TEAM: Milwaukee Brewers
BORN: October 16, 1961 Miami, AZ
HEIGHT: 6′ **WEIGHT:** 185 lbs.
BATS: Left **THROWS:** Left
ACQUIRED: Signed as a free agent, 9/83

Stapleton entered the 1988 season being looked upon as one of the Brewers' bullpen regulars. What resulted was an average year that obscured his exciting debut in late 1987. Stapleton won two of the four games he appeared in during his inaugural campaign, and his ERA was an admirable 1.84. Last year, however, was all downhill. The Brewers, contenders until the last week of the 1988 season, will be nurturing a youthful pitching corps for another pennant run. The return of Stapleton could be an important asset in that effort.

After two brief major league seasons, Stapleton remains an untried commodity. Based on his lack of experience, his future is harder to predict. Until he can post a full season in the majors, stay away from investing in his cards, even priced as commons. Our pick for his best 1989 card is Score.

TERRY STEINBACH

	BA	G	AB	R	H	2B	3B	HR	RBI	SB
1988	.265	104	351	42	93	19	1	9	51	3
Life	.276	232	757	111	209	35	4	27	111	4

POSITION: Catcher
TEAM: Oakland A's
BORN: March 2, 1962 New Ulm, MN
HEIGHT: 6'1" **WEIGHT:** 195 lbs.
BATS: Right **THROWS:** Right
ACQUIRED: Ninth-round pick in 6/83 free-agent draft

Steinbach had a fine season, considering that he missed 58 games due to an injury. His limited efforts helped the A's to the American League championship, and his early accomplishments helped him capture a spot on the American League All-Star Team. Steinbach's crucial home run earned him the game's MVP award. His defensive abilities are underrated, considering that he only learned the position of catcher in 1986, after coming up through the A's system as an infielder. If Steinbach is healthy in 1989, he may finally get to display his full talents.

Steinbach's 1989 cards should sell for around a dime, considering the renewed popularity of the A's and all of their players. Pick up his cards while they're cheap. As Steinbach improves, his card values will soar. Our pick for his best 1989 card is Fleer.

DAVE STEWART

	W	L	ERA	G	CG	IP	H	R	BB	SO
1988	21	12	3.23	37	14	275.2	240	111	110	192
Life	80	65	3.75	321	31	1303.0	1195	599	525	881

POSITION: Pitcher
TEAM: Oakland A's
BORN: February 19, 1957 Oakland, CA
HEIGHT: 6'2" **WEIGHT:** 200 lbs.
BATS: Right **THROWS:** Right
ACQUIRED: Signed as a free agent, 5/86

After an undistinguished decade in organized baseball, righthanded Stewart had accomplished little with three big league clubs. But in 1987, he had a surprising 20-13 season with the Athletics, and repeated his success in 1988 with a career-high 21-12 campaign, enhanced by 192 strikeouts. He also lowered his ERA to 3.23 in 1988 from 1987's 3.68 ERA. He was among league leaders in several categories and was a top contender for the Cy Young Award (finishing fourth) for the second straight year. At age 32, Stewart proved that his comeback is no fluke. This big forkballer should be a regular winner for years to come.

Stewart's convincing 1988 effort should boost his 1989 cards to 10 cents each. He'll never be a Hall of Famer, considering that he has not yet won 100 games. But his turnaround could increase his card prices to a quarter, if he keeps on winning. Our pick for his best 1989 card is Topps.

DAVE STIEB

	W	L	ERA	G	CG	IP	H	R	BB	SO
1988	16	8	3.04	32	8	207.1	157	76	79	147
Life	131	109	3.37	324	96	2251.2	1994	941	797	1331

POSITION: Pitcher
TEAM: Toronto Blue Jays
BORN: July 22, 1957 Santa Ana, CA
HEIGHT: 6′1″ **WEIGHT:** 195 lbs.
BATS: Right **THROWS:** Right
ACQUIRED: Fifth-round pick in 6/78 free-agent draft

Stieb remained the dean of the Toronto pitching staff in 1988. His victories were the most since his 1984 season, and his ERA was the lowest since his league-leading mark of 2.48 in 1985. Stieb claimed eight complete games and four shutouts during his fine campaign. A perennial All-Star, he is one of the American League's most proven winners. Because he's played for only one pennant winner in his career, he isn't sufficiently recognized for his success. While this isn't justified for Stieb, it could be a bonus for card investors.

Stieb's 1989 cards won't be more than a dime. He will be closing in on 200 wins and 2,000 strikeouts. All it would take would be one Cy Young Award to triple the value of his cards. Buy before that happens. Our pick for his best 1989 card is Topps.

KURT STILLWELL

	BA	G	AB	R	H	2B	3B	HR	RBI	SB
1988	.251	128	459	63	115	28	5	10	53	6
Life	.248	363	1133	148	281	54	13	14	112	16

POSITION: Shortstop
TEAM: Kansas City Royals
BORN: June 4, 1965 Thousand Oaks, CA
HEIGHT: 5′11″ **WEIGHT:** 175 lbs.
BATS: Both **THROWS:** Right
ACQUIRED: Traded from Reds for Danny Jackson and Angel Salazar, 11/87

All it took was a change of scenery for Stillwell to have one of his best seasons ever. He joined the Royals after two years with Cincinnati. He set career highs for himself with ten homers and 53 RBIs. Although he missed more than 30 games, Stillwell proved that he could handle the position of shortstop on a full-time basis. He fielded his territory well, making just 13 errors all season. The Royals have been needing a solid hitter at shortstop for years, and it seems that he is the answer. At age 23, Stillwell should be a fixture there for many years.

Here's a chance to get the jump on other investors. Stillwell is a young, underrated shortstop with tons of potential. Get his 1989 card while it's priced at under a nickel. Our pick for his best 1989 card is Fleer.

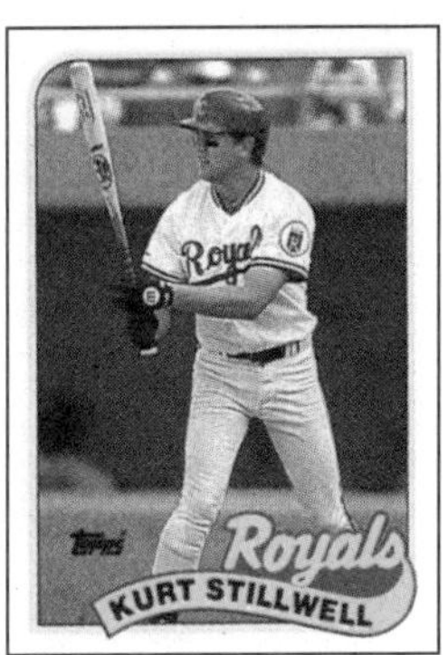

TODD STOTTLEMYRE

	W	L	ERA	G	CG	IP	H	R	BB	SO
1988	4	8	5.69	28	0	98.0	109	70	46	67
Life	4	8	5.69	28	0	98.0	109	70	46	67

POSITION: Pitcher
TEAM: Toronto Blue Jays
BORN: May 20, 1965 Sunnyside, WA
HEIGHT: 6′3″ **WEIGHT:** 190 lbs.
BATS: Left **THROWS:** Right
ACQUIRED: First-round pick in secondary phase of 6/85 free-agent draft

Stottlemyre was probably the hardest thrower in the Triple-A International League. That's good because fastballers get to the major leagues; that's bad because that's his only pitch, and one-pitch hurlers don't have long big league careers. In 1988 at Triple-A Syracuse, the righthander went 7-1, with 51 Ks in $48\frac{1}{3}$ innings. With Toronto in '88, he lost twice as many as he won and spent some time on the disabled list. Stottlemyre's dad Mel had a long pitching career and is currently pitching coach for the Mets. Todd could be in the majors quite a while with his talent.

At age 23, Stottlemyre has plenty of time to come up with a better breaking ball and an off-speed pitch to complete his arsenal. His 1989 cards will sell in the 25- to 35-cent range. Our pick for his best 1989 card is Topps.

DARRYL STRAWBERRY

	BA	G	AB	R	H	2B	3B	HR	RBI	SB
1988	.269	153	543	101	146	27	3	39	101	29
Life	.266	823	2885	501	768	143	28	186	548	165

POSITION: Outfield
TEAM: New York Mets
BORN: March 12, 1962 Los Angeles, CA
HEIGHT: 6′6″ **WEIGHT:** 190 lbs.
BATS: Left **THROWS:** Left
ACQUIRED: First-round pick in 6/80 free-agent draft

Strawberry followed his stunning 1987 season with another sparkling effort in 1988. He led the National League in home runs with 39 and was among league leaders in various other categories. No one seemed to notice that Strawberry's average slipped almost 20 points. It's a small price to pay for being a league-leading power hitter like Strawberry. He has never hit fewer than 26 homers a year in his six-year career. Behind all the hype is truly one of this decade's best ballplayers. In this coming season, another peak performance will establish Strawberry as the best in the league.

Strawberry's 1989 cards will sell for about 35 to 45 cents each. If you can pick them up at that price, do it. They could go for more than 75 cents each if he has a fast start in 1989. Our pick for his best 1989 card is Topps.

FRANKLIN STUBBS

	BA	G	AB	R	H	2B	3B	HR	RBI	SB
1988	.223	115	242	30	54	13	0	8	34	11
Life	.222	473	1274	155	283	42	7	55	163	28

POSITION: First base
TEAM: Los Angeles Dodgers
BORN: October 21, 1960 Laurinburg, NC
HEIGHT: 6'2" **WEIGHT:** 209 lbs.
BATS: Left **THROWS:** Left
ACQUIRED: First-round pick in 6/81 free-agent draft

Stubbs became the Dodgers' starting first baseman after Pedro Guerrero was traded to St. Louis in mid-season. Stubbs had his lowest number of home runs since his 1984 debut with the Dodgers. He has never been a high-average hitter. The best he's ever done was a .233 effort for 129 games in 1987. Instead, Stubbs specializes in home runs. He paced the 1986 team with 23 home runs, and added 16 more in 1987. Stubbs did steal a career-high 11 bases in 1988, the fourth-highest on the club.

Stubbs struck out approximately once for every four at-bats in 1988. His 1989 cards should be a nickel apiece, but they're not great investments. Stubbs needs to hit at least .250 with at least 20 homers a year before investors will take his cards seriously. Our pick for his best 1989 card is Topps.

B.J. SURHOFF

	BA	G	AB	R	H	2B	3B	HR	RBI	SB
1988	.245	139	493	47	121	21	0	5	38	21
Life	.269	254	888	97	239	43	3	12	106	32

POSITION: Catcher
TEAM: Milwaukee Brewers
BORN: August 4, 1964 Bronx, NY
HEIGHT: 6'1" **WEIGHT:** 190 lbs.
BATS: Left **THROWS:** Right
ACQUIRED: First-round pick in 6/85 free-agent draft

Surhoff didn't match the statistics he posted during an impressive 1987 rookie season, but he managed to convince fans that he can handle the full-time catching duties for the Brewers. After being platooned in 1987 with Bill Schroeder, Surhoff saw action in an additional 24 games in 1988. His second-year offense totals were somewhat deflated, but he showed the all-around ability that convinced the Brewers to bring him up after just two minor league seasons. He led all A.L. backstops with 21 stolen bases. At age 24, Surhoff is just starting to establish himself as one of baseball's finest receivers.

Expect Surhoff's 1989 cards to be selling as high as a quarter. If you can find them cheaper, buy. His cards could climb to 35 cents if the Brewers win their division. Our pick for his best 1989 card is Score.

RICK SUTCLIFFE

	W	L	ERA	G	CG	IP	H	R	BB	SO
1988	13	14	3.86	32	12	226.0	232	97	70	144
Life	117	92	3.83	317	59	1880.0	1783	872	775	1252

POSITION: Pitcher
TEAM: Chicago Cubs
BORN: June 21, 1956 Independence, MO
HEIGHT: 6'7" **WEIGHT:** 215 lbs.
BATS: Left **THROWS:** Right
ACQUIRED: Traded from Indians with Ron Hassey and George Frazier for Joe Carter, Mel Hall, Don Schulze, and Darryl Banks, 6/84

Sutcliffe's 1988 mark of 13-14 obscured his 12 complete games and two shutouts in 226 innings of work. Still, he slumped from his 18-10 record of 1987, when he came within a hair of winning his second Cy Young Award. Sutcliffe's best year ever was his 16-1 outing with the 1984 Cubs, as he led the team to its first pennant since 1945. He had won four games earlier that year with the Tribe, giving him his only 20-game winning season ever. In 1988, he paced the Cubs with 144 strikeouts, giving up only 70 bases on balls and finishing with a 3.86 ERA. With a little more run-scoring support, Sutcliffe could be a big winner again for the Cubs in 1989.

Sutcliffe's 1989 cards will be a nickel or less. They're a good investment, especially if Sutcliffe can once again reach the 20-game mark. Our pick for his best 1989 card is Topps.

BRUCE SUTTER

	W	L	ERA	G	SV	IP	H	R	BB	SO
1988	1	4	4.76	38	14	45.1	49	26	11	40
Life	68	71	2.84	661	300	1040.2	879	370	309	861

POSITION: Pitcher
TEAM: Atlanta Braves
BORN: January 8, 1953 Lancaster, PA
HEIGHT: 6'2" **WEIGHT:** 195 lbs.
BATS: Right **THROWS:** Right
ACQUIRED: Signed as a free agent, 12/84

Possibly the biggest highlight in the Braves' dismal 1988 season was the triumphant return of relief ace Sutter. He missed 1987 due to elbow surgery, but came back strongly in 1988. Sutter led the Braves in saves, and reached the 300-save level for his career before the season ended. He holds the N.L. season record for saves with 45, and has led the league in saves on five occasions. He trails only Rollie Fingers (341 saves) and Rich Gossage (302 saves) in career saves. With two more strong seasons, Sutter will get even closer to Hall of Fame election.

Incredibly, some dealers might sell Sutter's card as a three-cent common. His 1989 issues are worth investing in, particularly if he retires after this season. Sutter has a strong shot for Hall of Fame election. Our pick for his best 1989 card is Topps.

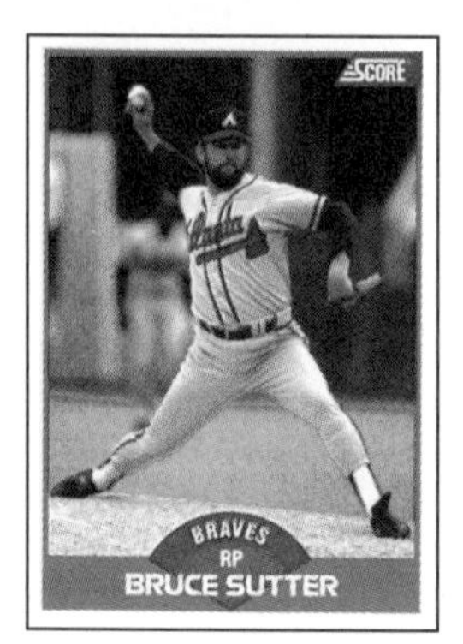

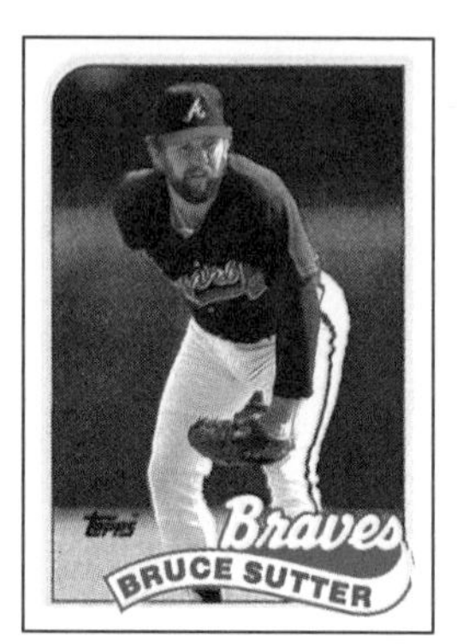

DALE SVEUM

	BA	G	AB	R	H	2B	3B	HR	RBI	SB
1988	.242	129	467	41	113	14	4	9	51	1
Life	.247	373	1319	162	326	54	9	41	181	7

POSITION: Shortstop
TEAM: Milwaukee Brewers
BORN: November 23, 1963
Richmond, CA
HEIGHT: 6′3″ **WEIGHT:** 185 lbs.
BATS: Both **THROWS:** Right
ACQUIRED: First-round pick in 6/82 free-agent draft

Sveum missed 33 games in 1988 and lost the chance to repeat his accomplishments from 1987. He assumed the starting shortstop duties for the Brewers in 1987. With 25 homers and 95 RBIs, it looked like he could join the ranks of hard-hitting shortstops like Cal Ripken and Alan Trammell. However, Sveum's output plummeted in 1988, as his homer and RBI totals nearly shrank by half. He made the most errors of any A.L. shortstop (27). His strikeout total (122) was second only to Rob Deer on the Brewers. Once Sveum gains more consistency in his play, he'll be considered among the best shortstops in the game.

After his 1988 tailspin, Sveum's cards should be no more than a nickel. Homer-hitting shortstops are a rare breed, and Sveum definitely has the potential for stardom. Our pick for his best 1989 card is Donruss.

BILL SWIFT

	W	L	ERA	G	CG	IP	H	R	BB	SO
1988	8	12	4.59	38	6	174.2	199	99	65	47
Life	16	31	4.89	90	7	410.2	478	255	168	157

POSITION: Pitcher
TEAM: Seattle Mariners
BORN: December 27, 1961 Portland, ME
HEIGHT: 6′ **WEIGHT:** 170 lbs.
BATS: Right **THROWS:** Right
ACQUIRED: First-round pick in 6/84 free-agent draft

Swift battled back from a year in the minors to regain a pitching spot with the 1988 Seattle Mariners. Despite his losing record, he earned six complete games and a shutout. His biggest problem remained too many walks. In his career, Swift's walks outnumber his strikeouts by 11. In 1984, Swift was a member of the U.S. Olympic team. Since his pro career began, he has endured time on the disabled list and a lack of control. Swift may have some fierce competition in his attempt to win a place on the team roster in 1989.

Swift's problems have been compounded by pitching for a low-scoring team that gives its pitchers few leads to work with. His career statistics are weak; his 1989 common-priced cards won't be worth the effort of investing. Our pick for his best 1989 card is Topps.

GREG SWINDELL

	W	L	ERA	G	CG	IP	H	R	BB	SO
1988	18	14	3.20	33	12	242.0	234	97	45	180
Life	26	24	3.83	58	17	406.0	403	194	97	323

POSITION: Pitcher
TEAM: Cleveland Indians
BORN: January 2, 1965 Fort Worth, TX
HEIGHT: 6'2" **WEIGHT:** 225 lbs.
BATS: Right **THROWS:** Left
ACQUIRED: First-round pick in 6/86 free-agent draft

Swindell rebounded from an elbow injury to lead the 1988 Indians in pitching. A second-half slump stopped him from winning 20 games, although his final record was 18-14 with a 3.20 ERA. His 1988 accomplishments included 12 complete games and four shutouts. Only Roger Clemens and Dave Stewart logged more complete games in 1988. Swindell is a hard-throwing lefty with only three games of minor league experience in 1986. If the Tribe wants to be a competitive team in 1989, they'll need another winning season from Swindell to do it.

Be ready to pay a quarter for Swindell's 1989 cards. That might seem high for such an inexperienced pitcher, but he will keep improving and his cards will keep gaining value. He could be one of the top A.L. hurlers in 1989. Our pick for his best 1989 card is Topps.

PAT TABLER

	BA	G	AB	R	H	2B	3B	HR	RBI	SB
1988	.282	130	444	53	125	22	3	2	66	3
Life	.291	856	2963	369	861	154	22	42	404	16

POSITION: Designated hitter; first base
TEAM: Kansas City Royals
BORN: February 2, 1958 Hamilton, OH
HEIGHT: 6'2" **WEIGHT:** 200 lbs.
BATS: Right **THROWS:** Right
ACQUIRED: Traded from Indians for Bud Black, 6/88

Tabler gave the Royals a versatile fielder and a dependable hitter when he was acquired in mid-1988. He was a long-time standout for the Tribe, playing both first base and the outfield. The Royals, however, are interested in turning him into a full-time designated hitter. Tabler, always a high-average performer, has a reputation for hitting well with the bases loaded. Although he's never been a power hitter by trade, he banged out a career-best 11 homers and 86 RBIs in 1987. Tabler, only age 31, will be a dynamic force in the 1989 Royals' offense.

Tabler's 1989 cards will start at a nickel. His cards would never make an investor rich, but they could go as high as 15 cents if the Royals win a pennant with his help. Our pick for his best 1989 card is Score.

FRANK TANANA

	W	L	ERA	G	CG	IP	H	R	BB	SO
1988	14	11	4.21	32	2	203.0	213	105	64	127
Life	188	174	3.48	474	130	3180.0	3025	1391	892	2189

POSITION: Pitcher
TEAM: Detroit Tigers
BORN: July 3, 1953 Detroit, MI
HEIGHT: 6'3" **WEIGHT:** 195 lbs.
BATS: Left **THROWS:** Left
ACQUIRED: Traded from Rangers for Duane James, 6/85

Tanana kept on winning as a member of the 1988 Tigers. He tied for the second-highest win total on the team with 14. Tanana's high ERA was partly due to yielding 25 homers. He first started his career as a young fireballer with the Angels in '73. His best season there was a 19-10 performance in 1976. Only one year earlier, he tied for the league lead in strikeouts with 269. Tanana seems to have found a home with the Tigers, where he should gain his 200th career win in 1989.

Tanana got little acclaim for his work with losing teams, and his 1989 cards won't sell for more than a nickel. Unless he could win 20 games for the first time in his career, his cards won't be going up in value for a long time. Our pick for his best 1989 card is Topps.

DANNY TARTABULL

	BA	G	AB	R	H	2B	3B	HR	RBI	SB
1988	.274	146	507	80	139	38	3	26	102	8
Life	.287	470	1681	262	483	98	13	88	313	22

POSITION: Outfield
TEAM: Kansas City Royals
BORN: October 30, 1962 San Juan, Puerto Rico
HEIGHT: 6'1" **WEIGHT:** 185 lbs.
BATS: Right **THROWS:** Right
ACQUIRED: Traded from Mariners with Rick Luecken for Scott Bankhead, Steve Shields, and Mike Kingery, 12/86

Tartabull's 1988 performance seemed like an instant replay of his superb 1987 season. He was just short on his chase for 30 home runs, ending with 26. He maintained his role as a chief run-producer for the Royals, driving in 102 and scoring 80. His batting average dropped more than 30 points in 1988, but no one seems to mind as long as he keeps hitting for power. He is the son of former major leaguer Jose Tartabull. In '87, Danny hit .309 and had 34 homers and 101 RBIs. He hit 25 homers and 96 RBIs in 1986, his first full season in the bigs. Tartabull and teammate Bo Jackson give Kansas City one of the most powerful outfield tandems of the future.

Tartabull's cards will sell in the neighborhood of 25 cents in 1989. Those prices could double if the Royals contend for the pennant. Our pick for his best 1989 card is Topps.

KENT TEKULVE

	W	L	ERA	G	SV	IP	H	R	BB	SO
1988	3	7	3.60	70	4	80.0	87	34	22	43
Life	94	87	2.77	1013	183	1284.1	1249	491	468	748

POSITION: Pitcher
TEAM: Philadelphia Phillies
BORN: March 5, 1957 Cincinnati, OH
HEIGHT: 6′4″ **WEIGHT:** 190 lbs.
BATS: Right **THROWS:** Right
ACQUIRED: Traded from Pirates for Al Holland and Frankie Griffin, 4/85

Tekulve is coming off what was for him an off-year. At age 41, he pitched in 70 games, the most on the Phillies' staff. He ended with a 3.60 ERA, a 3-7 record, and four saves. In 1987, Tekulve appeared in 90 games—the oldest pitcher (40) to ever lead the league in that category—and he had a 6-4 record. A big league pitcher for 15 years, he was a 27-year-old rookie when he broke in with the Pirates in 1974. In his 20-year pro career, he started just 15 games, all in the minors. Tekulve was the mainstay of the Pirate relief corps from 1975 through 1984.

Tekulve's 1989 cards are sleepers because one day his relief exploits might earn him a niche in the Hall of Fame. His cards cost a nickel apiece. Just put them away as speculation. Our pick for his best 1989 card is Score.

GARRY TEMPLETON

	BA	G	AB	R	H	2B	3B	HR	RBI	SB
1988	.249	110	362	35	90	15	7	3	36	8
Life	.277	1681	6434	780	1781	268	98	52	603	237

POSITION: Shortstop
TEAM: San Diego Padres
BORN: March 24, 1956 Lockey, TX
HEIGHT: 5′11″ **WEIGHT:** 193 lbs.
BATS: Both **THROWS:** Right
ACQUIRED: Traded from Cardinals for Ozzie Smith, 2/82

Templeton had one of the shortest seasons of his career in 1988. He has been one of baseball's most durable shortstops since he broke in with the Cardinals in 1976. However, Templeton missed 52 games in 1988. His hitting suffered as a result. His power stats were the lowest since 1985. Templeton once was one of the National League's flashiest shortstops. In 1979, he led the National League with 211 hits and was the first player ever to obtain 100 hits each batting lefthanded and righthanded. At age 32, Templeton is showing definite signs of slowing down.

Templeton needs to play around 150 games and rediscover his hitting groove if he wants to stick with the Padres. Currently, his 1989 cards are a nickel or less. Until Templeton plays a full season again, avoid investing in his cards. Our pick for his best 1989 card is Fleer.

WALT TERRELL

	W	L	ERA	G	CG	IP	H	R	BB	SO
1988	7	16	3.97	29	11	206.1	199	101	78	84
Life	73	71	3.94	189	42	1267.0	1250	615	514	631

POSITION: Pitcher
TEAM: San Diego Padres
BORN: May 11, 1958 Jeffersonville, IN
HEIGHT: 6'2" **WEIGHT:** 205 lbs.
BATS: Left **THROWS:** Right
ACQUIRED: Traded from Tigers for Chris Brown and Keith Moreland, 10/88

Terrrell had an uncharacteristically bad season in 1988 with the Tigers. His 7-16 record is an all-time low, even worse than his 8-8 performance with the Mets in 1983. Terrell did maintain his reputation as a long-distance performer, working more than 200 innings for the fifth consecutive season. His 11 complete games led the Tigers in that category. The Padres must have lots of hope for Terrell, because they sacrificed two starting infielders to get him. The move should be successful for Terrell, because he's been out of the National League for four years and many hitters won't remember his pitches.

Terrell's 1989 cards will be a nickel or less. Although he has a fair lifetime record, we'd recommend investing in his cards. Both Terrell and the Padre team in general should have surprising success in 1989. Our pick for his best 1989 card is Fleer.

SCOTT TERRY

	W	L	ERA	G	CG	IP	H	R	BB	SO
1988	9	6	2.92	51	1	129.1	119	48	34	65
Life	10	8	3.86	90	1	198.1	198	93	74	106

POSITION: Pitcher
TEAM: St. Louis Cardinals
BORN: November 21, 1959 Hobbs, NM
HEIGHT: 5'10" **WEIGHT:** 190 lbs.
BATS: Right **THROWS:** Right
ACQUIRED: Traded from Reds for Pat Perry, 8/87

Terry spent part of last season as a Cardinal starter and part of it as a reliever. The end result was a 9-6 record, a 2.92 ERA, and three saves in 51 appearances. It was a satisfying season for him because, honestly, time was beginning to run out on his career. Signed by the Reds as an outfielder in 1980, the Cincinnati organization opted to take advantage of Terry's strong arm, and he split time between the mound and the outfield, batting .238 and going 3-3 with six saves and a 4.25 ERA in Class-A ball in 1983. Terry's strong arm should help the Cards in 1989.

Terry's cards are commons at the moment. He is a novelty, in that he's a solid hitter as well as a good pitcher. Unfortunately, there's little collector interest in such novelties. Our pick for his best 1989 card is Topps.

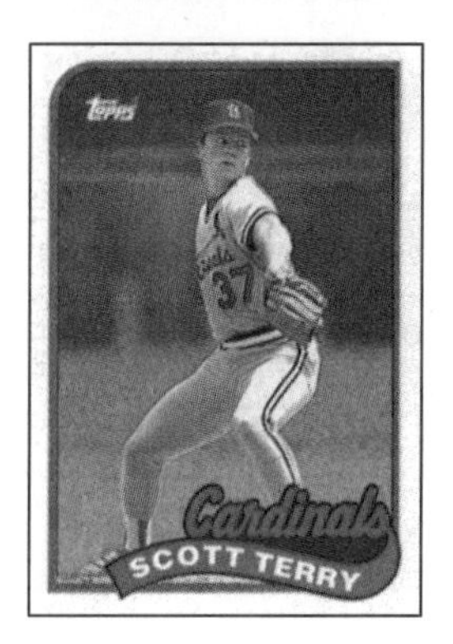

MICKEY TETTLETON

	BA	G	AB	R	H	2B	3B	HR	RBI	SB
1988	.261	86	283	31	74	11	1	11	37	0
Life	.233	369	992	109	231	37	2	33	118	10

POSITION: Catcher
TEAM: Baltimore Orioles
BORN: September 16, 1960
Oklahoma City, OK
HEIGHT: 6′2″ **WEIGHT:** 195 lbs.
BATS: Both **THROWS:** Right
ACQUIRED: Signed as a free agent, 4/88

Tettleton split the 1988 Baltimore Orioles' catching duties with Terry Kennedy and produced one of the best seasons of his career. Tettleton hit a career high of 11 home runs and 37 RBIs. He ranked behind only Cal Ripken, Jr., and Eddie Murray for the O's home run lead. Also, Tettleton had a personal-best .261 batting average. He's a fine fielder, as evidenced by only three errors during 1988. Baltimore will be looking for any help for its shaky offense in 1989. In the quest for more power, Tettleton may get more playing time this year.

Tettleton's prior statistics read like those of most second-string catchers. His 1988 efforts could be a turning point in his career. However, wait until Tettleton lands a starting job before investing in his common-priced cards. Our pick for his best 1989 card is Topps.

TIM TEUFEL

	BA	G	AB	R	H	2B	3B	HR	RBI	SB
1988	.234	90	273	35	64	20	0	4	31	0
Life	.265	596	1931	270	511	130	8	49	240	9

POSITION: Second base
TEAM: New York Mets
BORN: July 8, 1958 Greenwich, CT
HEIGHT: 6′ **WEIGHT:** 175 lbs.
BATS: Right **THROWS:** Right
ACQUIRED: Traded from Twins with Pat Crosby for Billy Beane, Bill Latham, and Joe Klink, 1/86

Teufel will finally get a shot at starting full-time for the Mets in 1989, which should end his perpetual state of unhappiness since being dealt to New York by the Twins in January 1986. He spent the last three seasons sharing second base with Wally Backman, who ironically was traded to the Twins in the off-season. In 1988, Teufel played in 90 games, batted .234, and drove in 31 runs from the right side of the plate. He was a regular with the Twins in 1984 and 1985. He hit .262 in 157 games in 1984 and .260 in 138 games in 1985. Teufel could find similar success with the Mets playing every day in '89.

Teufel's career so far is that of a utilityman. Look for his 1989 cards in the commons box. They could be a find if he becomes a fixture. Our pick for his best 1989 card is Topps.

BOBBY THIGPEN

	W	L	ERA	G	SV	IP	H	R	BB	SO
1988	5	8	3.30	68	34	90.0	96	38	33	62
Life	14	13	2.81	139	57	214.2	208	75	69	134

POSITION: Pitcher
TEAM: Chicago White Sox
BORN: July 17, 1963 Tallahassee, FL
HEIGHT: 6′3″ **WEIGHT:** 195 lbs.
BATS: Right **THROWS:** Right
ACQUIRED: Fourth-round pick in 6/85 free-agent draft

Thigpen set a White Sox club record for saves in 1988, with 34. His fine season wasn't enough to carry the entire club, however, because all the rest of Chicago's bullpen put together a total of only eight saves. Thigpen, meanwhile, finished more than 90 percent of the games he appeared in. In 1987, he saved 16 games and was 7-5 (all in relief), with a 2.73 ERA. It's possible that the White Sox could get another urge to convert Thigpen into a starter. If so, they may be erasing the potential of one of the league's future relief stars.

Less than 5 cents should get you a 1989 Thigpen card. Because he is one of the main elements in the fortunes of the White Sox, his cards could bring long-term gains. Relief pitchers, however, usually don't bring high short-term profits Our pick for his best 1989 card is Score.

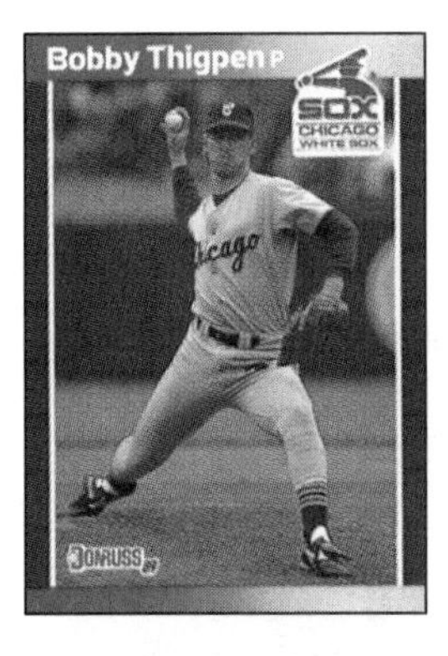

ANDRES THOMAS

	BA	G	AB	R	H	2B	3B	HR	RBI	SB
1988	.252	153	606	54	153	22	2	13	68	7
Life	.247	352	1271	115	314	50	4	24	141	17

POSITION: Shortstop
TEAM: Atlanta Braves
BORN: November 10, 1963 Santo Domingo, Dominican Republic
HEIGHT: 6′1″ **WEIGHT:** 185 lbs.
BATS: Right **THROWS:** Right
ACQUIRED: Signed as a free agent, 12/81

Thomas was second only to Dale Murphy in games played for the 1988 Braves. Thomas played in 153 contests in 1988, a pleasant turnaround from his injury-shortened season of 1987. He was one of the finest power-hitting shortstops in the N.L. last season. Thomas had the fifth-best average on the team (.252) and was third on the team in home runs (13). He got his first crack at starting in 1988 after sharing the job with Rafael Ramirez for two seasons. He should be a regular on the Brave team for many years. Thomas and Ronnie Gant give Atlanta a good, young double-play combination.

Solid-hitting shortstops are a rare breed, so Thomas might have the inside track on stardom. Invest in his 1989 cards, which should be a nickel or less. Our pick for his best 1989 card is Fleer.

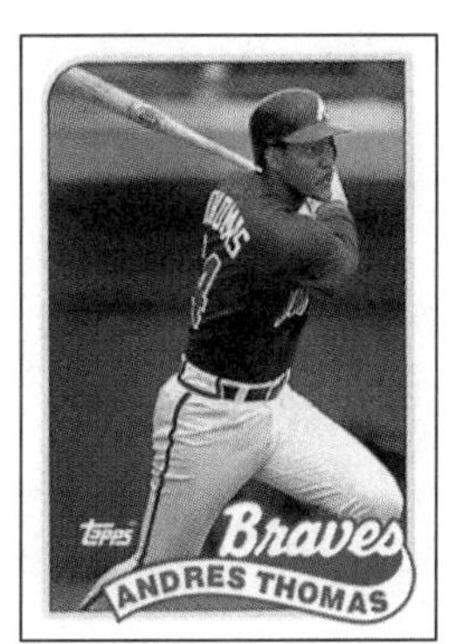

MILT THOMPSON

	BA	G	AB	R	H	2B	3B	HR	RBI	SB
1988	.288	122	378	53	109	16	2	2	33	17
Life	.288	466	1485	210	428	57	14	17	109	105

POSITION: Outfield
TEAM: Philadelphia Phillies
BORN: January 5, 1959 Washington, DC
HEIGHT: 5′11″ **WEIGHT:** 160 lbs.
BATS: Left **THROWS:** Right
ACQUIRED: Traded from Braves with Steve Bedrosian for Ozzie Virgil and Pete Smith, 12/85

Thompson split center field duties with Bob Dernier in 1988, and between them, center field was the most consistent spot in the Phils' lineup. Thompson batted .288, exactly at his lifetime mark. He also scored 53 runs and stole 17 bases. In 1987, he hit a career-high .302 in 150 games for the Phillies. He also stole 46 bases and scored 86 runs. Thompson hit .251 for the Phils his first season with them, in 1986. He came to Philadelphia in the Steve Bedrosian deal in December 1985. Thompson is one of those extremely fast players who covers a lot of ground in the field and can bunt his way on base.

Thompson's career seems destined to be that of a role-player; consequently his cards will never gain any premium value. Our pick for his best 1989 card is Topps.

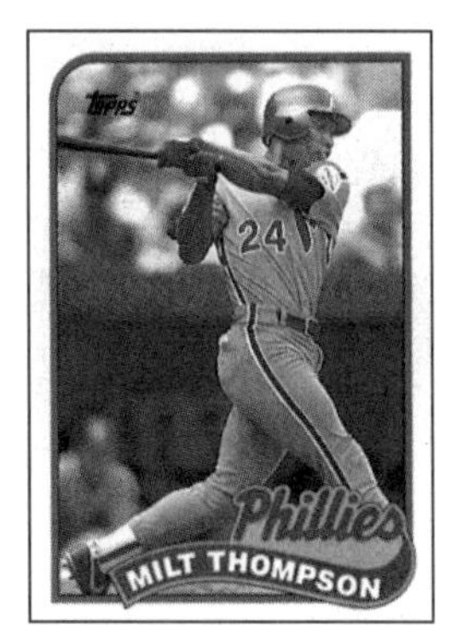

ROBBY THOMPSON

	BA	G	AB	R	H	2B	3B	HR	RBI	SB
1988	.264	138	477	66	126	24	6	7	48	14
Life	.266	419	1446	201	385	77	14	24	139	42

POSITION: Second base
TEAM: San Francisco Giants
BORN: May 10, 1962
West Palm Beach, FL
HEIGHT: 5′11″ **WEIGHT:** 170 lbs.
BATS: Right **THROWS:** Right
ACQUIRED: First-round pick in 6/83 free-agent draft

Minor injuries have slowed the progress of Thompson, the Giants' promising second baseman, during the past two seasons. He hit .264, with 66 runs scored, seven homers, and 48 RBIs in 1988. While not a base stealer, his 14 swipes tied him for second on the Giants. His steady defense helped start a club-record 183 double plays in 1987. He hit .262 in '87. In 1986, he made the jump from Double-A to the team's starting lineup. He hit .271 that year, with 73 runs scored. Steady defense and scrappy hitting continue to be the reasons San Francisco counts on Thompson at second base.

Thompson's 1989 cards will be priced as commons. His current stats don't merit huge price climbs for his cards, so investing heavily isn't recommended. His tenacious attitude, however, could change things. Our pick for his best 1989 card is Donruss.

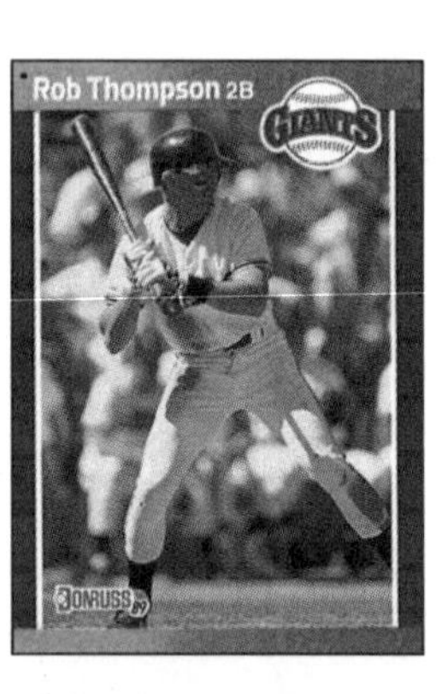

DICKIE THON

	BA	G	AB	R	H	2B	3B	HR	RBI	SB
1988	.264	95	258	36	68	12	2	1	18	19
Life	.269	776	2403	300	647	112	26	34	213	120

POSITION: Infield
TEAM: San Diego Padres
BORN: June 20, 1958 South Bend, IN
HEIGHT: 5′11″ **WEIGHT:** 175 lbs.
BATS: Right **THROWS:** Right
ACQUIRED: Signed as a free agent, 2/88

Thon made a remarkable comeback in 1988. In 1984, he was hit in the eye with a pitch, and though he had come back, his numbers had slowly decreased every season. He was released by the Astros after the 1987 season, and the Padres took a chance on him. Thon came through, with a .264 average and 36 runs scored. He had been a top-quality shortstop with the Astros prior to his injury. His best season for Houston was in 1983, when he hit .286, with 81 runs scored, 20 homers, 79 RBIs, and 34 stolen bases. Thon may never reach those numbers again, but he has achieved success with the Padres.

Thon's 1989 cards, unfortunately, will sell for less than a nickel. If he proceeds with his recovery, though, his stature and his card values will continue to increase. Our pick for his best 1989 card is Fleer.

GARY THURMAN

	BA	G	AB	R	H	2B	3B	HR	RBI	SB
1988	.167	35	66	6	11	1	0	0	2	5
Life	.238	62	147	18	35	3	0	0	7	12

POSITION: Outfield
TEAM: Kansas City Royals
BORN: November 12, 1964
Indianapolis, IN
HEIGHT: 5′10″ **WEIGHT:** 175 lbs.
BATS: Right **THROWS:** Right
ACQUIRED: First-round pick in 6/83 free-agent draft

Since Bo Jackson decided that baseball was more important than football, there was no room for Thurman in the Kansas City outfield. Thurman is a speedster, and he covers acres of territory in the outfield with the best of them. In 1988 at Omaha, his average slipped to .251 (he hit .293 the year before), but he's still very much in the Royals' 1989 plans. In a 1987 cameo with the Royals, Thurman hit .296 and five home runs. In 1988, however, he hit below .200 in limited action with the big club. Thurman has speed and some power, and he could be an important addition to the Royals' 1989 pennant hopes.

Look for Thurman's 1989 cards to open around a dime—or even in the commons box. If his potent bat of 1987 returns, his card values will soar. Our pick for his best 1989 card is Topps.

FRED TOLIVER

	W	L	ERA	G	CG	IP	H	R	BB	SO
1988	7	6	4.24	21	0	114.2	116	57	52	69
Life	8	13	4.24	50	0	205.2	212	107	104	141

POSITION: Pitcher
TEAM: Minnesota Twins
BORN: February 3, 1961 Natchez, MS
HEIGHT: 6′1″ **WEIGHT:** 170 lbs.
BATS: Right **THROWS:** Right
ACQUIRED: Traded from Phillies for Chris Calvert, 2/88

When Les Straker went down with a sore arm early in 1988, the Twins gave the ball to Toliver. He responded with an admirable outing. He finished the season at 7-6, with a 4.24 ERA, 114⅔ innings pitched, and 69 strikeouts. Toliver had great stats at Triple-A Portland before he was recalled by Minnesota. He was 7-2, with a 3.13 ERA, four complete games, 54 strikeouts, and only 35 bases on balls in 95 innings of work. In 1987 at Triple-A Maine, Toliver was 6-9, with a 4.62 ERA. He was recovering from a broken arm, which he suffered during the '86 season. The Twins hope that Toliver will be back in 1989 to be a fifth starter.

Toliver's 1989 cards will open in the 5-cent range. He still needs to prove that he can pitch effectively over a complete major league season. Our pick for his best 1989 card is Topps.

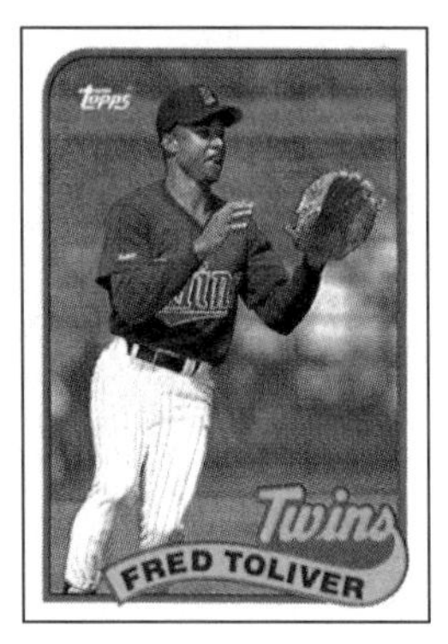

JIM TRABER

	BA	G	AB	R	H	2B	3B	HR	RBI	SB
1988	.222	103	352	25	78	6	0	10	45	1
Life	.234	178	585	56	137	13	0	23	91	1

POSITION: Outfield; designated hitter
TEAM: Baltimore Orioles
BORN: December 26, 1961 Columbus, OH
HEIGHT: 6′ **WEIGHT:** 195 lbs.
BATS: Left **THROWS:** Right
ACQUIRED: 21st-round pick in 6/82 free-agent draft

Traber played in a career-high 103 games with the 1988 Orioles, but he enjoyed only limited success. His ten home runs were the fourth most on the Orioles last season. His average was a so-so .222, but he drove in 45 runs, his best ever. Every team loves homers, and Traber could be a major producer. Therefore, he should get another chance with the O's in 1989. Between 1984 and 1988, he had bounced between Baltimore and Triple-A Rochester, unable to win a full-time job in the bigs. If he gets a starting job and plays a full season, Traber might produce some awesome statistics.

Traber's 1989 cards will be a nickel or less, a good price for speculators who believe that he could be a future home run king. Our pick for his best 1989 card is Fleer.

ALAN TRAMMELL

	BA	G	AB	R	H	2B	3B	HR	RBI	SB
1988	.311	128	466	73	145	24	1	15	69	7
Life	.290	1568	5694	884	1650	272	46	133	678	177

POSITION: Shortstop
TEAM: Detroit Tigers
BORN: February 21, 1958
Garden Grove, CA
HEIGHT: 6′ **WEIGHT:** 170 lbs.
BATS: Right **THROWS:** Right
ACQUIRED: Second-round pick in 6/76
free-agent draft

Trammell played his usual brand of quality baseball in 1988, his 11th full season in the majors. He led all Tiger regulars in batting average (.311), hits (145), and RBIs (69), an unusual feat for a shortstop. If he maintains his momentum, Trammell is just two seasons away from the 2,000-hit club. When he was put into the cleanup spot in 1986, he hit a career high .343, with 28 homers, 105 RBIs, and 109 runs scored. He may battle for another batting title soon if his hitting remains constant. Trammell, at age 31, has many good years ahead of him, years in which he'll help uphold the team's role as a perennial contender.

Trammell's 1989 cards should sell in the quarter range, and are worth accumulating at that price. He appears closer to Hall of Fame induction every year. Our pick for his best 1989 card is Topps.

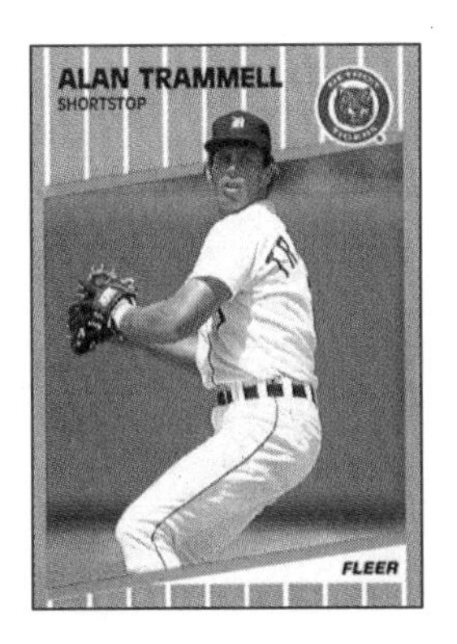

JEFF TREADWAY

	BA	G	AB	R	H	2B	3B	HR	RBI	SB
1988	.252	103	301	30	76	19	4	2	23	2
Life	.270	126	385	39	104	23	4	4	27	3

POSITION: Second base
TEAM: Cincinnati Reds
BORN: January 22, 1963 Columbus, GA
HEIGHT: 5′10″ **WEIGHT:** 170 lbs.
BATS: Left **THROWS:** Right
ACQUIRED: Signed as a free agent, 1/84

Treadway became a Red regular in 1988 and, though he batted around .250 all year, observers say he is the best of all the young infield talent that the Reds now have—including Chris Sabo and Barry Larkin. He has been a .300 hitter for most of his baseball career and in 1987, when the Reds recalled him from Triple-A Nashville, he hit a lofty .333 in 84 trips to the plate. At Nashville in 1987, Treadway batted .315 with 28 doubles, five triples, seven homers, and 59 RBIs. For the 1986 Double-A Vermont Reds, Treadway batted .336. In 1985, at Class-A Tampa, he notched a .309 average.

Treadway seems to be entrenched at second base for Cincinnati. His 1989 cards will open in the 25- to 30-cent range. That is too much to pay for a .250s hitter. Our pick for his best 1989 card is Donruss.

MANNY TRILLO

	BA	G	AB	R	H	2B	3B	HR	RBI	SB
1988	.250	76	164	15	41	5	0	1	14	2
Life	.263	1763	5911	595	1554	239	33	61	571	56

POSITION: Infield
TEAM: Chicago Cubs
BORN: December 25, 1950 Monagas, Venezuela
HEIGHT: 6′1″ **WEIGHT:** 165 lbs.
BATS: Right **THROWS:** Right
ACQUIRED: Traded from Giants for Dave Owen, 12/85

Trillo remained a constant performer for the Cubs in 1988. He played in 76 games, hitting .250 while playing all of the infield positions. He had his best season as a jack-of-all-trades for the Cubs in 1987. That year, he hit .294, with eight home runs, 26 RBIs, 27 runs scored, and eight doubles while playing in 108 games. Trillo first played in the big leagues in 1973 for the A's. Since that time, he has played with the Cubs, Phils, Indians, Expos, Giants, and the Cubs a second time. Trillo remains an experienced hand for Chicago.

Trillo's 1989 cards will be priced at 3 to 5 cents. Although he seems to get better with age, he still is not a starter. His cards probably will not gain in value. Our pick for his best 1989 card is Topps.

JOHN TUDOR

	W	L	ERA	G	CG	IP	H	R	BB	SO
1988	10	8	2.32	30	5	197.2	189	60	41	87
Life	105	68	3.18	250	49	1636.1	1540	647	439	916

POSITION: Pitcher
TEAM: Los Angeles Dodgers
BORN: February 2, 1954 Schenectady, NY
HEIGHT: 6′ **WEIGHT:** 185 lbs.
BATS: Left **THROWS:** Left
ACQUIRED: Traded from Cardinals for Pedro Guerrero, 9/88

Tudor came to the Dodgers late in the 1988 campaign and shored up L.A.'s pitching staff when Fernando Valenzuela was ailing. Tudor finished the year with a 10-8 record; his success made him the only active National League pitcher with at least ten victories in each of the past seven seasons. With a hard-hitting Dodgers team behind him, Tudor now has the backing needed to match his 1985 accomplishments: 21-8 record and a 1.93 ERA. Tudor gained his 100th career win in 1988, and should find lots more in 1989.

Tudor's 1989 cards will sell as commons. He may not be Hall of Fame material, but even one 20-game season could increase the value of his cards. Investors should settle for limited returns and sell quickly. Our pick for his best 1989 card is Score.

WILLIE UPSHAW

	BA	G	AB	R	H	2B	3B	HR	RBI	SB
1988	.245	149	493	58	121	22	3	11	50	12
Life	.262	1264	4203	596	1103	199	45	123	528	88

POSITION: First base
TEAM: Cleveland Indians
BORN: April 27, 1957 Blanco, TX
HEIGHT: 6′ **WEIGHT:** 195 lbs.
BATS: Left **THROWS:** Left
ACQUIRED: Purchased from Blue Jays, 3/88

Upshaw won the starting first baseman's job during his first year with the Indians in 1988. The veteran had spent several seasons with Toronto, but had been squeezed out of a job by rookie Fred McGriff. In 1988, Upshaw produced 11 homers and 50 RBIs for the Tribe, one of his lowest outputs in recent years. In 1987, he hit 15 homers and 58 RBIs in Toronto. His best season ever was in 1983, when he clubbed 27 homers, 104 RBIs, and a .304 average. Upshaw should adjust to his new surroundings and rebound to his past form in 1989.

Upshaw hasn't come close to reproducing his illustrious 1983 season. He should do better with the Tribe in 1989, but don't expect miracles. His 1989 cards cost a nickel or less, and seem questionable, considering that Upshaw is 31 years old. Our pick for his best 1989 card is Fleer.

JOSE URIBE

	BA	G	AB	R	H	2B	3B	HR	RBI	SB
1988	.252	141	493	47	124	10	7	3	35	14
Life	.247	548	1750	187	432	61	17	14	137	57

POSITION: Shortstop
TEAM: San Francisco Giants
BORN: January 21, 1959 San Cristobal, Dominican Republic
HEIGHT: 5′10″ **WEIGHT:** 156 lbs.
BATS: Both **THROWS:** Right
ACQUIRED: Traded from Cardinals with Dave LaPoint, Gary Rajsich, and David Green for Jack Clark, 2/85

Uribe is one of the top defensive shortstops in the National League. He and Robby Thompson combined to execute a league-leading and club-record 183 double plays in 1987. Uribe has a pretty good bat, too. He hit .252 in 1988, with ten doubles, three homers, 35 RBIs, and 47 runs scored. Uribe's best season at the plate, however, was in '87. He hit .291 that year and had 44 runs scored and 12 stolen bases in 95 games. The Giants were thinking about placing him in the leadoff spot, except that his on-base average wasn't high enough. But Uribe is established as the Giant shortstop.

Uribe's 1989 cards will sell as commons. Although he is a great fielder, card collectors don't place a premium on glovework. He'll have to raise his average to over .300 to make an impact. Our pick for his best 1989 card is Score.

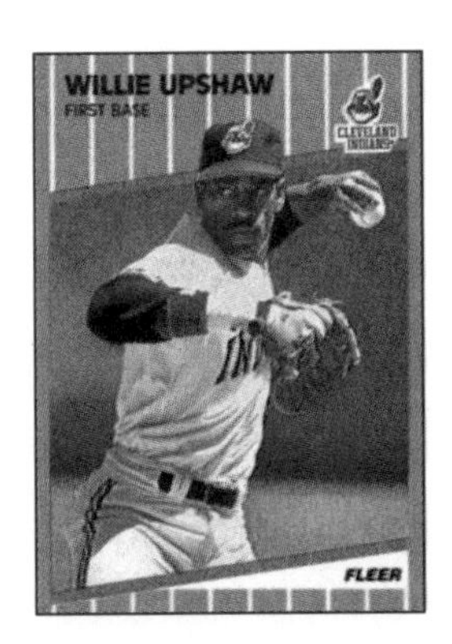

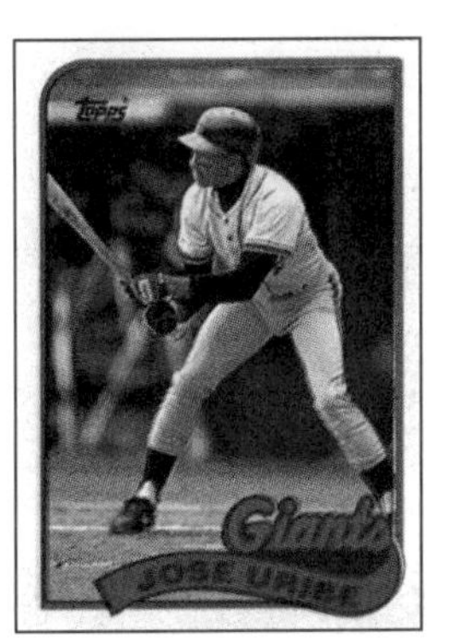

FERNANDO VALENZUELA

	W	L	ERA	G	CG	IP	H	R	BB	SO
1988	5	8	4.24	23	3	142.1	142	71	76	64
Life	118	90	3.16	267	99	1948.0	1691	780	740	1528

POSITION: Pitcher
TEAM: Los Angeles Dodgers
BORN: November 1, 1960 Sonora, Mexico
HEIGHT: 5′11″ **WEIGHT:** 180 lbs.
BATS: Left **THROWS:** Left
ACQUIRED: Purchased from Yucatan of the Mexican League, 7/79

Valenzuela had been an ironman pitcher until 1988. He had a string of 255 consecutive starts before injuring his shoulder. He had his first down year in '88. He was 5-8, with a 4.24 ERA, 64 strikeouts, and $142\frac{1}{3}$ innings pitched. Valenzuela seemed on the road to Cooperstown. He was the only pitcher in history to win the Cy Young Award and Rookie of the Year in the same season (1981). He has had only one 20-win season, but he's always been among the N.L. leaders in Ks, complete games, and ERA. Valenzuela is one tough ballplayer, and he should work back into the Dodger rotation sometime in 1989.

Surprisingly, Valenzuela's 1989 cards are available for 10 to 15 cents. The lefthander has definite Hall of Fame potential, and investing a few bucks in his cards could bring nice profits. Our pick for his best 1989 card is Topps.

DAVE VALLE

	BA	G	AB	R	H	2B	3B	HR	RBI	SB
1988	.231	93	290	29	67	15	2	10	50	0
Life	.245	254	764	85	187	36	5	28	126	2

POSITION: Catcher
TEAM: Seattle Mariners
BORN: October 30, 1960 Bayside, NY
HEIGHT: 6′2″ **WEIGHT:** 200 lbs.
BATS: Right **THROWS:** Right
ACQUIRED: Second-round pick in 6/78 free-agent draft

Valle is both talented and unlucky. The Mariner backstop had some hefty power stats for his limited number of appearances in 1988. However, after battling for the role of starting catcher, injuries have cut into Valle's playing time during the last two seasons. He labored in the minor leagues for six seasons beginning in 1978 before he got his shot with the M's. He is a constant power threat and a decent defensive player. All Valle needs is his health and a full season to prove that he's capable of posting some All-Star numbers.

Valle's 1989 cards will be commons. Make a minor investment at that price, then sell quickly when he makes it through his first full season and gets some recognition. If he hits 20 or more homers, his cards could quickly climb to the 10-cent mark. Our pick for his best 1989 card is Fleer.

ANDY VAN SLYKE

	BA	G	AB	R	H	2B	3B	HR	RBI	SB
1988	.288	154	587	101	169	23	15	25	100	30
Life	.273	832	2663	399	726	138	48	87	386	168

POSITION: Outfield
TEAM: Pittsburgh Pirates
BORN: December 21, 1960 Utica, NY
HEIGHT: 6′1″ **WEIGHT:** 190 lbs.
BATS: Left **THROWS:** Right
ACQUIRED: Traded from Cardinals with Mike LaValliere and Mike Dunne for Tony Pena, 4/87

Van Slyke found full-time work with the Pirates during the 1987 season, after spending four years of uncertainty with the Cardinals. In St. Louis, Van Slyke juggled five different positions. But for the '87 Bucs, he used steady glovework to claim the center fielder's post. At year's end, he led the Pirates in 11 offensive categories. Local media dubbed Van Slyke the team MVP, and local fans voted him "Most Popular Pirate." In 1988, he posted career highs in runs, triples, home runs, and RBIs. If the Pirates can battle for the division title again in 1989, Van Slyke will continue to harvest much-deserved praise for his ability.

Incredibly, Van Slyke's cards are still sold as commons by most dealers. Buy now. If Van Slyke leads the Bucs to 1989 postseason play, the payoff will be fast. Our pick for his best 1989 card is Fleer.

GARY VARSHO

	BA	G	AB	R	H	2B	3B	HR	RBI	SB
1988	.274	46	73	6	20	3	0	0	5	5
Life	.274	46	73	6	20	3	0	0	5	5

POSITION: Outfield
TEAM: Chicago Cubs
BORN: June 29, 1961 Marshfield, WI
HEIGHT: 5′11″ **WEIGHT:** 175 lbs.
BATS: Left **THROWS:** Right
ACQUIRED: Sixth-round pick in 6/82 free-agent draft

Varsho was recalled from Iowa two-thirds of the way through the 1988 campaign, and he impressed the Cubs' management by batting close to .300 for the balance of the season. Varsho was batting .278 for Triple-A Iowa when the call came to report to Wrigley Field. After two seasons at Double-A Pittsfield in 1985 and '86, he was promoted to Iowa for 1987. He was impressive there, with a .302 average, nine homers, 48 RBIs, and 37 stolen bases. He is a fast flychaser with a good arm, and with the opening created by Rafael Palmeiro's trade, Varsho could find a spot in the Cub outfield in 1989.

Varsho's 1989 cards open in the 10- to 15-cent range. Wait to see if he starts for Chicago before investing at that price. Our pick for his best 1989 card is Topps.

FRANK VIOLA

	W	L	ERA	G	CG	IP	H	R	BB	SO
1988	24	7	2.64	35	7	255.1	236	80	54	193
Life	104	81	3.87	236	47	1597.0	1604	762	474	1076

POSITION: Pitcher
TEAM: Minnesota Twins
BORN: April 19, 1960 Hempstead, NY
HEIGHT: 6′4″ **WEIGHT:** 210 lbs.
BATS: Left **THROWS:** Left
ACQUIRED: Second-round pick in 6/81 free-agent draft

While the Twins team didn't repeat as world champions, Viola duplicated another masterful season in 1988. After taking home an MVP trophy from the 1987 World Series, the southpaw lugged the Cy Young Award back to the ranch in 1988. He was 24-7, with a 2.64 ERA. He led the A.L. with a .774 winning percentage. He paced Minnesota in wins, strikeouts, ERA, and shutouts. Viola highlighted his year by breaking the 100-win barrier for career victories. He has won at least 16 games for five straight years. Following a second straight banner year, Viola has proven that he'll be an A.L. pitching mainstay for years to come.

Suddenly, collectors have taken notice of the Twins, and Viola's card values are rising steadily. Buy quickly. His 1989 cards could reach 25 cents by the start of the season. Our pick for his best 1989 card is Topps.

OZZIE VIRGIL

	BA	G	AB	R	H	2B	3B	HR	RBI	SB
1988	.256	107	320	23	82	10	0	9	31	2
Life	.244	727	2242	256	547	83	6	97	305	4

POSITION: Catcher
TEAM: Atlanta Braves
BORN: December 7, 1956 Mayaguez, Puerto Rico
HEIGHT: 6′1″ **WEIGHT:** 205 lbs.
BATS: Right **THROWS:** Right
ACQUIRED: Traded from Phillies with Pete Smith for Steve Bedrosian and Milt Thompson, 12/85

Virgil maintained his streak of playing in 100-plus games during his 1988 season with the Braves. The Atlanta starting catcher since 1986, he appeared in 107 contests in '88, ending with a .256 average, nine homers, and 31 RBIs. Those totals were his lowest since 1983, when he played in just 55 games for the Phillies. Virgil, the son of former major leaguer Ozzie Virgil, Sr., first rose to fame with the Phillies in 1984. He hit .261, with 18 homers and 68 RBIs that year. With the late 1988 acquisition of catcher Jody Davis, it seems like Virgil's days with the Braves may be numbered.

Virgil, a two-time All-Star, hits with power and fields well. Wherever he winds up in 1989, his cards are good investments at a nickel or less. Our pick for his best 1989 card is Donruss.

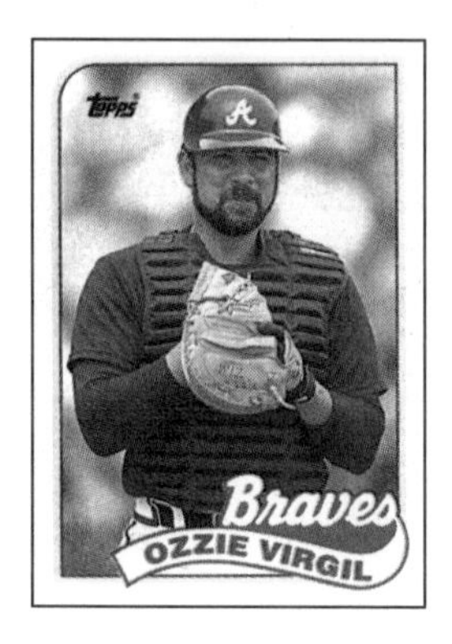

JIM WALEWANDER

	BA	G	AB	R	H	2B	3B	HR	RBI	SB
1988	.211	88	175	23	37	5	0	0	6	11
Life	.218	141	229	47	50	8	1	1	10	13

POSITION: Infield
TEAM: Detroit Tigers
BORN: May 2, 1961 Chicago, IL
HEIGHT: 5'10" **WEIGHT:** 160 lbs.
BATS: Both **THROWS:** Right
ACQUIRED: Ninth-round pick in 6/83 free-agent draft

Walewander finished his first full season in the major leagues as a part-time player for the Tigers. He hit .211 in 1988, with 11 stolen bases and 23 runs scored. He played 54 games for Detroit in 1987, hitting .241. He is seen as the eventual replacement for longtime Detroit second baseman, Lou Whitaker. Walewander possesses similar fielding ability, though he hasn't proven that he can hit as well. At Triple-A Toledo in 1987, he hit .271, with 12 RBIs, 27 runs scored, and 18 stolen bases. After being drafted in 1983 out of Iowa State, he led the Appalachian League in stolen bases, with 35. If Walewander can improve his hitting, he can be the heir to Whitaker's second base throne.

Walewander's 1988 cards will sell in the 5-cent range. He'll need to pull up his average for any significant ascent in that value. Our pick for his best 1989 card is Score.

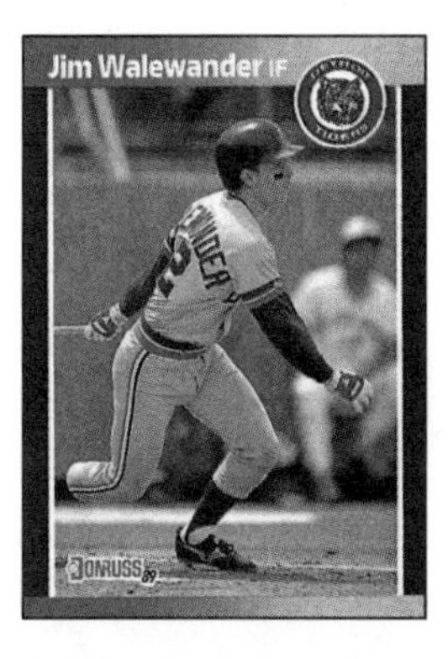

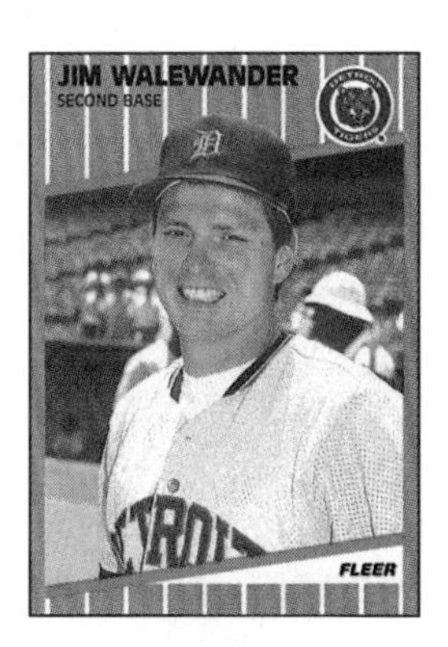

BOB WALK

	W	L	ERA	G	SV	IP	H	R	BB	SO
1988	12	10	2.71	32	1	212.2	183	75	65	81
Life	54	44	3.83	198	9	903.1	877	436	357	485

POSITION: Pitcher
TEAM: Pittsburgh Pirates
BORN: November 26, 1956 Van Nuys, CA
HEIGHT: 6'4" **WEIGHT:** 217 lbs.
BATS: Right **THROWS:** Right
ACQUIRED: Signed as a free agent, 4/84

Walk has established himself as one of the Pirates' most reliable starters. He was 12-10, with a 2.71 ERA in 32 games for Pittsburgh in 1988. He began his big league career in 1980 with a bang. He was 5-1 at Triple-A Oklahoma City when the Phillies brought him up. A fierce competitor, Walk got caught up in the pennant race and went 11-7 in 27 games as a starter. He was 24 years old when Phils manager Dallas Green handed him the ball and told him he'd pitch the opening game of the 1980 World Series. Walk responded with a 7-6 win over the Royals, and the Phils went on to become world champions. Walk continues to be a money pitcher for the Pirates.

Walk's 1989 cards will sell as commons. They will probably not be actively sought by investors. Our pick for his best 1989 card is Score.

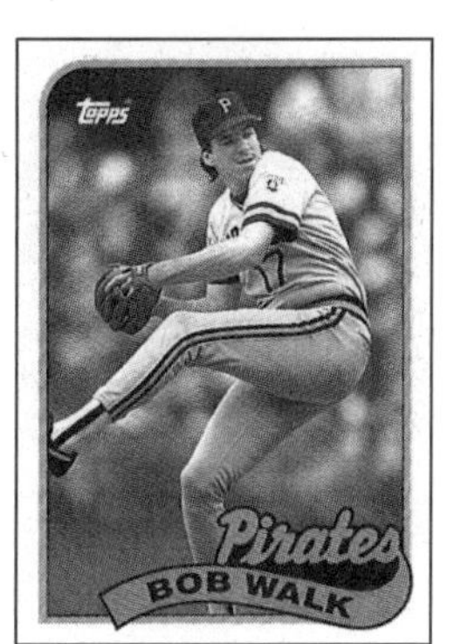

GREG WALKER

	BA	G	AB	R	H	2B	3B	HR	RBI	SB
1988	.247	99	377	45	93	22	1	8	42	0
Life	.267	762	2592	341	691	150	19	108	416	18

POSITION: First base
TEAM: Chicago White Sox
BORN: October 6, 1959 Douglas, GA
HEIGHT: 6'3" **WEIGHT:** 205 lbs.
BATS: Left **THROWS:** Right
ACQUIRED: Drafted from Phillies, 12/79

Walker's 1988 season was stopped when he suffered a seizure in July. He has a rare brain virus that was threatening his baseball future. Walker did play in 99 games in 1988, concluding with a .247 average, eight homers, and 42 RBIs. He had his best season in 1987, when he hit .256, with 27 homers, 94 RBIs, 85 runs scored, and 33 doubles. In 1985, he smashed 24 home runs and 92 RBIs. He hit in double figures in home runs for five seasons for the ChiSox before 1988. Walker is one of the power sources for Chicago, and he will be given every opportunity to come back.

Walker's 1989 cards are commons. He is tough, but his condition clouds his baseball future. If he returns to his previous production, his cards are bargains. Our pick for his best 1989 card is Donruss.

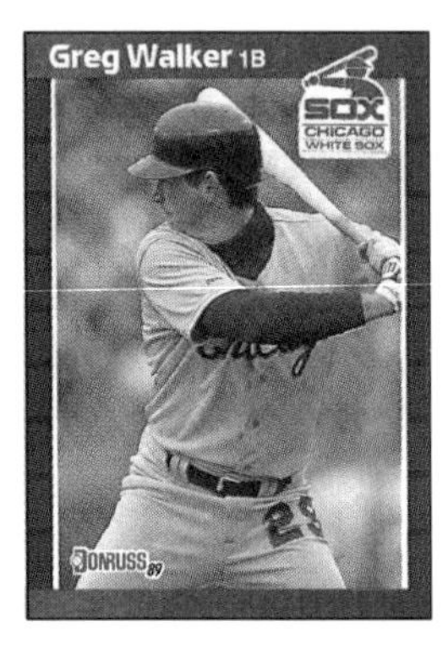

TIM WALLACH

	BA	G	AB	R	H	2B	3B	HR	RBI	SB
1988	.257	159	592	52	152	32	5	12	69	2
Life	.261	1151	4216	479	1100	230	24	148	598	37

POSITION: Third base
TEAM: Montreal Expos
BORN: September 14, 1957
Huntington Park, CA
HEIGHT: 6'3" **WEIGHT:** 200 lbs.
BATS: Right **THROWS:** Right
ACQUIRED: First-round pick in 6/79 free-agent draft

Now that Mike Schmidt is in the twilight of his career, Wallach is arguably the best third baseman in the National League. His numbers slipped a bit in 1988, but his .257 average, 12 home runs, and 69 RBIs combined with his fielding would still earn him the starting nod on just about any club. Wallach's 1987 stats, when he hit .298 with 26 home runs and had 123 RBIs, kept him in the thick of the MVP race that season. A clutch hitter and dangerous with runners on base, he tied for the league lead with 16 game-winning RBIs in 1987.

Wallach's cards are currently underpriced at 10 to 15 cents. He may turn out to be a good speculative buy in that price range. Third basemen who are that good are hard to find. Our pick for his best 1989 card is Score.

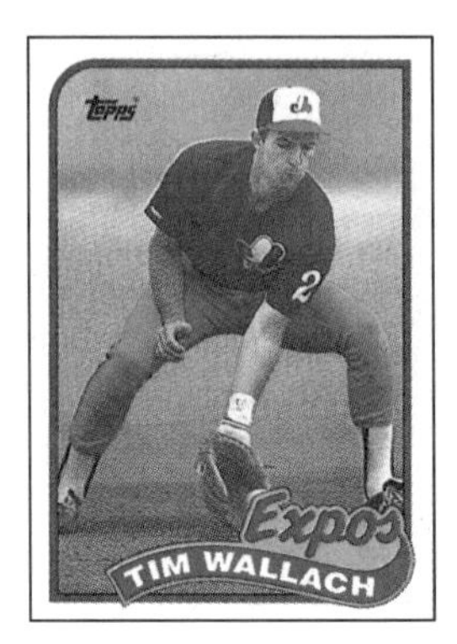

DUANE WARD

	W	L	ERA	G	SV	IP	H	R	BB	SO
1988	9	3	3.30	64	15	111.2	101	46	60	91
Life	10	5	4.20	88	15	141.1	140	72	84	110

POSITION: Pitcher
TEAM: Toronto Blue Jays
BORN: May 28, 1964 Parkview, NM
HEIGHT: 6′4″ **WEIGHT:** 205 lbs.
BATS: Right **THROWS:** Right
ACQUIRED: Traded from Braves for Doyle Alexander, 7/86

In his first full season with the Blue Jays, Ward reeled off a dazzling string of relief outings. He had massive control problems in previous late-season trials with Toronto in 1986 and 1987. However, 1988 was Ward's year to shine. He logged team-high 64 appearances while gaining nine wins and 15 saves. His control returned, and he finished 32 of the games he appeared in. The only reliever with more strike-outs in 1988 was Boston's Lee Smith, who notched 96. At age 24, Ward should get better and better with more experience.

Ward's cards should sell as commons in 1989. If you can buy them for three cents or less, do it. Sell for a hefty short-term gain as soon as the Blue Jays win a pennant or Ward gets national attention. Our pick for his best 1989 card is Score.

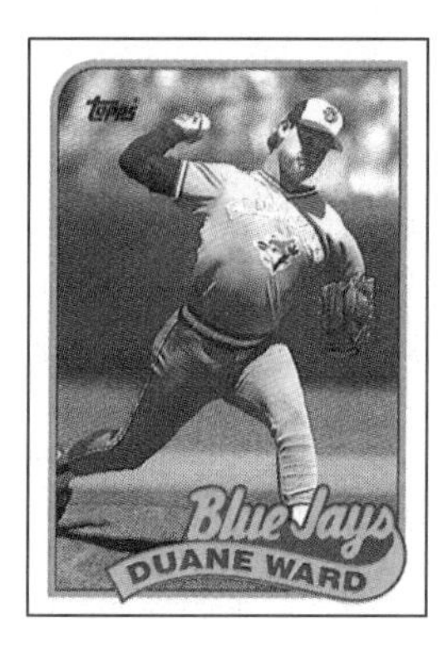

GARY WARD

	BA	G	AB	R	H	2B	3B	HR	RBI	SB
1988	.225	91	231	26	52	8	0	4	24	0
Life	.279	1068	388	535	1083	174	37	112	521	80

POSITION: Outfield
TEAM: New York Yankees
BORN: December 6, 1953
Los Angeles, CA
HEIGHT: 6′2″ **WEIGHT:** 210 lbs.
BATS: Right **THROWS:** Right
ACQUIRED: Signed as a free agent, 12/86

Ward saw a reduction in his playing time in 1988, and his offensive stats suffered. He hit only .225 while playing in 91 games. In 1987, his first season with the Yankees, he hit .248, with 16 homers and 78 RBIs. The former Minnesota outfielder had his best season at the plate for the 1982 Twins. Ward hit .289, with 28 homers, 33 doubles, 91 RBIs, and 85 runs scored. He has a powerful arm, and he led the A.L. in outfield assists with 24 in 1983. The Yankees hope that Ward recaptures some of his past glory, so that he can start again in their 1989 outfield.

Ward's 1989 cards will sell in the 5-cent range. If he puts up the numbers that he is capable of, and thereby leads the Yankees to a pennant, his cards could sell for much higher. Our pick for his best 1989 card is Score.

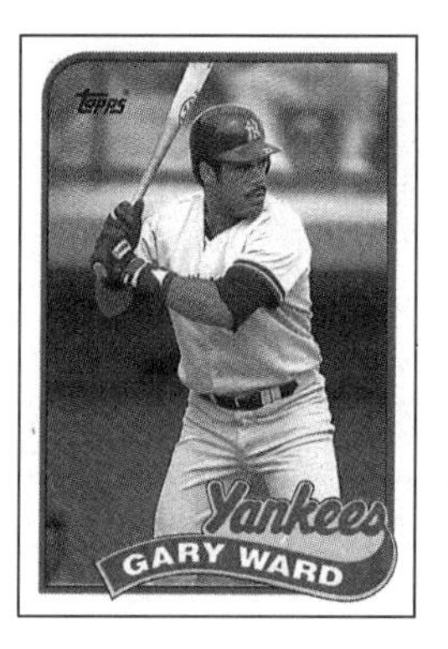

CLAUDELL WASHINGTON

	BA	G	AB	R	H	2B	3B	HR	RBI	SB
1988	.308	126	455	62	140	22	3	11	64	15
Life	.280	1757	6255	866	1751	314	64	150	773	295

POSITION: Outfield
TEAM: New York Yankees
BORN: August 31, 1954 Los Angeles, CA
HEIGHT: 6′2″ **WEIGHT:** 193 lbs.
BATS: Left **THROWS:** Left
ACQUIRED: Traded from Braves with Paul Zuvella for Ken Griffey, 6/86

Washington seemed to turn his career around with the 1988 Yankees. He appeared in 126 games, his most since 1982 with the Braves. Washington hit .308, and he hadn't hit .300 since 1975, his first full season with Oakland. Washington's 1988 success included big gains in home runs and RBIs. He had 11 homers, his most since 1985, and 64 RBIs, his most since 1982. The 34-year-old outfielder has endured a seesaw career that featured stopovers with the Rangers, White Sox, and Mets before joining the Braves. Washington's recent hitting heroics could land him a starting spot in 1989.

Washington has never reached the heights of stardom others predicted for him. His 1989 cards will be a nickel or less. Because he has never reeled off great consecutive seasons, his cards are risky. Our pick for his best 1989 card is Topps.

MITCH WEBSTER

	BA	G	AB	R	H	2B	3B	HR	RBI	SB
1988	.260	151	523	69	136	16	8	6	39	22
Life	.276	573	1933	302	533	87	32	40	185	106

POSITION: Outfield
TEAM: Chicago Cubs
BORN: May 16, 1959 Larned, KS
HEIGHT: 6′1″ **WEIGHT:** 185 lbs.
BATS: Both **THROWS:** Left
ACQUIRED: Traded from Expos for Dave Martinez, 7/88

Dealt to Chicago during the 1988 season, Webster had another solid season. He finished the season with a .260 average, six home runs, and 39 RBIs. He was tied for the team lead in triples, with eight, and stole 22 bases. In 1987 with the Expos, Webster had 53 extra-base hits, including a career-high 15 homers, and 63 RBIs. He stole 33 bases and gave Montreal a solid defensive job in both right and center. He hit .290, with a league-leading 13 triples for the Expos in 1986 in 151 games. Webster is the speedy, good hitting center fielder that the Cubs have been missing for years.

There is little likelihood of any investment potential in Webster's cards. His 1989 cards are in the commons pile. He would need an exceptional season for his cards to gain in value. Our pick for his best 1989 card is Topps.

BILL WEGMAN

	W	L	ERA	G	CG	IP	H	R	BB	SO
1988	13	13	4.12	32	4	199.0	207	104	50	84
Life	32	36	4.46	104	13	640.0	670	345	149	274

POSITION: Pitcher
TEAM: Milwaukee Brewers
BORN: December 19, 1962 Cincinnati, OH
HEIGHT: 6′6″ **WEIGHT:** 220 lbs.
BATS: Right **THROWS:** Right
ACQUIRED: Fifth-round pick in 6/81 free-agent draft

Wegman posted his second straight double-digit winning season for the Brewers in 1988. He won a career-best 13 games, compared to his 12 victories last season. He also had four complete games and a shutout in '88. Wegman, who had his ERA above four for the third consecutive year, can thank the potent Brewers offense for providing him with some leads to work with. He always seems like a willing worker for Milwaukee, as he's registered more than 190 innings in the last three campaigns. If Wegman can lower his ERA a bit, he might be ready to aim for 20 victories in 1989.

Wegman is only 26, and he seems to get better with age. His cards sell as commons now, but will gain in price as soon as he approaches a 20-win season. Our pick for his best 1989 card is Topps.

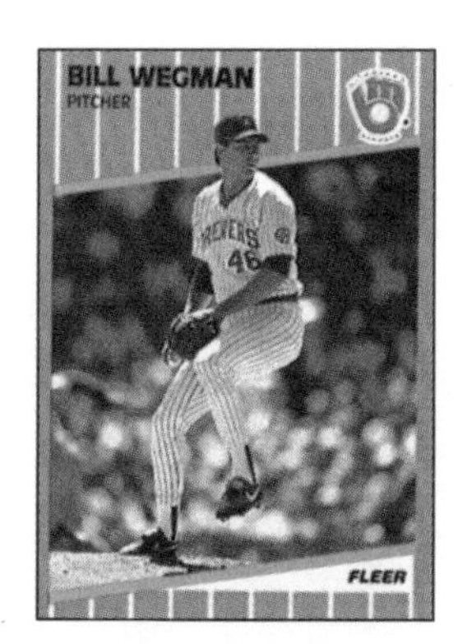

WALT WEISS

	BA	G	AB	R	H	2B	3B	HR	RBI	SB
1988	.250	147	452	44	113	17	3	3	39	4
Life	.262	163	478	47	125	21	3	3	40	5

POSITION: Shortstop
TEAM: Oakland A's
BORN: November 28, 1963 Tuxedo, NY
HEIGHT: 6′ **WEIGHT:** 175 lbs.
BATS: Both **THROWS:** Right
ACQUIRED: First-round pick in 6/85 free-agent draft

Teams aren't supposed to win with rookies at shortstop, but Weiss and the Oakland A's made a mockery of that theory in 1988. Weiss burst on the scene late in 1987, batting .462 for Oakland after his recall from Tucson. Obviously, his offensive flurry in '87 made an impression. With the A's in '88, Weiss made all the plays and batted .250. He was voted the A.L. Rookie of the Year, following in the footsteps of teammates Jose Canseco and Mark McGwire. Weiss had an interesting 1987 season, too: He began the year at Double-A Huntsville, where he was voted the league's premier shortstop, hitting .285. Promoted to Triple-A Tacoma, he hit .263 and played solid defense.

Weiss' 1989 cards will open in the 35- to 40-cent range. If he improves his average in 1989, expect those prices to double. Our pick for his best 1989 card is Topps.

BOB WELCH

	W	L	ERA	G	CG	IP	H	R	BB	SO
1988	17	9	3.64	36	4	244.2	237	107	81	158
Life	132	95	3.20	328	51	2064.2	1868	809	646	1450

POSITION: Pitcher
TEAM: Oakland A's
BORN: November 3, 1956 Detroit, MI
HEIGHT: 6'3" **WEIGHT:** 193 lbs.
BATS: Right **THROWS:** Right
ACQUIRED: Traded from Dodgers with Charlie Spikes and Jack Savage for Jesse Orosco, Alfredo Griffin, and Jay Howell, 12/87

Welch, a ten-year Dodgers veteran, joined the Athletics in 1988 and responded with his best performance in six seasons. The righthander was 17-9, with a 3.64 ERA. He has won in double figures seven times in his 11-year big league career. Welch signed with the Dodgers in 1977, making the major league roster after only a couple of minor league seasons. In 1978, the Dodgers rookie struck out Reggie Jackson to save game two of the World Series. Teaming with another former Dodger hurler, Dave Stewart, Welch has made the A's look like the league's team of the future.

Welch should be a vital component in future pennant drives by the A's. His cards are sound investments at 10 cents apiece, although some dealers may ask for a quarter each if Welch opens well in 1989. Our pick for his best 1989 card is Donruss.

DAVID WELLS

	W	L	ERA	G	SV	IP	H	R	BB	SO
1988	3	5	4.62	41	4	64.1	65	36	31	56
Life	7	8	4.42	59	5	93.2	102	50	43	88

POSITION: Pitcher
TEAM: Toronto Blue Jays
BORN: May 20, 1963 Torrance, CA
HEIGHT: 6'1" **WEIGHT:** 225 lbs.
BATS: Left **THROWS:** Left
ACQUIRED: Second-round pick in 6/82 free-agent draft

In his first full season, Wells provided a lot of relief to the Blue Jays. He finished 15 of the 41 games he appeared in. The lefty provided Toronto with a balanced bullpen. He could be the team's lefthanded stopper in the future, based on his 1988 performance. Wells has been toting a bloated ERA during his two seasons in Toronto, and could become much more effective if his average were down around 3.00. His high strikeout totals are encouraging marks any reliever would welcome. Wells will get lots more work for the Blue Jays in 1989, and could gain long-term employment there with another similar season.

Cards of Wells should be under a nickel in 1989. To be safe, wait for a second consecutive season of success before pursuing any of his cards. Our pick for his best 1989 card is Fleer.

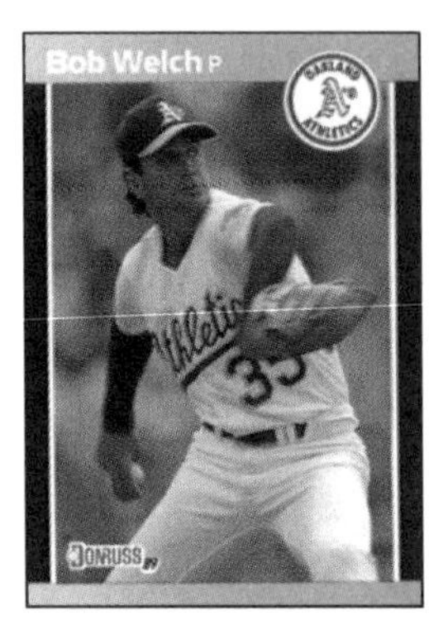

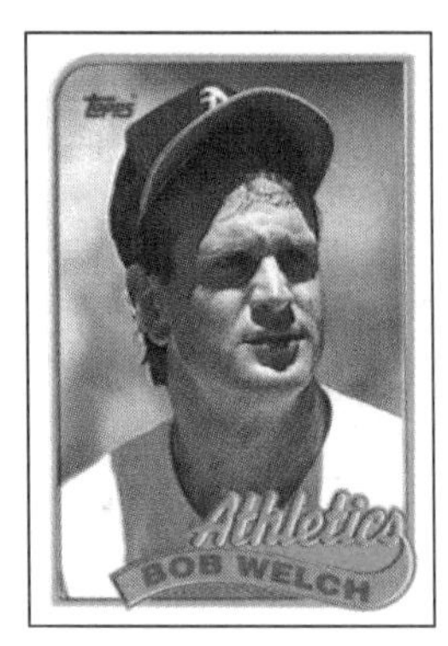

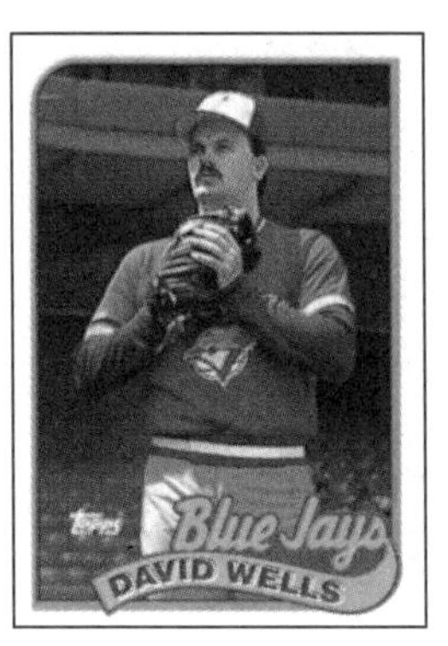

DAVE WEST

	W	L	ERA	G	CG	IP	H	R	BB	SO
1988	1	0	3.00	2	0	6.0	6	2	3	3
Life	1	0	3.00	2	0	6.0	6	2	3	3

POSITION: Pitcher
TEAM: New York Mets
BORN: September 1, 1964 Memphis, TN
HEIGHT: 6'6" **WEIGHT:** 205 lbs.
BATS: Left **THROWS:** Left
ACQUIRED: Fourth-round pick in 6/83 free-agent draft

The pitching-rich Mets had the luxury of bringing West along slowly, and experts agree that he'll probably open the 1989 campaign on the big league staff. He fashioned a 12-4 record and 1.80 ERA at Triple-A Tidewater in 1988. West was rated the Double-A Texas League's best pitching prospect in 1987, and the third best prospect in the Triple-A International League in 1988. The lefty had a 2.81 ERA at Double-A Jackson in 1987. He went 10-3 with a 2.91 ERA and 101 Ks in 93 innings at Class-A Columbia in 1986. West's late-season showing with the Mets in 1988 (1-0 and a 3.00 ERA) has convinced most observers that he's in the big leagues to stay.

West's cards will open in 1989 in the 15- to 25-cent area. Don't invest too heavily until he is in the New York rotation. Our pick for his best 1989 card is Donruss.

LOU WHITAKER

	BA	G	AB	R	H	2B	3B	HR	RBI	SB
1988	.275	115	403	54	111	18	2	12	55	2
Life	.279	1547	5712	888	1591	258	57	121	636	110

POSITION: Second base
TEAM: Detroit Tigers
BORN: May 12, 1957 Brooklyn, NY
HEIGHT: 5'11" **WEIGHT:** 160 lbs.
BATS: Left **THROWS:** Right
ACQUIRED: Fifth-round pick in 6/75 free-agent draft

One reason that Detroit wins season after season is that they have "strength up the middle." Whitaker and Alan Trammell have been the Tiger double-play combination since the late '70s. Whitaker played in only 115 games in 1988, but he still managed 12 homers and 55 RBIs in 403 at-bats to go with his .275 average. He has been an All-Star five times, and he was voted Rookie of the Year in 1978. In 1987, he hit .265, with 16 homers and 59 RBIs. With four more good seasons, he could crack the 2,000-hit and 200-homer barriers. Whitaker has been tops among second basemen for a decade.

Whitaker's 1989 cards will be in the 5- to 15-cent range. That is a good price, because if he tops 2,000 hits and 200 homers, he could find a place in the Hall of Fame. Our pick for his best 1989 card is Donruss.

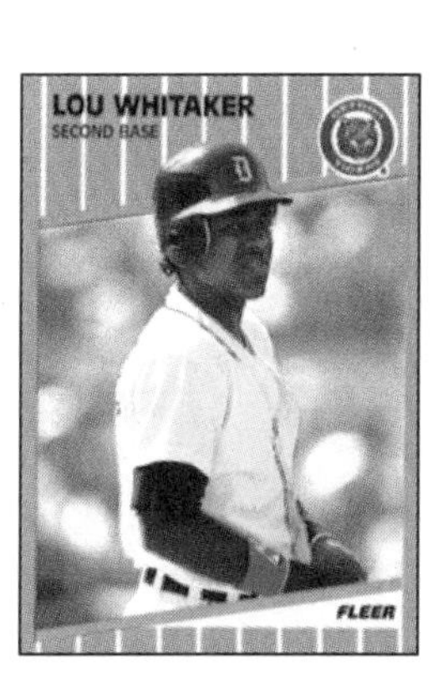

DEVON WHITE

	BA	G	AB	R	H	2B	3B	HR	RBI	SB
1988	.259	122	455	76	118	22	2	11	51	17
Life	.260	331	1152	194	299	56	8	36	141	58

POSITION: Outfield
TEAM: California Angels
BORN: December 29, 1962 Kingston, Jamaica
HEIGHT: 6'1" **WEIGHT:** 170 lbs.
BATS: Both **THROWS:** Right
ACQUIRED: Sixth-round pick in 6/81 free-agent draft

White missed 40 games in 1988, and both his stats and the Angels suffered. California, missing his bat, finished 75-87. White's totals were a far cry from his 1987 output of 24 homers and 87 RBIs. His power and speed give him the potential for stardom only if he brings his batting average closer to .300. The 26-year-old speedster swiped 17 bases in 1988, a total that's sure to increase when he is in action for a full season. California's chances of becoming a contender again will revolve around having a healthy White in the lineup.

White's 1988 cards were selling at 30 cents last fall, but that total could fall due to his atypical season. Try to acquire his cards at a quarter or less for the soundest investment. Our pick for his best 1989 card is Donruss.

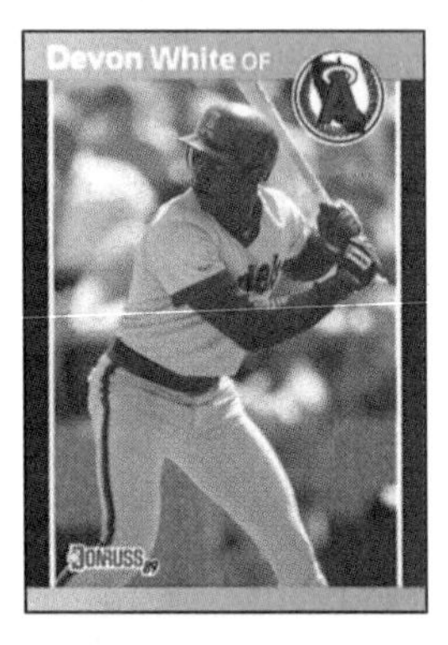

FRANK WHITE

	BA	G	AB	R	H	2B	3B	HR	RBI	SB
1988	.235	150	537	48	126	25	1	8	58	7
Life	.257	2107	7200	858	1847	371	56	156	829	174

POSITION: Second base
TEAM: Kansas City Royals
BORN: September 4, 1950 Greenville, MS
HEIGHT: 5'11" **WEIGHT:** 175 lbs.
BATS: Right **THROWS:** Right
ACQUIRED: Signed as a free agent, 7/70

White's 16th major league season produced some uncharacteristic slumps for the Royals' long-time second baseman. He hit just .235, his lowest since 1976. His eight homers were his fewest since 1980. White, an eight-time Gold Glove winner, kept his defensive prowess in 1988. He made just four errors all season long. He is known as the most successful graduate of the Royals' experimental baseball academy of the 1970s. He played in his 2,000th big-league game in 1988, and will likely surpass the 2,000-hit plateau in 1989. White is an example of continued excellence in baseball.

Incredibly, White's 1989 cards are valued at the bargain prices of a nickel or less. Those prices could go up fast if the Royals return to postseason play. Our pick for his best 1989 card is Score.

ED WHITSON

	W	L	ERA	G	CG	IP	H	R	BB	SO
1988	13	11	3.77	34	3	205.1	202	93	45	118
Life	92	97	4.05	374	22	1706.1	1734	848	586	982

POSITION: Pitcher
TEAM: San Diego Padres
BORN: May 9, 1955 Johnson City, TN
HEIGHT: 6'3" **WEIGHT:** 195 lbs.
BATS: Right **THROWS:** Right
ACQUIRED: Traded from Yankees for Tim Stoddard, 7/86

Whitson had his first winning campaign in three years with the 1988 Padres. He won 13 games, the most since his 14-8 season with the 1984 National League Champion Padres. Whitson kept his ERA at 3.77, and walked only 45 in 205⅓ innings, while striking out 118. For the Padres in 1987, he was 10-12, with a 4.73 ERA and 135 strikeouts. He spent a season and a half with the Yankees before returning to San Diego in mid-1986. He also saw stints with the Giants, Indians, and Padres before going to New York as a free agent. Whitson should return to lead the Padres' starting rotation in 1989.

Whitson's 1989 cards should be three cents or less. Don't forget that he has a lifetime losing record and a career ERA over 4.00. His cards are risky investments. Our pick for his best 1989 card is Score.

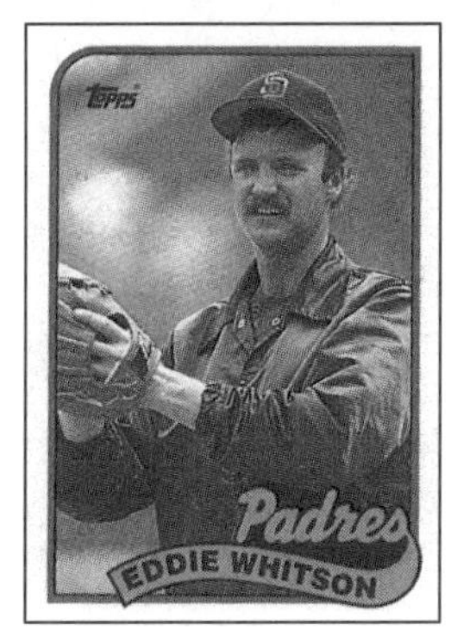

ERNIE WHITT

	BA	G	AB	R	H	2B	3B	HR	RBI	SB
1988	.251	127	398	63	100	11	2	16	70	4
Life	.251	1097	3147	386	791	142	14	121	468	17

POSITION: Catcher
TEAM: Toronto Blue Jays
BORN: June 13, 1952 Detroit, MI
HEIGHT: 6'2" **WEIGHT:** 205 lbs.
BATS: Left **THROWS:** Right
ACQUIRED: Selected from Red Sox in 1976 expansion draft

A lack of playing time was the only problem Whitt had with the 1988 Blue Jays. He had one of his best seasons ever both at bat and in the field. He nearly repeated his 1987 stats of 19 homers and 75 RBIs, but he got 48 fewer at-bats last season. Whitt made only four errors in 127 games behind the plate. He made his major league debut with the 1976 Red Sox. At age 36, no one can question his ability as a power hitter. The only question involves Whitt's stamina, and whether he can continue the grueling task of catching at least 120 games a year much longer.

Whitt's cards are priced as commons. His cards are questionable long-term investments. However, his cards could reach a dime or more if he helps Toronto capture a pennant. Our pick for his best 1989 card is Donruss.

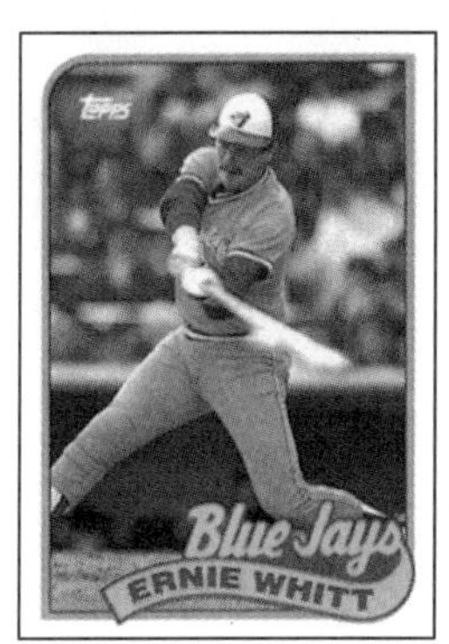

CURTIS WILKERSON

	BA	G	AB	R	H	2B	3B	HR	RBI	SB
1988	.293	117	338	41	99	12	5	0	28	9
Life	.255	610	1591	185	406	50	18	3	106	53

POSITION: Infield
TEAM: Chicago Cubs
BORN: April 26, 1961 Petersburg, VA
HEIGHT: 5′9″ **WEIGHT:** 161 lbs.
BATS: Both **THROWS:** Right
ACQUIRED: Traded from Rangers with Mitch Williams, Paul Kilgus, Steve Wilson, Luis Benitez, and Pablo Delgado for Rafael Palmeiro, Drew Hall, and Jamie Moyer, 12/88

Wilkerson becomes the utility infielder for the Cubs in 1989. He spent another season of double-duty, playing both second base and shortstop for the 1988 Rangers. He used to be the starting Texas shortstop until Scott Fletcher joined the team. Wilkerson led the Rangers with a career-high .293 average. His 99 hits were the most he had since 1984, when he played in 153 games. In 1987, he hit .268 in only 85 games for the Rangers. Wilkerson, who has been with the Rangers since 1983, put together the type of season that might help the Cubs retool for the pennant run in 1989.

Wilkerson's cards are easily available at a nickel or less. However, don't consider investing unless he can get an every-day job in Chicago. Our pick for his best 1989 card is Fleer.

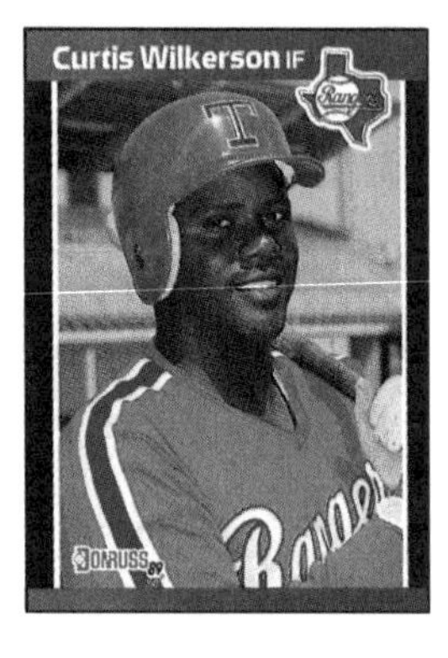

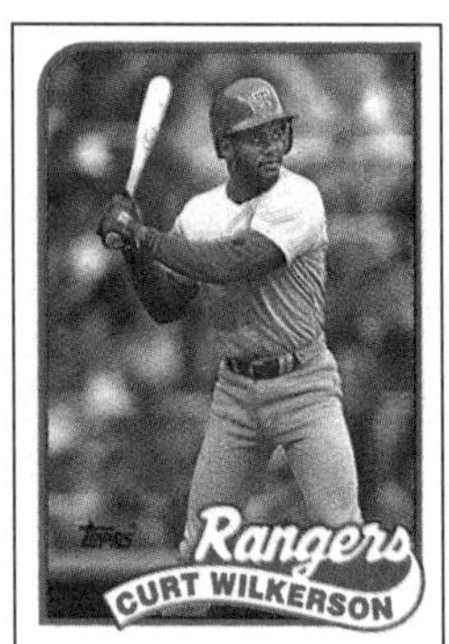

FRANK WILLIAMS

	W	L	ERA	G	SV	IP	H	R	BB	SO
1988	3	2	2.59	60	1	62.2	59	24	35	43
Life	21	11	2.88	291	7	400.0	348	157	181	281

POSITION: Pitcher
TEAM: Cincinnati Reds
BORN: February 13, 1958 Seattle, WA
HEIGHT: 6′1″ **WEIGHT:** 180 lbs.
BATS: Right **THROWS:** Right
ACQUIRED: Traded from Giants for Eddie Milner, 1/87

Williams was an active member of the 1988 Reds' bullpen. He appeared in 60 games, acting as a set-up pitcher for stopper John Franco. Williams had a 2.59 ERA and a 3-2 record in 62⅔ innings pitched. He had a perfect record in 1987, going 4-0. He pitched 105⅔ innings, with a career-high 85 appearances. He began his career in 1984 with the Giants and had a remarkable rookie season. He was 9-4 that year, with a 3.55 ERA, three saves, and 91 strikeouts in 106⅓ innings. Williams continues to be a reliable right-handed middle reliever for the Reds.

Williams 1989 cards will be commons. The only chance for his cards to gain in value would be if he were converted to a starting role, which could happen. But don't invest in his cards if he stays in middle relief. Our pick for his best 1989 card is Score.

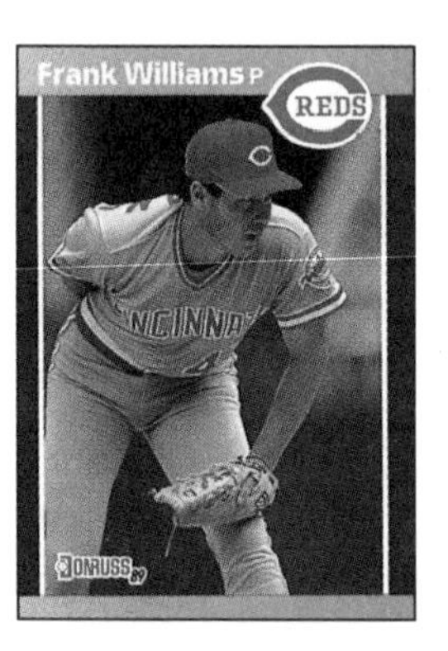

KEN WILLIAMS

	BA	G	AB	R	H	2B	3B	HR	RBI	SB
1988	.159	73	220	18	35	4	2	8	28	6
Life	.232	204	642	68	149	22	4	20	79	28

POSITION: Outfield
TEAM: Chicago White Sox
BORN: April 6, 1964 Berkeley, CA
HEIGHT: 6'1" **WEIGHT:** 184 lbs.
BATS: Right **THROWS:** Right
ACQUIRED: Third-round pick in 6/82 free-agent draft

Williams was back at home in center field for the White Sox in 1988, after they tried to convert him into a third baseman. The experiment was a failure. Williams appeared in only 73 games in 1988, and his average suffered for it. Still, he displayed his power-hitting even in a shortened season. He clubbed eight homers and 28 RBIs. The year-long slump was a turnaround from his 1987 achievements. In 1987, Williams hit .281, with 11 homers, 50 RBIs, and 21 stolen bases. If Williams can hit for a decent average, he'll be a mainstay in future White Sox lineups.

Expect 1989 cards of Williams to sell for a nickel or less, based on his 1988 problems. Smart investors will gamble on his rebound and snatch up his cards. He has lots of time to establish a star career. Our pick for his best 1989 card is Score.

MATT WILLIAMS

	BA	G	AB	R	H	2B	3B	HR	RBI	SB
1988	.205	52	156	17	32	6	1	8	19	0
Life	.195	136	401	45	78	15	3	16	40	4

POSITION: Third base
TEAM: San Francisco Giants
BORN: November 28, 1965 Bishop, CA
HEIGHT: 6'2" **WEIGHT:** 205 lbs.
BATS: Right **THROWS:** Right
ACQUIRED: First-round pick in 6/86 free-agent draft

Baseball America rated Williams among the Triple-A Pacific Coast League's top ten prospects in 1988. At Phoenix in '88, he batted .271, with 12 home runs and 51 RBIs. The converted shortstop has spent much of the past two seasons shuttling between the majors and Triple-A, as he learns how to hit a big league breaking ball and make better contact. At Phoenix in '87, Williams hit .289. He broke into pro baseball in 1986 at Class-A Everett; in just one season he made exceptional progress and won a job on the Giants' 1987 opening day roster. The Giants see Williams as their third baseman of the future, and experts have labeled him a "can't miss" prospect.

Williams' 1989 cards will sell in the 15- to 20-cent range. His cards are good bets for future appreciation. Our pick for his best 1989 card is Topps.

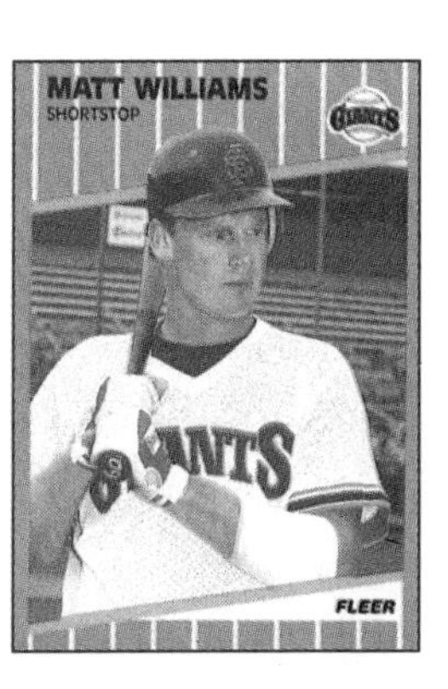

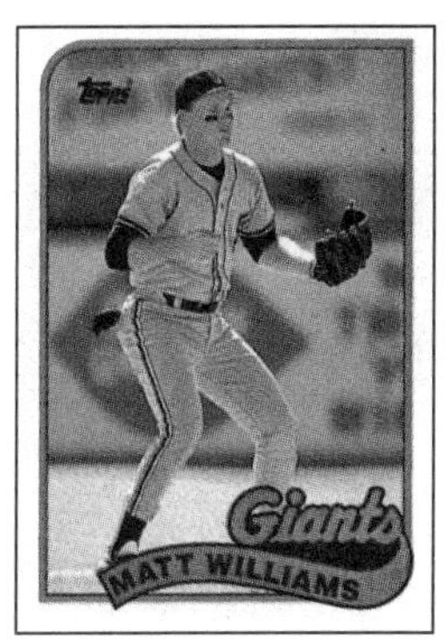

MITCH WILLIAMS

	W	L	ERA	G	SV	IP	H	R	BB	SO
1988	2	7	4.63	67	18	68.0	48	38	47	61
Life	18	19	3.70	232	32	274.2	180	124	220	280

POSITION: Pitcher
TEAM: Chicago Cubs
BORN: November 17, 1964
Santa Ana, CA
HEIGHT: 6′4″ **WEIGHT:** 200 lbs.
BATS: Left **THROWS:** Left
ACQUIRED: Traded from Rangers with Curtis Wilkerson, Paul Kilgus, Steve Wilson, Luis Benitez, and Pablo Delgado for Rafael Palmeiro, Drew Hall, and Jamie Moyer, 12/88

Williams was the main reason that the Cubs were willing to send the N.L.'s second highest batting leader (Rafael Palmeiro) to Texas. Despite his ERA and losing record, Williams remained the top lefty in the Rangers' bullpen in 1988. He racked up a career-best 18 saves and was third in the American League in appearances. In 1986, his rookie year, Williams led the A.L. in appearances (80), setting an A.L. record for rookies. In 1987, he pitched in 85 games. The Cubs needed a closer, and Williams has a chance to be the savior for them in 1989.

Williams' 1989 cards are priced as commons. He has averaged more than one strikeout an inning, an attractive statistic that makes his low-priced cards appealing investments. Our pick for his best 1989 card is Topps.

MARK WILLIAMSON

	W	L	ERA	G	SV	IP	H	R	BB	SO
1988	5	8	4.90	37	2	117.2	125	70	40	69
Life	13	17	4.45	98	5	242.2	247	129	81	142

POSITION: Pitcher
TEAM: Baltimore Orioles
BORN: July 21, 1959
Corpus Christi, TX
HEIGHT: 6′ **WEIGHT:** 155 lbs.
BATS: Right **THROWS:** Right
ACQUIRED: Traded from Padres with Terry Kennedy for Storm Davis, 10/86

Williamson's 1988 efforts suffered with the rest of the Orioles' pitching staff. Used both in starting and relief roles, he logged two complete games as a starter and finished 11 games as a reliever. He was third on the club in strikeouts. While with the Padres' Triple-A team in 1986, Williamson tied for the Pacific Coast League lead with 16 saves. In 1987, his 61 mound appearances as a rookie set a Baltimore record. It's a good bet that Williamson will see lots more work with the pitching-thin Orioles in 1989.

At age 29, Williamson could be too old to accumulate impressive lifetime statistics as a reliever. Based on his prior record and the uncertain ability of the 1989 Orioles, his common-priced cards aren't sound investments. Our pick for his best 1989 card is Score.

GLENN WILSON

	BA	G	AB	R	H	2B	3B	HR	RBI	SB
1988	.256	115	410	39	105	18	1	5	32	1
Life	.267	945	3337	359	891	169	22	77	402	26

POSITION: Outfield
TEAM: Pittsburgh Pirates
BORN: December 22, 1958 Baytown, TX
HEIGHT: 6′1″ **WEIGHT:** 190 lbs.
BATS: Right **THROWS:** Right
ACQUIRED: Traded from Mariners for Darnell Coles, 7/88

Wilson played only ten games for the Pirates before undergoing surgery on his right knee. He got back into the Pirate lineup in late August, hitting .270, two homers, and 15 RBIs to end his year on an up note. Traded by the Phillies to the Mariners last spring, he came back to the N.L. in the deal that sent Darnell Coles to Seattle. Wilson was batting .250 for the M's when he was traded. Never a long-ball hitter, his career high in home runs was 15 in 1986. The Pirates hope for a return to the form that saw Wilson drive in 102 runs for the 1985 Phils.

Wilson's card values have dipped in recent years, and his 1989 cards will be found among commons. They are not investment material for now. Our pick for his best 1989 card is Topps.

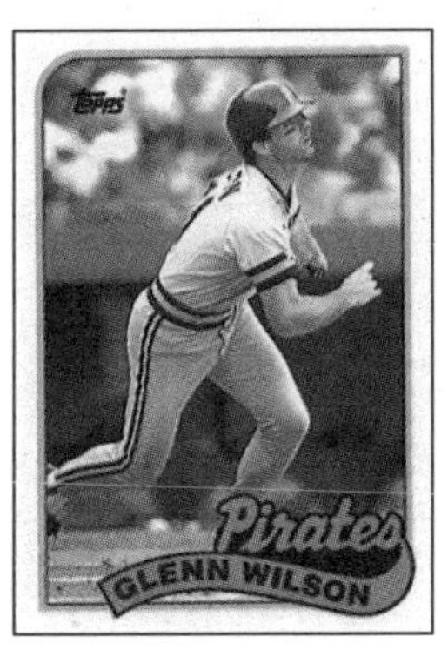

MOOKIE WILSON

	BA	G	AB	R	H	2B	3B	HR	RBI	SB
1988	.296	112	378	61	112	17	5	8	41	15
Life	.281	1036	3778	570	1061	160	61	57	324	274

POSITION: Outfield
TEAM: New York Mets
BORN: February 9, 1956 Bamberg, SC
HEIGHT: 5′10″ **WEIGHT:** 170 lbs.
BATS: Both **THROWS:** Right
ACQUIRED: Second-round pick in 6/77 free-agent draft

Platooned with Lenny Dykstra for the past two seasons, Wilson has made no secret of his desire to be traded away from the Mets. On the other hand, the Mets are in no hurry to unload Wilson. Last year he saw action in 112 games, batting .296, eight homers, and 41 RBIs. Wilson had a career-high 638 at-bats in 1983, tops in the N.L., while batting .276. His best homer year was 1984, when he hit ten. In 1987, he hit his career-high batting average of .299 in 124 games. Wilson may be able to seal the center field job on an every-day basis with a good spring training in 1989.

Wilson had flirted with stardom, but even playing in New York didn't help. There is no premium attached to the value of his cards. Our pick for his best 1989 card is Fleer.

WILLIE WILSON

	BA	G	AB	R	H	2B	3B	HR	RBI	SB
1988	.262	147	591	81	155	17	11	1	37	35
Life	.292	1560	6109	953	1782	211	123	35	424	564

POSITION: Outfield
TEAM: Kansas City Royals
BORN: July 9, 1955 Montgomery, AL
HEIGHT: 6'3" **WEIGHT:** 195 lbs.
BATS: Both **THROWS:** Right
ACQUIRED: First-round pick in 6/74 free-agent draft

Wilson, at 33 years old, still can tear it up. His speed and defense were highlights in the 1988 season of the Royals. He tied for the A.L. lead in triples, with 11. Wilson's 35 stolen bases led the Royals and raised his career total to 564. In 147 games, he committed just four errors in the outfield. In 1987, he hit .279, with 97 runs scored and 59 stolen bases. In 1986, he popped nine home runs, a career best, while hitting .269. He scored a career-high 133 runs in 1980. With continued fine play from Wilson, the Royals could be solid contenders in 1989.

At his current pace, Wilson can break the 2,000-hit barrier in early 1990. He still has several good seasons to look forward to. His 1989 cards, at a nickel or less, are promising investments. Our pick for his best 1989 card is Topps.

DAVE WINFIELD

	BA	G	AB	R	H	2B	3B	HR	RBI	SB
1988	.322	149	559	96	180	37	2	25	107	9
Life	.287	2269	8421	1314	2421	412	74	357	1438	209

POSITION: Outfield
TEAM: New York Yankees
BORN: October 3, 1951 St. Paul, MN
HEIGHT: 6'6" **WEIGHT:** 220 lbs.
BATS: Right **THROWS:** Right
ACQUIRED: Signed as a free agent, 12/80

Winfield had one of the greatest seasons of his career in 1988, blunting criticism from team owner George Steinbrenner and keeping the Yankees in the pennant race all season long. After a slow start, it looked like Winfield would be best remembered in 1988 for his controversial autobiography. But his bat heated up later, and he hit .322, with 25 homers and 107 RBIs. At age 36, he led the Yankees in virtually every offensive category. Winfield could play a vital role with the team for another three to five years, giving him a shot at reaching the 3,000-hit and 450-homer plateaus.

Winfield's 1989 cards will be about 25 cents apiece, which is too expensive for investment purposes. Hang on to any of his cards found in wax packs. He surprised everyone in 1988; he might do it again. Our pick for his best 1989 card is Topps.

HERM WINNINGHAM

	BA	G	AB	R	H	2B	3B	HR	RBI	SB
1988	.232	100	203	16	47	3	4	0	21	12
Life	.237	466	1074	108	255	36	16	11	99	75

POSITION: Outfield
TEAM: Cincinnati Reds
BORN: December 1, 1961
Orangeburg, SC
HEIGHT: 5′11″ **WEIGHT:** 180 lbs.
BATS: Left **THROWS:** Right
ACQUIRED: Traded from Expos with Jeff Reed and Randy St. Claire for Tracy Jones and Pat Pacillo, 7/88

Winningham ended his three-year stay with the Expos with a mid-season move to the Reds. He played part-time and appeared in 100 games in 1988. His average hovered around the .230s, as usual, but he stole 12 bases. Winningham was a defensive asset for Cincinnati, making only one error all season. He started his career in the Mets' system, but got only a brief trial with them in late 1984. He hit .407 in 14 games, but was traded to Montreal the next season. If Winningham could hit even in the .260s, he might have a chance at a starting position.

Winningham's 1989 cards will be three cents or less. Because of his low average and his part-time status, his cards are not safe investments. Our pick for his best 1989 card is Fleer.

BOBBY WITT

	W	L	ERA	G	CG	IP	H	R	BB	SO
1988	8	10	3.92	22	13	174.1	134	83	101	148
Life	27	29	4.74	79	14	475.0	378	269	384	482

POSITION: Pitcher
TEAM: Texas Rangers
BORN: May 11, 1964 Arlington, VA
HEIGHT: 6′2″ **WEIGHT:** 200 lbs.
BATS: Right **THROWS:** Right
ACQUIRED: First-round pick in 6/85 free-agent draft

Witt finally made a major league impression with the 1988 Texas Rangers. In 55 previous starts, the once-erratic righty only logged one complete game. A mid-season trip to the minors turned Witt's career around, and he went on to pace Texas with 13 complete outings and his first two career shutouts. His control returned after leading the American League in walks for the past two seasons. Witt's 1988 8-10 record was blighted by his team's sputtering offense, fourth worst in the league. Still, the marked turnaround of this 1984 Olympian is just a glimpse of Witt's unlimited potential.

Witt's 1989 cards will sell for less than a nickel apiece. He could become one of the league's 20-game winners. Daring collectors will gamble on his cards. Our pick for his best 1989 card is Fleer.

MIKE WITT

	W	L	ERA	G	CG	IP	H	R	BB	SO
1988	13	16	4.15	34	12	249.2	263	130	87	133
Life	100	89	3.68	271	65	1725.0	1661	798	595	1146

POSITION: Pitcher
TEAM: California Angels
BORN: July 20, 1960 Fullerton, CA
HEIGHT: 6′7″ **WEIGHT:** 192 lbs.
BATS: Right **THROWS:** Right
ACQUIRED: Fourth-round pick in 6/78 free-agent draft

Witt didn't have his usual outstanding season in 1988, but his record could have improved if he had received more offensive backup from the Angels. Nevertheless, he was among American League leaders in innings pitched. He tied Greg Swindell for second in the league for complete games with 12. Witt has anchored the Angels staff for the last five years now. His losing mark was his first since 1983, when he was used both in starting and relief assignments. Watch for a rebound from Witt if the Angel offense improves in 1989.

If Witt carries on for another decade, he could put together some statistics worthy of Hall of Fame consideration. His cards are long-shot investments at 10 cents. The payoff would come as soon as Witt wins 20 games. Our pick for his best 1989 card is Score.

TRACY WOODSON

	BA	G	AB	R	H	2B	3B	HR	RBI	SB
1988	.249	65	173	15	43	4	1	3	15	1
Life	.239	118	309	29	74	12	2	4	26	2

POSITION: Infield
TEAM: Los Angeles Dodgers
BORN: October 5, 1962 Richmond, VA
HEIGHT: 6′3″ **WEIGHT:** 215 lbs.
BATS: Right **THROWS:** Right
ACQUIRED: Third-round pick in 6/84 free-agent draft

Woodson appeared in a career-high 65 games for the 1988 Dodgers. The Dodgers used this adept fielder both at third and first base last season. He debuted with the Dodgers in 1987, and raised his average to a career-high .249 in 1988. His first major league highlight was a big one. His initial home run was a blast off none other than Nolan Ryan. In just two seasons of part-time appearances, Woodson hasn't displayed awesome abilities. Still, he is only 26 years old and could blossom with time. With a good spring training, Woodson might challenge Jeff Hamilton for the starting third baseman's job.

Woodson's 1989 cards should be a nickel or less. See if he gets more playing time in 1989 before investing. Our pick for his best 1989 card is Topps.

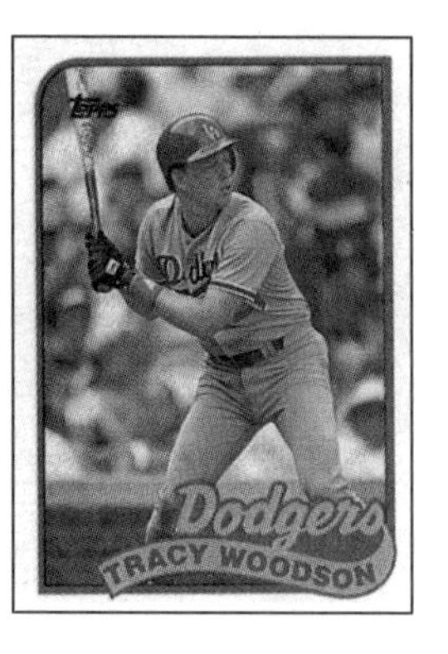

TODD WORRELL

	W	L	ERA	G	SV	IP	H	R	BB	SO
1988	5	9	3.00	68	32	90.0	69	32	34	78
Life	25	25	2.58	234	106	310.0	258	97	116	260

POSITION: Pitcher
TEAM: St. Louis Cardinals
BORN: September 28, 1959 Arcadia, CA
HEIGHT: 6'5" **WEIGHT:** 215 lbs.
BATS: Right **THROWS:** Right
ACQUIRED: First-round pick in 6/82 free-agent draft

Worrell is the only Cardinal ever to post three consecutive seasons of 30 or more saves. After several seasons of limited success as a starter in the minors, his 1985 mid-season debut as a reliever helped the Cardinals to the National League title. In 1986, he was named N.L. Rookie of the Year. In 1988, Worrell saved more than 40 percent of the Cardinal victories. He had 32 saves, an ERA of 3.00, and 78 strikeouts in 90 innings. For the last three years, Worrell has been among the finest relievers in the league.

Worrell may have a stunning career ahead of him if his arm holds out. However, due to the chance of a career-ending arm injury, which hard-throwing relievers are prone to, his cards would be risky purchases at more than 15 cents apiece. Our pick for his best 1989 card is Score.

CRAIG WORTHINGTON

	BA	G	AB	R	H	2B	3B	HR	RBI	SB
1988	.185	26	81	5	15	2	0	2	4	1
Life	.185	26	81	5	15	2	0	2	4	1

POSITION: Third base
TEAM: Baltimore Orioles
BORN: April 17, 1965 Los Angeles, CA
HEIGHT: 6' **WEIGHT:** 160 lbs.
BATS: Right **THROWS:** Right
ACQUIRED: First pick in secondary phase of 6/85 free-agent draft

For all of the Orioles' troubles in 1988, they still seem to have a wealth of good young infielders. Worthington appears to be next in line. When he hit .300 for Class-A Hagerstown in 1986, there was thought given to promoting him directly to the big club in 1987. However, Worthington spent the '87 campaign at Triple-A Rochester, where he played an excellent hot corner and batted .258, with seven homers and 50 RBIs. At Rochester in 1988, Worthington hit .244, 16 homers, and 73 RBIs. Defensively, he has the necessary skills: He goes left and right, plays the slow roller, and has a strong arm.

He may not be Brooks Robinson, but Worthington appears to be the next Oriole third baseman, making his cards good buys. His 1989 cards will be 15 to 20 cents. Our pick for his best 1989 card is Topps.

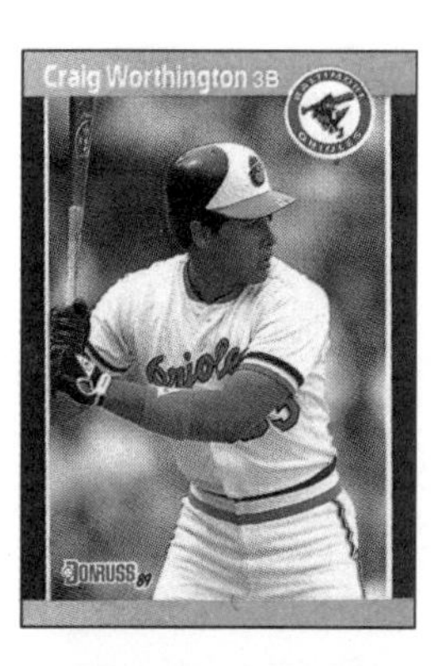

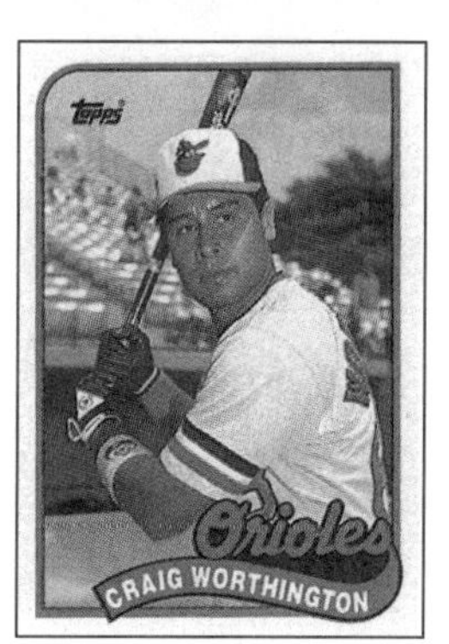

MARVELL WYNNE

	BA	G	AB	R	H	2B	3B	HR	RBI	SB
1988	.264	128	333	37	88	13	4	11	42	3
Life	.251	723	2165	252	543	86	24	29	186	71

POSITION: Outfield
TEAM: San Diego Padres
BORN: December 17, 1959 Chicago, IL
HEIGHT: 5′11″ **WEIGHT:** 185 lbs.
BATS: Left **THROWS:** Left
ACQUIRED: Traded from the Pirates for Bob Patterson, 4/86

Wynne had one of the best seasons of his career with the 1988 Padres. Even as a backup outfielder, he had career highs in both homers (11) and RBIs (42). Wynne, who came up through the Mets' system, briefly held a starting outfield job with the Pirates. He played in 154 games in 1984, finishing with a .266 average, 174 hits, and 24 stolen bases. In 1987, he hit .250, with two homers, 24 RBIs, and 11 stolen bases. His speed and defense help him serve the Padres in various ways. Wynne will see lots of playing time again in 1989.

Wynne's 1989 cards should be three cents or less. It's not safe to invest in his cards until he gets a starting outfield post, because he'll never get the needed at-bats to prove himself. Our pick for his best 1989 card is Fleer.

RICH YETT

	W	L	ERA	G	CG	IP	H	R	BB	SO
1988	9	6	4.62	23	0	134.1	146	72	55	71
Life	17	18	4.98	100	3	311.0	327	184	143	180

POSITION: Pitcher
TEAM: Cleveland Indians
BORN: October 6, 1962 Pomona, CA
HEIGHT: 6′2″ **WEIGHT:** 187 lbs.
BATS: Right **THROWS:** Right
ACQUIRED: Traded from Twins with Jay Bell, Curt Wardle, and Jim Weaver for Bert Blyleven, 8/85

Yett won a career-high nine games for the 1988 Indians. He was used primarily as a starter in 1988, which may explain the improvement in his performance. In 1987, he was 3-9 before ending the season in the minors. He bounced around in the Minnesota farm system from 1980 through 1984 before getting traded to the Tribe in 1985. The big righthander pitched in 39 games for the Indians in 1986, going 5-3 with one save. The Indians hope that his recent improvement is due to the fact that he was placed in one role. Yett's best bet seems to be sticking to starting in the future.

Yett's 1989 cards will be priced at three cents or less. He is relatively young and hasn't proven himself. Wait to invest in his cards. Our pick for his best 1989 card is Topps.

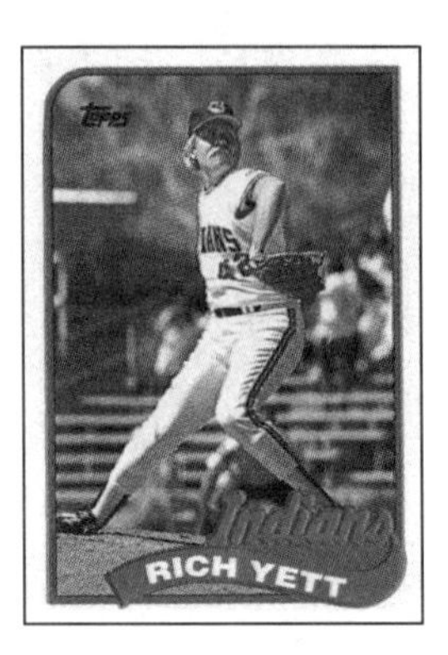

CURT YOUNG

	W	L	ERA	G	CG	IP	H	R	BB	SO
1988	11	8	4.14	26	1	156.1	162	77	50	69
Life	46	33	4.27	133	14	721.0	724	375	209	374

POSITION: Pitcher
TEAM: Oakland A's
BORN: April 16, 1960 Saginaw, MI
HEIGHT: 6′1″ **WEIGHT:** 180 lbs.
BATS: Right **THROWS:** Left
ACQUIRED: Fourth-round pick in 6/81 free-agent draft

Young won in double digits for the third consecutive season in 1988. After two straight 13-win seasons in 1986 and 1987, he got 11 victories in 1988. His ERA was the highest among A's starters last season, and there was concern about the condition of his arm. Young, in just 26 starts, logged only one complete game. He was a rookie sensation in 1984, when he registered a 9-4 season in 20 appearances. Since then, several injuries have taken their toll. Young needs to last an entire season in 1989 to prove he can still handle the rigors of starting pitching.

Young's cards are available at three cents or less, something that can't be said for many A's in 1989. Don't invest in his cards until the doubts about his health (and his future) are gone. Our pick for his best 1989 card is Topps.

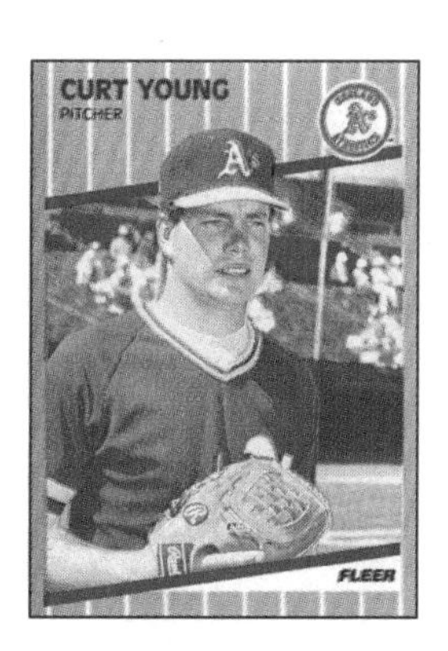

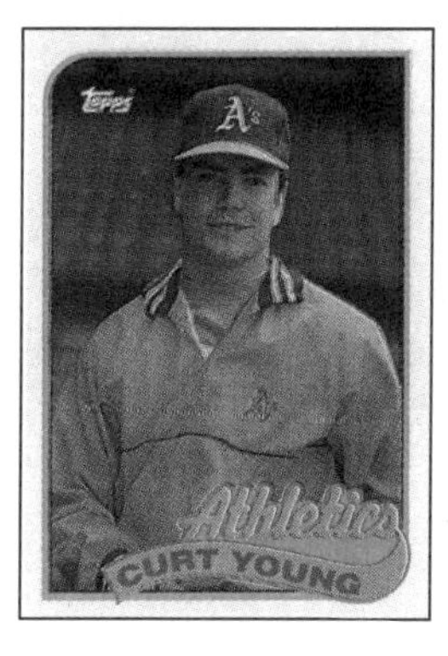

GERALD YOUNG

	BA	G	AB	R	H	2B	3B	HR	RBI	SB
1988	.257	149	576	79	148	21	9	0	37	65
Life	.278	220	850	123	236	30	11	1	52	91

POSITION: Outfield
TEAM: Houston Astros
BORN: October 22, 1964 Tele, Honduras
HEIGHT: 6′2″ **WEIGHT:** 185 lbs.
BATS: Both **THROWS:** Right
ACQUIRED: Traded from Mets with Mitch Cook and Manny Lee for Ray Knight, 8/84

Young has become a hot commodity in Houston in 1988. This young speedster broke the Astros' single-season stolen base mark of 61 set by Cesar Cedeno in 1977. Young led the 1988 Astros in triples and stolen bases, and played near-flawless defense in center field. He got his first chance in the Astros outfield in 1987 when Billy Hatcher was injured, and when Hatcher came back he found he was in left field. Young was acquired from the Mets in 1984 in a deal for Ray Knight. Young could challenge as the best leadoff hitter in the N.L. if he improves his on-base percentage.

Young's 1989 cards would be a good deal at 10 cents or less. If his batting average improves, his speed could carry him to stardom. Our pick for his best 1989 card is Fleer.

MIKE YOUNG

	BA	G	AB	R	H	2B	3B	HR	RBI	SB
1988	.206	83	160	15	33	14	0	1	14	0
Life	.249	603	1781	242	443	80	6	71	230	21

POSITION: Outfield
TEAM: Milwaukee Brewers
BORN: March 20, 1960 Oakland, CA
HEIGHT: 6′2″ **WEIGHT:** 204 lbs.
BATS: Both **THROWS:** Right
ACQUIRED: Traded from Phillies for Alex Madrid, 8/88

Young struggled in his first season with the Phillies, hitting .226 in 146 at-bats. Philadelphia traded him to the Brewers, and Milwaukee used him as a fourth outfielder in 1988. A former Baltimore outfielder, Young seemed set as an Oriole after the 1985 season, when he hit .274, 28 home runs, and 81 RBIs. But his stats slid from that year, and he found himself being used as trade fodder. With Jeffery Leonard no longer a Brewer, Young has an exceptional opportunity to put his career back on track in 1989.

Young's 1989 cards will be priced as commons. His cards are risky, but gamblers may want to invest a few dollars in them, hoping that he can post numbers similar to his 1985 stats. Our pick for his best 1989 card is Donruss.

ROBIN YOUNT

	BA	G	AB	R	H	2B	3B	HR	RBI	SB
1988	.306	162	621	92	190	38	11	13	91	22
Life	.290	2131	8293	1234	2407	443	102	187	1021	207

POSITION: Outfield
TEAM: Milwaukee Brewers
BORN: September 16, 1955 Danville, IL
HEIGHT: 6′ **WEIGHT:** 170 lbs.
BATS: Right **THROWS:** Right
ACQUIRED: First-round pick in 6/73 free-agent draft

Each year, Yount is quietly approaching the exclusive 3,000-hit club. In less than four more seasons, he'll have conquered the challenge. Yount nearly matched his previous year's totals in 1988. He hit .306, with 13 homers and 91 RBIs. He led the Brewers in RBIs and games played, helping the team hold its own in a four-team race that went down to the wire. In 1987, he hit 21 homers, with 103 RBIs, 99 runs scored, and a .312 batting average. If Yount played for the Mets or the Yankees, he'd be immortal. But playing in Milwaukee, he remains an unheralded hero who will be a key to the 1989 team.

Yount is a good choice for the Hall of Fame. His 1989 cards will be 25 cents each, and investors will reap large dividends if Yount gets elected to Cooperstown. Our pick for his best 1989 card is Fleer.